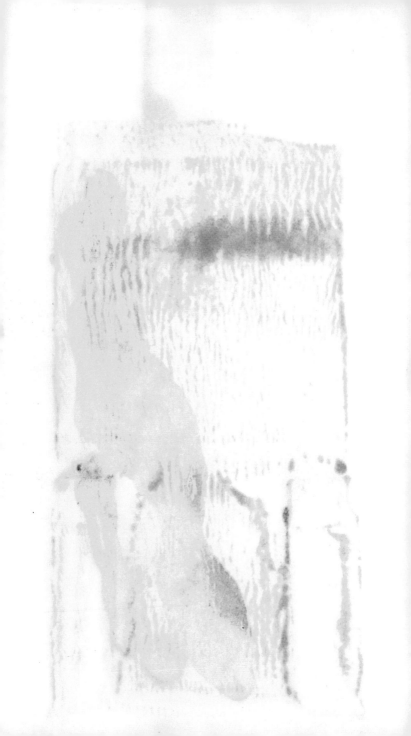

THE SOCIAL IDEAS
OF AMERICAN EDUCATORS

WITH NEW CHAPTER ON
THE LAST TWENTY-FIVE YEARS

by

Merle Curti

About the Book

The present-day demands for a reassessment of American education, for a tougher school program, can be understood only in terms of a wider frame of reference than the sudden awakening to the achievements of Soviet science and technology. In point of fact, several basic forces in American life in large part accounted for the growing emphasis over the decades on the "life-adjustment" programs, that is, homemaking, community activity, the driving of automobiles, vocational and and personal guidance, and interpersonal and inter-group relationships. In becoming increasingly corporate in character American life and values stressed the importance of teamwork, of conformity to the group norm, of reducing conflict in personal and group relations. This was summed up in such slogans as "other-directedness," "the organization man," and "togetherness." The emphasis on the group and on togetherness, though a natural outgrowth of our own American experiences, helped to prepare us to look with more favor on Russian methods of education. Perhaps, many said, America also needed to concentrate more heavily on scientific and technical training to meet national needs. It was taken for granted in many circles that the supreme national need is to dominate or at least hold the balance in world politics and also, for military reasons, to achieve leadership in the mastery of outer space.

AMERICAN
HISTORICAL ASSOCIATION

INVESTIGATION OF THE
SOCIAL STUDIES IN THE SCHOOLS

• •

STAFF

A. C. KREY
Chairman, Director of the Investigation

G. S. COUNTS
Research Director

W. G. KIMMEL
Executive Secretary

T. L. KELLEY
Psychologist, Advisor on Tests

COMMISSION ON DIRECTION

THE SOCIAL IDEAS
OF AMERICAN EDUCATORS

AMERICAN HISTORICAL ASSOCIATION
COMMISSION ON THE SOCIAL STUDIES

THE SOCIAL IDEAS
OF AMERICAN EDUCATORS

WITH NEW CHAPTER ON
THE LAST TWENTY-FIVE YEARS

by

Merle Curti

Professor of History,
The University of Wisconsin

1971

LITTLEFIELD, ADAMS & CO.

Totowa, New Jersey

PREFACE

This is the tenth volume of the Report of the American Historical Association Commission on the Social Studies in the Schools. As the title indicates, it presents a history of the social ideas of leaders in education from the beginning of our history. This work is closely related to the preceding volume by G. S. Counts, *The Social Foundations of American Education*. It shares with that work the recognition of tradition, accepted ideals and social habit as powerful forces in contemporary education. As the preceding work sought to discover these forces in the detailed development of the activities of American society, this work seeks to find them in the social ideas of leaders in American education. The general plan for both volumes was worked out by G. S. Counts as Director of Research in conjunction with the Executive Committee of the Commission and approved by the Commission.

The execution of this task required some one familiar with the broad field of American history who was also somewhat familiar with education, an unusual combination of interests. The Commission was therefore fortunate in prevailing upon Professor M. E. Curti of Smith College, who had made the intellectual and social history of the United States his special field of study, to undertake this work. The authorities of Smith College very graciously consented to grant him leave of absence for the year necessary to complete the task.

The author submitted the outline of his work to the Commission for criticism and suggestions. A first draft of the volume when completed was likewise submitted to all members of the Commission for criticism. The author has indicated in his foreword his indebtedness for aid in the preparation of this volume. In large measure, however, he was forced to do pioneer work. Certain high spots were adequately documented, but for the most part he had to pursue his search without much guidance, and for the more recent developments he had to rely in considerable measure upon oral testimony.

Having complied with the request of the Commission in undertaking the task, the author likewise complied with its desire to have the work available on time though this demand prevented the fuller exploration of the many ramifications of the theme. Despite his regrets, however, he has succeeded in blazing a wide trail through the whole subject which others as well as himself may follow as circumstances permit. As such it marks a distinct contribution to the social and intellectual history of the nation.

A. C. Krey, *Chairman.*

ACKNOWLEDGMENTS

It would be difficult adequately to express my appreciation of the contributions made by many persons to this study. I especially wish to express my gratitude to the following educators who discussed with me either their own work or some of the problems of this report: Professor John Dewey, Professor E. L. Thorndike, Professor George S. Strayer, Professor William H. Kilpatrick, Professor William Bagley, Professor Goodwin Watson, Dr. Charles Allen, Dr. Charles Prosser, Dr. Howard Wilson, Dr. Lura Oak, Miss Flora Cooke, Dr. William Carr, the Rt. Rev. Patrick Joseph McCormick, Father George Johnson, Mr. Charles Lischka, Dean Dwight Oliver Wendell Holmes, Dr. Charles Henry Thompson, Professor I. W. Howerth, and Professor Charles McMurray. Dr. Charles Wesley, Dr. Peter Guilday, Dr. William H. Burnham, Dr. H. D. Sheldon, Father Edward Jordan, Dr. John S. Brubacher, and others also extended courtesies for which I am grateful. I wish to thank the following publishers for permission to use quotations from their publications: Henry Holt and Company, Houghton Mifflin Company, Longmans, Green and Company, Doubleday, Doran and Company, D. Appleton-Century Company, and Harper and Brothers.

Professor Will S. Monroe very graciously permitted me to use, under the most favorable circumstances, his rich collection of Barnard papers and shared with me his wide knowledge of Barnard. Mrs. Edna Shepard put at my disposal unpublished letters of Colonel Francis W. Parker. Dr. Anna Blair gave me permission to read her thesis, "Henry Barnard, School

Administrator," and Miss Ada Cass Heffron kindly sent me her unpublished "Sketch in Appreciation of the Life and Work of Francis W. Parker." I am also very grateful to Miss Mary Dunham, Librarian of Smith College library, and to the staff of the library, for many kindnesses, and to Miss Mary Pardee Allison for proofreading.

Several friends and colleagues each read one or two chapters of my manuscript and offered valuable criticism. For such help I am grateful to Professor Newton Arvin, Professor Gail Kennedy, Dr. S. McClellan Butt, Professor Viola Barnes, Dr. Fulmer Mood, Dr. Howard Beale, Professor James Gibson, Professor and Mrs. H. U. Faulkner, and especially to Professor and Mrs. G. W. Allport and Professor and Mrs. Louis Hunter. My wife, Dr. Margaret Wooster Curti, who read the entire manuscript critically, offered invaluable criticism and suggested fruitful lines of inquiry.

I am also under very deep obligations to the Commission for its more than generous support of this investigation. Many of its members at the Princeton meeting in November, 1932, made valuable suggestions in regard to subject matter and method of treatment. Mrs. Margaret Harding as editorial assistant gave valuable final aid in the preparation of the manuscript. To Dr. Charles A. Beard, Professor A. C. Krey, Dean Guy Stanton Ford, Professor Jesse Newlon and Professor George S. Counts I am especially grateful for criticism, advice, suggestions, and encouragement. It was the pioneer work of Dr. Counts in relating educational thinking and practice to economic and cultural forces in American life which first suggested to me the general method of approach used in this research.

I am under very special debt to my former pupil and research assistant, Miss LaWanda Fenlason. Miss Fenlason helped in collecting materials, made preliminary reports on certain topics, checked the footnotes, and read the entire manuscript, making invaluable suggestions and criticisms. Without her loyal and indefatigable help the report could not have been prepared in the time at my disposal.

NORTHAMPTON, MASSACHUSETTS,   MERLE E. CURTI.

INTRODUCTION

An historical analysis of the social thought of American educators may be useful in the work of clarifying the purposes of the social studies in this time of rapid social change. The social ideas of teachers and administrators to whom any recommendations of the Commission on the Social Studies must be entrusted for execution are a product and a part of the stream of ideas expressed and handed on by previous educators. The things which American educators in the past have deemed necessary, possible, and desirable, to use Professor Beard's phrase, may be assumed to have had some influence on the social philosophy of the men and women to whom the recommendations of the Commission are addressed. In asking the educators of today to think of education in relation to statesmanship the Commission may, on the basis of this report, indicate the extent to which there is a precedent for such a conception of education. It may also call attention to certain historical factors which have furthered or limited that conception.

Leading educators have not only formulated a professional point of view and technique. Whether or not they are aware of it, they have also developed a social philosophy, confused or clearly designed. This social philosophy has been influenced by certain factors, such as the time and place in which they have lived, the class to which they have belonged, the current of ideas about them, and the social and economic tensions which have touched their interests and aroused their sympathies or antipathies. These factors, together with their own personal temperaments, have not only conditioned their social thinking, but have also provided them with standards of judgment. Consciously or unconsciously, they have applied these standards of judgment to far-reaching social problems. Much of the confusion and inconsistency in the social thinking of educators has been due to the fact that they have been for the most part unaware of their own frame of reference, or the complex which, grounded in the realities of time and place, has governed their conception of "the necessary, the possible, and the desirable."

However different the social objectives outlined in the report of the Commission are in many respects from those of most of the educators studied in this investigation, there is nevertheless much in common between them. A knowledge of the expectations, successes, and disappointments of the men and women who have been outstanding in the upbuilding and direction of the American schools may help to furnish incentives and warnings for those who now have at heart the social purposes of the schools in the transition to a new society.

A broad meaning has been given in this report to the term "social ideas." In the more or less definite attitudes which people take toward their everyday contacts with their fellows, social ideas are revealed. The individual's intellectual and emotional responses to his family, his own social group, and his country, to the more privileged and the less privileged classes, to the church and to his recreational and intellectual activities, and to humanity in general—all these roughly make up the substance of his social ideas. Yet all ideas, being social in origin, have, in a certain sense, social implications; and sometimes the social implications of what appear to be purely individual or abstract ideas are even more important than specific attitudes toward social relationships and problems.

Any discussion of the social ideas of American educators, therefore, should include the social implications of their philosophical and psychological principles and of their pedagogical and administrative work. It is, of course, obvious that quite different social implications may often be seen in a given word or act, and that a writer's own point of view and standard of values and judgments will, however much he be on his guard, affect the interpretations he makes.

If social ideas are related to the cultural and economic interests of individuals and groups, it is important to try to trace relationships between given social ideas explicit or implicit in the writings of educational leaders, and the complex and changing interests of American life. Yet this is no easy task, for the relation between social ideas and specific interests is often an indirect and subtle one, frequently modified by the temperament of the individual as well as by personal, social, and political influences.

No attempt has been made, in the present study, to classify social ideas definitely and to treat all of these systematically for every educator and every period. The conceptions treated and the length and character of the treatment have varied widely according to the interests of the thinkers dealt with and the material available. But it is possible to indicate the leading topics which were kept in mind during the investigaton, and which served as a general guide.

The social ideas which have been selected for special study have been, first of all, those which have to do with the purposes of elementary and secondary education. Even the conception of education as an individual matter, as a means of enriching the child's life, of preparing him for some vocation or profession, or of enabling him to survive in competition with his fellows, implies significant social attitudes. When educaton is more formally thought of as a matter of the individual's relation to the organized social and economic structure, the purposes of education fall, with many qualifications to be sure, into three categories: education to perpetuate the existing pattern of economic and social arrangements; education to modify or reform the established system; and education to completely reorganize affairs in such a way that a future differing fundamentally from the past and present may be achieved. We shall see how the character of these more explicitly social purposes of education has differed from period to period, as well as from individual to individual. We shall also inquire to what extent educators as a group have shared the social beliefs of conservatives, liberals, or radicals, and whether they have in general tended to lead, to follow, or to resist the exponents of social change.

Another group of social ideas important in this study is that involved in attitudes toward those we may call the underprivileged—toward the Negro, the Indian, and foreign immigrants; toward women (especially in certain periods); and toward laborers. Attitudes toward nationalism and internationalism have been treated, involving ideas about war and peace and patriotism, about a distinctively American culture, and about the rôle of the United States in the society of nations. The concept of individualism, as well as ideas about socialism and collectivism, is also part of the picture. Cultural ideas or values as such—ideas about the use of leisure, the place of art and learning and the good life generally—have received consideration, but these have usually been discussed in connection with the general aims of education. Ethical and religious ideas have been dealt with in discussing attitudes toward the growth of secularization in American life, the rôle of the church and the state in education, and the problem of character training in the schools. These general classes of ideas may be said to comprise those most important in the social thinking of leading educators.

While particular attention has been given to the more specifically social ideas of American educators and to their conception of the social aims of education, the social implications of their points of view on the curriculum, classroom methods, and administration have also been considered, though not systematically and formally.

The problem of selection of educators has of course been difficult. Partly because of the character of the work of the Commission, and partly because of the limitations of time and space, leaders whose major work was in the field of higher education, such as Charles W. Eliot, have been excluded. Although the importance of leaders in higher education who have also been concerned with the schools, and especially with the relationship between the schools and the universities, has been recognized, the recognition has been incidental rather than systematic. This exclusion of leaders of higher education is, it need hardly be said, open to the criticism that the social ideas of those concerned with elementary and secondary schools have been affected by institutions of higher learning and by the men who have presided over them and taught in them.

The educators selected for analysis have been chosen on the ground that they seemed to be both representative and influential. The selection was partly guided by consultation with many students of American education and by reference to the work of others, and partly by the amount and character of the source material available. A recent investigation of the National Education Association, which listed the leading non-living educators of America, included all but one of those chosen for a detailed analysis in this report. Ideally, educators who wrote little but whose acts were of consequence should find a place in such an investigation. The historian, however, unless he has the time and facilities for very extended investigation, is for the most part limited by available written documents, and such limitation has influenced selection in the present study.

No systematic effort has been made to evaluate the influence of the social ideas of the educators chosen. Even the approximate influence of social ideas can be objectively determined only by a study of the legislation or institutions in which they became embodied, or by the extensive use of questionnaires. Such a study was not only impossible in the time available, but also, in the opinion of many members of the Commission, outside the scope of this investigation. No claim is made, therefore, that the social ideas of the educators studied in this report were shared by educators in general. Indeed, further research might modify somewhat the general pattern as well as the interpretations and conclusions. In view of the relatively short time available for its preparation, this study makes no claim of being in any sense finished in character. It is, on the contrary, frankly tentative and exploratory. For this, as well as for other reasons, many outstanding contemporary educators have not been included. Much light is thrown on the social beliefs of a large number of contemporary educators by Harper's *Social Ideas of American Educators,* an investigation which made admirable use of the questionnaire method. Those interested in a more detailed analysis of the social ideas of living educators than is to be found in the present volume may consult Norman Woelfel's *Molders of the American Mind,* a monograph which appeared after this report had been submitted to the Commission.

The problem of organization of material proved to be even more difficult than that of selection. The social ideas of American educators might be treated in either of two ways. On the one hand, it would be possible to organize the material in topical or chronological form, subordinating the social ideas of particular individuals to the selected problems. Since social historians have with much justification reacted against the conventional over-emphasis on biography, and since much is to be gained by tracing the origin, development, and fate of ideas in relationship to existing conditions and to other ideas, a strong argument could be made for such an organization. But the topical treatment makes it difficult to evaluate the rôle which an individual's temperament, occupational and class affiliations, and ideological equipment play in influencing his social philosophy. The history of a man's ideas is part and parcel of the story of his life, and his ideas at any period of his life can be adequately appreciated only in the light of his whole personality. These and other considerations resulted in the adoption of an organization combining the topical with the biographical treatment.

Not only has an effort been made to determine the extent to which the social and intellectual environment of given educators colored their social philosophy, but the importance of determining in what measure they have transcended their economic and intellectual background in their social thinking, and in consequence modified that background, has not been overlooked. Yet there are so many imponderables involved in any effort to determine the dynamic character of social ideas and ideals in modifying the conditions which influenced them that caution is necessary in any effort to gauge such reciprocal relationships.

A consistent and conscientious desire to be as objective as possible has governed this investigation. Whether or not the historian is aware of it, his life has given him, as it has given to every one, a special point of view, which influences him in his historical work. It would seem to be impossible for a historian to make a study of social ideas without being influenced by his own social philosophy. This must be especially true of any study that is interpretative rather than merely descriptive in character. In spite of its limitations, this study, it is hoped, presents a reasonably accurate analysis of the social hopes and fears of some outstanding American educators.

CONTENTS

PAGE

PREFACE—A. C. KREY   vii

ACKNOWLEDGMENTS   ix

INTRODUCTION   xiii

THE LAST TWENTY-FIVE YEARS   xxv

PART I

I. COLONIAL SURVIVALS AND REVOLUTIONARY PROM-
ISES, 1620-1820   3

II. NEW CONFLICTS AND A NEW SOLUTION, 1800-1860   50

III. EDUCATION AND SOCIAL REFORM: HORACE MANN   101

IV. HENRY BARNARD   139

V. THE EDUCATION OF WOMEN   169

SUMMARY   194

PART II

VI. THE SCHOOL AND THE TRIUMPH OF BUSINESS
ENTERPRISE, 1860-1914   203

VII. EDUCATION IN THE SOUTH   261

VIII. THE BLACK MAN'S PLACE: BOOKER T. WASHING-
TON, 1856?-1916   288

IX. WILLIAM T. HARRIS, THE CONSERVATOR, 1835-1908 310

X. BISHOP SPALDING, CATHOLIC EDUCATOR, 1840-1916 348

XI. FRANCIS WAYLAND PARKER, DEMOCRAT, 1837-1902   374

XII. G. STANLEY HALL, EVOLUTIONIST, 1846-1924   396

XIII. WILLIAM JAMES, INDIVIDUALIST, 1842-1910   429

XIV. EDWARD LEE THORNDIKE, SCIENTIST, 1874-1949   459

XV. JOHN DEWEY, 1859-1952   499

XVI. POST-WAR PATTERNS   542

CONCLUSION   581

BIBLIOGRAPHICAL NOTES   593

INDEX   601

THE SOCIAL IDEAS
OF AMERICAN EDUCATORS

THE LAST TWENTY-FIVE YEARS

A quarter of a century has gone by since the publication of *The Social Ideas of American Educators*. At the time it appeared the book was generously praised as a pioneer study and, though long out of print, it has continued to be read and cited. In making it again available it seems proper to include a brief retrospect of the main developments in the social thinking of spokesmen of American education in the past twenty-five years.

The quasi-biographical organization that seemed appropriate when the book was written is not so suitable for the treatment of the period since the 1930's. For in the decades since then no two, three or four figures have exerted the influence or given the leadership of a Harris, an Eliot, a Thorndike, or a Dewey in the preceding half century. It is true that some of those who commanded nation-wide attention in the mid-1930's continued to write about education. One thinks of George S. Counts, John L. Childs, Harold Rugg, William H. Kilpatrick, Robert M. Hutchins, and of Dewey himself, who spoke in telling ways almost until his death in his ninety-fourth year. It is also true that new voices, representing the liberal arts as well as professional education, have been heard and have carried weight. James B. Conant, A. Whitney Griswold, Howard Mumford Jones, Gilbert Highet, Jacques Barzun, Arthur E. Bestor, Jr., Theodore Brameld, David Riesman, and Paul Woodring come readily to mind. Also to be included is John W. Gardner, president of both the Carnegie Corporation and of the Carnegie Foundation for the Advancement of Teaching.

The fact that it is hard to single out any of these leaders

as comparable to some of their predecessors in an earlier period is related to many circumstances. One, no doubt, has been the increasingly specialized interests of educational administrators and theorists. The whole school business became so big and so complex, and professional training so narrow, that the educator's approach was more and more restricted. Another explanation has been the growing tendency to attack intellectual problems through the joint efforts of members of committees. This of course has not been an entirely new procedure. But one is put to it to think off-hand of earlier committee pronouncements that commanded as much public attention as have the Harvard report on general education, the various statements of the Educational Policies Commission of the N.E.A., the recommendations of President Truman's Commission on Higher Education, and the injunctions of President Eisenhower's White House Conference.

Still another explanation of the difficulty of identifying two or three commanding educational leaders has been the increased lay participation in the formulation of educational aims and of ways of realizing them. An especially interesting example of the combined lay factor and committee approach to the discussion of the social aspects of education has been the work of the National Citizens' Commission for the Public Schools. Chartered in 1946 as the result of a suggestion of President Conant and the initiative of the Educational Policies Commission, the new organization enjoyed the effective leadership of its president, Roy M. Larsen of Time, Incorporated. The National Citizens' Commission for the Public Schools stimulated men and women all over the country "to define good education and encouraged them to bring their own local schools up to the standards they themselves set." The leadership urged participants to work actively to make the best in education available to every American child on completely equal terms and, as a means to that end, to arouse in each community the "intelligence and will to improve our public schools."[1]

Another related example of the more active interest of citizens in education is the recent publication of the Rockefeller Brothers Fund, a special studies project report entitled *The Pursuit of Excellence. Education and the Future of America*.[2] This was the result of an effort to assess the chief problems and opportunities that are apt to face the United States over the next decade and a half. Its thesis was summed up in the statement that "our society will have passed an important milestone of maturity when those who are the most enthusiastic proponents of a democratic way of life are also the most vigorous proponents of excellence." To these examples of lay participation in educational thinking might be added the publication of a large body of widely read articles and books about education from the hands of such men and women as Agnes Meyer, Fred M. Hechinger, and Admiral H. G. Rickover.

In discussing the social ideas implicit or explicit in educational writing and practice over our whole history, I pointed out again and again the dominant trends and minor eddies in the American economy and society and the influence these shifting forces had on the social thinking of educational leaders. These trends and eddies included the transfer of western civilization to our shores and its modification by the westward movement, immigration, and the slavery controversy, as well as the shift from a commercial-agrarian to an industrial-urban economy and culture, and the vast consequences of civil and world war.

[1] *National Citizens' Commission for the Public Schools. Historical Document Series* (New York, no date, 8 volumes), I, p. 2.
[2] *The Pursuit of Excellence. Education and the Future of America.* Special Studies Project Report V, Rockefeller Brothers Fund (New York, 1958), ix, 7.

I also took into account the impact on the social ideas of those deeply concerned with education, of such movements of thought as Puritanism, the Enlightenment, humanitarianism, Romanticism, evolutionary theory, scientific measurement, and nationalism and democracy. It still seems to hold that all these developments in the economy and culture were so interdependent with the social attitudes of educators that one could not attribute autonomy either to ideas or to economic and social forces, could not say which were causes and which were effects.

To say this is not to say that were I to write the book today the presuppositions and treatment would be exactly what they were then. It is possible that some of the analyses of issues, as these were developed in *The Social Ideas of American Educators,* were too sharply defined, that they reflected too markedly the mood of the early nineteen thirties, a time when almost everyone was very much aware of the interplay of conflicting interests and ideas. It is now fashionable in historical circles to play down the conflicts in our past, to emphasize a more or less constant homogeneity. This tendency no doubt reflects the understandable search for stability and continuity in a time of world-wide revolutionary changes. The current fashion seems to me to have sometimes resulted, in historical writing, in over-corrective interpretations. Today it seems to be as hard as I admitted it was in the preface to my book, to overcome and transcend the impact of the prevailing intellectual fashions and existing situations.

If the method of relating ideas and interests without giving a determining role to either was essentially sound, one might begin a brief retrospective glance at the last twenty-five years by asking what have been the chief social and economic changes that have furnished a background for the thinking of those who have written in these years about American education and its social implications. Most students would agree in emphasizing the economic recovery from the great depression, the implementation of the New Deal, and the expanding powers of the federal government. Of obvious importance has been the challenge of totalitarianism in Italy, Germany, and Japan and the second world war, problems associated with American leadership of the non-communist world in the "cold war," including the fear of Communism, and the issues of civil and minority rights and intergroup relationships at home. On a different level has been the so-called communications revolution. All these have played important parts in educational operations, including pressures for the expansion of the school plant, the growth in enrollment in schools and colleges, and the recruitment, training, and pay of an adequate teaching force. These social and political developments have also influenced the social thinking of educational spokesmen.

Of importance in greater or lesser degree have been movements of thought and feeling associated with these economic, social, and political developments. Most historians would probably agree that social thinking about education has been only slightly influenced, so far, by neo-Thomism (at least outside Catholic circles), neo-orthodoxy, logical positivism, and existentialism.[3] It may of course be too soon to sense, let alone assess, such influences as these movements of thought may be exerting on education.

In the last quarter of a century three major movements of thought that had already become familiar in educational discussion continued, in quite different ways, to figure in the social thinking of those articulately concerned with education.

[3] Note should be taken of John Redden and Francis Ryan, *A Catholic Philosophy of Education* (1942), Jacques Maritain, *Education at the Crossroads* (1943), Henry P. Van Dusen, *God in Education* (1951), Israel Scheffler, ed., *Philosophy and Education* (1958) and George F. Kneller, *Existentialism and Education* (1958).

One, obviously, has been the continuing emphasis, indeed, an increasing emphasis, on science and technology
in our culture, including our education. It is not necessary
to belittle the importance and truly great achievements
of the natural sciences to note that in many eyes the premi-
ums put on scientific achievements and the applications
of these, undermined the humanities. Of late there has
indeed been a growing realization that the decline of the
humanities has carried its hazards. Vigorous voices, including those of well known scientists, have called attention
to the importance of the humanities not only in enriching
individual lives but also in preserving and extending
ethical and social values highly necessary in a free society.[4]
It is too soon to say what the public response will be.

Another continuing movement in thought and culture has
been neo-Marxism. The direct or positive influence of this
and of the world-wide revolutionary movements associated with it had never been of great importance in
American educational thought. Outside two or three metropolitan centers only a very small number of teachers looked
with sympathy on Marxism even at the height of the great
depression. True, it was common for the Hearst press, the
professional patriotic organizations, and the National Association of Manufacturers to denounce as "Marxists" and
"Reds" the leaders of the *Social Frontier* magazine and its
successor, *Frontiers of Democracy*. But Marxism was only
one, and certainly not the most important factor in the
social thinking of this group.

By the mid-nineteen forties Marxism had ceased to have
any significance in a positive way for the thinking of this

[4] Two able but quite different kinds of defense of the humanities
were Gordon Keith Chalmers' *The Public and the Person* (Chicago,
1952), the social implications of which re-enforced the new conservatism, and Howard Mumford Jones' brilliantly democratic championship of the humanities in *One Great Society. Humane Learning
in the United States* (New York, 1959).

or any other group of educational leaders. The antithesis between almost everything that the Soviet Union stood for and the democratic values to which the *Social Frontier* group was dedicated, was increasingly clear. And the achievements of the New Deal and, presently, the promises of the Fair Deal, together with a high level of prosperity, confirmed faith in the American democratic means of moving toward an ever greater measure of social and economic equality and well-being.

On the other hand, the indirect and negative impact of Marxism and the revolutionary movements associated with it was of far-reaching importance on the thinking and feeling of those concerned with education in a social context. It was plain that freedom of teaching and learning was in grave danger as McCarthyism swept on, and resistance seemed at best to be timid and ineffective. The danger was exemplified by the methods often used by Congressional committees in probing into the past beliefs and affiliations of students and teachers, by the enactment in many states of special teachers' loyalty oaths, and by the insistence of citizens' pressure groups that school text-books be "purged" of anything that raised questions about American political and economic institutions and purposes. Even the United Nations and UNESCO were anathema to many such groups.

Educational circles reacted in several ways to this situation. The path for one clearly defined position was prepared by the *Social Frontier* group in the later 1930's when it insisted that there was no place for Communists in the American Federation of Teachers. Building on this, Sidney Hook and others during the McCarthy era urged that the distinction between "heresy" and "conspiracy" is a major one. In other words, liberal and radical dissent was one thing, something to be defended and even welcomed, while Communist rejection of democratic means and values was something very different. The rigid, doctrinaire controls over the mind, it was argued, were too tight to enable a Communist teacher to play his role with the integrity and effectiveness that his position required. Another view, espoused by the American Association of University Professors, maintained that mere association with Communist "fronts" or even with the Party itself as long as it remained a legal organization, was not sufficient ground for the dismissal of a teacher. Competence to teach must be the criterion in each individual case. But this view met with widespread opposition both within the educational profession and in the country at large.

Whatever the differences between educators over the issue of Communism and academic freedom, there was pretty general agreement among educators on the need of opposing the irresponsible tendency to label as communists anyone with ideas different from those of the majority. It was clear to many at the time that the extent of genuine disloyalty was vastly exaggerated. It is not possible to say how many teachers and students were frightened into an unwilling conformity or distraught by fear, anxiety. and insecurity—or still are. Nor is it possible to say that the whole issue, as it was resolved in favor of the moderate position, has been permanently solved. Many have certainly learned that freedom of teaching within the democratic frame is indispensable in a democratic society. But one cannot be sure how well the lesson has been learned, or whether a sufficient number of Americans have learned it to prevent another crisis similar to the McCarthyism of the early nineteen fifties.

In still other ways the influence of Marxism and the world revolution associated with it played an indirect influence on the social thinking of those concerned with education. The great gulf between Communism and the western form of democracy has led to the "cold war." This in turn has been in part responsible for the conservative mood of America in the post-war era. It has expressed itself, so far as education goes, in many ways. One has been the closer relations between American business and education. Educational discussion has had little to say about corporations that suggests an older, frequently critical view. And corporations have given generously to institutions of learning, especially to the liberal arts colleges, partly on the ground that in a time of continuing government expansion into all walks of life it is important to strengthen private and voluntary agencies. But the chief example of the relation between the conservative mood of the country and educational thinking has been the retreat of the idea that the school can and should take the lead in initiating and implementing social reform. This idea, it will be recalled, received much publicity in the 1930's when it was a main tenet in the thinking of George S. Counts and the *Social Frontier* group.

It is true that most of this group did not entirely repudiate the position they once so boldly championed. It was reflected, for example, in the mellow exposition of American education and civilization which Counts wrote in 1952. And in *The Challenge of Soviet Education,* the major work of Counts in the last decade, Americans were called on to meet the challenge presented by the amazing advances in Soviet education, all of which reflected the conviction that education is an all-embracing instrument of political control and of building a completely communist mind and society.[5]

The most vigorous and original exponent of the idea that education could and should improve the social order has

[5] George S. Counts, *Education and American Civilization* (New York, 1952), and *The Challenge of Soviet Education* (New York, 1957). See also John L. Childs, *American Pragmatism and Education* (New York, 1956).

been Theodore Brameld. In addresses and in systematic writings he has carried on the tradition with important modifications. He has called his position "reconstructionism." It holds that public education, informed with new findings in the behavioral sciences, especially anthropology and psychology, should take sides with forces all over the world that are struggling to make full use of science and technology to create an abundant life for all peoples. While recognizing the existence and indeed the necessity of conflict, Brameld holds that it can be carried on within the frame of democratic means and values. To some the position which was so clearly developed in such papers as "Education for the Emerging Age" seemed to rely too optimistically on the promise of the behavioral sciences and the world revolutionary situation. But the thoughtful attention given to Professor Brameld's writings indicates that the constructive potentialities in the situation as he analyzed them could not be ignored.[6]

The prevailing position, nevertheless, is that social reform is largely or even solely the business of adult citizens. The only proper role of the school in social reform is that of preparing the child in the classroom to make intelligent judgments when he becomes a voting participant in decision-making. This is to be done by supplying the young with accurate information, by pointing to the ways in which further information can be gathered, and by developing habits of careful thinking and judgment. This view has been popularized by Professor Paul Woodring, among others.[7] In some, though by no means in all

[6] Theodore Brameld, *Patterns of Educational Philosophy* (New York, 1950), *Philosophies of Education in Cultural Perspective* (New York, 1955), *Toward a Reconstructed Philosophy of Education* (New York, 1956), *Cultural Foundations of Education* (New York, 1957), and "Education for an Emerging Age" in *The Humanist*, 1957, no. 3.

[7] Paul Woodring, *"Let's Talk Sense About Our Schools* (New York, 1953), and *A Fourth of the Nation* (New York, 1957), 119-126.

respects, this position in its relation to education and social reform, resembles the neo-Thomistic view of education which also attaches great importance to intellectual discipline. But neo-Thomism also emphasizes the importance of a humanistic content much richer than that of the so-called essentialists.[8]

One further indirect result of Marxism and the world of revolution of our time must be mentioned. Long accustomed to regarding themselves as superior to any other people in "know-how," Americans were deeply shaken when, in the autumn of 1957, it was clear that the Russians had an edge on us in the use of atomic power in space technology. The American press teemed with articles blaming our backwardness on our education: the schools had not been sufficiently vigorous in teaching mathematics and the sciences. Much general support was forthcoming to those who had long claimed that American education in general was too soft, that it catered too much to the whims and immediate interests of the young, that it had become enmeshed in a superficial, even frivolous "life-adjustment" program.[9] Education, which President Conant of Harvard had said as early as 1948 was a matter of survival, was now proclaimed to be the indispensable means by which the United States could regain and keep supremacy over the Russians in science and technology. Many commentators felt that it was necessary to imitate the Soviet Union's

[8] Robert M. Hutchins, *The Conflict of Education in a Democratic Society* (New York, 1953) and *The Democratic Dilemma in Freedom, Education, and the Fund* (New York, 1956), 138 *ff.* Hutchins proved a staunch champion of academic freedom, a matter of social importance in any period and one of great importance in the changes taking place in America and in the world in the last quarter of a century.

[9] A widely used text which expounds the position under attack is Florence B. Stratemeyer, Hamden L. Forkner, Margaret G. McKim, and A. Harvey Passow, *Developing a Curriculum for Modern Living* (New York, 1957).

system of "hard" educational training.[10] Others agreed in holding that supremacy in science and technology could alone insure victory in the "cold war" and that American education must look to this major obligation. Some also insisted that America must in addition prove her civilization to be superior to that of the Communist world in political, cultural, and philosophical terms.

The present-day demands for a reassessment of American education, for a tougher school program, can be understood only in terms of a wider frame of reference than the sudden awakening to the achievements of Soviet science and technology. In point of fact, several basic forces in American life in large part accounted for the growing emphasis over the decades on the "life-adjustment" programs, that is, homemaking, community activity, the driving of automobiles, vocational and personal guidance, and interpersonal and intergroup relationships. In becoming increasingly corporate in character American life and values stressed the importance of teamwork, of conformity to the group norm, of reducing conflict in personal and group relations. This was summed up in such slogans as "other-directedness," "the organization man," and "togetherness." The emphasis on the group and on togetherness, though a natural outgrowth of our own American experiences, helped to prepare us to look with more favor on Russian methods of education. Perhaps, many said, America also needed to concentrate more heavily on scientific and technical training to meet national needs. It was taken for granted in many circles that the supreme national need is to dominate or at least hold the balance in world politics and also, for military reasons, to achieve leadership in the mastery of outer space.

[10] See Fred M. Hechinger, *Big Red School House* (New York, 1959).

In responding to those values which pressure groups and parents themselves often demanded, professional educators were also influenced by two movements of thought which had become important in the decades after the First World War. One was a body of psychological and psychoanalytical theories and findings which emphasized the adjustment of the individual to his environment. Another was the movement known as progressive education. To be sure, John Dewey himself never advocated life-adjustment as the key to school activities despite the fact that many critics of life-adjustment programs thought so. But many educators did cite Dewey and his interpreters as authority for life-adjustment programs even when they misunderstood and misapplied his teachings.

No one can doubt that the main body of psychological, psychoanalytical and clinical writings contributed a good deal to the understanding of human motivation and behavior. Nor can one doubt that, from some angles of vision, these theories as they were applied proved to be wholesome and beneficial to a great many growing children and adolescents. The point is clear enough when the widespread concern over juvenile delinquency is considered. Social workers, civic leaders, and parents looked with considerable sympathy on the therapeutic responsibilities of the school, particularly when Evan Hunter's *The Blackboard Jungle* and Harrison Salisbury's *The Shook-up Generation* dramatized the issue. The feeling that "getting tough" with uprooted adolescents promised less than intelligent understanding and love, gave support to the life-adjustment programs. So did the search for activities which might motivate these adolescents more effectively than the traditional program of studies.

At the same time psychological and clinical emphases also supported the tendency in our culture to other-directedness, to conformity, to getting along by following the cue of the group. To a certain extent conformity is of course necessary both in the interest of the individual and of society. But in some cases the emphasis or over-emphasis in education on adjustment must have checked the full development of individual potentialities, with a consequent loss for a deeply rich personal growth and for social contributions of importance. In any case, the emphasis on adjustment, working with basic forces in our mid-twentieth century economy and culture, has militated against the doctrine of education for social reform.

But it was not this effect that troubled most of the critics of the American public school both before and after Sputnik.[11] At least as early as the 1930's Robert M. Hutchins argued that the intellectual content of the curriculum had been dangerously watered down by the core curriculum which broke up traditional subject disciplines into units allegedly functional to life-solving problems. The core curriculum and the growing emphasis on life-adjustment had, Hutchins and a growing number of fellow-critics held, done even worse. The movement had deprived everyone subject to it of the basic human right of developing to the full whatever intellectual capacities he had. Whether these critics spoke of themselves as classicists or as perennialists or as essentialists, they agreed that training for immediate needs such as personal hygiene, homemaking, and participation in community interests, gave support to regrettable anti-intellectual forces in American life. The American school, they claimed, had become little more than an "educational wasteland." It was responsible for "the diminished mind." On the positive side, these critics urged a return to an emphasis on the 3-R's, on the basic intellectual disciplines of mathematics, language, and science. Such

[11] C. Winfield Scott and Clyde M. Hill brought together representative criticisms in an anthology, *Public Education Under Criticism* (New York, 1954).

an emphasis, they insisted, must replace the prevailing one of training partly for immediate needs and for life-adjustment, if the American people were not to be further deprived of their rights to the great heritage of systematic knowledge and of intellectual discipline. After Sputnik, these arguments seemed to have an even wider appeal.[12]

In general the critics blamed John Dewey and the progressive education movement, and the professional educationists who had blindly followed in the path marked out, for the sad state of affairs. If Johnny couldn't read, it was their fault. If the city school in the slum or near-slum was a blackboard jungle, John Dewey or William H. Kilpatrick and their disciples were to be blamed. It is true that some followers of Dewey, in the name of progressive education, misunderstood his teaching, ignored his warning that experiences are not all equally valuable, that the teacher must play a positive, constructive role, that reflective thought is an indispensable part of any worth-while activities program. It is also true that some disciples of Dewey and of progressive education ignored the emphasis he had put, not on mere adjustment to environment as it was, but to those parts of the environment that promised to bring out the best potentialities in children and thus to promote the reconstruction of the whole environment in the interest of better individuals and a better society. It is further true that many professional educators justified the life-adjustment programs even when they fell far short of what Dewey had in mind. But critics failed to see, as I have

[12] In addition to the Scott and Hill anthology, see, for an elaboration of these criticisms, Arthur E. Bestor, *Educational Wastelands* (Urbana, 1953), "Anti-Intellectualism in the Schools," *New Republic*, Jan. 19, 1953, and *The Restoration of Learning* (New York, 1955); Albert Lynd, *Quackery in the Public Schools* (Boston, 1950) and Admiral H. G. Rickover, *Education and Freedom* (New York, 1959). For a quite different presentation and discussion of the criticisms see Vivian T. Thayer, *Public Education and Its Critics* (New York, 1954).

noted before, that this approach seemed a promising means
of motivating and of helping "the beat generation." They
also failed to see that it was often the parents, not John
Dewey, who demanded that the schools teach good manners, hygiene, the home arts, safe driving, that they provide
guidance and direct community activities. Too often the
critics did not realize that in no country did the local
community and parents have as great an influence on the
schools as in America. All these points were made in the
more sensible and balanced replies to the critics of the
public school.[13]

There is, in any effort to evaluate the social ideas explicit
and implicit in the criticism of the life-adjustment emphasis
in American education, another side of the coin to be
considered. For the emphasis on personal relations in
living has, together with other factors, strengthened one
of the most affirmative social developments in education.
This has been the invigorated effort in our time to realize
more fully the American tradition of equality of opportunity
for minority groups—for the recent immigrants, for Jews,
for Negroes. The issue of desegregation in public education is, of course, only one phase of the larger movement
for insuring civil and human rights. The roots of this
movement lie deep in American history, as *The Social
Ideas of American Educators* clearly showed. In our own
time, as in earlier periods, the movement for equality of
opportunity has been strengthened by an awareness of the
inconsistency between our professions of equal human
rights for minority groups and the actualities ("the American dilemma"). That awareness owes something to the

[13] For representative replies on the part of educators see R. Will
Burnett and Harold C. Hand, "Two Critiques of Educational Wastelands," *Progressive Education,* vol. 31, no. 3 (Jan., 1954) and *Educational Theory,* vol. 4 (Jan., 1954), Hollis L. Caswell, *The Attack
on the Schools* (Teachers College, Columbia University, 1958).

awkward position which denial of equal opportunities to some has placed us in during our post-war effort to give effective leadership to the "free world" in the struggle against Communism. But this awareness of the American dilemma and the feeling that something should be done to narrow the gap between professions and practice actually rests largely on the conscientious convictions and efforts of countless men and women. These range from little known people in minority and majority groups to the Bureau for Intercultural Education, a pioneer venture which produced a number of basic studies and initiated many school projects.[14] Of importance was the leadership given by Franklin and Eleanor Roosevelt, Harry S. Truman, and, above all, the Supreme Court.

The maintenance of segregated schools in seventeen states was justified on many grounds, hygienic and social as well as "racial." The constitutional justification was found in the famous *Plessy v. Ferguson* case of 1896 in which the Supreme Court held that state legislation requiring segregated transportation facilities did not violate the Fourteenth Amendment if these facilities were equal. The gradual shift from this position was reflected in a series of decisions which required state supported professional schools to admit qualified Negroes. In 1954, in five decisions involving segregation in public schools in four states and the District of Columbia, the Supreme Court unanimously rejected the "separate but equal doctrine." It is noteworthy that the opinions cited a considerable body of social science writings in support of the legal reasoning of the justices. The Supreme Court placed the responsibility for desegregating public schools "with all deliberate speed" on local communities. These decisions were a milestone in

14 Leaders in this movement have included W. H. Kilpatrick, Stewart Cole, and L. J. Stiles.

the long struggle for equal opportunity for all people regardless of race and status.

The struggle since 1954 to spell out the directives of the Supreme Court has been a turbulent one. White Councils have been pitted against the National Association for the Advancement of Colored People, to name only two organizations that have figured in the struggle. Every case, in effect, differed from every other. Sometimes schools have been closed to make the process of desegregation impossible; sometimes they were closed after a few Negroes had been admitted. Occasional incidents of violence have taken place. The greatest differences emerging were those between the border states where, with the exception of Virginia, desegregation in general has proceeded as well as could be expected, and the Deep South where, in 1959, no Negroes had been allowed to go to any white public school and where laws and other devices reflected a determined effort on the part of the whites in control to have things their way.

On all sides the discussion has been charged with high emotional content. To quote the words of a Kentucky educator, the early stages of the struggle clearly showed that "integration is more important to Negroes than the white man realizes, and segregation is more important to whites than the Negro realizes."[15] If a distinguished Negro sociologist, Ira De A. Reid, was right in thinking that it was possible to overstress law and law enforcement, and that personal, group, and cultural interplay and understanding were even more important, then a big burden is thrown on education, broadly conceived as fostering cooperation, and mutual adjustment and appreciation.[16]

[15] Don Shoemaker, ed., *With All Deliberate Speed* (New York, 1957), p. 203.
[16] Ira De A. Reid, "Integration Reconsidered," *Harvard Educational Review*, vol. 27, pp. 85-91 (Spring, 1957).

On various occasions in our history, as *The Social Ideas of American Educators* made clear, the question of the proper relations between public schools and religion has been a concern of educational leaders. In the past quarter of a century this problem continued to be one that concerned Jewish, Catholic, and Protestant religious organizations, public school administrators and boards of education, state legislatures, the courts, and Congress itself. The growing American interest in religion, which marked the years following the second world war, provided a new context for discussion and decision.[17]

In an effort to diminish further the gap between those parts of the country in which reasonably good schools rested on a prosperous economy and those in which it proved hard to provide adequate local support for public schools, the movement for federal aid was revived. In the discussions thus evoked religion as well as traditional states rights issues figured. On at least two occasions bills for substantially increasing the federal aid given to schools for special purposes passed the Senate despite opposition. In the House the opposition was stiffer. Many expressed the conviction that federal aid should be provided parochial schools, or at least that federal funds might be used for bus transportation of parochial school pupils, for non-religious textbooks, and for health services. But many stubbornly opposed such provisions. The conflict contributed to the defeat of the proposal, to which opposition was also made on the ground that federal support of schools endangered local control (an issue to which Southern members of Congress were especially sensitive).

The controversy over federal aid to private schools also of course involved the larger issue of the traditional

[17] Scott and Hill, *Public Education Under Criticism*, pp. 128-148; Vivian T. Thayer, *Religion in Public Education* (New York, 1947) and *The Attack Upon the Secular School* (Boston, 1951).

American separation of church and state. This issue figured in the efforts of many religious leaders and many parents to have religion recognized as part of the public school program. Some favored non-sectarian instruction in the history and general significance of religion in civilization; others wanted to have the King James version of the Old Testament read daily, with the saying of nonsectarian prayers; still others wanted to have ministers, priests, and rabbis come to the public schools to teach children of their flocks. All these experiments were tried in one or another locality. But many parents and educators opposed all of them on the ground that each in some way violated the constitutional provision for religious freedom and endangered the historic separation of church and state. The Supreme Court finally ruled that if there was no element of compulsion, public school authorities might send pupils at the request of parents to church or synagogue for special instruction during school hours. If interest in religion continues to increase the whole issue may again become a matter of discussion and decision.

Thus in the past quarter century the lively discussion of the social implications of education has continued a long tradition. It is possible to regard the differences and conflicts as regrettable confusion. Or they may seem an unhappy exception to the consolidation of American thought and values which is taking place as we fight Communism. Many take this view. It is also possible to agree still with the analysis John Dewey made in 1939 when he wrote: "All social movements involve conflicts which are reflected intellectually in controversies. It would not be a sign of health if such an important social interest as education were not also an arena of struggles, practical and theoretical."[18]

[18] John Dewey, *Experiences and Education* (New York, 1939), v.

PART 1

I

COLONIAL SURVIVALS AND REVOLUTIONARY PROMISES

1620–1820

In most Parishes are *Schools* (little Houses being built on Purpose) where are taught *English* and *Writing;* but to prevent the sowing the Seeds of Dissention and Faction, it is to be wished that the *Masters* or *Mistresses* should be such as are approved or licensed by the Minister, and Vestry of the Parish, or Justices of the County.
—Hugh Jones, *The Present State of Virginia*—1724.

Even under the best forms [of government], those entrusted with power have, in time, and by slow operations, perverted it into tyranny; and it is believed that the most effectual means of preventing this would be, to illuminate, as far as practicable, the minds of the people at large . . . whence it becomes expedient for promoting the publick happiness that those persons, whom nature hath endowed with genius and virtue, should be rendered by liberal education worthy to receive, and able to guard the sacred deposit of the rights and liberties of their fellow citizens, and that they should be called to that charge without regard to wealth, birth or other accidental condition or circumstance.
—Thomas Jefferson, 1779.

I

Even as late as a hundred years ago American schools still bore the characteristic impress of the colonial era. In spite of the growth of secular interests and influence, in spite of the development of political democracy, the schools two hundred years after the founding of Jamestown and Massachusetts Bay reflected the class prejudices and the religious interests of colonial society. This was true notwithstanding the fact that from region to region and even from neighborhood to neighborhood there were great differences in the character of the schooling provided. New currents of thought and a variety of unique experiences had only slightly modified the practices prevailing in the schools and the ideas which their directors cherished regarding their social function. So stubborn was the colonial inheritance that it seriously interfered with the educational plans and democratic aspirations of Revolutionary patriots, idealistic humanitarians, and educational reformers who desired to broaden the basis of the public schools and to endow them with new social and cultural functions.

The colonial conception of schools as instruments for the preservation of religious faith and existing economic and social arrangements was rooted in old-world tradition and practice. When the English-speaking colonies were planted, sons of the nobility and wealthier gentry in the mother country were educated in the classics at the great endowed public schools; those of the relatively well-to-do middle classes learned their three R's, religion, and a certain amount of Latin at the parish grammar schools; and at least a handful of the offspring of the very poor attended a few charity schools. The vast number of poor children, however, were bound out as apprentices to learn a trade and, incidentally, the tenets of religion and piety, with perhaps a little reading to promote that end. Religious conformity and the maintenance of the existing authority characterized educational efforts. In other countries which supplied immigrants to the thirteen colonies education was similarly influenced by religious purposes and by class inequalities. It was therefore natural that these forces characterized the first educational institutions in America.

In the colonies institutionalized religion and the class structure of society, the two main forces that determined the character of schooling, were closely related. Whether Anglican or Congregationalist, the church recruited its clergy for the most part from the privileged order and was in turn supported by the more substantial farmers, planters, and merchants. In New England this virtual identity of the dominant religious group with the ruling class was undermined if not broken after the Puritan theocracy began to lose its power in the late seventeenth century; and such parsons as Cotton Mather and Jonathan Mayhew did not then hesitate to denounce the crown authorities with bitter words. It is also true that even in the provinces in which the union of church and ruling group continued, an occasional church-conscious ecclesiastic like Commissary James Blair fought not only the colonial assembly but even the provincial governor. But in spite of such exceptions, church and ruling class were in general intimately associated; and such cleavages as existed did not keep clergy and men of substance from standing shoulder to shoulder when, as in Bacon's Rebellion, the lesser folk threatened the existing order.

The clergy, anxious to promote such learning as was necessary to advance God's kingdom, appealed to planters and merchants to support the educational work of the church as equally beneficial to them. "As contempt of Religion and the Laws is a sure mark of a declining Nation; so new Colonies and Societies of Men must soon fall to pieces, and dwindle to nothing, unless their Governours and Magistrates interpose, to season betimes the Minds of such new people with a sense of Religion, and with good and vertuous Principles," was the warning of Doctor Thomas Bray, the most energetic spirit in the Anglican Society for the Propagation of the Gospel in Foreign Parts.[1]

[1] Thomas Bray, "Apostolick Charity, Its Nature and Excellence Consider'd, etc.," in *Rev. Thomas Bray: His Life and Selected Works Relating to Maryland,* ed. by Bernard C. Steiner (Maryland Historical Society, Fund Publication No. 37, Baltimore, 1901), p. 78.

Doctor William Smith, an earnest worker for education and the church, later appealed for funds with which to educate the Germans of Pennsylvania on the ground that "without education it is impossible to preserve the spirit of commerce. . . . Liberty is the most dangerous of all weapons, in the hands of those who know not the use and value of it. . . . In a word, commerce and riches are the offspring of industry and an unprecarious property; but these depend on virtue and liberty, which again depend on knowledge and religion."[2] He believed that the English language, together with writing, something of figures, and a short system of religious and civil truths and duties, taught by the method of the catechism, was all the education necessary to secure "the people" in the needed virtues; the less necessary branches of literature should have quarterly fees laid upon them to prevent the vulgar from spending more time upon them than was necessary.[3]

In the early Massachusetts and Connecticut colonies, where gentlemen shared authority with the clergy in the theocratic governments, those entitled to be called "Mister" were particularly ready to support the clerically inspired schools, including Harvard College. Quite naturally they saw much in the argument that to insure the obedience of goodmen, goodwives, and servants, these must be able to read the capital laws on which rested the rule of clergy and gentlemen. But in the other colonies also leading people recognized the value of a knowledge of laws and of civic and moral duties, such as was instilled by the essentially religious instruction. Whether members of the theocracy of New England, the Dutch Company of New Netherlands, or the royal government of the

---

[2] James P. Wickersham, *A History of Education in Pennsylvania, Private and Public, Elementary and Higher* (Lancaster, Pa., 1886), p. 66.
[3] *Ibid.*, p. 67.

Carolinas, rulers esteemed the services of religion and of education.[4]

Moreover, the frequent requirement that servants as well as children should be instructed in the elements of religious knowledge, especially where placed beside the provision for punishment of the unruly, makes it appear likely that persons of substance believed servants less prone to give trouble when imbued with the moral principles of Christianity through schooling in the Bible and the catechism.[5] If such instruction could make the restless, wretched, and often well-nigh unmanageable underlings more temperate, more industrious, more virtuous, in short, more content with their station, it had a tangible and immediate as well as an eternal value. To planters who hesitated to teach their Negro slaves the elements of Christianity the bishop of London gave the assurance that its principles did not jeopardize outward bondage. Indeed, "so far is Christianity from discharging Men from the Duties of the Station and Condition in which it found them, that it lays them under stronger Obligations to perform those Duties with the greatest Diligence and Fidelity, not only from the Fear of Men, but from a sense of Duty to God, and the Belief and Expectation of a future Account."[6]

Another circumstance that throws light on the support given by the privileged secular class to clerically controlled education is the fact that this education included some specific features tending to promote the prosperity of planters and merchants.

[4] Elsie W. Clews, *Educational Legislation and Administration of the Colonial Governments* (Columbia University Contributions to Philosophy, Psychology, and Education, Vol. VI, Nos. 1–4, New York, May, 1899), pp. 200, 480–85.

[5] *Ibid.*, p. 223; Marcus W. Jernegan, *Laboring and Dependent Classes in Colonial America, 1607–1783* (Chicago, 1931), pp. 92, 109–10, 148.

[6] David Humphreys, *An Historical Account of the Incorporated Society for the Propagation of the Gospel in Foreign Parts. Containing their Foundation, Proceedings, and the Success of their Missionaries in the British Colonies, to the Year 1728* (London, 1730), p. 266.

Some of the very laws which in New England provided for schools as a safeguard against "the fiery Darts of Satan" also obliged parents to train their children in useful trades lest, by becoming paupers, they should become burdens to the well-to-do of the community. The libraries that good Doctor Bray labored so untiringly to build up contained books of practical knowledge on such matters as agriculture, gardening, and the like, to aid men "through the Mazes and Labyrinths of this World," to rest and happiness in the other.[7] The Society for the Propagation of the Gospel in Foreign Parts made a point, in much of its educational work in the eighteenth century, of offering a training that would promote the economic usefulness of child apprentices. They were taught not only honesty and respect toward their superiors, but the art of writing a plain hand in order that they might be usefully employed and, in many instances, enough arithmetic to enable them to cast accounts.[8]

Even after the dissolution of the alliance between clergy and higher provincial authorities in certain colonies, education, remaining largely under the control of the dominant church, continued to serve the interests of secular authorities and the more important persons in the community. Thus in many of the Dutch villages of New York under the English rule, even up to the Revolution, the Reformed Dutch Church and the Dutch school were supported and controlled by the local gentry.[9] During the Leisler Rebellion in New York, 1689–91,

[7] Thomas Bray, "An Essay Toward Promoting All Necessary and Useful Knowledge both Divine and Human, etc.," in *Rev. Thomas Bray: His Life and Selected Works*, p. 53.

[8] William Webb Kemp, *The Support of Schools in Colonial New York by the Society for the Propagation of the Gospel in Foreign Parts* (Teachers College, Columbia University, Contributions to Education, No. 56, New York, 1913), p. 58.

[9] William H. Kilpatrick, *The Dutch Schools of New Netherland and Colonial New York* (United States Bureau of Education, Bulletin No. 12, 1912), p. 18.

a movement that provoked the fears and vindictive anger of the governing aristocracy, one village schoolmaster who supported the cause of the people was ousted from his position by the minister and church council, while another who espoused the side of the conservatives was sustained in office by the local minister and justice of the peace, backed by an order from the governor, despite the efforts of the townspeople to remove him.[10]

In 1686 Edward Randolph, who with great difficulty was trying to force New England taxpayers to abide by the decrees of the Board of Trade and thereby replenish British coffers, testified to the service which the clerically controlled schools had rendered the colonial ruling class. Urging the need of undermining the resistance of the local aristocracy to British authority, he warned the home government that "till there be provision made to rectifye the youth of this country, there is noe hopes that this people will prove loyall."[11] Randolph implied that where Puritan schoolmasters were indoctrinating the young with loyalty to the local governing entente of clergy and gentlemen, royalist teachers could inculcate good imperialistic doctrines.

With the rise of the new and more worldly commercial aristocracy and with the challenge of Puritan control by the Andros regime and by the extension of suffrage to non-church members under the new charter of 1691, clerical predominance in New England was shaken. Cotton Mather, in lamenting the passing of the good old times when the Puritan parsons and church members had things their own way, made it quite clear that the school had been an instrument for maintaining the pre-eminence of the godly and regarded its decline as a major

[10] *Ibid.*, pp. 194–95, 210.
[11] *The Hutchinson Papers* (The Prince Society Publications, Albany, N. Y., 1865), Vol. II, p. 295.

cause of all the black and sad omens that descended on New England.[12] Jonathan Edwards, fiery divine who wished to recall men to the stern Puritan faith of their fathers, proposed that for the furthering of the ends sought by the leaders of the Great Awakening, schools be endowed in poor towns and villages in order not only "to bring up children in common learning," but also to promote their conviction and conversion, and their training in "vital piety."[13] Yet the close relation between church and state in New England and the grip of the Puritan clergy upon the schools were by no means broken by the end of the seventeenth century. In Connecticut, where the conservative clergy longest retained power in secular affairs, a law was enacted in 1742, during the revivals, to prohibit the educational work of the challenging "New Lights." It stated that "the erecting of any other schools, which are not under the establishment and inspection aforesaid, may tend to train up youth in ill principles and practices, and introduce such disorders as may be of fatal consequence to the public peace and weal of this Colony."[14]

In colonies where the alliance between church and state had never been so firmly cemented, education in the hands of the various religious sects was used as a strategic weapon for increasing political power or preserving the group from the encroachment of hostile practices and principles. This use is well illustrated in Pennsylvania during the eighteenth century. There the Quakers, surrounded by peoples of differing

[12] Cotton Mather, *Magnalia Christi Americana* (Hartford, 1820), Vol. I, p. 499.
[13] *The Works of President Edwards* (New York, 1843), Vol. III, p. 416.
[14] Clews, *op. cit.*, p. 106. For the relation between church and state in Massachusetts during the first half of the eighteenth century see Susan Martha Reed, *Church and State in Massachusetts 1691-1740* (University of Illinois Studies in the Social Sciences, Vol. III, No. 4, Dec., 1914). For the effect of the administration of Andros upon the schools see Viola F. Barnes, *The Dominion of New England* (New Haven, 1923), pp. 131-32.

customs and practices, were concerned that their own children should be provided with schools where Quaker belief and conduct would be taught them. Finding their political supremacy severely contested, they looked with fear upon efforts of the royalist clergyman and college provost, William Smith, to capture the support of the non-resisting German settlers for the war party by establishing schools among them under the auspices of the Society for Propagating Christian Knowledge among the Germans in America.[15]

If the clergy sought and won the support of other interests in their educational work, and used the schools to cement their alliance with the ruling class, they kept the control of these institutions pretty much in their own hands, at least during the seventeenth century, and even in the eighteenth only partially surrendered their influence. In 1688 an order was issued in Virginia warning all schoolmasters to appear at the next meeting of the General Court to present testimonials of their competency and proof "that they were upright and sober in their lives, and conformable in their religious opinions to the doctrines of the Church of England."[16] A similar law was passed in 1654 by the General Court of Massachusetts Bay, which charged the officers of the college and the selectmen of the several towns "not to admit or suffer any such to be continued in the office or place of teaching, educating or instructing of youth or children in the college or schools,

[15] Thomas Woody, *Early Quaker Education in Pennsylvania* (Teachers College, Columbia University, Contributions to Education, No. 105, New York, 1920), pp. 21–23; Wickersham, *op. cit.,* pp. 85, 73, 63–64. For the schools of other groups, see David Murray, *History of Education in New Jersey* (United States Bureau of Education, Circular of Information, No. 1, 1899), p. 11; Wickersham, *op. cit.,* p. 17; Stephen B. Weeks, *History of Public School Education in Delaware* (Department of the Interior, Bureau of Education, Bulletin No. 18, 1917), p. 11.

[16] Philip Alexander Bruce, *Institutional History of Virginia in the Seventeenth Century* (New York, 1910), Vol. I, p. 334.

that have manifested themselves unsound in the faith, or scandalous in their lives, and not giving due satisfaction according to the rules of Christ."[17] Teachers in New England were in general required throughout the eighteenth century to secure clerical approval before assuming their functions,[18] and there is little evidence to suggest that this was not the case elsewhere. However lacking in piety and the true spirit of religion tutors in the planting families and teachers in the "old field schools" of Virginia may have been, they probably conformed outwardly to the tenets of the established church.

Indeed, it is not too much to say that religious indoctrination, Calvinistic, Anglican, or Catholic, continued to be the practice throughout the colonial period. When Ezekiel Cheever died in 1708 after having schooled New England's sons for seventy years, Cotton Mather eulogized him in these words: "He so constantly *Pray'd* with us every *Day,* and Catechis'd us every *Week,* and let fall such Holy *Counsels* upon us; He took so many Occasions, to make *Speeches* unto us, that should make us Afraid of Sin, and of incurring the fearful Judgments of God by Sin; That I do propose him for *Imitation*."[19] Christopher Dock, a Mennonite teacher in Pennsylvania for almost fifty years, imbued his pupils with the tenets of his faith and composed a teaching manual strongly religious in spirit.[20] William Huddleson, who spent half his life in New York City in the service of the Society for the Propagation of the Gospel in Foreign Parts, faithfully taught the tenets of

17 Walter Herbert Small, *Early New England Schools* (Boston, 1914), pp. 90–91.

18 *Ibid.*, pp. 91 *et seq.*

19 "Cotton Mather's Tribute to Ezekiel Cheever," *Old South Leaflets,* Vol. VIII, No. 177, p. 4.

20 This manual is to be found in Martin G. Brumbaugh, *The Life and Works of Christopher Dock, America's Pioneer Writer on Education* (Philadelphia and London, 1908).

the Anglican Church, as did other teachers of the Society, while Jesuits and Ursulines in their scattered convent schools instructed the young in the doctrines of Roman Catholicism.[21] From the Reverend William Tennent's "log college," founded about 1726 in New Jersey, young men, trained for the evangelical preaching of Presbyterianism, went forth with enthusiasm for both education and religion.[22] Down to the Revolution teaching materials in all schools continued to be of a strongly religious and sectarian temper.[23]

Even the growing secularization of life, apparent in the seventeenth century and greatly furthered in the eighteenth by the rise of a new commercial class and the political discussions occasioned by the struggles with England, only partly modified the religious character of the schools. Some of the skepticism which captured Yale students at the end of the eighteenth century must indeed have corrupted the faith of the schoolmasters, who without difficulty could obtain and read Tom Paine's *Age of Reason*. Doubtless there was some basis in fact for President Timothy Dwight's hysterical fear of the "atheism" which he, together with other devout Congregationalist divines, attributed to a plot on the part of such old-world Jacobin groups as the Bavarian Illuminati. But this skepticism and worldliness of the Revolutionary period, which evoked so many protests on the part of the pious, was checked by the wave of religious enthusiasm which the revivals of the early eighteen hundreds quickened not only on the frontier but on the seaboard as well.

[21] Kemp, *op. cit.,* p. 83; J. A. Burns, *The Catholic School System in the United States* (New York, 1908), pp. 70 *et seq.*

[22] Archibald Alexander, *Biographical Sketches of the Founder and Principal Alumni of the Log College* (Princeton, N. J., 1845).

[23] For a discussion of the whole subject see A. A. Holtz, *A Study of the Moral and Religious Elements in American Education up to 1800* (Menasha, Wis., 1917).

Although the wave of revivals and religious reaction against deism hardly made their influence felt much before 1800, a number of circumstances in the preceding years must have assured conservatives that the church was still a friend. The New England clergy as a class felt slight sympathy for Daniel Shays, and godliness as well as law and order seemed to be vindicated when his rebellion was routed. It may not have meant that there was anything like an explicit alliance between ruling class and religion when the uncouth frontiersmen of western Pennsylvania were encouraged by their parsons, as well as by Washington's God-fearing bayonet, to pay their whiskey tax and defer to the authority of the commercial lords, nascent industrialists, and other respectable property-owners who had rallied to the support of the Federalists. Too much might be made of the fact that Noah Webster, father of American school texts, abandoned his revolutionary Jacobin principles and his agnosticism at about the same time and became converted to conservative Federalism in politics and to orthodox Calvinism in religion. Yet these considerations suggest that however deistic the propertied class of the Federalist period may have been, it had some reason to regard religion as an ally when onslaughts were made against property. Certainly in New England conservatives could thank the orthodox clergy for railing against Jefferson and his "atheistic" cohorts in the campaign of 1800. Those who feared that the Jeffersonian victory might jeopardize the privileges of the mercantile class could not have been entirely indifferent to the religious awakening which seemed to have been sent by God Himself to counteract the dangerous power of those who had expressed sympathy with the heretical ideas of Tom Paine and the Jacobin revolutionists.

The galvanization of religion was associated with the rise of new economic forces—the development of the frontier, the revitalization of slavery, and the growth of the factory system. There was need for reconciling the evils and hardships wrought by these new forces with the democratic ideals of the revolutionary period which the election of Jefferson seemed to have revived. Such a sect as Unitarianism might seek in some measure to face existent human ills, but in its broad sweep religion was still otherworldly—and a religion which emphasized preparation for another world tended to make the troubles of this life seem less important. Harsh battles with the wilderness were to be fought, and faith in God and zeal for His word would fortify many a pioneer in his desperate struggles on the borderland. Arduous work was to be done in the new textile and boot factories and in the black foundries, and many a hand would find solace in religion, and courage to endure his twelve or more daily hours and his scanty wages. Many a factory owner would unconsciously sense the stabilizing effect of the churches and sincerely feel that he was enriching the spiritual lives of his employees. Henry Barnard observed that men of ample means began "to feel the luxury of doing good, to see that a wise endowment for the relief of suffering, the diffusion of knowledge, . . . and the spread of religious truth is in the best sense of the term a good investment—an investment productive of the greatest amount of the highest good both to the donor and his posterity, and which makes the residue of the property from which it is taken, both more secure and more valuable."[24] In the South many a slaveowner who had more than half accepted the eighteenth century philosophy of doubt would in good faith pay respect to a clergy which made no bones of blessing slavery when the cotton gin made it seem not only profitable but indispensable. While there was not an explicit entente between religion and

[24] *American Journal of Education*, Vol. I (Jan., 1856), p. 203.

the economically dominant class, each drew strength from the other.

Thus it was that, in spite of the decline of the colonial religion which had so long dominated education and in spite of the plain and widespread signs that American life was becoming increasingly secular, religion, energized by an association with new and friendly economic forces, continued to shape much that the schools were doing on the eve of the educational revival of which Mann and Barnard were to be the leaders.[25] When President Monroe took possession of the White House in 1817, many of the colonial laws revealing the religious purpose of education, the pious character of the curriculum and methods of instruction, and ecclesiastical influence in the control of schools, continued to mold the daily routine of pupils and teachers. Even some of the new laws enacted after the Revolution, which had put a premium on civic values, left to the church a large measure of control in the supervision of schools.[26] Not until the middle of the century was the colonial practice abandoned of granting public subsidies to educational institutions more or less controlled by religious groups.

Although Massachusetts forbade sectarian teaching in public schools in 1827, such teaching survived elsewhere until the middle of the century and even later.[27] Prayers and scriptural readings were almost universal. Textbooks continued to inculcate respect for organized religion. The notoriously religious character of the *New England Primer* was, to be sure, less

[25] De Tocqueville during his visit of 1831 was very much impressed by the prevalence of the Christian religion in the United States, which he contrasted with the unbelief in France, and by the universal conviction that religion was indispensable to the maintenance of republican institutions. *Democracy in America* (London, 1889), Vol. I, pp. 307–19.

[26] Samuel Windsor Brown, *The Secularization of American Education* (Teachers College, Columbia University, Contributions to Education, No. 49, New York, 1912), p. 155.

[27] *Ibid.*

marked in the editions appearing after 1800. Soon even these more secular editions, as well as the psalters, testaments, and Bibles which had generally served colonial children in their reading lessons, were being replaced by the new spelling books and readers. But the most popular of these new texts also sought to instill religious principles. As late as 1848, Webster's *Elementary Speller,* of which a million copies were being sold annually, was outspoken in its religious character. Children who studied this famous "blue-back" learned that "God governs the world with infinite wisdom," makes the ground to bring forth fruit for man and beast, and is to be worshipped with prayer on beginning the day and before retiring at night. They were also told that the laws of nature are sustained "by the immediate presence and agency of God," and that hence they were never to complain of unavoidable calamities. Further, they were taught that the immortality of the soul had been rarely disputed; that the Scriptures were to be examined "daily and carefully"; that pastors did not like to see vacant seats in church, and that the devil is the great adversary of man. "We are apt to live forgetful of our continual dependence on God," and it should never be forgotten that it is a solemn thing to die and appear before Him for judgment.[28]

Other schoolbooks were likewise vehicles for religious indoctrination. Jonathan Fisher's *The Youth's Primer* (Bluehill, Maine, 1817) illustrated the letter "Y" with

> Take ye my Yoke
> So Jesus spoke
> Borne with delight
> 'Tis easy quite.

This book drilled into its readers not only orthodox belief

[28] Noah Webster, *The Elementary Spelling Book* (New York, 1848), *passim.*

but a fatalistic readiness to accept human suffering without complaint.[29] Caleb Bingham's *The Columbian Orator,* more secular than many texts by reason of the Jeffersonian principles of its compiler, included descriptions of the creation of the world, Christ's crucifixion, and other religious pieces such as Dwight's "On the General Judgment Day," More's "David and Goliath," and Milton's "Christ Triumphant over the Apostate Angels."

Nor was it in the school texts alone that religious feeling and teachings survived even long after Mann and Barnard had begun their work. The educational periodicals, particularly the *Academician* (1818–1820), the *American Journal of Education* (1826–1830), and the *American Annals of Education and Instruction* (1831–1839), paid their respects to the importance of the moral and religious elements in education; and Barnard's *Journal* paid no less tribute.[30] One of the first manuals for teacher training, Hall's *Lectures* (1829), laid down the judgment that whoever "regards it as a matter of indifference, whether his children can read the sacred Scriptures understandingly or not, whether they form their moral taste from the writings of inspired men or heathen philosophers, must be considered as not realizing his own moral accountability."[31]

The founders of the Western Institute and College, which profoundly influenced education in the Ohio Valley in the thirties, spared no pains to denounce the ideas of Voltaire, Volney, and Diderot, whose "licentious books" were considered to have brought on the Revolution in France and made of that country "one vast charnel house." No nation can become and remain free, said one contributor to the transactions of

[29] Clifton Johnson, *Old-Time Schools and Schoolbooks* (New York, 1904), p. 95.

[30] *American Journal of Education,* Vol. I (Jan., 1856), p. 139.

[31] Arthur D. Wright and George E. Gardner, *Hall's Lectures on School Keeping* (Hanover, N. H., 1829), p. 53.

the Institute, unless its people is trained in "a sound, Christian education."[32] Another educational leader in the West, B. P. Aydelott, maintained that "the Christianity of the Bible is the salvation of our country" and must be taught in the schools if pride, prejudice, selfishness, and worst of all socialism and Fourierism are not to triumph.[33] The first essential of a sound system of public education, remarked Caleb Mills, the father of Indiana's schools, is that its moral basis be the word of God.[34] In addressing a group of Ohio teachers William H. McGuffey, compiler of the famous "Readers," urged his audience not to incur the charge of being enemies of their country by teaching "the crude notions and revolutionary principles of modern infidelity," inasmuch as Christianity was the religion of our land and the bulwark of our peculiar institutions.[35]

Protestantism, dominant by inheritance from our colonial past, and reinforced by an alliance with new economic and social interests, was not the only form of Christianity to strengthen religion as a force in the thought and feeling of the American people and as an influence on their schools. When the great migration of Catholics from Ireland and the Continent began in the thirties, both an ecclesiastical hierarchy and an embryonic parochial school system capable of indefinite expansion were already being organized. Although Protestants and Catholics were to come into bitter conflict, and although parochial education was to complicate the problem of establishing free public schools, the growth of Catholicism none

[32] *Transactions of the Western Literary Institute and College of Teachers,* 1837, pp. 39, 59.

[33] B. P. Aydelott, *Our Country's Evils and Their Remedy* (Cincinnati, 1843), pp. iv–v, vi. Aydelott was an Episcopalian minister living in Cincinnati.

[34] *Third Annual Report of the Superintendent of Public Instruction for the State of Indiana* (1855), pp. 13–14.

[35] Wm. H. McGuffey, "On the Duties of Teachers and Parents," *Transactions of the Western Literary Institute and College of Teachers* (1835), p. 138.

the less counteracted in part the new secularizing tendencies. Catholicism, no less than Protestantism, gave support to the new industrial, commercial, and planting interests which were competing for the control of the country.

In view of the deep roots of religion in the American past, and in view of its useful functions on a new economic stage, we shall not be surprised to find it playing a very important part in the social thinking of the educational leaders of the pre-Civil War period. We shall see that even those reformers who most sincerely wished to separate the older idea of Christian charity from that of public schools were unable to disentangle the two strands which had been woven together so closely. We shall see that the great desire for moral and religious education, the controversy over the reading of the Bible in the schools, the problem of whether sectarian or non-sectarian religion should be taught, were in part a protest against competing secular tendencies in American life; and that the vigor of the secular protest is to be understood in relation to the renewed vitality which religion itself enjoyed. We shall see, too, that as in the colonial period, there was a fairly general conviction that a chief aim of schooling is to provide the necessary basis of instruction in religion. No great educational leader before the Civil War would have denied that intellectual education was subordinate to religious values. None would tolerate any non-Christian beliefs in the schools.

Moreover, this Christian spirit in education, with its insistence on the religious and the moral, continued to be directed to the upholding of "established institutions." Educational leaders, almost in the same breath, talked of religion, morals, and the preservation of American institutions. Doubtless many who thus associated these words were not conscious of the fact that they were thereby throwing their weight on the side of duly constituted authority, the dominant economic and political organization of society. They were certainly in most cases unaware that by so doing they were in reality taking sides against the underprivileged. As individuals their intentions were humane and sincere, but they belonged to or were allied with a controlling class which, less obviously but no less certainly than in the colonial period, utilized religion to serve its ends.

II

The class society, which, with religion, molded the character of colonial education, also proved to have remarkable survival power, even though it was materially modified by the democratic forces of the Revolution and the frontier. There were two distinct schemes of education in the colonies, though these overlapped in certain places and at certain times. But it is in general true to say that one scheme of education served the gentle and well-to-do folk—the merchants, planters, clergy, and lawyers; and that the other served the common people. For the most part children of the better classes began their education, if they lived in the South, with private tutors or in one of the endowed "free schools," though they might occasionally attend one of the "old field schools" in which perhaps children of the poorer folk might also be learning the elementary branches. New England, with its town schools required by law and often maintained, at least in part, by general taxation, established a precedent for the free school of the nineteenth century. But in colonial times, many children of the better-off learned their first lessons in private dame schools. They sometimes attended the town schools for reading and writing together with poorer children; but the frequent practice of levying charges upon the parents, which the town paid for the children of the poor, prevented real equality in the school. Private schools, which always existed alongside the writing schools, came to be more numerous after the Revolution when New England public schools were at their lowest ebb.[36]

Such overlapping as there might be in the education of the better classes and the poorer folk was to be found, however, only on the elementary level. The New England grammar or "Latin" schools were never popular institutions; they were "conceived, supported, and perpetuated by the few."[37] When they declined toward the end of the colonial period, their place was taken by private academies in which the ancient and modern languages continued to be taught as the badge of culture and social status. As for the colleges, they were far removed indeed from the lower classes. They were attended by the sons of the professional, merchant, and planting classes, and had the effect of perpetuating class distinctions as well as preparing favored youth for the church or the semi-cultured life of the great plantations.

But the class character of colonial education appears in its starkest outlines when we consider the provisions made for orphans, the offspring of indentured servants, and the children of the very poor. These were bound out as apprentices, sometimes when they were infants in arms, sometimes when four or five years old. The purpose of the apprenticeship system, whether voluntary or forced, was primarily economic, although humanitarian, educational, and religious motives were not alien to it.[38] Cheap labor was scarce throughout the colonial period, and the apprenticeship system provided the better established classes with help at an almost negligible cost. More-

---

[36] Small, *op. cit.*, pp. 311 *et seq.*   [37] *Ibid.*, p. 31.
[38] Jernegan, *op. cit.*, pp. 170–71; R. F. Seybolt, *Apprenticeship and Apprenticeship Education in Colonial New England and New York* (Teachers College, Columbia University, Contributions to Education, No. 85, New York, 1917), *passim.*

over, it also furnished skilled artisans, a class greatly needed in a new society. It was further designed to prevent the rise and growth of a "Barberous, Rude or Stubborn" class of servants that would prove "Pests enstead of Blessings to the Country"[39] and particularly to free the well-to-do from the burden of pauper relief.

As regards educational features, the indentures provided that masters, in addition to teaching apprentices an "honest calling profitable to the Publick," should see that they were taught "to Reade & Rite" and sometimes to "Cypher and Cast Accounts," as well as the principles of Christianity.[40] Day and evening schools were kept for this purpose, the master paying a fee for the tuition of his apprentice if he himself were unable to teach the required subjects. In the southern and middle colonies these schools were maintained, for the most part, by philanthropic societies or foundations, generally sponsored by the established church or by a religious sect. In New England the town itself frequently provided such schools.

But this elementary education, useful though it was to its recipients, was marked by its class character: it was charity education for the poor who were unable to take care of themselves. In a variety of ways it served to support the existing order. The ability to read was not only necessary to lead a religious life, but to pursue certain humble and useful callings, and to know the "capital laws" of the land, which laid down the penalties for runaway servant apprentices and otherwise sanctioned the arrangement of classes and the existing inequalities of wealth. Moreover, the apprentices were taught to respect their superiors and the sons of their superiors who were conning Latin verbs and acquiring the other requisites of the

[39] Jernegan, *op. cit.*, p. 98.
[40] Seybolt, *op. cit.*, p. 95, for the compulsory character of the educational features.

culture and polish that characterized the class to which they
belonged. Though masters might sincerely cherish the well-
being of their apprentices, and though these dependents might
through the training they received lead a more decent life and
in some cases advance with less difficulty into the privileged
group, on the whole the system, in its educational as well as
in its economic aspects, tended to perpetuate the class society
of which it was the product.

The Revolution, by abolishing primogeniture and entail, by
separating church and state in several states,[41] by breaking up
some of the great landed estates in still others, and by arousing
democratic enthusiasm for the "rights of man," had, of course,
some of the earmarks of a social revolution. The frontier, too,
was contributing substantially to a liberalization of suffrage, an
equalization of opportunity, and a more democratic outlook
everywhere. But as if both the Revolution and the pushing
back of the line of settlement required so much energy that
little was left for other public enterprises, elementary education slumped and only very faintly responded to the ideas of
'76. Had the more radical elements dominated during the
formative years of the new republic, it is possible that the
caste character of the schools might have been undermined, at
least to some extent. But the conservatives stabilized their privileges and built the state, and although educational theory did
reflect the fervor of our own and the French Revolution, school
practice did not substantially change its class character.

In some respects, it must be confessed, the situation for the
common people was, by the eighteen-twenties, perhaps even

[41] In Virginia, at least, confiscated church glebes were pooled into a "literary" fund for the promotion of the education of the poor. William A. Maddox, *The Free School Idea in Virginia before the Civil War* (Teachers College, Columbia University, Contributions to Education, No. 93, New York,
1918), p. 43.

worse, so far as educational opportunity went, than in the colonial period. This was because, with the rise of the factory system in the Northeast and the extension of slavery in the South, the old apprenticeship system declined.[42] Although the book education it provided had been meager and although it bore the stigma of pauperism, still it did offer the more gifted and enterprising apprentices a tool by which their social and economic status might be bettered. It is true that, with the decline of the apprenticeship system, new educational substitutes were found in the infant and the Lancastrian schools, the cheapness and economy of which were praised by De Witt Clinton, governor of New York, and especially in the Sunday schools, which were at first designed primarily to afford secular instruction to the children of those too poor to attend other schools. These new institutions, however, bore the stigma of pauper and class education quite as much as those in which colonial apprentices had learned to read the religious writings and capital laws which made clear the duties of their station.[43]

Numerous illustrations of the survival of the colonial class system of education, diluted in some respects and modified in others, can be found in the early state laws and educational practices. As late as 1834 whatever public aid was given to elementary education in Pennsylvania was confined to the poor, many of whom refused to accept it because to do so was to advertise their pauperism. So inadequate was the system that at least 100,000 voters in that state were unable to read.[44] In

[42] Paul Douglas, *American Apprenticeship and Industrial Education* (Studies in History, Economics and Public Law, Vol. XCV, No. 2, Columbia University, New York, 1921), p. 54.

[43] In Virginia, and perhaps elsewhere, the Sunday schools may have promoted indirectly the political ideal of common schools by bringing together rich and poor in the name of religion. Maddox, *op. cit.*, pp. 31, 40.

[44] *Report of the Joint Committee of the Two Houses of the Pennsylvania Legislature on the Subject of a System of General Education* (Harrisburg, 1834).

1805.New York City possessed practically nothing but parochial and private schools, and as late as 1828 more than 24,000 children between the ages of five and fifteen were in no school of any description.[45] The situation was even worse in Delaware,[46] New Jersey,[47] and Maryland.[48]

In Virginia the handful of free school foundations, so far as they survived the Revolution, hardly touched the masses, and the same was true, with few exceptions, of the old field schools. Jefferson's Bill for the More General Diffusion of Knowledge, which would have eradicated the dual, parallel systems for the education of the rich and poor, had failed of adoption.[49] The act of 1818 made primary education a gift to the destitute, "to those willing to accept the brand of pauperism in a social system based on wealth and caste."[50] The planting aristocracy, alone fully aware of its needs, had obtained in the university all it wanted. In other southern states, and even across the Appalachians, conditions were not substantially different. Indiana, having created Vincennes University in 1807, waited until 1824 before enacting a general school law. It was not until 1852, 1853, and 1855 that Indiana, Ohio, and Illinois made their public schools free of all tuition.

The class character of education was easily discernible in New York and even in New England where the habit of paying taxes for the support of public schools had early been formed.[51] In the eighteen-twenties children of the better-to-do classes were still beginning their education in private dame

[45] Frank Tracy Carlton, *Economic Influences upon Educational Progress in the United States, 1820–1850* (Bulletin of the University of Wisconsin, No. 221, Madison, May, 1908), p. 98.

[46] Weeks, *Education in Delaware,* pp. 26, 160–61.

[47] Murray, *Education in New Jersey,* p. 29.

[48] Maddox, *op. cit.,* p. 6.

[49] Roy J. Honeywell, *Educational Work of Thomas Jefferson* (Harvard Studies in Education, No. 16, Cambridge, 1931), pp. 14 *et seq.*

[50] Maddox, *op. cit.,* p. 90.   [51] Carlton, *op. cit.,* p. 89.

schools.[52] They continued it in private academies which Samuel Adams, as early as 1795, had feared would detract from the value of the common school and lead to class distinctions between rich and poor.[53] In 1843 James Henry, a New York educator, spoke of the private schools and "misnamed academies" as places where favorites of fortune, believing themselves "of nobler origin and of higher race than the common masses of humanity," sent their offspring, while "equally deserving children of honest manual labor" were sent to common schools, both children and schools "neglected and uncared for."[54]

The neglect of common schools in the pre-Civil War period was indeed striking. In 1837 Barnard estimated that 10,000 children of the rich and educated in Connecticut were receiving good instruction in private schools at an expense greater than that appropriated for the other 60,000 or 70,000 in the state.[55] When Mann began his educational labors in Massachusetts during the same year, he found the disproportionate expenditure for private schooling almost as great. Moreover, a large proportion of the children of that state were receiving no schooling at all, or a mere smattering.[56] Some thousand districts, or one-third of all, did not even possess schoolhouses. In Connecticut, as late as 1867, a member of the state board of education declared that "able men among us" still held that the state had no right to educate any but paupers. In that year "hundreds of thousands" of children in Henry

[52] For an interesting description of a Boston dame school in 1825 see Small, *op. cit.*, p. 185.

[53] George H. Martin, *The Evolution of the Massachusetts Public School System; a Historical Sketch* (New York, 1894), p. 128.

[54] James Henry, *An Address upon Education in the Common Schools* (Albany, 1843), p. 24. Delivered at Cooperstown, Sept. 21, and repeated by request at Johnstown, Oct. 17, 1843.

[55] *American Journal of Education*, Vol. V, p. 153.

[56] "The First Annual Report of the Secretary of the Board of Education," in *The Common School Journal*, Vol. I (1839), pp. 262–63, 253–54.

Barnard's state were kept away from school by the degrading practice of the rate bill, which marked as paupers children whose parents were unable to pay tuition charges.[57] Only one-half of the school children of New England were given free education in 1840, one-seventh of those in the Middle States, and one-sixth of those in the West.[58]

Differences in curricula distinguished private schools from those for the children of common men. While spelling, writing, and reading were taught in every elementary school, with arithmetic, grammar, and geography beginning by 1820 to find a place, more socially and professionally useful subjects, as well as the "frills," were to be found chiefly in private institutions. Composition, history, rhetoric, and in some cases natural philosophy, surveying, bookkeeping, and oratory, the last indispensable for a political career, were available in many of the select institutions. For those favored youth of the middle class who attended the private academies there were the ancient and modern languages, which still, as in colonial times, set one off from the common herd. No wonder that the *Old Farmer's Almanac* advised its readers not to send their children to the academy, an inappropriate place for a farmer's lad! "Fun, frolick, and filigree are too much practiced at the academies for the benefit of the farmer's boy."[59] At about the same time the conservative and pious Timothy Dwight excoriated the fashionable and useless as well as "irreligious" education meted out to upper-class girls.[60]

There was less difference in the social status of the teachers of

[57] Edgar W. Knight, *Public Education in the United States* (Boston, 1929), p. 156.

[58] *Statistical View of the United States; A Compendium of the Seventh Census, 1850* (Washington, 1854), pp. 150–51.

[59] G. L. Kittredge, *The Old Farmer and His Almanac* (Cambridge, 1924), pp. 228–29. The date is 1808.

[60] Timothy Dwight, *Travels in New England and New York* (New Haven, 1821), Vol. I, Letter XLVIII, pp. 514–18.

the moneyed people and the poor. While favored daughters of planters and merchants often received an "elegant" education from the cultured Ursulines and aristocratic ladies of the Sacred Heart, and while sons of Boston gentlemen learned their Latin from accomplished and esteemed teachers, still children of the upper classes as well as those of the more humble ranks were not infrequently taught by men of low social standing. Moreover, just as indentured children had sometimes learned their letters from the Anglican clergy, so pupils in some Lancastrian schools might look up to an accomplished headmaster, although their actual work was under the direction of older pupils. Students at the district schools, whose teachers were commonly regarded as social failures and vagabonds, were sometimes favored by a poor but ambitious young man for whom teaching was but a temporary stepping stone to a more honored career.[61]

Less difference was also to be found in the methods of teaching in the schools for the masses and in those for the favored groups than in the character of the respective curricula. Yet the pedagogy inherited from the colonial period, emphasizing as it did dogmatism, authoritarianism, and memorization,[62] and aiming to impose "good order" by fear and physical brutality, was more suitable to a class society than to a republican one that claimed to be democratic. It is true that a greater degree of spontaneity was to be found in the relatively small number of schools which, after the first decade of the nineteenth century, were influenced by the teachings of Pestalozzi. Protests against the current emphasis on authoritarianism,

[61] Clifton Johnson, *Old-Time Schools and Schoolbooks,* pp. 119 ff.; Elmer Ellsworth Brown, *The Making of Our Middle Schools* (New York, 1903), pp. 110, 250.

[62] Francis Wayland, President of Brown, did not remember "anything approaching an explanation" while in school. James O. Murray, *Francis Wayland* (Boston, 1891), p. 10.

which savored so much of the privileged social order of the past, were to be found in the educational periodicals of the eighteen-twenties. "Reason, the distinguishing attribute of our nature," remarked a writer in the *American Journal of Education* in 1828, "should not be debased by the inculcations of authority, or the deceptions of prejudice and error."[63] After describing the prevalent mechanical character of instruction, a contributor to the *American Annals of Education and Instruction* observed, in 1831, that such instruction had no use other than to make machines. "If it be allowable in any country, it is utterly out of place in one where men are called to *act* in government of themselves, to examine the qualifications and measure of men who are to decide their fate and that of their families. He that *gives* or *encourages* such instruction as this, is among the most *dangerous enemies of his country,* for he is undermining the very basis of its freedom, and preparing and accustoming men to obey, in blind ignorance, the dictates of those who go before them."[64] Another contributor maintained that "the great object to be kept in view in all our efforts for the instruction and government and education of the young, should be to lead them as early and as rapidly as possible, to *self-instruction, self-government,* and *self-education.*"[65]

While such "progressive" writers, influenced by Pestalozzi,[66] generally included all children in their pleas for a less mechanical pedagogy in which self-direction might play a part, they

[63] *American Journal of Education,* Vol. III (June, 1828), p. 370.

[64] *American Annals of Education and Instruction,* Vol. I (Dec., 1831), p. 577.

[65] *Ibid.,* Vol. II (April 1, 1832), p. 161. James Carter, *Letters to the Hon. Wm. Prescott, LL.D., on the Free Schools of New England* (Boston, 1824), maintained that the triumph of inductive logic was but half complete until it was carried into the subject of education; and that "the object of the school was not so much to give knowledge as to develop the powers of the mind so that it can secure knowledge at a future period," pp. 65, 67.

[66] *Post,* pp. 65–67, 99, 123–24, 143.

would probably have shared the feeling expressed in an article in the *Academician* which held that "the indefinite variety of relations in which men stand to each other, require a corresponding variety of accomplishments, to enable them to fill their respective stations with respectability and satisfaction to themselves, and with advantage to the community to which they belong."[67] In general, the significance of these criticisms of existing pedagogy lay in the fact that they were protests against what was almost a universal practice—a practice inherited from the colonial period and one which, as we have seen, was more suitable to a class society than to a democratic way of life.

While schoolbooks continued to instill into the minds of the young the time-honored belief that learning and knowledge were a panoply whereby mankind might be secured against "the fiery Darts of the Devil," schooling came more and more to be regarded as a necessary means for social and economic advance. Society was more flexible than it had been. The rising middle class, whose values Benjamin Franklin so well symbolized, was associating learning with worldly success and demanding a more utilitarian type of knowledge and morals. Aware that there were others more privileged than they, the middle class and even the very poor nevertheless believed in the possibility of securing fame and wealth, and looked upon knowledge as a means to that end rather than as the path to Heaven. Advertisements indicate that by the eighteenth century evening schools—the "business colleges" of the colonial period—were teaching practical mathematics, bookkeeping, and such modern languages as foreign commerce required.[68]

[67] The *Academician*, Vol. I (June 18, 1818), p. 98.
[68] R. F. Seybolt, *The Evening School in Colonial America* (University of Illinois, Bureau of Educational Research, Bulletin 24), pp. 12, 28–29, 31, 39, 55.

Schoolbooks also very clearly reflect these utilitarian morals and middle-class aspirations. Even *The New England Primer,* which had furnished endless "spiritual Milk for Babes," held up a more worldly motive for learning letters:

> "He who ne'er learns his ABC
> Forever will a blockhead be.
> But he who learns his letters fair,
> Shall have a coach to take the air."[69]

"Reading" books of the eighteen-twenties were including stories of poor boys who by honesty and industry "made good" and won respectability, prominence, and wealth. In John Franklin Jones's *Analytical Spelling Book* (New York, 1823) we have in the story of Frank Lucas a forerunner of the Alger legend. The kind benefactor who rewards the deserving poor lad is likewise the theme of one of the sketches in Worcester's *A Second Book for Reading and Spelling.*[70]

The ubiquitous Webster's *Elementary Spelling Book,* of which over twenty million copies were sold between 1782 and 1847, with many used over and over again—this speller translated into terse sentences a social philosophy appropriate to a system which attached great value to acquiescence on the part of the poor in their poverty and at the same time promised ultimate success to those who would practice the virtues of frugality, industry, and submissiveness to moral teachings and to God's will. This philosophy held that if there were no pain, misery, misfortune, or danger, then patience, humanity, fortitude, and prudence would be but empty names and that consequently man's duty is patient submission "to the evils of life and calm acquiescence in the disposition of divine provi-

---

[69] Paul Leicester Ford, ed., *The New England Primer* (New York, 1899), p. 101.
[70] Johnson, *op. cit.,* pp. 215–18, 244–45.

dence which suffers no more evils to take place in the system than are necessary to produce the greatest possible good."[71]

Webster's social philosophy included the astute doctrine that real power always consists in property, and held that "the laborious and saving, who are generally the best citizens, will possess each his share of property and power."[72] His Federalist sympathies were evident in his indignation at the refusal of Shays's followers to pay their taxes; and he laid down the illuminating doctrine that "the best way to redress grievances is for every man, when he gets a sixpence, instead of purchasing a pint of Rum or two ounces of tea, to deposit his pence in a desk, till he has accumulated enough to answer to calls of the Collector."[73] Although an early friend of antislavery, by 1820 Noah Webster had so modified his views that he regarded discussion of so controversial an issue inexpedient, disturbing to peace and order, and inimical to "the harmony of society." He even fortified his position by recalling that Christ had not authorized his disciples to "persevere in preaching, in opposition to *public sentiment.*"[74]

With such views it is not surprising to find in the speller maxims inculcating respect for property rights and honest labor, the virtues of poverty, and contentment with one's lot, as well as an aristocratic conception of charity. Children were told that property was acquired by industry and economy, that only a few were rich enough to keep a coach, and that it was "the meanest of all low tricks to creep into a man's inclosure

[71] Emily E. F. Ford, *Notes on the Life of Noah Webster* (New York, 1912), Vol. I, p. 72. (Webster's Diary, March 13, 1784.)

[72] *Ibid.,* Vol. II, pp. 458–59. "The system of the great Montesquieu will ever be erroneous, till the words property or land in fee simple, are substituted for virtue, through his Spirit of the Laws."

[73] *Ibid.,* Vol. I, p. 118. (Webster to Timothy Pickering, Aug. 10, 1786.)

[74] *Ibid.,* Vol. II, p. 482. Webster probably has reference to Matthew 10: 16–23.

and take his property." They were also told that modest gains were likely to be more durable than greater ones, that money should be invested rather than hoarded, that if a farmer were only wise he could contrive by honest labor to procure a good living. They were further taught that charitable societies exhibited "proof of much benevolence," that beggars "would rather beg than work," and that paupers were poor people supported by a public tax. Fragments of time were not to be wasted and exact accounts were to be kept. There was a warning note in the statement that men often toiled all their lives to get property which their children squandered and wasted. Temperance was inculcated by a dozen or more maxims, one of which contended that there was "a near intimacy between drunkenness, poverty, and ruin." Other half-truths, equally fitting to a society in which some had more and others less, were read and re-read by American youth who learned their letters from the old "blue-back."

III

A brief examination of the educational ideas of Benjamin Franklin and Thomas Jefferson and the pretentious schemes of ardent and enlightened nationalists will illustrate the practical limitations of even the more democratic educational thought of the late eighteenth and early nineteenth centuries, when liberalism, the principles of '76, and the influence of the back country were challenging the established order. Both Franklin and Jefferson had slight sympathy with ecclesiastical sanctions, authoritarianism, privilege, and aristocracy; both advanced educational ideas with social implications that were hostile to much of the religious and class character of existing practice; both were truly prophets and destined to have great influence on American education: and yet both were limited and circumscribed by their class affiliations.

Although as the child of a poor tallow chandler and soap boiler Franklin did not associate with the young sons of Boston's ministers, lawyers, and merchants, he was none the less proud of the fact that Cotton Mather made honorable mention of the substantial and respectable character of some of his kin, and that his forefathers in England had been able to retire comfortably from business after securing a competence.

As a member of the middle class which was pushing ahead, Franklin had slight respect for the exclusive and aristocratic education that prevailed in the colleges. While working as an apprentice-printer he heaped ridicule on Harvard, dominated as it was by wealth, privilege, and "the useless classics," and sharply remarked in his brother's paper, the *New England Courant,* that rich men's sons went to college because they were rich, often found themselves unable to mount "the throne of learning," and got their degrees only because they were rich enough to pay poor students for help.[75] All his life, both in his formal writings on education,[76] and in his private references to it, he showed scant sympathy for the classics, which he thought of as useless tags of theological, aristocratic, and barren learning.

Franklin's own conception of education was pragmatic and utilitarian, and designed to promote the interest of the ambitious middle class. He would not train the young in the frivolous arts and graces, the dead tongues, and all the other empty badges of the aristocratic past; he even cast aside whatever, like music, dancing, and art, possessed mere æsthetic value.

[75] "A Letter on the Temple of Learning," in A. H. Smyth, ed., *The Writings of Benjamin Franklin* (New York, 1907), Vol. II, pp. 9–14.

[76] Professor Thomas Woody has conveniently edited the chief educational writings of Franklin in *Educational Views of Benjamin Franklin* (New York, 1931).

It was his purpose to train youth to "serve the public with honor to themselves, and to their country," and to fit them for successful careers in business. Like Locke, he regarded the formation of useful habits as more important than the mere acquisition of knowledge. The subjects he valued were, therefore, those conducive to success in politics, which the aristocracy could no longer hope to monopolize, and those advantageous in business, a career which the middle class had made its own. Good morals, especially the virtues of temperance, order, industry, and frugality, the usefulness of which his own experience had given evidence; good English, so necessary a distinction between the middle and lower class folk; mathematics, accounts, the history of commerce, natural philosophy, mechanics, the principles of good health, and whatever else was necessary to fit one for business or profession—these were the subjects he valued above all others.[77]

Franklin's devotion to experimental science, and the important place it took in all his educational projects, characterized middle-class utilitarianism. The old order had ruled by authority, inheritance, and tradition; the new middle class would rule by reason, intelligence, and the wealth that was regarded as its just and natural reward. Moreover, the practical applications of science promised to make agriculture, commerce, and industry more profitable, and everyday life more comfortable, an important value for those who had not customarily lived in wealth and ease, and who, however religious, did not underestimate the practical importance of the sojourn here

[77] "Proposals Relating to the Education of Youth in Pennsylvania" (1749), "Constitutions of the Public Academy," Woody, op. cit., pp. 149 et seq. In "A Petition of the Left Hand to those who have Superintendence of Education" (1778) Franklin pleaded for the equal training of both hands and anticipated Froebel's idea of the free industrial training of the hands and the even development of all bodily organs and functions. F. N. Thorpe, Benjamin Franklin and the University of Pennsylvania (Bureau of Education, Circular of Information, No. 2, 1892), p. 155.

below. When it came to fixing a curriculum for the "academy" which with other wealthy men Franklin founded, he had to make concessions to their aristocratic notions concerning the value of the classics. But he himself never modified his belief that the best education was practical and scientific—an education which was the most serviceable one for the children of the middle class. It would enable youth the better to follow the advice

> "Get what you can, and what you get hold,
> 'Tis the stone that will turn all your lead into gold."

Realizing what inadequate educational opportunities existed for the lower ranks of the middle class, Franklin attached great importance to self-education. If he read Locke's treatise on education—and this environmentalist was widely read and influential in America—he must have agreed with him in the contention that while a few men attain excellence by virtue of their own endowments, most people are what they are by reason of the training and discipline which they receive or with which they provide themselves. Franklin's own career had shown what could be done without the aid of school and college. With the help of a few good books and Socratic discussions in self-improvement clubs he had acquired reputation, praise, and honors as a great philosopher and scientist. It was natural for him to glorify the advantages of self-education, especially since by so doing he was able to compensate for some of his shortcomings—his own inability, for example, to feel at home in a French conversation and to write in that language to his distinguished friends.[78]

Firmly believing in self-improvement, he won to its support

---

[78] Thorpe, *op. cit.*, pp. 108–9.

countless Americans who generation after generation read in
his autobiography the convincing story of his own successful
education and perhaps as a consequence were less ready to
support free and universal schooling and a broad conception
of the necessity and usefulness of formal education.[79] Self-
education may have made an unconscious appeal by reason of
the fact that it asked little of wealth in the form of taxes and
endowments, and yet appeared to be sufficiently democratic
to permit boys in the lowest social strata to apply it to themselves. The exceptionally talented ones might, indeed, do so;
and, so far as the privileged were concerned, their own sons,
mediocre as well as gifted, were assured of an education
which would further their advancement and set them apart
from their social inferiors.

Franklin, though an adherent of the enlightened philosophy
of Defoe, Hume, Swift, Fontenelle, Montesquieu, Quesnay,
and Voltaire, and though a "father" of the Revolution, subscribed to the prevalent attitude of the leading people toward
the education of the poor. Far from ever visioning a democratic, state-supported, and universal education for all children, Franklin rested content with the private charitable
institutions characteristic of a class society. Yet he was more
of a humanitarian and democrat than many of his contemporaries. His devotion to the "general welfare" was genuine.
His respect for work, especially for that of skilled mechanics,
had led him to announce, as early as 1729, that labor was the

---

[79] Woodbridge, for one, suggests (*American Annals of Education and Instruction,* Vol. VI, May, 1836, p. 239) that the Poor Richard idea of education
had a restricting and unfortunate influence. Governor Joseph Haslet told the
Delaware legislature in 1813 that a man possessing "the rudiments of education may improve himself by his own assiduity. Some of the greatest characters
have made themselves in this way." Weeks, *Public School Education in Delaware,* p. 22. David C. Cloyd maintains that Franklin did not believe that self-
education was the best type, but merely an adequate one of which all could
avail themselves. *Franklin's Educational Ideal* (Boston, 1902), p. 26.

measure and creator of wealth.[80] He had seen so much of poverty, and his class had historically been so discriminated against, that he sincerely cherished humane sentiments toward the most unfortunate members of society.

Thus, for instance, like the Quakers who probably influenced him, he spoke out against Negro slavery and sympathized with the efforts of such philanthropists as Doctor Bray and Anthony Benezet to provide the blacks with some sort of elementary education. He proposed that each orphan in the charity school he was responsible for founding be paid, on leaving, what he had earned in excess of his keep, rather than have the institution profit from the exploitation of his labor.[81] In short, the general welfare was best promoted by providing the under-privileged with incentives for self-help and self-education in morals—especially in thrift.

The middle class of Franklin's time not only subscribed to the doctrines of humanitarianism and of self-help, and applauded the business virtues and increasing uses of science, but championed nationalism as well. As early as 1753 Franklin proposed what might be called a policy of Americanization through education. Convinced of the political need for emphasis on the teaching of English in the German settlements of Pennsylvania, he even went so far as to issue a warning to the effect that the preservation "of our language and even of our government" was precarious unless English schools were established among German-speaking groups.[82] Thus Franklin conceived of education as an agency of societal control—

---

[80] W. A. Wetzel, *Benjamin Franklin as an Economist* (Johns Hopkins Studies in Historical and Political Science, 13th Series, Vol. IX, Baltimore, 1895), p. 30; Lewis J. Carey, *Franklin's Economic Views* (Garden City, N. Y., 1928), pp. 41–43. For Franklin's final views see Carey, p. 165.

[81] "Hints for Consideration Respecting the Orphan School-Houses of Philadelphia" in Woody, *op. cit.*, p. 238.

[82] Woody, *op. cit.*, pp. 112–15.

specifically, as an instrument to secure the political and cultural supremacy of his own racial group. On the eve of the Revolution he gave evidence of his nationalist conception of education by experimenting with a reformed and more suitably American orthography; and later he encouraged Noah Webster in his plan for strengthening American nationalism through a more thoroughly national type of educatio

Today this all sounds familiar and ordinary. Yet the significance of Franklin's educational and social philosophy would be only partly appreciated if its revolutionary character is not taken into account. The middle class which his thought so well represented was, in mid-eighteenth century America, a revolutionary class: it was creating not only a new economic structure; it was also creating new cultural values which were competing with those inherited from the feudal past. Now that middle-class ideals have so triumphantly molded our civilization, it is easy to forget that at one time they represented change, progress, and revolt against much that the existing order held sacred.

Franklin proved a veritable John the Baptist for Jefferson, whose educational thought was even more characteristic of eighteenth century liberalism than was that of the author of *Poor Richard*. Jefferson's scheme, outlined while he was governor of Virginia in the Bill for the More General Diffusion of Knowledge (1779),[83] bore, at least implicitly, the marks of a class society. Yet the framer of the Declaration of Independence, inspired by hostility to an entrenched aristocracy and by faith in universal education as a necessary instrument of democratic republicanism, advocated a system of schools and higher institutions which went considerably farther than Franklin's ideas toward breaking down class bar-

[83] Paul L. Ford, ed., *The Writings of Thomas Jefferson* (New York, 1892–99), Vol. II, pp. 220–29.

riers in education. For all their shortcomings when measured by twentieth-century concepts of democracy, Jefferson's proposals were in their day truly revolutionary.

Jefferson, it will be remembered, did not believe in the absolutely equal abilities of all men, but rather in an aristocracy based on talent and virtue. His educational scheme consequently provided for recruiting from the masses such individuals as were exceptionally gifted for leadership. He intended, as he put it, to rake from the rubbish such geniuses as would otherwise, for lack of nourishment, be unable to develop their capacities and serve society as trained leaders.

To secure that end there were to be, in the wards into which it was planned to divide Virginia for the purposes of elementary education, local schools open free for three years to all white children, male and female. Each year an overseer was to choose from the approximately ten schools under his charge the boy of greatest promise from among those whose parents were unable to provide further instruction. These chosen boys were to be sent to secondary schools in larger areas. At the end of the year, a third of the least promising of the publicly supported scholars were to be discontinued; and at the end of the second year all were to be sent home except the one of greatest ability. The latter might remain for an additional four years along with the sons of parents who could afford to pay tuition. A selected number of these prize boys were then to attend William and Mary College for three years at public expense. This provision for the selection of talented youths is similar to the plan Condorcet proposed to the French revolutionary government.

Jefferson's quest for genius among the poor was far more democratic than anything that existed then, or was for a long time to exist. At least every poor child was to be offered an elementary schooling in an institution which did not bear the stigma of pauperism; a fraction of the sons of the less-well-to-do might enjoy a secondary education, or part of one; while a very small proportion could aspire to collegiate training. But this scheme was far from democratic. According to even the liberal standards of those days it would have been unthinkable, of course, that Negroes should be included in the plan, or that girls should be offered educational opportunities equal to those of boys. One might, however, expect that such a brilliant radical as Jefferson was would recognize certain other shortcomings. But his intense individualism and devotion to *laissez-faire* theory led him to oppose compulsory school attendance; and many of the most ignorant and lowly might fail to see the advantage of sending their children to school, even though literacy be made a test of franchise. Perhaps the greatest qualification of the democracy of his scheme, however, lay in the fact that it failed to take account of the ability of the wealthy to maintain their status by providing *all* their children with educational advantages, irrespective of their native ability. They could enrich the lives of even the more mediocre of their children by providing instruction more suitable to their talent than that provided the average child of the poor who attended for three years the elementary free school. Considering the lack of knowledge at that time regarding the influence on school performance of very early environmental handicaps, it was hardly to be expected that Jefferson could take account of such factors, though they might well mean that many a poor child would be condemned to inferior training and status for no lack of native ability or fault of his own.

Another evidence of the class character of Jefferson's educational philosophy is to be found in his scale of values, both as regards the character of subject matter taught and the relative importance of higher and elementary instruction. It is somewhat surprising that Jefferson, distrusting as he did the artisan class and pinning his faith to the small farmer folk, still made no special provision for further training of those children who were to enter into the "business of agriculture."[84] It is strange that so much emphasis was put on a purely literary training in the elementary schools, and even, for the most part, in those of the next level,[85] since such training could be of little direct benefit to common folk struggling on the less fertile soils and to frontiersmen with their peculiar problems.

To the extent that Jefferson wished to open the cultural riches of civilization to *all* children and to break down a false educational division between rich and poor, his emphasis on literary subjects was indeed democratic. But in failing to provide for such useful instruction as agriculture, a matter in which he was much concerned, his curriculum was scarcely designed to promote the economic well-being of the common people, on which depended in considerable measure their political influence, their practical intelligence, and their social position. Moreover, the strict division that he made between those who, after passing the elementary years, were to labor and those who were to learn, would prevent all but a very few of the poorer folk from securing a broad cultural education. It is significant too that while Jefferson kept alive for fifty years the ideal of universal elementary education, free to all alike and bearing no stigma of pauperism, and while in theory he regarded schools for the people as more important than a university, yet in actuality he devoted his major efforts, particularly after his retirement to Monticello, to the founding of an essentially exclusive institution of higher learning.

[84] "Letter to Peter Carr, September 7, 1814," in Honeywell, *op. cit.*, p. 223.
[85] *Ibid.*, pp. 10, 38. The utilitarian purpose which Jefferson ascribed to higher education makes a striking contrast to the literary emphasis which was put on the elementary and secondary curricula.

The most telling test of the degree to which Jefferson's educational theory was truly democratic and capable of resisting the aristocratic social system of Virginia lies in its relation to his theory of democracy and to the actually existing facts. A foe of centralization and of bureaucracy, Jefferson believed that participation in and administration of the local free schools by the immediate community would provide the common people with general enlightenment and political training—the instruments necessary for the banishing of the evil spirit of tyranny and oppression. The individual was to develop his capacities by direct participation in government, and in turn government was to be democratized and its democratic character perpetuated. It was Jefferson's way of insuring the direction of government by the governed rather than by the landed aristocracy.

Jefferson is thus the first American to emphasize public education as an instrument for the realization of democracy and for the furthering of social reform. He regarded education as the only certain means of promoting human happiness and the freedom and democracy for which he stood. He also thought of it as the necessary means by which federalism and sectarianism—those two tormenting bugbears—were to be checked. He even regarded his Bill for the More General Diffusion of Knowledge, taken along with the abolition of entail and primogeniture, as a sufficient program for "striking at the root of the landed aristocracy": by nourishing the talented poor, public education was to prepare them "for defeating the competition of wealth and birth for public trusts." It was he who set forth the idea, to be so persistent in American educational thought, that a single system of schools would close the gap between rich and poor.

The faith Jefferson put in democratic education as the means by which democracy was to be realized suggests that of John Dewey. But Dewey was to contend against Jefferson's aristocratic conception of a division of the people into two classes—the vast majority of laborers, whose function required merely an elementary education; and the learned class, made up of the talented poor, trained at public expense, and the wealthy, who retained a share of directive power in matters of state, cultivated their plantations, and appreciated the cultural achievements of the truly learned.

Jefferson's educational philosophy had limitations even more significant than these class implications. The course of events during the fifty years in which he kept his educational plan before the public, *viz.,* the years between 1778 and 1826, proved that he put too much trust in enlightened self-interest, which he mistakenly thought would prompt the people of a ward to establish and improve its schools. More important, his theory did not adequately take into account the existing inequality of wealth which, as the Federalists saw so clearly, lay at the bottom of political power. Although not afraid of revolution, Jefferson preferred to check tyranny, oppression, and the ruthless rule of an aristocracy by a periodical renewal of the social compact.[86] In thinking that general enlightenment would compel that renewal and the imposition of more democratic provisions, he did not calculate the influence of wealth on political action—an influence that not only prevented Jefferson's educational plan from being given a trial, but, as we shall see, was often to interfere with the hope of other educators that a democratic school system would effect needed social change.

The failure of Jefferson's plan,[87] which with all its short-

[86] Dumas Malone, "Thomas Jefferson," *Dictionary of American Biography,* Vol. X, p. 19.
[87] The act of 1796 and that of 1818 virtually defeated the distinguishing features of Jefferson's plan.

comings far transcended in its democratic features most existing educational theory and all actual practice in those days,
was due to a variety of circumstances.[88] It was partly the result
of the priority that Jefferson himself gave to the university, but
to a greater extent it was to be laid at the door of partisan
politics, sectional antagonisms, the slavery controversy, and the
decline of the revolutionary enthusiasm which, years before,
had abolished primogeniture, entail, and an established church.
But the failure was, after all, chiefly to be fastened on the
shoulders of the dominant and conservative classes, who resented the idea of taxation for public purposes and objected
to the mingling of their own sons "in a vulgar and suspicious
communion" with those of Tom, Dick, and Harry.[89] Feeling
no need for public elementary schools for its own children, the
ruling class remained content with the university to which it
might send its sons.[90] Thus did a relatively democratic con-

---

[88] The influence of the Jeffersonian educational ideal on practical educational
programs outside his own state seems to have been slight, although there are
some traces of it. Thus Archibald D. Murphey, an early but none too successful champion of common schools in North Carolina, looked upon the children
of indigent parents as valuable, undeveloped resources and urged that the state
take to its bosom all children of the poor, feed, clothe, and teach them, and
even provide university training for those who gave proof of mental excellence
and future usefulness. M. C. S. Noble, *A History of the Public Schools of
North Carolina* (Chapel Hill, North Carolina, 1930), pp. 50–51. An address
by a committee of the Georgia Convention of Teachers in 1833 asked whether
it was consistent with republican principles to put into the hands of a part of
the people so powerful a weapon as that of knowledge, while the rest were
without its mighty influence. "Rail as we may against the aristocracy of other
countries, there is no aristocracy so perfect as that of wealth and knowledge.
Those who monopolize the knowledge of a country, will be its governors in
fact, whatever may be the constitution and laws." *American Annals of Education and Instruction,* Vol. III (Dec., 1833), p. 563. Many of the ideas of De
Witt Clinton, the New York governor who did so much to promote education
in the state, likewise suggest Jeffersonian influence, though some of his opinions
are more conservative.

[89] Maddox, *op. cit.,* pp. 184–85.

[90] *Ibid.,* pp. 53, 187. Chief Justice John Marshall was exceptional in thinking that, whatever importance attached to the university, the primary schools
were "objects of deeper interest." Marshall to Mercer, April 7, 1827. Cham-
berlain MSS., Boston Public Library.

ception of education, which in part was designed to defeat aristocracy, come to defeat at the hands of that class. Whether this planting aristocracy, which the Civil War finally demolished, could have been transformed into an aristocracy of talents by Jefferson's educational project, remains a subject for conjecture. Actually, the colonial inheritance of class structure and class education survived.

While Jefferson's theory of education was colored by intense sectional and, particularly, state loyalty, some of his contemporaries drew up schemes markedly influenced by patriotic nationalism.[91] Indeed, this insistence on the necessity of a distinctively American system of education characterized much of the educational thought of the early national period.

This conception found striking expression in the dissertations submitted to the American Philosophical Society, which in 1795 held a prize essay contest designed to promote an American system of education. All the essays assumed that the peculiar genius of American institutions required a unique type of education, and almost all of them maintained that the nation was the most effective unit for educational administration and for furthering the development of a truly national culture by means of institutions of learning. Most of the writers favored a highly centralized control of the schools, which were to be universal, free, and open to girls as well as to boys. Above all, the national system of schools was to inculcate in the youth of America loyalty to its institutions, purposes, and ideals.

It was thought that the purpose of American nationalism, which the schools were to promote, was fundamentally humane

[91] It should be pointed out that, cosmopolitan though Jefferson was in his intellectual interests and associations, and deficient as he knew higher education in America to be, he was sufficiently nationalistic to believe that young Americans would better study at home, since Europe would corrupt their Americanism. Jefferson to J. Banister, Oct. 15, 1785, in the *Writings of Thomas Jefferson* (Washington, 1903), p. 186.

and enlightened. Practically all the essays took for granted in good eighteenth-century fashion the doctrine of the indefinite perfectibility of man and institutions. Practically all of them favored the sciences and utilitarian subjects as against the traditional disciplines, which were regarded as aristocratic relics of an outworn past. Inspired in part by the ideas of French revolutionists, they too desired to seek human welfare and social progress through education. Moreover, the full and free development of every individual was to be promoted, in order that a true democracy might be realized. These writers thus identified the liberalism, humanitarianism, and belief in the idea of progress, which characterized a large body of eighteenth-century thought,[92] with the peculiar destiny and promise of America.

Since this American nationalism was none too strong, and faith in the ideal of a democratic and universal education suited to a democratic and enlightened society neither widely pervasive nor very influential, there was question as to how far these blue prints would be used in the building of an educational structure. There were obstinate difficulties in the way. One was the intense sectional antagonism inherited from colonial days. The followers of Jefferson would never stomach all this high nationalism, centralization, and integrated planning. Even those who sincerely boasted of their nationalism—people like Noah Webster—in reality were trying to impose Yankee speech and ideals and values on the rest of the country. In the second place, the democratic aspects of this thought, which visioned the continuous remaking of society through science and education, clashed with long-established class and religious concepts of education.

[92] For an excellent summary of these schemes see Allen Oscar Hansen, *Liberalism and American Education in the Eighteenth Century* (New York, 1926).

These colonial survivals were so strong and so fixed as seriously to threaten the success of bold and forward-looking plans inspired by faith in the radical doctrines of the eighteenth century, doctrines which these idealists fused and confused with American nationalism. Yet however far patriotic nationalism was to fall short of establishing a truly democratic and secular education, and however slight was to be its effect in wiping out the colonial legacies of class distinction and religious influence in the schools, it had begun a long course of development. It was to mingle with new forces, to contribute with them to the modification of old legacies, and to help condition the social ideas of our first great educational leaders.

II

NEW CONFLICTS AND A NEW SOLUTION
1800–1860

Efficient universal education, that makes men producers as well as consumers, is the surest guarantee of progress in the arts of peace —is the mother of national prosperity. . . . Let us make our education brave and preventive. Politics is an afterwork, a poor patching. . . . We shall one day learn to supersede politics by education. What we call our root-and-branch reforms . . . is only medicating the system. We must begin higher up, namely in Education.
                                        —RALPH WALDO EMERSON.

I

The years between the War of 1812 and the struggle for southern independence were not placid ones. In spite of what the second war with England and the declaration of the Monroe doctrine did to safeguard the young republic against the dangers of old-world encroachments, the very life of the nation seemed, in a real sense, to be at stake. As threats from Europe decreased, dangers from internal cleavages multiplied. On more than one occasion sectional antagonisms threatened to tear the federal government to pieces. Many solutions for achieving an integrated nationality were offered. Some thought it could be best promoted by a federal system of internal improvements, such as roads, canals, and railways. Others preferred to lean on sectional bargains and compromises. Still others were convinced that national unity could best be won by diverting attention from domestic antagonisms. They urged the need of a big navy and tried to involve the government in a crusade to foment revolutions in Europe for the overthrow of monarchies and the substitution of republics modeled on our own.

Closely associated with the problem of consolidating national-ism was the insistence on the part of many writers, artists, and scientists that America declare and win its cultural indepen-dence from Europe. Some visioned a new literature, differing in style and substance from that of feudal Europe. Others went so far as to encourage the development of a distinctively American language. Artists demanded that their colleagues emancipate themselves from the shackles binding them to the traditions of the great masters of the Old World. Even scientists declared that it was their duty to develop a distinctively Amer-ican science.

There were, however, many obstacles in the way of all these dreams. Cultural independence generally follows, rather than precedes, economic independence, and America still required European credit, labor, and markets. Besides, the larger sec-tions, "shadowy images of European nations," aspired to re-gional cultures which often ran counter to the ideal of a national cultural independence.

The aristocracy of wealth was called on to face new chal-lenges to its power. On the one hand the landed gentry and the older mercantile classes in the North were forced to make concessions to the rising industrialists whose interests often ran counter to their own. On the other hand, the well-to-do and powerful, whatever the source of their wealth, saw new dan-gers to their position in the rise and discontent of the common man. Universal suffrage was not conceded in the eighteen-twenties without pressure. The unruly mob that invaded the White House when Jackson was inaugurated in 1829 seemed to symbolize a new power. Labor troubles in the seaboard cities aroused resentment. Many among the privileged class called to mind the violence which had destroyed the old aris-tocracy in France and frankly confessed their own fears. They saw danger in the anti-rent war, the attacks on the judiciary, and the repudiation of public and private debts, in the Dorr war and the Nat Turner slave insurrection, in the abolition mobs and the anti-Catholic riots. Men of position shuddered at the thought that they might be forced to see the overthrow of republican institutions which had hitherto safeguarded their status.

However mistaken the privileged were in their fears, they did not invent them out of whole cloth. The common man, remembering the promises of the Declaration of Independence, and oppressed by real grievances, demanded concessions. In his efforts to improve his position, however, he met obstacles that seemed all but overwhelming. While he won the suffrage, he found that it did not market his goods at prices which assured him even a measure of economic stability. He found that the vote did not enable him to wring higher wages and shorter hours from the industrial owner in whose factories he toiled; that it often failed to prevent his creditor from foreclosing mortgages; that it did not even provide him, if he were truly down and out, with the slender outfit which was indispensable for going west and taking up cheap land. He found that the right to go to the polls did little to change the conditions of life in the dismal slums that arose in seaboard cities; that it did not effectively change the conditions which made it imperative for him to send his children, underfed and puny, to work in factories; that, in short, universal suffrage was not a sesame opening the doors to a good life. Although the common man did not realize that the mushroom growth of industrial capitalism favored a stratification of society quite opposed to the spirit of the Declaration of Independence, the burdens to which it committed him weighed none the less heavily on his shoulders. They were not lightened by the buoyant optimism which characterized so much of the talk that has come down to us from that day.

If the common man tried, sometimes successfully, to use his ballot to remedy his grievances, women did not enjoy even that recourse. They were not merely disenfranchised. As late as the third decade of the nineteenth century married women were legally incapable of controlling their own property. If they worked for wages, fathers and husbands could sequester them. Professions were for the most part barred to them. The type of education permitted them was restricted and vastly inferior to that of men. Custom forbade them from even speaking in public in behalf of those worse off than themselves.

The spread of slavery created a series of harassing problems. When the invention of the cotton gin enabled vast quantities of cotton to be cheaply prepared for the textile mills, the slave system took on a new economic importance. For the apologetic and paternalistic attitude of the Revolutionary period was substituted a bold defense of the "peculiar institution." The rationalizations evoked in its defense paralyzed free and honest thinking. The shadows it cast over the purity of family life were concealed as well as they could be. But it was impossible to conceal the fact that, in advancing westward, the plantation system, based as it was on slavery, crowded poorer whites onto less fertile soil and condemned those who did not own Negroes to an inferior and even precarious way of life.

But the heightening of class distinctions was not the only way in which slavery travestied the Declaration of Independence. It condemned a whole race to a static if not a degrading condition. Whoever spoke out against Negro slavery in a bold and uncompromising way was excoriated by those who, North as well as South, profited directly or indirectly from its existence. Only when the slavocracy threatened the interests of important groups in the North did it become respectable to denounce it and advocate its limitation.

In these stirring years of conflict and opportunity for the new America, people all over the country looked to educators as well as to political and other leaders for guidance and for help. How did educators look upon these pressing social problems of their country? What solutions did they advocate and help bring about?

II

In spite of our cultural dependence on Europe, patriotic nationalism did succeed in diminishing the British character of our school education. Motivated by an ardent patriotism and a desire for profits, textbook makers denounced slavish dependence on the schoolbooks of the mother country. In his *Introduction to Arithmetic,* published in 1796, Erastus Root urged the use of the American money system in reckoning, rather than the English. "Their mode is suited to the genius of the government, for it seems to be the policy of tyrants to keep their accounts in as intricate, and perplexing a method as possible; that the smaller number of their subjects may be able to estimate their enormous impositions and exactions. But Republican money ought to be simple and adapted to the meanest capacity."[1] Caleb Bingham announced in the foreword of his "readers" that preference had been given to publications thoroughly American in spirit. The strongly national character of the selections in John Pierpont's *The Young Reader* was due to his conviction that succeeding generations could not uphold our unique institutions unless they understood them. Lyman Cobb in 1831 appealed for support for his

[1] Clifton Johnson, *Old-Time Schools and Schoolbooks,* p. 306.

school texts on the ground that they were more patriotic than their English competitors.[2]

But it was Noah Webster who gave the strongest expression to the patriotic spirit. As early as 1783 he attacked the Latin domination of the English language and pleaded for its Americanization in both spelling and idiom. Although his extreme reforms failed, Webster did succeed in providing an important basis for a national culture by standardizing the polyglot spelling which prevailed and by extending that standard over the whole land. His texts at the same time inculcated republican precepts and instilled a knowledge of and respect for American forms of government.[3]

III

While the writers of schoolbooks were waging the war for cultural independence from Europe, other educational leaders urged the necessity of furthering popular intelligence in general, and a system of free public schools in particular, as the best means of preserving the new republican institutions. Had Napoleon not demolished the French Republic, Americans might have been less worried about the security of their own experiment. But the chaos and the resulting despotism served as a warning, and they redoubled their zeal for education as the only means of perpetuating republicanism and remedying its defects. James Madison, in observing that a "popular gov-

[2] Rudolph R. Reeder, *The Historical Development of School Readers and of Method in Teaching Reading* (Columbia University Contributions to Philosophy, Psychology, and Education, Vol. VIII, No. 2, May, 1900), pp. 45–46, 48.

[3] The preface of Webster's *Elementary Spelling Book* constantly maintained that competing texts were endangering the success of his patriotic aim, and that Americans must guard against vulgarizations that were creeping in. "To diffuse an uniformity and purity of language in America, to destroy the provincial prejudices that originate in the trifling difference of dialect and produce reciprocal ridicule, to promote the interest of literature and the harmony of the United States, is the most earnest wish of the author, and it is the highest ambition to deserve the approbation and encouragement of his countrymen." *Ibid.*, p. 31.

ernment without popular information or the means of acquiring it, is but a prologue to a farce or tragedy, or perhaps to both," was expressing a point of view shared by Washington, Jefferson, John Adams, John Jay, the Clintons, Francis Marion, and a host of other men who helped lay the foundations for the new nation.[4]

This faith that popular intelligence could secure and perpetuate republican institutions was derived in part from the later eighteenth-century notion that education was a function of the state rather than of the church or private enterprise.[5] In part it was an application of the idea which John Locke and his followers had advanced regarding the malleability of human nature: if the human mind was originally empty and passive, if native endowments were of slight importance, then the acquisition of habits, or education, was an almost omnipotent force for shaping human society. Helvetius and other French writers cherished this idea, and Condorcet, who believed in the indefinite perfectibility of mankind, proposed to the French Republic a plan of education for the realization of its principles.

When De Witt Clinton in 1826 advised the legislature of New York that "a general diffusion of knowledge is the precursor and protector of republican institutions, and in it we must confide as the conservative power that will watch over our liberties and guard them against fraud, intrigue, corruption and violence,"[6] he was expressing a powerful but none the less vague dogma which meant different things to different men. For many the meaning of the idea was admirably inter-

[4] Washington, Hamilton, and Madison favored the establishment of a national university for the political training of American youth.

[5] Even such a doctrinaire advocate of the theory of *laissez faire* as Adam Smith conceded the right and duty of the state to instruct the mass of the people.

[6] *American Journal of Education,* Vol. I (Jan., 1826), p. 58. For similar sentiments from public men see S. S. Randall, *History of the Common School*

preted by Josiah Quincy, mayor of Boston and president of Harvard, who held that a republic combined in itself the elements of anarchy, revolution, and despotism, and that one or another of these tendencies was certain to become predominant unless the state provided that every child was educated to obey law and authority, to resist political corruption and the wiles of demagogues, and to take an intelligent share in the burdens to which his citizenship committed him.[7]

Those patriots to whom anarchy was a more dreadful evil than dictatorship emphasized the function of public education as a preventive of social disintegration. In no part of the world, wrote George Emerson in the popular manual for teachers, *School and Schoolmaster,* was submission to the authority of the law so important as in the United States, for unless all its people were accustomed from their earliest years to submit to authority and law, the republic could hardly endure.[8] Alonzo Potter, prominent in educational circles in Massachusetts and New York and subsequently Episcopal bishop of Pennsylvania, warned against the insidious notion that the people cannot err: when such a siren song lulled the land to sleep, then the republic would become a mere ghostly beacon by which the prejudiced would warn the whole world against free institutions.[9] In equally picturesque words an Ohio educator predicted lugubriously that if the burning tide of violence and anarchy were not put down, the country would

System of the State of New York (New York, 1871), p. 13; *The Academician,* Vol. I (Feb. 7, 1818), p. 16; Thaddeus Stevens, "Speech Against the Repeal of the School Law" (1835) in *Report of the Commissioner of Education* (1898–99), Vol. I, pp. 518–24.

[7] *Common School Journal,* Vol. X (Aug. 1, 1848), p. 223.

[8] George Emerson, Part II, *School and Schoolmaster* (New York, 1873), p. 353.

[9] Alonzo Potter, Part I, *School and Schoolmaster,* p. 129. For Bishop Potter's educational work see M. A. De Wolfe Howe, *Memoirs of the Life and Services of the Rt. Rev. Alonzo Potter, D.D., LL.D.* (Philadelphia, 1871), p. 70.

be reduced "to one vast moral desert, tenanted only by the savage beast and the poisonous serpent."[10]

Others feared that the republic was more likely to succumb to a dictatorship than to anarchy, and with equal zeal insisted that public education alone could save the nation from so dire a fate. Representing this sentiment was a writer in the *Academician* who urged the value of public schools for insuring the people against the "artifices of the crafty and aspiring demagogue or king."[11] In similar language other writers maintained that the triumph of demagogues and military leaders would be checked by that intelligent use of the ballot which education alone could insure.[12]

In addition to the conviction that the perpetuation of republican government depended on public education, the belief was also widely held that schools could weed out corruption, inculcate the proper standards for public office and jury service, and promote the ability of the citizen to judge wisely of measures and men.[13] William C. Woodbridge, the editor of the *American Annals of Education and Instruction,* demanded the immediate, vigorous, and unremitting efforts of school men to close the floodgate of corruption and to arrest the torrent of public immorality,[14] while a writer in the *New York Teacher* insisted that children should be taught that the selling of votes was treachery differing only in degree from that of Arnold.[15]

[10] The Reverend B. P. Aydelott, "Address on the Duties of Citizens," in *Transactions of the Western Literary Institute and College of Teachers* (1839), p. 54.

[11] *Academician,* Vol. I (Feb. 7, 1818), p. 14.

[12] Potter, *School and Schoolmaster,* p. 69; *American Annals of Education and Instruction,* Vol. II (Sept. 1, 1832), p. 445.

[13] Edward Everett, *Importance of Practical Education and Useful Knowledge* (Boston, 1840), pp. 337–38.

[14] *American Annals of Education and Instruction,* Vol. I (Aug., 1830), p. 326.

[15] *New York Teacher,* Dec., 1852, pp. 87–88.

It was easier to formulate objectives than to work out concrete methods by which education was to perpetuate republican institutions. Almost without exception, however, educational writers pinned their faith to moral education as the means of effecting that end. Since they believed that a republic could not survive unless its citizens were virtuous as well as intelligent, they never tired of condemning mere intellectual training. Charles Brooks spoke for many others when he observed that if the mind alone of a sagacious boy were educated, he would very likely menace republican institutions by growing up to be either the ringleader of an agrarian faction or the head of a mob.[16]

If there was trafficking in votes, then teach children to be honest, and such trafficking would cease. Thus ran the argument of educational leaders in those days. If there was political corruption, teach them honor, and political corruption would vanish. If there was danger of demagogism, eliminate the prevalent practice of emulation from the schoolroom. It was urged that appeals to emulation, an incentive much used in Lancastrian schools, kindled a passion for honor and power, which was seldom repressed and which endangered the very foundations of republican government.[17] Rid the schoolroom of emulation, it was said, and there would be few to resort to questionable manœuvres in the later race for popularity, few to elevate themselves by bringing about the downfall of others.[18] Above all, children must be taught to entertain the deepest horror of fraud and falsehood; they must be persuaded to resolve that, through their life, their faith, when once plighted, whether

[16] Charles Brooks, *Elementary Instruction* (Quincy, 1837), p. 15. For Brooks's educational work see *Dictionary of American Biography*, Vol. III, pp. 74-75.
[17] W. C. Woodbridge in *American Annals of Education and Instruction,* Vol. I (Sept., 1831), p. 420.
[18] A. D. Wright and G. E. Gardner, *Hall's Lectures on School Keeping,* pp. 144-50.

in public or private contracts, whether in affairs of a personal or political nature, must be held sacred and irrevocable.[19]

For most educational writers an important part of moral training was the inculcation in the schoolroom of respect for authority in order to prevent the anarchistic dissolution of republican society. Some teachers, like George Emerson and A. Bronson Alcott of Boston, did indeed try to train children for their responsibilities in a republic by encouraging them to learn in the schoolroom the art of self-government,[20] but they were exceptional. Far more representative was Jacob Abbott, father of Lyman Abbott and writer of innumerable highly moral stories for boys. It was his conviction that the maintenance of rigid discipline and authority in the schoolroom was by far the best means of inculcating respect for law and order.[21] The vast majority of teachers tried to follow his precept.

All this faith in moral instruction, it is clear, was characteristic of the dominant American belief in and practice of individualism. The eighteenth-century doctrine that human nature was so malleable that good conduct could be insured merely by providing abstract moral instruction was an engaging, though from our contemporary point of view, a naïve conviction. But no one questioned it, except utopian socialists and economic radicals who did not write educational treatises or condition the ideals of school teachers. Difficult though it is to gauge the effect of the prevalent reliance on moral instruction, we cannot say that it has not contributed to the realization of its objectives. Americans did not succumb to dictators, except in national

[19] Potter, *School and Schoolmaster*, p. 66.

[20] George Emerson, *Reminiscences of an Old Teacher* (Boston, 1878), p. 53; A Bronson Alcott, *The Doctrine and Discipline of Human Culture* (Boston, 1836), *passim*.

[21] Jacob Abbott, *The Teacher, Moral Influences Employed in the Instruction and Government of the Young* (New York, 1856), pp. iii–iv, 70.

emergencies like the Civil War and the World War, and even then the word "dictator" was seldom spoken. Nor did Americans abandon republicanism for downright anarchy and revolution. Perhaps we might have been plagued by even more Tweed rings and Teapot Domes had it not been for all that moral instruction patiently and reverently taught by generations of schoolmasters and schoolma'ams. However that may be, the American doctrine of the power of good individuals to weed out graft and political corruption from public life, slender though its perennial harvests appeared to be, was not abandoned. It was, indeed, to become a blind spot for generation after generation of Americans.

In addition to the emphasis laid on the implanting of good morals as the primary means of safeguarding the republic, educational writers also called attention to the need for definite political and civic instruction. Some recommended the cultivation of habits of careful inquiry, so that each person might think independently and vote intelligently.[22] More typical was Jacob Abbott, who thought that a teacher was employed for specific purposes—the interpretation of the will of his employers—and that he therefore had no right to wander away from that purpose. The limitations of this conception may be inferred from the fact that while Abbott thought a teacher in a republic might explain and commend the principles and blessings of a republican government, he would not be justified in doing so under a monarchy[23]—in other words, he could lead his students only to accept, not to question, the existing order.

Almost all educators advocated the teaching of the Constitution. American history, federal, state, and local, found many advocates, for it was felt that if children could be taught to appreciate the struggles of their fathers in achieving the bless-

[22] Potter, *School and Schoolmaster*, p. 69.   [23] Abbott, *op. cit.*, p. 178.

ings of civil freedom, their heirs might be more apt to perform their duty in preserving the heritage.[24] Teachers were charged with the duty of inspiring in their pupils a love of country and conformity to its institutions and ideals. A policy of Americanization for immigrants was formulated. "Our policy as a State," wrote the superintendent of public instruction in Indiana in 1853, "is to make of all the varieties of population among us, differing as they do in origin, language, habits of thought, modes of action, and social custom, one people, with one common interest."[25]

It was, however, an "unadulterated love of country" rather than a critical understanding of national shortcomings and proposals for remedying them that the schools were to inspire. With few exceptions, little can be found in the texts of the period that was likely to promote a constructive type of patriotism. Nothing like the call to integrity which Thoreau sounded in his essay on civil disobedience, and which Lowell boldly proclaimed in the *Biglow Papers,* found its way into textbooks or educational guides. It is true that a few voices were raised to further peaceful rather than warlike methods of settling future controversies in which the country might be engaged;[26] that sometimes a plea for justice to the Indian invaded the textbooks;[27] and that there were occasional sugges-

[24] *American Journal of Education,* Vol. I (Jan., 1826), p. 53; Vol. III (April, 1828), pp. 244–45; *Hall's Lectures,* pp. 72–74; *American Annals of Education and Instruction,* Vol. II (Oct. 1, 1832), pp. 505–9. Abraham Lincoln, in a communication dated New Salem, Illinois, March, 1832, urged the importance for every citizen of sufficient instruction to enable him "to read the histories of his own and other countries, by which he may duly appreciate the value of our free institutions," J. W. Cook, *Educational History of Illinois* (Chicago, 1912), p. 43.

[25] W. C. Larrabee, *Second Annual Report of the Superintendent of Public Instruction, Indiana,* 1853, p. 31.

[26] George Emerson, *History and Design of the Institute of Instruction* (Boston, 1849), Vol. I, pp. 1–2; Reeder, *op. cit.,* pp. 53–54; M. E. Curti, *The American Peace Crusade, 1815–1860* (Durham, 1929), pp. 49, 50, 51.

[27] Caleb Bingham, *The Columbian Orator* (Boston, 1812), p. 272.

tions of national shortcomings. But on the whole there prevailed an attitude of reverence and respect for what had been achieved and for what was established, rather than one of critical independence.

IV

The high-sounding nationalism which inspired so much educational thought in the period after the Revolution should not, however, conceal the plain fact that localism and regionalism actually held the stage. Even the amazing spread of internal improvements and means of communication—roads, canals, railways, postal facilities, and telegraph—only partly broke down the isolation of American life. If the men and women who crossed the Appalachians took with them much of the mental and emotional equipment of their old homes, they also acquired from pioneer conditions characteristics which set them off in many ways from their former neighbors. The growth of the plantation system based on Negro slavery was at the same time sharpening the differences between the South and the rest of the country. In the Northeast the rise of the factory system and the coming of the immigrants stamped new peculiarities on that region.

The spokesmen of each section represented the interests of its dominant class and half convinced themselves and even persuaded certain others that they stood for the welfare of the whole nation. But they knew what they were about when they made bargains with each other for the support necessary to push their pet legislation through Congress. The words of national patriotism which fell from their lips for the justification of their acts did not blind them to the cleavages existing between sections and even within them. To promote an actual solidarity in their sections and to cover the cleavages and class antagonisms that often proved embarrassing, they urged the need of a regional type of education.

Thus regionalism played an important part in the social thinking of educational leaders, and tended to impede the development of a nationalistic program of education. When the editor of Buchanan's *Journal of Man* declared that the time must come "when the mighty West, with its bold and liberal population, shall exhibit the power of new thoughts and high aspirations (too daring for the old),"[28] he was expressing a sentiment shared by almost every Westerner who could frame his feelings in literary form.[29] In such an emotional climate it was natural for the ministers and teachers who were most vocal in furthering educational work to proclaim the necessity for a truly Western system of schools and higher institutions of learning.[30] In their school journals, in their meetings, and in legislatures, they insisted on the need for an educational system that would express the peculiar spirit of the West and promote its distinctive interests.

In part this attitude was due to their realization of the heterogeneous character of the new country, and to their hope that an educational system would promote its solidarity. In part their demand for a distinctively Western school system merely expressed the sectional self-consciousness of the trans-Appalachian region. These Westerners confidently believed their new home was to be the scene of progress and a great future; they exuberantly thought of it as a place where a new start was to be made, where the fetters of the past were to be thrown off, where a

[28] *The Journal of Man*, Vol. I (June, 1850), p. 191.

[29] For Western self-consciousness see *The Western Monthly Review*, Vol. I (July, 1827), p. 133; Vol. II (June, 1828), p. 12; F. L. Mott, *A History of American Magazines, 1741–1850* (New York, 1930), p. 660.

[30] Some ministers, it is true, disparaged school learning. Father Bangs, one of the characters in James Hall's *Legends of the West* (Philadelphia, 1833), p. 43, regarded it as the "most prolific source of human misery and mental degradation."

more democratic and humane civilization was to be built; where each individual would have a chance to realize a rich and full development. These grandiose aspirations may be thought of partly as compensatory for the actual hardships of the frontier, partly as good politics, and partly as propaganda to attract settlers. But whatever their origin, these regional ambitions had a considerable influence on educational thought.

Trans-Appalachian educators insisted that a uniquely Western school system must be democratic and universally inclusive. They spurned the idea prevalent in some of the older states that public schools were devices of philanthropists to aid paupers. Although sectarian interests defended parochial institutions, there was general enthusiasm for public schools which taught "true religious and moral principles." There was also the feeling that, since society was in the making, schools must be immediately responsive to social needs. Utilitarian and practical values were regarded more highly than classical and cultural ones. From the Ohio valley to the Mormon settlement in Utah,[31] science and its applications were deemed highly useful and desirable. Some of the discussions in the Western Literary Institute and College of Teachers expressed enthusiasm for Pestalozzian pedagogy on the ground that its greater spontaneity and concreteness peculiarly suited the West and promised to further the realization of its ideals.[32] This self-consciousness did not close Western eyes to the best in educational practice and theory elsewhere, but rather stimulated interest in other systems that might furnish new ideas. For example, the Ohio legislature commissioned Calvin E. Stowe in 1836 to examine

[31] John A. Widtsoe, ed., *Discourses of Brigham Young* (Salt Lake City, 1925), 390–91, 393.
[32] *Transactions of the Western Literary Institute and College of Teachers;* Allen Oscar Hansen, *Early Educational Leadership in the Ohio Valley* (Journal of Educational Research Monographs, ed. B. R. Buckingham, No. 5, Bloomington, Ill., 1923), *passim.*

the Prussian system, and the resulting report greatly influenced education in all parts of the country.

Western provincialism found vigorous expression in the demand for textbooks suited to Western character. Enterprising publishers and authors with an eye to the main chance contended that Eastern schoolbooks were effete and undemocratic, and lacking in frontier materials and the point of view that Western children required. In announcing *The Western Reader,* which was published at Cincinnati in 1833, its compiler, James Hall, boasted of its peculiarly Western themes and added that it was a "work of Western origin and manufacture; having been prepared in this city expressly for the use of our schools, and published here by means of our own workmanship and materials." In like vein the *Western Farmers' Almanac* for 1845 evaluated existing school texts and found most of them wanting in "the freshness and appropriateness" congenial to Western minds.[33]

If such thinking retarded the sentiment of nationalism in educational circles, it did not entirely succeed in its main objective. Notwithstanding such patriotic appeals to Western sectionalism, and in spite of the impetus given to public education by the Western land grants, the actual up-building of public school systems encountered many obstacles. Few lessons were learned from the educational experiment at New Harmony, Indiana, where in 1826 Robert Owen and William Maclure, both bent upon regenerating society in the interest of the producing classes, turned to Pestalozzian practices and teachers for aid. There, from the tender age of two, children were cared for and instructed by the community. After their years at an infant play school, a forerunner of the Froebel kindergartens,

[33] Ralph Rusk, *The Literature of the Middle Western Frontier* (New York, 1925), Vol. I, pp. 265–66; *Western Farmers' Almanac* (Lexington, Ky., 1845), Vol. VI, p. 31.

they entered the higher school where classics were spurned and practical trades constituted an essential part of the program. The aim of instruction, much as in modern progressive education, was to teach only what the children could understand, making use of concrete objects and avoiding the abstract, and to banish fear and all artificial reward and punishment from the classroom, appealing instead to the natural interests of the children. Girls, on equal footing with their brothers, received the benefits of this free and comprehensive education, a system of instruction, it should be noted, entirely secular. But schools of equal freedom and utility did not spring up under the stimulus of its example.[34]

As a matter of fact, the over-confident enthusiasm for schools, even for characteristically Western schools, was not shared by all frontiersmen. Each class or group of people in the new country had its own attitude toward education. The most migratory frontiersmen, getting along as they did by virtue of their boldness, skill, and strength, saw little need for schooling, and either opposed or ignored educational plans and movements. Although a school was to be found in the vicinity of David Crockett's boyhood home, he was proud of the fact that at the age of fifteen he was still ignorant of his letters.[35] The more stable pioneers who settled down on farms were apt to look favorably on efforts to establish free public schools, particularly if they had migrated from regions where such institutions existed. But the cramping circumstances of their life, the battles against the wilderness, the struggles for markets, and the fear of burdensome taxes often combined to narrow their minds and even to inspire their opposition to free schools. Some, less

[34] See George B. Lockwood, *The New Harmony Movement* (New York, 1905), pp. 209–93; and Will S. Monroe, *History of the Pestalozzian Movement in the United States* (Syracuse, N. Y., 1907), pp. 101–26.

[35] *The Autobiography of David Crockett* (New York, 1923), pp. 28–36.

godly than those around them, feared that the influence of the clergy would be strengthened by the schools in which they seemed suspiciously interested. Others, ignorant and not ashamed to be, suspected the "larnin" of their better educated neighbors—for even frontier communities did not long remain without class distinctions.[36] Such factors checked the aspirations of the expansive would-be architects of a uniquely Western school system. They also tended to counteract the positive contributions that the frontier was making toward public education—the impetus from land grants[37] and the general conviction that education was necessary to prevent disastrous consequences from the Western-achieved victory of manhood suffrage.

Eastern interests, moreover, were determined to have a voice in the shaping of Western schools. Conservative bankers, merchants, and industrialists, fearing that their pocketbooks would be emptied by the repudiation of loans, the wild-cat banking, and the inflation schemes of Western democracy, looked on public schools and colleges as a means of teaching frontier folk sound economic doctrines. Especially after the thirties there came to be a growing realization on the part of Easterners that the future power of the country would be concentrated in the West,[38] and that if there was to be any insurance against frontier attacks on property rights, the time had come to act. Moreover, South Carolina's nullification of the tariff act suggested the desirability of finding an ally in the West, and aid to the

[36] Henry Barnard during his educational tour in the West noted that the appeals of demagogues in the legislature were chiefly responsible for the deficient state of education. Barnard to Mann, Feb. 13, 1845, Mann Papers.

[37] The provision in the ordinances of 1785 and 1787 setting aside certain sections of land for the support of schools seems to have been due as much to a desire on the part of land promoters and speculators to enhance their profits by speeding up settlement as to philanthropic interest in education. *Journal of Education,* Vol. XXXIX (March 29, 1894), p. 200.

[38] *American Annals of Education and Instruction,* Vol. V (May, 1835), p. 232.

educational institutions beyond the Appalachians was regarded as an appropriate step to that end.

These were the thoughts in the mind of Edward Everett, representative of the conservative business interests of New England, when in 1833 he appealed to Boston capitalists for contributions to an Ohio institution of learning. "We can," he advised, "from our surplus, contribute toward the establishment and endowment of those seminaries, where the mind of the West shall be trained and enlightened. Yes, sir, we can do this; and it is so far optional with us, whether the power, to which we have subjected ourselves [the West] shall be a power of intelligence or of ignorance; . . . a reign of darkness, or of light. . . . Let no Bostonian capitalist, then, let no man, who has a large stake in New England, and who is called upon to aid this Institution in the center of Ohio, think that he is called upon to exercise his liberality at a distance, toward those in whom he has no concern. . . . They ask you to contribute to give security to your own property, by diffusing the means of light and truth throughout the region, where so much of the power to preserve or to shake it resides."[39]

In another plea for similar support, equally outspoken and equally representative, the orator declared that "the learning, religion, and the living ministry bestowed on the great West by these Colleges, unite in special benefit to mercantile morality and hence to the safety and value of business engagements there formed. Eastern merchants have an especial and increasing concern in the commercial integrity of this immense market for Eastern industry. However lightly men think of religion and of the culture attending it, they are 'terribly in earnest' as to the counterfeits and cheats which irreligion and ungodliness impose on them. They forget that like the pillars of Hercules, Education and Religion define and defend the path of trade.

[39] Everett, *Practical Education*, pp. 169–170.

. . . These colleges thus plead, to every enlightened merchant, his own self-preservation."[40] The Beechers and Horace Bushnell used similar arguments in their efforts to enlist financial support for Western educational enterprises, while conservatives in the West itself appealed to the East for educational help lest this nation "grow up under the predominating influence of ignorance and fanaticism, anarchy, and misrule."[41]

As pioneers streamed westward, Easterners, alarmed at their exhausted lands and at the draining away of their factory hands, turned to education to solve the difficulty, with the now characteristic American faith in its efficacy. They urged the improvement of educational opportunities in the East as a bait to keep the restless and ambitious from crossing the mountains. In a report presented to the Massachusetts legislature in 1835, A. H. Everett, the chairman of the committee on education, urged support of the movement for public high schools in order to check the disastrous effects of westward migration. Let the voters, he urged, "seek to increase the amount of light *among every class of citizens,* that this ancient state may maintain by their intelligence, that influence which they are rapidly losing by the increase of population in other parts of the Union."[42]

Although such arguments for the support of public education were familiar to all regions which suffered from competition with the rich, new Western lands, they were perhaps most thoroughly elaborated in North Carolina. As early as 1833 the Reverend John Armstrong urged the support of manual

[40] Quoted by Donald Tewksbury, *The Founding of American Colleges and Universities before the Civil War* (Teachers College, Columbia University, Contributions to Education, No. 543, New York, 1932), pp. 12–13.
[41] Catharine Beecher, *The True Remedy for the Wrongs of Woman* (Boston, 1851), p. 200; *American Annals of Education and Instruction,* Vol. V (Feb., 1833), p. 82.
[42] *American Annals of Education and Instruction,* Vol. V (April, 1835), p. 181.

and agricultural education, on the ground that if the people were informed of the possibilities of North Carolina they would not succumb to the fever of emigration which was inflicting so serious an evil on the state.[43] In the *North Carolina Reader,* prepared by Calvin Wiley, the great educational leader of that commonwealth,[44] children were told that the state in which they lived possessed great resources, and that if these were developed by intelligence and industry, natives need no longer look beyond the limits of the state for wealth, happiness, and fame. If universal education became a fact, then the strength lost by westward migration would be regained, and new prosperity found. "Let the sun of universal education shine upon it [North Carolina], and the matchless resources of the State, by works of improvement, be made to minister nutriment to its wants, and soon its bright blossoms will imparadise the soil from which its sturdy trunk has sprung, and its green, unfading foliage furnish umbrageous retreats for the weary of the earth."[45] Public education would not only enable the resources of North Carolina to be made profitable; it would also bind together the discordant sections of the state, resuscitate the dormant life of the people and create in them public spirit and a love of home;[46] it would even generate a new, noble, and honored people, armed with varied, sublime, and unfailing pleasures, and refreshed by sparkling fountains in their midst.[47]

[43] Reverend John Armstrong, "Labor System of Education," reprinted in C. L. Coon, *North Carolina Schools and Academies, 1790–1840, A Documentary History* (Raleigh, 1915), pp. 755–56.

[44] Calvin Wiley was of Scotch-Irish ancestry, studied law, wrote novels, edited newspapers, felt called upon to preach, studied theology, edited the *North Carolina Journal of Education,* was elected in 1850 as a Whig to the legislature, and from 1853–66 was superintendent of the public schools of North Carolina.

[45] C. H. Wiley, *The North Carolina Reader* (Philadelphia, 1851), p. 222.

[46] *North Carolina Journal of Education,* Vol. I (Jan., 1858), pp. 12–13; Wiley, *North Carolina Reader,* No. 3 (New York, 1859), p. 4.

[47] *North Carolina Reader* (1851), p. 76.

V

The sectional self-consciousness which the Old South expressed in educational matters was even more pointed than that of other sections. As the North began to outstrip her in population, in industry, and in wealth, leaders below the Mason and Dixon line urged the need of an educational awakening to redress the balance. When the educational statistics in the census of 1840 revealed the sluggishness of the public school movement in the South, its spokesmen gave evidence of sensitiveness and in some places bent their efforts to improve affairs.[48] As antagonism toward the North developed, the demand for educational independence from that section became widespread. In 1821, when the Missouri question inflamed men's passions, Jefferson warned against the danger of sending Southern boys to Northern colleges, where they were subjected to pernicious political doctrines.[49] A decade later Harriet Martineau commented on the boasts of Southern members of Congress regarding the increase in the number of their educational institutions, which, they asserted, would soon be sufficient to free the South from collegiate thraldom to the North.[50]

This sentiment became very strong during the fifties, when such periodicals as *De Bow's Commercial Review* and the *Southern Literary Messenger* launched a spirited crusade for

[48] For a Northerner's comparison see Frederick Law Olmsted, *A Journey in the Seaboard Slave States* (New York, 1904), Vol. II, p. 176. For a Southerner's comparison see H. R. Helper, *The Impending Crisis* (New York, 1857), pp. 398–99. William Gregg, a South Carolinian manufacturer, deprecated the fact that two-thirds of the poor whites with whom he came in contact were illiterate. Broadus Mitchell and George S. Mitchell, *The Industrial Revolution in the South* (Baltimore, 1930), p. 6.

[49] Roy J. Honeywell, *The Educational Work of Thomas Jefferson*, pp. 150–51.

[50] Harriet Martineau, *Society in America* (New York, 1837), Vol. I, p. 135.

educational independence from the North. It was pointed out that Southern youths in Northern institutions were in danger of being corrupted by anti-slavery propaganda. If Southern institutions were to be strengthened, Southern students must be kept at home. If the South was to develop an economic independence, industrial and commercial education must be promoted.[51] If Southern art and letters were to flourish, Southern educational institutions must thrive. Champions of cultural independence demanded liberal support for higher institutions of learning that the South might attain the heights of a cultural renaissance.[52]

Indignation was expressed that Southern children should be forced to use Northern school texts, which were not only written without reference to their needs and wants but were full of attacks on Southern institutions. In 1853 the Southern commercial convention at Memphis recommended to the citizens of the states represented "the education of their youth at home as far as practicable, the employment of native teachers in their schools and colleges, the encouragement of a home press, the publication of books adapted to the educational wants and the social condition of these states, and the encouragement and support of inventions and discoveries in the arts and sciences."[53] The following year a committee was appointed by the commercial convention in Charleston to further the publication of Southern textbooks.[54] Southern patriots and defenders of the sanctity of slavery pointed out the passages in Northern texts that breathed hostility to Southern institutions or conveyed "the most unjust and insidious comparisons," and feared that

[51] *De Bow's Commercial Review*, Vol. VII (Sept., 1849), pp. 222–26.
[52] *Southern Literary Messenger*, Vol. XXII (April, 1856), p. 243; Vol. XXIV (Nov., 1856), pp. 387–91.
[53] *De Bow's Commercial Review*, Vol. XV (Sept., 1853), p. 268.
[54] *Ibid.*, Vol. XVII (Nov., 1854), pp. 509–10.

these false ideas would array their own children "against the established ordinance of God."[55]

Nor was the usefulness of education in the event of conflict overlooked. In 1856 Calvin Wiley warned Southerners to be prepared for contingencies, for "surely, if the awful crisis that many dread should come, the South cannot well afford to spare any effort which has a tendency to unite the people, to pervade their minds with common sentiments, and to qualify all classes for co-operative, enlightened and manly action in the day of trial."[56]

In spite of the protests against the "educational peonage" of the South, little was actually done to make effective the demand for educational independence. True, Southern colleges flourished in the fifties as they never had, and it became less common to send young men to the North.[57] Yet, for all the progress made in two or three states and in the larger cities, and for all the exaggerations regarding the educational superiority of North and West, a truly Southern system of public schools was not achieved. It was natural for exponents of the theory of *laissez faire* to regard education as a matter for private enterprise—an attitude more easily entertained by reason of the bewildering multiplication of sectarian seminaries and academies.

But the fundamental cause for the sluggishness of the public school movement in the ante-bellum South lay in the paralyzing effect of a stratified society built on sharp class lines, with Negro slavery as the base of the pyramid. In almost every Southern state intra-sectional conflicts, which on analysis often prove to be class struggles, made the development of a truly

[55] *Ibid.,* Vol. XVIII (May, 1855), p. 661.

[56] Calvin Wiley, *Fourth Annual Report of the Superintendent of Common Schools of North Carolina,* 1856, pp. 13–14. See also *North Carolina Journal of Education,* Vol. III (Jan., 1860), pp. 57–58.

[57] E. Merton Coulter, *College Life in the Old South* (New York, 1928), pp. 234–41.

social and public consciousness impossible. For that reason the plea that in a country where slavery was a permanent institution the white race must maintain intellectual and moral, as well as social and political, elevation, fell on deaf ears.[58] In some places both rich and poor believed that it was injurious for their children to associate together in common schools—such was the blighting effect of slavery, which divided the whites into the class that owned blacks and the class that did not.[59] Jealous of the aristocrats, the common folk spurned as an earmark of the ruling group the education which that group denied them. Even the rural character of the South, with its sparse, widely scattered population,[60] so unsuited to public schools, was itself partly the result of the fact that slavery restricted the economic structure to plantation agriculture. These were the stubborn facts that ironically blasted the hopes of those who desired a truly Southern system of education to safeguard the "peculiar institutions" of the South.[61]

VI

The Northeast, enjoying as it did a traditional educational system, felt less called upon than the South and West to agitate for distinctive schools. Yet it took pride in the fact that its teachers and tutors supplied the needs of other sections, and that its migrating people established across the Appalachians insti-

[58] *Report of the Superintendent of Common Schools of North Carolina for 1862*, p. 17.
[59] Wiley in *North Carolina Journal of Education*, Vol. III (Sept., 1860), p. 277.
[60] Edgar Knight, *Public Education in the South* (Boston, 1922), p. 264, regards the rural character of Southern life as a very important reason for the slow development of a public school system.
[61] Letters among the Mann Papers, especially one from Ed. Jarvis, dated Louisville, Ky., Feb. 25, 1840, and in the Wilkins Updike Papers, especially one from Henry Barnard, dated Columbus, S. C., April 30, 1848, substantiate the foregoing interpretation.

tutions comparable to those in the seaboard states. As we have seen, sectional self-consciousness also expressed itself in the conviction that support must be given the Western institutions in order to secure the property interests of the East, and in the respect inculcated by textbooks for "the New England virtues." Efforts to fit the incoming immigrant into the established order without disturbing it, though also evident in the West, seemed particularly desirable in the Northeast. There were new forces shaping the patterns of American social and economic life. Although their impact was felt throughout the country, they centered in the Northeast and there found early and striking educational expression.

Of these forces none was so important as the rise of the factory system and industrial capitalism. It was industrialism that lured country folk to the city and, together with the rich lands of the West, beckoned European immigrants, many of whom settled down in the seaboard towns. By clinging to their old-world customs, and especially to Catholicism, these immigrants aroused the opposition of older Americans, many of whom felt that their own national institutions were imperiled. Industrialism created a new laboring class that demanded privileges and aroused the fear of conservatives. Industrialism also gave rise to new social problems such as the slums, the increase of crime, and the weakening of family ties, evils that the South was not slow to detect and denounce. The new industrialism conditioned in many respects the character of education and the social thought of its leaders.

Although industrialists were divided on the question of tax-supported public schools, a number regarded them as essential to the well-being and prosperity of the country. Thaddeus Stevens, who made two fortunes out of Pennsylvania iron, urged his colleagues in the legislature to support the measure for free public schools, since they would cost less than half as much as private schools and afford much better instruction.[62] No outstanding industrialist was more ardent in befriending public education than Abbott Lawrence. If we were to compete successfully with the manufacturers of Great Britain, warned this great man of affairs, we must spare no effort to increase the general level of intelligence through education.[63] Productive and remunerative factories required skill in the use of tools and machines, resourcefulness and invention; hence universal popular education as well as special technical schools were indispensable. Lawrence contributed from his own purse to both.[64] Healthful prosperity, he wrote to William Rives of Virginia, could be best furthered by a system of public instruction and by the promotion of manufacturing establishments. "Let your common school system go hand in hand with the employment of your people; you may be quite certain that the adoption of these systems at once, will aid each other."[65] Other industrialists lent their pens, purses, and influence to the cause of education with the conviction that by so doing they were advancing their own prosperity and that of the country.[66]

In his argument that public schools promoted industrial prosperity Alonzo Potter spoke the sentiments of many educational leaders. Education, wrote this author of the widely known manual, *School and Schoolmaster,* makes men more efficient as producers and as preservers of property, and thus

[62] Stevens, *Speech in Defense of the Pennsylvania Free School System,* 1835, p. 519.

[63] Hamilton Andrews Hill, *Memoir of Abbott Lawrence* (Boston, 1884), pp. 115–16.

[64] Hon. Nathan Appleton, *Memoir of the Hon. Abbott Lawrence* in Collections of the Massachusetts Historical Society, Series 4, Vol. IV (Boston, 1858), p. 506.

[65] *Letters from the Hon. Abbott Lawrence to the Hon. William C. Rives of Virginia* (Boston, 1846), pp. 6–7. Letter of Jan. 7, 1846.

[66] *Niles' Weekly Register,* an organ of manufacturing interests, frequently showed interest in the cause of public education.

"multiplies the ways in which they can be employed with profit to themselves, and with advantage to the community." Moreover, he continued, a laborer whose mind has been disciplined by culture "works more steadily and cheerfully, and therefore more productively, than one who, when a child, was left to grovel in ignorance and idleness." Nor must sight be lost of the fact that an educated workingman was more "fruitful in expedients." Believing that education afforded "the most certain and effectual means of developing the industrial resources of a country, and promoting its growth and prosperity," Potter favored its liberal support,[67] and like Lawrence urged the need of general and specialized education to make our competition with England more effective. If there was any doubt in regard to the pecuniary advantages to be gained from free public schools, the example of New England was reassuring: for she was proof that "education is unspeakably more important than a luxuriant soil, fine climate, or noble rivers."[68] Other voices were raised to encourage the teaching of mercantile arithmetic and bookkeeping in order that industrial and commercial prosperity might be furthered.[69]

When financial crises struck the country, education was urged as both preventive and remedy. The poverty so obvious after the debacle of 1837, some argued, was to be chiefly ascribed to ignorance. Education, by cultivating energy and enterprise, would curb improvidence, idleness, and intemperance. A trans-

[67] Potter, *School and Schoolmaster,* pp. 112–20, 148.

[68] *Ibid.,* pp. 122–23, 117. This was an argument frequently heard. See, for example, Robert Rantoul, Jr., "The Education of a Free People," 1839, in *Memoirs, Speeches and Writings of Robert Rantoul, Jr.* ed. by Luther Hamilton (Boston, 1854), p. 140.

[69] President Joshua Bates, of Middlebury College, probably expressed a fairly widespread upper-class opinion when in 1818 he advocated only elementary education for the masses, fearing that "a more refined education and a highly cultivated taste, by dividing the attention, might even unfit a man for excellence and energy in everyday pursuits." *Academician,* Vol. I (May 19, 1818), p. 83.

planted New Englander, Caleb Mills, had no doubt that such a state as Massachusetts, whose mental development had converted "the solid ice into bank notes," transmuted the ever enduring granite into gold, and converted "the banks of Newfoundland into banks of discount and circulation," would have no "lack of wisdom and resources to conduct her enterprises to a successful issue."[70] Disciplined intellects and cultivated hearts, continued this pontifical authority, were the best palliatives for financial disorders and a more substantial basis for prosperity than the millions of California.[71] In 1859 a writer in the *New York Teacher* related in great detail the bearings of education, particularly instruction in the social sciences, on the financial disasters besetting the country. A knowledge of the recurrence of crises and of the advantage of prudence in expenditure and investment would, it was argued, diminish the number of paupers, idlers, police officers, insolvencies, and bankruptcies, and guarantee a normal and virtuous state of society.[72]

But it was not only prosperity that industrialists were led to expect from public education. Anxious to wring support for public schools from propertied interests then opposed to taxation for such a purpose, educational spokesmen warned them of the dangers to property rights from universal suffrage, Jacksonian democracy, and even, possibly, revolution—any of which might result if the masses were left undisciplined by education. If the rich would enjoy security against hostile legislative attacks on corporation franchises; if they would put an end to the mob violence which was already attacking property; if they would curb "men of warm passion and little reason," vindictive and dangerous workingmen, restless and vicious frontiersmen—they could do no better than to lend support to the move-

[70] *Fifth Annual Report of the Superintendent of Public Instruction, Indiana* (1856), p. 54.
[71] *Ibid.*   [72] *New York Teacher* (Oct., 1859), p. 53.

ment for free public schools.[73] A writer in the conservative *North American Review* drew from Dorr's rebellion the lesson that the security of the established order depended on whether the masses were instructed or remained untaught, saying that the manufacturers might well tremble in the presence of the large masses of uninstructed population which were growing up around them, and see it written everywhere with a distinctness which none could comprehend as well as they, that it was only by educating this population that their business would prosper and their lives and property be secure.[74] This is by no means an exceptional statement.

Equally typical is the remark of John Armstrong, who in an address on education delivered in North Carolina in 1833 declared: "When Revolution threatens the overthrow of our institutions, everything depends upon the character of the people. If they are ignorant, they will surrender themselves to the control of their passions, and submit to be guided by noisy political fanatics."[75] In his report for 1847 the secretary of the Maine state board of education minced words no less in putting the question, "What surer guaranty can the capitalist find for the security of his investments, than is to be found in the sense of a community morally and intellectually enlightened?"[76] Another spokesman for the teaching profession observed that "to the owner of property, no economy is more important than that which shall reform those who have it in their power to plunder and destroy."[77]

No efforts were spared to convince men of wealth that public education was preferable to revolution and its only certain

[73] For a characteristic statement of this argument see James G. Carter, *Letters to the Hon. Wm. Prescott, LL.D., on the Free Schools of New England*, pp. 51–52.
[74] *North American Review*, Vol. LXVII (July, 1848), p. 254.
[75] Coon, *North Carolina Schools and Academies*, p. 751.
[76] *Common School Journal*, Vol. IX (Nov. 16, 1847), p. 339.
[77] *American Annals of Education and Instruction*, Vol. II (Jan., 1832), p. 43.

preventive. The French Revolution and its Napoleonic after-math profoundly influenced the social thought of American educators. They believed that the excesses of the Revolution would have been prevented had the French enjoyed mass education, but failed to appreciate the efforts of the revolutionists to give the masses what the privileged regime had denied them.[78] Furthermore, the lawlessness and mob violence of the thirties, startling enough in themselves, were interpreted by educators as threatening revolution. The Dorr war, the anti-rent struggles, anti-foreign and anti-Catholic riots in the East, the Aroostook war and the abolition riots—all at various times aroused apprehension and led to efforts to counteract revolutionary sentiment. Francis Gray, for example, in a lecture given in 1832 before the American Institute of Instruction, argued the failure of modern revolutions to effect beneficial and permanent social changes, and the suffering which attended such upheavals. He went on to observe that since men trained in a given society could not administer or enjoy one totally different, the "improvement of education has come to be regarded by many as the first certain and safe step to all radical and permanent improvements in the condition of men."[79]

A committee of Congress had similar fears. Under a government like ours, where everybody had the vote, it was dangerous, members reported, to leave the masses illiterate, because some master spirit might, in a day of crisis, "exercise a fatal control."[80] Could anyone remain complacent, asked a writer in

[78] *American Journal of Education,* Vol. I, p. 757, editorial "Retrospect" at the end of the volume (1826); *Transactions of the Western Literary Institute and College of Teachers,* 1837, pp. 39, 58; Potter, *School and Schoolmaster,* p. 126; Howard Mumford Jones, *America and French Culture* (Chapel Hill, N. C., 1927), p. 482.

[79] *American Annals of Education and Instruction,* Vol. III (Jan., 1833), p. 3.

[80] *American Journal of Education,* Vol. I (April, 1826), p. 226. The quotation is from a report of the House Committee on the Public Lands on the occasion of a resolution instructing them to inquire into the expediency of using the national domain to further common schools in the several states.

the *American Annals of Education and Instruction* in 1835, when "a few self-appointed individuals have undertaken to seize, abuse, and even execute the objects of their vengeance, and destroy their property, as *'their'* sense of justice should dictate—and even to attack those who attempted to sustain the laws?"[81]

Lax morals, educators maintained, were responsible for repudiation of debts, for bankruptcies, and for the tendency to evade responsibilities. Character training, it will be remembered, was held to be an even more important goal of schooling than intellectual discipline. "Is not the merchant also interested to the full amount of his stock in trade, in the intelligence and integrity of the community in which he does business? Would he find so large a share of his profits engulfed in the whirlpool of bad debts, if the people were honest? Can the manufacturer invest his capital with equal security among an ignorant and vicious people, that he would in an intelligent and virtuous community?" asked Caleb Mills. Did not public schools in a community contribute, he went on, to the enhanced value of real estate, to the increasing productiveness of capital? Would a railroad or a telegraph running through a region whose inhabitants, "induced by designing men to believe that such monopolies were hostile to their interest, should obstruct the cars, remove the rails, or cut the wires, be as productive, or the market value of its stock be as high, as it would be, if such an improvement was situated in a section of the country distinguished for its provision for the education of the whole rising generation without distinction?"[82]

Much was also made of the necessity of educating the work-

---

[81] *American Annals of Education and Instruction,* Vol. V (Oct., 1835), p. 467.

[82] Caleb Mills, *Second Address on Popular Education to the Legislature of Indiana,* 1847, reprinted in *Indiana Historical Society Publications,* Vol. III (1905), pp. 447–48.

ingmen in particular, as well as people in general, in order to prevent labor uprisings. The manager of a Lowell mill testified that in times of agitation on account of some change in regulations or wages, he always looked to the most intelligent, best educated, and most moral for support, and seldom met disappointment. The ignorant and uneducated, on the other hand, were "generally found the most turbulent and troublesome, acting under the impulse of excited passion and jealousy."[83] If attacks on property and security by "lewd fellows of the base sort" were to be put down, if the artful attempts of demagogues to array the poor against the rich were to be checked, then, argued B. P. Aydelott, correct schooling of the masses must be supported in order to refute in their minds the foolish and mischievous notion that there should be an "equality of condition."[84]

No one was more exercised about the dangers which the rising tide of labor threatened to the security of wealth than Frederick A. Packard, who persistently opposed Mann in his fight against sectarianism in the schools. This minister furthered the interests of the Sunday school movement and concerned himself with other educational matters. He painted a black picture in his *Thoughts on Popular Education* (1836). Popular licentiousness and violent excitement had trampled on the sanctions of judicial authority, knocked down the constitutional guarantees that safeguarded the franchises of corporations, and endangered all law and decency. As if he were speaking directly to men of wealth he exclaimed: "And then, forsooth, when these same boys come up into the ranks of apprentices and journeymen, without the intelligence or moral restraint which a good education would have supplied, and are

[83] "Education in Its Relation to Health, Insanity, Labor, Pauperism and Crime," in *Educational Tracts*, Vol. II (prepared by Henry Barnard, n. p., n. d.).
[84] B. P. Aydelott, *Our Country's Evils and Their Remedy*, pp. 12–13.

found at the head of mobs, and strikes, and trades' unions; speech-makers at riotous assemblies, and ringleaders of agrarian and atheistical clubs; when war is made upon the peace and order of communities, and law, with all its forms, and sanctions, and ministers, is set aside; and especially when the hand of their lawless violence is laid on the mansions, and luxuries, and treasure-houses of the rich; the arm of power must be raised, and held up by military force; the police dockets must be crowded; and, in the direct and remote influence of such a state of things, our prisons and penitentiaries will overflow, and the public purse be emptied for the support of their degraded and miserable tenants. . . . Under such institutions as ours . . . not a child can come to years of maturity, uneducated, without harm to us—to you—to the whole republic."[85]

The desire to provide an education for the working classes which would make them more readily acquiesce in the established order of political and particularly economic life, was not, of course, uniquely American. Lord Brougham, prominent English Whig who took the leading rôle in promoting education for "the people" of his country, clearly saw the conservative potentialities of popular education. "The interests of both [working classes and their superiors] are deeply concerned in sounder views being taught them; I can hardly imagine, for example, a greater service being rendered to the men, than expounding to them the true principles and mutual relations of population and wages; and both they and their masters will assuredly experience the effects of the prevailing ignorance upon such questions, as soon as any interruption shall happen in the commercial prosperity of the country, if indeed the present course of things, daily tending to lower wages as well as profits, and set the two classes in opposition to each other,

[85] F. A. Packard, *Thoughts on Popular Education* (Philadelphia, 1836), pp. 1, 36–37.

shall not of itself bring on a crisis."[86] Adam Smith, an earlier spokesman for the dominant commercial and business interests, had counseled education, for "an instructed and intelligent people are always more decent and orderly than an ignorant and stupid one" and are "less apt to be misled into any wanton or unnecessary opposition to the measures of government."[87]

The position of these men indicates that the movement for the education of the masses was not merely a democratic movement peculiarly at home in republican America. It was in part a product of the industrial capitalism rapidly becoming dominant throughout the western world. We tend today to think of our American system of public schools as having been founded out of a great zeal for the welfare of the plain people. But actually this zeal was tempered by zeal for the welfare of the employers of labor, by zeal for maintaining the political and social *status quo*. These economic motives were frankly recognized in the days of the founding. Now, however, looking back, we tend to rationalize, and to recognize only the more idealistic motives, which were of course also operative.

Appeals to the self-interest of men of wealth to educate the masses recur with monotonous frequency in the writings of educators throughout the second quarter of the century. Nor were the appeals merely general. Even in the teachers' manuals effort was made to persuade instructors of youth to inculcate respect for property rights and the existing order. David Page, whose *Theory and Practice of Teaching* inspired over 10,000 teachers, and for fifty years was regarded as the one indispensable book for those who kept school, emphasized the duty of instructing children with regard to "the sacredness of all prop-

---

[86] Henry Lord Brougham, "Practical Observations upon the Education of the People, 1825," in *Sketches of Public Characters* (Philadelphia, 1839), Vol. II, pp. 45–46.
[87] Adam Smith, *Wealth of Nations* (London, reprint of 1812 ed.), p. 621.

erty."[88] Respect for property, wrote George Emerson in his *School and Schoolmaster,* must be taught in school, where it can be better inculcated than anywhere else, since the school is a "miniature community."[89] Similar lessons, as we have seen, were taught by Noah Webster's *Elementary Speller.* Sometimes educators assumed a special responsibility for combating tendencies hostile to order and security. Stern opponents of lax discipline in family and school, for example, attributed much of the lawlessness and mob violence to the undermining of family and school authority, and to the "new freedom" of children. They argued that disobedience on the part of the child to parent and teacher must be checked if the social evils resulting from such degeneracy of family and school government were to be eliminated.[90]

Public men similarly urged conservative interests to support tax-maintained public schools as a preventive of social upheaval and hostile attacks on property. Daniel Webster, spokesman of industrial Massachusetts, held that universal suffrage would mean the dispossession of the wealthy were it not for the democratic division of property in the United States. Yet he supported public schools on the ground that, among other things, they would serve as a police system by which property, the peace of society, and the political fabric would be secured against "the slow but sure undermining of licentiousness" and "open violence and overthrow."[91] Another representative of conservative interests, Edward Everett, favored educating mechanics, since

[88] David Page, *Theory and Practice of Teaching* (Syracuse, 1893), p. 362.

[89] Emerson, *School and Schoolmaster,* pp. 350–51.

[90] Albert Picket, Address, *Transactions of the Western Literary Institute and College of Teachers* (1836), p. 39; *American Annals of Education and Instruction,* Vol. V (Oct., 1835), p. 469.

[91] Daniel Webster, "First Settlement of New England," address at Plymouth, Dec. 22. 1820, in *The Works of Daniel Webster* (Boston, 1853), Vol. I, pp. 38, 41–42; and Address in the Massachusetts Constitutional Convention, cited by Carter, *Letters to Hon. Wm. Prescott,* p. 49.

"an intelligent class can scarce be, as a class, vicious."[92] Chief Justice Marshall also relied on the education of the masses to prevent the development of a serious labor problem, although he foresaw that after free lands were exhausted, education might prove unequal to the task.[93] Similar arguments were used by many governors in their appeals to legislatures for the support of free public schools.[94]

However outspoken in favor of education some industrialists, rich merchants, and landowners were, and however impressed others must have been by the foregoing arguments, many continued to oppose tax-supported public schools. As late as 1850 Samuel J. May, of Syracuse, New York, begged Horace Mann to address an approaching convention because the free school law was being attacked by "certain wealthy individuals and monied institutions."[95] A wealthy citizen of Watertown, New York, thought that the free school law differed little from the poor law, the purpose of which was to fill the belly and cover the back of the indigent at the expense of the taxpayer.[96] Others thought that the children of the poor would grow up idle and lazy if education were provided free of charge. They feared that free schools would pauperize their beneficiaries in much the same way as some opponents of unemployment insurance in our own time fear dire consequences from such social legislation. Still others regarded free public education as an entering wedge of agrarianism and

[92] Everett, *Practical Education*, p. 83.
[93] Albert J. Beveridge, *The Life of John Marshall* (Boston, 1919), Vol. IV, pp. 471–72.
[94] For example: David S. Reid, governor of North Carolina, in M. C. S. Noble, *A History of the Public Schools of North Carolina*, p. 189; T. Worthington, governor of Ohio, *The Academician*, Vol. I (Jan. 30, 1819), p. 239; Report to the legislature of Illinois, cited in *American Annals of Education and Instruction*, Vol. V (April, 1835), p. 173.
[95] May to Mann, May 21, 1850, Mann Papers.
[96] Frank T. Carlton, *Economic Influences upon Educational Progress in the United States, 1820–1850*, p. 60.

socialism. Some were alarmed lest tax-supported schools infringe on the liberty of individuals who had hitherto provided private education for their own children. In Rhode Island the prejudice of respectable members of the legislature against a tax to support public schools was so great that they declared it would be resisted at the point of a bayonet.[97]

There were even those who rested their hostility to free common schools on the ground that they strengthened the spirit of democracy and broke down class barriers. Why should men of wealth, it was asked, be required to pay for the schooling of those "who were better suited to their station without it?"[98] Culture, it was urged, depended on leisure, and leisure in turn was impossible without a small wealthy class.[99] As to the contention that the education of workers would promote the prosperity of industrialists, some argued openly that their prosperity depended rather on an abundant supply of labor "comparatively uneducated."[100] Representative of a considerable body of opinion was the conviction of "intelligent gentlemen" familiar with the "most respectable manufacturing establishments," who in answer to an appeal for support of practical instruction to workers, replied that the "only way to get along with such ignorant people is to keep them from mischief by keeping them constantly employed."[101]

In view of such opposition of wealthy men to tax-supported education, while supplying their own sons with the best, it is

[97] *Ibid.*, pp. 59–62.
[98] Richard G. Boone, *A History of Education in Indiana* (New York, 1892), p. 123.
[99] Philip R. V. Curoe, *Educational Attitudes and Policies of Organized Labor in the United States* (Teachers College, Columbia University, Contributions to Education, No. 201, New York, 1926), p. 33.
[100] Editorial, *Philadelphia National Gazette,* Aug. 25, 1830, cited in *Documentary History of American Industrial Society,* ed. by John R. Commons and associates (Cleveland, 1910), Vol. V, pp. 113–14.
[101] *American Annals of Education and Instruction,* Vol. III (June, 1833), pp. 257–58.

small wonder that leaders of the rising labor movement condemned capitalists for monopolizing knowledge. Nor is it surprising, in the light of the extravagant claims made on behalf of education, that they expected great benefit for their own class could they but attain free schools for their children. As Stephen Simpson put it, "we seem to have resuscitated from the tomb of time the very spirit of the feudal ages, in the breast of certain bigots, intolerants, aristocrats, and narrow-minded monopolists of knowledge, who seem as averse to giving the people light, as they are to paying them for their labor in hard money."[102] A Boston labor leader, Seth Luther, pictured the miserable body of workers, "ruined by the neglect of education, rendered miserable in the extreme, and incapable of self-government; and this by the grinding of the rich on the faces of the poor, through the operations of cotton and other machinery."[103] Both Simpson and Luther insisted on free and universal schooling as necessary to the well-being of the laboring classes. Simpson declared that it was mainly to education that the working class must turn for redress of that "perverted system of society, which dooms the producer to ignorance, to toil, and to penury, to moral degradation, physical want and social barbarism."[104]

Robert Dale Owen, an active leader in the labor struggles of New York about 1830, likewise regarded a national, equal, and practical system of education as "the only redeemer of our suffering country from the equal curses of chilling poverty and corrupting riches."[105] When Robert Rantoul, Jr., a friend of labor, told a group of workingmen that "with free schools, and a free press, improved as both of them ought to be, and must be, if we duly prize our peculiar privileges, we need have

102 Cited by Carlton, *op. cit.*, p. 64.
103 Seth Luther, *Education of Workingmen,* cited by Carlton, p. 48.
104 Stephen Simpson, *A Manual for Workingmen,* cited by Carlton, *op. cit.,* p. 49.
105 *Ibid.,* p. 56.

no fear of the aristocratical tendencies of accumulated masses of capital," he was expressing a belief common among working people.[106]

Labor newspapers and conventions reiterated and elaborated the demand for free public education, which became one of the most important planks in the workingmen's parties in the years 1828 to 1831.[107] To a less extent the trades unions in the following decades continued to advocate tax-supported schools. While it would be too much to say, as some writers have claimed, that public education was wrung from the privileged classes by the pressure of American labor, its contributions to the cause were not unimportant. Workers educated their own class to appreciate the value of free public schools, contributed to the popularization of the movement among legislators and the general public, and "sold" the idea that a voting citizen could not discharge his obligations without a minimum of education and leisure for self-improvement.[108]

But even within the ranks of the early labor movement some questioned the wisdom and expediency of depending upon education to improve the status of workingmen. It is not clear whether these skeptics were suspicious of the efforts of educators to convince capitalists that free schools were the best means of perpetuating their own position and power. But it would be strange if they did not note the fact that in the struggles between workers and owners many leaders of education appeared to be serving the interests of the latter.

In any case, it was plain at least to Thomas Skidmore, a left-wing New York leader, that the "benefit of education" would not inevitably secure the food and clothing and comfortable

[106] *Memoirs of Robert Rantoul, Jr.*, p. 137.

[107] Curoe, *op. cit.*, pp. 8–21. Some workingmen's groups favored the improvement of existing public schools; others wanted communistic boarding schools; some insisted on a utilitarian type of training.

[108] *Ibid.*, p. 33.

homes which the workers needed. "If they [political physicians] be sincere in their belief that such education is so very indispensable as a previous step in this enjoyment; and that the people are not now sufficiently instructed, let me ask them how, under present circumstances, is it ever *possible* to give it? Is a family, where both parents and children are suffering daily, in their animal wants; where excessive toil is required to obtain the little they enjoy; where the unkind and the unfriendly passions, generated by such a wretched condition of things, reign with fell sway: is such a family in a situation to receive instruction? . . . let all remember, that those who undertake to *hold back* the people from their rights of property, as shown in this work, until *education,* as they call it, can first be communicated . . . either do not understand themselves, or pursue the course they *are* pursuing, for the purpose of diverting the people from the possession of these rights; that they may be held in bondage, even yet longer."[109] Thus spoke a forerunner of Marx more than thirty years before the publication of *Capital.*

Among the friends of the labor movement Horace Greeley expressed the same point of view. "I would not if I could conceal from you my conviction that, before Education can become what it should and must be, we must reform the Social Life whence it proceeds, whitherto it tends," he wrote in his *Hints Toward Reforms.* "To the child daily sent out from some rickety hovel or miserable garret to wrestle with Poverty and Misery for such knowledge as the teacher can impart, what true idea or purpose of Education is possible?"[110] On other occasions, too, Greeley insisted that education should not be regarded as a substitute for social reform. Until a "vast and per-

[109] Thomas Skidmore, *The Rights of Man to Property! Being a Proposition to Make it Equal Among the Adults of the Present Generation* (New York, 1829), p. 369.
[110] Horace Greeley, *Hints Toward Reforms* (New York, 1853), p. 219.

vading" improvement had been made in the social and physical condition of mankind, education could never be what it ought to be or elevate the worker to a higher level.

Would subsequent events justify the criticism of Skidmore and Greeley? Free schools were achieved, and many working-class children profited from them. Some, no doubt, left the ranks of their class because of the advantages school had provided them. But a working class remained. Low wages, unemployment, insecurity remained. Clearly the free public school has not fulfilled the hopes of early labor leaders and "redeemed our suffering country from the equal curses of chilling poverty and corrupting riches." Nor have our free schools and our free press removed all danger from "the aristocratic tendencies of accumulated masses of capital."

It is clear that friends of labor exaggerated the benefits education would bring to the wage earner. One reason why the labor movement in this country has been so backward, as compared with European movements, is quite probably to be found in the extravagant faith of the masses in popular education. The public school with its free opportunities of cultural advancement for all, along with the frontier offering free or cheap land for many who needed it—the existence of these two paths of advancement may well have been the chief of the factors in America which blinded labor to the existence of its fundamental problems. To the extent that educational leaders remained indifferent to or unaware of their responsibilities for improving the condition of the masses, to the extent that the free public school provided actually an education limited in content and aim to the standards and outlook of the owning class which conceded it—to that extent it may be said that the warnings of Greeley and of Skidmore were justified.

In some respects the reactions of educators to the arguments of labor suggest that in the struggle between the proletariat and the industrialists their sympathies were with the latter. As we have seen, they spared no pains in endeavoring to persuade men of wealth that free schools promised security to property. In commenting on Seth Luther's address on education a writer in the *American Annals of Education and Instruction* took exception to many of the arguments made by that labor leader. Far from being objects of pity, workers, according to this writer, ate better food than the wealthy, slept more soundly, sweetly, and unbrokenly, suffered less from changes of temperature, and pursued occupations "more favorable to morals, and quite as much so to healthy intellectual development." He denounced Luther for insinuating that capitalists calculatingly monopolized education for the training of drones, vampires, and young men who "spend their time in patching up the present state of things and lord it over others."[111]

Another early advocate of education took workingmen to task for claiming that their labors alone created wealth and for denouncing as non-producers those who supplied them, by incessant activity of mind, with the opportunity and instruments of labor. But he agreed with Adam Smith that the working masses if instructed would be more decent and orderly, "more respectable and likely to obtain the respect of their lawful superiors" and therefore "more disposed to respect those superiors."[112] The editor of the *American Annals of Education and Instruction,* in reprinting an English article advising education of the worker so that he might "learn to look upon the distinctions of society without envy" and be "taught to understand that they are open to him as well as to others, and to respect them for this reason," observed that these remarks were

[111] *American Annals of Education and Instruction,* Vol. III (June, 1833), pp. 255, 258–59.
[112] *Ibid.,* Vol. III (Dec., 1833), pp. 565–66.

hardly less applicable to the United States than to England.[113] Even Alonzo Potter, who felt that Providence had not condemned any person to a dull round of toil, such as life-long heading of nails and pointing of pins, and who conceded that every one had the right to better his status through schooling, nevertheless regarded education as the means of inspiring workers to perform the most humble duties with "unfaltering fidelity."[114]

Other educational leaders gave evidence of more sympathy with the problems of labor even if they did not advance realistic solutions. It was a frequent argument that common schools, by bringing together all classes of children, the rich with the poor, would eliminate class distinctions, which Jacksonian democracy had not been able to vanquish.[115] It was thought that the poor would learn decorum and cleanliness from the rich, who in turn would appreciate sympathetically the wants and deprivations of their fellows of the same age.[116] C. G. Memminger, an orphan who became a public leader and ardent exponent of free public schools in South Carolina, contended that "the bringing together the children of the rich and poor will benefit both, by removing from one any disposition to arrogance and self-will, and from the other the spirit of envy and jealousy."[117] Calvin Wiley and Caleb Mills argued

[113] "The Necessity of Educating the Poor," *ibid.*, Vol. VI (April, 1836), pp. 163–64.

[114] Potter, *School and Schoolmaster*, pp. 145, 148.

[115] It is of interest to note that Henry Lord Brougham, English exponent of education and conservative economic indoctrination of the people, similarly held that if the working classes could read and had cheap editions available the "marked line of separation between the two classes" would disappear. Brougham, *Practical Observations upon the Education of the People*, 1825, in *Sketches of Public Characters*, p. 44.

[116] Report of the trustees of the New York Free-School Society in *American Journal of Education*, Vol. I (Aug., 1826), p. 462.

[117] Mattie Crouch Kneece, *The Contributions of C. G. Memminger to the Cause of Education* (Bulletin of the University of South Carolina, No. 177, Feb. 15, 1926), p. 25.

in much the same way, the latter observing that public schools humbled aristocratic pride, refined plebeian roughness, rebuked haughty insolence, and thus assimilated the various discordant materials and rendered the body politic homogeneous in character and sympathy.[118]

Not everyone, however, shared this general faith in the power of the public schools to dissolve social differences. The Reverend B. O. Peers, who was commissioned by the legislature of Kentucky in 1829 to visit the schools of Connecticut, concluded that the public schools actually accentuated social distinction, since education in the free public schools had been so cheapened that all who were able refused to accept it, even as a gratuity. If knowledge is power, then, asked this shrewd clergyman, how can the unsuspected ascendancy of the rich be more effectually secured than by putting off the poor in means, with the present of a poor education?[119]

By giving rise to a new set of social evils the growth of industrialism in the Northeast was a very important factor in the development of a wave of humanitarian agitation which still further accentuated the differences between New England and the Middle States on the one hand and the rest of the country on the other. This humanitarian movement, of which the crusade for tax-supported and improved public schools was in part an expression, was, to be sure, more than a mere protest against the social evils resulting from the expansion of the factory system. Back of it was the conviction of eighteenth-century philosophers that human misery was irrational, unnecessary, and remediable; the concern of Rousseau for the welfare of all

[118] *North Carolina Journal of Education,* Vol. III (Sept., 1860), p. 277; Mills, *Sixth Address on Popular Education to the Legislature of Indiana* (1852), p. 585. For other evidence that educators in the West, where society was presumably democratic, urged public schools to break down class distinctions, see Carlton, *op. cit.,* p. 51.

[119] *Barnard's American Journal of Education,* Vol. V (June, 1858), pp. 135–37.

mankind; the evangelical faith and zeal of certain types of Christianity; and also a quite special set of conditions in the states in which industrialism was making its most rapid headway.

In the America of the early eighteen hundreds the old, harsh, and rigid Puritan faith had declined. Unitarianism, with its emphasis on the brotherhood and the divinity of man, could not but be interested in the lot of man on earth. Social morality became in the minds of many people a substitute for the older and now weakened religious sanctions. The children of the ministerial class, moreover, saw the hold their group had exercised on public life rapidly vanishing. For the most part, the humanitarian agitators came, not from the new industrial class which was making up to sixty per cent profit annually from its shops and factories, but rather from the ministerial, farming, and commercial classes—groups with less pecuniary interest in the conditions which aroused their indignant sense of human injustice, and at the same time conscious of the fact that a new type of power was superseding their own.

Of sensitive temperament, the humanitarians who enlisted in the crusades against slavery, war, intemperance, imprisonment for debt, and harsh penal conditions, and who battled heroically for the rights of women, the insane, and the underprivileged, saw plenty in the factory towns and cities to arouse their wrath. Living conditions in the slums were revolting. In 1849 Doctor Henry Clark found one small Boston cellar inhabited by thirty-nine persons, and this was typical of the whole district into which the Irish immigrants had crowded. The section was reported as being a "perfect hive of human beings without comforts and mostly without common necessaries." In many cases men, women, and children were huddled together like brutes without any regard to sex, age, or sense of decency. Small wonder, it was felt, that the average length of life of the Irish in Boston was not over fourteen years. In the "hub of the universe" Doctor C. E. Buckingham saw the salt tides pouring into miserable backyards from all four sides to the depth of a foot. In Lowell, which was regarded as an exemplary factory town, one building centrally located—and it was not unique—was occupied by a store and 120 families. Sometimes two families lived in the same room. The Reverend Henry Wood knew of numerous cases in the same city where from six to ten persons lived in a single room and sometimes slept in the same bed. The Society for the Improvement of the Condition of the Poor pointed out in 1853 that the almost incredible slums of New York were so profitable that a return of 100 per cent interest was not uncommon.

Wages and standards of living were indecently low. Horace Greeley estimated that in 1845 two-thirds of the population of New York City lived on barely a dollar a week for each person subsisting thereon. This was at a period when prosperity reigned and when business and wealth were expanding in an almost breathless fashion. Yet in one month it was estimated that there were 20,000 unemployed in the metropolis alone. At the same time the prosperous Lowell mills declared an average dividend of 12 per cent and cut wages in exactly the same proportion.

In the recurring periods of depression, conditions were much worse. That of 1837 left one-third of the working population of New York City unemployed. In 1833 one person out of every eight in the metropolis was a public pauper, and in 1844 it was thought that the number exceeded 51,000. Matters were not much better in New England. In a letter of 1846, Mr. Abbott Lawrence stated that the wages of mill operatives had risen from $1.75 to $2.00 a week, but neglected to point out that the increase was only a partial return after an earlier cut. The cost of living was rising. Already company stores demanded exorbitant prices from their employees. A manager in Holyoke found his hands "languorous" in the early morning, and got 3000 more yards of cloth a week by working them without breakfast. It was hardly a golden day for the plain people.[120]

Children were whirled into the maelstrom. Replies to questions sent to the city authorities of all the factory towns in Massachusetts in 1825 showed that not one town claimed less than eleven hours of toil for child workers from six to seventeen years of age, and only two reported so short a day. In 1833 a report of a committee of the New England Association of Farmers, Mechanics and other Working Men exposed the fact that two-fifths of all persons employed in New England factories were children between seven and sixteen; that hours were from daylight to eight in the evening; and that the only opportunity for them to obtain an education was on Sunday, or after eight on week days.[121] At Hope Factory in Rhode Island, workers, more than half of whom were children, toiled fifteen or sixteen hours a day. In the same state, where conditions were worse than in Massachusetts, small, half-clothed children went to work and came home by dark, and as late as 1853 their numbers were increasing. Yet President Monroe in the midst of the "era of good feeling" congratulated factory owners on the "fall in the prices of labor, so favorable to the success of domestic manufacturers," and many agreed with Alexander Hamilton that children were better off in mills and shops than at home or in school. *Niles' Weekly Register,* an organ of industrialists and merchants, calculated the wealth that

[120] These figures are taken from Norman Ware, *The Industrial Worker* (Boston, 1924).
[121] F. C. Ensign, *Compulsory Attendance and Child Labor* (New York, 1921), p. 38.

could be made if all children were put to work in factories.[122]

It was against such degradation that humanitarians protested. Shocked at the conditions in the slums, the rising tide of crime, the disintegration of the family, and the prevalence of drunkenness and crass forms of immorality, many turned to the movement for tax-supported public schools to remedy conditions. In so doing they were following the example of the great humanitarian educators of Europe, who looked to education for the solution of the problem of poverty. Inspired by Rousseau, Pestalozzi sought to show how sense-impressions, physical activity, and the acquisition of industrial skill would alleviate the condition of the poorest classes, whose children would thus acquire sound moral character and a self-respecting contentment with their lot. If neither Pestalozzi nor his even less democratic associate Fellenberg sought to break down class alignments through education, they did believe and attempt in their experiments to prove that the proper sort of education could advance the humanitarian ideal of eliminating the worst types of degradation among the masses of the poor.[123] The fame of Pestalozzi's and Fellenberg's humanitarian devotion to education as a means of remedying the condition of the poor reached American shores and aroused a good deal of interest.[124]

Stimulated by the crying evils of industrialism and reenforced by the example of European educational thought and experiment, the movement for more and better schools enlisted greater support than any of the humanitarian reforms

[122] Knight, *Education in the United States,* pp. 177–79.
[123] Johann Heinrich Pestalozzi, *How Gertrude Teaches Her Children* (Syracuse, 1898), Letter I, pp. 29–80; Letter IV, pp. 124–34; Letter X, pp. 220–27; Letter XII, pp. 256–66. J. A. Green, *Life and Work of Pestalozzi* (Baltimore, pref. 1912), pp. 23, 47, 266.
[124] William C. Woodbridge, "Letters from Hofwyl" in most issues of *American Annals of Education and Instruction,* Vols. I and II (Aug., 1830, to Dec., 1832). See also John Griscom, *A Year in Europe* (New York, 1823); and Will S. Monroe, *Pestalozzian Movement in the United States* (Syracuse, 1907), *passim.*

designed to wipe out the social miseries born of industrial capitalism. The problems it created, and which the hordes of immigrants who came to build railroads, dig canals, and mine coal and iron accentuated, were to be solved by education. Public schools were to give every son of toil a chance to better himself, to withstand the temptation of the dram shop, the lure of the brothel, the binding grip of the slum. Public schools were to realize the dream of the Revolutionary fathers. The direct action and militancy they had appealed to was now to give way to the method of the schoolroom.

III

EDUCATION AND SOCIAL REFORM:
HORACE MANN

What Rousseau as a writer was to the emotions of the France of his day, Horace Mann as a doer was to the practical situation of the United States in his time.

—JOHN DEWEY.

I

Perhaps more influential than any of the other factors which determined the social philosophy of Horace Mann was the character of his early environment. It was that of thousands of other boys who grew up in rural New England in the first years of the nineteenth century—an environment governed by poverty, hardship, and denial, and inspired by sobriety, thrift, and godliness. His body was over-strained by work that was too hard for him, and as a result he suffered all his life from poor health.[1] His soul was tortured by the harsh and horrible sermons of the Calvinist minister who presided over the village church, and though he early accepted the more humane tenets of Unitarianism, he never entirely freed himself from the shadow those sermons cast over him. Until the end of his life he was inclined, as he himself said, to hold fast to intense and extreme views—to make too serious matters of small ones, and to be absorbed, incited, and stimulated by really serious ones to a degree that his physical constitution was unfitted to bear.[2]

Mann had toiled too hard and learned too well the lessons of

[1] Mann to his wife, May 25, 1850, Mann Papers.
[2] Mann to his sister, May 30, 1848, Mann Papers.

his austere and high-minded home to cherish culture that did not have a utilitarian value: thus all his life he regarded fiction as prejudicial to the "attainment of solid science" and as productive of permanent injury to the mind. He had struggled against obstacles sufficiently to prize the advantages of education: until he was fifteen his own schooling had yearly amounted to a mere pittance of eight or ten weeks, and his teachers could hardly have been poorer than they were. But his parents taught him that knowledge was an instrument for doing good, and that benevolence ranked high in the scale of virtues, so that, as he remembered later, all his "boyish castles in the air had reference to doing something for the benefit of mankind."

Without the moral earnestness absorbed in his formative years, it is doubtful whether Horace Mann could have sufficiently overcome the handicaps of poverty and slender schooling to enter Brown University, as he did in 1816. The many college essays still preserved among his manuscripts reveal the influences that were further molding his mind and character. Although devoted to New England, which he cherished as probably "the most favored community since the creation of man," he was at the same time inspired by patriotic enthusiasm for the young republic, and he took pleasure in defending its institutions and aspirations against the tyranny and treachery of the Old World. He even had high words of praise for the American navy, though he was later to spare nothing in his denunciation of war.

Almost everything he wrote in these years at Providence bore the impress of the strong utilitarian influence to which early surroundings and natural bent committed him. Life in his native Massachusetts town, named for Benjamin Franklin and prizing a library given by that philosopher, had put a premium on the useful as well as the austere virtues. While in college Mann, when he was not mastering the classics, devoted himself to such things as nature study and more practical methods of learning languages. He was, indeed, already showing a leaning toward the utilitarian disciplines that was to lead him, in his later career as an educator, to defend such practical studies as arithmetic, drawing, surveying, nature studies and, especially, physiology, and to maintain that the school which failed to prepare its pupils for the work of field, shop, forum, and desk fell short of its true goal.[3] But even in these college years it was plain that his utilitarianism was of no narrow sort, and those best acquainted with his student work would not have been surprised to see that his later educational reports insisted that school work must not merely train skilled craftsmen but rather intelligent men who understood "the principles upon which their work proceeds" as well as its social, economic, and cultural implications.[4]

Mann's humanitarian interests were particularly apparent in his college essays. The cause of temperance found in him an ardent champion. He welcomed the oppressed immigrant who sought our shores, and calculated the material and spiritual contributions which he brought with him. He justified the separation of church and state and defended the freedom of the press. He championed the cause of democratic education; a national university had no appeal for him since it threatened

[3] Mann prepared, or helped prepare, more practical texts in arithmetic, physiology, and hygiene, and in other ways contributed, specifically, to furthering utilitarianism in the schools. H. Mann and Pliny E. Chase, *The Primary School Arithmetic* (Philadelphia, 1851), p. vi; *Lecture on the Best Mode of Preparing and Using Spelling Books*, 1841; *The Study of Physiology in the Schools* (New York, 1869). For the high place assigned to science in education and in life see Horace Mann, *A Few Thoughts for a Young Man . . .* (Boston, 1850), pp. 47–50.

[4] Mann Papers, Miscellaneous 1779–1827, especially "Natural History," "Value of Knowledge" and "To Improve Language Teaching." For the later development of his educational utilitarianism, which suggests that of John Dewey, see the Annual Reports of 1839 and 1842 in *Life and Works of Horace Mann,* ed. by Mary Mann (Boston, 1865–68), Vol. III, pp. 35–36, 130.

to promote distribution of knowledge solely among the wealthy, who alone could afford to attend such an institution. In one of his essays he declared that "there is by nature little, or perhaps no distinction among men with respect to their original powers of intellect. The seeds of knowledge, of refinement, and of literary excellence are implanted with a liberality, nearly or completely equal, in the mind of the ignorant peasant, and in the mind of the most profound philosopher."[5] Popular education was therefore necessary if the seeds implanted by the impartial hand of nature in the mind of the illiterate peasant were to germinate.

Thus Horace Mann opened his heart and mind to every generous and humane thought and feeling. Fittingly enough, he achieved the climax of his liberal thinking in his commencement oration, "The Progressive Character of the Human Race."[6] Visioning the day when education should lift human society to a lofty position, when philanthropy should succor the wants and relieve the woes of the race, when free institutions, guaranteed by popular schools, should abolish oppression, the enthusiastic orator committed himself unreservedly to the humanitarian movement that was invading New England.

A Puritan reformer, spotless in character and heroic in benevolence, Horace Mann was ready, after supplementing his college training by a little teaching and by legal study, to take the field in behalf of his convictions. Elected a member of the Massachusetts legislature from the town of Dedham, he made a notable defense of the principle of religious freedom. He also championed the cause of better treatment for the insane and was chiefly responsible for the establishment of the state hospital at Worcester. Desiring to help the drunken wretches exploited by the dram shops, he induced the legislature in 1836

[5] "Self-Improvement," Mann Papers, Miscellaneous, 1779–1827.
[6] *American Journal of Education*, Vol. V (Dec., 1858), p. 614.

to enact a law making it a crime to drink in public.[7] A society for the prevention of pauperism formed in Boston in 1836 found in the representative from Dedham an intelligent friend.[8] Believing that the Negro and white child were alike in capacity for enjoying physical pleasures and for suffering physical pain, he defended the right of handicapped black children to attend special educational institutions along with whites.[9] As a member of the Prison Discipline Society, Mann helped popularize the idea that prisons should be reformatory rather than merely penal.

In these crusades it was necessary to fight the mercenary selfishness which opposed the expenditure of public money for human welfare. Sometimes Mann satisfied himself by merely excoriating so unchristian a policy as that, for example, which set in motion the whole agency of the state to recover stolen property and to punish the culprit, but which at the same time neglected the infinitely more important task of rehabilitating the character of the thief. "Surely things could never be so in a community where the love of virtue had practical ascendency over the love of money—where, in the price-current of public opinion, souls were of more value than silver or gold."[10] Yet on other occasions, adopting a more pragmatic course, he attempted to convince stubborn vested interests that the reform they opposed would actually redound to their own profit. Thus he tried to persuade the grocers who profited from the sale of intoxicating drink that they would earn greater profits if ardent spirits were outlawed, since customers would as a result be more efficient in their work and able to buy a greater

[7] Elizabeth Palmer Peabody, *Reminiscences of William Ellery Channing, D. D.* (Boston, 1880), p. 383; John Krout, *Origins of Prohibition* (New York, 1925), p. 145.
[8] Mann to Miss Peabody, Oct. 4, 1836, Mann Papers.
[9] Mann to Miss Peabody, Aug. 24, 1833; Mann to his sister, June, 1845, Mann Papers.
[10] *Common School Journal*, Vol. VII (Jan. 1, 1845), p. 14.

number of other commodities. Moreover, it was not to be forgotten, he told the recalcitrant grocers, that their very business in ordinary merchandise depended on the general security
of property which was dangerously jeopardized by prevalent
drunkenness.[11] In view of the opposition Mann encountered
in all his reform activities, and his consequent efforts to meet
the dollar argument in kind, a contemporary judgment that
his "evangelical piety" blinded him to the actual wickedness
of the world was not altogether true.[12]

II

The educational work in which Horace Mann enlisted in
1837 was only another expression of his humanitarian zeal.
In view of the sad plight of the common schools of Massachusetts, it was not strange that he decided their improvement
was a more pressing and important matter than prison reform,
the treatment of the insane, pauperism, and temperance. While
it was true that in the decade preceding 1837 something had
been done to improve the schools, much remained to be accomplished. Until James Carter, a teacher and a member of the
legislature, by reason of his vigorous writings and active work
brought about certain improvements in 1826 and 1827, the
common schools had received almost no legislative attention,
protection, or bounty for almost forty years. It was, indeed,
hardly an exaggeration when Carter declared in 1826 that if
legislative policy did not change, common schools would become extinct in another twenty years.[13] The state had shifted
the responsibility for the upkeep and supervision of the schools
to the towns; the towns had passed it on to the local dis-

[11] Horace Mann, *Remarks upon the Comparative Profits of Grocers and Re-
tailers, as Derived from Temperate and Intemperate Customers* (Massachusetts
Temperance Society Publications, 1st series, No. 1, Boston, 1834), pp. 12 *et seq.*
[12] Samuel Downer to Mann, June 18, 1850, Mann Papers.
[13] James G. Carter, *Essays upon Popular Education* (Boston, 1826), p. 41.

tricts; and the districts had shifted it to individuals. In 1826 barely a third of the children of suitable age had opportunity to attend public school, and actually did attend, for some portion of the year.[14] Moreover, the schools were incredibly deficient. Instructors often were unable to do simple sums in multiplication and division, and in 1837 some three hundred teachers were driven out of their schools by unruly and riotous pupils over whom, in spite of the prevalent use of the whip, they were unable to keep any semblance of order. Yet Massachusetts led in educational matters—probably in no state were conditions better.

In the revival of common school education Horace Mann, who served during the years 1837 to 1848 as secretary of the State Board of Education, played a leading rôle the influence of which penetrated far beyond Massachusetts.[15] Much, it is true, had been done in the decade preceding his appointment to the secretaryship. James Carter had preached the gospel of better support for the common schools, state supervision, the establishment of normal schools, better teaching methods, and the paying of higher salaries to attract better men.[16] It was largely due to his energy and persistence that the bill drafted by his pen for the establishment of the State Board of Education was finally passed by the legislature in 1837. In view of the pioneer work of Carter there was some truth in the assertion that Mann was an educational follower rather than a leader. Yet none of Mann's predecessors stirred the great body of the public as he was to do. As John Dewey has said, Mann stood, and stood most effectively, "for letting the democratic spirit,

[14] *Ibid.*, p. 57.
[15] C. Roy Aurner, "Iowa a Debtor to Horace Mann," *Journal of Education*, Vol. LXXVIII (Oct. 2, 1913), pp. 315–16; Barnard's address on the occasion of Mann's death, *Proceedings of the First Annual Convention of the American Normal School Association, Trenton, N. J., Aug. 19, 20, 1859*, p. 111.
[16] Carter, *op. cit.*, and *Letters to the Hon. William Prescott, LL.D. on the Free Schools of New England, passim.*

in all its ethical significance, into the common elementary schools, and for such a complete reorganization of these schools as would make them the most serviceable possible instruments of human development."[17]

It was at great personal sacrifice that Mann undertook the difficult work of popularizing the cause of better common school education. But he did not share the feeling of many of his friends that he had made a mistake in giving up a lucrative legal practice and membership in the legislature to undertake a badly paid and thankless task. A true humanitarian, he was convinced that it was better to do good than to enjoy profit and honor. "If I can be the means of ascertaining what is the best construction of [school] houses, what are the best books, what is the best mode of instruction; if I can discover by what appliance of means a non-thinking, non-reflecting, non-speaking child can most surely be trained into a noble citizen, ready to contend for the *right,* and to die for the *right;* if I can only obtain and diffuse throughout the state a few good ideas on these and similar subjects, may I not flatter myself that my ministry has not been wholly in vain?"[18]

To effect these ends Mann resorted to all the techniques of publicity familiar in his day and even invented some that were hardly known. He organized teachers' conventions and institutes and inspired those who kept school with his own educational and social philosophy. He founded and edited the *Common School Journal* to further the same end, and to enlighten and win the public to the cause. He organized and administered normal schools; he studied methods of education abroad; he encouraged educational leaders throughout the West and South. Most important of all, he wrote the famous reports, which, covering a wide variety of subjects, exerted great influ-

[17] John Dewey, *The Educational Situation* (Chicago, 1902), p. 59.
[18] Horace Mann to Lydia B. Mann, July 16, 1837, Mann Papers.

ence on educational thought and practice.[19] In all this work he did not spare himself. "From the time I accepted the secretary-ship, on January 1, 1837 until May 1848, when I tendered my resignation," he wrote, "I labored in this cause an average of not less than fifteen hours a day; from the beginning to the end of this period I never took a single day for recreation, and months and months together passed without my withdrawing a single evening to call on a friend."[20]

Nor was his path a smooth one. Without justification, bigots like Frederick Packard[21] and Matthew Hale Smith miscon-strued his efforts to execute a state law which forbade the teach-ing of sectarianism in the common schools and, in spite of all he did to promote the reading of the Bible and the teach-ing of non-sectarian religion, denounced him as an atheist who crowded religious instruction out of the schools.[22] In spite of the fact that no one could have been more non-partisan in public office, politicians sought to undermine his position. His measures of state supervision, desperately needed though they were, alarmed local interests which resented any interference. Worst of all, in one of the most notorious controversies of the

[19] In these reports Mann considered a wide variety of subjects, many of which were so forward-looking that his discussion of them is still interesting and important. He concerned himself with what would today be thought of as school statistics, administration, supervision, consolidation of rural districts, hygiene, and school architecture; and, believing that school reform is always schoolmaster reform, he advocated teacher training, better salaries, and more secure tenure. Mann also in these reports advanced reasons for more liberal support of public education, and especially upheld the position that the spirit of co-operation and democracy should be developed by the public schools. For recent appreciations of the reports see *School and Society*, Vol. XIV (Sept. 3, 1921), pp. 109–15, and the *Journal of the N. E. A.*, Vol. XIX (Nov., 1930), p. 265.

[20] William A. Mowry, *Recollections of a New England Educator, 1838–1908* (New York, 1908), p. 167.

[21] Cf. ante, pp. 83–4.

[22] Raymond B. Culver, *Horace Mann and Religion in the Massachusetts Public Schools* (New Haven, 1929), Chap. 12. Mann also expected regular church attendance on the part of normal school students. Mann to Pierce, Aug. 6, 1846, Mann Papers.

day, thirty-nine Boston schoolmasters denounced him for his criticisms of their teaching methods and for their scandalous abuse of corporal punishment.[23]

High-strung and sensitive, Mann fought back, unsatisfied until, as Theodore Parker said, he had crushed his enemies as he would obliterate mosquitoes. But he paid a price. "Can you," he asked his friend Doctor Jarvis, "do anything for a man's brain that has not slept for three weeks? I can feel the flame in the center of my cranium flaring and flaring around just as you see that of a pile of brush burning on a distant heath in the wind. What can be done to extinguish it?"[24] But it was moral earnestness and staunchness of purpose, inherited from his Puritan forebears, and humanitarian faith in the divine character of the cause that, quite as much as the physician's anodyne, provided the needed strength in all his vicissitudes.

To understand Mann's educational and social philosophy one must bear in mind the fact that, shortly after assuming the office of secretary of the Massachusetts Board of Education, in 1837, he became a convert without qualification to the doctrines of phrenology. This was a system of psychology, philosophy, and ethics which attracted, at least for a time, such persons as William Ellery Channing, Ralph Waldo Emerson, Walt Whitman, Charles Sumner, and Henry Ward Beecher, as well as a number of prominent physicians. For the rest of his life Mann kept up a close correspondence with George

[23] Of the twenty-five pamphlets printed to defend or attack Mann, the following are representative: George B. Emerson, *Observations on a pamphlet entitled "Remarks" on the Seventh Annual Report of Hon. Horace Mann* (Boston, 1844); (Rev. Leonard Withington) *Penitential Tears, or a Cry from the Dust by "the Thirty-one" Prostrated and Pulverized by the Hand of Horace Mann* (Boston, 1845); *Rejoinder to the Reply of the Hon. Horace Mann . . . to the "Remarks" of the Association of Boston Masters upon his Seventh Annual Report* (Boston, 1845).

[24] Mann to Jarvis, Feb. 10, 1844, Mann Papers.

Combe, the foremost representative of phrenology after Spurz-
heim died in Boston in 1833. He regarded phrenology as the
greatest discovery of the ages, recommended its study to teachers,[25] referred to it constantly in his lectures on education, and
modified some of his own attitudes as a result of its influence
on him.

Having accepted phrenology, Mann could no longer hold
that all men were created with equal intellect and moral capacities, for the essence of phrenology was its insistence on
the unique differences in the propensities of individuals.
Though some were endowed with more highly developed
propensities for evil than others, they might weaken these
tendencies by suitable means, just as those blessed with the
more admirable propensities might cultivate them. Though
the basic propensities such as acquisitiveness, which gave rise to
unchecked grasping for gold, and destructiveness, which supported the institution of war, could never be completely obliterated in the members of the human race, who possessed them
in varying measure, they might be effectively checked by the
conscious cultivation of such counteracting propensities as
benevolence. Since the phrenologists advocated education, especially training in the proper laws of health and morals, Mann's
acceptance of their doctrines re-enforced his zeal for the new
work he had undertaken and committed him to bend every
effort in behalf of hygienic instruction, and, above all, character
training. As we shall see, his enthusiasm for phrenology also
influenced his thinking on some of the most fundamental social
problems of the day.

[25] Mann to Lydia Mann, Nov. 9, 1838, Mann Papers; *A Few Thoughts for
a Young Man,* p. 83.

III

Equipped with loyalty to the New England virtues of thrift, individual integrity, and respectability, quickened with zeal for humanitarianism, and strengthened in purpose by his acceptance of phrenology, Mann gradually developed his social and educational philosophy. It was, to be sure, in large measure conditioned by the specific problems that confronted him. First of all it was necessary to convince the people of Massachusetts that further financial support for the common schools was indispensable if they were to function at all effectively. Thus we find him constantly endeavoring to prove that universal education would promote prosperity. As his experience in the temperance movement had taught him, it was well to appeal to self-interest; and this conviction was strengthened by the emphasis that phrenology placed on the basic importance of the propensity of acquisitiveness.

Since the opposition to the improvement of the public schools was made up of a "few wealthy leaders, with many times more their own number of ignorant and deluded followers,"[26] Mann addressed his appeals particularly to men of substance. He assembled abundant statistics to prove that educated labor was far more productive and profitable than ignorant labor. He solicited and published the testimony of factory managers and successful industrialists to add to the impressiveness of figures. After a visit to the Lowell mills in 1841, preparatory to a famous report on the economic value of education, Mann wrote that his object was to show that "education has a market value; that it is so far an article of merchandise, that it may be turned to a pecuniary account: it may be minted, and will yield a larger amount of statutable coin than common bullion."[27]

[26] *Common School Journal*, Vol. IX (March 15, 1847), p. 95.
[27] [Mary Tyler Peabody Mann], *Life and Works of Horace Mann*, Vol. I, p. 151.

The famous fifth report, originally published in 1842, was a direct and plausible appeal to industrialists to support public education.[28] Circulated to the number of 18,000 copies by the New York legislature, translated into German, and cited again and again in school periodicals and in the addresses of educational leaders, this report enlisted from an imposing number of prominent and well-to-do citizens in Massachusetts the testimonial that Mann was to be regarded as a benefactor to humanity for having demonstrated so convincingly that "the aim of industry is served, and the wealth of the country is augmented, in proportion to the diffusion of knowledge."[29]

Though this idea of the money value of education was in keeping with the thought of the times and had been stated by others before Mann, it was he who first really popularized it, he who gathered evidence that convinced the skeptical. Years later John D. Philbrick, a distinguished educational authority, observed that Mann's fifth report had "probably done more than all other publications written within the past twenty-five years to convince capitalists of the value of elementary instruction as a means of increasing the value of labor."[30]

In his private letters no less than in his public statements Mann appealed directly to such men as the Lowells, the Appletons, the Lawrences, and other industrialists for contributions to support educational work. Although Edward Dwight made possible the founding of a normal school, for the most part the capitalists, while vouchsafing sympathy with public schools, found one or another reason for not donating funds.[31] On one occasion, after applying for contributions to Dwight, the

[28] *Life and Works,* Vol. III, pp. 92–128.
[29] Letter to Mann, Boston, Jan. 13, 1845, Mann Papers.
[30] National Teachers' Association, *Journal of Proceedings and Lectures, Chicago, Aug. 5, 6, 7, 1863,* p. 56. The Mann Papers contain abundant evidence of the influence of the fifth report.
[31] A. Lawrence to Mann, Dec. 8, Dec. 19, 1842, Mann Papers.

two Appletons, and the three Lawrences, Mann indignantly wrote to a friend: "No one of them would give a cent, . . . and I will live by tapping my own veins and sucking the blood, before I will ever ask any one of them for a cent. . . . There is no hyperbole in the old comparison about a rich man's getting into heaven and a camel's going through the eye of a needle."[32]

It may well have been partly because of the rebuffs he encountered in his appeals to the rich that Mann developed a theory of wealth which suggests that of St. Paul and Thomas Aquinas. According to this theory property, though in general the result of an individual's ability or that of his forefathers, is a relative and not an absolute right. Mann held that wealth had been created in the past by the ability of man to apply intelligence to the exploitation of natural resources. As a consequence, it was actually social intelligence or education which, by enormously multiplying the effectiveness of this process, really created "value" or wealth. It followed that property owners in any given generation were indebted to the social intelligence of the past. They could pay the debt only by regarding themselves as stewards of wealth for future generations, who by every consideration had an equal right to employ social intelligence for the further exploitation and enjoyment of natural resources.[33] It was therefore an obligation on the part of contemporary capitalists to cease exploiting the public lands for private profit and to set them aside for the support of such socially useful institutions as insane asylums and schools.[34] As stewards of wealth it was also their duty to tax the riches which

[32] Mann to Cyrus Pierce, June 6, 1846, and to his wife, June 22, 1848, Mann Papers.

[33] *A Few Thoughts for a Young Man*, pp. 51 *ff.*; *Common School Journal*, Vol. IX (May, 1847), pp. 139–43; and, especially, the Annual Report for 1846, in *Life and Works*, Vol. III, pp. 536 *et seq.*

[34] Horace Mann to his wife, June 17, 1849, Mann Papers.

the intelligence of the past had created in order that the cumulative body of learning might be transmitted through schools for the future creation and enjoyment of wealth. This concept of the duties of property owners tended to qualify Mann's allegiance to industrial capitalism and to modify his individualist philosophy by the doctrine of social obligation.

Indeed, Horace Mann was by no means blind to the evils of capitalism, nor did he remain silent before the ruthless exploitation by which capitalists overrode human rights. Once he had determined to give up his position with the Board of Education, he became increasingly outspoken in his criticism of the growing "extremes of opulence and poverty." Deprecating our vainglory and overgrown pride, his alert eyes saw many rotten spots in our civilization. When Southerners in Congress insisted that the slave trade was justified because it civilized Africans by exposing them to our superior American civilization, Mann, who had entered the House of Representatives in 1848 as successor to John Quincy Adams, retorted that this country was one of the dark spots of the earth. In our cities "the rich and strong live upon the poor and the weak, almost as much as in the waters on which they are situated, the great fishes eat up the little ones. When some one asked John Jacob Astor how so many men found business in the city of New York, his reply was: 'They cheats one another, and they calls that business.' The wealthy have more houses than they can live in, the costliest furniture, wardrobes, equipages, libraries, and all that art or nature can produce, while thousands of the children of the same Heavenly Father, around them, are houseless and shelterless, naked and hungry. Such is the type of civilization which our example proffers to Africa."[35]

In his final report to the Massachusetts Board of Education

[35] *Cong. Globe*, XXV, Append., 1st sess. 32d Cong., p. 1073, Aug. 23, 1852.

and in an address entitled *A Few Thoughts for a Young Man,* given in 1849, Mann used equally vigorous language to condemn the increasing inequalities of wealth and the cupidity, fraud, and robbery of the rich men of America. The millionaire, he maintained, was as "dangerous to the welfare of the community, in our day, as was the baronial lord of the Middle Ages. Both supply the means of shelter and of raiment on the same conditions; . . . both use their superiority to keep themselves superior. The power of money is as imperial as the power of the sword; and I may as well depend upon another for my head, as for my bread. The day is sure to come, when men will look back upon the prerogatives of Capital, at the present time, with as severe and as just a condemnation as we now look back upon the predatory Chieftains of the Dark Ages."[36] There could be no equity in the allotments which assigned to one man but a dollar a day, with working, while another had an income of a dollar a minute without working. Indigence was no part of the eternal ordinances of Heaven; inequality in the distribution of wealth was responsible for privations and suffering.[37]

For trade practices that violated the laws of the land and human rights, Mann had only the severest condemnation.[38] On one occasion he compared the ruthless money brokers and interest-takers to wreckers who, after throwing out a rope to a drowning man, extorted all they could wring from their victim before drawing him in. In stinging words he excoriated rich capitalists who, in the interest of profits, every day of their lives violated tariff laws and liquor laws, and then had the cheek to rave about violations of the fugitive slave law.[39] Nor

---

[36] *A Few Thoughts for a Young Man,* pp. 57–58.
[37] Report for 1848, *Life and Works,* Vol. III, p. 664.
[38] "An Address to an Institute of Merchants," Mann Papers, Miscellaneous, 1828–1843.
[39] *Cong. Globe,* XXIII, Append., 2d sess., 31st Cong., p. 248, Feb. 28, 1851.

did he fail to indict Webster and Northern manufacturers, though more strongly in private correspondence than in public speech, for bartering with representatives from below the Mason and Dixon line for tariff favors in exchange for the extension of human slavery.[40] "The truth is," he recorded, "the slave-power of the South and the money-power of the North have struck hands. The one threatens the Union, the other yields, professing to be in fear of the Union, but really for the purpose of obtaining the profits of trade and of getting a new tariff."[41]

Mann's outspoken criticism of industrial and commercial capitalism provoked bitter denunciations. Charles Astor Bristed published a pamphlet in which he tried to refute Mann's insinuations that wealth meant oppression, that capitalists were responsible for the shame of prostitution, that the rich man's patronage of art was hardly conducive to its progress, and that the factory worker was the slave of the factory owner. He declared that Mann was preaching socialist dogma and falsely inflaming the imagination of the people.[42] The press was not slow to take up the controversy between Mann and the grandson of John Jacob Astor,[43] and Charles Sumner found evidence that the conservative political enemies of Mann in Massachusetts were circulating Bristed's pamphlet in their campaign against him when he stood for re-election to Congress.[44]

Such condemnation of the abuses of wealth was accompanied, and even preceded, as one would expect, by genuine expressions

[40] Horace Mann, *Speech on the Fugitive Slave Law*, delivered at Lancaster, Mass., May 19, 1851 (Pamphlet, n. p., n. d.), p. 14.
[41] *Life of Horace Mann*, pp. 315, 354–55; Mann to Samuel Downer, June 18, 1850, Mann Papers.
[42] Charles Astor Bristed, "Letter to Horace Mann, May 15, 1850," in *Pieces of a Broken-Down Critic Picked up by Himself* (Baden-Baden, 1859), Vol. IV, pp. 17–24.
[43] *Littell's Living Age*, Vol. XXVI (July 13, 1850), pp. 49–52.
[44] Charles Sumner to Mann, July 7, 1850, Mann Papers.

of sympathy with the underdog. Humanitarian that he was, Mann's soul cried out against the shame, squalor, and social injustice that he detected on his European tour in 1843.[45] When he read the first report of the British Children's Employment Commission on "Colliery Serfs" his heart rebelled at the indignity suffered by the victims of the coal operators.[46] If the villein of the Middle Ages had no spot on the earth on which he could live, unless one were granted to him by his lord, the factory hand had no employment, and therefore no bread, unless the capitalist would accept his employment. Indeed, the condition of the modern operative was worse than that of the serf of feudal times, since even that harsh system provided for relief in sickness and old age.[47]

Nor was Mann blind to matters in his own Massachusetts.[48] Shocked by the vice, crime, pauperism, and misery in the urban slums he spoke out clearly against such things.[49] He even went so far as to say that the laboring hands of men, women, and children created more value than the capital that employed them. He paid tribute to the workers who built piers and wharves that enriched our commerce, turned the bed of the ocean into dry land for the enlargement of our cities, and drove the tireless machines that kept us comfortable and warm. Since these workers were paid barely enough to eke out their miserable existence, could we not at least, Mann urged, recompense them in part by providing free education for their children,

---

[45] *Life of Horace Mann*, pp. 109, 177, 202, 216.
[46] *Common School Journal*, Vol. IV (July 1, 1842), p. 201.
[47] Report for 1848, *Life and Works*, Vol. III, p. 667.
[48] *Ibid.*, pp. 666 *et seq.*
[49] Mann, in preparation for the Annual Report for 1847, which was largely devoted to the relation between crime and education, sent a circular to Calvinistic educators committed to the idea of total depravity, asking whether they thought education could prevent crime. They agreed that, under the conditions Mann outlined, it would do so in the great majority of cases. *Ibid.*, pp. 569–89.

even though they themselves felt no discontent under their privations?[50] His final educational message to the state was a protest against an economic development which had come to mean that "with every generation . . . some new privation is added to poverty."[51]

Further than that Horace Mann did not go; nor had he gone even that far during most of the years as secretary, when his first purpose was to gain support for the public schools. Unlike such an exceptional friend of education as Robert Rantoul, Jr.,[52] he did not raise his voice in defense of labor's right to organize and strike. On the contrary, as we shall see, he reserved his most bitter words for the mob violence so often associated with such unpleasant and dangerous affairs as labor troubles. He may even have shared the ambiguous view of his close friend, Doctor Samuel Gridley Howe, who while wishing that laborers might work but six or eight hours daily, maintained that a ten-hour day legally enacted would, by establishing a harmful guardianship and protection, emasculate the worker.[53]

As for children in factories, Mann contended in his report for 1839, despite his belief that society had the right and duty to shoulder responsibility for all children,[54] that their labor, if supplemented by some schooling, could be "converted from a servitude into a useful habit of diligence."[55] In almost his last report Mann did recommend education for all children from four to sixteen, ten months a year, enforced by the state

[50] *Common School Journal,* Vol. II (Feb. 15, 1840), pp. 50–51. The only interest Mann showed in education for adult workers was the support given to the movement for mechanics' institutes and lyceums in his report for 1839, *Common School Journal,* Vol. II (April 15 and May 1, 1840), pp. 122, 139–41.

[51] Report for 1848, *Life and Works,* Vol. III, p. 664.

[52] Merle Curti, "Robert Rantoul, Jr., the Reformer in Politics," *New England Quarterly,* Vol. V (April, 1932), pp. 264–80.

[53] Laura E. Richards, ed., *Letters and Journals of Samuel Gridley Howe* (Boston, 1909), Vol. II, p. 385.

[54] Horace Mann, *Lectures on Education* (Boston, 1845), pp. 69–70.

[55] Report for 1839, *Life and Works,* Vol. III, p. 9.

upon recalcitrant parents and made possible to the offspring of the very poor by state grants of aid to their parents.[56] But a student of child labor, in evaluating Mann's services, has concluded that he made no serious effort to solve the problem of providing school opportunities for child workers in factories.[57] Although Mann doubtless convinced many social and political leaders of the evils of non-attendance at schools, he was responsible for no remedy for these abuses.

With such views on problems affecting the amelioration of the lot of the worker, Mann quite naturally condemned the theories of "revolutionizers," who held that "some people are poor because others are rich," as dangerous and utterly impracticable.[58] Naïvely thinking that socialists intended "to divide all property equally, and when they have spent their share, to divide again,"[59] he regarded such doctrines as incompatible with the fundamental propensity of acquisitiveness, which provided the mainspring of human behavior.[60] Believing an educated body of men could never remain "permanently poor," he could not be expected to sympathize with means other than schooling for righting economic injustices.

Mann saw no fundamental conflict of interest in American society, in spite of his indictment of capital and his pity for labor. Although, to a degree, he understood and even commended "fellow-feeling for one's class or caste," he did not hold class struggle to be an inescapable element of industrial capitalism.[61] The fact that he himself, a poor handicapped boy, had somehow got through Brown University, become a successful

[56] Report for 1847, *ibid.*, pp. 592–636.

[57] F. C. Ensign, *Compulsory School Attendance and Child Labor*, pp. 47, 50–51.

[58] Report for 1848, *Life and Works*, Vol. III, pp. 669–70.

[59] Horace Mann, *Lectures on Various Subjects* (New York, 1859), p. 184.

[60] *Cong. Globe*, Append., 1st sess., 30th Cong., p. 835, June 30, 1848.

[61] *Life and Works*, Vol. III, pp. 669–70.

.awyer, and enjoyed a career in the legislature and in Congress, doubtless influenced his belief. He did not quite confuse the ideal of a classless society with its actuality, but his great confidence in education prevented a critical analysis of realities. Conscious that exploitation of labor existed, aware that social and economic justice was sadly lacking, he failed to see the roots that produced the weeds.

While Mann rejected the program of the labor movement and of the socialism of his day, he believed that the machine, which made possible the rise of industrialism, would greatly further social justice. As early as 1827, when the legislature was discussing the question of a subsidy to a railroad, he urged its support on the ground that machinery was "an enlargement of human power" and that the mechanical arts promised the amelioration of man's lot. He begged his listeners to note that in ancient times oppression was based on the inability of man adequately to supply his own wants, with the result that he sought superiority over his fellows. The toils of the vassal thus ministered to the pleasures of the lord. But the machine, he continued, would harness the forces of nature, supply all man's wants, relieve the distress of the unfortunate, and finally effect an end to poverty itself.[62] Though in later years he saw that machines brought great hardships of their own making, it did not occur to him that possibly the social evils he decried might be an inevitable part of industrialism when its machines were controlled by private groups for the sake of profit.

IV

But in holding that the invention of machines promised the elimination of the social ills of industrial capitalism, Mann, like his fellow educators, relied chiefly on free public schools to

[62] Mann Papers, Miscellaneous, 1779–1827.

achieve that end. Not that he visioned an economic democracy: the old-time New Englander in him spoke when he insisted that whatever is really and truly valuable might be possessed by all and possessed in exhaustless abundance, because real values were moral and intellectual, and therefore every one with a "competence" or decently moderate income, might enjoy them.[63] But pauperism was indeed a foe to the good life, and Mann held that, along with the obvious ills of industrialism, it might be eliminated within two or three generations by more and better public schools. Moreover, he even believed that education would rid the earth of that "all-comprehending misanthropy, the Law of Caste, which includes within itself every form of iniquity, because it lives by the practical denial of Human Brotherhood."[64] By providing every child with the independence and the means for resisting the selfishness of other men, education, "beyond all other devices of human origin," was "the great equalizer of the conditions of men—the balance wheel of the social machinery."[65]

All these things, and more, were to be accomplished, not by any sort of education, but by a particular kind, character training. By applying the principles of phrenology, moral instruction in the schoolroom would nourish the propensities that expressed themselves in righteous and humane behavior, and restrain the "ravenous and tyrannizing" ones that led to selfishness and indifference to human suffering. By instilling the principles of temperance, the school would remove from society the drunkenness which Mann believed to be the chief cause of degradation and poverty—he went so far on one occasion as to attribute four-fifths of all pauperism to the direct or indirect

[63] *Lectures on Education*, pp. 57, 58.
[64] Horace Mann, *"Inaugural Address," Dedication of Antioch College* (Boston, 1854), pp. 116–17; *Life and Works*, Vol. III, pp. 669–70.
[65] Report for 1848, *Life and Works*, Vol. III, p. 669.

effects of liquor.[66] By implanting benevolence in the heart of the child, education would start the future philanthropist on his road. By curbing such propensities as avarice, self-esteem, and acquisitiveness, education would influence the future industrialist to eschew inhumane and unrighteous practices even though his profits might be curtailed. If wealth were not forever talked about before children as the chief prize of life, would we see such throngs making haste to be rich, with all the consequences of fraud and dishonor? If the child were taught the dignity and healthfulness of voluntary labor, together with the meanness of living on the unrequited services of the weak and defenseless, could he ever bear to live a life of pampered indolence secured by a hundred other lives?[67] In short, Mann's moral earnestness and faith in individualism led him to believe that, were character training resorted to in accordance with the principles of phrenology, the old-time New England virtues of honesty, frugality, and uprightness would prevail even in a changing and unfriendly world.

Like so many of his contemporaries, Mann denounced the prevalent resort to emulation in the schoolroom. The passion for praise and place in which it had resulted was, he thought, largely responsible for the "madness and profligacy" of the political and social rivalries that convulsed the land.[68] Nothing, indeed, so degraded the "social affections" as the practice of emulation, bartering as it did the morals of a child for arrogance, and for love of precedence and attainment.[69]

It is to Mann's credit that he recognized the inadequacy of the old dogmatic way of imparting moral instruction. From Pestalozzi, whose educational and social philosophy in so many respects resembled his own, he learned that it was better to

[66] Horace Mann, *Two Lectures on Intemperance* (New York, 1859), p. 22.
[67] Annual Report for 1848, *Life and Works,* Vol. III, p. 707.
[68] *Lectures on Education,* p. 104.   [69] *Life and Works,* Vol. III, p. 386.

appeal to the affection rather than to the fear of the child. From the Swiss master he also learned that the inductive method was vastly superior to the old formal and sterile technique that piled dogma on dogma. "Unfortunately," declared Mann in 1838, "education amongst us at present consists too much in *telling,* not in *training,* on the part of parents and teachers; and, of course, in *hearing,* and not *in doing,* on the part of children and pupils."[70]

From the point of view of the America in which he lived the educational remedy Mann proposed for the social evils was a fairly natural and logical one. Not only his fellow educators, but the great bulk of American citizens turned deaf ears to the arguments of labor leaders and Fourierists who insisted that the evils of industrial capitalism were inherent in the system itself. It was natural for Americans, with their inventive genius, and possessed of the great treasure house of Western lands, to believe that the chance to "get ahead" and secure at least a modest competence was destined to be virtually a permanent opportunity, particularly if all were aided on their way by a free education.[71]

Nor was Mann alone in failing to take into account the consideration that many of the poorest urban workers and run-down Eastern farmers did not possess even the modest means necessary to go West and take up land. He was also unaware of the fact that even on the frontier in his own day a master class of speculators and creditors exploited a large number of poor folk struggling against great odds. If he was not discouraged by the failure of industrial capitalism, as it advanced in its course in England, to greatly improve the lot of the common man, it was because the mother country had

[70] *Lectures on Education,* pp. 93, 95.
[71] *Life and Works,* Vol. III, pp. 430–31.

not provided the universal education with its moral indoctrination which he deemed indispensable to the elimination of the evils of industrial capitalism.

Mann should not be judged harshly for overemphasizing the ameliorating rôle of education. Confidence in the efficacy of the school as a means of effecting social change was then in its heyday. Education on a large scale had not been tried for a sufficiently long time to disprove his belief that it would vanquish crime, the excesses of profit-making, and even poverty itself. Finally, the unqualified acceptance of education as a means of remedying social evils was the natural corollary to the dominant belief in individualism which Mann, like almost everyone else, shared. The pseudo-science of phrenology confirmed his abiding faith in the importance of the individual. This doctrine of individualism was at the same time quickened and reinforced both by the frontier process and by industrial expansion, at that time the two most vital forces in American life.

Nevertheless it remains true that just as the eighteenth century rationalists made too much of the power of reason, so Mann and his contemporaries overemphasized the effectiveness of morality implanted by education. He did not realize that general training alone in such abstract virtues as honesty, uprightness, and integrity could not, in the majority of cases, compete successfully with incompatible practices in the everyday world, particularly because the situations there varied enough from those in the schoolroom to throw even the best-intentioned off their guard. He failed to understand that in a competitive system based on production for profits alone, the temptation to forego "the inner check" and then to rationalize violations of the moral code was too strong for the vast bulk of mankind. Above all, by refusing to permit his teach-

ers to bring certain controversial questions into the schoolroom
and by his inconsistent position on indoctrination against specific social evils Mann deprived moral instruction of such vitality as it might otherwise have enjoyed in its battle against the
allies, Mammon and slavery.

Mann found admirable pedagogical reasons to support his
position on indoctrination. As early as 1825, in an oration at
Providence, he had maintained that the fundamental maxim
of true education was not so much "to inculcate opinions and
beliefs, as to impart the means of their correct formation."[72]
What was worse, he asked on a later occasion, than to have
children see but parts of the truth? Truth-seeking required
an impartial and discriminating ability to circumnavigate a
problem, to see it in all its completeness. Moreover, if there
must be associations among men whose tendency it was to promote alienation and discord, the school, at least, should be
"sacred from the ravages of the spirit of party and unblasted
by the fiery breath of authority."[73]

Although he believed that truth was absolute, yet the method
of obtaining it must be pragmatic. "All plans for reform and
improvement which appear to the eye of reason to be safe and
useful," he remarked, "or which have been successfully tried
elsewhere, are entitled to a fair trial among ourselves; and if
they are found to pass this ordeal successfully, should be
adopted." The whole history of human advancement was one
of innovation upon the then existing state of practice and belief, and we could not be "circumscribed within the range of our
fathers' ideas, any more than we can use their old instru-

[72] Horace Mann, *Oration delivered at Providence, Sept. 6, 1825* (Providence,
1825), p. 22.
[73] *Common School Journal,* Vol. III (Jan. 1, 1841), pp. 1–16. In a lecture
at Concord Mann delighted Emerson by declaring that "we should think on
oath." *Journals of Ralph Waldo Emerson,* ed. by E. W. Emerson and W. E.
Forbes (Boston, 1909–14), Vol. IV, pp. 361–62. Entry of Nov. 16, 1837.

ments."[74] His method, in short, was that of trial and error, or tentative and cautious experiment, even though he did not, with all his enthusiasm for science, clearly grasp all the implications of the scientific method. He believed that the great axioms of life must ever be demonstrated anew, that maxims in conduct, truth, and morals must ever be re-examined, since "truth could not be defined either by law, or perpetuated by power, authority, or wealth without endangering it."[75]

It was this devotion to truth and this conviction that dogmatism was incompatible with it that led Mann, when his colleagues in Congress declared that the Compromise of 1850 was a "finality" which made any further discussion of it unpatriotic, to make one of the finest defenses of freedom of discussion that America has ever heard. In ringing words he exclaimed that this was a "free country, except when a man wishes to vindicate the claims of freedom"; that free speech was not to be confined to one side of a question; that truth alone could conquer if the right of minorities to criticize were not suppressed; and finally, that, however enormous the crime of treason against the government was, he for one held "treason against free speech and free thought to be a crime incomparably greater."[76] It was the desire to develop in children a love of truth more powerful than devotion to dogma, fortified by his own belief in freedom of religious opinion, which made Mann so obstinate an enemy to those who would use the schools for sectarian religious teaching.

[74] *Life and Works*, Vol. V, pp. 282–84. Mann emphasized the necessity of learning all the facts pertinent to any problem to be solved. "Error often could arise, not from any mistake in our judgment upon the premises given, but from omitting views, as much belonging to the subject as those which are considered. . . . Thus error becomes the consequence of seeing only parts of the truth."

[75] *Life and Works*, Vol. II, p. 104.

[76] *Cong. Globe*, Vol. XXIII, Append., 2d sess., 31st Cong., pp. 237–49, Feb. 28, 1851.

However admirable the principles underlying Mann's opposition to indoctrination, he was far from consistent in adhering to them. Although he did not urge definite pacifist teaching in the schools, as head of the Massachusetts schools he made
known his conviction that war is wicked and unjustifiable,
wasteful, and inhumane. He apparently believed that education
by strengthening the intellect and developing sentiments of
universal brotherhood would rear a generation for whom the
"insane illusions of martial glory" would hold no attraction and
the heroism of battle would appear but "a horror and an abomination." But he condemned the histories in school libraries for
their emphasis upon wars, military heroes, and all the trap-
pings of battles: if school children were to read history it must
be rewritten.[77] The wisdom and expediency of abstaining
from alcoholic liquor, however, was so self-evident to Mann
that he did not hesitate to except temperance from his general
rule that as secretary he should not make "any direct or indirect
interference" in behalf of the great reformatory movements of
the age.[78]

On an even more significant matter, Mann entirely approved
of indoctrination. Like other educators and professional men
of his time he not only denounced the violence which he saw
in such affairs as the anti-rent war in New York, the anti-
Irish mobs, and the Dorr rebellion, but he also insisted that
school children should be indoctrinated against the use of
rebellion to change "laws and rulers." Education, he argued,
would and should prevent the masses from resorting to violence, and school children should be taught to despise the use

[77] *Lectures on Education*, p. 242; *Life and Works*, Vol. III, pp. 15–17, 425–
26, 646. Although Mann recognized that the institution of war was based on
the innate propensity of combativeness, he nevertheless believed that war was
destined to become obsolete. For one of his strongest indictments of war see
"A Few Thoughts on the Powers and Duties of Women," 1853, in *Lectures on
Various Subjects*, pp. 85–86.
[78] *Two Lectures on Intemperance*, pp. 10–12.

of bullets for effecting social change. "Had the obligations of the future citizen been sedulously inculcated upon all the children of the Republic, would the patriot have had to mourn over so many instances where the voter, not being able to accomplish his purpose by voting, has proceeded to accomplish it by violence; where, agreeing with his fellow-citizens to use the machinery of the ballot, he makes a tacit reservation, that, if that machinery does not move according to his pleasure, he will wrest or break it?"[79] The condition of society was to be but the embodiment of the mighty will of the people, and "if greater care be not taken than has ever heretofore been taken, to inform and regulate that will, it will inscribe its laws, all over the face of society, in such broad and terrific characters, that, not only whoever runs may read, but whoever reads will run. . . . Should besotting vices and false knowledge bear sway, then will every wealthy and every educated, and every refined individual and family, stand in the same relation to society, in which game stands to a sportsman!"[80]

Mann's advocacy of indoctrination against the use of violence on the part of the underdog is significant partly because he failed to see that violence on the part of the underprivileged might be due to sufferings and evils which made them desperate. But its greater significance lies in the fact that it was not on pacifist grounds that Mann opposed violence and advocated indoctrination against it. On the contrary, he thought that our forefathers had been justified in using violence to overthrow the authority of Great Britain, and he expressed great sympathy with the revolutionists of '48, whose use of violence for the overthrow of autocracy he defended. "The time has fully come when the despot, not the patriot," he wrote, "should feel the executioner's steel or lead. . . . If the oppressed demand

[79] Report for 1848, *Life and Works,* Vol. III, p. 696.
[80] *Lectures on Education,* pp. 142–43.

their inalienable and Heaven-born rights of their oppressors and this demand is denied . . . [they] should say to the oppressor, 'Give *me* liberty, or I will give *you* death.' "[81] But the oppressed whom he had in mind were the racial and national groups under respectable, middle-class leaders like Kossuth— for whose fortunes he inquired on his deathbed. Violence for the emancipation of the wage-slave, for the underprivileged at home, this he could regard only with horror; but violence for the purposes of national self-determination was a different matter. Nor did his opposition to violence prevent him from declaring that he preferred a civil war or a servile war, or "anything that God in His providence shall send," to an extension of the boundary of slavery.[82] Unstinted violence was permissible in a conflict between slavery and freedom; but violence on the part of the white underdog was so great a horror that the school was to oppose its mighty force against such a possibility.

But the full import of Mann's position on indoctrination and the relation it bears to the efficacy of his demand that moral education effect social reform can be appreciated only by an examination of his attitude toward the problem of anti-slavery teaching in the schools. Though he expressed uncompromising opposition to slavery even before his election to Congress in 1848, he was greatly exercised when Samuel J. May, whom he had appointed to the headship of a normal school, took his students to an abolitionist meeting. Mann informed the normal school head that a teacher had no more right to make abolitionists out of his students than he had to convert them to Unitarianism. He was equally concerned when he learned that

[81] *Cong. Globe,* Vol. XXV, Append., 1st sess., 32d Cong., p. 1075, Aug. 23, 1852.
[82] *Ibid.,* Vol. XXII, 1st sess., 31st Cong., p. 260, March 11, 1850; *Life of Horace Mann,* p. 288.

May was intending to deliver a lecture on abolition in Boston. "I have further plans for obtaining more aid (for the schools)," he wrote May, "but the moment it is known or supposed that the cause is to be perverted to, or connected with, any of the exciting party questions of the day, I shall never get another cent."[83] Not only might the wealthy industrialists like the Dwights refuse to make any contributions at all, but the cotton Whigs and pro-slavery Democrats in the legislature, who for economic reasons dared not alienate Southern planters, might withdraw their support. Abolitionism, it must be remembered, was the communism of its day, and the schools dared not flirt with it in any way lest they seem to jeopardize the established order. To exist at all, they must fit into the system to which they were functional. Though the evils of that system, whether slavery or the abuses of profit-making, must be opposed, the opposition must be indirect, general, and vague.

Thus Mann was hardly free to think out either an educational or a social philosophy which could challenge the *status quo* in any fundamental way. He was free merely to attack certain features of the existing order—crime, ignorance, ill-health, pauperism, features which, he warned, were both a burden to taxpayers and a menace to their interests. It was as if Mann were unconsciously trying to tell the dominant class what must be done to make its position more advantageous and secure. It would be unfair to suggest that in taking this stand he was failing to consider the underprivileged, with whom, as we have seen, he felt a genuine sympathy. He was convinced that the course he advocated, the popularization of education, would redound to its advantage quite as much as to that of the upper class. By the necessity of his humanitarian individual-

[83] *Life of Horace Mann,* pp. 168–72; *Memoir of Samuel Joseph May* (Boston, 1873), pp. 177–79.

ism and by reason of the situation in which he found himself, Mann was obliged to hold that the misery of the poor farmers and workers was not due to anything inherent in the established social and economic order. He explained their condition as due merely to their lack of knowledge of the laws of the universe, physical, intellectual, and moral laws which the privileged class better understood and obeyed.

Whatever the limitations imposed by the framework within which he worked, Mann did hold up the ideal that the true interests of the schoolroom were identical with the great interests of society—an ideal which John Dewey was much later to advocate with telling force. "The former is the infant, immature state of those interests," said Mann, "the latter their developed, adult state. As 'the child is father to the man,' so may the training of the schoolroom expand into the institutions and fortunes of the State." The educational statesman was to plan for society, to "study out the eternal principles which conduce to the strength, wisdom, and righteousness of the community; to search for those principles as for hidden riches; to strive for them as one would strive for his life, and then to form public institutions in accordance with them."[84] The aim of education was to fit children for society as well as for a rich personal life: the two aims were in fact inseparable. "As each citizen is to participate in the power of governing others, it is an essential preliminary that he should be imbued with a feeling for the wants, and a sense of the rights, of those whom he is to govern. . . . It becomes, then, a momentous question, whether the children in our schools are educated in reference to themselves and their private interests only, or with a regard to the great social duties and prerogatives that await them in after-life. Are they so educated that, when they grow up, they

[84] Report for 1848, *Life and Works,* Vol. III, pp. 649–51.

will make better philanthropists and Christians, or only grander savages?"[85]

If the privileged classes thought that they had no direct interest in the general condition of the community, Mann warned, they need do no more than look into the jails, prisons, poorhouses, and the like, and they would see that in the social state, not even "the purest virtue can secure happiness, or an immunity from danger, to any one class, while vice abounds in another. . . . The favored classes may think they occupy favored apartments in the ship but, if it does founder, the state-room will go down with the steerage."[86] In short, our advanced state of civilization had evolved many complicated questions respecting social duties, and it was consequently necessary to educate a generation of men able to decide great and eternal questions, not on narrow, selfish, and opportunistic grounds, but in accord with truth and the genuine interests of humanity.[87]

Mann not only, like Dewey, insisted on education for social purposes, but he also urged education for a changing world. The earlier educator noted that mankind was, in the first half of the nineteenth century, passing rapidly through a transition state. The idea that the world was made, and life given, for the happiness of all, and not for the ambition, pride, and luxury of the few, was rapidly forcing recognition, to the point, even, that a virtual revolution in human affairs was taking place. Governments, laws, and social usages were rapidly dissolving and recombining in new forms. In the rapid evolution of the idea of human rights, we might either accelerate or postpone the transition; we might make it a peaceful and efficient change, or we might postpone it and make it a calamitous one.

85 Report for 1845, *ibid.*, Vol. III, p. 422.
86 *Two Lectures on Intemperance*, p. 100.
87 *Lectures on Education*, pp. 50, 52.

Our attitude toward education, Mann thought, would decide what our rôle would be in the changes that the world was experiencing and would inevitably continue to experience to-morrow and the day after. "The history of the future is to be widely different from that of the past. The stream of time is changing its direction. . . . We must prepare ourselves to move with safety through the new realms we are now enter-ing."[88] Although human nature itself did not change, Mann contended that the same human nature might be made to yield opposite results. Education must provide a generation of "sober, wise, good men, to prepare for coming events, to ad-just society to the new relations it is to fill, to remove the old, and to substitute a new social edifice, without overwhelming the present occupants in ruin."[89]

It is clear that Mann's social and educational philosophy was opposed to a romantic "escape" doctrine. No ivory towers for this teacher and his disciples! They were to remain in the world, confront selfishness, wickedness, and ignorance, at what-ever personal peril, and subdue or extirpate them, or die in the attempt.[90] Mann would have a brotherhood of teachers, bound together by their devotion to one object, "a desire to reform the world, to re-impress upon the heart of man the almost obliter-ated image of his Maker."[91]

Of all the great questions with which education was to grap-ple, none was more important in Mann's eyes than that of democracy itself. Accepting political democracy as an inevi-table and desirable development, he shared the view of all his fellow educators that it could succeed only if it were accom-panied by educational and intellectual democracy, and hence

[88] *Common School Journal,* Vol. II (Jan. 1, 1840), p. 5.
[89] *Ibid.,* Vol. IV (April 1, 1842), p. 99.
[90] Remarks at the Dedication of the Bridgewater Normal School, Aug. 19, 1846, *Life and Works,* Vol. V, p. 218.
[91] "The Motives of Teachers," Mann Papers, Miscellaneous, 1844–1847.

pinned his faith to a free and universal school system. For the class system of education in which the children of the wealthy attended superior private schools he had only condemnation. The most effective remedy was to improve the public schools to such an extent that they equaled or surpassed private institutions.[92]

Popular education was as necessary to check the excesses of democracy as it was to insure its successful achievements. Sharing the alarm of conservatives lest universal suffrage cause people to throw off the restraints of authority and invite anarchy, Mann turned to universal education as the best insurance against mobocracy, confiscatory legislation, threats to judicial supremacy, and the spoils system which Jacksonism held so dear. So he shouldered new burdens on the schools, advising them to teach, not a ritualistic patriotism of oath-taking and flag-saluting, but the true principles of the Constitution and good citizenship.[93] As if to prove the sincerity of his own preachings regarding the duty of the East to tame and civilize the West, he spent his last four years in the trying and heroic work of administering the newly founded Antioch College in Ohio.[94]

V

In spite of all that Mann said about the duty of the school to effect social change and to secure human justice, he nevertheless believed that in times of crisis education was inadequate to check wickedness. To prevent slavery from spreading into the territories was a short-run job to be fought by agitation and

[92] Lectures and Reports on Education, *Life and Works*, Vol. II, pp. 410–11.
[93] The report for 1848 is partly devoted to political education, *Life and Works*, Vol. III, pp. 686–701.
[94] For Mann's fear of the frontier and sense of obligation to extend education westward see "Fourth of July Oration, 1842," *ibid.*, Vol. IV, p. 364, and *Dedication of Antioch College*, pp. 13–16.

on the political front. "Our motto used to be, 'the cause of education, the first of all causes,'" he observed in his farewell to the teachers of Massachusetts. "Recent events, however," he went on, "have forced upon the public attention the great truth, that before a man can be educated, he must be a free man."[95] Delay, waiting on education, particularly in view of the fetters that tied the schools in matters of great moment, might well mean that 600,000 square miles of territory would be cursed—for how long who could say—with the political, economic, and moral blight of slavery.

So, notwithstanding the fact that he had always held partisan politics in low esteem,[96] Mann resigned his educational office in 1848 and accepted an election to Congress.[97] Casting to the winds the expediency that had characterized his administration of the Massachusetts schools, he made, in four notable speeches, every indictment against slavery that could be made. He anticipated every argument that Helper was to make in his *Impending Crisis,* pointing out how slavery held the South in economic and cultural peonage to the North; how it fettered its industrial development; how it prevented the growth of free public schools; how it contaminated private and public morals; how it betrayed our foreign relations into inhumane, reactionary, and un-American policies; how it polluted our free institutions and endangered our American experiment; showing, in short, that it was an institution, local in character, outworn in function, barbarous in nature, with which no compromise could be made.[98]

He who had bade Samuel J. May hold his tongue now poured

[95] *Common School Journal,* Vol. X (Dec. 15, 1848), p. 384.
[96] *Life of Horace Mann,* pp. 340, 346.
[97] *Ibid.,* p. 271; Mann Papers, 1848, *passim;* B. A. Hinsdale, *Horace Mann, and the Common School Revival in the United States* (New York, 1911), pp. 233–34. While Barnard regretted Mann's decision to quit education for politics, a great many of his educational colleagues approved his decision.
[98] *Cong. Globe,* Append., 1st sess., 30th Cong., pp. 832–41, June 30, 1850.

out words of gall on those who would suppress his right to say what he would about the blight of human bondage. He who had defended the property rights of capitalists against the attacks of the ignorant mob now denounced Webster for his compromises with the slavocracy, the more execrable because of the bribes taken in the form of tariff favors for selfish industrialists. He who had preached the sanctity of law now preached the doctrine that human law was binding only when it did not conflict with the "higher law" God had implanted in man's conscience—and he himself before the whole land flouted the idea of obeying the Fugitive Slave Act. Now he saw clearly that laws could not be considered except in relation to the prejudices, the social and moral backgrounds of their makers, their interpreters, and their executors. He who had mercilessly condemned appeal to violence on the part of white underdogs now openly advocated civil war as preferable to an extension of slavery.

In temporarily giving up the work of education for the political arena Mann found greater freedom to fight against human slavery than he had seen fit to grant himself and his educational associates. It is not within our province to compare the contributions to the abolition of slavery made by the schools on the one hand, and by the forum and battlefield on the other. Nor is it within our province to evaluate Mann's educational influence in curbing the ways of industrial capitalism. Yet it is of primary significance that he leaned far less heavily in fact than in theory on the inspiring doctrine that it was the function of education to effect social reform. If at first he thought the schools could effect reforms within a relatively short time, the fact that he deserted education for politics to fight slavery shows that he must have come to feel that at least this reform would come very slowly if left to education alone.

The moral tradition of New England Puritanism, the creed of humanitarianism, the teachings of what seemed to be a scientific and advanced psychology, all contributed to quicken Mann's indignation at the social injustice he saw and to convince him that public education could remedy it. Yet Horace Mann as an educator was bound in all he did, or permitted others to do, by the framework of the system in which he worked. That system, moreover, was responsible for the limitations which narrowed his vision and, even within the non-revolutionary area of reform, paralyzed his freedom of action in fighting vested interests on which the schools depended for support. Although he hated chattel slavery, he felt that as an educator he could not speak out against it; although he had set his heart against the ruthlessness of the surging tide of capitalism, it is significant that his bitterest attacks on wealth were made after his work as state secretary was over, and that he never did question the system itself, but only abuses within it.

Mann the idealist was inconsistent in many ways; his principles and his practice sometimes were quite divergent, and his methods of combating social evils changed with circumstances and with the years. But his social vision remained undimmed to the end, and all his work in the educational field was an effort to introduce into that field a more humane and democratic spirit. In the last address that he made after seven years of struggle and bitter disappointment at Antioch he concluded, "I should like to live again, to enroll myself anew in a fifty years' campaign, and fight once more for the glory of God and the happiness of humanity." Whether, had that boon been granted him, he would have modified his technique for achieving his ends, none can say. The historian can merely try to determine what his successors learned and failed to learn from their first really great educational leader.

IV

HENRY BARNARD

I am ambitious of being remembered . . . because of some
service, however small, done to the cause of humanity in my day
and generation; but I am more desirous to deserve, at the end of life,
the nameless epitaph of one in whom mankind lost a friend, and
no man got rid of an enemy.

—Henry Barnard, 1855.

I

"You are my guide, my hope, my friend, my fellow-laborer
and fellow-sufferer in 'the cause' "—so wrote Henry Barnard to
Horace Mann.[1] It is true that the social and educational philosophy of the writer of these generous words resembled in many
points that of the Massachusetts leader. Like him, Barnard
very early interested himself in various humanitarian movements. Elected as a Whig member of the Connecticut legislature in 1837, Barnard sponsored legislation designed to improve the condition of all sorts of unfortunate groups—the blind
and the deaf, the insane, and the inmates of jails and prisons,
as well as degraded paupers.[2] The lyceum movement, inaugurated shortly before he began his public career, found in
him an energetic and loyal friend. If Barnard was less enthusiastic than Mann about the "vandal work" of the temperance
crusaders,[3] he was as friendly as the latter toward the peace
movement, declaring in an address in 1834 before the Connecti-

[1] Barnard to Mann, Louisville, Ky., Feb. 13, 1843, Mann Papers.
[2] *American Journal of Education,* Vol. I (1856), p. 667; Bernard C. Steiner,
Life of Henry Barnard (Dept. of Interior, Bureau of Education Bulletin, 1919,
No. 8), pp. 24, 28, 29.
[3] Barnard to E. R. Potter, Hartford, Feb. 22, 1852, Barnard MSS., Monroe
Collection.

cut Peace Society that the "weight of universal popular intelligence" favored the settlement of international differences before war was declared and demanded the "arbitration of neutral powers before appealing to brute force."[4] Like Mann, Barnard held in high regard "liberty of thought, speech, occupation, and political action."[5] His zeal for the education of women equaled that of his colleague, and as an educational administrator he did a good deal to advance the cause of civil service reform.[6] In the field of education itself he devoted a longer time than Mann to the advance of "the cause," and once having deserted politics to serve education, he was never again tempted into the political arena.

But in certain respects Barnard was decidedly more conservative than his friend. His interest in almost every reform except education waned. Although he had visited the Count de Sellon, one of the most distinguished pacifists of the early nineteenth century, and was much impressed by his teachings,[7] he came to show more and more friendliness towards military institutions. As Commissioner of Education he prefaced the "Papers on Military Education" with the remark that since there was much practical value in the military element he did not oppose a moderate amount of drill in the schools. He even wrote a eulogistic memorial account of "The Home, the Arm, and the Armory of Samuel Colt," which not only contained no criticism of the manufacture of arms but praised Colt for supplying honest labor to working men, and compared his

[4] *American Journal of Education,* Vol. XXVIII (1878), p. 228; also views for addresses, undated, Barnard MSS., Watkinson Collection.

[5] *American Journal of Education,* Vol. VIII (June, 1860), p. 409.

[6] *Proceedings of the First American Normal School Convention, Aug. 19, 20, 1859,* p. 105; memorandum, undated, Barnard MSS., Watkinson Collection; O. C. Boynton, West Point, Jan. 13, 1864, to Barnard, Barnard MSS., Monroe Collection; *American Journal of Education,* Vol. XXX (March, 1880), p. 213.

[7] M. E. Curti, *American Peace Crusade, 1815–1860,* pp. 66, 135; Henry Barnard, *Récit d'une visite à la Fenêtre* (Geneva, 1837), *passim.*

ideal of a matchless firearm to that inspiring the noble genius of the sculptor.[8] Although he had no great heart for the Civil War, there is nothing to show that he desired to use the schools as a means of influencing the young against war.

While it is true that Barnard early befriended the cause of Negro education and was sufficiently lacking in race prejudice to enlist an enviable tribute from at least one black man,[9] he took a much more conservative stand on the slavery question than Mann. It was not only that he defended the harmless project of colonization of free Negroes in Africa at the very time that Garrison was holding high the banner for universal emancipation. In the very year when Mann was denouncing slavery in Congress in words that made a Southern sympathizer speak of him as a "scoundrel," Barnard was being royally entertained in South Carolina. Only a few years before he had been offered the superintendency of schools in New Orleans and in Charleston.[10]

Finally, although Barnard saw many of the evils of industrial capitalism, he never exposed its sins in the pitiless way that Mann did. Unlike the Massachusetts educator, he did not stop with mere appeals to men of wealth to support education in their own interest and to further their own security. As we shall see, he was not averse to the inculcation of the principles of capitalism.

[8] *American Journal of Education*, Vol. XI (March, 1862), pp. 313–14; Henry Barnard, *Armsmear; the Home, the Arm, and the Armory of Samuel Colt* (New York, 1866).
[9] *American Journal of Education*, Vol. XXXII (1882), pp. 912–14; *Connecticut Common School Journal*, Vol. I (June, 1839), pp. 165–66; E. D. Bassett to Barnard, Jan. 21, 1897, Barnard MSS., Monroe Collection.
[10] Meredith King, Charleston, July 10, 1848, to Barnard, Barnard MSS., Monroe Collection; J. S. Copes, New Orleans, May 17, June 6, July 26, 1847, *ibid*. As late as 1856 a prominent South Carolinian, C. E. Memminger, wrote to Barnard that he was highly regarded in the South in spite of prevalent sensitiveness and prejudice against Northerners. Memminger to Barnard, Aug. 1, 1856, *ibid*.

If one looks for an explanation of these differences, one is struck by the fact that Barnard was far more religious, in a conservative sense, than Mann. Both, it is true, had as children learned from the Westminster Catechism that human nature was depraved, and that but little could be expected from it. But while Mann gave up Calvinism for the optimistic Unitarianism with its humanitarian interests, Barnard accepted the creed of the Episcopalian Church and in marrying a Catholic still further circumscribed himself by a conservative religious creed. Thus he lacked a critical attitude toward the Bible and interpreted freethinking as a weak desire to hide from the demands of conscience and from the reality of human depravity.[11] He lumped together as the opposite of all religion freethinkers, atheists, deists, and rationalists.

Indeed, the whole problem of education was for Barnard associated with Christianity. Christ was the first great teacher, and the desire to read and understand his teachings had given the original impetus, in both Protestant Germany and Puritan New England, to the movement for universal education. Barnard often spoke of the need of creating a priesthood of teachers since education was primarily not a matter of intellect but rather one of training in reverence for God and the principles of His religion. He always spoke with high consideration of the Sunday schools, and recommended teaching in them as excellent preparation for the duties of the schoolroom.[12]

Although, like Mann, Barnard regarded moral training as the first essential in public education, his conception of character formation was more definitely orthodox and more specifically religious. He did not, indeed, interpret moral training exclusively in terms of religion, but the Bible held a conspicu-

[11] *American Journal of Education,* Vol. XXXII (1882), pp. 1066–67.
[12] *Connecticut Common School Journal,* Vol. I (Oct., 1838), pp. 19–20.

ous place in its achievement. As head of the schools of Connecticut he printed an account of various methods by which the Bible could be used in the classroom for reading, for the study of history and geography, and as the regulating law for students and teachers. He believed that increased light "on the principles of sound education" could not fail to establish the place of the Bible in every classroom.[13] He urged the inclusion of history in the school curriculum because, when studied by the aid of the Bible, it showed "plainly and magnificently the existence, character and attributes of God."[14] In outlining a program of educational work in Rhode Island, he recommended that no applicant be considered for a teaching position who spoke discreditingly of the Bible.[15] When his fundamentalist conception of rationalism and deism is recalled, it is clear that Barnard's attitude tended definitely toward continuing the influence of the colonial religious inheritance.

Barnard's devotion to conventional religion meant, in the first place, that he had scant sympathy for either the doctrines of the eighteenth-century rationalists or for those of Rousseau, intellectual positions which in many respects challenged the *status quo*. Believing as he did in the imperfection of man and in his predominant importance as a social unit, it is likely that Barnard, in accepting some of the educational doctrines of Rousseau and of his follower Pestalozzi,[16] drew a rather sharp line between them and the radical implications of the *Social Contract*. Certainly the Connecticut leader had little respect for the common man, unless he were first educated; and his horror of mobs and the whims and lawlessness of the populace knew

[13] *Ibid.* (Sept. 1, 1838), p. 15. [14] *Ibid.* (March 15, 1839), p. 113.
[15] *Journal of the Rhode Island Institute of Instruction,* Vol. II (Nov., 1847), p. 245.
[16] Barnard visited Fellenberg and his schools at Hofwyl, and devoted much effort to familiarizing American educators with his ideas. Steiner, *Henry Barnard,* p. 23.

no bounds. Moreover, the religious groups with which he was affiliated took a notoriously conservative position on slavery and other forms of social injustice, and this fact doubtless confirmed Barnard's willingness to refrain from arousing the ill will of those high in authority.

Even more important, perhaps, in explaining the social conservatism of Barnard than his devotion to conventional religion was the fact that, unlike Mann, he did not have to struggle with poverty to secure an education and a start in life. His father, a man of means, was able to provide his son with a knowledge of the best social usages. Young Barnard was sent to a private school and to Yale, with ample means to purchase books and with the leisure to read them. Besides, he enjoyed the advantages of an extensive journey in the South and, on graduation from college, spent the years 1835 and 1836 abroad, where he met some of the most distinguished men of the day. Although he studied law, it was apparently not necessary for him to earn his living by its practice.

Barnard's friends and acquaintances included some of the wealthiest men of America. "No other man can carry the wealthy and powerful but you," wrote a friend of popular education in Rhode Island when he seemed for a moment to be faltering in the cause. "The rest of us can do the small work, but you can stir the strong men and no one else can."[17] As Barnard's own financial interests included sawmills and water works in New England, real estate in New York, and investments in Western lands, there was reason for his ability to understand men of means. Indeed, his private fortune was ample enough to permit him to spend more than $40,000 for the educational publications he edited—an expenditure which,

[17] Wilkins Updike, Kingston, R. I., to Barnard, July 4, 1845, Barnard MSS., Monroe Collection.

with various reverses, brought him almost to poverty before he lived out his long life of eighty-nine years.[18]

II

With this background, it was natural for Barnard to begin his public career by denouncing Jackson in an address delivered in 1831 in Hartford, his native city. Sharply condemning Jacksonian democracy for defaming the sacred judiciary and for its onslaughts against sound money and the national bank, Barnard saved his most biting indictment for the enemy's attacks on the protective tariff, "upon the strength of which a vast amount of property has been invested in manufacturing industry."[19] In the midst of the depression of 1837, when palliative measures threatened vested interests, Barnard, now a member of the Connecticut legislature, fought every effort to weaken the power of the courts, which he frankly recognized as the guardians of property against the "frenzy of popular excitement."[20]

It was perhaps because of his own interests and associations that Barnard minced no words in painting, both in his private papers and published writings, what would now be called a class struggle. His eyes beheld with fear the sordid drudgery, misery, crime, and potential revolt which lurked about the crowded quarters of city districts. In a book of notes, presumably intended for a speech or lecture, he sounded a warning against the danger inherent in the volcanic mass of

[18] *American Journal of Education,* Vol. XXX (March, 1880), p. 224; James L. Hughes, *Henry Barnard* (Hartford, 1896); Anna Blair, Henry Barnard, School Administrator (Yale doctoral dissertation, 1931, unpublished), pp. 19–20.

[19] "Address to the National Republican Young Men of Hartford County," Barnard MSS., Watkinson Collection; Barnard to Doctor Todd, Washington, Feb. 11, 1833, *ibid.*

[20] "Remarks of Mr. Barnard of Hartford in the House of Representatives, May 23, 1837, on the proposed amendment to the constitution," *ibid.*

146

workers, who might not only usurp the judicial and executive power of society but through violent mobs destroy property itself. The working class was "a mighty power, and there is a physical strength slumbering in their arms in peaceful times and a greater and more terrible than mere strength of muscles in their uninformed intellect and uninstructed heart, which is liable at any time to be called into exercise."

We may think, he continued, that in its blindness "we can with safety drive it [the working class] to grind at the mill for our pleasure and convenience—but we must take care how we sport with its awakened feelings lest the spirit of vengeance and of strength return upon it, and it bow itself mightily against the pillory of your unrighteous system and destroy the social structure, though itself perish."[21] Alarmed at "all the elements of anarchy, revolution, and crime," which had been apparent, and which even as he wrote seemed to lie "weltering in the bosom of society" waiting to be let loose and scatter desolation, Barnard declared that it was time for awakened capitalists, patriots, and Christians to set the social house in order.[22]

It would be unfair to Barnard to suggest that he had no human regard for the underdog apart from a desire to render him harmless. He did not hide his belief that industrialism endangered the well-being of women and children.[23] His reports as well as his lectures abound with indictments of the badly ventilated and poorly lighted dwellings in the slums.

---

[21] Book of notes, Barnard MSS., Watkinson Collection.

[22] Views for lectures, *ibid.; Journal of the R. I. Institute of Instruction,* Vol. I (Dec., 1845), p. 37; *Report of the Superintendent of Common Schools in Connecticut* (1851), p. 13.

[23] *Connecticut Common School Journal,* Vol. I (June, 1839), pp. 165–66; Henry Barnard, *Legal Provisions Respecting the Education and Employment of Children in Factories* (Hartford, 1842), *passim; Journal of the R. I. Institute of Instruction,* Vol. I (March, 1846), p. 133; *Report,* 1851, p. 12: Ensign, *op. cit.,* pp. 87–92.

They reveal his awareness of the relation between long, dull hours of work and the craving for excitement which so often led to drunkenness and crime.[24] He commended Gallaudet, a philanthropist who centered his efforts in the education of the deaf, for having seen "the difficulty, if not the impossibility of cultivating the Christian virtues and graces, amid the filth and discomfort of cellars and garrets, and even of such as the destitute generally occupy" and for having realized that after ten or twelve or fifteen hours' work the laborer had no elasticity of mind or body, no time or energy to profit even from sermons and lectures.[25]

Barnard believed that the *status quo* might be preserved if the worst abuses were removed; but he also sincerely desired the well-being of the masses. While it would be too much to say that he visioned a society in which there were no classes and no class distinctions, he did desire an order in which personal dignity, virtue, and merit would be reverenced regardless of wealth and rank, in which there should be "no populace, no common people," but where all ranks and occupations of men would enjoy the pleasure of taste and imagination, respectful manners and correct morals.[26] He not only believed that this could be done without disturbing the social and economic status of the privileged classes; he even thought that, in spite of differences of wealth and social position, the rich and the poor might truly understand each other and share in common many, and particularly cultural, experiences. While Barnard, like Jefferson, would provide means by which the most gifted of the poor might advance into the privileged classes, and while he sometimes described in glowing terms how, by the educational

[24] *Journal of the R. I. Institute of Instruction,* Vol. I (Jan., Feb., 1846), p. 72; *Report,* 1851, p. 33.
[25] Henry Barnard, *Tribute to Gallaudet* (Hartford, 1852), p. 55.
[26] Views for lectures, Barnard MSS., Watkinson Collection.

ladder, the top might be reached from the bottom, he did not conceal his belief that the great mass of the urban workers in such industrial areas as Rhode Island would remain in the economic class of their parents. But he thought that, however humble their circumstances, it was possible for them to lead decent and happy lives and to participate with the well-to-do in the cultural values created by the past.[27]

Barnard saw that the removal of at least part of the existing class prejudice was indispensable if such an end were to be won. For that reason he bitterly attacked the class structure of the schools which was a part of our colonial inheritance. Fearing the disastrous results of class antagonism, he vigorously opposed private academies and favored the movement for public high schools in order that children of rich and poor might join hands and come to a mutual understanding. His indictment of the private school deserves quotation:

"It classifies society at the root, by assorting children according to the wealth, education, or outward circumstances of their parents into different schools; and educates children of the same neighborhood differently and unequally. These differences of culture, as to manners, morals and intellectual tastes and habits, begun in childhood and strengthened by differences in occupation, which are determined mainly by early education, open a real chasm between members of the same society, broad and deep, which equal laws and political theories cannot close."[28] "The children who attend the private school at home, or go abroad to the academy or boarding school, associate almost of necessity together, and thus, with the enjoyment of superior advantages, and the influence of exclusive association, they grow up with a feeling of superiority every way at war with their own usefulness and the peace of society. On the other hand, the children of the district school feel more or less the depressing influences of their inferior advantages, and imbibe feel-

[27] *Journal of the Rhode Island Institute of Instruction,* Vol. I (Jan. and Feb., 1846), pp. 75–78; *Report,* 1851, pp. 37–40.
[28] *Journal of R. I. Institute of Instruction,* Vol. I (Dec., 1845), p. 38; *Report of the Superintendent of Common Schools in Connecticut* (1850), pp. 33–34.

ings of jealousy, if not of hostility, towards their more fortunate neighbors."[29]

If private schools could be eliminated, and children of all classes attend common institutions, the poor would feel that, "whatever may betide them, their children are born to an inheritance more valuable than lands or shops, in the free access to institutions where as good education can be had as money can buy at home or abroad."[30] Nothing, he maintained, would do more to undermine the jealousy which the poor felt for the rich than to realize that the children of the two classes started life from the same platform and enjoyed equality in the benefits of education.[31]

Barnard did not seek to realize this end through a system of schools open to all without charge. He held that parents able to pay tuition for their children should support the public schools in that way as well as by paying taxes. The town or state should assume the burden of tuition only for the child whose father was too poor to pay the rates.[32] If Barnard failed to see that such an arrangement might defeat his purpose of breaking down class antagonisms by making children conscious of the arbitrary distinctions between rich and poor, he did propose other measures more likely to achieve his ideal. To secure equality of opportunity, he advocated a policy of giving larger appropriations of state funds to the smaller and poorer school districts. Wholesale higher education did not come within his scheme, but he suggested that scholarships be established to permit the gifted poor to enjoy the advantages of college and university.

[29] *Connecticut Common School Journal,* Vol. II (May, 1840), p. 215.
[30] *Report,* 1850, p. 31.
[31] Book of notes, Barnard MSS., Watkinson Collection.
[32] Barnard to Potter, June 15, 1894, and notes for lecture, Barnard MSS., Watkinson Collection; Steiner, *Henry Barnard,* p. 89.

Although Barnard thought that class antagonism and the danger of conflict between rich and poor might be greatly reduced, if not eliminated, by a system of public schools in which children would be indifferent to distinctions of dress and in which they would act as a "band of brothers, bound by the tenderest ties of love,"[33] he was too realistic to pin all his faith to the influences of a common education. Indeed, while he sometimes spoke as if the schools were to regenerate society,[34] he seems also to have recognized the fact that certain forces entirely outside their sphere might be equally potent, or more so, in remedying conditions. Aware of the woeful deficiency in our schools at the end of the colonial period, Barnard frankly stated that the great figures of the Revolutionary era owed very little to them. In explaining the greatness of these men, he was compelled to recognize the complexity of the forces conditioning the development of the individual. The daily routine of the child, which in most cases endowed him with robustness, patience of toil, resoluteness, perseverance, and fertility of resource, family training, the influence of church and Bible, the observation of man and nature, debates over public questions, books in the village library, and, especially, the newspaper, all nourished qualities of inestimable consequence.[35] If the school was to help weed the "moral jungle," it must not attempt so complex a work single-handed.

Holding that the regeneration of the unfortunate classes involved the "harmonious co-operation of earnest philanthropy, missionary enterprise and sanctified wisdom," Barnard urged the wealthy and intelligent classes to make their own influence pervade and transform the slums. They might begin by con-

---

[33] *Connecticut Common School Journal*, Vol. II (Oct., 1839), p. 47.
[34] Views for lecture, Barnard MSS., Watkinson Collection; *Tribute to Gallaudet*, p. 60; *American Journal of Education*, Vol. I (1856), p. 735.
[35] *American Journal of Education*, Vol. XXXII (1882), pp. 816–18.

structing model tenement houses for rental at a moderate profit, and thus wipe out one of the worst eyesores and dangers. Equally important was the construction of attractive and convenient schoolhouses with libraries, lecture and conversation rooms, as well as facilities for harmless amusement. Not only must they send their children to these schools, but they themselves must frequent them and partake in their activities. These broadly educational institutions, suggestive of the modern social settlement, were to provide the opportunities by which the well-to-do and the poor were to come to know and understand each other. By such means the gulf between the classes would be closed; in this manner would be remedied a situation which "must ever be accompanied with contempt, exclusiveness, and apprehension on one side, and on the other with envying jealousies, curses not loud but deep, and occasionally with outbreaks which will carry the desolation of a tornado in their track."[36]

It cannot be claimed that Barnard, sincere though he doubtless was in advocating such methods to achieve his ideal, was unaware of the fundamental criticisms which the socialism of his day launched against such a program. Elijah P. Grant, a college friend and frequent correspondent, challenged in unmistakable terms the conception to which Barnard devoted his life-long efforts. "I hope," he wrote to his old classmate, "to see you get engaged in some more efficient project for the regeneration of society than *common schools,* for until you are, I am persuaded that your labors will be almost in vain."[37] But Grant, in spite of all his efforts, apparently failed seriously to interest his educational friend in Fourierism, though at one time Barnard

[36] *Journal of the R. I. Institute of Instruction,* Vol. I (Jan., Feb., 1846), pp. 49, 75–77; *Report,* 1851, pp. 26, 35–40.
[37] E. P. Grant to Barnard, Sept. 1, 1843, Barnard MSS., Watkinson Collection.

was on the point of advancing money for the Ohio Phalanx which Grant organized in 1844.

It is worth asking why Barnard did not accept the idea that fundamental economic changes were a necessary prelude to the social and cultural values he desired, for in rejecting the arguments of his socialist friend, Barnard shared the deep and abiding faith that educators, as well as the American people at large, have placed in ameliorative and particularly in educational efforts to achieve social improvement. It is possible, in the first place, that Barnard and his educational associates were influenced by their study of and regard for Pestalozzi, who believed that every person could become fully rounded and developed in spite of exterior circumstances. In the second place, Barnard, like most of his fellow educators, came from and shared the views of the more privileged class. The son of a well-to-do man, he had come fairly easily by the cultural equipment he wished the poor to share. While he realized that it would be impossible for the most degraded and overworked laborers to profit from such opportunities as might be offered, he failed, perhaps because of his own high regard for cultural values, to understand the necessity for their substantial basis in material goods. Nor did he see all the obstacles in the way of achieving a cultural democracy in a prevailing economic aristocracy. With the limitations imposed on him by his own environment and associations he could not have been expected to see the force of the argument that the culture he so much valued, being a class culture, could not easily be imposed on a class which had not shared in creating it.

An equally important reason, perhaps, for the failure of Barnard and his contemporary educational colleagues to respond to the socialist contention that the public school was an inadequate road to social justice and cultural equality lay in the basic philosophy of individualism to which almost all Americans in that day subscribed. This philosophy, which found favorable soil in an economy governed by the idea of *laissez faire* and by the ideals of industrial capitalism, and which was greatly invigorated by the frontier experience, held that the really worthy individual, regardless of his status, could, by self-help, achieve at least a competency adequate to permit him to enjoy the better things of life. It is to Barnard's credit that, unlike certain more enthusiastic but less realistic apostles of individualism, he did not contend that American life in urban centers was such as to permit the lower classes to move out of their rank. But, along with almost everyone else, he did think that, if one were industrious, punctual, and frugal, if one had perseverance, and if one were respectful of property, law, and God, the existing social order provided him with abundant opportunities for living an eligible life. It is hardly necessary to observe that this social philosophy, however much in accordance it may or may not have been with realities, seemed reasonable to the privileged class. It minimized their social responsibilities and saved their consciences from smarting too much when they beheld the "moral jungle" with its squalor, misery, and suffering. It was, furthermore, sufficiently plausible to capture the bulk of the lower classes who, with proper encouragement, proved quite willing to subscribe to it.

Barnard, with his typically American individualism, thus defended the existing order of industrial capitalism, whose sores he would have healed by a classless education and a philanthropic co-operation between rich and poor. The America of which he approved was the America of Poor Richard:

"In this country, the art of acquisition is pretty well understood; for which we are indebted, mainly to the necessities of a poor but intelligent ancestry, and the possession of rich but undeveloped material and facilities, but in no small degree to the maxims of POOR RICHARD, which, by household and schoolbook repetition, have become inwrought into the texture of every American mind."[88]

This statement introduces a series of quotations on thrift and the use of money, which Barnard attempted to popularize through the *Journal*. They constituted "sound" attitudes toward a subject concerning which he believed the young of both sexes and all conditions needed to "form clear conceptions and practical aims." Industry, frugality, regard for money, and the association of wealth and character distinguish the maxims of which Barnard approved.[39]

In spite of the fact that Barnard was in theory devoted to the ideal of an open-minded method of inquiry, in practice he seems to have sanctioned what was virtually the indoctrination of the teachers of youth with capitalistic theory. Had Barnard excluded from the *American Journal of Education* all material directly pertinent to capitalism (as he did exclude material on the slavery and temperance questions) there would be no ground for this statement, even though his own bias had incidentally manifested itself. The *Journal* contains few discussions of capitalism, but there can be slight doubt about the purpose and character of these discussions. Moreover, the two most

[88] *American Journal of Education,* Vol. XXIII (1872), p. 249.

[39] Poor Richard admonishes the reader to promote industry, cultivate frugality, and master idleness and small unnecessary expenses. Lord Bacon proclaims the advantage of a comfortable amount of honorably obtained riches and advises that one divide up investments between "gains certain" and "adventures." Pope praises the gentleman of small fortune who is generous to the common folk of the town. Henry Taylor condemns as superficial the philosophy which teaches contempt for money, advises that one save for a purpose and at death so distribute one's estate that it will make a moderate addition to moderate fortunes. Lord Edward Bulwer Lytton identifies the acquisition and use of money with character: Money is power; associate toil with something dear to your affection, like a mother's comfort or the possession of a bride, for it will strengthen you in economy; never endorse a neighbor's note unless you can afford to give him the money. *Ibid.,* pp. 249–72.

definitely propagandist articles were printed also in *Papers for the Teacher,* a sort of manual which Barnard edited while agent of the regents of normal schools in Wisconsin, and which he prefaced with the statement that the volume contained "a number of papers which he may deem worthy of study and preservation by the Teachers of Wisconsin."[40] That Barnard did not live up to his idea of promoting a spirit of inquiry in education is clear from the fact that while he saw fit to publish materials with a definitely pro-capitalistic bias, he did not print any of the contemporary socialistic criticisms which, by reason of his acquaintance with one of the leading Fourierists, must have been familiar to him. Even in an article on Robert Owen, prefaced by editorial remarks regarding his educational practices, practically nothing was said about Owen's challenge to conventional capitalism and his socialistic experiment in America.[41]

Even more illuminating, however, are the two articles, "Education, A Preventive of Misery and Crime," from a prize essay of the British schoolmasters' association, and "Elementary Instruction in Economical Science," extracts from a paper by Charles Knight, which proposed education in political economy as a remedy for the extensive organization and strikes of workingmen in London. The first article demands that the teacher acquaint himself with the causes of misery by visiting homes of poverty: in one he will find a father unemployed because he was not always punctual, and hence was the first to be let off in slack times; in another he will discover that the head of the

---

[40] *Papers for the Teacher,* 2d series: *Object Teaching and Oral Lessons on Social Science and Common Things* (New York, 1860), introduction. The two articles are Edward Campbell Tainsh, "Education, A Preventive of Misery and Crime," *Object Teaching,* pp. 116–32; *American Journal of Education,* Vol. XI (March, 1862), pp. 77–93; and "Elementary Instruction in Economical Science," *Object Teaching,* pp. 105–15; *American Journal of Education,* Vol. X (March, 1861), pp. 105–15.

[41] *American Journal of Education,* Vol. XXVI (July, 1876), pp. 403–16.

house is a drunkard; and in a third, that the bread-earner, while now incapacitated by illness, had failed to lay by savings for a rainy day. In other words, the chief causes of poverty were held to be extravagance, ungoverned passion, tardiness, and ignorance; under this last category was included "destitution resulting from a strike which was engaged in with a view of bettering their condition." The schoolmaster's duty was to instill correct virtues, impress youth with its duties, train them in right habits, and impart knowledge of proper social relationships.

"As a *capitalist* he should so employ his capital as to produce that which society most wants in the greatest possible quantities, and at the smallest possible cost. He should select those laborers who can best help him in making his capital productive, those whose qualifications are the highest, who can produce most in proportion to the wages paid them. He should endeavor to turn their labor to the best account, availing himself of every aid that lies within his reach. In so doing, he will be the benefactory of society. . . . As his own special reward he will obtain large profits.

"As a *laborer* he should endeavor to cultivate in himself those qualities, to attain that knowledge and skill which will make his services most acceptable to the capitalist. He should serve his employer faithfully, bringing all his intelligence to bear upon his work. He will then serve society by making capital upon which he is employed as productive as possible, and will earn for himself the reward of high wages. If his wages be lower than desirable, he should seek for the means of obtaining higher, taking care, at the same time, not to engage in strikes, or any other means, whose real tendency is the opposite of the one sought for. Should there be no means of *immediately* obtaining higher wages, he should endeavor to increase his productiveness as the only means of increasing the store out of which wages are paid, and of obtaining for himself a large share of that store."[42]

Barnard's editorial remarks which prefaced the second article suggest his willingness to indoctrinate school children and

[42] *Object Teaching,* pp. 129–30.

artisans in mechanics' institutes with definitely capitalistic economics in order to prevent strikes and labor troubles.[43] The paper itself included a catechism designed to help the teacher provide the proper economic truths to workers or their children. Among the questions and answers the following show the tenor of the whole:

Q. Suppose a capitalist in employing his capital makes large profits, would that harm the working man?

A. No. There would be more capital to pay wages.

Q. Which is best, that capitalists be saving or wasteful?

A. Saving.

Q. Why?

A. (After several attempts, a boy said) If wasteful men, they would consume and have less capital.

Q. But if they were not wasteful, what would happen?

A. There would be more capital to earn capital hereafter.

Q. Are you sorry, then, that capitalists should have great profits?

A. Glad.

Q. Why does the foreman get more than the laborer?

A. Because the foreman's work is of more value than the laborer's.

Q. There are differences of character as well as of skill between two workmen. Why do capitalists run after men, and will give them very high wages for skill, and a combination of good qualities?

A. Capitalists give wages to workmen in proportion to their productiveness.

Q. If there are two boys starting in life, one the son of a man who has accumulated capital, the other of a man who has not, shall I be right in saying that the boy without this advantage can never be a capitalist?

A. No.

Q. But what is to make him a capitalist?

A. Saving.[44]

This instruction, the author notes, together with lectures of the same import, would go far toward producing a happier and

[43] *Ibid.,* p. 105.   [44] *Ibid.,* p. 109.

more contented population, and it would further put an end to the chronic state of feverish hostility between capitalists and laborers. Although an editor does not necessarily share the views of the writers whose articles he publishes, it seems clear that Barnard was willing to popularize apologies for the dominant economic system without in any way suggesting the criticisms with which his socialist friend, Elijah Grant, had made him familiar.

If further evidence were needed to indicate that Barnard was on the whole friendly toward industrial capitalism it is to be found in the fact that, although he held the virtues of rural America in high regard, he measured success, even for his rural countrymen, in terms of achievement in industry and commerce.[45] Furthermore, while he condemned vanity and ruthlessness when displayed by men of great fortune, he defended rather than criticized the pursuit of wealth as such.[46] He appreciated the benefactions which men of wealth conferred upon the cause of education. Believing that the improvement of educational institutions depended upon the liberality of men of means, he saw no objection to the resulting dependence of such institutions on those who supported them. In making proposals for the reorganization of St. John's College, the presidency of which he accepted in 1866, he recommended that, in the interest of increasing endowment, those who contributed gifts of money for the establishment of chairs might name members to fill vacancies in the board of directors.[47]

If Barnard sincerely supported the existing economic order, he was a reformer in the field of education itself. It is true that the major reform he advocated, an increasing emphasis upon

[45] *Report of the Superintendent of Common Schools in Connecticut,* 1853, p. 181; *American Journal of Education,* Vol. XXX (March, 1880), p. 207.
[46] *Ibid.,* Vol. I (Jan., 1856), pp. 202–3; Vol. II (Aug., 1856), p. 33.
[47] *Ibid.,* Vol. XVI (Sept., 1866), p. 547.

utilitarian disciplines in the curriculum,[48] favored rather than militated against the new industrial order which was rapidly becoming dominant. Nonetheless, in opposing the prevailing emphasis on book learning and in urging that education promote whatever was practical and useful, Barnard was an innovator and a prophet. It is without doubt these qualities that in large part explain the influence that he exerted on the educators of his own day. While it is true that his plans for adult as well as for common school education aimed to universalize cultivation in taste and intellect, still he did a great deal to further in the schools whatever was practical, whether the principles of health, agriculture, commerce, or mechanics.[49] Education, in short, was to serve the actual needs of the community.[50]

One of the great practical services which Barnard thought universal education would render—and one of the arguments continually used to gain support for the public schools—was the promotion of industrialism. Even elementary training in the rudiments of knowledge and the basic moral virtues would, by rendering the common laborer more fruitfully industrious, efficient, and frugal, enable American industry to compete the better with countries where workingmen were ignorant.[51] His scheme of moral instruction, as we have seen, provided for the inculcation of habits of industry, frugality, and respect for property, habits of definite utilitarian value in the America of

[48] Barnard came under the influence of the doctrines of utilitarianism in his early youth. On his return from Europe in 1836, he said that individual happiness in America was "bound up with the greatest good of the greatest number. Every man must at once make himself as good and useful as he can, and help at the same time to make everybody about him, and all whom he can reach, better and happier." Steiner, *Henry Barnard*, p. 28.

[49] *Connecticut Common School Journal*, Vol. II (Aug., 1839), p. 11. Also, "Common School Education Should be Practical," *ibid.*, Vol. I (March 15, 1839), p. 113.

[50] *Report of the Commissioner of Education*, 1867–68, pp. xvii, 831.

[51] *Report*, 1851, p. 41.

Barnard's day. From many obscure and humble homes, education was expected to call forth inventive talent, productive skill, and intellectual taste, which would multiply workshops and increase the general wealth.[52]

Recognizing that the world of applied science was a rapidly changing one, Barnard believed that a practical education was necessary to its successful and rapid development. He was keenly interested in what the high schools and special institutions could do to aid the nation's industries.[53] If everyone were taught the laws of natural science, inventions would be multiplied. An increase in the number of technical schools would, he thought, contribute to the same end and at the same time enhance production. Barnard recommended that high schools teach "such studies as navigation, bookkeeping, surveying, botany, chemistry, and kindred studies which are directly connected with success in the varied departments of domestic and inland trade, with foreign commerce, with gardening, with agriculture, the manufacturing and domestic arts."[54] Even the president of a literary institution, like St. John's College, should, Barnard thought, understand the "bearing of science on the existing industries of the country."[55] Although these ideals of education were somewhat less revolutionary than when Benjamin Franklin championed them, they were still sufficiently novel to make Barnard something of an educational radical.

Patriotism must be added to the influences which religion, humanitarianism, class background, and utilitarianism exerted on Barnard's social and educational thought. Like so many

[52] *Report,* 1850, pp. 29–30.
[53] *American Journal of Education,* Vol. XXII (Jan., 1871), p. 9; Henry Barnard, "Education and Educational Institutions" in *First Century of National Existence* (Hartford, 1874), p. 403; Steiner, *Henry Barnard,* pp. 69, 81, 91.
[54] *Report,* 1850, p. 28.
[55] Barnard to Judge Mason, undated, Barnard MSS., Watkinson Collection.

other educators, he preached the necessity of cultural independence from Europe. As early as 1828, he took James Fenimore Cooper to task for his degrading imitation of Scott and for his failure to quicken his writings with "some touch of the freedom and independence of his country."[56] Although no one did so much to familiarize his countrymen with the educational thought and practice of Europe, Barnard never recommended the blind adoption of old-world ideals and practices. In spite of his cultural patriotism, however, the fact that he devoted thousands of pages of the *American Journal of Education* to European education must have helped to prolong our dependence on European example.

One of Barnard's strongest convictions was that the historic deeds and words of his countrymen must be engraved on the conscience of subsequent generations, that they might be prepared to preserve the heritage of the past.[57] Barnard's evaluation of the American heritage, though less critical than that of Mann, was more typical of the feelings of his fellow educators and of the American people. While Mann defined patriotism as love of the human beings thronging our vast domains and a willingness to work for a better life for their descendants,[58] Barnard thought of it rather in terms of the more conservative and martial traditions. While Mann observed that the Revolution was not merely a transfer of sovereignty from England to America, but a crusade for the regeneration of mankind from the binding fetters of body and mind,[59] Barnard found compensation for the fact that the struggle had closed the schools in the "stirring exhibitions of heroic patriotism" which surrounded children at that time.[60] With a consciousness of the "black

[56] *New England Weekly Review,* July 28, 1828, in Watkinson Collection.
[57] *Connecticut Common School Journal,* Vol. I (March 15, 1839), p. 113.
[58] [Massachusetts] *Common School Journal,* Vol. IV (Jan. 1, 1842), p. 8.
[59] *Life and Works of Horace Mann,* Vol. IV, pp. 341 *et seq.*
[60] *American Journal of Education,* Vol. XXXII (1882), p. 783.

spots" in American civilization, Mann nowhere expressed the general enthusiasm for "the American mission," to which Barnard paid tribute in glowing words. "Here on these shores," he wrote, "the claims of humanity in its broadest sense are recognized in the government under which we live. From the first hour our history opened on the rock of Plymouth, all that gives value to human life, security to human happiness, protection to personal rights, to private property and public liberty has been wrought out by the agency of institutions, created by and for the benefit of the people themselves."[61]

With this type of patriotic devotion to his country it was natural for this leader to urge that the schools impress sentiments of patriotism on the mind of the child. Desiring to have civics taught in the common school, Barnard, while secretary of education in Connecticut, complained of the lack of a good textbook on the subject. Unlike Mann, who deprecated history as a school subject because of its glorification of war, Barnard hoped to see it, along with a course on the state and national constitutions, in every high school.[62] He advised that a fit test for the exercise of the suffrage would be the intelligent reading of the Constitution.[63] In making suggestions for the reorganization of St. John's College, he proposed that all candidates for the Bachelor's or Master's degree should be examined in law and public economy, covering the constitutions of the state and the country, as well as the "law of the citizen and man of business."[64]

Although Barnard paid tribute to Jefferson along with Madi-

61 Views for lectures, Barnard MSS., Watkinson Collection. For a discussion of "the American mission" see Merle Curti, "Young America," *American Historical Review,* Vol. XXXII (Oct., 1926), pp. 34–55.

62 *Connecticut Common School Journal,* Vol. I (June, 1839), p. 169; *Report,* 1850, pp. 28, 58.

63 *Report,* 1851, p. 27; *Connecticut Common School Journal,* Vol. I (June, 1839), p. 157.

64 *American Journal of Education,* Vol. XVI (Sept., 1866), p. 544.

son, Hamilton, and Washington, and even interpreted the Constitution as a guaranty that all men "not only *shall be,* but shall be *fit to be* voters, jurors, witnesses, legislators and judges of legislation,"[65] one searches in vain in his writings on civic patriotism for any suggestion of the concept—which Mann upheld—that obedience and subordination were due not merely to the law, but to the law of God written in the heart.[66]

III

Unlike Mann, Barnard did not think that any crisis in the welfare of humanity could ever be sufficiently important to justify an educator in quitting his own work to fight on the political front. After a brief term in the Connecticut legislature, Barnard consistently subordinated political life to that of labor in the educational field. He deplored Mann's entry into politics in 1848, and in 1856 was not enough interested in politics to cast a vote.[67] On the eve of the Civil War he wrote to Senator Dixon that if the senator and his colleagues would help "the humble teacher in the 80,000 schools of the land in the great work of educating the next generation in . . . an abiding respect for law and the meaning and sanctity of such words as patriotism, justice, duty, . . . then your successors will have a better time in administering the great interests of the American people, however divided and subdivided into confederacies, nations, and states."[68] Yet Barnard did not think that education had any specific responsibility for breaking down sectionalism. Patriot though he was, his conviction that education must be nonpartisan led him to introduce the second issue of

[65] Views for Lectures, Barnard MSS., Watkinson Collection.
[66] *Life and Works of Horace Mann,* Vol. III, p. 456.
[67] Barnard to E. R. Potter, Hartford, April 7, 1856, Barnard MSS., Monroe Collection.
[68] Barnard to Dixon, March 22, 1861, Barnard MSS., Watkinson Collection.

the *American Journal of Education* in 1856 with the declaration that the causes of sectional animosities lay outside the field of educational effort and discussion.[69] In taking the attitude that the educator must be nonpartisan Barnard was only carrying to a logical development the point of view that made Mann put the clamps on Samuel J. May when he took his normal school students to an antislavery meeting.

While it was as a member of the Connecticut legislature that Barnard began his work for educational reform, he sincerely tried to eschew politics in his administrative work. Contrary to generally accepted opinion, the first battle for better schools and for teacher training had been virtually won before Barnard consummated the victory in the Connecticut legislature. The first bill that he brought forward in the legislature to better the school system was introduced at the suggestion and request of a fellow legislator who belonged to the opposite and majority party, the Democratic. The bill which he brought forward and which passed the following year was carried with almost unanimous consent. It is true that after four years, during which Barnard presided over the newly established supervisory commission, the progressive legislation was swept away by a Democratic legislature[70] and that his bitter resentment against the "demagogues" knew no bounds.[71] When he returned in 1849 as commissioner of education he managed to steer a neutral course and succeeded in not antagonizing any important political interest. As a matter of fact, the ardent Whig of 1837 had quietly become, by 1856, a less enthusiastic Democrat.

[69] *American Journal of Education,* Vol. I (Jan., 1856), p. 139.

[70] A number of reasons have been assigned for this reversal: party politics and complications, opposition of the propertied interests that opposed general taxation for the support of the schools, and the feeling that little had been achieved to improve the education offered in the public schools. The real elements of support and opposition are obscure.

[71] Barnard to Mann, Hartford, May 29, June 11, 1842, Mann Papers.

The situation in Rhode Island in 1842, when Barnard took the position of commissioner of public schools, presents many undercurrents of social significance. Although the Dorr war, which had just been brought to an end, is generally interpreted as a demand for wider franchise and a more equitable distribution of representation, a good deal of evidence suggests strongly that the disturbance had much deeper roots than is generally supposed. To the significant statement of the writer in the *North American Review* that the new educational policy was wisely recognized by manufacturers to be the only certain security for their property rights,[72] there is to be added the testimony of Barnard's reports and the whole tone of the *Journal of the Rhode Island Institute of Instruction,* which he edited during the six years of his residence in Providence.

Both the reports and the *Journal,* while obviously designed to enlist the co-operation of all factions, left no doubt that the education of the new generation was in part designed to secure existing governmental institutions. In referring to qualifications for teachers, Barnard made it clear that while the political opinions of candidates were not to be taken into account, "their manner of expressing such belief, or maintaining it," was of importance. "If that manner is in itself boisterous and disorderly, intemperate and offensive, it may well be supposed to indicate ungoverned passions, or want of sound principles of conduct which would render its possessor obnoxious to the inhabitants of the district, and unfit for the sacred duties of a teacher of youth."[73]

It is true that the leading men of both parties favored the reorganization and increased support of public education. Dorr, however, had been more actively engaged in the work of pub-

[72] *North American Review,* Vol. LXVII (July, 1848), p. 254.
[73] *Journal of the R. I. Institute of Instruction,* Vol. II (Nov., 1847), p. 245.

lic education than any of his opponents, and his constitution
went further than that of the conservatives in the support it
promised for improved common schools.[74] At the same time
the leaders of the anti-Dorr party, such men as President Wayland of Brown, E. R. Potter, Wilkins Updike, John Kingsbury, and Governor James Fenner, were likewise committed to
the cause of more general and efficient support of public schools.
The bill providing for the reorganization of the school system
passed in both houses without a dissenting voice. Since it was
impossible to name a Rhode Islander to the new office of commissioner, Barnard was called in to increase and improve the
number of common schools.

Although Barnard was confronted by a good deal of apathy
and some real opposition, he succeeded in winning the aid of
many men of ample fortune and in consolidating the victory
for the principle of better public schools.[75] When he retired
in 1849 he was congratulated on "the successful prosecution
of an enterprise, which at the outset . . . seemed hopeless, and
which in its prosecution encountered hindrances and difficulties
under which almost any other man would have been thrown
into despair."[76] In even more striking words Elisha R. Potter,
who succeeded Barnard when ill health led him to resign,
testified that, although old prejudices and antagonisms ran
high, the first Rhode Island commissioner of education managed to secure the support of all parties, who found it possible
to work harmoniously together under his unselfish and enthusiastic leadership.[77]

[74] Charles Carroll, *Public Education in Rhode Island* (Providence, 1918),
pp. 120–23.
[75] *American Journal of Education*, Vol. I (1856), p. 725; E. R. Potter to
Barnard, Kingston, Jan. 29, 1847, March 4, May 10, June 8, 1849, Barnard
MSS., Monroe Collection.
[76] John Kingsbury to Barnard, undated, *ibid*.
[77] Elisha R. Potter to ex-Governor Thomas of Maryland, Washington, D. C.,
Jan. 10, 1867, Barnard MSS., Watkinson Collection.

Barnard encountered plenty of trouble in his subsequent administrative work as president of the University of Wisconsin and of St. John's College, and as the first United States Commissioner of Education. Yet he sincerely tried to work outside party lines and he honestly believed that his attitude toward the political and economic struggles of the American people was disinterested. The admiring or the casual reader of his reports, his educational journals, and his private papers might be tempted to believe that Barnard succeeded in his efforts. What could be more disinterested than his vigorous efforts to provide teacher training and well supervised schools for rich and poor alike? What could be more aloof than his work for better school architecture and for the more liberal support of every type of educational institution? What could be more objective than the mass of articles in the fifty-two volumes of the *American Journal of Education* describing educational thought and practice at home and abroad? The very fact that Barnard was reluctant to publish any comprehensive exposition of his own ideas, together with his pronounced historical, not to say antiquarian, interest, would tend to confirm the belief that his contributions lay in administration, popularization of the free school idea, and educational journalism, rather than in the sphere of educational and social philosophy; and that, consequently, it was relatively easy for him to practice his ideal of neutrality and aloofness.

Yet, as we have seen, Barnard was neither neutral toward nor aloof from many of the most lasting struggles and antagonisms of his time. When a small but persistent band of pacifists proclaimed the doctrine that war shall be no more, Barnard, though sympathetic with their position, lent his authority to perpetuating the war system. When his co-worker Horace Mann suggested a patriotism of humanity, he affirmed rather his countrymen's belief that America was the best place in which to have been born and in which to live. When his friend Elijah Grant tried to enlist his support for an experiment designed to illustrate the superior advantages of a socialistic society, he gave no heed but provided materials by which teachers could strengthen their pupils' faith in the virtues of capitalism.

Barnard's ideal of the good citizen was that of the man who toiled industriously and frugally his whole life, and stoically accepted reverses with the conviction that the will of God was recorded in the past history of mankind, and that it would also guide the future ever onward without the necessity of rebellion or revolution. His work was thus not so completely that of a neutral as he thought. Even the great sincerity and humanity which characterized his efforts to improve the daily lot of degraded and impoverished Americans and to provide them with some part of culture did not mitigate the fact that these measures were in large part designed to remove the menace of a "populace."

On the other hand, in the educational practices which he favored, Barnard was a reformer. He desired to make education functional to the actual life and needs of the people in an age that was becoming industrialized. No one worked with greater consistency, devotion, and sacrifice for the improvement of educational standards and for the extension of educational opportunities to the underprivileged. To schoolmen in his day he was a pioneer and the architect of a new and more useful educational structure. His ideal, conservative in its social and liberal in its professional aspects, was in large measure the product of major forces in American life, and is to be regarded as critically and as sympathetically as those forces themselves.

V

THE EDUCATION OF WOMEN

In the great art of Teaching we shall find
Its best exponent is a female mind.
                              —CHRISTOPHER C. COX.

I have longed to be permitted to labor where the expenses would
be less than they are here, so that more of our daughters could reap
the fruits.

                              —MARY LYON.

I

While girls as well as boys profited from the common school
revival for which Barnard and Mann waged so many battles,
social and cultural discrimination against women was so pronounced during the first half of the nineteenth century that the
problem of their education was in many respects a unique one.
Although in the decade before the Civil War some states conceded to women the right to control their own property, the
war that freed the slaves found half of the white race still
fettered by many economic, political, and educational restrictions.

The welfare of their eternal souls and the requirements of
practical affairs which many women were called on to manage
assured a goodly proportion of colonial girls enough education
to enable them to read and write, and, in exceptional cases, to
figure. Nowhere were secondary schools, to say nothing of colleges, open to them. Their work, even when not confined to
their own hearths, required little book learning. Consequently
they were trained for the state of matrimony, which economic

169

necessity forced on almost every girl. This training was secured from their mothers, or, if they were indentured, from
their mistresses. In New England girls learned their letters at
dame schools and, in exceptional cases, enjoyed restricted opportunities in the elementary town schools. As late as 1820 the
mayor of Boston closed the first school opened to girls on the
ground that it would bankrupt the city to educate them.
Thanks in part to the Quaker and Moravian attitude toward
women, there was somewhat greater educational opportunity,
so far as the elementary level was concerned, in some of the
middle colonies. In the South, particularly as the eighteenth
century advanced, well-to-do families felt increasingly called on
to provide their daughters with such embellishments as music,
dancing, and French, talents that eligible young gentlemen,
according to the fashion, increasingly demanded. With some
exceptions, it was not until the period of the Revolution that
men of wealth in the North provided their daughters and
expected from their wives the showy graces dispensed by masters of riding, dancing, music, and French.

Thus at the time when the Declaration of Independence was
challenging the old aristocratic order, the education of women
was coming to be differentiated according to the class to which
they belonged. Girls in the lower economic strata continued to
be thought fortunate if they learned their letters and a pittance
of figures. Those of the more privileged group began to acquire, either from private masters or from the so-called "adven-
ture" schools, or from female seminaries, the polite and elegant
education appropriate to their station. Capability in the household, an ideal cherished by almost everyone in the colonial
period, was increasingly relegated to the middle and lower
classes.

It was not until the period of the Revolution that anyone

ventured to suggest that women should be educated in anything save the fundamentals and the arts of embroidery, music, dancing, and French. The performance of domestic duties, the management of household affairs, participation in social life—these made no very great demands on the intellect of women. This fact, quite as much as Aristotelian, Pauline, and feudal traditions, explained why few people would have questioned Governor Winthrop's judgment that women should content themselves with the feminine skills and refrain from meddling in "such things as are proper for men, whose minds are stronger." As late as the struggle for independence Mrs. John Adams regretted that it was fashionable to ridicule "female learning."

But new ideas were in the air, and they anticipated new conditions which were to provide opportunities for experiment. Mary Wollstonecraft's *Vindication,* republished in Philadelphia as early as 1794, was only a specific application to women of the eighteenth-century idea of natural rights, the rationality of all human beings, and the doctrine of humanitarianism. Within three decades an imposing number of men and women, in promulgating a new concept of woman's education, suggested that American soil was favorable for a more humane and enlarged idea of the intellectual capacity and social responsibility of women. Several factors, no doubt, had helped break the barrier. Some were of an ideological character; others sprang from new facts and concrete exigencies.

Difficult though it is to measure the influence of changing intellectual points of view, their importance can hardly be questioned. While few women ventured to express in writing the notion that the Revolutionary principles ought logically and in justice to be applied to their sex, all the talk about natural rights and all the revolt against tradition and authority must have given women a new importance. Quakerism, always emphatic in its insistence on the ministerial equality of the sexes, likewise provided favorable leaven. When the faculty psychology developed it was difficult not to apply to women its basic principle that, whatever the character or strength of innate faculties, training and discipline insured their growth. The new enthusiasm for humanitarian crusades also infected women. While men reformers were at first chary about admitting them to the work of the "cause," the more zealous and open-minded welcomed their aid. Often handicapped by convention, which kept women from speaking in public, the more persistent and far-sighted feminine reformers were forced to advocate not only greater freedom to address meetings but also an opportunity to increase their knowledge and understanding. Yet as late as 1837 a Philadelphia mob, incensed by the fact that the Grimké sisters were to speak in public, burned the hall. In 1840 American women delegates to the first world anti-slavery convention were refused seats on the floor in spite of William Lloyd Garrison's indignant protest.

These new ideas regarding the intellectual capacity and responsibility of women were able to transform cramping and stubborn tradition by reason of new actualities which were tending in the same direction. While the frontier process retarded the development of culture, it demanded from women an equal sharing of hardships and won increased respect for their abilities. It was hardly an accident that the first co-educational colleges sprang up in the West. At the same time the progress of industry gradually substituted machine-made products for the elaborate embroideries that consumed so much of the training and time of women of the leisure class, and paved the way for the introduction of more solid disciplines in their education. Most important of all was the demand for cheap teachers which the development of the public school movement created. Until the second quarter of the nineteenth century, women seldom taught in the elementary schools save during a short summer term designed for the younger children. As the frontier and the factory provided men with new opportunities for making money, and as the length of the school term increased, women, who were able and willing to work for much smaller pay than men, found their way into the schoolroom. When the movement for improved quality of teaching developed, academies, female seminaries, and normal schools provided them with special training and better intellectual opportunities.

Another very important factor in the changing attitude toward the education of women was the growth of the lyceum movement. Eight years after Josiah Holbrook founded the first lyceum at Millbury, Massachusetts, in 1826, more than 3000 of these pioneer institutions for adult education could be found east of the Alleghanies, and their migration westward was not long postponed. Women as well as men heard some of the most distinguished public figures of the day discuss not only literary and cultural but political subjects. The lyceum was not only an important agency in the transmission of culture westward: it provided women with intellectual opportunities and helped break down the barriers the past had erected against their education. The same end was also promoted by new typographical processes which cheapened the cost of newspapers and periodicals.

In spite of the fact that the more exceptional factory girls in Lowell saved their pennies for lyceum courses, and in spite of the opportunity which the public school awakening provided for daughters of farmers and artisans, the education of women continued to be governed by class considerations. Only the better-to-do could afford to send their daughters to the private academies and female seminaries which sprang up in the first half of the nineteenth century. High schools open to girls were so exceptional in the period before the Civil War as to make little difference in the situation.

It is true that some leaders in the education of women made efforts to provide for poor girls. On the whole the Catholic orders which founded schools for girls did rather better in this respect than the proprietors of private Protestant seminaries. Mother Duchesne, the foundress of the first American academy of the order of the Sacred Heart, never abandoned the hope she entertained when she went to Louisiana that her work might be chiefly among the lowly; but when she died in 1852 her order was for the most part educating the daughters of the wealthy. Her successor, Mother Hardey, gave some attention to the education of the poor; and Mother Seton and the Sisters of Charity likewise cherished that purpose. But on the whole the Catholic orders reached only the daughters of the middle and upper classes. The education afforded in their institutions, so far as it was not religious, could benefit only girls of the leisure class. The Protestant female seminaries catered with even fewer exceptions to the well-to-do classes. When Mary Lyon founded Mount Holyoke Female Seminary in 1837 one of her principal purposes was to break the monopoly the upper classes had enjoyed in educating their daughters: her institution was frankly intended to make possible an education for the middle classes.

To understand the significance of the work of reformers in women's education it is necessary to understand the character of the institutions patronized by the well-to-do. Many of the seminaries aimed primarily to produce an accomplished young woman who might embellish the home and the society of her husband.[1] The teaching was designed to promote taste and propriety, and to provide a veneer of artificial graces and a superficial knowledge of drawing, painting, modern languages, and music. Serious Puritans like President Timothy Dwight were horrified at the way in which the frothy smatterings of this and that embellishment crowded out the teaching of morals and religion.[2]

Some seminaries, it is true, pretended to offer a bewildering variety of more imposing intellectual disciplines, such as the natural sciences, history, geography, and even mathematics and classics. But there was great popular prejudice against any study that threatened to "unfit women for family and social duties." Geography was opposed on the ground that it would make girls dissatisfied with home and anxious to travel. When in 1829 a girl was publicly examined in geometry in New York a cry of disapproval was heard all over the land.[3]

Leaders of reform insisted that female schools tried to teach too many subjects and failed to teach very much in any one.[4] Regulation of the number and sequence of studies pursued was entirely lacking. One might choose at will mythology, chirography, uranography, mezzotint, calisthenics, or flourishing; French alone was an indispensable "ribbon for external covering." While certain institutions were less guilty of indulging in "fripperies of filigree," external accomplishment was in general the desideratum. Equipment was scanty, teachers were overburdened, and, since profits were seldom invested in endowment, the permanence of most of the female seminaries was precarious.

[1] Thomas Woody, *A History of Women's Education in the United States* (New York, 1929), Vol. I, p. 96.
[2] Timothy Dwight, *Travels in New England and New York*, Vol. I, pp. 512–19.
[3] A. W. Calhoun, *A Social History of the American Family* (Cleveland, 1918), Vol. II, p. 89.
[4] Woody, *History of Women's Education*, Vol. I, p. 410.

II

Even before the first group of notable women began their pioneer work to improve the education of their sex, a broader and more utilitarian training was advocated. Doctor Benjamin Rush, in an essay entitled *Thoughts upon Female Education* (1787), considered it proper for American girls to be educated for the specific functions imposed on them by American life. Women must help their husbands guard and steward their property, and should therefore know bookkeeping. They must, in view of the lack of servants in the New World, be trained in domestic affairs and should to that end understand something of chemistry and natural philosophy. Finally, since the success of republican institutions depended on the ability of men to fulfil their political obligations, mothers must be able to teach their sons such subjects as English language and grammar, writing, geography, biography, and history.[5] Other writers on education in the early national period substantially agreed with the famous medical leader.

Early in the nineteenth century De Witt Clinton, governor of New York, encouraged more advanced education for girls.[6] But the most vigorous early attack on the "ornamental or superficial acquirements" in the training of young women came from Charles Burroughs and was popularized by the *American Journal of Education*.[7] Encouraging a type of education that would call into exercise all the faculties of the soul, Burroughs pointed out the function of woman's education in advancing

[5] Harry G. Good, *Benjamin Rush and His Services to American Education* (Berne, Ind., 1918), pp. 226–34. Rush also approved of instruction in vocal music, dancing, poetry, and moral essays, as well as instruction in the Christian religion.

[6] E. A. Fitzpatrick, *The Educational Views and Influence of De Witt Clinton*, pp. 52, 121–24.

[7] *American Journal of Education*, Vol. III (Jan., 1828), pp. 53–58.

not only personal happiness but the good of society. Thomas Gallaudet at about the same time attacked the one-sided memory training prevalent in female education and advocated the practical application of knowledge in the everyday life of the girl who had received it.[8] William Russell, editor of the *American Journal of Education* (1826–1831), and William C. Woodbridge, of the *American Annals of Education* (1831–1839), greatly promoted the newer concept of a more serious education for women by hospitably opening their journals to its discussion and by their own advocacy of normal schools for girls.[9]

The attitude of Horace Mann and Henry Barnard toward women's education was sufficiently in advance of the major currents of their times to rank them as pioneers. Neither sympathized with the extreme advocates of women's rights, and both discouraged women from aiming to secure suffrage and equal opportunity with men in all professions. But both believed that women had a divine mission to teach; that they were not only cheaper but superior instructors of youth, inasmuch as they understood the child's mind and were able better than men to follow its movements and to lead it more gently and effectively along the right paths.[10] Both subscribed to the doctrine that if only one sex could be educated, women should have that advantage. At the least, women must have equal educational advantages with men. "The rulers of our country need knowledge (God only knows how much they need it!)" Mann declared, "but mothers need it more; for they determine, to a great extent, the very capacity of the rulers'

---

[8] *Ibid.* Vol. III (March, 1828), pp. 178–87.
[9] Prospectus, *American Journal of Education*, Vol. I (Jan., 1826), p. 3; *American Annals of Education and Instruction*, Vol. I (Sept., 1830), pp. 421–23; Vol. III (Jan., 1833), p. 25.
[10] Horace Mann, *Lectures on Education*, p. 73.

minds to acquire knowledge and to apply it."[11] Both believed
that education was necessary if women were to co-operate effectively in humanitarian reforms, and both agreed that education
was a more effective instrument for righting the wrongs of
women than agitation and suffrage.

Barnard not only fathered the kindergarten, but like Mann
faithfully labored for state normal schools and for teacher
training. Both were doubtless influenced by Pestalozzi in
the high regard they held for women as teachers of the young;
a regard that led them to champion more serious and advanced education for women. Yet in spite of such a generous
spirit, and in spite of all they did to advance the lot of women
in the teaching profession, it was not until 1866 that the
National Teachers' Association admitted women to membership on the same terms as men.[12]

III

The women who led the reform for the education of their
own sex belonged to the middle class, and for the most part
planned and worked for the training of girls from either the
wealthy or fairly well-to-do groups. Emma Hart Willard came
from good New England stock. Her father, who held liberal
religious views and discussed with his young daughter both
metaphysics and politics, must have been a man of substance.
She married a physician who held an important political office
in Vermont. She was forced to take charge of a school in
1814 by reason of financial misfortune, but she later made sufficient profits from the seminary she founded at Troy in 1821, and
particularly from her textbooks, to live more than comfortably.

[11] Horace Mann, "A Few Thoughts on the Powers and Duties of Woman,"
1853, in *Lectures on Various Subjects,* p. 65; Henry Barnard in *Journal of the
R. I. Institute of Instruction,* Vol. I (Dec., 1845), p. 35.

[12] National Teachers' Association, *Addresses and Journal of Proceedings of
Tenth Annual Meeting* (Cleveland, Aug. 17–19, 1870), p. 93.

She traveled extensively and hobnobbed with the wealthy and distinguished personages of her day. In formal attire, wearing silver slippers, she was even presented to the French queen.[13]

Catharine Beecher belonged to an even more distinguished family. Her father, Lyman Beecher, was one of the best known Congregational ministers in New England. Although at the time of her birth in 1800 the family was poor, she enjoyed by reason of its social position both prestige and unusual cultural advantages. She early counted among her best friends the children of Litchfield's most distinguished families. In her later years she shared in the glory that her sister, Harriet Beecher Stowe, and her brother, Henry Ward Beecher, brought to the family.[14]

Mary Hardey left behind the advantages of her father's wealthy Louisiana plantation when in 1821 she entered the convent school at Grand Coteau, and before many years began her great work of making the order of the Sacred Heart prosper.[15] Likewise Mother Elizabeth Seton, who established an order of the Sisters of Charity in Maryland in 1809, belonged to one of the most wealthy and distinguished families in Philadelphia, although through misfortune she came to know the hardships of poverty.[16]

Mary Lyon, the founder of Mount Holyoke Female Sem-

13 She proudly recorded that Her Majesty's cloak was of identical style with her own recent purchase. Emma Willard, *Journal and Letters from France and Great Britain* (Troy, New York, 1833), pp. 100–101. For biographical material see Alma Lutz, *Emma Willard, Daughter of Democracy* (Boston, 1929); Willystine Goodsell, ed., *Pioneers of Women's Education in the United States: Emma Willard, Catharine Beecher, Mary Lyon* (New York, 1931); and John Lord, *The Life of Emma Willard* (New York, 1873).

14 Mae Elizabeth Harveson, *Catharine Esther Beecher: Pioneer Educator* (Philadelphia, 1932).

15 Mary Garvey, R.S.C.J., *Mary Aloysia Hardey, Religious of the Sacred Heart, 1809–1886* (New York, 1925).

16 Charles I. White, *Life of Mrs. Eliza A. Seton* (3d ed., Baltimore); Agnes Sadlier, *Elizabeth Seton, Foundress of the American Sisters of Charity, Her Life and Work* (New York, 1905); Louise Malloy, *The Life Story of Mother Seton* (Baltimore, 1924).

inary, was born on a poor Massachusetts farm. She alone of the group knew the bitter struggles of poverty and, with one exception, was the only pioneer in woman's education to make special efforts to provide an education that girls of the middle class could afford. "My thoughts, feelings, and judgments," she wrote in 1833, when she had decided to give up her work with Miss Zilpah P. Grant in the expensive seminary at Ipswich, "are turned toward the middle classes in society. . . . To this class in society would I devote directly, all the remainder of my strength (God permitting)—not to the higher classes, not to the poorer classes. This middle class contains the main springs and main wheels, which are to move the world."[17]

In 1819 the movement for the education of women was invigorated by the arrival of the notorious Scotch feminist, Frances Wright, who for a number of years entered into various struggles for social justice. Although she had enjoyed the advantages of upper-class British society, she was exceptional among the women pioneer educators in her championship of schools for the common people. Believing that the failure to provide for the education of women put them at the mercy of all who would prey on their ignorance and credulity, she advocated the educational emancipation of women in the broadest sense of the word.

As early as the eighteen-twenties this courageous feminist preached the doctrine of birth control, demanded the legal right of women to their own property, and insisted on their intellectual emancipation from the dogmas of religion and the authority of tradition. Denouncing the unequal distribution of wealth as the cause of urban misery, she favored free boarding schools maintained by the state as an effective means of defeating class control of culture and government. Quixotic though

[17] Edward Hitchcock, *The Power of Christian Benevolence as Illustrated in the Life and Labors of Mary Lyon* (Northampton, 1851), p. 178.

some of her activities seemed, Frances Wright represented the advance guard of women pioneers of educational reform and emancipation.[18]

What the other women advocates of education thought of the position their sex should assume in society resembled more nearly the ideas of Mann and Barnard than those of Frances Wright. Inspired by religious principles, the women pioneers of education believed that their sex was called on to advance God's kingdom on earth. Even Emma Willard, less pious than Catharine Beecher and Mary Lyon, invited the terrifying evangelist, Finney, to save the souls of the charges under her care at the Troy Female Seminary. Her *Universal History* was intended to strengthen the truths of sacred scripture, and she was properly repelled by such "atheists" as Rousseau, Voltaire, and their popularizers.[19] Though she believed that her sex should stand for Christian principles, she was too much a woman of affairs to devote herself as whole-heartedly as had Mary Lyon and Catharine Beecher to the religious education of women.

At the beginning of her labors Mary Lyon wrote to her mother that in undertaking her educational venture at Mount Holyoke she had thought much more constantly, and felt much more deeply "about doing that which shall be for the honor of Christ, and for the good of souls," than she had ever done in her life.[20] The next year she confided to her family her conviction that the institution she was building and others like it were necessary instruments for the conversion of the world. To insure its success the founder trudged over the hill farms of western Massachusetts, pleading, arguing, begging for support for the seminary, sometimes, in her zeal, refusing to take

[18] William Randall Waterman, *Frances Wright* (New York, 1924).
[19] Emma Willard, *Universal History in Perspective* (New York, 1845), pp. 34, 436.
[20] Hitchcock, *op. cit.*, p. 192.

her foot off the wheel of a wagon or a rake until the farmer she was soliciting had promised to give at least a portion of his crop to the cause at South Hadley. For the seminary was to be a delightful spot for those "whose heart has stirred them up to use all their talents in the great work of serving their generation and of advancing the Redeemer's Kingdom."

In spite of the fact that the curriculum included geography, history, and sciences, the avowed purpose of even the literary subjects was to form Christian character. The young ladies were subjected to yearly revivals and urged to serve Christ's cause in distant lands. In the religious devotion Mary Lyon inspired lay the seed for the social service work of the women of subsequent generations. As missionaries, as pious, God-fearing mothers, and as "benevolent, self-denying female teachers," the students of the seminary were to advance the Kingdom of God.

Catharine Beecher, no less religious than Mary Lyon, saw even more explicitly the social implications of the Christian and moral training she wished all young women to enjoy. "I have ever considered *intellectual* culture as subordinate to the main end of education, which is the formation of that character which Jesus Christ teaches to be indispensable to the *eternal* well being of our race," she wrote to Horace Mann.[21] In an outline on the inculcation of moral and religious virtues she urged the study of Bible verses as an important means of teaching girls their social duty. Possessing the Puritan conscience, Catharine Beecher furthered the work of conversion in her first school at Hartford with such zeal and strenuousness that even her pious and ecclesiastical father cautioned her to use more gentleness and moderation.[22]

[21] Catharine Beecher to Horace Mann, Aug. 20, 1847, Mann Papers.
[22] *Autobiography, Correspondence, etc., of Lyman Beecher, D.D.* (New York, 1865), Vol. II, p. 63.

If the Protestant pioneers of women's education desired to train Christians, Catholic leaders bent every effort to that end and spared neither pain nor sacrifice. The injunction "Remember Mother's first and last lesson to you: see God in all things," characterized the educational philosophy of Mother Seton.[23] Mother Hardey of the order of the Ladies of the Sacred Heart used human knowledge merely as a useful instrument to direct young souls to His love. Governing by tact, patience, and kindness, she sought to develop in her charges all the Christian virtues. "I really do not know why," she said, "but it is an historical fact that the elevation of woman has always been the infallible sign and the measure of the whole race."[24]

These pioneers recognized, however, that women must live in this world as well as prepare themselves and others for the next. In varying degrees all the leaders of the educational awakening desired to prepare their sex for social responsibilities. They were one in believing that woman's first duty was in the home. As Christian wives and mothers they were to advance the well-being of the members of their family, so they regarded "solid" and practical subjects with greater favor than the frothy accomplishments that prevailed in so many of the female seminaries.

Emma Willard, who had always been accepted by her family, husband, and friends as an intellectual equal, desired to have women become companions rather than satellites of their husbands. She favored instruction in science and higher mathematics. By precept if not by example she deplored feminine subservience to fashion. She spoke in behalf of simple, homely virtues, and wished girls to be preserved from contempt of use-

23 Joseph B. Code, *A Daily Thought from the Writings of Mother Seton* (Emmitsburg, 1929).
24 Garvey, *op. cit.,* p. 248.

ful labor. She hoped that "ladies of fortune, like wealthy agri-culturists, might find that to regulate their business was an agreeable employment."[25]

Catharine Beecher was even more outspoken in her insistence that a woman's education should prepare her for the career of wife and mother. To further that end she championed physical training to promote health and advocated the teaching of the domestic arts in female institutions of learning. When Vassar was founded, she was particularly critical of the new ideal of patterning the curriculum of women's colleges on those prevailing in men's institutions. She upheld the intellectual character of domestic work, and declared in words that have a modern ring that "a problem in arithmetic or geometry is far more interesting, and therefore more quickening to the intellect, when it is directly applied to some useful, practical purpose."[26] If proper training were supplied, then domestic work would assume its true and rightful dignity. Catharine Beecher was trying to dispel the degradation of caste which was coming to be associated with kitchen and household duties, and to recall women to their proper work. She never wearied of attacking the notion that "to be a lady is synonymous with being waited upon."

Like John Dewey, Miss Beecher denounced the separation of classes based on differing occupations and types of training. Daughters of wealth would sharpen their intellectual faculties by engaging in household tasks. By having all classes engage in productive labor, and by affording a similar education to all classes, caste barriers would be broken down.[27] "Young

[25] Emma Willard, "A Plan for Improving Female Education" (1819) in Goodsell, *op. cit.,* pp. 77–78.

[26] Catharine Beecher, *Woman Suffrage and Woman's Profession* (Hartford, 1871), p. 125.

[27] Catharine Beecher, *The Evils Suffered by American Women and Children: the Causes and the Remedy* (New York, 1847), p. 6.

girls can be taught at school," she wrote to Horace Mann, "many things that will secure future domestic comfort and thrift."[28] Above all she urged the prime importance of physiology and the laws of health, ventilation and the "proper selection of healthful and nutritious food," since the health of the family rested in large part on the mother's shoulders.[29]

Meanwhile at Mount Holyoke Female Seminary Mary Lyon was trying to give concrete expression to the feeling she confided to her mother, "O how immensely important is this work of preparing the daughters of the land to be good mothers!"[30] While the provision that every girl must share in the daily household work of the seminary was designed to lower the tuition rate sufficiently to enable poorer girls to attend and to weaken the widespread prejudice against female education, Mary Lyon was in substantial agreement with Catharine Beecher on the proper and necessary rôle of domestic knowledge in every woman's education.

Catholic educators were not far behind in the emphasis they put on training for the duties of family. "Your little mother, my darlings," Mother Seton told her pupils, "does not come to teach you how to be good nuns or Sisters of Charity; but rather I would wish to fit you for that world in which you are destined to live; to teach you how to be good mistresses and mothers of families. Yet, if the dear Master selects one among you to be closer to Him, happy are you! He will teach you Himself."[31] While Mother Hardey and the ladies of the Sacred Heart watched out for the health of their charges, cultivated their minds, and corrected their faults, they attached less importance to specific training for the home than certain other

[28] Catharine Beecher to Mann, Aug. 20, 1847, Mann Papers.
[29] Catharine Beecher, *Letters to the People on Health and Happiness* (New York, 1855); *Woman Suffrage*, pp. 21–25.
[30] Hitchcock, *op. cit.*, pp. 190–91.
[31] White, *Life of Mrs. Seton*, p. 344.

orders.[32] Mother Caroline Friess, first commissary-general of the school sisters of Notre Dame, for instance, emphasized from the start the need of a more practical education for girls which would make them strong, brave, self-reliant, and useful.[33]

Devoted though the women pioneers in education were to the ideal of training girls for their domestic duties, they also attached great importance to the preparation of teachers. Some, aware of troublesome social problems, believed that properly trained teachers could help in their solution. Catharine Beecher, who had not seen fit to marry after the tragic death of her betrothed, did not want women forced into matrimony when their hearts were against it. She thought that in teaching the maternal capacity might find social expression. Moreover, trained women teachers could, she was convinced, help solve vital social problems, for "all must see that the surest as well as the most peaceful method of bringing to an end all social evils, all wrong, and all injustice, is to train the young children of our nation 'to do justly, to love mercy, and to walk humbly with God.' "[34]

Properly trained women teachers, Miss Beecher believed, would not only prevent the violence and revolution which, like other educators, she feared so much; they would also soften sectional antagonisms and promote true national solidarity.[35] Sharing with many conservative Easterners a fear of the agnosticism, and of the political and economic heterodoxy of the West, she labored all her life to establish schools beyond the Alleghanies and to send out women teachers for the common schools of that vast and threatening region. "We all concede,"

[32] Garvey, *op. cit., passim.*
[33] Right Reverend Monsignor P. M. Abbelen, *Mother Caroline Friess* (St. Louis, 1893), pp. 17–18.
[34] *Evils Suffered,* p. 15.
[35] *Ibid.; American Women, Will You Save Your Country?* (New York, 1845), p. 30.

she wrote to Mary Lyon, "that the grand experiment for liberty and self-government for this nation and for the world, is to be made [in] the coming fifty years, and that too, mainly *at the West*."[36] No missionary could have shown greater zeal than did Catharine Beecher in her efforts to save the West through schools and trained women teachers.[37]

This sister of Henry Ward Beecher also saw evils nearer home. Unlike so many visitors to the Lowell mills, she was not carried off her feet by the fact that some of the women operatives edited literary magazines and attended lyceum lectures. Denying that the mills brought any benefit to her sex, she insisted, on the contrary, that the long hours, the low pay, and the hard working conditions could only degrade women. She condemned capitalists for making "monstrous profits" from the exploitation of poor females, and she did what she could to expose the "shocking" conditions and the suffering of women factory hands.[38]

Her remedy was to train female factory workers as teachers, send them to keep the common schools of the West, and fill their places in the factories with the schoolmasters they relieved.[39] Unrealistic though this solution was, she finally succeeded in 1852 in founding the American Women's Education Association to further her plan. Her energy in trying to give the idea a trial testified to her conviction that in the fight against evil, actions were as necessary as words.

Although Emma Willard at times seemed to share Catharine Beecher's faith that if America were to be saved educated women must take the leading rôle in the work of salvation,[40]

36 Catharine Beecher to Mary Lyon, Walnut Hills, O., n. d., Barnard MSS., Monroe Collection.
37 Catharine Beecher, *The True Remedy for the Wrongs of Women* (Boston, 1851), p. 200; *American Women*, p. 106.
38 *Evils Suffered*, pp. 6, 7–9.
39 *Ibid.*, p. 9; *True Remedy*, pp. 33–34.   40 Lutz, *op. cit.*, pp. 221–22.

she did not teach her students to question the traditional belief in masculine responsibility for the social and political problems of the day. Though she herself was active in the peace movement and expressed opinions on politics, slavery, and other affairs of moment, she did not encourage her students to consider such things as politics, temperance, and abolition. In common with other educators, however, she deplored the dangers which threatened the permanence of republican institutions, and warned wealthy girls against "vain amusements and the snares and follies of luxury," which were in her mind associated with the decline of republics.[41] Yet in the emphasis she put on history and geography, in her nominal advocacy of training women factory hands for teachers,[42] in her promotion of universal peace, and by her concern with public matters, Emma Willard doubtless aided in breaking down the narrow boundaries of women's interests and efforts.

The single-hearted devotion of Mary Lyon to God and to the immediate educational work at hand made her less interested in public questions than were the outspoken Catharine Beecher and the charming and brilliant Emma Willard. There is no evidence that the founder of Mount Holyoke was particularly concerned with the social and economic questions of the day or that she expected her students to be. But the ideal that educated women were to serve others, and the Christian type of training for which she stood, were factors that paved the way for the participation of a later generation of women in social welfare activities.

One searches in vain the biographies and writings of the Catholic pioneers of women's education for explicit statements regarding their own social opinions or those that they thought proper for their pupils to cherish. The religious communities

[41] *Ibid.*   [42] *Ibid.*, p. 195.

reflected to a considerable degree the social attitudes of their surroundings. Slaves served in the Southern convent schools of the ladies of the Sacred Heart, who thus accepted the prevailing institution. Charity and personal benevolence, with a modest aloofness from pressing public questions, characterized the social ideal of Mother Hardey and the other leaders who directed the Catholic education of girls.

The women educational pioneers were slightly in advance of most of their sex in their attitude toward its position in society, but considerably behind the leaders of the woman's rights movement.[43] None of the women educators, save Frances Wright, approved the militant agitation for the legal, political, and economic emancipation of women. Catharine Beecher wrote, as late as 1840, that "Heaven has appointed to one sex the superior, and to the other the subordinate station, and this without any reference to the character or conduct of either. It is therefore as much for the dignity as it is for the interest of females, in all respects to conform to the duties of this relation."[44]

Emma Willard urged the cheaper pay at which women would instruct the young as one reason for state support of female seminaries—an argument not uncommonly used to break down the opposition of reluctant taxpayers during the years when women were being paid one-half to three-fourths less than men, sometimes as little as fifty cents a week and "board around."[45] Women educators were deaf to the argument made in a teachers' meeting in 1852 by Susan Anthony, who, in answering the objection that teachers were not so highly

43 For a representative statement of the attitudes of the more conservative male educational leaders toward the social function and training of women see Alonzo Potter, *School and Schoolmaster*, pp. 55–56.

44 *Woman Suffrage*, pp. 176 *et seq.*; Calhoun, *A Social History of the American Family*, Vol. II, p. 84.

45 *A Plan for Improving Female Education*, p. 72: Woody, *History of Women's Education*, Vol. I, p. 491.

respected as ministers, doctors, and lawyers, observed: "It seems to me you fail to comprehend the cause of the disrespect of which you complain. Do you not see that so long as society says woman has not brains enough to be a doctor, lawyer, or minister, but has plenty to be a teacher, every man of you who condescends to teach tacitly admits before all Israel and the sun that he has no more brains than a woman?"[46]

It is also true that, sheltered as they were, the women educational pioneers, Frances Wright always excepted, took in general a somewhat more conservative stand on the public questions of the day than did the men who led the educational awakening in the first half of the last century. Neither Catharine Beecher nor Emma Willard, for example, held very advanced views on the slavery controversy. While her sister wrote *Uncle Tom's Cabin,* Miss Beecher wielded her vigorous pen in denouncing the extreme anti-slavery position of the Grimké sisters and, after early contending that women ought not to participate in the work of the anti-slavery societies, said little or nothing on that crucial question.[47] Emma Willard, though identified with the American Colonization Society and for a time, at least, convinced that slavery was wrong, never ventured into the ranks of the abolitionists. In fact, her plan of 1862, designed to settle the slavery question, proposed a regulated servitude and even suggested that God had deliberately intended the black race to serve physically weak white women.[48]

The most outspoken pioneers in woman's education agreed with Mann and Barnard that public schools were indispensable instruments for the repression of social upheaval. In her efforts

[46] Ira Husted Harper, *The Life and Work of Susan B. Anthony* (Indianapolis, 1898), Vol. I, p. 99.

[47] Catharine Beecher wrote with satisfaction to Barnard, on Dec. 1, 1845, that her anti-abolition book had secured her much good will in the South. Barnard MSS., Monroe Collection. See also Harveson, *op. cit.,* pp. 196–99.

[48] Lutz, *op. cit.,* pp. 243, 254–57.

to enlist the support of Governor Slade of Vermont Catharine Beecher reminded him that free common schools promised to save our republic from "the ruin of an ignorant populace."[49] If children were taught to rule their passions and to control themselves by reason, religion, and law, the catastrophe that demagogues had brought to France at the time of the Revolution might be avoided.[50] When, late in life, the daughter of Lyman Beecher spoke well of limited woman suffrage, she stipulated the necessity of granting it only to educated women who paid taxes; this might "rectify the mistake made so extensively in giving this power to *all men,* however ignorant and vicious."[51]

Miss Beecher explicitly upheld the aristocratic idea that it was necessary for men to be placed in "different stations, higher and lower, by differences in goodness, habits, learning and wealth," and that education was necessary to insure in every grown person as well as in every child the duty of subordination to their superiors in station.[52] Thus she accepted the ideal of democracy with even greater qualifications than those imposed by Barnard. Emma Willard too seems to have shared the prevalent view that education must inculcate respect for law if republican government was to be sustained.[53]

On the question of peace and war Emma Willard alone took a forthright position. Although Catharine Beecher held that no employment was so wicked as that of war, attended as it was by "everything low, brutal, unchristian, and disgusting," she

[49] Catharine Beecher to Governor Slade, Nov. 14, 1845, Barnard MSS., Monroe Collection.

[50] Catharine Beecher, *Educational Reminiscences and Suggestions* (New York, 1874), pp. 210–32; *American Women,* pp. 31, 67–68.

[51] *Reminiscences,* p. 201.

[52] Catharine Beecher, *Moral Instructor for Schools and Families* (Cincinnati, 1838), p. 122. Emma Willard, after being presented to the Queen of France, argued in behalf of paying deference to power where power is united to noble faculties. *Journal and Letters,* p. 101.

[53] *Universal History,* pp. 493–94.

did not align herself with the organized friends of peace.[54] Emma Willard, on the other hand, in spite of her ardent patriotism, merits an honored place among the early advocates of peace, having been attracted to the cause as early as 1820, only five years after the founding of the first peace societies. In an address to teachers in Washington in 1850, she urged that children be sent to petition the government against civil war.[55] When conflict seemed imminent, she favored a policy of conciliation, and in February, 1861, brought to Washington a petition in which 4000 ladies prayed for a peaceful settlement of the issue. Later she called on Elihu Burritt, the well-known peace leader, and sought help for her plan providing for a permanent juridical tribunal at Jerusalem.

Mary Lyon did not commit herself, apparently, on the issue of peace and war. The Catholic sisters who devoted themselves to education likewise maintained silence, though in the Civil War Mother Hardey engaged in relief work, and committed to God the conflicting interests and affections which interfered with the work of her order.[56]

But if the women educators did not take so advanced a social position as Mann, they were, in view of the status of their sex at that time, surprisingly aware of some of the faults in the existing order, and hospitable toward the ideal of a better society. If Emma Willard refused to discuss socialism with Robert Owen,[57] Barnard also closed his ears to its message. If Catharine Beecher proposed an unrealistic solution for the ailments of the industrial capitalism that brought women into factories, she agreed with Mann on the necessity of curbing the profit system when it jeopardized human interests and rights. If Mary Lyon and Mother Hardey did not see the relation between an educated womanhood and the broader social

[54] *Evils Suffered*, p. 10.   [55] Lutz, *op. cit.*, p. 248.
[56] Garvey, *op. cit.*, p. 238.   [57] *Journal and Letters*, p. 308.

problems, they carried the doctrine of training righteous and Christian individuals as far as most men who gave their primary attention to education.

Without the work of these women, progress in the education of their sex would have been made, for a long line of educators from Benjamin Rush to Horace Mann and Henry Barnard urged the need of equipping women for taking charge of the common schools. But the work of Catharine Beecher and of Emma Willard, who, after leaving Troy Seminary in the hands of her son and daughter-in-law, devoted herself to improvement of the common schools in Connecticut, greatly accelerated the newer ideal that women should be educated, not merely to adorn and embellish fashionable society, but also for broader social functions and for specific utilitarian tasks. Without the proof that women were capable of pursuing the more "solid" studies which Emma Willard, Catharine Beecher, and Mary Lyon furnished in their seminaries, it would have been even more difficult than it was to break down the obstacles in the way of founding Vassar, Wellesley, and Smith.

The broader outlook with which the pioneers of women's education provided the more favored members of their sex contributed materially to the important rôle women came increasingly to take in social, philanthropic, and public problems. At the same time these leaders, aware of the dangers with which factories threatened the home, invigorated the old ideal of domestic capability with more scientific knowledge of the principles of health and household economy. They did much to make the learned lady acceptable to masculine taste and prejudice. In short, they pointed out how women might be better fitted for their conventional rôle and at the same time opened to them, cautiously to be sure, new avenues of social usefulness.

SUMMARY OF PART I

Between 1820 and 1850 educational leaders were engaged primarily in a battle to secure more adequate public support and supervision of the common elementary school. Although aided by the early New England tradition of collective responsibility for the training of children, they were handicapped by colonial survivals—by sectarian influences in education and by a class system of schools. Other powerful forces also contended against them; but before the outbreak of the Civil War it was clear that, except in the South, they had won the struggle for state supported and state supervised public education. While the public schools in 1860 had not by any means broken down the caste system of education, they had dealt it an effective blow. If religion was still taught it was no longer definitely sectarian. Catholics had not, as we shall see, abandoned their efforts to secure public support for their parochial schools. But on the whole the elementary schools were administered and controlled by secular authority.

The battle for improved public schools also involved the necessity of attacking the dominant *laissez-faire* philosophy, which, in spite of the early New England tradition, still looked on education as a private rather than a public matter. It is true that this philosophy continued to dominate the thinking of Americans on almost every matter except public education, and even in that category the victory was far from complete. But the way had been prepared for the acceptance of the idea of public responsibility for all manner of important concerns that involved the well-being of individuals, particularly of individuals discriminated against by existing social arrangements and inequalities of wealth. Educators in fighting for the recognition of responsibility for public education also had to face the stubborn opposition to taxation of property for its support. In some cases property interests were forced by popular pressure to surrender; but in general they voluntarily made concessions, especially when they were persuaded that public education would redound to their own advantage.

Another force equally strong in its opposition to the state control of public schools was the localism which looked suspiciously on anything that threatened to impose limitations on neighborhood control. Wealthier local units did not want to be taxed for the support of schools in less fortunate districts, and only slight progress was made in state taxation. Local opposition did in part give way to the demand for state supervision of textbooks, the qualifications of teachers, the length of the school term, and other educational standards. But in spite of the development of transportation and communication, which was undermining localism in so many respects, opposition to state authority over the neighborhood control of schools had by no means disappeared in 1860. In fact even as late as the opening of the twentieth century the fight had not been completely won.

But despite all opposition, systems of state schools were constructed—even in the West, where pressing problems of building a material civilization retarded cultural achievement. Special obstacles, such as scarcity of taxable wealth and grinding poverty, added to the difficulties of educational leaders in the new country. These disadvantages, however, were not so formidable as those against which their Southern colleagues labored. In the cotton kingdom slavery and the resulting caste system blocked substantial progress.

In the victory of the principle that it was the duty of the state to extend to all children the facilities of free schools, educators were the leaders. They were, it is true, greatly aided by public men like Jefferson, De Witt Clinton, and James G. Carter; and often the ranks of labor came to their support. Occasionally wealthy men like James Wadsworth of New York and Edward Dwight of Massachusetts made substantial contributions to the cause. But the leadership of such people as Mann, Barnard, Catharine Beecher, Calvin Wiley of North Carolina, John Pierce of Michigan, Caleb Mills of Indiana, and John Swett of California was the most important single factor in weighting the scales on the side of victory. In winning that victory they profited greatly from the example of Prussia, from the influence of humanitarianism and utilitarianism, and from economic interests which looked favorably on their cause.

In the period during which the chief problem of educators was to secure more adequate support for public schools it seemed especially necessary to steer a neutral course toward controversial problems, to avoid offending powerful interests on whose support educational leaders depended. Partly because of this circumstance, and partly because the educational leaders themselves often came from the privileged classes, they were less neutral than they themselves believed. By keeping silent on the issue of slavery they were in effect supporting the institution. By appealing to the wealthy for support of the schools on the ground that popular education would insure the *status quo* against social upheaval, repudiation of debts, and even revolution, they were in fact taking sides with the privileged who stood to lose by such measures—measures which, it was conceded, might bring the masses into power.

Horace Mann and Catharine Beecher were exceptional in speaking out against the evils of industrial capitalism. Other educational leaders apparently thought it wise to maintain the more non-committal attitude of Barnard on such questions. But it should be pointed out that the issue of free public schools was itself a controversial question, and that in supporting common schools against the opposition of dominant interests even these more conservative educational leaders did fundamentally challenge the *status quo*.

If educators avoided alienating powerful interests on all controversial questions save that of the schools, they nevertheless urged the general social importance of public education. Almost every educator agreed with Mann and Barnard that free schools would promote general prosperity, and made the most of that argument. Almost all of them contended that popular education would eliminate such social evils as crime, poverty, intemperance, and the more crass and, from a traditional standpoint, indefensible practices of industrial and financial capitalism. They all agreed, moreover, that it was necessary to safeguard republican institutions against monarchy, mobocracy, and revolution itself. They also urged, somewhat more cautiously, that the free common school would break down the barriers of caste and promote a true democracy by equalizing opportunity for every rank of life. Stimulated by faith in the dominant idea of progress, they looked to public education as the chief instrument for realizing a middle-class utopia in which morality and religion would be respected; in which every citizen would be law-abiding, orderly, industrious, frugal; in which there would be no crime and no pauperism; in which property and life would be secure. Some also visioned an equality of cultural advantages for all classes, whatever their economic status.

In contending for these social ideals American educational leaders were in advance of important conservative interests in American life. Great Southern planters, although prone to excoriate the abuses of Northern capitalism, defended the caste system prevalent in their own region and often bitterly criticized the social ideals of educators; certainly they did little to promote the public school which, according to its friends, would achieve such ideals. While the Lawrences, the Lowells, and the Appletons, as well as other important Northern industrialists, posed as friends of the common schools and generously endowed technological and even adult education, their reluctance to support the common schools and normal institutions aroused the wrath of Horace Mann. Spokesmen of the frontier West did not all agree with Abraham Lincoln who, as early as 1832, declared that education was "the most important subject which we as a people can be engaged in." In general, Western pioneers were, in spite of their idealism, frequently more conventional in their social philosophy than the educational leaders. Self-help, and government favors in the form of roads, tariffs, and repudiation schemes often appealed to them as more promising roads to utopia than public education.

At least one group stood for more radical social ideas than the educational leaders, and even it shared many of the aspirations of Horace Mann and his more conservative colleagues. That group was made up of the more militant labor leaders and the utopian socialists. Declaring that free schools could not alone effect the more equitable distribution of wealth which they insisted was a prerequisite to the utopia visioned by the educators, they charged the Manns and the Barnards with putting the cart before the horse. But, save as critics, they did not count for much in American life.

Few educational leaders saw as clearly as Mann the limitations imposed on the schools as a means of social reform. He alone laid down his educational work, which imposed restrictions on his zeal for anti-slavery, and fought for social justice in the political arena. Educators as educators were not free to contend for principles certain to alienate those whose support was indispensable for the very existence of the public school system.

An equally powerful consideration blocked the possibility of using schools as an effective agency for fundamental social change, and that is the fact that social purposes in the public which controlled the common schools were divergent and contradictory. Like most Americans, educational leaders assumed that a solidarity of interests existed when in fact cleavages and antagonisms were merely covered up by surface talk about harmony. While many in the interest of cultural independence from the old world desired to have the schools assume distinctively American characteristics, they at the same time were eager to adopt from Europe educational theories and practices. While many others expected the common school to promote national unity, they often, consciously or unconsciously, also expected it to develop a particular regional culture at the same time.

Above all, the privileged classes expected the free public school to increase wealth, secure their property, and prevent revolution, while the lower classes thought that popular education would break down class barriers, lift them into the ranks of the rich and bring about, in short, substantial equality. Could the schools do both? Could they leave the wealthy with all their economic power and privileges and at the same time enable the masses to enter the upper ranks without jeopardizing the position of those already on the top? Could all stand on the top of the pyramid?

Almost every interest in America was sufficiently articulate to develop some idea, catchword, or program instrumental to the realization of its ambitions. However mutually antagonistic, virtually all interests looked to public education as the means of furthering specific and contradictory ends. It was this failure to see that education could not serve contradictory interests that lay at the bottom of its ineffectiveness as a solution for the varied social problems of the pre-Civil War period. The Civil War was an admission that education had failed to achieve nationalism. Henry Barnard, in the middle of that struggle, insisted that if there had only been more support for the public schools, the catastrophe would have been prevented. But in point of fact other forces, and among them blood and iron, were called on to effect the victory of nationalism over sectionalism; though after the war the schools helped to consolidate the victory.

Yet in the field of education some social progress was made in the pre-Civil War period. A blow had been struck at the educational class system. Religious influences had largely given way to secular ones. Educational doors had been partly opened to women. On the other side of the ledger there were, indeed, many failures written down. But after all, it was too soon to indict popular education for having failed to rid the country of intemperance, materialism, crime, pauperism, and the evils of the slum. In view of the obstacles that had to be met it was a great deal to have achieved the bare establishment of the public school system as a social institution. The future would determine how boldly and realistically other educational leaders would face the old problems, and how clearly they would discern new ones. The years to come would tell how skillfully they would devise improved methods within the framework of the established school system for realizing the social vision of the founders; and what new forces would oppose their efforts.

PART II

VI

THE SCHOOL AND THE TRIUMPH OF BUSINESS
ENTERPRISE 1860–1914

The business man has, of course, not said to himself: "I will have the public school train office boys and clerks for me, so that I may have them cheap," but he has thought, and sometimes said, "Teach the children to write legibly, and to figure accurately and quickly; to acquire habits of punctuality and order; to be prompt to obey, and not question why; and you will fit them to make their way in the world as I have made mine!"

—JANE ADDAMS, 1897.

However successful organized labor has been in many ways, it has never succeeded in directing the education of its children. Capital still prepares the school books and practically controls the school systems of the world.

—ROGER BABSON, 1914.

I

The years between the Civil War and the World War saw the disappearance of some of the problems that had troubled the American people and their educational leaders in the preceding period. By 1890 the process of winning the West from the Indian was a closed chapter. Long before that the freedom of the slave had been written into the supreme law of the land. If many sore spots in republican and democratic institutions remained unhealed, almost everyone proudly believed that the American experiment, having justified itself in the eyes of the world, had ceased to be a mere experiment. European encroachments and the danger of entangling alliances no longer aroused serious anxiety. If swarms of immigrants and the clash of sectional rivalries warned patriots that nationalism had not been completely achieved, the surrender of Lee at Appomattox was commonly interpreted as the triumph of national unity.

Yet many old problems remained. While industrial and financial capitalists, having crushed the slavocracy and enacted much legislation favorable to their own interests, seemed to be in the saddle, their path was not altogether smooth. Unsatisfied with their share of this world's goods, they continued to vie with each other in bitter struggles for increased profits. Having allied with Western farmers to defeat the Southern planters, they now had to resume their former watchfulness lest the agrarians jeopardize their financial interests. Though they might continue to supply their factories with cheap European labor, they had to concern themselves even more definitely than before the Civil War with the demands of workers. Goaded by conditions in factories and sweatshops, and by the use of troops and other repressive measures to prevent effective protest, laborers resorted in increasing measure to organization, strikes, and the use of violence. Even the feeble growth of socialism and anarchism alarmed people of substance, who feared that social upheaval was lurking around the corner.

In addition to the survival of economic conflicts which a new setting sharpened and embittered, other problems connected with the growth of industrialism remained. The city lured the country folk in ever increasing numbers to its factories, shops, and offices, and the years between the Civil War and the World War saw the Americans virtually transformed from a rural into a predominantly urban people. Long before Roosevelt's country life commission made its report in 1909, thoughtful men had viewed with alarm the rural problems which in part resulted from the depletion of population in the country areas. The amazing growth of the cities themselves accentuated many of the problems that had concerned Barnard and Mann.

Among the questions inherited from the ante-bellum period were those concerned with the status of women and the place of religion in public education. Much remained to be done before women could claim even a part of equal opportunity with men. They were still handicapped in social and economic as well as in political relations. Religious interests had the task of strengthening their fortifications against the old enemy, secularization.

Problems that were relatively new also appeared. Changing economic and cultural modes undermined the traditional American family. The emancipation of the slave gave rise to a different Negro problem. It looked as if the old-world peasantry were to be duplicated in the rise of a tenant farmer class. With the extinction of free lands there was no longer even a partial avenue of escape for the less well-to-do and the discontented. As business became ever more integrated, there was less and less opportunity for the ambitious to climb the industrial ladder. Powerful interests combined, with the result that the individual of inferior economic status was virtually helpless when thrown into competition with those on the top. Wealth, organizing itself on a huge scale, resorted to wholesale methods of bribery and corruption; and not a few thoughtful men began to fear for the permanence of traditional American democracy. New methods of controlling the distribution of information and the organization of opinion enabled pressure groups to foist their programs on a helpless public. Increasing competition with other industrial nations hurled us into the maelstrom of world politics and competition for empire with all the problems involved in its defense by diplomacy, armies, and a great navy.

In general the application of science to everyday life brought increased health and happiness to the masses. But when "poison for profit" stalked out of the chemical laboratory it was clear that even science, under the tutelage of business enterprise, might create as well as solve problems. New and perplexing issues were introduced by the expansion of machine technology. Such revolutionary developments in science as the concept of evolution undermined old faiths and moral sanctions.

These problems, old and new, would, in their relation to the schools, have taxed educational leaders had they had no other work to do. But in point of fact their hands were already full. While the period before the Civil War marked the victory of the principle of state systems of tax-supported and publicly controlled free elementary schools, in reality a bare scaffolding had been erected. The fight against a class system of education had not been won.[1] As late as 1890 the average length of schooling for each individual in the nation, including higher and special education, was but four and a half years; many children, of course, received far less than that. During the first part of the period it was even necessary to build in both the South and the new West the framework of a system of elementary schools. In addition, the high school movement, which had barely begun when South Carolina seceded, had to be extended, and the old arguments against taxation for public education required new answers. Correlations between secondary schools and the new state universities must be worked out. The pioneer labors of early educators who had insisted on the duty of the schools to

---

[1] Although not taking a common view, G. W. Howison of California wrote in 1893 that the state could not consistently take measures that "would compel the parents to submit to one mingled contagion, children of every grade of morality and immorality, coarseness and refinement, uncleanliness and cleanliness, high social development and low." To avoid risks of social contagion the state should not only authorize but encourage private and select schools. *Ed. Rev.*, Vol. V (May, 1893), pp. 432–33.

provide for the training of defective children must be carried on. Stimulated by the hordes of immigrants who came from Europe, the Catholic hierarchy was working out a system of parochial schools, asking for state support, and, in the eyes of many, jeopardizing the very existence of the public secular school.

Much also remained to be done for professional standards and for the improvement of physical equipment. Wretched school-houses, a menace to decency and a defiance to the new principles of hygiene, must be replaced by more adequate structures. Something must be done to break down the opposition of tax-payers to expenditures for such purposes. Rural schools, almost hopelessly inferior to those of cities, demanded attention. The training of teachers, in which only a beginning had been made, required both extension and improvement. Pay was still scandalously low. Only a small proportion of teachers were included in the professional organizations which earlier educators had worked so hard to found.

New intellectual currents, together with practical exigencies, demanded changes in the curriculum. The old conflict between the bookish and traditional subjects and those of utilitarian value had not been resolved; and the influence of Herbert Spencer, a champion of the cult of the useful, was to be measured against that of the conservatives. The theory of evolution pushed biology into the schools, stimulated the cult of child study, and virtually refashioned the psychology which had conditioned so much that was done in the classroom. In warning against the traditional view that the social order was fixed and unchanging, the work of Darwin also gave support to those who held that a changing society necessitated more attention to the social studies; and the new discipline of sociology contributed to the same end. The American followers of Herbart, who during the '90s led in the criticism and reorganization of the conventional curriculum, deprecated the importance of the classics and insisted that the schools be brought into more intimate relation with the actualities of the everyday world. The Herbartians helped to secure a larger place in the curriculum for literature, history, and economics as well as for practical subjects such as cooking and typewriting.[2]

These provocative intellectual currents also required changes in methods of teaching and discipline as well as in the curriculum. The theory of evolution, together with other factors, helped to emancipate the child from the old Calvinistic dogma of original sin, an idea which had condemned the young in school to a blind and brutal discipline. By emphasizing individual differences the doctrine of Darwin also challenged the lock-step organization, the stereotyped recitation, and the demand for rigid conformity. In a similar way the Herbartian psychology, with its doctrine of apperception, put a damper on the old memorizing methods, diminished the importance of the textbook, and attached greater importance to arousing the interest of the child than to disciplining his will. The rise of the "new psychology" of Wundt, Dewey, and James, which with that of Herbart undermined the old faculty psychology, demanded revolutionary changes in the technique of teaching. Stimulated by Galton, Joseph Mayer Rice and J. McKeen Cattell turned the attention of educators to tests and scientific measurements. As we shall see, all these matters had important social implications.

In their efforts to solve these technical problems, in part

2 Charles A. McMurry, *The Elements of General Method Based on the Principles of Herbart* (New York, 1904), p. 9; *Special Method in Geography* (New York, 1907), pp. 7 *et seq.;* Frank M. McMurry, *How to Study and Teaching How to Study* (Boston, 1909), p. 43; Charles De Garmo, *Herbart and the Herbartians* (New York, 1896), p. 241; *Principles of Secondary Education,* Vol. I, *The Studies* (New York, 1907), Chap. II, p. 161.

handed on by the past and in part raised by new intellectual movements, educators had plenty to do. But, as we have seen, they had always been expected to help solve grave social problems as well as to attend to the immediate duties of their craft. Would educators, so far as they thought in social terms, merely continue to advocate public schools and moral training as the best means of remedying the defects of democracy and the shortcomings of our social and economic order, and as the surest preventive of violence, lawlessness, and revolution? Would they consciously align themselves with one group or would they try to steer a neutral course? Would they initiate reform, follow others who aimed to improve matters, or remain aloof from such efforts?[3]

II

Having loyally supported the Federal Government in its struggle with the Confederacy,[4] educational leaders proclaimed their willingness to help consolidate the victory which Union arms had won for the dominant economic system of the North. Crushed though the Southern aristocracy was, many educators in the days of reconstruction shared the fear of the "Radical Republicans" that, unless safeguards were erected, the Civil War might have to be fought over again. Richard Edwards, president of Illinois Normal University, told the National Teachers' Association in 1865 that the teacher must finish

[3] Although a wide variety of materials has been consulted, the following discussion is for the most part based on the reports of the Commissioner of Education, and the opinions of those who spoke in the annual meetings of the National Education Association and through the pages of the *Educational Review*.

[4] For examples see John Swett, *Public Education in California* (New York, 1911), pp. 146–47; and J. W. Cook's *Educational History of Illinois* (Chicago, 1912), p. 127, for Newton Bateman's Civil War activities.

what the soldier had so well begun.[5] Public education, declared the president of the association, was "the chief unifying process on which we can rely for a permanent peace."[6] J. P. Wickersham of Pennsylvania feared that unless the South were speedily educated the haughty slave lords would legislate slavery back into existence, annul the confiscation laws, and even make the United States government assume the debt of the Confederacy.[7] If his ardent concern for the welfare of the emancipated Negro, which led him to declare that the former slaveowners should be rooted out "as western farmers do the stumps in their clearing," was scarcely typical of the meetings that followed, his desire to extend the school system to the South was in harmony with the efforts of educators throughout the century. In addresses and resolutions, the National Education Association throughout the period urged Congress to appropriate money to help the South remove its educational handicaps.

The connection between the well-being of investments, sound finance, and business enterprise and the campaign for Southern education was sometimes clearly recognized by the spokesmen of education. In 1882 the prominent New York lawyer and reformer, Dexter Hawkins, urged that the development of education in the South would enable that section to bear a larger proportion of the national taxes.[8] The Reverend A. D. Mayo, an even more devoted friend of Southern education, declared that Northern capital could be attracted and Southern resources properly developed only if the working masses

[5] *National Teachers' Association, 6th Annual Meeting, Harrisburg, Aug. 16, 17, 18, 1865*, p. 276.
[6] *Ibid.*, pp. 232, 234.   [7] *Ibid.*, pp. 290–94.
[8] Dept. of Superintendence, N. E. A., *Proceedings*, 1882 (Circular of Information, Bureau of Education, No. 2, 1882), p. 54. For additional evidence see *Report of the Commissioner of Education*, 1870, p. 7.

were educated in skill and dependability.[9] In a more detailed study we shall enquire into the extent to which enthusiasm for the education of the Negro was prompted by economic motives.

Educational leaders consciously or unconsciously spoke and acted in ways calculated to aid nationalism in its victory over the Indians, as well as in its triumph in the South. Before settlers could occupy Western lands and enable the newly built railways to pay dividends to Eastern investors the Indians had to be removed from the plains and tamed on reservations. Although early educational leaders had occasionally raised their voices in behalf of Indian education,[10] it was not until the end of the Civil War that a leading spokesman advocated settling the Indian problem by means of schools rather than by war. In his report for 1870 John Eaton, commissioner of the newly established federal Bureau of Education, urged that, quite apart from Christian and philanthropic considerations, it would be cheaper to educate than to fight the Indians.[11]

In 1885, after the government had begun to pass more liberal appropriations for Indian education and to transfer it from the missionaries to federal control, the National Education Association passed a resolution heartily commending the efforts made to solve the Indian problem "by educating the young Indians out of the savagery of their parents into the industries and attainments of civilization."[12] Indian education began to appear on the Association's programs, and R. H. Pratt and

[9] Reverend A. D. Mayo, *Industrial Education in the South* (Bureau of Education, Circular of Information, No. 5, 1888), p. 13.

[10] In spite of the pioneer work of educating the Indian which is associated with such men as John Eliot, Robert Boyle, Jonathan Mayhew, and Jonathan Edwards, leading educators paid little attention to the problem. As early as 1820 Governor Clinton did, however, recommend education for the Indian; and Catharine Beecher protested against the cruel treatment of the red men.

[11] *Report of the Commissioner of Education*, 1870, pp. 22–27. The bureau did not have control over the educational work among the Indians.

[12] N. E. A., *Proceedings*, 1885, pp. 20–21.

General Armstrong demonstrated that the Indian, if properly trained, could become self-sufficient on his reservation.[13] Increasingly educational leaders agreed on the advantages to all concerned if the Indian could be trained in agriculture, craftsmanship, the wearing of the white man's apparel, and the reading of the white man's books. If educators were belated in proposing schools as a substitute for the sword in solving the Indian problem, they nevertheless rendered aid to the nation by assisting the government in the work of civilizing the subdued red man.

III

Education also played at least a minor part in the conflict between Western farmers and Eastern industrialists and financiers. In one sense the Morrill Act of 1862, which provided for the support of agricultural education by setting aside public land for that purpose, was a concession on the part of the industrial East to its agrarian ally in the common crusade against the Southern planter. But for some time the concession was a barren one. In spite of the good intentions of such pioneer educators as William Watts Folwell, who became president of the University of Minnesota in 1869,[14] the Morrill funds were for the most part administered, throughout the seventies and eighties, in a casual and indifferent manner. In many state institutions, in the West as well as in the East, a single professorship in agriculture or perhaps a summer course was the most that was done; experimental farms and profes-

[13] *Ibid.*, 1884, pp. 17, 177–80; 1890, p. 39; 1895, pp. 80–86; 1900, pp. 682–92; *Ed. Rev.*, Vol. X (Nov., 1895), pp. 325–30; Vol. I (Jan., 1891), pp. 57–59; *Report of the Commissioner of Education*, 1885–86, p. xviii; 1912, Vol. I, pp. 420–28; 1931, pp. 1 *ff*.

[14] Solon J. Buck, ed., *William Watts Folwell, The Autobiography and Letters of a Pioneer of Culture* (Minneapolis, 1933), pp. 189–90. Folwell took the lead in securing state aid for the secondary schools of Minnesota.

sional agricultural education developed slowly. This was in part due to the academic traditionalism of educators, and in part to the indifference and skepticism of the farmers themselves.

In educational matters the countryside fared badly indeed in comparison with urban regions. Farmers were not unaware of the disparity, but they were not unanimous in looking to education as the best remedy for the problems they faced during this period of industrialization. Traditionally they had been indifferent and even hostile to the battle for better schools.[15] The limited curriculum of the country school had little to offer the farmer in carrying on his daily work and in solving his problems. Discussions in the lyceum and in agricultural periodicals in considerable measure took the place of school instruction in agricultural subjects.[16]

But with the disappearance of free lands agrarian groups increasingly appreciated the importance of better education if their children were to enjoy equality of opportunity with city boys and girls, and if the growth of a caste civilization were to be prevented. The Grange took an active interest in securing better texts, more adequately trained and better paid teachers, and the introduction of specifically agricultural subjects. In its convention in 1887 the Farmers' Alliance also included in

[15] For examples of the attitude of farmers toward public schools see F. T. Carlton, *Economic Influences Upon Educational Progress in the United States, 1820–1850*, pp. 83–84, and W. E. Chancellor, *Our Schools; their Administration and Supervision* (Boston, 1904), pp. 294–95. For a brief summary of the disparity between rural and urban schools at the end of the World War see *School and Society*, Vol. XVI (Aug. 19, 1922), pp. 197–98.

[16] Most of the pre-Civil War agricultural education was furthered by agricultural societies and by such outstanding leaders as Edmund Ruffin. See, for example, Ruffin's *Premium Essay on Agricultural Education* (Richmond, 1853). Early arguments for the introduction of agricultural subjects into the common school curriculum may be found in *Transactions of the Western Literary Institute and College of Teachers* (1836), pp. 204 *et seq.*; *New York Teacher* (March, 1860), pp. 257–59; N. E. A. *Proceedings*, 1875, pp. 10 *et seq.* R. R. Reeder, *The Historical Development of Early School Readers*, describes the place of agriculture in school readers, pp. 54–55.

its demands the "promotion of industrial and agricultural education." Such an agrarian leader as Ignatius Donnelly of Minnesota, who introduced into Congress the bill for the organization of the federal bureau of education and who favored national support for Southern schools, distinguished himself as an advocate for better public school education, free textbooks, and other improvements.[17] But the general attitude of the militant farmers was expressed by the Populists who, while sympathetic with "every proposition which will tend to make men intelligent, virtuous, and temperate," nevertheless regarded educational measures as secondary in importance to agitation and legislation in solving pressing agrarian problems.[18]

Disturbed by the militancy of certain agrarian movements and aware of the inadequate school advantages in rural areas, educational leaders urged the expansion of the country school. There were of course various humanitarian reasons for urging such expansion, but one may detect also the influence of social and economic attitudes. Some educators explicitly argued that farmers' grievances might in this way be removed and the danger of political and direct action be reduced. Granges and "other popular upheavals," declared an educational leader in 1875, "are ineffectual because too late to rectify evils that should be prevented by thorough education and careful training in early life."[19] One state superintendent expressed what was probably a fairly common point of view when in 1892 he told the National Education Association the duty of the teacher in the Populist uprising. "When the farmers demand special

[17] E. W. Fish, biographical sketch of Ignatius Donnelly, in *Donnelliana: An Appendix to Caesar's Column* (Chicago, n. d.), pp. 53–54, 57, 85.

[18] *What is Populism, an Exposition of the Principles of the Omaha Platform* (Salem, Ore., 1895); C. H. Bliss. ed., *The Populist Compendium: References for Reformers* (Auburn, Indiana, 1894), Vol. I, No. 1, p. 78.

[19] W. F. Phelps, principal of the State Normal School, Winona, Minn., N. E. A., *Proceedings*, 1875, p. 11.

legislation in their behalf; when they propose to form into a political party by virtue of their occupation; when they expect the government to purchase their surplus produce and store it; when they demand the unlimited issuing of paper money without any funds to redeem it; then citizens, and especially teachers, will respectfully differ with them; but when they strive to improve their social, intellectual, and financial condition, every one may well contribute his share towards the consummation."[20]

In the critical campaign of 1896, Nicholas Murray Butler called upon the teachers to oppose Bryan, whom he denounced as a demagogue seeking to inflame men's passions and base desires by asserting that the nation was divisible into sections or classes whose interests were antagonistic. "If there be any single teacher who, for local, personal, or economic reasons, feels any temptation to vote in company such as this," Butler admonished his readers, "we ask him, before preparing his ballot, to read *twice* this extract from the resolutions adopted by unanimous vote with tremendous enthusiasm by the National Education Association at Asbury Park in 1894: '. . . At such a time we deem it our highest duty to pronounce enthusiastically, and with unanimous voice, for the supremacy of law and the maintenance of social and political order. Before grievances of individuals or organizations can be considered or redressed, violence, riot, and insurrection must be repelled and overcome.' "[21]

Nor was such support to captains of industry in their contest with agrarianism apparent only in the clash with Populism.

[20] Henry Raab, *ibid.* (1892), pp. 571 *et seq.*

[21] *Ed. Rev.,* Vol. XII (Nov., 1896), pp. 404–6. The president of the N. E. A. in 1896 declared that the free public school "will make the decision at the ballot-box next November, a decision which shall be in accord with national honor and true economic principles." Newton C. Dougherty, N. E. A., *Proceedings,* 1896, p. 86.

More than twenty years later the leaders of rural education were congratulated for urging American farmers to base their case on "enlightened judgment" and for trying to implant in them a feeling of social solidarity—achievements that would serve as "a bulwark against which waves of selfish class interests might spend themselves in time of stress."[22] Dean Russell of Teachers College at that time urged a rural education which would make a happy, contented farmer, rather than one which would send country boys to the factory, turn them over to the tender mercies of the trade union, and perhaps lead them to socialism and anarchism.[23]

This desire to keep the rural boys and girls upon the farm and to prevent their bringing additional problems to the crowded streets of the cities, which were finding abundant cheap labor in the hordes of immigrants, was increasingly common among educators as the startling rapidity of urbanization became evident.[24] It was even urged that rural life be made more attractive and rural schools improved, on the plea that the depletion of country population, by leaving fewer hands to carry on farming, was raising the cost of food products.[25]

While educators were disturbed by the effects of "the rural problem" upon the city, they were even more concerned with the cultural and economic plight of the farmer. They believed that the farmer was moving to the city in part to give his children the better advantages of the urban schools.[26] They

[22] Thomas J. Smart, *School and Society*, Vol. X (Nov. 8, 1919), p. 542.

[23] James Earl Russell *Good Housekeeping*, March, 1914, reprinted in *The Trend in American Education* (New York, 1922), pp. 173-74.

[24] W. Carson Ryan, *Report of the Commissioner of Education*, 1913, Vol. I, p. 9; L. H. Bailey, *Ed. Rev.*, Vol. XX (Nov., 1900), p. 381. Much earlier certain educators such as Henry Barnard and Alonzo Potter had praised the country virtues and tried through the country schools to prevent the movement to the cities. *Report*, 1851, p. 28; Potter, *School and Schoolmaster*, pp. 56-57.

[25] *Report of the Commissioner of Education*, 1913, Vol. I, p. 9.

[26] George H. Betts, *New Ideals in Rural Schools* (Boston, 1913), p. 13.

deplored the poverty of social activities among the rural population.[27] They hoped that tenant farmers, recruited from southern and central Europe, could be made into self-reliant, land-owning citizens after the pattern of the older America.[28]

To meet these needs of rural life, educators offered improvements in country schools. They accepted the criticism that the schools actually led away from country life by teaching subjects that prepared pupils only for city jobs, and made efforts to introduce materials that would attract country boys and girls to the life of their fathers and would be useful to them in that vocation.[29] The school, some maintained, must become the active center of an awakened rural community life.[30]

In regard to the cause and cure of the farmers' economic difficulties, educators in general accepted uncritically the point of view of financiers and industrialists. They assumed that the agrarian ills would be cured if production were increased and cheapened by a greater knowledge and skill in the farming process.[31] The end of the era of free lands gave added emphasis to that point of view. So close was the interrelation between industry and agriculture, educators were told, that great captains of industry and financiers awaited with anxiety the first official crop predictions.[32] Beginning in 1906 Rockefeller money, in providing for demonstration farms and agents, gave support to the idea that the agricultural problem might be

[27] *Ibid.*, pp. 14, 26–35.
[28] Ellwood P. Cubberley, *Rural Life and Education* (Boston, 1914), pp. 55–56, 106–7.
[29] John M. Gillette, *Constructive Rural Sociology* (New York, 1913), pp. 246 *et seq.;* H. Updegraff, *Ed. Rev.*, Vol. XLI (Feb., 1911), pp. 139–40; *Report of the Commissioner of Education*, 1906, Vol, I, pp. xxxiii–xxxiv.
[30] Betts, *op. cit.*, vi; Ellwood P. Cubberley, *The Improvement of Rural Schools* (Boston, 1912), p. 15; Herbert Quick, N. E. A., *Proceedings*, 1912, pp. 250–57.
[31] H. L. Russell, University of Wisconsin, N. E. A., *Proceedings*, 1910, p. 108; John W. Zeller, *ibid.*, p. 245.
[32] John A. Lapp, *School and Society*, Vol. I (May 8, 1915), p. 652.

solved, not by effecting more equitable marketing and distribution of profits, but by efficiency in production. In 1914 the Smith-Lever Act allocated federal funds for educational extension work of a similar character.

Only very rarely did an educator suggest that the problem of the farmer was not one of greater production, but rather one of marketing his produce at a fair and profitable price; and when such a suggestion was made, it fell upon deaf ears.[33] While educators were anxious to ameliorate the farmers' lot, they had only disapproval for any real challenge, such as the Populists represented, to the dominant and prosperous lords of the city.

IV

It was common for educators to show an even greater sympathy with the position of industry and finance in its struggles with labor than in the tension between conservative wealth and the farmer. Hardly an annual meeting of the National Education Association was concluded without an appeal on the part of leading educators for the help of the teacher in quelling strikes and checking the spread of socialism and anarchism. Commissioners of education and editors of educational periodicals summoned their forces to the same end.

Strikes were condemned as inexcusable attacks on the social order. In 1877 the president of the National Education Association, in commenting on the railroad strikes, declared that the public school alone had saved the country from the terrors of the French Commune and that the outbreaks might have been entirely prevented had the workers been trained "to think

[33] William R. Callicotte, N. E. A., *Proceedings,* 1909, pp. 971–72. Another uncommon view among educators was that of Arland D. Weeks, of North Dakota Agricultural College, who held that improvement of rural life depended first upon economic legislation favorable to farmers. *Ed. Rev.,* Vol. XL (Oct., 1910), p. 230.

as well as to toil."[34] In his report for the same year John Eaton, Commissioner of Education, insisted that the school could train the child to resist the evils of strikes and violence and declared that capital should "weigh the cost of the mob and the tramp against the expense of universal and sufficient education."[35] When President Cleveland broke up the Pullman strike with federal troops, the National Education Association commended him for his wisdom and firmness. Condemning "riot, incendiarism, and conspiracy" as un-American methods of settling social problems, the resolution insisted that order must be restored before wrongs could be considered.[36] In no instance, apparently, did the Association take cognizance of the causes of the strikes or suggest other realistic means for the solution of grievances. It appears that violence in strikes was not condemned when used by owners of factories and railroads or by the government.

With such hostility toward strikes educators naturally expressed horror of socialism, anarchism, and communism, using the terms almost interchangeably. A. D. Mayo, New England's educational missionary to the South, declared that communism was "the pit that yawns below every state whose masses are groping through the perilous labyrinth of mental confusion and labor without brains" and that the wealthy class could least afford to advocate a narrow and selfish policy in public education.[37] In his presidential address in 1881 James H. Smart, admitting that it was reasonable for the poor man, particularly after middle age, to demand a "division of property," declared that the free school did more "to suppress the

[34] M. A. Newell, N. E. A., *Proceedings,* 1877, pp. 6 *et seq.*
[35] *Report of the Commissioner of Education,* 1877, p. viii.
[36] N. E. A., *Proceedings,* 1894, pp. 34–35.
[37] A. D. Mayo, *Building for the Children of the South* (Washington, 1884), p. 7.

latent flame of communism than all other agencies combined."[38] At the same meeting another speaker declared that "men stand aghast at the prophetic rumblings of an unreasoning and relentless communism . . . a more serious thing . . . than many of us dare speak above our breath." He concluded that there was no use in deploring the powerlessness of the schools to eradicate communistic tendencies "so long as teachers are taken so largely from classes whose narrow means force them to adopt teaching to gain their bread, and are then denied such social recognition as will alone occasion that cultivation of the graces which will give power to hold the best born to their best level and to raise others toward that best level."[39] After the assassination of McKinley, Nicholas Murray Butler, editor of *The Educational Review,* declared that it was the licensing of lunacy rather than the guaranteeing of freedom of speech to permit the public to discuss anarchy, a thing which was "settled forever."[40] Again and again educators denounced radical doctrines and offered education as the best preventive and cure.

Educators did not rest content with merely pointing out the duty of the school to counteract challenges to the established order. They also advocated specific methods by which the school could lessen unrest and insure the dominance of sound economic principles. Some thought that the extension of the high school would provide the more intelligent son of the worker with an education that would enable him to find an honorable and profitable place within the existing industrial system, and prevent him from becoming an agitator.[41] "The high school education detects and exposes the fallacies of

[38] N. E. A., *Proceedings,* 1881, p. 12.

[39] Honorable D. F. De Wolf, *ibid.,* pp. 61–64.

[40] *Ed. Rev.,* Vol. XXII (Oct., 1901), pp. 320–23.

[41] *Report of the Commissioner of Education,* 1877, p. lxxxv; *Journal of Education,* Vol. I (Feb. 6, 1875), p. 66.

socialism; the poor learn that they have an interest in respecting the property of the rich, and that their powers and their labors are also real property, which require to be respected in turn," J. E. Seaman told the national body of educators in 1885.[42]

An increasing number of educators advocated manual training and industrial education as the best specific means of counteracting radicalism on the part of the working masses. Senator Justin Morrill of Vermont, in a speech delivered in 1876, urged the Senate to support practical education in order that the worker, by obtaining the higher wages awarded to skilled labor, might steer his way clear from "the imported barbarous despotism reigning over our trade unions."[43]

Although educators continued to develop more specifically the idea of moral training,[44] as the period advanced they turned their attention increasingly to the social sciences as means by which schools might inculcate respect for law and order, and suspicion for the doctrines of socialism and anarchism. As early as 1877 Honorable M. A. Newell, superintendent of public instruction in Maryland, declared that the elements of political economy, the nature and the relations of money, capital, labor, and wages, could be made as accessible to the young as the elements of grammar and arithmetic.[45]

It became increasingly common as years passed for educators to insist that children should be made to see the mutual interdependence of capital and labor; to appreciate the necessity of co-operation, rather than conflict; and to realize that

[42] N. E. A., *Proceedings*, 1885, p. 176.

[43] Justin S. Morrill, *Educational Fund: Speech in the Senate of the United States*, April 26, 1876 (Washington, 1876), p. 17.

[44] For example, "Moral Training in the Public School," N. E. A., *Proceedings*, 1886, pp. 128–38; *Ed. Rev.*, Vol. XI (Feb., 1896), pp. 134–35; Resolutions of N. E. A., *Proceedings*, 1887, p. 47; 1905, p. 43; 1907, p. 30; 1908, pp. 37, 38.

[45] N. E. A., *Proceedings*, 1877, p. 12.

there was no inherent opposition between the two.[46] In 1915 President Eliot, in urging the teaching of economics in secondary schools, warned against the great danger to civilization should the government come to be controlled by the masses of people whose ideas on the subject of capital and labor were "crude, mistaken, or perverse."[47] Decrying the tendencies of the masses to succumb to assaults on capital, sound money, and "radical changes in our system" Frederick Speirs of Philadelphia also advocated the teaching of economics in school.[48] Although certain voices were also raised in behalf of the teaching of history as a means of solving problems of capital and labor,[49] the more typical view was expressed by a committee of the National Education Association which in 1895 recommended that the teacher of American history confine herself to the colonial and early national period.[50] To the very close of the century the political, military, and constitutional point of view virtually excluded the economic and social.[51]

These were the services that educators gave to the leaders of business in their contests with the workers. If, as we shall later see, the spokesmen of education did not entirely ignore

[46] George Gunton, editor of Gunton's Magazine (earlier, Social Economist), was one of the earliest influential voices to popularize this view, and particularly the argument that a higher standard of living for laborers would benefit manufacturers by increasing the wants of the working class. Gunton was interested in education and even addressed the N. E. A. on the desirability of teaching social economics in the public schools. Wealth and Progress (New York, 1887); "Need of Political Education," Gunton Institute Bulletin, Vol. II (Sept., 1898), pp. 45–57; Gunton's Magazine, Vol. XXI (Aug., 1901), pp. 140–50.

[47] School and Society, Vol. I (Jan. 2, 1915), p. 3.

[48] N. E. A., Proceedings, 1901, pp. 137–43.

[49] E. A. Bryan, President of the Washington State Agricultural College, N. E. A., Proceedings, 1899, pp. 186–96; Homer H. Seerley, President State Normal School, Cedar Falls, Iowa, ibid., 1898, pp. 77–82; Wilbur F. Gordy, Hartford, ibid., pp. 70–77; George E. Howard, Stanford University, Ed. Rev., Vol. XIX (March, 1900), p. 262.

[50] Committee of Fifteen, Ed. Rev., Vol. IX (March, 1895), p. 256.

[51] John Elbert Stout, The Development of the High-School Curricula in the North Central States from 1860 to 1918 (Chicago, 1921), p. 181.

the interest of labor, they gave more attention to providing a training of which business men, large and small, could thoroughly approve. To promote the efficiency of business at home and to enable it to compete with foreign rivals for markets, commercial and other special types of education were advocated and gradually developed. As early as 1871 Commissioner Eaton, while complimenting the private business colleges for their work, advocated the introduction of commercial subjects into the public school system.[52] Ten years later he was able to report "an increasing consciousness of the imperative necessity for this training" among public school authorities.[53] By familiarizing educators with the status of commercial education in Europe his successors likewise used their influence to further the movement.

Stimulated by the special section which the educational congress at the World's Fair devoted to commercial education, by the American Bankers' Association, and by such financial leaders as Frank Vanderlip, educators increasingly recognized the need of business for special training.[54] It was clearly realized that the success of the commercial high schools would "depend on their ability to get and hold the favorable regard of business men" and the willingness of educators to defer to them in questions of subject matter and methods of teaching.[55] At the turn of the century President Eliot recommended that education assume the task of promoting trade by training consuls better able to contend with our rivals and by otherwise contributing to the development of alert, inventive,

[52] *Report of the Commissioner of Education,* 1871, p. 54; 1873, pp. viii, xxxv; 1875, p. lxii.

[53] *Ibid.,* 1882–83, p. civ.

[54] N. E. A., *Proceedings,* 1893, pp. 788 *et seq.; Report of the Commissioner of Education,* 1895–96, Vol. I, p. 721; Frank A. Vanderlip, *Addresses on Commercial and Technical Education* (New York, 1905), pp. 21–38, 5–17.

[55] *Supplement to the Fifth Yearbook of the National Herbart Society,* 1899, p. 212.

and successful merchants.[56] The National Education Association seriously began to consider the problem of commercial education about 1900, and by the end of the period the Bureau of Education created a special department in its interest.

It was also recognized that the introduction of drawing and design into the public schools possessed utilitarian as well as artistic value. Joseph White, secretary of the Massachusetts Board of Education, noted as early as 1871 that such subjects promised to improve the quality of our manufactures; while Commissioner Eaton, in commenting on the increasingly intense competition with foreign producers, likewise thought that the teaching of art subjects in the schools would greatly advance the interests of manufacturing. The international exhibits at Philadelphia in 1876 and at Chicago in 1893 impressed educators with the "economic importance of various applications of art to industry."[57] Although a great deal was said in the earlier period about the value of art education in securing markets against our competitors, as our manufacturers established their markets and technological changes in industry diminished the importance of the artisan, more emphasis was placed on the æsthetic and moral values of the arts in school work.[58]

It would indeed be unfair to imply that even the educators who most explicitly advocated commercial subjects on the ground of their service to business were unmindful of the interests of school children. Educators were aware of the fact that many pupils stayed in school only because they shared their parents' belief that industrial and commercial subjects would best enable them to "get ahead." If schoolmen failed to see

[56] Charles W. Eliot, *Ed. Rev.*, Vol. XVIII (Dec., 1899), pp. 416–24.
[57] *Report of the Commissioner of Education*, 1871, pp. 38–39; 1873, p. ci; 1876, p. cxl.
[58] *Ibid.*, 1905, Vol. I, Chap. X; 1909, Vol. I, p. 6.

that the proficiency of pupils in commercial and industrial subjects might in actuality serve those already on the top and even stifle the capacities of school children, they were merely no better judges of trends and needs than the parents of their pupils.

While educators pointed out the importance of commercial and art training in competing with other industrial nations for markets, they were not active in the movement for imperialism in the way that some intellectual groups were.[59] In opposing the martial spirit that led to the war with Spain, Nicholas Murray Butler, as editor of *The Educational Review*, wrote that educators might well hang their heads in deepest shame if the verdict of history should be that the United States closed the nineteenth century with a preventable war.[60] Once war was declared, however, they rallied to the support of the government. The National Education Association resolved that, much as the war was to be deplored, "the teachers of the United States recognize that it has been entered upon in the most unselfish spirit and from the loftiest motives. The cause of freedom and humanity, and the solidarity of both the American people and the Anglo-Saxon races is vastly increased by such an armed contest."[61] If educators were not very critical in their analysis of the causes of the war, they showed a willingness to assume the responsibility of preparing the American people for its imperial obligations and of co-operating with government authorities in the upbuilding of school systems in the new colonies.[62]

With high-mindedness and a good deal of disinterestedness

[59] Julius Pratt, "The 'Large Policy' of 1898," *The Mississippi Valley Historical Review*, Vol. XIX (Sept., 1932), pp. 219–42.
[60] Editorial, *Ed. Rev.*, Vol. XV (May, 1898), pp. 515–16.
[61] *Ed. Rev.*, Vol. XVI (Sept., 1898), p. 204.
[62] *Ibid.*, pp. 204–6; N. E. A., *Proceedings*, 1900, p. 31; Honorable John Ross, *ibid.*, 1898, p. 44.

educators embarked on the task of aiding the government in Americanizing the newly acquired possessions by teaching the natives English, respect for American institutions, and the steady, industrious habits of the Yankee. It was urged that education was a cheaper and more effective way of pacifying the Filipinos than the sword, and even military authorities in the Islands welcomed the aid of teachers.[63] Doctor David P. Barrows, Bernard Moses, and John Eaton, in organizing schools in the new possessions, emphasized the importance of industrial and agricultural education. While occasional references were made to the advantages to American trade and industry that might be expected from such a policy, more importance was attached to providing an education for the Filipinos which would fit them for ultimate self-government and which would elevate the masses from ignorance and laziness.[64] The Commissioner of Education reported in 1914 that in the industrial work the commercial side had been kept in view, but that the purpose had never been to exploit in any way the productive capacity of the pupils.[65]

While sincere effort was made not only in the insular possessions but also in Alaska to provide an education for the natives which would improve their material and cultural status,[66] they were also expected to become good Americans. Only five years after we acquired Porto Rico visiting educators were thrilled to see the young islanders singing lustily "My country, 'tis of thee"

[63] *Ed. Rev.*, Vol. XXII (Oct., 1901), p. 227; Vol. XXV (March, 1903), p. 239; *Report of the Commissioner of Education*, 1900–1901, Vol. I, pp. l–liii.

[64] *Ed. Rev.*, Vol. XXVII (March, 1904), p. 235; *Report of the Commissioner of Education*, 1909, Vol. I, Chap. V, especially pp. 284–85. See especially Wm. H. Taft, "American Education in the Philippines: A Contrast to English and Dutch Colonial Policies," *Ed. Rev.*, Vol. XXIX (March, 1905), pp. 264–85, and "The Relation of Education to Democratic Government," N. E. A., *Proceedings*, 1910, pp. 71–78.

[65] *Report of the Commissioner of Education*, 1914, Vol. I, p. 645.

[66] *Ibid.*, 1913, Vol. I, pp. xlvi–xlvii; 1913, Vol. II, p. xii; 1909, Vol. II, Chap. XXX; 1905, Vol. I, Chap. XV.

and saluting the Stars and Stripes.[67] Thus did educational experts, without always being fully aware of the implications of their acts, help insure the success of what was regarded as an enlightened and beneficent chapter in the history of imperialism.

Besides these new services which education rendered industrialism during the period, leaders of the schools continued, as in pre-Civil War days, to impress upon the rich the benefits of education in promoting prosperity and increasing wealth. Commissioner Eaton brought forward elaborate evidence in 1870 to prove, as Mann had done some twenty-five years before, that the public schools encouraged inventiveness, rendered labor more productive, and enriched industry.[68] Others pointed out that education also created new desires and thereby stimulated new industries. Nicholas Murray Butler was quoted as having said that "where the public term is the longest, there the average productive capacity of the citizen is the greatest." While President Eliot thought that the influence of the educational system on business enterprise and profit was indirect, President Angell of Michigan believed it to be both positive and direct.[69] In 1904 the Mosely Educational Commission reported to the British Government that on the whole both teachers and industrial leaders regarded education as a powerful contributory cause of the remarkable economic progress of the past thirty years and an essential condition of its maintenance.[70]

Employers, whatever their indifference to the benefits of schooling when they made use of child labor in beet fields and in factories, nevertheless gave much evidence of their appreciation of the economic values of education and of the services of

[67] Ibid., 1904, Vol. I, p. 942.
[68] Report of the Commissioner of Education, 1870, pp. 38–53.
[69] Reports of the Mosely Educational Commission to the United States of America (London, 1904), p. 307.
[70] Ibid.

its leaders.[71] Education was considered a good investment. Among the benefactors of the public schools were Henry Frick, John D. Rockefeller, George Peabody, John F. Slater, Robert C. Ogden, Andrew Carnegie, Elbert H. Gary, and Pierre S. Dupont.[72] In 1880 it was pointed out with pride that such great capitalists as Astor and Stewart gladly paid taxes for the education of the sons and daughters of poor laborers.[73] A few merchants and manufacturers in the North at the end of the period testified in public that they were willing to be taxed for the improvement of schools in the South because of the sure markets that would result.[74]

This interest shown by leaders of finance and industry in the schools, as well as other influences of the industrial order, did not leave the schools untouched. In general educational leaders were duly grateful for the benefits bestowed by men of substance, great or small. The Commissioner of Education in 1896 told superintendents that they would find their best support in conservative business leaders.[75] In 1899 the National Education Association expressed its hearty appreciation to all the noble men and women who, by their gifts and endowments, were adding so much to the upbuilding of elementary and higher education.[76] Only one speaker in the meetings of the National Educational Association seems to have taken the position that there was something incongruous in the accep-

[71] *Ed. Rev.*, Vol. XXV (March, 1903), p. 225.

[72] George Harvey, *Henry Clay Frick: The Man* (New York, 1928), pp. 345–49; John D. Rockefeller, *Random Reminiscences of Men and Events* (London, 1909), pp. 176–77; Ida M. Tarbell, *The Life of Elbert H. Gary* (New York, 1925), p. 312; *School and Society*, Vol. V (April 14, 1917), p. 438; Leonard P. Ayres, *Seven Great Foundations* (New York, 1911). In addition to these donors, the Reports of the Commissioner of Education list a great number of other prominent men of wealth who aided education; see, for example, *Report*, 1903, Vol. II, Chap. XXIX.

[73] *American Journal of Education*, Vol. XXX, (Sept., 1880), p. 820.

[74] John Dewey, *Pictorial Review* (Aug. 31, 1930), pp. 65–66.

[75] *Report of the Commissioner of Education*, 1895–96, Vol. I, p. xxiii.

[76] N. E. A., *Proceedings*, 1899, p. 31.

tance of huge sums of money from capitalists, many of whom came by their fortunes in questionable ways. "The schools," declared S. Y. Gillan, editor of *The Western Teacher,* "suffer for the want of money, and the slums continue a growing menace because the owners of swollen fortunes—stolen fortunes—are the beneficiaries of special privileges. And we in our simplicity allow them to hold these privileges untaxed and to practice their religion, which is to get all they can and to keep all they get except those sums which they use for debauching public morals and which we advertise under the euphemism of 'gifts' to education."[77] But his remarks were met by silence. Many years later John Dewey gave the same idea a wider hearing.[78]

V

In at least one important category business enterprise exerted a direct influence upon the schools. In 1902 Dewey pointed out that publishing houses not only affected the textbooks but also influenced the course of study. New subjects were introduced because "some publishing firm, by a happy coincidence, has exactly the books which are needed to make that study successful," while on the other hand old ones that should have been entirely replaced were retained because of the vested interest behind them.[79] When California and Kansas undertook to

[77] N. E. A., *Proceedings,* 1907, p. 165.

[78] John Dewey, *Individualism Old and New* (New York, 1930), p. 89. For an early view of Dewey on academic freedom in relation to the subsidizing of education by wealth see *Ed. Rev.,* Vol. XXIII (Jan., 1902), pp. 1–14. William E. Chancellor declared that it was perilous for a teacher to be even a conventional expounder of the system "by which business men maintain their hold on us all." *School and Society,* Vol. II (Nov. 6, 1915), pp. 670–71.

[79] John Dewey, *The Educational Situation* (Chicago, 1902), p. 38. For additional evidence of the way in which business influenced or attempted to influence the curriculum see *Ed. Rev.,* Vol. XVIII (Nov., 1899), pp. 378–86; *Report of the Commissioner of Education,* 1900–1901, Vol. I, Chap. VII; 1898–99, Vol. I, Chap. XVIII; and especially John Dewey, "Learning to Earn," *School and Society,* Vol. V (March 24, 1917), pp. 331–35.

publish textbooks the argument was made in educational circles that no state should engage in an undertaking that could be safely left to private effort, since such state activity discouraged authorship and competitive publishing effort and brought a train of other evils.[80]

But doubtless the influence of business on the social outlook and on the policies of educators was largely indirect. Educators accepted, in general, the business man's outlook and consciously or unconsciously molded the school system to accord with the canons of a profit-making economic system. In contrasting educational methods with those of factories, George H. Martin, secretary of the board of education in Boston, noted the crude, unscientific, and wasteful character of the former.[81] As early as 1911 the achievements of Taylor in scientific factory management were associated with the movement for efficiency in education.[82] Efforts were made, by introducing specialized classes, tests, measurements, and new administrative methods, to reduce the waste, speed up the rate of promotion, and increase the efficiency of the schools. "The condition of our schools before about 1890," wrote a leading authority, "was that of a manufacturing establishment running on a low grade of efficiency."[83]

More and more educators, in speaking in terms of efficiency, revealed the influence of business enterprise on their objectives and techniques. With a note of pride one educator wrote that

[80] John Franklin Brown, "State Publication of School Books," *School and Society*, Vol. II (Oct. 2, 1915), pp. 474–85. See also G. Stanley Hall, *Educational Problems* (New York, 1911), Vol. II, p. 572.

[81] N. E. A., *Proceedings*, 1905, p. 821.

[82] J. George Becht, principal of the State Normal School, Clarion, Pa., *ibid.*, 1911, p. 221.

[83] Ellwood P. Cubberley, *Public Education in the United States* (Boston, 1919), p. 378. "The public schools of the United States are, in a sense, a manufactory, doing a half-billion dollar business each year in trying to prepare future citizens for usefulness and efficiency in life."

"the whole drift of present educational thinking is to produce the efficient man, the man related by forceful needs to the world without."[84] William H. Maxwell, superintendent of the New York City public schools, declared that "in a community in which every man had been trained to his highest efficiency the evils of monopoly and poverty would be alike impossible."[85]

In 1900 the president of the National Education Association, Oscar T. Corson, asserted that "the real educational leaders of the age whose influence will be permanent are those who have the business capacity to appreciate and comprehend the business problems which are always a part of the educational problem." He advised that care be exercised "lest we go too far in the modern movement of separating the business and educational management of our schools, and thereby develop the false idea that business and education have nothing in common."[86] It was in the spirit of business practice that a writer on classroom management asserted that on the part of the teacher *"unquestioned obedience* is the first rule of efficient service." The teacher must remember that her relation to her superiors was "entirely analogous to that in . . . the army, navy, governmental departments, great business enterprises."[87] It was even suggested that in devising a hierarchy of teachers, principals, supervisors, and superintendents educators were copying the stratified and feudal society which business leaders were threatening to consolidate.[88] In the great attention which many school authorities gave to the movement for establishing savings banks in the schools for the encouragement of thrift, a move-

[84] James Branch Taylor, *Ed. Rev.,* Vol. XIX (March, 1900), p. 248.
[85] N. E. A., *Proceedings,* 1905, p. 60.   [86] *Ibid.,* 1900, pp. 58–59.
[87] William Chandler Bagley, *Classroom Management* (New York, 1907), pp. 262, 265. A visiting English educator, Anna Burstall, commented on the influence of American business and factory methods on school administration. *Impressions of American Education in 1908* (New York, 1909), pp. 290–91.
[88] William Estabrook Chancellor, *Our Schools, Their Administration and Supervision* (Boston, 1910), pp. 106, 108, 109.

ment sponsored by leading bankers, educators still further demonstrated the influence of financial capitalism on their procedure and methods.[89]

Thus from the days following the surrender at Appomattox, education rendered assistance to industrial and financial capitalism in its struggles with other groups, and helped to promote the spirit of business enterprise which captured America's middle class as well as her captains of industry and finance. Education, in turn, was affected by business methods and purposes. Despite these allegiances, the majority of educators subscribed to the principle of a classless society and advocated greater equality of educational opportunity to achieve that end. They were probably seldom conscious of having a class bias— they were simply supporting the order of things which, as they had grown up in it, seemed inevitably right.

VI

As in the early national period, education was still thought to be the great means of bringing about a democratic and a happy society. The argument that the public school would break down class barriers by bringing together on an equal footing children of rich and poor continued to be heard.[90] In the contest for the extension of the high school and the kindergarten the plea was again and again made that such measures were

[89] Public attention was attracted to this idea as early as 1876 though savings banks were not actually introduced into the schools before 1885. By 1910 such banks existed in 108 cities. In 1916 the Bankers' Association of America launched a campaign to encourage the spread of the movement. See *Report of the Commissioner of Education,* 1888–89, Vol. I, pp. 655–61; California Bankers' Association, *Thrift in Education: A Source Book of Materials with Suggestions for Study in Connection with the Teaching of Thrift* (Los Angeles, 1931); W. Espey Albig, *A History of School Savings Banks in the United States and Its European Beginnings* (New York, 1928).

[90] A. P. Marble, N. E. A., *Proceedings,* 1875, pp. 22–32; C. J. Baxter, *ibid.,* 1898, p. 310; Resolutions, *ibid.,* 1900, p. 31.

necessary to prevent the development of a caste system.[91] When the movement for industrial education was put on foot, some of its stoutest friends maintained that it would achieve the classless society which American life had long promised.[92] Others, like Judd and Dewey, sounded the warning that industrial schools, particularly if separated from those preparing for the professions and leadership in business, would accentuate existing differences.[93]

In advocating more extensive educational opportunities to bring about a classless society educators unconsciously admitted the existence of classes. Yet, in their desire to prevent class conflict, many at the same time insisted that there was no antagonism between various groups and preached in and out of season the existence of a solidarity of interest.[94] As Professor Coe has pointed out, they thus substituted the doctrine that there ought not to be a class struggle for an inquiry into the actual tensions in society. The effect of this substitution was to leave the causes of tension almost untouched, and to provide a "specious justification for whatever element in society happened to have the economic upper hand, and a specious condemnation of opposing elements."[95]

The ideal of a classless society, if tenaciously held by educators, might be expected to influence them in various ways. It might lead them to revolt against the support they were giv-

[91] For example: John Hancock, N. E. A., *Proceedings,* 1879, p. 15; J. W. Dickinson, *ibid.,* pp. 22, 26; J. E. Seaman, *ibid.,* 1885, p. 177; Grace Everett Barnard, *ibid.,* 1907, p. 460.
[92] For example: Henry S. Pritchett, *Ed. Rev.,* Vol. XXIII (March, 1902), p. 300; Herbert Stebbins, *ibid.* (May, 1902), p. 466.
[93] *Cf. post,* Chaps. XV, XVI.
[94] Richard T. Ely was exceptional in pointing out that what was needed in the teaching of economics in high school was not "namby-pamby talk about a non-existent harmony of interests, but a presentation of the real facts of life with their conflicts of interests and all their requirements in the way of self-control, obedience, and command." *Ed. Rev.,* Vol. XX (Sept., 1900), pp. 155–56.
[95] George A. Coe, *Educating for Citizenship* (New York, 1932), p. 164.

ing to industrial capitalism and to endeavor to transform society into a quite different and economically democratic order. Or it might make them attempt to reform such contradictions of democracy as the disenfranchisement of women, the exploitation of child labor, the graft in city politics. Having seen to what extent educators as a group aided business in its struggles with its rivals, we should not expect to find many following the more radical path. But efforts at reform might well be expected of educators since they, as a body, were not of the most privileged class and since their task of building the school system was still, as in the earlier period, something of a crusade for collective responsibility and social control, and thus allied them with the more liberal elements of the community. Before examining the social philosophy of the most outstanding leaders, it may be well to determine whether or not educators as a group led or followed in the reform movements which were frankly aimed to palliate evils of the existing order without seriously affecting its basic character.

VII

Of all the sores within the existing system one would suppose child labor to have come closest home to educational leaders. In addressing the National Education Association in 1905 Jane Addams took its members to task for not having given greater help in past campaigns against child labor, and called on them to take a more militant stand in the future.[96] In the surprisingly few addresses on this subject before the Association, there was a tendency to blame the parents' greed and laxness for the violations of existing child labor laws and compulsory school attendance regulations, an attitude the more understandable because the indictment of parents was so often true. Lawton

[96] N. E. A., *Proceedings*, p. 260.

B. Evans, superintendent of schools in Augusta, Georgia, declared in 1904 and again in 1911 that mill authorities generally permitted children to work only because of the pressure of the insistent parent, and no one arose to suggest that if parents were better paid, they might be more apt to keep their children in school.[97] Even the rather belated resolutions which the National Education Association passed on child labor implied that parents were more responsible than operators for its existence.[98] In writing of the marked advance made in the first two decades of the twentieth century in anti-child labor legislation and in compulsory school attendance laws, E. P. Cubberley admitted that such social legislation was due more to the efforts of groups interested in improving the physical and moral welfare of children than to educators themselves.[99]

In view of the fact that they so generally shared the social views of business men, educators could hardly have been expected to help develop a class conscious and militant educational movement among adult workers, or even to have sponsored the proposals of laborers who desired to improve their status without overturning the existing order. It was left to labor to elaborate its own educational program and to make known what it desired.

Although the National Labor Union, the Knights of Labor, and the American Federation of Labor, which successively dominated the workers' movements during this period, differed somewhat in their educational programs, all agreed on certain essentials. Wages and conditions of labor, not the public schools, were, of course, their first consideration. William H. Sylvis, a pioneer in the organization of the iron

97 *Ibid.*, 1914, pp. 244–49; 1911, p. 178.
98 *Ibid.*, 1907, p. 29; 1908, p. 37. The first resolution on child labor and compulsory school attendance seems to have been passed in 1902. *Ibid.*, 1902, p. 26.
99 Cubberley, *Public Education*, p. 380.

moulders and the National Labor Union, insisted that as long
as workingmen were compelled to labor to the point of excessive
fatigue to keep the wolf from the door, they could not be expected to improve their general intelligence and culture, or
even to take full advantage of such educational opportunities
as existed. Additional mechanics' institutes, reading and lecture rooms, desirable though they were for self-improvement
during leisure time, could be of little significance until they
were accompanied by an eight-hour day.[100]

In the early eighties demands were made for the effective
abolition of child labor and compulsory school attendance in
common schools.[101] The A. F. of L. asked for higher standards
of compulsory education with increasing definiteness as the
years passed.[102] This organization did not greet with enthusiasm, as did the Knights of Labor, the introduction of practical
studies, such as manual training, into the school curriculum.
Jealous of its control over the skilled labor market, it somewhat
hesitantly approved industrial education in the public school
system, and insisted that this instruction should not be controlled in the interests of employers.[103]

The A. F. of L. in 1903 formally indicted the point of view
that taught workers to be content with their lot and that
argued from the exceptional instance of the worker who rose

[100] James C. Sylvis, *The Life, Speeches, Labors and Essays of William H.
Sylvis* (Philadelphia, 1872), pp. 97, 113. Sylvis assumed that labor was the
real source of all wealth, denied the identity of interests between labor and
capital, and demanded the militant organization of workers as well as political
action.
[101] Philip R. V. Curoe, *Educational Attitudes and Policies of Organized Labor in the United States* (Teachers College, Columbia University, Contributions
to Education, No. 201, New York, 1926, pp. 81, 107.
[102] *Ibid.*, p. 107.
[103] Gompers as early as 1889 opposed public trade schools on the ground
that they would create scabs. Gompers to Emil Applehagen, Duluth, Feb. 16,
1889, Gompers MSS., A. F. of L. Headquarters. I am indebted to Miss Phyllis
Freeman for this reference. See also *Industrial Education,* published by A. F.
of L. (Washington, 1910), pp. 14–15.

out of his class. Instruction, it was urged, must promote the idea that the hope of workers lay in the elevation of the working class as a class. Greater attention to the social studies was requested, and texts in use in those subjects were criticized for failing to give due importance to the dignity and services of labor.[104] Yet in emphasizing the training of skilled workers the A. F. of L. left largely out of account the economic and cultural well-being of the mass of unskilled laborers.

At the very end of the period Samuel Gompers advocated before the National Education Association the view which Dewey had popularized: he insisted that education should provide so wide an understanding of the relation of one's work to society that no vocation could become a rut and no worker could be shut off from a full and rich life in his work itself.[105] The Federation also consistently worked for a larger measure of federal support for education, the representation of labor on boards of education, and, after 1902, for better wages for teachers and for their affiliation with organized labor.[106]

Even such left-wing groups as Socialists, Anarchists, and the I. W. W. offered a criticism of the existing system of schools and presented a philosophy of education which, however thorough-going and opposed to the existing economic order, contained suggestions to which educators might listen. The Socialists and Anarchists, considering the schools to be entirely dominated by the capitalist class, which used them for indoctrinating the rising generation with its own economic views, did not expect the schools to contribute appreciably to the realization of their utopias. Yet the Anarchists demanded less regimentation and greater individual freedom, while the Socialists desired, even under capitalism, free clothes and free

[104] Curoe, *op. cit.*, p. 113.
[105] N. E. A., *Proceedings*, 1916, p. 182.
[106] Curoe, *op. cit.*, pp. 126 *et seq.*, pp. 137 *et seq.*

lunches to enable the poorest people to keep their children in the public schools.[107]

Educators were not entirely indifferent to the needs of the working class and to the programs of its spokesmen. Although some maintained that the schools should simply teach the worker to accept his place, do his job like a man, and find satisfaction in the thought that by earning his bread he was contributing to the well-being of society,[108] others believed that with more adequate educational opportunities laborers would be able to improve their position. The Emersonian demand that the dignity of labor should be recognized in the school was frequently re-echoed in educational circles.[109]

To demonstrate the money value of education to the individual statistical studies began to appear. Though open to serious criticism because of the factors which were not considered, these studies all tended to confirm the belief that in providing the lower classes with education those who directed and supported the schools were helping the child of the worker to improve his status.[110] Like Jefferson, educators believed that the public school gave the more gifted child of the lower class an opportunity to rise to the level above him. Though this point of view neglected the economic and cultural claims of the average child of the working class, it was thoroughly in accord with the American doctrine that the best man gets to the top.

Finally, educators said a good deal about the cultural values

107 John S. Gambs, *The Decline of the I. W. W.* (New York, 1932), pp. 156–57; *Ed. Rev.*, Vol. XV (Jan., 1898), pp. 1–16.

108 For example, George H. Howison, "What the Public School Should Teach the American Laborer," N. E. A., *Proceedings*, 1888, pp. 243–49, and W. N. Ackley, "The True American Idea of Labor," *ibid.*, pp. 238–43.

109 For example: Samuel T. Dutton, *Ed. Rev.*, Vol. XII (Nov., 1896), pp. 343; Henry S. Pritchett, *ibid.*, Vol. XXIII (March, 1902), pp. 297–98.

110 A. Caswell Ellis, *The Money Value of Education* (Bureau of Education, Bulletin No. 22, 1917), p. 44.

which the schools provided to the children of even the humblest origin. Notwithstanding this emphasis, however, the great majority of those who passed through the public schools regarded education as "a narrowly practical tool with which to get bread and butter enough to eke out a restricted life."[111] Few took very seriously the criticism of Simon N. Patten who, in 1911, challenged educators to show how the teaching of morality and culture without a definite increase in income profited the underprivileged or improved public morality and general culture.[112]

More specific efforts were also made to help the worker. It was hoped that the kindergarten would give children in the slums a somewhat better start in life.[113] In spite of the opposition of the Knights of Labor to the high school, which was regarded as an institution for the middle classes, educators contended that the extension of the secondary school would enable the child from the lower ranks to prepare himself for positions of leadership in the ranks of business and even in the professions.[114] In urging factory owners to follow the example of the National Cash Register Company, which provided its help with rest rooms, a library, lectures, entertainments, and even free lunches, George Bicknell argued that "the class struggle and the question of proper distribution of wealth would be solved."[115] In similar vein, and not without opposition, others urged teachers and school authorities to make the school a philanthropic and useful social centre for the material and cultural

[111] John Dewey, *The School and Society* (Chicago, 1900), pp. 42–43.
[112] F. C. Ensign, *Compulsory School Attendance and Child Labor*, pp. 85, 233.
[113] For example: N. E. A., *Proceedings*, 1896, pp. 496–97; *Report of the Commissioner of Education*, 1878, pp. lxxvi–lxxvii; 1914, Vol. I, p. xviii.
[114] N. E. A., *Proceedings*, 1873, pp. 23, 31; 1879, p. 26; *Report of the Commissioner of Education*, 1886–87, p. 1019; *Ed. Rev.*, Vol. II (July, 1891), p. 136.
[115] *Inland Educator* (Sept., 1899), pp. 65–69.

elevation of the working class.[116] In rare instances attention was called to the economic distress that drove children out of the school and into the factory; and in 1905 William Maxwell, superintendent of the New York schools, in speaking of the malnutrition of school children, urged boards of education to provide noonday lunches at the lowest possible cost.[117] In a very restricted way a few such experiments, socialistic though they seemed to some, were begun.

Something was also done to meet the contention of labor that the curricula of the schools should be more practical. Realizing that the more classical high school studies could not greatly interest nor equip children of the lower classes, efforts were made as the period advanced to introduce more useful subjects. The voice of Franklin still echoed. Many advocates of industrial schools sincerely believed that such schools would promote the well-being of the laboring class. The indictment that the schools taught a sterile culture which had served the middle class in the past, but which offered little of practical value to the rising lower classes, was heard with increasing frequency after 1905.[118]

Even a beginning was made in what might be called adult education. Whether or not in response to the demands of the militant trade unionist, William Sylvis, as early as 1870 Commissioner Eaton took a real interest in the development of evening classes for employees, and some progress was made in that direction.[119] Educators encouraged the development of

[116] Lucia Stickney, N. E. A., *Proceedings*, 1899, pp. 388–92; Howard Rogers, *Ed. Rev.*, Vol. XXX (Sept., 1905), p. 135.

[117] Maxwell, *A Quarter Century*, p. 402.

[118] *Report of the Commissioner of Education*, 1915, Vol. I, pp. 223–24; N. E. A., *Proceedings*, 1914, p. 130.

[119] *Report of the Commissioner of Education*, 1870, pp. 53–55, 439–47; 1875, p. clxiv. See also the presidential address of Thomas W. Bicknell, N. E. A., *Proceedings*, 1884, pp. 65 *et seq.;* resolution, *ibid.*, 1905, p. 43. Henry Leipziger of New York City was a pioneer in bringing adult education into the school system, *ibid.*, 1904, pp. 284–94.

public libraries,[120] and the achievement of university extension work, however little it meant to the mass of workers, was due almost solely to educational pioneers.[121] Encouragement was also given to the Chautauqua movement. Although it reached only the middle classes, it popularized a meliorism which called attention to the conditions of the working poor, the advantages of better housing, profit-sharing, and other reforms beneficial to working people.[122] If few laborers profited directly from these efforts to develop adult education, Thomas Davidson, who founded Bread-Winners' College in the slums of New York in 1898, reached a larger number. However drastically he chided his class for their Marxist leanings, he made the culture of the past seem attractive to many who earned their living by the sweat of their brows.[123]

Rarely did educators in the seventies and eighties express sympathy with the militant struggles of workers. The Reverend A. D. Mayo was apparently alone in declaring that the best thing about the groping, superstitious, and downtrodden laboring man was his discontent, "even if it flare up sometimes into violence and threatens society itself; for of all the pitiful sights on God's earth, the most deplorable is a grown man content with such a deplorable lot as the life of the ignorant laborer must be in this land, in this age of liberty and light."[124]

Equally exceptional was the more militant and consistent

---

[120] *Report of the Commissioner of Education,* 1873, pp. lxxxviii–xciv; 1874, pp. lxxxix–xcii; 1886–87, p. 901; 1903, Vol. I, Chap. XVIII.

[121] *School and Society,* Vol. XII (July 10, 1920), pp. 31 *et seq.; Ed. Rev.,* Vol. II (Oct., 1891), pp. 220–30; N. E. A., *Proceedings,* 1891, p. 37.

[122] J. H. Vincent, *The Chautauqua Movement* (Boston, 1886), pp. v–viii, 4–5, 9, 13–14; C. R. Henderson, *The Social Spirit in America* (Meadville, Pa., 1897), pp. 26–27, 68–69, 101–2, 104–5, 107–10, 135–36, 173; Richard T. Ely, *The Strength and Weakness of Socialism* (New York, 1894, 1899); N. E. A., *Proceedings,* 1879, p. 16; 1880, p. 5.

[123] Thomas Davidson, *Education of the Wage Earners* (Boston, 1904), pp. 43–45, 190 *et seq.*

[124] A. D. Mayo, *American Brains in American Hands* (Manhattan, Kansas, 1885), pp. 7–8.

position of Margaret Haley of Chicago, a pioneer in the movement for teachers' unions and for their affiliation with the
A. F. of L. Miss Haley, a classroom teacher, declared before
the National Education Association in 1904 that public school
teachers must recognize the fact that their struggle to maintain the efficiency of the schools through better conditions for
themselves was part of the same great struggle which manual
workers had been making for humanity through their efforts
to secure living conditions for themselves and their children.
She unequivocally called on the public school to aid the workers in their struggle to secure a more equitable distribution of
the products of their labor. The school must fight political corruption, even when "good business men" were at the back of it.
The anarchy which should be feared in America, she asserted,
was "the anarchy which sends the railroad and corporation
lobby to the legislatures and to the taxing bodies—yes, even
to the bench." She took pride in the services of the unionized
Chicago teachers in disclosing the robbery perpetrated by the
five public utility corporations and in forcing them to return
"some of the stolen millions."

Miss Haley also fought the tendency toward "factoryizing
education"—a tendency which, she argued, made the teacher
an automaton, a mere factory hand who was expected to carry
out orders without question. Such servility, together with inadequate pay and insecure tenure, militated against efficient
teaching and the protection of the child and of society. If the
ideal of democracy, which placed humanity above commercialism and the machine and which demanded the full expression of life for every human being, Miss Haley insisted, were
not carried by educators into the industrial field, then the
ideal of industry would triumph in the school.[125]

[125] Margaret Haley, "Why Teachers Should Organize," N. E. A., *Proceedings,* 1904, pp. 145–52.

But most educational leaders, as well as the rank and file of teachers, remained deaf to such appeals as that of this outspoken Catholic woman. Influential authorities argued that the unionization of teachers was prompted by selfish devotion to class interest and by the unbridled ambition of a small coterie of teachers who made their bread and butter out of agitation. They argued that affiliation with the A. F. of L. was the prostitution of the well-being of all children to the interests of the laboring class.[126] One metropolitan superintendent asserted that, whatever the conditions under which they worked, no worthy teacher would ever feel justified in going out on strike.[127] Ellwood P. Cubberley wrote that teachers' organizations might unintentionally but nevertheless seriously interfere with the proper and effective working of school administrative officers.[128] Though progressive administrators tolerated and even encouraged teachers' councils as a substitute for teachers' unions, John Dewey was almost alone among educational leaders in blessing the union movement and in contributing to its development.[129]

Without committing themselves to the Socialist doctrine that the existing industrial order must be entirely remade along fundamentally democratic and collectivist principles, a handful of educators went further than the conservative labor unions in their criticisms of the existing order and in their advocacy of a more equitable distribution of wealth in the interest of the underprivileged. As early as 1888 the attention of the National Education Association was called to pressing evils in the distribution of capital. "Colossal fortunes by the side of hopeless

[126] *Ed. Rev.*, Vol. XXX (Nov., 1905), pp. 344–74; *School and Society*, Vol. X (Nov. 8, 1918), pp. 535–38.

[127] William H. Maxwell, *Ed. Rev.*, Vol. XXV (Feb., 1903), p. 163.

[128] Introduction, John C. Almack and Albert R. Lang, *Problems of the Teaching Profession* (Boston, 1925), p. vi.

[129] John Dewey, "Professional Organization of Teachers," *American Teacher*, Vol. V (Sept., 1916), pp. 99–101.

and terrible poverty is evidence of blundering not in production but in distribution, in education, and consequently in government and religion," declared R. K. Buehrle, of Lancaster, Pennsylvania. With proper education it was possible, Buehrle thought, to prevent the rise of monopoly and to effect greater justice in the distribution of goods. The school, especially through the historical and social sciences, must demonstrate the scientific and political necessity of realizing in fact the Christian slogan, "Bear ye one another's burdens." This was the only suggestion, apparently, within the ranks of the Association that anarchism might be due to something besides moral depravity. But even this criticism of the existing economic order ascribed its shortcomings to man's moral and spiritual nature, and stopped short of a diagnosis of fundamental strains and cleavages.[130]

Three years later another lonely and even apologetic voice called on the teaching body to utilize the school for the reform of an industrial system which had bred slaves as well as tramps.[131] Before the turn of the century I. W. Howerth, influenced by Lester Ward and the Fabians, indicted in an uncompromising fashion a profit-making economy and demanded the substitution of a democratic and co-operative for a competitive and ruthlessly unjust society.[132] In 1908 Edgar James Swift, in his provocative book, *Mind in the Making,* urged the need of a survey to demonstrate the "inherent antagonism of our industrial system to education." He declared that the schools must correct the defects in the economic order if they were to do even their specifically educational work.

130 N. E. A., *Proceedings*, 1888, pp. 173–82.
131 S. Jones, *ibid.*, 1891, p. 101.
132 I. W. Howerth, "The Social Aim in Education," *Fifth Yearbook of the National Herbart Society*, 1899, pp. 69–108; *Ed. Rev.*, Vol. XX (Nov., 1900), pp. 346–56; Vol. XXIII (April, 1902), pp. 355–70; *Work and Life: A Study of the Social Problems of Today* (New York, 1913).

Every educator, he continued, must know enough about the distribution of wealth and the income of society to enable him to understand how matters could be arranged to permit all children and all youths to receive a full education.[133] But such positions were very exceptional—a fact that makes the social thinking of John Dewey the more significant.[134]

Since isolated voices were raised within educational circles and were re-enforced by well-known writers outside the field, the conservatism of the directors of the public schools appears even more striking. Many must have been familiar with the teachings of Henry George, who denied that the existing education enabled a man to use his natural powers effectively and insisted that, under the prevalent economic system, it could not possibly exert so magical an influence. At best education could raise wages, he declared, only so far as it made men discontented with a state of things which condemned producers to a life of toil while non-producers lolled in luxury.[135] The almost equally well-known Henry D. Lloyd urged a new type of school for the realization of a more equitable social order. Let the unemployed, he argued, be put into communities where the youth could produce food, raw materials, and manufactures, in a spirit of true play and real education.[136] Thus might education promote a more just social system and at the same time provide an experience similar to that Dewey had advocated a few years earlier.[137]

[133] Edgar James Swift, *Mind in the Making* (New York, 1908), pp. 305–6, 325–26. On June 18, 1932, Professor Swift wrote the author that he was and had long been a Socialist.

[134] *Post,* Chap. XV.

[135] Henry George, *Progress and Poverty* (Garden City, N. Y., 1919), p. 306.

[136] Henry Demarest Lloyd, *Wealth Against Commonwealth* (New York, 1894), p. 534; *Mazzini and Other Essays* (New York, 1910), pp. 224–25; *Man, the Social Creator* (New York, 1906), pp. 179–80, 198.

[137] The criticism of the class character of higher education made by Edward Bellamy in *Looking Backward* (Boston, 1888, 1889), pp. 66, 221, must have been known to educators, also.

VIII

If educators on the whole turned a deaf ear to the more thoroughgoing demands of organized labor and the Socialists, and if they paid slight attention to Henry George and H. D. Lloyd, their efforts to promote the health of school children did fall as a greater blessing on the poor than on those better able to provide medical care, playgrounds, and healthful environment for their boys and girls. The interest of school administrators and teachers fairly closely followed the agitation for generally better physical well-being. Even before Herbert Spencer's gospel of the responsibility of education for good health reached America in the 1860's, Mann, Barnard, and their colleagues had pointed out the relation of school architecture to the health of children and had taken steps to facilitate instruction in hygiene.[138] About the same time that Spencer's emphasis on health stirred up American educators, Dio Lewis was carrying on an effective propaganda for putting physical culture into the schools; and, after 1880, his work was continued by others.[139]

Beginning with its first report in 1868 the Bureau of Education begged administrators to realize the importance of school hygiene and instruction in the principles of health, and at the same time acquainted them with the type of medical inspection of schools that European countries had already inaugurated.[140] The Committee of Fifteen, in making its report on curricula

[138] *Ante,* pp. 111, 159; *American Annals of Education and Instruction,* Vol. V (1835), *passim;* Vol. VII (Nov., 1837), pp. 515–16; Caleb Mills, *Address,* 1847, pp. 449–50; Charles Brooks, *Elementary Instruction* (Quincy, 1837), pp. 5–8.

[139] Doctor E. M. Hartwell, "On Physical Training," *Report of the Commissioner of Education,* 1903, Vol I, Chap. XVII.

[140] *Report of the Commissioner of Education,* 1868, pp. xiii–xiv, 823; 1872, p. lxxvii; 1873, p. cxxv; 1875, pp. cliv–clxiv; 1876, pp. clvii–clxi; 1880, pp. ccl–cclv; 1881, p. cxvi; 1884–85, pp. clx–clxii; 1887–88, p. 179; 1891–92, Vol. I, pp. xix–xx; 1909, Vol. I, pp. 7–9.

in 1895, recommended some form of daily exercise, amounting to one hour each week, and weekly oral lessons in natural science which should include physiology and hygiene, with special reference to the effects of stimulants, as required by state laws.[141] Both the National Education Association and the profession's periodicals gave some attention to the problem.[142] But the prevalent doctrine of *laissez faire,* the difficulty of finding funds, and possibly the tendency of educators to talk rather than to agitate and demand, prevented a great deal from actually being done.

It was not until 1894 that medical inspection was begun in American schools in any thoroughgoing manner, and as late as 1905 it was provided for in only fifty-five cities.[143] When the second international congress of school hygiene met in 1907, the United States was only scantily represented, and physicians took a more active rôle than did educators.[144] But within the next half dozen years the White House Conference on Child Health and the eugenics movement stimulated interest. Headway was made in providing for dental inspection, general physical examination, and remedial measures for defective vision and hearing.[145] Meanwhile educators had begun to realize the importance of giving special attention to defective children; and gradually the idea gained acceptance that the public schools must assume responsibility for their training.[146] Toward the

[141] Committee of Fifteen, *Ed. Rev.,* Vol. IX (March, 1895), pp. 261–62.

[142] In 1895 the N. E. A. inaugurated the new department of physical education, which, according to its spokesman, "raised the 'new idea' from the orphanage of 'faddism' to the dignity of a child of education." *Proceedings,* 1895, p. 946.

[143] *Report of the Commissioner of Education,* 1911, Vol. I, pp. 19–20.

[144] *Ibid.,* 1907, Vol. I, Chap. X.

[145] *Ibid.,* 1911, Vol. I, pp. 19–20; Luther Halsey Gulick and Leonard P. Ayres, *Medical Inspection of Schools* (New York, 1908).

[146] *Report of the Commissioner of Education,* 1902, Chap. XLVII; *Ed. Rev.,* Vol. IV (June, 1892), pp. 16–26; Vol. III (April, 1892), pp. 348–54; Vol. XVIII (June, 1899), pp. 15–22; Vol. XLIV (June, 1912), pp. 62–69; N. E. A., *Proceedings,* 1908, pp. 345–85.

end of the period a beginning was made in sex instruction.[147]

In support of all this extension of school activity it was argued that social maladjustments now made it impossible to thrust the entire responsibility for the health of children on parents. It was also pointed out that the rapid urbanization of American life required schools to assume many of the functions that could safely be left to nature in a simpler society. A good deal was also said about the necessity of removing physical impediments if children were to be made responsive to the educative process. Some even maintained that if the state was to be perpetuated it must assure its wards the physical well-being upon which their mental ability and their morals so largely depended.

An important stimulus to the introduction of physiology in the curriculum came from the pressure of the anti-alcohol crusaders. Though the pre-Civil War educators favored temperance instruction, early teaching was moral and general rather than scientific in character. About 1878 Mary Hanchett Hunt, an ardent advocate of abstinence, conceived the idea of engrafting on the school system graded lessons in hygiene and temperance. As a result of effective lobbying every state by 1901 required such instruction in the schools. Even before 1892, when she began to edit *School Physiology,* a journal for teachers, Mrs. Hunt had stimulated publishers to prepare texts in physiology intended to indoctrinate children with fear of the effects of alcoholic liquor. As early as 1884 the National Education Association expressed profound satisfaction with the efforts of the W. C. T. U. to secure instruction in physiology "with par-

---

147 *Ed. Rev.,* Vol. XLI (Jan., 1911), pp. 42–59; *School and Society,* Vol. I (Jan. 2, 1915), p. 7; J. E. Russell, *The Trend in American Education,* p. 173; Jane Addams, *McClure's Magazine,* Vol. XXXVIII (June, 1912), pp. 338–44; *Eighth Yearbook of the National Society for the Scientific Study of Education,* 1909. Much approval was expressed when the Chicago Board of Education vetoed Ella Flagg Young's proposal for sex instruction in the schools. *Ed. Rev.,* Vol. XLVI (Oct., 1913), pp. 318–19.

ticular reference to the effects of alcoholic stimulants upon the human system."[148] The movement was also sponsored by the commissioners of education;[149] and although some opposition was expressed,[150] on the whole prohibitionists found responsive friends in the directors of the public schools.

It was asserted in temperance quarters that the victory of their principles would lessen crime,[151] a problem that had long remained a thorn in the flesh of educators. The early arguments that crime would disappear if everyone received common schooling[152] proved somewhat embarrassing, since it was plain that such predictions were hardly borne out by the facts. Nevertheless the first commissioners of education brought forward evidence to prove that there was a positive correlation between crime and the lack of school education.[153] Others, however, urged that more specific and effective moral education alone could diminish or remove crime.[154] Still others contended that the failure to vitalize play by providing swimming pools, playgrounds, and the like, was responsible for much anti-social behavior on the part of children and laid the foundations for later crime.[155] It was also urged that an effective

[148] N. E. A., *Proceedings*, 1884, p. 15. Frances Willard had addressed the N. E. A. in 1875, urging teachers to make themselves a force in the temperance movement. *Ibid.*, 1875, pp. 181–86.

[149] *Report of the Commissioner of Education*, 1883–84, p. xli; 1889–90, Vol. I, p. xx; 1902, Vol. II, Chap. VI, pp. 695–742.

[150] *Ed. Rev.*, Vol. XXIII (March, 1902), pp. 233–49; *ibid.*, Vol. XXIV (Oct., 1902), p. 323.

[151] N. E. A., *Proceedings*, 1884, p. 70.

[152] For example: Francis Lieber, *Remarks on the Relation between Education and Crime in a letter to the Right Reverend William White* (Philadelphia, 1835); Caleb Mills, *An Address to the Legislature of Indiana*, 1847, pp. 494–96, 437; *New York Teacher* (Dec., 1852), p. 73; Cyrus Pierce, *Crime: Its Cause and Cure* (Boston, 1854), *passim*.

[153] *Report of the Commissioner of Education*, 1872, pp. 586–95; 1874, pp. cx–cxx; 1877, pp. cciii–ccv; 1898–99, Vol. II, Chap. XXVIII; 1893–94, Vol. II, Chap. XIV.

[154] N. E. A., *Proceedings*, 1875, pp. 118–20.

[155] N. E. A., *ibid.*, 1909, pp. 737–43.

damper might be put on crime by checking truancy through effective compulsory attendance laws and by multiplying juvenile courts, which would work with the schools.[156]

IX

Although the peace movement was as old as the temperance crusade, its exponents found greater difficulty in persuading educators to respond favorably to its pressure. It was not until the United States, by participating in the Hague conferences, seemed to give more than lip service to international peace, that its friends succeeded in thoroughly committing the National Education Association to the cause. In 1907 a resolution was passed calling on teachers to study the work of the Hague Conference and of the peace societies.[157] A few years later the Association formally endorsed the American School Peace League; and by 1915 the Bureau of Education was circulating 100,000 of its bulletins, which were designed to furnish materials for commemorating the opening of the first Hague Conference—Peace Day.[158] In 1910 the National Education Association expressed profound satisfaction with President Taft's overture for the settlement by arbitration of "all differences whatever between nations."[159] A hearing was also given to such outstanding foes of war as David Starr Jordan, the Baroness von Suttner, and William Jennings Bryan.[160]

The peace program of the schools emphasized international friendship, arbitration, and restriction of armaments—the tenets, in short, of the more conservative wing of the peace move-

[156] *Ed. Rev.,* Vol. XXXIII (April, 1907), pp. 374–85.

[157] N. E. A., *Proceedings,* 1907, pp. 30–31, 58–62. A somewhat favorable resolution was passed in 1895, *ibid.,* 1895, p. 32.

[158] *Report of the Commissioner of Education,* 1905, Vol. I, pp. l–li; *School and Society,* Vol. I (April 3, 1915), p. 495.

[159] N. E. A., *Proceedings,* 1910, p. 36.

[160] *Ibid.,* pp. 61–71; 1912, pp. 316–19; 1916, pp. 77–79.

ment. Arguments were indeed made in behalf of history texts that devoted less space to wars and showed their destructive effects, but little headway was made in securing their adoption.[161] Nothing at all was said of the relationship between economic factors and war. Moreover, such progress as was made in securing peace instruction in the schools counted for little when weighed in the balance with the uncritical patriotism that was being taught everywhere with increasing intensity.[162] The distinguished historian, John Bach McMaster, expressed a common view when in 1898 he declared that history should be so taught as to convince students that as a people we had been animated by the highest and noblest ideals of humanity, and that there was no land "where the people are so prosperous, so happy, so intelligent, so bent on doing what is just and right as the people of the United States."[163]

Considering the increasing number of women who filled the teaching ranks, educators might have been expected to champion the movement for the further emancipation of that sex. Driven by economic and social forces the influence of women in American life greatly increased during this period, but educators hardly led in the efforts to cast off the shackles of tradition. President Eliot long supported the conventional view which put their intellectual ability below that of men;[164] and many agreed with G. Stanley Hall in thinking that

[161] Wilbur F. Gordy, *ibid.*, 1909, pp. 88–91; *Ed. Rev.*, Vol. XXXVIII (Sept., 1909), pp. 181–86. For a statement of the program of the American School Peace League, founded by Fanny Fern Andrews, see her article in *School and Society*, Vol. IV (Aug. 5, 1916), pp. 194–97.

[162] For example, see Andrew S. Draper, *Ed. Rev.*, Vol. I (Jan., 1891), p. 29; N. E. A., *Proceedings*, 1892, p. 248; Wm. A. Mowry, *Proceedings of the International Congress of Education* (Chicago, 1893), pp. 273–78; Robert Blair, *Some Features of American Education* (Dept. of Agriculture and Technical Instruction for Ireland, Bulletin No. 8, Misc. Series, 1904), p. 17; *Reports of the Mosely Educational Commission to the United States of America*, p. 298.

[163] *Fourth Yearbook of the National Herbart Society*, 1898, pp. 29–30.

[164] Thomas Woody, *History of Women's Education in the United States*, Vol. I, p. 88.

their proper sphere was still in the home. If women not only constituted the largest part of the teaching profession but also made use of the increasing opportunities to secure higher education, their place in the meetings of the National Education Association and in the professional periodicals was not proportionate to their numbers and training.

Here and there one did speak up rather plaintively in defense of her drably dressed colleagues who were, largely for economic reasons, driving men out of the lower ranks of the profession.[165] Perhaps, in view of the humble economic status of the average woman teacher, she counted for as much as any one might expect. In 1910 the typical woman teacher came from a family whose income was about $800 a year and, in earning slightly more than half that amount, was on a lower economic level than the skilled manual worker.[166]

It was not until 1909 that a woman reached a position of influence in the profession. In that year Ella Flagg Young, a pioneer in progressive education, became superintendent of the Chicago schools, and two years later she was made the first woman president of the National Education Association despite the report of the committee on nominations, which favored a man. At the session over which she presided the cause of woman's suffrage was officially endorsed by the Association. On the whole, in spite of the reliance on women to conduct the schools, those who directed them and spoke for education did little to advance the movement for the greater equality and well-being of those who taught the young.

[165] "Pretty Dresses on $350 a Year," *Common School Education*, Vol. I (June, 1887), pp. 231–32.

[166] Lotus D. Coffman, *The Social Composition of the Teaching Population* (Teachers College, Columbia University, Contributions to Education, No. 41, New York, 1911), p. 80.

X

Confronted by the harmful effects on the schools of the scandalous graft and corruption in politics, educational leaders spoke out against political jobbery. In 1891 the civil service reformer, George William Curtis, asked superintendents to work for the extension of the merit system to public education;[167] and eight years later the National Education Association, in a unanimous resolution, attacked the prevalent practice of political interference with the schools.[168] A few educators stand out for their courageous and persistent fights against the "rings" which tainted the administration of the schools with fraud and graft. Among these John Swett of California and William H. Maxwell of Brooklyn and New York are representative.[169] While a professional periodical now and then came to the support of a political reformer like Theodore Roosevelt[170] and attacked Tammany outright,[171] Margaret Haley's vigorous fight against the tax-dodging franchise corporations in Chicago was exceptional.[172]

Most educators preferred to attack the problem of political corruption through the safer medium of character education or citizenship training in the schools. If it seemed to a few cynics and Socialists that all Theodore Roosevelt's talk about righteous men making for righteous politics was twaddle, educators were not of their number. They not only held up the righteous president as an example, but redoubled their own efforts to

[167] N. E. A., *Proceedings*, 1891, pp. 481–93.
[168] *Ibid.*, 1899, p. 31.
[169] John Swett, *Public Education in California*, Chaps. IX, X, pp. 205 *et seq.*, pp. 239 *et seq.*; N. M. Butler, preface to Maxwell, *A Quarter Century*, p. vii.
[170] *Inland Educator* (Aug., 1899), p. 4.
[171] *Ed. Rev.*, Vol. XV (Feb., Mar., 1896), pp. 196, 300–6.
[172] Dr. A. E. Winship, "A Woman's Victory for Schools," *Everybody's Magazine*, Vol. VII (Oct., 1902), pp. 393–96.

train up a generation imbued with his moral fervor and pugnacity.

The Herbartians were foremost among educators who believed that the reform of the individual was the chief task of the school and that individual morality would be an all-sufficient cure for the social injustice of the day. They worked out methods of teaching morals through literature and history.[173]

This ideal of the good man who is also an intelligent citizen, which was upheld by the Herbartians and many others, while certainly an ideal of considerable social value, placed too much confidence in knowledge as power. It also over-simplified the relation of the good citizen to social and economic forces in the face of which he, as an individual, was impotent, in spite of his knowledge and goodness. It likewise held a danger of diverting the good will of upright citizens into merely moral and individualistic channels of action when a program of social action was needed. By centering attention upon the development of moral quality in men and women, it overlooked, of course, the possibility that the existing system itself might be immoral.

As an educational goal, this ideal looked to the solution of social problems *in the future*. The educational emphasis on character, derived from the Christian religion, was originally directed toward achieving eternal salvation rather than toward bettering the here and the now. Transferred to the problems of social improvement, the technique of character training militated against immediate action, either through organized political pressure or through revolution. Considering the gen-

[173] Frank McMurry, in *First Yearbook of the Herbart Society*, 1895, p. 62; Charles De Garmo, *Herbart and the Herbartians*, p. 113; *Interest and Education* (New York, 1904), p. 82; *Principles of Secondary Education*, Vol. III: *Ethical Training* (New York, 1910), p. 24; Charles McMurry, *The Elements of General Method*, p. 9.

eral optimism of the American people, their belief in the future, their certainty that however bad things might be, they were not so bad as elsewhere and would certainly become better tomorrow, this emphasis on character education was not merely escapist. It was a faith that arose from fundamental convictions of the great body of American people, and it corresponded to a social program not generally questioned until the helplessness and disillusionment that followed the crash of 1929.

Underneath most of the civic education lay the assumption that corrupt practices were to be laid at the door of unscrupulous men, and that they could be weeded out of public life if the schools taught individual integrity, a higher code of political ethics, and, above all, respect for law.[174] As the immigrant hordes multiplied, there was an increasing tendency to blame the newcomers for the gravest abuses of political corruption; and the Americanization movement, which the schools adopted, was welcomed with naïve faith.[175] More realistic exponents of citizenship training felt that greater headway could be made if children were given some insight into the actual problems of municipal housekeeping in their own community.[176] Some urged the duty of encouraging pupils to look forward to a political career, thus to prevent saloon keepers and demagogues from monopolizing public offices. Others insisted that more could be accomplished if children were taught to be nonpartisan and to see the flaws of all parties and politicians.

Here and there a voice was raised against such superficial diagnoses and prescriptions for cure. But even the exposures of

[174] For typical examples from the voluminous literature see Andrew S. Draper, *Ed. Rev.*, Vol. I (Jan., 1891), pp. 26–32; *Report of the Commissioner of Education*, 1914, Vol. I, Chap. XVIII; N. E. A., *Proceedings*, 1903, p. 30; 1907, pp. 181–91; 1908, p. 37.

[175] *Report of the Commissioner of Education*, 1870, p. 36; N. E. A., *Proceedings*, 1886, pp. 222–28; 1891, pp. 294–97.

[176] Richard Jones, *Ed. Rev.*, Vol. XI (March, 1896), p. 234; J. Lynn Barnard, N. E. A., *Proceedings*, 1913, pp. 84–90.

the muckrakers in the first decade of the twentieth century seem to have affected only slightly the thought of those concerned with instruction in citizenship. President Eliot did not appreciate the offer of Lincoln Steffens to teach Harvard boys how to become better bosses.[177] It was, moreover, relatively rare when someone deprecated the superficial character of the flag-saluting type of citizenship training.[178] Judging from subsequent literature, the address of Jane Addams before the National Association in 1897, in which she pointed out some of the relations between industrial exploitation of the immigrants and corruption, made but slight impression.[179] Toward the end of the period Angelo Patri presented a comparatively realistic and sympathetic picture of the life back of the immigrant school child.[180] But except for a few spirits like Margaret Haley, Henry Linville, I. W. Howerth, and John Dewey, the most prominent educators in this period do not seem to have recognized the shallowness of a civic instruction that overlooked the unsavory matters connected with the fortune-making of great and respectable men of wealth. In spite, even, of the increasing emphasis on the social studies, few of their exponents seem to have faced the more fundamental causes of corruption in public life.[181]

As *laissez faire* gave way in a somewhat piecemeal and unsatisfactory way to the new doctrine of public responsibility and

[177] *The Autobiography of Lincoln Steffens* (New York, 1931), p. 608.

[178] Ira W. Howerth, *Ed. Rev.*, Vol. XLIV (June, 1912), pp. 13-24.

[179] N. E. A., *Proceedings*, 1897, pp. 104-12; *Ed. Rev.*, Vol. XXIX (March, 1905), pp. 245-63.

[180] Angelo Patri, *A Schoolmaster of the Great City* (New York, 1917), pp. 68 *et seq.*, 124 *et seq.*

[181] Occasionally a political scientist such as Jeremiah W. Jenks suggested some of the relationships between big business and political graft. *Second Yearbook of the National Herbart Society*, 1896, pp. 177 *et seq*. Although not speaking for the entire Herbartian movement, De Garmo, one of its leaders, at times demanded that moral and civic education be directed against such practices as watering stock and stealing franchises, and against whatever

control over individual enterprise, educators were called on to consider the social bearing of the training that the schools gave. Under the spell of the high individualism of Rousseau and Spencer and the equally individualistic psychology of William James and G. Stanley Hall, they were in fact engaged in developing the capacity of the individual and of adjusting him to society. It is true that some followed William T. Harris in attaching great importance to social values; but these were static values and education was intended to prepare the individual to appreciate and preserve existing institutions without inquiring whether or not they actually fulfilled the functions they were presumed to fulfil.

Between the social emphasis of William T. Harris and that of John Dewey, who charged the school with the remaking of society in order to permit the realization of a truly inclusive and democratically co-operative individualism, there was a world of difference. The turning point in the conflict between these two points of view regarding the social purpose of education came in the nineties—at the very time when the Populists seemed, by virtue of their defeat in 1896, to have failed to force a greater measure of social control over unscrupulous profit-making enterprise. Perhaps, thought a few educational pioneers, an entirely new type of school might succeed in effecting some of the democratic reforms which an aroused social consciousness demanded.

The philosophic justification for the new emphasis on the social purpose of education was in part provided by Auguste Comte and Lester Ward.[182] Throughout the eighties Ward

in public morality, held over from the older exploiting frontier days, jeopardized the means of subsistence for large classes of the population. See his *Principles of Secondary Education,* Vol. III, pp. 51–52, 53–54, 113, 149–50; and his demand that the teacher expose the need of reform, in *Religious Education,* Vol. III (Oct., 1908), p. 128.

[182] Elsa Kimball, *Sociology and Education* (Columbia University Studies in History, Economics and Public Law, New York, 1932).

was insisting that the lower classes were the intellectual equals of the upper classes, who had culturally disinherited those beneath them. Asserting that every economic class had a wide and equal range of mental capacity among its members, Ward attributed stratification almost entirely to social environment and social heritage, and advocated an equitable distribution of knowledge to effect general social improvement. Declaring that inequality in the distribution of information and knowledge necessarily resulted in "the cleavage of society into an exploiting and an exploited class," Ward believed that this cleavage and exploitation could be removed, and social reform made effective, only through truly democratic education.[183] While in some respects there was little new in this idea that knowledge must be shared by all alike, it did shoulder education with the responsibility of changing the social environment as well as molding individuals.

Although in 1891 it was in order to apologize for introducing so extraneous a matter as sociology into the meetings of the National Education Association,[184] an increasing number of voices, led by Colonel Francis Parker, spoke in terms of social responsibility. They insisted that education had merely trained the child to guard successfully his own personal ends and advance his own selfish interests, instead of equipping him to live co-operatively in an interdependent society. While some who spoke in terms of sociology still contended that it was man, not environment, that needed to be remade, others maintained the contrary. The school, they said, must so change its discipline, its curriculum, its pedagogy, and its entire spirit as to meet the social needs of community life. True individualism, it was argued, meant enriching each life with the possessions

---

[183] Lester Ward, *Applied Sociology* (Boston, 1906), p. 93.
[184] Jones, N. E. A., *Proceedings,* 1891, p. 101.

of all, not enabling one person to compete with another. "It is a bad thing," President Hadley of Yale said in 1904, "to encourage the individual to think that his success and his happiness are the ultimate ends for which he is to work."[185] It was further said that the school must arouse in the pupil a feeling that he was part of one great whole, that no man liveth unto himself, and that happiness could be found only in a sense of social responsibility, service to others, and regard for their well-being.

Although there was frequently a tendency to talk of social values in a nebulous and unrealistic way, the very fact that emphasis was shifting from the ideal of an education which fitted one to "get ahead" or at best to appreciate and identify himself with existing social institutions, to one which charged the individual with a sense of social responsibility, marked a necessary first step. Of course if educators persisted in offering the glittering platitudes of social responsibility without analyzing the underlying obstacles, if they refused to attack specific problems, no matter how dangerous to vested interests, then this first step would prove merely a stop-gap for saving appearances without really affecting the *status quo*.

In furthering a more realistic analysis John Dewey was not altogether alone. But it was very unusual for educators to be thus in the vanguard. With few exceptions, they not only advanced social ideas thoroughly in keeping with the existing system of profit-making industrialism; they also aided it in its struggles with farmers and workers. Even within the framework of the capitalistic system, educators in this period between Lincoln and Wilson failed to lead in reforms for the remedying of obvious social disorders. In excuse they might have pleaded that they must first complete the rearing of the school

185 *Ed. Rev.*, Vol. XXVIII (Nov., 1904), p. 332.

structure—their predecessors had been able merely to lay the foundations. But even in the rearing of the structure, particularly in providing room for the poor whites and the newly emancipated blacks, important social problems were involved.

VII

EDUCATION IN THE SOUTH

Nobody never comes in here and nobody never goes out. My paw just growed up and never knowed nothin' and so did his paw afore him. Sometimes when I be hoeing corn on the mountain side, I looks up the creek and down the creek and wonders if there ain't nobody never comin' to larn me nothin'.
—Quoted in N. E. A., *Proceedings,* 1908.

Doctor Curry represents, in his personal feelings and ways of thinking, all that was best in the life of the Southern white people.
—Booker T. Washington.

I

Secession and civil war struck a blow at the rather promising movement for free public schools in some parts of the Old South. In spite of hostile forces this movement, under the leadership of men like Calvin Wiley, William F. Perry, the first superintendent of schools in Alabama, and Governor Henry Wise of Virginia was making headway and, in the view of one authority, was actually on the eve of victory.[1] In the first two years after the surrender of Lee, when reconstruction was in the hands of the moderate party, Southern leaders made a brave effort to provide educational systems in which even the blacks were not to be entirely overlooked. In Virginia William Ruffner actually began and later effected the organization of a system of public schools.

When, however, the "radical" congressional policy of reconstruction triumphed, the agitation for free public schools was so much identified with the carpetbag leadership and with

[1] Edgar W. Knight, *Public Education in the South,* pp. 266–67, 307–8.

racial equality that the disenfranchised planters were embittered and the poor whites antagonized. Southerners resented the missionary "schoolmarms" from the North who taught the Negro Yankee songs and "pernicious" ideas of racial equality. They were horrified at the expenditures which the scalawag and carpetbag regimes lavished on the schools as well as at the notorious cuspidors and free restaurant service in legislative halls, abuses which they seldom thought of comparing with the scandalous corruption of the Tweed ring in New York. Moreover, so far as the new public schools were co-racial, they were boycotted by the whites. Even when the carpetbag governments collapsed, the reinstated dominant group, struggling with bitter poverty, continued to think with scant respect of the public school systems which the constitutions of the "radical" period had set up.

But it was not bitter winds only that blew down from the North.[2] In 1866 George Peabody, a Massachusetts money broker who had, apparently by somewhat questionable means,[3] accumulated a large fortune in London, announced his purpose of endowing Southern common school education. He had lived in the South, laid the foundations of his fortune there, and contracted many friendships. Aware of the needs of that section, he determined to encourage intellectual, moral, and industrial education among Southerners, without other distinction

[2] The wise and prudent Reverend A. D. Mayo, editor of the *New England Journal of Education,* and lecturer in the South on public education in the early eighties, did much to break down opposition to taxation for public schools. See his *Building for the Children in the South* (Washington, 1884) and J. L. M. Curry's judgment on his work. Curry to R. C. Winthrop, July 14, 1881, Curry MSS., Vol. II.

[3] L. L. Wallis, writing to Curry from Baltimore, Dec. 12, 1892, says that in investigating Peabody's life he "became acquainted . . . with details, of the truth of which there was no mistake, and which were very far from being agreeable, or consistent with that side of him and his life which the public knew." Hence in a memorial address on Peabody he had made general reflections upon the giving of rich gifts by rich people. Curry MSS., Vol. X.

than "their needs and the opportunities of usefulness to them."

The Peabody Fund, which was administered by conservative gentlemen, Southern as well as Northern, initiated an era of better feeling between the two sections. It became an effective agency in the South in promoting concord and in cultivating a broad and generous patriotism.[4] While the work was not, at least directly and consciously, motivated by economic considerations, it had the effect of enlisting the co-operation of members of the dominant Southern class with men of finance in the victorious North. Whether or not the improvement of Southern education which resulted from it actually encouraged the investment of Northern capital in the South cannot be easily determined; but the argument was made that such capital would not flow southward unless education insured order and trained a skilled and reliable working class.

It was Doctor Barnas Sears, the successor of Mann in the secretaryship of the Massachusetts Board of Education and subsequently president of Brown University, who, as first agent of the Peabody Fund, molded the policy that governed its administration. To disarm opposition to public schools, no funds were allocated to systems established on the co-racial basis. To stimulate Southern authorities to help themselves, funds were granted on condition that a larger sum was raised by taxation than that granted by the foundation. It was calculated that the chief benefit should come, not from what the fund itself gave, but from what it stimulated the South to do for itself. Helping those who helped themselves seemed, from every point of view, a sound maxim. A special effort was made to concentrate on the establishing of a few model schools and on teachers' training institutions. When Doctor Sears died in

[4] J. L. M. Curry, *A Brief Sketch of George Peabody, and a History of the Peabody Education Fund Through Thirty Years* (Cambridge, 1898), pp. 18 *et seq.*

1880, Southern superintendents and public men testified to his rare insight into the needs of the South and his influence in stimulating wise and proper action. A man of scholarship and broad culture, full of enthusiasm and yet prudent, Sears offended few and, apart from his influence in breaking down opposition to public schools, did much to strengthen better feeling between the two sections.[5]

From the time when he succeeded Sears until his death in 1903 Jabez Lamar Monroe Curry was the best known and most influential figure in Southern education. His own life represents the adjustment of the old agrarian and caste civilization of the South to the new and more democratic order which followed the defeat of the Confederacy. Southern in birth and training, Curry was a gentleman of the old school.[6] Brought up on an Alabama plantation, he studied at the University of Georgia, and was graduated in the class of 1843. The curriculum emphasized the classics and mathematics, but some attention was paid to political economy and moral philosophy. Current issues were vehemently discussed in the debating clubs, and young Curry, a disciple of Calhoun, took an active part.[7] After taking his degree, he went to study law with Story at Harvard, and in Massachusetts his interest in public education was first aroused. The work of Horace Mann enlisted his admiration and awakened a deep and lasting interest. As a candidate for the legislature of Alabama in 1847, he spoke in favor

[5] Barnas Sears, Address before the Constitutional Convention of Virginia, Jan. 23, 1868, *Proceedings of the Trustees of the Peabody Educational Fund*, Vol. I (Jan., 1868), pp. 63 *et seq.; ibid.*, Vol. II, Appendix, pp. 373–432; *ibid.*, Vol. III, Appendix, pp. 423 *et seq.* For the best brief account of Sears's educational work see J. L. M. Curry, *ibid.*, Vol. III (Oct., 1881), pp. 5 *et seq.*

[6] For Curry's evaluation of the culture of the Old South see his "The South in the Olden Time," Southern History Association *Publications*, Vol. V (Jan., 1901), pp. 35–48.

[7] For student life at the University of Georgia in Curry's undergraduate days see *The Autobiography of Joseph Le Conte* (New York, 1903), and E. Merton Coulter, *College Life in the Old South.*

of public schools and as a member of the committee on education sustained Judge A. B. Meek's bill to establish an educational system for the state.[8]

An ardent Southerner, Curry identified himself with the fortunes of the governing class. His state sent him to Congress in 1856 and *The New York Tribune* recognized in him a powerful addition to the pro-slavery group in the national lawmaking body. Convinced that abolition would spell the economic and moral ruin of the South, he early championed the cause of secession and ably upheld it on constitutional grounds. As a member of the Confederate Congress he favored a vigorous prosecution of the war and finally joined the army. While he came, in later life, to regard slavery as a curse, he never changed his views in regard to the constitutional right of secession, and in many writings sympathetically interpreted the Old South and became one of the most able apologists for its struggle for independence.[9]

Deeply religious and lofty in his spiritual life, Curry, once the war ended, devoted himself to the work of the Baptist Church and to the cause of education. As president of a small denominational college in Alabama he traveled up and down the South giving public lectures in behalf of college and general education, which he believed to be the most promising way of rehabilitating his crushed and impoverished section. In persuading towns to pass resolutions as early as 1866 in behalf of education for the blacks he was in advance of many of his contemporaries. Disgusted with reconstruction politics in Alabama he removed to Richmond, married a wealthy and socially prominent lady, taught literature and law at Richmond

[8] J. L. M. Curry, "My Educational Life," notebook A, Curry MSS.
[9] J. L. M. Curry, *Principles, Acts, and Utterances of John C. Calhoun* (Chicago, 1898) *passim; The Southern States of the American Union* (New York, 1894), *passim*.

College, and continued to write, talk, and work in behalf of his church and education.[10]

Although a good deal had been done for education in the South when Curry became general agent for the Peabody Fund in 1881, much remained to be accomplished. Impatience with taxation for education, poverty, and indifference still blocked the effective execution of the newly established systems of education.[11] Proceeding cautiously, Curry journeyed all over the South. He talked with governors, and again and again addressed legislatures when public education needed particular support or even seemed to be in danger. His political and social standing gave weight to his words. He pushed, lubricated, smoothed away difficulties; he advised, encouraged, and strengthened public men and school officials. His reports to the Peabody trustees and his manuscript papers alone can picture the extent of his activities—long journeys, innumerable addresses, and a stream of letters to individuals and communications to the press. Fourteen times he refused the presidency of as many different colleges and universities—so important did his work for public education seem to him. In administering the funds under his direction he was judicious; in organizing the work entrusted to him he was statesmanlike. It would be hard to estimate the extent to which he broke down indifference and opposition to state-supported schools, not only among legislators and the public generally, but even in church and college circles. When in 1890 he was named agent of the fund established by John Slater of Connecticut for the encouragement of Negro education, his activity became even more extensive.

Curry's papers include many testimonials and appreciations.

10 Edwin Anderson Alderman and Armistead Churchill Gordon, *J. L. M. Curry, A Biography* (New York, 1911), pp. xii–xiii.
11 J. L. M. Curry to Robert Winthrop, March 14, 1881, Curry MSS., Vol. II; *ibid.*, Vol. XV.

His close contacts with leading business men and educators in the North enabled him to interpret the South to the rest of the nation; and he was an interpreter of the North to his own people. He was praised by John D. Rockefeller and J. P. Morgan, by Booker T. Washington and by William T. Harris, by President Hayes and by President Cleveland, by Theodore Roosevelt and by Woodrow Wilson. Andrew D. White considered his work greater "than anything any person could do in any political position in the United States,"[12] while the Reverend A. D. Mayo, a well-informed and active friend of Southern education, thought that during the period of Curry's active work "no man, certainly in the South, and possibly in the Union, occupied a more responsible position in the development of popular education."[13]

Curry's educational philosophy was derived in part from the individualist tradition to which he subscribed, in part from the humanitarian and reform tenets which he shared with Mann, and in part from the exigencies of the environment in which he worked. Idealist and individualist that he was, he believed that the function of education was to enable its recipient to develop his full powers and to live abundantly. Complete living meant for him self-preservation, parentage, citizenship, the refinements of life, and Christian duty and service. While he did not expect the public school to solve the most difficult social problems, he did believe it could promote prosperity, alleviate racial friction, and help to resolve the conflict between capital and labor. Above all he believed that it promised to rehabilitate the South, to preserve the best of its old culture and to adjust it to the new civilization with which it must integrate itself.[14]

[12] Curry to Winthrop, Feb. 5, 1883, quoting a letter from White, Curry MSS., Vol. IV.
[13] *Ibid.*, Vol. XV.
[14] *Texas Journal of Education* (March, 1881), p. 149, in Curry MSS., Vol. II.

To fulfil its purposes education, insisted Curry, must be universal, because man's needs are universal. The failure to ascertain and to develop natural aptitudes for industries or for special avocations, begat waste, unhappiness, poverty. Every individual, therefore, had a right to the most complete education a state could give. Such an education was alike necessary to his enjoyment of himself and to the well-being of his fellows. If one were to be surrounded by and incapable of rising above boorish, coarse, and vulgar men and women, life would cease to be worth living.[15] Moral character, the training of all the people, and the gospel of social sympathy, these were the tenets to which he subscribed and which he believed public education would further.

Curry's attitude toward the events which followed Appomattox was that of his class. Unable to see the deeper economic and cultural conflict that the deeds of reconstruction expressed, he regarded the whole dreadful affair as a battle between passionate and vindictive politicians, conscientious and patriotic fanatics, disgraceful thieves and vulgar rascals.[16] For him the overthrow of carpetbag and Negro rule was a victory of the strength, patriotism, intelligence, and idealism of the South over ignorance, superstition, and fanaticism.

But once white rule was restored, Curry used his great influence to further reconciliation between the two sections and particularly to tie more closely the bonds between men of wealth in the North and men of standing in the South. He believed that the new South was to reclaim and adapt the Jeffersonian principles of individual freedom, states' rights, and public edu-

[15] Curry's address to the General Assembly of Virginia, May 2, 1890, in *Proceedings of the Trustees of the Peabody Educational Fund,* Vol. IV (Oct., 1890).

[16] *The Southern States,* pp. 232–33; Curry to Winthrop, Aug. 2, 1882, July 4, 1888, Oct. 11, 1895, Curry MSS., Vols. III, VI, and XII; "Claims of the Hour on the Young Man," Lecture, 1867, *ibid.,* Vol. II.

cation to a new nationalism embodying the best tradition of ante-bellum days. We need no discord, he liked to tell the sons and daughters of the Confederacy, no nursing of old wounds, no separate political existence.[17] Let the resurrected South reinvigorate the true constitutional principles of states' rights, the abdication of which, he rather naïvely believed, was responsible for the graft and the spoils which blackened public life.[18]

Let the pure Anglo-Saxon stock of the Southland, Curry urged, use its influence in federal councils to check the immigrant invasion, which threatened our Protestant and traditionally American culture. Let the South safeguard our friendship with England by putting a damper on the injection of the question of Irish home rule into our politics and our foreign relations.[19] Above all, let the South serve as a conservative bulwark against assaults on the foundation of public and private credit and financial integrity—let it cast its weight with the industrial East rather than with the inflationists and the upstart demagogues who in the South seemed to betray its culture and its conservative past.[20]

When President Cleveland, as an evidence of confidence in the patriotic loyalty of the reconstructed South, appointed Curry in 1885 as minister to Spain, he temporarily laid down his educational work and served his country on a foreign stage. Life in an aristocratic and Catholic land confirmed Curry's faith in American democracy, his zeal for separation of church and state, and his enthusiasm for the new Union.[21] A Confederate veteran, he spoke out against the dangers of huge armaments

[17] Speech before the Sons of the Confederacy, *Richmond Dispatch*, July 2, 1896.
[18] *Principles, Acts, and Utterances of John C. Calhoun*, pp. 25–27.
[19] Curry to Winthrop, Aug. 24, 1885, Sept. 23, 1886, July 4, 1887, Curry MSS., Vols. V and VI; *The Southern States*, pp. 246–47.
[20] *Ibid.*, p. 247; Speech before the Sons of the Confederacy, *loc. cit.*
[21] Curry to Winthrop, Madrid, July 4, 1887, Curry MSS., Vol. VI.

and the false glories of war.[22] He rejoiced to see American ideas "pervading, uplifting, and regenerating the Old World."[23] His friendship for Spain, his hatred of war, and his constitutional scruples against expansion led him ardently to oppose the Spanish-American War.[24] Yet, like so many other educators, he publicly paid tribute to the patriotic purposes that it called out, to the high citizenship that it developed, and to the bonds it cemented between North and South.[25]

Notwithstanding his devotion to the doctrine of states' rights and his incessant warnings against the dangers of centralization, Curry joined the crusade which was designed to secure federal funds for the public schools of the South.[26] In a public address, which was later circulated among the members of Congress, Curry urged support for the bill that Senator Henry Blair of New Hampshire was sponsoring—a bill providing for the appropriation of federal funds for public schools in proportion to the illiteracy existing in the several states. In this address Curry summarily dismissed the idea that such an act would be unconstitutional and argued that universal education was the most effective way of realizing the Jeffersonian maxim that the best government was the one which governed least. If every-

[22] Curry to Winthrop, Jan. 19, 1887, Aug. 24, 1888, *ibid.;* Address before the Peabody Normal School, Nov., 1892, *ibid.,* Vol. X; J. L. M. Curry, "National Aid to Education," Appendix to Charles Warren, *Illiteracy in the United States in 1870 and 1880* (Bureau of Education, Circular of Information No. 3, 1884), pp. 97–98.

[23] Speech before the Centennial Exposition Board, Dec. 4, 1888, clipping from *The Washington Post,* Curry MSS., Vol. VII.

[24] William T. Harris to Curry, April, 1898; W. C. Wilson to Curry, April 19, 1898, *ibid.,* Vol. XII.

[25] *Principles, Acts, and Utterances of John C. Calhoun,* pp. 22–23; *Proceedings of the Trustees of the Peabody Educational Fund,* Vol. V (Oct. 4, 1898), p. 315.

[26] *Proceedings of the Trustees of the Peabody Educational Fund,* Vol. III (Oct., 1883), pp. 100 *et seq.* Both Ignatius Donnelly and Justin Morrill were early exponents of this idea. See Morrill's speech delivered in the Senate April 26, 1876, *The Educational Fund* (Washington, 1876).

one were educated, then government would have less need of enacting laws and enforcing harsh regulations to protect life and property. If there were no illiteracy, political fraud would be reduced to a minimum because governmental agents would realize that they were being carefully scrutinized by their constituents. In short, the best limitation to the encroachments of government on the individual lay in universal education.

Curry also urged that illiteracy was a menace not only to free institutions, but to the republic itself. "Such a mass of illiteracy as we have is worse than foreign invasion, incites domestic violence, gives supremacy to bad appetites, and is a perpetual menace to the life and well-being of republican institutions." Through no fault of their own, he urged, the emancipated Negroes were too poor to pay taxes, and the South too impoverished to provide the necessary education to keep them from succumbing to the false ideas of demagogues.

As if to make a stronger appeal to the industrial North, Curry argued that universal education, particularly industrial training, was indispensable if industry were to be promoted and capital to be accumulated and made secure. He approved the requirement in the Blair bill that the disbursement of federal funds should be based on the amount of illiteracy in a state and that it should be contingent on an equal contribution from state and local revenues. The apologist for states' rights even went so far as to concede a certain amount of federal direction and oversight of the funds granted by the central government. Thus almost a hundred years after the educational planners of the post-revolutionary period advocated national support for public education, a powerful voice from the traditionally *laissez-faire* South spoke in its behalf. The idea that the individual should be for the most part left to shift for himself was slowly giving way to the concept of the state as the trustee for all its citizens.[27]

In addition to making speeches in behalf of federal aid Curry appealed to Southern representatives in Congress to support the Blair bill and again and again went to Washington to lobby in its behalf.[28] He provided Congressmen with material for speeches in behalf of the bill, he solicited the support of the press, he answered all manner of objections. Senator Blair himself wrote that no one had contributed more to the success of the bill. Although his zeal brought him much criticism, Curry continued year after year to work for the triumph of the measure. More than once it seemed on the point of victory.[29]

A variety of reasons account for the failure of the movement for federal aid to Southern education. Although Bayard, Carlisle, and Samuel J. Randall, its most powerful opponents, grounded their opposition on constitutional theory, and although many Southern opponents criticized it for similar reasons, Curry suspected that race prejudice in the South and a fear that the educated Negro could be less easily manipulated in elections had more influence on adverse action than had constitutional scruples.[30] Another factor, he thought, was the widespread talk about the prosperity of the New South.[31] Some Southern support was alienated by reason of the fact that Senator Blair, at a critical juncture in Virginia politics, came to the aid of the "readjuster" Malone, a man whose repudiation policy and appeal to the poorer whites was thoroughly hated by

[27] "National Aid to Education," p. 94.
[28] Curry to Winthrop, Jan. 12, 1882, March 27, 1882, April 10, 1884, Curry MSS., Vols. III and IV.
[29] The bill passed the Senate in 1884, 1886, and 1888 but was defeated by the House. It was defeated by the Senate in 1890. In 1885 President Hayes noted in his diary that a majority of Northern and Southern, Democratic and Republican, senators favored the bill.
[30] Curry to Winthrop, Sept. 1, 1886, Curry MSS., Vol. V.
[31] Curry to Winthrop, Jan. 11, 1890, *ibid.*, Vol. VII.

Southern aristocrats.[32] In addition, Catholic opposition to all federal aid for public schools seems to have been a factor in the defeat of the bill.[33] In any case, the failure of the proposal was a great disappointment and a real defeat for Curry.

If in pleading with the great men of the North to subsidize Southern education Curry stretched the constitutional principles he had inherited from the Old South and which he in general continued to defend, he maintained a traditionally aristocratic attitude toward the agrarian unrest and political upheavals of the eighties and nineties. While favoring the breaking up of the plantations to permit the development of a peasant or tenant class,[34] he failed to understand the causes of the hardships that farmers suffered. Repudiation, which was anathema to his sound money principles, was laid at the door of ignorant voters misled by demagogues; and he wrote to his conservative Northern friend, Robert C. Winthrop, that a century would hardly suffice to "wipe out the deep damning stain."[35] He even suggested that the Peabody Fund be drawn upon to reward Florida, a state which, unlike Mississippi, had not succumbed to the "scourging pestilence" of repudiation.[36]

In spite of his opposition to the Farmers' Alliance and to the Tillman movement, he brought himself to say little in the open and to co-operate whenever he could with those "powers that be" for the advancement of public education.[37] In addressing

[32] Curry to Winthrop, Oct. 31, 1889, *ibid*.
[33] Winthrop to Curry, Nov. 13, 1889, *ibid*.
[34] "Speeches, Reports," Curry MSS., Vol. F.
[35] Curry to Winthrop, Feb. 5, 1883, Feb. 16, 1883, Feb. 25, 1883, Curry MSS., Vol. IV.
[36] Curry to Winthrop, May 25, 1889, *ibid.,* Vol. VII.
[37] Curry to Winthrop, Aug. 1, 1890, Dec. 11, 1890, March 28, 1891, March 15, 1892, *ibid.,* Vols. VIII and IX; Tillman to Curry, Dec. 12, 1896, *ibid.,* Vol. XII; Speech before the legislature of North Carolina, Jan. 21, 1891, in *Proceedings of the Trustees of the Peabody Educational Fund,* Vol. IV (Oct., 1891), pp. 322 *et seq.* Many of the Farmers' Alliance conventions in the South favored the extension and improvement of free public schools.

the Farmers' Alliance of North Carolina he admitted that the unequal distribution of wealth might occasionally require remedial legislation, but insisted that domestic economy, thrift, and education in practical matters of everyday life were of greater importance. "The remedy for agricultural depression, bad roads, the discontent and thriftlessness of youth, for many of the ills of which we complain," Curry declared in public addresses, "is a well sustained school system."[38]

It was not only in his opposition to the politics of repudiation that this educator gave evidence of his conservative sympathies. Although the industrial development of the South had not led to much labor unrest in that section before his death in 1903, Curry was as much alarmed by the growth of the single tax movement and by the noise which Socialism and Anarchism made as were his Northern colleagues. Writing in *The Independent* he declared that the conduct of the railroad strikers in 1877 was atrocious, and deserved "prompt repression, at any sacrifice."[39] Admitting that the strikers had grievances, that unions *per se* were not wrong, and that capital had not been "proverbially unselfish," he nevertheless declared that workers were not justified in preventing others from taking their places. He also observed that the workers had, during good times, spent money lavishly on drink and luxury and hence were in part at fault when wage cuts brought actual suffering. The vote for Henry George in the mayoralty campaign in 1886 gave him "no little uneasiness." He wrote to Winthrop that the condemnation of the Chicago anarchists, more than anything which had occurred since Appomattox, had vindicated our republican institutions in the eyes of Europe. He feared, however, that the release of part of them would nullify the

[38] *Proceedings of the Trustees of the Peabody Educational Fund*, Vol. V (Oct., 1897), p. 306.
[39] *The Independent*, Aug. 23, 1877.

effect.[40] He hoped that the "discontent among our working men, the spirit of lawlessness so widespread . . . will be restrained from running to extreme and revolutionary length."[41] Although he expressed sympathy for the men who made up Coxey's "idiotic, perhaps wicked army," he would punish its leaders.[42]

In Curry's opinion, the institution of private property was necessary in order to provide motives for industrious work. Take away property, he declared, and there would be no motive for work beyond the bare minimum necessary for subsistence. Believing in "the inalienable right of every human being to the fullest and completest moral and intellectual development," he at the same time told the legislature of Alabama that "socialism, agrarianism, communism, so far as they mean partition of property, are absurd and criminal, for all true civilization rests on the security of property."[43]

In view of the fact that the industrialization of the South did not begin much before 1890 and that ten years later Curry congratulated that section on its freedom from strikes and from "the lawlessness of organized assertive labor,"[44] it is important to ask why he was so much concerned by the labor disturbances in the North. His anxiety may in part have been due to sympathy for his friends and associates who were prominent in industrial enterprise. It may in part be ascribed to his Jeffersonian dislike of the proletariat, and to his *laissez-faire* individualism, which he felt to be endangered by collective action on the part of labor. It may have been in part due to the fact that, since he had committed himself in at least a moderate way

[40] Curry to Winthrop, Nov., 1886, Curry MSS., Vol. VI.
[41] Curry to Winthrop, Dec. 2, 1887, *ibid.*
[42] Curry to Winthrop, April 18, 1894, *ibid.*, Vol. XI.
[43] Address before the General Assembly of Alabama, Dec. 2, 1896, Curry MSS.
[44] "The South in the Olden Time," p. 47.

to the industrialization of the South, he feared the introduction of a new labor problem in his beloved homeland.

Whatever the cause of his attitude toward labor, strikes, and Socialism, Curry abandoned the pre-Civil War indifference of his section to industry and partly identified himself with the New South. Unlike Jefferson, he came to believe that a purely agricultural country could not be powerful and prosperous, and he looked with friendly eyes on the invasion of Northern capital to exploit Southern resources. In the interest of more leisure, greater utility and profit he urged farmers to adopt agricultural machinery.[45] He declared that "capital follows the schoolhouse" and, as we shall see, supported vocational education in order to further the adjustment of the South to the new industrial civilization.

Yet Curry's objections to Socialism and aggressive organized labor on the one hand and his encouragement of industrialism in the South on the other did not mean that he was charitable toward every aspect of industrial capitalism. Believing that "wealth in excess is a serious evil" he had harsh words for the tendency of legislative bodies to pamper banks, corporations, railroads, and manufacturing by special legislation. "Instead of guarding against the undue influence of wealth, or the tendency to favoritism, governments have rather helped and strengthened" the wealthy who had been constituted into a privileged class.[46] It was against the encroachments of this class that organized labor revolted and Socialism protested. To counteract radicalism, the powers of government had been unwisely extended and consolidated even further. He was convinced that this unwarranted departure from the strict con-

[45] "Speeches, Reports," Curry MSS., Vol. F.
[46] J. L. M. Curry, "The Classes Against the Masses," *The Baptist Quarterly Review,* Vol. X (April, 1888), pp. 142 *et seq.*

stitutional principles of limited governmental powers lay at the root of all our troubles.

While Curry, pious and evangelical as he was, believed that a Christian education could go far toward alleviating the abuses of which capital and labor were guilty,[47] he also felt that proper teaching must lead the American people back to the Jeffersonian principles of limited government. "The government," he declared, "has nothing of property or rank or special favors to bestow" on either capital or labor. It could merely protect what man had. Education must rehabilitate and insure the victory of the only safe principle of government: no preferences to corporations, special interests, or any class; and no extension of governmental powers save by constitutional amendment. Thus Curry proposed education in the Jeffersonian maxims of restricted power of government as a solution for the complex problems of an economic system appreciably different from that of the early republic.[48]

If, in spite of his support of the Blair bill, Curry did not substantially modify his ante-bellum faith in strictly limited governmental powers, he did, in accepting industrialism for the South, somewhat change his scale of values. In the period immediately after the war, his educational speeches suggest the cultural appreciations of Jefferson rather than the more prosaic and useful ideals of Franklin. He emphasized the æsthetic values and criticized the unpoetical, selfish, and utilitarian devotion to the philosophy of Poor Richard. In the urbane

[47] Address to Y. M. C. A., Portsmouth, Va., Oct. 20, 1889, Curry MSS., Vol. VII; Address to the General Assembly of Virginia, Feb. 4, 1892, in *Proceedings of the Trustees of the Peabody Educational Fund*, Vol. IV (Oct., 1892).

[48] *Ibid.*, Vol. V (Oct., 1894), pp. 78–79; *Principles, Acts, and Utterances of John C. Calhoun*, pp. 2–5; lecture, 1884, Curry MSS., Vol. V; "Recent Tendencies in Free Political Institutions," *ibid.*, Vol. XIII.

spirit of the culture of the Old South he pleaded for grace, refinement, and beauty in public and private dwellings and in every common walk of life.[49]

But after the early eighties Curry seldom made an address which did not recommend the incorporation of industrial training into the school system. Although he sometimes pointed out the educational advantages of breaking down the traditional separation between doing and knowing,[50] and although he sometimes cited Spencer as an authority for the value of the useful in the schools, he also put great emphasis on industrial education to promote the economic advancement of the masses of Southerners, white and black. Realizing that they must earn their bread by hard labor, he thought that the schools should, through special vocational training, equip them with habits of individual thrift, skill, and insight into the use of machinery, and with the ability to earn better wages as skilled workers. Such an education, he believed, would not only benefit its recipients but contribute to material prosperity and to social quiet.[51]

Although Curry thought that industrial education would help alleviate the Negro problem, he often despaired of its solution. Like Southerners in every walk of life, he assumed that the supremacy of the white race was both inevitable and desirable. He thought the enfranchisement of the blacks had been an "indescribable blunder" and a curse to the whole nation as well as to the Negroes and the South, although he did come to look with some favor on an educational requirement for

[49] Notes for an address, 1875 or 1876, Curry MSS., Vol. I.
[50] Address before the General Assembly of Alabama, 1897, clipping, Curry MSS., Vol. XII.
[51] *Proceedings of the Trustees of the Peabody Educational Fund,* Vol. III (Oct., 1883), p. 125; *ibid.,* Vol. IV (1888–1892), p. 399; Speech at Raleigh Fair, Oct. 23, 1894, Curry MSS., Vol. XI; *Address before the General Assembly of South Carolina,* Dec. 13, 1894 (Columbia, 1895), p. 8.

exercising the suffrage.[52] The achievements of a handful of
Negroes did not impress him with the capacity of the race for
improvement.[53] Yet he felt that religion, humanity, and the
material interests of both races dictated the effort to provide the
Negro with such an education as might regenerate him in his
personal, home, and religious life, as well as in his political
life.[54]

But he was too much a product of the Old South to be very
sanguine about what education could do for the black. "Fitting
the Negro for citizenship, putting him into a moral and intellectual and economic condition, so as to accumulate property
and take on some of the refinements of civilization," he wrote
to Winthrop, "seems so hopeless an undertaking that one has
to throw himself upon the All-Knowing and All-Just, when he
sees how feeble and inadequate are the remedies to correct what
seem to be incurable evils."[55]

With such convictions, it is to the credit of Curry that he not
only spoke out against lynching[56] but that he did a good deal
for Negro education. When, in the early eighties, a movement
was inaugurated for restricting the use of school money to the
race which provided it through taxation, he pointed out that
this would deprive the Negro of almost all public support for
his schools. When he was not able to prevent this measure from
coming up in legislatures, he threatened to refuse to allocate
Peabody money to communities in which such a practice pre-

[52] *The Southern States,* pp. 238–39; "The South in the Olden Times," pp.
46–47.
[53] J. L. M. Curry, *Difficulties, Complications and Limitations Connected
with the Education of the Negro* (Baltimore, 1895), pp. 9–10.
[54] Address to the legislature of North Carolina, Jan. 21, 1891, *Proceedings
of the Trustees of the Peabody Educational Fund,* Vol. IV, pp. 330–31.
[55] Curry to Winthrop, June 18, 1894, Curry MSS., Vol. XI.
[56] *Address before the General Assembly of Georgia,* Oct. 31, 1893 (Atlanta,
1893), p. 4.

vailed.[57] Moreover, as general agent of the Slater Fund, he promoted the education of the black at a time when any association with such work was still regarded as a social stigma in many Southern cities. When he died the principal of Hampton Institute spoke for a great many in declaring that no one had done as much for the colored race as J. L. M. Curry.[58]

Important though the achievements of Curry were, the task confronting him was too great for any one man. Working with other forces, however, he did contribute to the democratization of an aristocratic society, to the reconciliation of two unfriendly sections, to the stimulation of community effort for public ends, and to the development of the public school system for blacks as well as for whites.

II

Stimulated in part by local conditions and in part by a group of enthusiastic Southerners and philanthropic Northerners, an educational awakening was under way toward the end of the century and continued in the following decades to exert a profound effect on the whole South. Although the Farmers' Alliance had upheld the idea of better support for free public schools, such influential leaders of Populism as Tom Watson of Georgia, in calling upon the poorer classes to revolt against the domination of the older aristocracy of wealth and culture, talked in terms of class hatred and militant political action rather than in terms of education.[59] When, with the defeat of

[57] Curry to Winthrop, July 23, 1883, Oct. 22, 1892, Curry MSS., Vols. IV and X.

[58] Curry MSS., Vol. XV. When Curry was made agent of the Peabody Fund a Negro paper, the *Virginia Star*, congratulated the race and spoke in high praise of Curry for his well-known friendship toward the Negro. *Ibid.*, Vol. II.

[59] William W. Brewton, *Life of Thomas E. Watson* (Atlanta, 1926). See also Thomas Watson, *Prose Miscellanies* (Thompson, Ga., 1917), pp. 14 *et seq.*, 86 *et seq.*

Bryan in 1896, conservatives gained the upper hand in many regions in the South, a new sense of social obligation for the well-being of the poor whites was felt in many circles. In one sense, this concern for the physical and economic advancement of the lower classes, this demand for the conservation of womanhood and manhood as well as childhood, this enthusiasm for democratic sharing of the values of health, comfort, and culture with the underprivileged, was stimulated by the industrial development and, perhaps, by the desire of some people of substance to consolidate their victory by granting concessions. But it was also due to the idealism of a group of men, among whom the most persuasive were E. C. Alderman, Charles Brantley Aycock, Edgar Gardner Murphy, and Walter Hines Page.[60]

The bugle call for the new movement was sounded at Greensboro in 1897 when Walter Hines Page, a native North Carolinian who had achieved distinction in Northern journalism, delivered an address, *The Forgotten Man,* which electrified the South. Roundly denouncing the entrenched ecclesiastical and political authorities for having failed to provide educational opportunities for the "forgotten man" and his family, Page declared that "our civilization has been a failure." Courageously demonstrating the intellectual as well as the economic backwardness of North Carolina, he called for generous public support to build a democratic system of schools in which the hands and head of every child were to be trained. Such a measure, he promised, would regenerate the social structure, lay the dead ghosts of the aristocratic and church-ridden past, and effect an enriching economic and cultural rehabilitation. Page, by dramatizing the melancholy, dull-faced "forgotten man" and his wife, provided a slogan and a challenge as well as

[60] For Murphy's educational philosophy see his *Problems of the Present South* (New York, 1916).

a rebuke. In subsequent addresses and articles he stimulated so much enthusiasm and support for public education that Abraham Flexner called him "one of the real educational statesmen of this country, probably the greatest that we have had since the Civil War."[61]

Page's plea for a truly democratic system of education to break down caste barriers, to achieve economic independence for the masses by the training of hand and mind, and to effect the social regeneration of the South, contained little that was new in American educational thought. But the times were ripe for a response to his enthusiastic gospel. The more aristocratic and conservative classes, aware that their position was menaced by the rough and tumble politics of such "demagogues" as the Tillmans, the Vardamans, and the Tom Watsons, appealing as they did to the class interests and prejudices of the poorer whites, were willing to make concessions to the democratic forces. The democracy symbolized by free public education was, in short, acceptable to such leaders as Charles Brantley Aycock, who had fought the Populists in North Carolina, stood out against Negro suffrage, and was welcoming the industrial development of the state.[62]

The educational awakening was greatly furthered by the widely varying services of two Northern men. The one was a business organizer, the other a teacher and an educational expert in the art and science of agriculture. Without the work of Robert Curtis Ogden and Doctor Seaman A. Knapp, the

[61] Burton J. Hendrick, *The Life and Letters of Walter Hines Page* (Garden City, N. Y., 1923), Vol. I, p. 85. See Page's *The Rebuilding of Old Commonwealths* (Garden City, N. Y., 1902), for a brief statement of his social and educational philosophy.

[62] R. D. W. Connor and Clarence Poe, *The Life and Speeches of Charles Brantley Aycock* (Garden City, N. Y., 1912). An engaging man, who himself remembered his mother marking a cross on a legal document in lieu of her name, Aycock achieved a signal success in his battle for better state support for public education. He fell dead while delivering an address on that subject.

educational movement would have been less dramatic and probably less effective.

Robert Ogden, son of a Philadelphia wool merchant, represents the type of successful business man who devotes time, thought, and money to a social cause that has captured his imagination.[63] Deeply religious, he was not content to regard money-making as an end in itself. Having, as the head of Wanamaker's stores, perfected an organization that worked "as smoothly and efficiently as a Genevan watch," he brought his moral idealism, his grasp of details, and his boldness of execution to the aid of Southern education. He thought of business in the broad terms of service. It included the gratification of tastes, the promotion of culture, human brotherhood, and happiness. Believing that the successful business man possessed a royal opportunity for socializing his initiative, his executive capacity, and his accumulated profits, he attempted to carry out a philosophy which, among other things, seemed to him to promise to nip Socialism in the bud.[64]

As early as 1871 Ogden was befriending Hampton Institute and encouraging its founder, General Armstrong, an old personal friend. As a member of the board of trustees he gave shrewd business advice as well as funds; and, what was equally important, he popularized its needs in the North by taking to Hampton Northern people of substance and influence. Ogden never gave up his faith in the value of first-hand impres-

[63] The best account of Ogden is the unpublished life by Professor Samuel C. Mitchell which, with Ogden's papers, is deposited in the Library of Congress. The published life is that of P. W. Wilson, *An Unofficial Statesman: Robert C. Ogden* (Garden City, N. Y., 1924).

[64] For Ogden's philosophy of social obligation and business idealism see his "Business Idealism," *The Business World,* Vol. XXV (June, 1905), pp. 277–81. For his attitude on Socialism see his letter to Frances Ogden Ide, July 17, 1912, Mitchell, *op. cit.,* p. 45. *The New York Times,* Jan. 14, 1912, sec. V, p. 4, contains an article in which he develops a moderate and qualified philosophy of profit-sharing.

sions and in the power of organizing friendships for social ends.

In 1898 Ogden took a leading part in the organization of what developed into the Conference on Southern Education. This conference, which annually brought together a great many distinguished bankers, manufacturers, educators, and journalists from all parts of the country, sired the Southern Education Board and contributed to the organization of the General Education Board. Financed by the Rockefellers, these boards made generous and far-reaching contributions to the educational development of that section. Another outcome of the conference held in 1898 was the "Ogden movement." Each year the merchant prince, who possessed a flair for publicity and for organizing friendships, chartered special trains which carried distinguished guests to the South. In selected places impressive educational conferences were held. Quickening the cause of education by stirring up enthusiasm and breaking down opposition to increased taxation for its extension, this movement became a driving social force. Ogden claimed that he was merely helping the South to help itself—that he was simply urging public education before the business men of the South as a business proposition. The criticism which arose on the part of certain Southerners who resented the Northern philanthropic and efficiently organized invasion did not discourage his efforts.[65]

If Ogden was motivated by economic considerations in his work for Southern education, his private papers do not reveal any such interest. In part he was moved by Christian idealism. In part he was motivated by a sense of the successful business

[65] For Southern criticisms of "the Ogden movement" see a letter of Rollen Sawyer to Ogden, Feb. 13, 1906, Ogden MSS., Ed. Ser., Vol. IV; and Edward Ingle, *The Ogden Movement: An Educational Monopoly in the Making* (Baltimore, 1908).

man's *noblesse oblige*. Just as the old feudal aristocracy developed a *noblesse oblige* which in effect served to perpetuate and even to endear it among those who did not participate equally in its advantages, so business entrepreneurs developed a sense of social obligation to those whose profits from the established economic structure were not so obvious. Ogden along with other beneficiaries and directors of the existing economic system assumed responsibility for bestowing what the system itself failed to provide directly for social need. Thus at the very time when industrialism was invading the South, its representatives in the North helped enterprising and idealistic Southerners to extend the blessings of free public schools as a means of solving social problems.

Although the work of Doctor Seaman Knapp for Southern education lies outside the schools, it is comparable to that of Walter Hines Page and Robert Ogden. As a professor of agriculture in the State College of Iowa Knapp gave an address in 1883 in which he attacked whatever merely trained the memory, developed the reasoning power, and provided useless academic information. "The great need of the many is a more scientific and practical knowledge of the common things of life." A lover of the common man, and a deep sympathizer with the average farmer for his tough lot, Knapp began his co-operative demonstration work among Texas farmers in 1903 in order to lighten their burdens. His thrilling victories over the boll weevil and his promotion of diversified farming were, in his mind, but a means to an end: he wanted the farmer to learn how to farm efficiently, how to nourish, clothe, and properly feed his family. He wanted him to emerge from the depths of poverty and insecurity to enjoy comfort and well-being. He believed that all this could be done if the farmer would learn that his occupation was a business and must be managed in a businesslike way.

When his work came to the attention of the General Education Board, that foundation financed an extensive campaign which Knapp directed. "Your mission," he told the farming masses of the South, "is to create a great common people and thus to readjust the map of the world." By means of demontration agents and demonstration farms, and by boys' and girls' clubs, he inspired confidence and hope; he introduced more efficient methods of farming; he demonstrated the educational and idealistic value of doing common things in an intelligent and scientific way. His ability to idealize material things and to spiritualize the commonplace, which would have delighted Emerson's soul, was rooted in American soil. Appealing to the American sense of neighborly co-operation, and to the spirit of rivalry among boys and girls and their parents, he gave proof of his theory that the child must learn farming, not from books, but from actual farming. He encouraged the fight against inefficiency, ignorance, and poverty, not only in order to furnish material well-being, but to lay the indispensable foundation for "spiritual and intellectual uplifting." In 1914 Congress recognized the economic and educational importance of Knapp's work by providing for its financial support and its systematic direction by the Department of Agriculture.[66]

Without doubt Knapp's educational work contributed not only to the improvement of farm crops but also to efficient mass production of farm produce. If his work failed to free the Southern farmer from mortgages and debts and to lay the foundation for a better life, if it even seemed to aggravate his problems by glutting the market with increased output and consequent lower prices, it may not have been in vain. It

[66] O. B. Martin, *The Demonstration Work: Dr. Seaman A. Knapp's Contribution to Civilization* (Boston, 1921) *passim.*

cannot yet be said whether it cleared the way for some successor to educate the efficient producer to the necessity of an
economic system in which a more equitable method of distribution might secure to him the fruits of his labor.

VIII

THE BLACK MAN'S PLACE: BOOKER T. WASHINGTON

1856?–1916

Just so soon as the white merchant finds that education is giving the Negro not only more wants, but more money with which to satisfy these wants, thus making him a better customer; when the white people generally discover that Negro education lessens crime and disease and makes the Negro in every way a better citizen, then the white taxpayer will not look upon the money spent for Negro education as a mere sop to the Negro race, or perhaps as money entirely thrown away.

—Booker T. Washington, *My Larger Education.*

I

In 1872 a young Negro boy with fifty cents in his pocket knocked at the door of Hampton Institute. Born a slave, he had, as a toiler in the salt and coal mines of West Virginia, known nothing but degradation and poverty in the turbulent years that followed emancipation. His mother was not one of the five or ten per cent of her race who could read, and it was only by heroic efforts that he had succeeded in learning his letters. The elementary schools for freedmen established in some places in the South by the missionary societies of Northern churches and by the Freedman's Aid Bureau had apparently not penetrated the mining region where he lived.[1] It was

[1] For an account of the educational work of the Freedmen's Aid Societies and the Freedman's Aid Bureau see George S. Dickerson, "History of Negro Education," and Julius H. Parmelee, "Freedmen's Aid Societies, 1861–1871" in *Negro Education* (Bureau of Education, Bulletins Nos. 38 and 39, 1916), Vol. I, pp. 244–95.

consequently not his fortune to learn his three R's from any of the courageous Yankee schoolma'ams who had gone South to educate the Negro. Had he come under the influence of one of these teachers, who were regarded by Southern whites as obnoxious and who sometimes saw their schoolhouses burned by the Ku-Klux, his later social philosophy might have been very different.[2] If it was true, as Southerners insisted, that these Yankee teachers were inculcating in the blacks pernicious ideas of racial equality and hatred toward their former masters, Booker T. Washington might have developed a militancy which would have altered his outlook on life. But he learned another lesson from his first great hero, the founder and head of the Hampton Institute.

General Samuel Chapman Armstrong had founded Hampton with the conviction that the only hope for the future of the South lay "in a vigorous attempt to lift the colored race by a practical education that shall fit them for life." He had learned from the experiences of the American missionaries in Hawaii, from whom he had sprung, the value of an education for less advanced peoples which, by training the hand for efficient industry, at the same time disciplined the mind and formed character. He taught his pupils that labor was a spiritual force, that physical work not only increased wage-earning capacity but promoted fidelity, accuracy, honesty, persistence, and intelligence. At a time when most Negroes who dreamed of education at all aspired to a knowledge, no matter how smattering, of Latin and Greek, and looked upon education as a substitute for the grinding toil of slavery, Armstrong at Hampton was teaching that the capacity to "make a living becomes enlarged

[2] See Walter L. Fleming, *Documentary History of Reconstruction* (Cleveland, Ohio, 1907), Vol. II, pp. 165 *et seq.*, for the attitude of Yankee teachers in the South, and for the reaction of Southerners to them.

into the capacity to make a life." At great personal sacrifice and with true missionary zeal he and his teachers, when Washington entered the school, were training selected colored youths to go out and lead their people by showing them how to acquire land and homes, vocations and skills; by teaching them to respect labor, especially skilled labor, and to appreciate the value that such work had for the making of character.

In the spirit of Dewey, the founder of Hampton had thus created a school which was a little world where education was to be identical with actual living and which was intended to become a potent and directing force in solving a great social problem. A new type of education was to prevent economic and political catastrophe for blacks and whites alike. "Education, to be effective for life," Armstrong declared, "must be, like the conduct of life itself, both alert and patient, beginning where people are, and creating character rather than comfort, goodness rather than goods. It must be won rather than given, and based on faith in labor as a moral force; it must inspire the will to serve rather than the will to get; it must be a struggle, not for life alone, but for the lives of others."[3]

General Armstrong's appreciation of Booker Washington's admirable qualities—his perseverance, diligence, optimism, and submission to authority—did not assure to that boy an easy road. Hard and exemplary janitor service, a part of the self-help that prevailed at Hampton, enabled him to earn his way. He had never before known what it was to sleep in a bed, to eat regular meals with a knife and a fork, and to take the most elementary care of his body. These things he learned, and, realizing their importance to the progress of his race, idealized.

[3] Francis G. Peabody, *Education for Life, The Story of Hampton Institute* (New York, 1919), p. 206.

Hampton taught other lessons. Booker T. Washington learned the full meaning of duty. Above all, General Armstrong imbued him with his own burning love of service to others, especially service to the black race. His doctrine that skill in labor was indispensable to the Negro was confirmed in Washington's mind when his awkwardness in waiting on table at a summer hotel brought him a cruel rebuff. Each obstacle that he overcame, however, strengthened in his mind the Hampton doctrine that personal success depended on one's ability to do some useful service that the world wanted. If this applied to the individual, it must also apply to his race.

In his first teaching experience in a small school in West Virginia Washington learned to apply the pedagogical principles which in a general way prevailed at Hampton and, in doing so, anticipated one of the most characteristic features of progressive education. Noting the listlessness of his pupils one hot June day, he prolonged their recess and by a happy accident discovered that in surveying the islands in a neighboring marsh the children learned their geography with a zeal entirely lacking when they pondered their maps and books. "For the first time the real difference between studying about things through the medium of books, and studying things themselves without the medium of books, was revealed to me."[4] Washington ever afterwards impressed on his associates the great importance of training pupils to study and analyze actual things, and to use what they had learned in the schoolroom in observing, thinking about, and dealing with the objects and situations of everyday life.

When, in 1881, Washington was called to found a normal institution at Tuskegee, he found no plant, no apparatus, and almost no money. Moreover, he found hostility on the part of

[4] Booker T. Washington, *My Larger Education* (New York, 1911), p. 133.

the white community. Save at Hampton, Negro education had largely been a bookish training which fitted the students for teaching and preaching; and it was widely feared that this would result in making blacks dissatisfied with manual work. To provide the means for building and maintaining the school, and to break down this prejudice, Washington was virtually compelled to fuse practical and intellectual training, thus anticipating the project method which Dewey popularized many years later. If there were to be buildings, students must construct them. If there was to be food, they must produce it, for few could pay for its purchase. If it was to be prepared, they must cook it. So students were taught arithmetic by figuring the cost of constructing and painting a building, by measuring an acre of land, by estimating the cost of producing and preparing a pound of pork. When the school, to meet its own and the community's needs, developed the industry of brick-making, an opportunity was provided for studying the history of the practical arts; and all these matters formed the basis of instruction in English composition.

When students co-operated in doing all the necessary work at Tuskegee and in providing the community with many of the products it needed, and especially when the surrounding area was included in this education through extension work, education was in fact closely tied up with life. Experience and necessity taught Washington that in education it is best "to stick close to the common and familiar things—things that concern the greater part of the people the great part of the time." Education became, in short, problem-solving; and the problems were created, not by artificial devices, but by the compelling necessities of existence. Thus in the struggle to find an education which would best meet the needs of his people, Washington gave the world a practical example of "a broader and more generous conception of what education is and should be than it had had before."[5]

In spite of the Hampton precedent, it was not an easy matter to popularize practical education. Armstrong's doctrine of the moral value of industrial training was of course reiterated, but to the ambitious young Negroes who desired to raise their status by acquiring the culture of upper-class whites it was not altogether convincing.[6] When classroom work was dropped for several days in order to prepare special exhibits and to put Tuskegee in apple-pie order for President McKinley's visit, there was much grumbling on the part of students. Dewey had not yet popularized his doctrine of the educational value of learning by doing useful and co-operative tasks, but Washington appeased his pupils by talking to them at length in very much the way that Dewey might have done.[7] It was not, however, until 1911, when the founder of Tuskegee visited the folk schools of Denmark, that he came fully to appreciate the broader cultural value of utilitarian education.[8] Meantime it was in his mind justified chiefly on the ground that it was necessary, not simply for the existence of Tuskegee, but for the solution of the race problem itself. It is his emphasis on the social significance of a purposeful education which lies at the heart of Washington's social philosophy and which makes him a great American educator.

Washington's emphasis on a practical education for the Negro is explained by his belief that, in order to break down racial prejudice and to achieve real progress for the black, the Southern white must be convinced that the education of the

[5] *Ibid.*, p. 312.
[6] Booker T. Washington, *Working with the Hands* (New York, 1904), pp. 22–23.
[7] Booker T. Washington, *Character Building* (New York, 1902), pp. 95–98.
[8] *My Larger Education*, p. 286.

former slaves was in the true interest of the South—in the interest, in short, of the Southern white himself. Far from appealing to disinterested motives, this black leader believed in the efficacy of appealing to the self-interest of the dominant whites. In their hands lay the granting or withholding of funds for Negro schools. In their hands, moreover, lay the administration of court justice and the alternative device of the rope and faggot —the year after Washington arrived at Tuskegee forty-nine black men were lynched, and in 1892, ten years later, the number was 155. In the hands of the ruling race, too, lay a thousand other matters which vitally affected the blacks. It was clear to Washington that the alliance with Northern whites during Reconstruction had failed to effect any permanent guarantees to his race; and it was equally clear that the more militant and aggressive behavior of the post-war days had provoked reaction and the violence of the Ku-Klux Klan. Where aggressiveness and militancy had failed, an appeal to the self-interest of the dominant whites might succeed. The founder of Tuskegee faced the facts and acted according to his light.

In his effort to enlist the sympathy and co-operation of the white community in Tuskegee Washington was surprisingly successful. His warning that white men, by holding blacks in the gutter, would have to stay there with them, was a compelling argument when it became clear that the whole community actually did profit by what was being done for the Negro. By providing skilled services and produce that Tuskegee needed, he broke down a great deal of the existing prejudice against Negro education. By encouraging the blacks to respect the law and to co-operate with white authorities in detecting crime and punishing it, he still further won the good will of the old master class. When he insisted that the great majority of his race did not expect or desire social equality, he still further disarmed the whites.

The astute Negro leader also did much to dispel the bugbear of black political domination. At first he said very little about the constitutional right of the Negro to vote. Only very cautiously and gradually did he come to advocate the desirability of permitting educated and property-owning blacks to exercise the right of suffrage. He declared that the Negroes should give up their political affiliations with the Republican party which had befriended them in Reconstruction and which they regarded as their emancipator. The Negro in the solid South should vote Democratic because that party was regarded as the true friend of the economic interests of the South, and by so voting he would still further ingratiate himself with the white people in their community. The principal of Tuskegee himself, having made it clear that he would vote only for Democratic candidates, had no trouble in casting his ballot.[9]

To his own people Washington preached the necessity of making themselves useful to the whites and thus securing their good will and the favors they alone could bestow. If the Negro learned how to cultivate the land so efficiently as to produce a larger acreage of cotton, the white farmer would not only respect him but chat with him on the methods he had so successfully used. If the black mastered a skilled trade, the white employer would value his greater usefulness and recognize the potential ability of the race economically to rehabilitate the South. If he accumulated property and paid taxes, if he was able to succeed in business and trade and even to lend money to the dominant race, no barrier of skin could keep the white from associating with him. If he gave up his desire to imitate the

[9] *My Larger Education*, p. 46.

upper-class whites by taking on a veneer of superficial polish and made himself valuable in terms of dollars and cents, he would in the long run win their respect and confidence and even break down their antipathy.

In season and out of season, therefore, Washington warned his people against the deadly sins of idleness, gambling, and drinking, and held up to them the ideals of industry, thrift, chastity, honesty, and earnestness. The Negro, he pleaded, could better afford to be wronged than the white man could afford to wrong him. Unlike the Russian, who hurled dynamite to right his wrongs, or the Frenchman who applied the torch of revolution, or the Indian who flew to his tomahawk, the "Negro must lie by, must be patient, must forgive his enemies, and depend for the righting of his wrong upon his midnight moans, upon his songs, upon his four-day prayers, and upon an inherent faith in the justice of his cause."[10]

In short, the black man was to cease depending upon the humanitarian friendship of Northerners and, by making himself indispensable to the ruling class at home, to work out his own salvation. He must never forget that for the race as for the individual the more discriminations and difficulties, the more steam was required to overcome them, and the greater the victory. If this optimistic philosophy was in part compensatory for the actual handicaps of the race, it nevertheless proved to be a dynamic force, giving courage and incentive to many who came under its spell.

Washington spared nothing to get a hearing for his social philosophy among Southern whites. Aware that his public words in the North would find their way South, he took care never to say anything in that section which he would not say at home. Southerners who attended the sessions of the Na-

10 N. E. A., *Proceedings*, 1896, p. 217.

tional Education Association in Madison in 1884 reported with approval the generous tribute he paid to the white people in Tuskegee for the sympathy they had shown toward his work.[11] When at last an invitation came to give a five-minute talk before a Southern audience, he thought it worth while to make a three-thousand mile journey in order to win the ear of those who directed matters south of the Mason and Dixon line.[12] It is said that he even paid $1000 to get a speech into *The Atlanta Constitution*. His great victory came in 1896 when, notwithstanding grave doubts as to the propriety of the invitation, he was asked to give an address at the opening of the Cotton States Exposition in Atlanta.

In the famous speech which Washington delivered on that occasion he translated his social philosophy into epigrammatic terms. The opportunity to earn a dollar, he declared, was more important to the Negro than the chance to spend it in the opera house. Pleading with the Negro to make himself useful to the South and with the white to cultivate a spirit of friendliness and fairness to the black in return for his economic contribution, Washington won great applause from the governing class for concluding that "in all things that are purely social we can be as separate as the fingers, yet one as the hand in all things essential to mutual progress."[13] Clark Howell of *The Atlanta Constitution* wired New York that the speech was one of the most notable that had ever been given to a Southern audience; it was "a revelation, a platform upon which blacks and whites can stand with full justice to each other." For the first time the white South listened seriously to a Negro, and the speech won new allies in the North as well.

[11] *Ibid.*, 1884, pp. 125–30.
[12] Booker T. Washington, *Up from Slavery* (New York, 1901), pp. 204–5.
[13] E. Davidson Washington, ed., *Selected Speeches of Booker T. Washington* (Garden City, N. Y., 1932), p. 34.

Subsequent lectures, articles, and books consolidated the position thus won. In view of the bids that the South was making for Northern capital, it was not without significance that the Negro educator declared in the Atlanta speech, as he had done before and continued to do, that his people had never engaged in strikes or given any labor trouble.[14] He announced that the hope of the Negro rested largely on such Southern leaders in finance and business as John M. Parker, a New Orleans cotton merchant who was quoted as saying that it was "important to the commercial progress of the country that the Negro should be treated with justice in the courts, in business, and in all the affairs of life."[15] So exemplary was Washington's behavior that J. L. M. Curry could observe that in fourteen years of intimate association with him he had never once known the Negro educator to say or to do an unwise thing.[16]

Regardless of the extent to which Washington succeeded in convincing Northern financial groups that industrial education of the Negro promised a skilled, docile, and cheap labor supply, and that racial friction would diminish, he certainly found it, after his reassuring speeches, less of a struggle to obtain endowment for his institution. Both the Peabody and Slater funds increased their subsidies; and the great railroad magnate Collis Huntington and such industrialists as Andrew Carnegie, H. H. Rogers of the Standard Oil Company, William H. Baldwin, and Robert Ogden discovered the value of the work which was being done at Tuskegee, and contributed to its exchequer.

In 1905 Ogden wrote that, in view of the ill effects of excite-

---

[14] *Ibid.*, p. 33; *The Educational and Industrial Emancipation of the Negro* (Brooklyn, N. Y., 1903), p. 14; *Up from Slavery*, p. 69.

[15] *My Larger Education*, pp. 60–61.

[16] John G. Brooks, *An American Citizen. The Life of William Henry Baldwin, Jr.* (Boston, 1910), pp. 226–27.

ment on the race question, *"peaceful patience* should control the utterances from Hampton"[17] and doubtless the same advice was given to Tuskegee. On one of the rare occasions when Washington referred to the race question, which he thought must be *"lived* down, not *talked* down," he took particular pleasure in Curry's praise of his remarks.[18] William Henry Baldwin, manager and vice-president of the Southern Railway, was, in Washington's words, "always particularly interested and even anxious that in all my public utterances I should say the right thing, and, above all, that I should say the helpful thing."[19]

Convinced that the Negro was at his best in the country and that he showed up worst in the city, Washington made every effort to persuade his people to acquire the farms on which they lived. Yet, as the years passed, he came more and more to sympathize with the Negro business man and to reverence the business ideal of life. In part this change was due to new associations. He learned to admire such men as H. H. Rogers, William Baldwin, Robert Ogden, and the Negro business leader, Charles Banks. In part, however, his increased interest in business was merely a recognition that American life was becoming urbanized and that business success offered the great road to advancement. He took it for granted that a people able to organize and conduct large business corporations, banks, insurance companies, and other forms of corporate enterprises was destined to survive and prosper.

If the Negro business man was successful, Washington felt that then prejudice and color could not long shut the race

[17] Ogden to Helen Ludlow, New York, June 15, 1905, Ogden MSS., Educational Series, Vol. I, Letters, 1886–1910.

[18] Washington to Curry, Oct. 24, 1898, Curry MSS., Vol. XII.

[19] Brooks, *op. cit.,* p. 247. It is the impression of Doctor W. E. B. DuBois that Baldwin openly stated that his plan was to train in the South two sets of workers, equally skilled, black and white, who could be used to offset each other and break the power of trade unions (personal interview).

out from a share in any of the responsibilities of the community in which they lived, or in any opportunity or position that a self-respecting people would desire to possess. "Our people," he declared, "must learn not merely the lessons of industry and thrift; they must also learn to employ corporate action for the achievement of their ends as individuals and a race, in the same way that the white man has learned to employ it."[28] He sponsored the National Negro Business League and in refutation of the charge that the race was lacking in thrift, executive talent, and organizing ability, cited with pride the success of colored men in business.

The black leader was merely accepting the dominant business philosophy of his day. Like most Americans, he did not ask how fortunes were made, nor question the ethics of the captains of industry and finance. Accepting the tenet that whenever the Negro failed to find steady employment, it was due to his shiftlessness, his unreliability, and his easy-going ways, he begged his people, in heart to heart talks, to cultivate the business virtues.

In plain words Washington reminded his race that one of their sins was their inability to handle other people's property honestly.[21] He held up for praise the successful boy who did a dollar's worth of work for fifty cents, was at hand before starting time, and stayed after the closing hour to ask the employer if there were not something more to be done before he went home.[22] The Negro was urged to anticipate the wants of his employer and to remember that it did not pay to do anything less than his very best. Above all, he was advised to accumulate a bank account. Frugality, industry, foresight, financial responsibility, and independence—these were prominent among

[20] Booker T. Washington, *The Negro in Business* (Chicago, 1907), p. 173.
[21] *Character Building*, p. 145.   [22] *Ibid.*, p. 211.

the virtues that Washington begged his people to cultivate as the surest means of getting ahead.

Believing that if the blacks knew something of the burdens borne by the masses of Europe they would realize that their own position was by no means unique or hopeless, as many had supposed, Booker T. Washington went to Europe in 1910 to study the "man farthest down." He came back with an optimistic message for his people. If they could have heard one race in Austria-Hungary denouncing another in the most virulent terms, they would realize that race prejudice was not a matter of color. Could they have visited with him the desolate slums of the great European cities, seen the degradation, the beggary, the unemployment, they would have seen sights, he declared, far worse than anything which existed in the Negro quarters of Southern cities or in the most wretched cabins in the countryside.

In Europe Washington found conditions bad indeed. There the overcrowded land was owned by a few great landlords; in the South, there was plenty for every one to own an ample farm. In Cracow, women toiled in the granite quarries. In Sicily existed moral degeneracy that made the Negro seem in comparison a model of virtue. In Bohemia, the Czechs, in addition to the discriminations inflicted on them by the ruling Germans, spoke a different language and adhered to a different faith: the Negro spoke the tongue and attended the church of the Southern white. However meager the educational opportunities of American Negroes, boys and girls shared them alike. In Europe, on the other hand, the women farthest down were burdened with additional discriminations because of their sex. In short, while the Negro had suffered as a slave and was still discriminated against, his position was by no means exceptional. Indeed, in some respects he fared better than the man farthest down in the Old World. In finding people lower still than they, Washington seemed to lift his own race to a higher level.

Although Washington found much evidence that the masses in Europe were getting ahead, he doubted whether trade unions, strikes, Socialism, and revolution could improve their lot. Wherever the governing classes had made concessions, wherever remedial measures and reforms had been granted, the spirit of revolution had subsided. While he admitted that he did not very clearly understand Socialism, he expressed doubt whether, human nature being what it was, the Socialist program could be realized in the way its adherents believed. It was the American individualist of the middle class, not the Negro, who spoke when he declared that as human capacities differed, so opportunities and rewards must also differ. As a Southerner he paid tribute to the *laissez-faire* theory that the best government was that which governed least; and as an American, he repudiated reform by revolution and by political machinery which directed and controlled the individual from the outside.[23] Neither his own race nor the substantial friends of Tuskegee could doubt where he stood. Possibly, however, there was something of an ironical warning in his statement that the dominant class in Europe had patriotically striven to strengthen the existing order by freeing it from the defects that endangered its existence.

In a truly American middle-class spirit this educator looked to philanthropy, collaboration between classes and races, and, above all, to education, to effect a great silent, peaceful revolution in the lot of the European masses. "The effect of this movement, or revolution as I have called it, is not to 'tear

[23] Booker T. Washington, *The Man Farthest Down* (New York, 1912), pp. 102–3.

down and level up,' in order to bring about an artificial equality, but to give every individual a chance to 'make good,' to determine for himself his place and position in the community by the character and quality of the service he is able to perform."[24] The industrial training which European governments provided for the masses confirmed him in his belief that he had done well to emphasize that type of education for his race.

Washington's social philosophy was, in fine, more typical of middle-class white Americans, whom he wanted his people to be like, than it was of the Negro as such. It is true that in appealing to former slaves and their offspring to eschew militancy and conflict with the whites in the effort to improve the status of the race, he capitalized the black man's way of getting along by laughing, dancing, and singing. But little was said about the qualities of gayety, humor, and wistful whimsicality, virtues and gifts which some thought might enrich and soften the driving, efficient, and machinelike ways of the American whites. On the contrary, Washington made simplicity, earnestness, frugality, and industry the great desiderata. One searches his writings in vain for any appreciation of the æsthetic and cultural values of the African background, of the "spirituals," or of the generally pleasant, easy-going ways of the black man. Although very occasionally he made a bow to the need of cultivating the beautiful, he resembled Franklin in paying much greater deference to whatever was useful and practical.

In other ways Washington was like the average American. His insistence on looking at the bright side of things, his devotion to getting ahead by self-help, his conviction that every one had his future in his own hands, that success came to him who

24 *Ibid.*, p. 385.

was worthy of it, and that the greater the obstacles, the greater the victory over them—all this characterized the thought and feeling of most Americans. Equally typical of the dominant psychology of the middle and upper classes was his denial of any conflict or cleavage of interest between worker and employer, white and black. His was the gospel of class co-operation. His boast that his race had never been guilty of declaring strikes was pleasant to Americans who loved to think that there could be no justification in such disturbances to decency and public order. His patriotic belief that, however bad conditions were for his race at home, the masses of Europe were even worse off, was likewise good American doctrine.

II

Characteristically middle-class though his social thinking was, it met with criticism. After the Atlanta speech, when Washington was accorded recognition as the leader of his race, Negroes took him to task for truckling to the dominant whites in the South. Some felt he should speak out more openly in regard to the violation of the civic rights of Negroes. Others lamented that his philosophy lacked the spirit of the Declaration of Independence. His complacency and his desire to give no offense seemed to many a betrayal of the best aspirations and hopes of the race.

Oustanding among his critics was Doctor W. E. Burghart DuBois. A graduate of Fisk and of Harvard, DuBois had studied at the University of Berlin and won distinction as a scholar and as a writer. What he especially resented was the overshadowing emphasis which Washington placed on industrial education. It seemed to obscure the legitimate desires of many Negroes for professional, literary, and artistic distinction. College education, which promised to teach the Negro the values and meaning of life, seemed relegated to a back place by all the insistence on training to get ahead in the trades, in farming, and in business. If the race was to have leadership, if Negroes were not to be simply more efficient hewers of wood and drawers of water, then, it was held, something more than industrial training was imperative. If the Negro were to win equality with the white, he must equal the white in culture, in creative scholarship, and in the arts. He must prize the best in his racial heritage; he must hold his head high, and stop turning the other cheek; he must, in short, cast off the psychology of the slave. Between these two ideals of education a bitter fight was waged. In spite of the passionate and tenacious sincerity that characterized both sides, each made concessions. But on the whole, at least among the leaders of the race who succeeded Washington, the point of view for which Doctor DuBois stood gained an increasingly important place.[25]

Yet, as Doctor DuBois himself later admitted, much could be said in defense of the position that Washington took. When he insisted that no end of talk would refute the evidence that the blacks did not equal in condition and capacity the majority of the whites with whom they came in contact, he added the significant remark that to insist that such was not the case was merely to admit that slavery had not been a handicap to the race.[26] While professional men were indeed necessary, and while culture must be kept in mind, the race for the time needed above all else the knowledge and skill which would insure the material necessities of life.

[25] After the death of Wallace Buttrick in 1926, the General Education Board reversed its former policy and began to promote cultural as well as industrial education of the Negro.

[26] *Character Building*, pp. 119–20.

Washington's position is better understood when it is remembered that he began his work when race hatred was at its height and when emotions were strained and tense. The temper of the times was against the black man. Washington felt that much could be gained if attention were diverted from the fear of whites for the integrity and supremacy of their race, a fear deeply ingrained by hundreds of years of experience as a master class. That fear might be diverted if the ignorant black could be made to seem a more serious danger than the educated Negro. The satisfaction of the stronger race that came from insults could perhaps best be undermined by the black if he capitalized his defensive sense of humor. If defiant passion were met with resistant passion conflict rather than conviction promised to result. A wise strategy would shift the proof of the capacity of the black race from the subjective to the objective plane. The emotional resistance of the whites to such objective proof must be swept aside, not by a frontal attack, but by a diversion—by allaying the fear of the dominant group that its self-interest and integrity were threatened by the lower.[27]

Education of the hands helped in fact to bridge the gap between slavery and freedom; it taught thousands of Southern whites to accept Negro education, not merely as a necessary evil, but as a possible social benefit. The good will that Washington won was at least partly responsible for increasing public support to Negro colleges and schools. But this support has remained to our own day both inadequate and unequal to that given the schools for white children. While in 1931 an average of $45.63 was spent by Southern states for the education of the white child, only $14.95 was spent for that of

[27] Charles S. Johnson, "The Social Philosophy of Booker T. Washington," *Opportunity,* Vol. VI (April, 1928), pp. 102–5.

the black. Of the total school expenditure in the South, only 10.7 per cent went to the Negro race.[28]

The industrial school was, nevertheless, realistic and not without victories in its practical object of aiding the black man to find a place in American life in which he could make a decent living as the foundation of culture. In the words of its early critic Doctor DuBois, "it tempered and rationalized the inner emancipation of American Negroes. It made the Negro patient when impatience would have killed him. If it has not made working with the hands popular, it has at least removed much of the stigma of social degradation. It has made many Negroes seek the friendship of their white fellow citizens, even at the cost of insult and caste. And thus through a wide strip of our country it has brought peace and not a sword."[29]

Yet, as Doctor DuBois has pointed out, industrial training did not keep the Negro farm population from decreasing; it did not enable the Negro artisan to gain proportionately in industry; it did not establish Negro business on a sound footing. Leaders of the movement ignored the fact that at the very time when the crusade for industrial training was being launched, the technological basis of industry was rapidly shifting from that of the skilled artisan to machine production. They failed to see that the machine, by invading the farm, was already beginning to push even the established farmer to the wall. They did not come to grips with the stubborn and fettering problem of tenantry. They were blind to the fact that in business a new technique of world-wide combination, the use of credit on a vast scale, and the rise of the mail order house and

28 Investment in school property in the South in 1931 averaged $120.09 for each white child and $29.62 for each colored child. The Negro schools had larger classes per teacher and a shorter school year. *Negro Year Book,* 1931–32 (Tuskegee Institute, Alabama, 1931), pp. 203–5.
29 W. E. Burghart DuBois, "Education and Work," *Journal of Negro Education,* Vol. I (April 1, 1932), p. 65.

chain store, was stacking the cards against the success of the Negro business man. Above all, they failed to see the weaknesses in the dominant industrial and financial system into which industrial education was trying to fit the Negro. They made the grave mistake of assuming that it was both sound and unchanging. In short, Washington failed to see the problem of democracy in industry; he failed to seek an alliance with the labor movement, or with any group that sought to remake the existing order along more equitable and more stable lines.

In view of the hostility of organized labor to the black and the general ineffectiveness of Socialism on the one hand, and the friendliness of men of great wealth on the other, it was, of course, entirely natural for Washington to take the stand he did. Moreover, there was much justification for his emphasis on the immediate amelioration of his race within the system that actually existed. Until collaboration with the dominant class among the whites had been proved to be ineffective as an instrument for elevating the race, it was natural to pin great faith to it. Even the majority of white educational leaders, far better equipped than a former slave to penetrate and to interpret events, did not see any fundamental inadequacies in the existing order.

With much mellowness and philosophical insight Doctor DuBois has criticized also the cultural type of Negro education which supinely imitated the white college and university. If it provided much intelligent leadership, it too had failed to comprehend the age for which it was presumably fitting its students. Like other colleges, it had often turned attention away from a disposition to study and solve fundamental economic and cultural problems.[30]

If the Negro were to fit into the existing system—and what

[30] *Ibid.*, p. 63.

could seem more natural and desirable to a former slave?—Washington offered a realistic approach to the problem. His ideas and his leadership were widely appreciated. Probably the most representative and influential educational leader of the period, William T. Harris, declared that Washington's solution for the Negro problem was of "so universal a character that it applies to the down-trodden of all races, without reference to color."[31] If in spite of his positive contributions in helping Negroes adjust themselves to a system, Booker T. Washington failed to criticize fundamental weaknesses within that system, his failure was hardly a personal one. He was merely accepting the prevalent American doctrine of self-help and the belief that the best man gets ahead, and, considering his background, it is not strange that he failed to see that this holds even less true for the humble Negro than for the average white man. The limitations of his social thinking were not, primarily, those of a Negro—they were those of the class which, on the whole, determined American values and governed American life.

[31] William T. Harris, *Addresses Delivered at the Inauguration of the Reverend John Gordon, D.D.* (Washington, D. C., 1904), p. 28.

IX

WILLIAM T. HARRIS, THE CONSERVATOR
1835–1908

Ninety-nine out of a hundred people in every civilized nation are automata, careful to walk in the prescribed paths, careful to follow prescribed custom. This is the result of substantial education, which, scientifically defined, is the subsumption of the individual under his species. The other educational principle is that of emancipation from this subsumption. This is subordinate, and yet, in our time, we lay more stress upon it than the other.

—WILLIAM T. HARRIS, *The Philosophy of Education.*

Already he was exerting a most profound influence upon the teachers and the public-school system of the entire country, and was quoted more frequently and with more approval by educational journals and by public-school teachers than any other American— not even excepting Horace Mann.

—JAMES H. CANFIELD, 1906.

I

While it was Barnard and Mann who laid the foundations of the American public school system, it was William T. Harris who presided over the rearing of the structure. His most important achievement, however, was to furnish American education with a philosophy which helped the rank and file to adjust their thought and feeling to new actualities without losing the sense of identity with older values and conditions.

When Harris was born in 1835, American nationality had not yet been consolidated; when he died in 1909, no important group seriously challenged it. When he was born, rural America was dominant; when he died, urban and industrial America was in the saddle. When Harris began his educational work, there was still abundant free land, with something approaching, roughly to be sure, economic opportunities for everyone; when he finished his work, the traditional opportunities for the individual were, while still celebrated, in fact very much limited. In 1835, most of the intellectual and social leaders of America believed in a personal God, the freedom of the will, and immortality. In 1909, the advance of science had to a considerable extent changed that faith. It was the work of Harris to aid his fellow Americans, and particularly educators, to accept the new order without entirely repudiating the old.

North Killingly, Connecticut, where Harris was born in 1835, was less than a hundred miles from both Boston and Hartford, where Mann and Barnard were then on the threshold of their active educational labors. The parents of Harris were well-to-do farmers, and members of the family were interested in the textile mills which by 1836 made Killingly the most important cotton manufacturing town in Connecticut. Harris was sent to private academies, including the famous Phillips Andover, and in 1855 entered Yale. He left after two years, not because of the inability of his parents to pay his tuition, but rather because he was dissatisfied with what Yale offered.[1]

Young Harris had caught the radical virus that had contaminated the solidity and complacency of New England. He became converted to phrenology, mesmerism, and the claims and promises of "natural science," repudiated a good deal of the orthodox Congregationalism with which he had been indoctrinated, and turned his back on the authoritarianism of the classics. While he did not, apparently, interest himself in Fourierism or any radical economic doctrines, he was nevertheless a

[1] Henry Sabin, "Reminiscences of William Torrey Harris," *Journal of Education*, Vol. LXXI (May 5, 1910), pp. 483–84; William T. Harris, "How I Was Educated," *The Forum*, Vol. I (Aug., 1886), pp. 552–61.

come-outer. Theodore Parker's writings led him to study German philosophy; and he became, and continued to his death, an ardent student of Kant, Fichte, and, above all, of Hegel.[2]

Whether it was the influence of Hegel, whom he discovered after migrating to St. Louis in 1857, or his rapid success as a teacher and administrator in the schools of that city, which sobered his radicalism, one cannot be certain. In any case, the idealism which had been nourished in him by transcendentalism (it was the reading of Bronson Alcott that undermined his faith in phrenology) flourished on the new-found German philosophy, and his opposition to the determinism and empiricism of Spencer became pronounced. The refusal of the editors of *The Atlantic Monthly* and *The North American Review* to publish a criticism of Spencer led Harris, when but thirty-two years old, to found in St. Louis *The Journal of Speculative Philosophy,* which he continued to edit through twenty-two volumes, and which familiarized many Americans with German idealistic philosophy, as well as with Greek thought, and their applications to æsthetics and the more practical problems of life. The agnostic and deterministic ideas of Spencer were proving popular in many circles, and the doctrines of Darwin were challenging the faith of orthodox Christians. Yet many Americans were eagerly seeking for a philosophic justification of faith in God, freedom, and immortality. Harris, by popularizing the absolute idealism of Hegel, provided them with able and authoritarian support for their cherished views.

The Hegelian philosophy which Harris made the basis of all his social and educational thinking[3] possessed the virtue of

[2] Harris to S. S. McClure, Sept. 7, 1887, Harris MSS., No. 863; "Books That Have Helped Me," *The Forum,* Vol. III (April, 1887), pp. 142–51.

[3] For a brief discussion of Harris's philosophy see John S. Roberts, *William T. Harris, A Critical Study of His Educational and Related Philosophic Views* (Washington, D. C., 1924).

being thoroughly optimistic and idealistic in character. It infused the world with a divine purpose and endowed the individual with a noble and immortal destiny. At the same time it justified the existing order and authorities by declaring that whatever is, is an inevitable stage in the unfolding of objective reason or the world spirit, and is therefore right. It seemed to lift the individual to a higher plane of self-realization without sacrificing the ideals of self-help and self-activity. At the same time it subordinated the individual to existing social institutions by maintaining that his true, spiritual self, which was constantly in conflict with his natural or physical self, could be realized only by adjusting himself to the divinely appointed environment and institutions that were in actual existence. This doctrine of spiritual self-realization or self-estrangement, as we shall see, was given important applications in the educational and social thought of Harris.

By the use of the dialectic method of resolving antitheses into higher syntheses, Hegelian philosophy also permitted the exploitation of science for social and economic purposes without sacrificing religion and the concerns of the spirit as ultimate values. In short, the right-wing Hegelianism to which Harris subscribed satisfied religious and idealistic aspirations, paid tribute to the cult of individuality and self-help, and at the same time subordinated the mass of individuals to existing institutions, which included the corporation, the city, and the machine, as well as religion and the national state. As we shall see, it also had a good deal to say about socialism and other protests against industrial capitalism.

It would be hard to overemphasize the importance which Harris attached to "spiritual values," both cultural and religious. Reared a Congregationalist, he had flirted for a time during his college days with naturalism and then, until his death, regularly attended the church of his fathers. In his mind philosophy supported the Christian religion; and the church, together with the state, civil society, the family, and the school, was a necessary and beneficent institution. Like its sister institutions, religion enabled the individual to come into harmony and cooperation with human society as a totality and to receive a share of the whole re-enforcing spiritual achievements of the race. As the basis of civilization, religion was a social process by which the intellect, will, and heart of the individual were strengthened. It held conservatively to monogamy and the integrity of the family; it provided charity for the weaklings of society; above all, it inculcated respect for private property and for law and order.[4]

In Christianity Harris also found a synthesis of the Oriental religions which virtually denied the here and now, individuality, and secondary causes, and the naturalism of Hume, Spencer, and his followers, who virtually dismissed everything except the here and the now, sense experience, and secondary causes. By synthesizing these two extremes, Christianity made room both for ultimate truth, first cause, and God, and for individual self-activity and the affairs of this world. Thus Christianity was an indispensable institution for securing the proper relationship between the individual and the universal, the temporal and the eternal.[5]

Yet Harris did not wish religious instruction to be given in public schools. The principle of religious instruction was authority; that of secular teaching, demonstration and verification. "It is obvious," he remarked, "that these two principles should not be brought into the same school, but separated as widely as possible." Religious instruction should be accompanied by

[4] Wm. T. Harris, "Social Culture in the Form of Education and Religion," *Ed. Rev.*, Vol. XXIX (Jan., 1905), pp. 18–37.
[5] *Ibid.*

reverence, solemnity, and, preferably, by ritualistic surroundings. In the experience of centuries, Harris thought, the church
had admirably learned its technique. Secular instruction in
parochial schools often suffered by virtue of carrying over the
religious method of authority, memorization, and symbols. Religious instruction in public schools, to meet the varied needs
and beliefs of all, had to be denatured into mere Deism.[6]

While the most important of the spiritual values which made
up the good life, religion was not the sole one: the higher
culture was also fundamental in Harris's *Weltanschauung*. In
theory, at least, he had no heart for a culture "belonging to a
class that rests like an upper layer upon the mass below, who in
turn have to spin and dig for them."[7] Assuming that American
industrial civilization provided and would increasingly provide
the mass of the people with an opportunity co-operatively to
subjugate the elements and win a competence on such easy
terms that the greater part of life might be devoted to higher
culture, Harris firmly believed that the common man was
destined to participate in "the realized intelligence of all mankind."[8]

Elementary education, which must be universal, was to give
to each child the tools by which he might participate in the culture of the race—grammar, literature and art, mathematics,
geography, and history. These were the "five windows of the
soul," which enabled the individual to appreciate the common
stock of ideas and cultural values that governed the social
organization and civilization of which he was a part. By these
"tool subjects" the child was to acquire the instruments for

[6] Wm. T. Harris, "Religious Instruction in the Public Schools," *Independent*,
Vol. LV (Aug. 6, 1903), pp. 1841–43.
[7] *A Statement of the Theory of Education in the United States by Many
Leading Educators* (Washington, D. C., 1874), p. 34.
[8] *Ibid.*, p. 35.

mastering the entire realms of nature and of mind. The vast technological and business developments which provided libraries and newspapers to the masses enabled them to master, independently of teachers and universities, the great cultural treasures of the past, even if they went no farther than the elementary school.[9]

As the utilitarian subjects pressed for an increasing place in the curriculum, Harris, while permitting moderate compromise, insisted on the value of the disciplinary and cultural studies. Although he did not ignore the new emphasis on hygiene and physiology and the demands for better ventilated and better lighted schools, he declared that the great purposes of the school had been and were still realized in dark, ill-aired log schoolhouses, in slum tenements rented for the purpose, and in the shanty school.[10] Emphasis on biological and physiological theory seemed to him an undue surrender to the physical nature of man, which education was primarily responsible for subordinating to the spiritual or true self.[11] The chief object of physical training was to put will into the muscles. But this could be overdone, and Harris always opposed the movement for abandoning the old-fashioned recess, which he believed necessary for relaxation, involving momentary surrender to caprice.[12]

In still other ways Harris defended the cultural and spiritual values in education and in life. Believing that Latin and Greek vocabularies and syntax provided students with the most effec-

[9] Wm. T. Harris, *What Shall We Study?* Reprint from *Journal of Education*, St. Louis, Vol. II (Sept., 1869), pp. 1–3.

[10] Wm. T. Harris, *The Danger of Using Biological Analogies in Reasoning on Educational Subjects* (Bloomington, Ill., 1902).

[11] *Annual Report of the St. Louis Public Schools*, 19th, 1872–73, p. 110.

[12] "Observations on Physical Training in and out of School," in Harris MSS.; Wm. T. Harris, *Recess* (*Popular Education Document*, No. 20, St. Louis, 1884), p. 8.

tive insight into the embryonic period of Western civilization and enabled them better to understand the forms and usages of their intellectual and moral being, he stoutly defended the classics.[13] As superintendent of the St. Louis schools and as the editor of a series of school readers he did a good deal to familiarize American school children with the great literary masterpieces of the past, and he was also an early champion of instruction in art. If he occasionally called attention to the advantage such training would give in the international competition for markets,[14] for the most part he advocated art instruction as a means of cultivating the feelings and curbing the appetites, and of so transcending the beauty of nature as to permit man to realize the divine.[15]

When the manual training movement was launched in the 1880's, Harris minimized its importance and denied that it possessed great intellectual value. His opposition was based in large part on his conviction that sense-training was less valuable than the Pestalozzians thought. "It is a false psychology which says we derive all our knowledge from sense-perception."[16] His view was that school education should develop the power to withdraw from the external world of the senses and to fix attention on forces and principles; it should also open the child's soul to the cultural treasures of the past. He denied that hand labor had any particular moral value, unless it resulted in products for the market place, thereby subordinating

[13] "On the Function of the Study of Latin and Greek in Education," address, Sept. 4, 1884, in Harris MSS.; Wm. T. Harris, "A Brief for Latin," *Ed. Rev.*, Vol. XVII (April, 1899), pp. 313–16.

[14] Wm. T. Harris, *Compulsory Education in Relation to Crime and Social Morals* (Washington, 1885), p. 13.

[15] Wm. T. Harris, "The Aesthetic Element in Education," N. E. A., *Proceedings*, 1897, pp. 330–38; "The Study of Art and Literature in the Schools," *Report of the Commissioner of Education*, 1898–99, Vol. I, pp. 687–706.

[16] *Education*, Vol. IX (May, 1889), p. 580.

the worker for the good of others and in turn enabling him to share in their production.[17] In expressing sympathy for the establishment of manual trade schools for children "unwilling to carry any further their purely cultural studies," Harris, somewhat in the spirit of Dewey, wished these schools to teach not merely the narrow skills and techniques, but the broader aspects of trade—its place in society and its relation to the traditions and needs of civilization.[18] Moreover, students in the trade schools, having acquired the tool subjects in elementary school, might through the newspaper and the public library continue to enrich themselves in cultural and non-technical values.[19] If he overlooked the fact that the newspaper was already in the nineties being transformed into a commercial and even sensational money-making venture, and if he neglected to see that cheap but profit-making amusements were already commercializing the scant leisure of workingmen, he nevertheless did not intend to condemn them to purely manual, technical, and material values.

The great emphasis that Harris attached to cultural and spiritual values, as well as to religion, made his defense of the machine, of the urbanization of American life, and of industrial capitalism, seem all the more rational and convincing. Indeed he was a pioneer in welcoming the application of science to the affairs of everyday life and in urging the introduction of the sciences into the school curriculum.[20] Recognizing the inevitability of the "machine age," and also aware of some of the contradictions to cultural and spiritual values it

17 *The Forum*, Vol. IV (Feb., 1888), p. 580.
18 Wm. T. Harris, "The Intellectual Value of Tool Work," *Scientific American*, supplement, No. 1598 (Aug. 18, 1906).
19 Wm. T. Harris, "The Printing Press as an Instrument of Education," *Education*, Vol. I (March, 1881), pp. 371–83; "What Shall the Public Schools Teach?" *Forum*, Vol. IV (Feb., 1888), pp. 573–81.
20 *St. Louis Report*, 17th, 1870–71, p. 173.

implied, Harris resolved the contradictions by the use of the dialectical method and his philosophic presuppositions.

Thus in tracing the development of machine industrialism in England, Harris dwelt on the benefits that the factory system had brought to laborers. "Instead of occasional seasons of work and most inadequate wages on farms, this population obtained in the newly-established mills of Manchester and Birmingham a constant employment and remunerative wages,—better dwelling, better food and clothing, and a plenty."[21] Actually, of course, the factory system also meant the substitution of wretched urban tenements and frightful slums for rural hovels, child labor under execrable conditions, technological unemployment, suffering during ever recurring crises and depressions— the creation, in short, of an industrial proletariat.

In resolving the contradictions between machine civilization and cultural values, Harris obscured the evils in accentuating the benefits. He never tired of explaining that machine industry, by substituting intelligent direction for brute force and by multiplying the commodities one man could produce, freed the worker from grinding toil and enabled him to share in the products of others. He pictured glowingly the leisure for the pursuit of culture which machine production provided for the laborer.[22]

Harris also emphasized the educational values of machine production. Instead of enslaving the individual, the machine, he contended, actually freed and elevated him. The machine required alertness of mind, versatility, and trained intelligence on the part of its directors; and education must develop these qualities. Harris was not disturbed by the monotonous routine

---

[21] *Education*, Vol. V (May, 1885), p. 444.
[22] N. E. A., *Proceedings*, 1898, p. 124; *Atlantic Monthly*, Vol. LXIX (June, 1892), p. 731; *The Educational Journal of Virginia*, Vol. XXII (Nov., 1891), pp. 519–23.

that new machinery was bringing to many former artisans, for he believed that the dull tending of these new instruments of production was a passing phase of industrialism. From the stage that "reduces the human being to a machine" would develop, "by a sort of dialectic necessity," the complete mechanization in which the machine would itself care for all tasks except those demanding intelligence and imagination.[23] Woman, with her alert intellect but weak physique, would particularly benefit from this development, achieving economic independence, freedom for her individuality, and a sense of fulfilling a necessary function in the larger economic order.[24] Harris was not troubled by the specter of technological unemployment, saying that the educated man would easily learn the operation of new machines.[25]

It is noteworthy that Harris sensed in the dominance of the machine certain contradictions to the values of the past which he cherished. These contradictions were, for him, banished by the certainty that the Hegelian process of development and synthesis would eliminate many and that education could dispel others. Education would enable the masses successfully to adjust to the demands of the machine and would teach them to utilize their new leisure by sharing the finest culture of the race. Harris was not impressed by the argument that, so long as the machine was controlled by the owning class and utilized for profits, many of its actual and potential advantages would be offset by such unfortunate consequences as uneven

[23] Wm. T. Harris, "Co-education of the Sexes," *Report of the Commissioner of Education,* 1900–1901, Vol. II, pp. 1241–47; N. E. A., *Proceedings,* 1898, pp. 124–25; *The Arena,* Vol. XVII (Feb., 1897), pp. 355–56; *St. Louis Report,* 19th, 1872–73, p. 130.
[24] Wm. T. Harris, "The Relation of Woman to the Trades and Professions," *Ed. Rev.,* Vol. XX (Oct., 1900), pp. 217–29; "Co-education of the Sexes," *loc. cit.*
[25] Wm. T. Harris, *Do the Public Schools Educate Children Beyond the Position Which They Must Occupy in Life?* (New Haven, 1882), pp. 34–35.

distribution of the increased wealth, commercialized culture for the released leisure of the masses, and overexpansion of industry with subsequent distress for the worker.

Harris was as energetic an apologist for the urbanization of American life as he was for the age of the machine. He believed that the city enabled the laborer to develop greater independence of opinion and action than did the country: both the parent and the employer in the city had to be less patriarchal than in the country.[26] But the city not only marked an important step in the emancipation of the individual; it also stimulated the development of the "directive power which regulates the national industry and prosperity."[27] Harris also rejoiced that the invasion of the daily newspaper into the country elevated its life toward that of city civilization, and hopefully observed that the application of the machine to agriculture, by releasing man power for industry and commerce, would compel the illiterate rural drudge to "climb up or else starve in his attempt to compete with the machine."[28]

In his defense of industrial capitalism Harris was even more confident than in his defense of the machine and the city. Despite his devotion to philosophy and his scant interest in money *per se*—he even refused to have his modest salary as Commissioner of the Bureau of Education raised during his incumbency—Harris was a practical man of affairs. When in 1880 he resigned his position as superintendent of the St. Louis schools, he was offered the vice-presidency of one of the largest white lead companies in the country.

To this philosopher the industrialist was a builder of civiliza-

[26] *Atlantic Monthly*, Vol. LXIX (June, 1892), p. 726; N. E. A., *Proceedings*, 1890, pp. 485–86.
[27] Address at the dedication of a new building for public school management on the fiftieth anniversary of the Board of Education of New York City, Harris MSS., No. 712.
[28] Speech at New Orleans, Dec. 28, 1898, Harris MSS.

tion. He believed that capitalism was thoroughly in accord with the highest law of existence, altruism, a law which religion, philosophy, and even science, as well as the tradition of the race, confirmed. Wealth, he said, was admirable because it enabled its possessor to grow good and wise and to become more helpful to his fellow men. He praised capitalists for their support of education and rejoiced that higher education, in turn, furnished industrialists with trained experts who stimulated the work of prospecting for natural resources, abroad as well as at home, and who also aided in the accumulation of wealth for the owning class by their work in developing transportation and manufacturing.[29]

Unlike Mann, Harris saw no objection to the accumulation of vast fortunes and rationalized and idealized the formation of trusts and mergers. Far from denouncing captains of industry for the practices involved, he pointed out how higher education could aid in carrying them out. In a lecture to women he favored their study of law so that they might be useful when the welfare of business necessitated the evasion of the anti-trust laws. The "captains of industry," he remarked, "depend on higher education to keep themselves out of jail, for great business combinations involve collisions of all kinds with other interests and must adopt legal precautions to avoid civil and criminal liabilities."[30]

Yet these very trusts which Harris accepted and approved in

29 "What Captains of Industry Owe the Higher Education," clipping, *The Patriot,* Jackson, Mich., Oct. 20, 1901, Harris MSS., No. 754. In an interview in *The Brooklyn Daily Eagle,* Aug. 16, 1899, Harris sought to refute the statement of Collis P. Huntington, the great railway magnate, that the average American boy was overeducated. *Ibid.,* No. 726. See also *Report of the Commissioner of Education,* 1902, Vol. I, pp. 951–52.

30 Wm. T. Harris, "Why Women Should Study Law," *Ohio Educational Monthly,* Vol. L (July, 1901), pp. 289–92. For a eulogy of the corporation see *Do the Public Schools Educate Children Beyond the Position Which They Must Occupy in Life?* p. 37.

reality submerged the middleman, the small business man. One might have expected Harris, as an individualist, to desire certain restrictions upon this consolidation. But although he admitted that inconvenience and even suffering and injustice might accompany the process, these considerations were dwarfed before the great economies made possible by big business. The savings effected by the elimination of the middleman enabled the capitalists to apportion "to the producers and consumers their quota of the benefit derived from reducing the expense of the middle term"—and in spite of their immense profits, Harris thought they made such a distribution. In addition, the capitalist's share of the savings permitted him to endow education more richly.[31]

But the defense which this great educational leader made of industrial ·capitalism was based on even more fundamental convictions. Private ownership of property and its corollary, production for profit, was for him necessary for the participation of the race in the benefits of the invention and productivity of individuals. Through private property and free competition "society gains constantly at the least expense."[32] They were also necessary for the freedom and development of the individual. The discovery of private property Harris described as "the discovery of the possibility of human freedom."[33] The property of the individual is his " 'dominum' and he can by its means gain self-respect and self-knowledge."[34] Without this institution Harris thought there could be no freedom of thought or action.

Although he prized highly the function of the capitalist class,

[31] *Report of the Commissioner of Education,* 1902, Vol. I, pp. 949–51; Harris to Lucia Ames, Dec. 20, 1895, Harris MSS., No. 380.

[32] Wm. T. Harris, *The Right of Property and the Ownership of Land,* read before the National Social Science Association, Sept. 10, 1886 (Boston, 1887), p. 148.

[33] *Ibid.,* p. 146.   [34] *The Forum,* Vol. VIII (Oct., 1889), p. 205.

Harris, as an educator, was greatly concerned over the dangers involved in the typical rearing given the offspring of the wealthy. He lamented that well-to-do mothers, eager to play a prominent rôle in "society," turned over their children to low-bred servants, who frequently spoiled them and thus deprived civilization of the directive ability which he thought such children inherited from their parents. Believing that the kindergarten could salvage these pampered children of the rich, a function he considered of at least equal importance with its power to redeem moral weaklings from homes of poverty and squalor, Harris was a pioneer in its behalf. St. Louis under his superintendency was the first American city to incorporate the kindergarten in the system of public schools.[35]

With the same end in view, Harris wrote President Benjamin Ide Wheeler of the University of California urging him to accept the presidency of Teachers College:

"New York has by far the larger number of the directors of the wealth of the United States. A peculiar problem has arisen in education in recent years through the fact that the children from wealthy families are possessed of unusual directive power and are consequently difficult to manage in ordinary schools. It must be admitted that most of the promising youth from these families are swept away on the tide of dissipation. The New York Teachers College has done more than any other institution to explore new means and methods by which this, a most important class of our population, important because it furnishes nearly all of the directive power to our industries—can save its children for the blessings of society. Turned in directions of selfish pleasure-seeking, the children of the wealthy do more than any other persons to irritate the masses of the American people and encourage the development of socialism and lines of political obstruction to the large enterprises of capital in the interest of productive industry. . . . In mentioning the great wealth of the trustees I have hinted that a

[35] Wm. T. Harris, "The Kindergarten as a Preparation for the Highest Civilization," *Atlantic Educational Journal*, Vol. VII (July–Aug., 1903), pp. 35–36; *Report of the Commissioner of Education*, 1896–97, Vol. I, p. 903.

phenomenal endowment of this institution is to be expected when it obtains for itself a universal recognition in the United States for the higher order of work which it will do."[36]

As a champion of industrial capitalism and the virtues that it prized, Harris accepted the doctrines of class co-operation and self-reliance. He sincerely believed that there were no conflicts of interest between any individual, whether factory worker or tenant farmer, and his employer or creditor. With equal conviction he upheld the gospel of self-help and ardently opposed any governmental activity which would make the individual less likely to take care of himself. "Help the poor and unfortunate to help themselves, and you elevate them towards human perfection, and the divine ideal. It is this principle, too, that makes clear to us what road leads to the surest amelioration of the evils of poverty and mendicancy. Education is the one sure road to help the unfortunate. Adopt all the cunning devices that social science has invented, and you cannot be sure that direct or indirect help of the poor does not undermine their self-respect and weaken their independence."[37] Thus Harris subscribed to the middle-class doctrine set forth by Franklin and cherished by President Hoover as "rugged individualism."

While it was the common thing for American educational leaders in this period to condemn organized opposition to capitalism, Harris went a good deal farther than his colleagues. Again and again he elaborated detailed refutations of all the criticisms of capitalism then current. Not on one, but on many occasions, Harris pleaded persuasively with his listeners or readers to have no faith in the teachings of Karl Marx and Henry George. His benevolence, his kindliness, his shrewd-

[36] Harris to Wheeler, Aug. 23, 1897, Harris MSS., No. 855.
[37] *Education*, Vol. IX (Dec., 1888), p. 215.

ness, must have made his unquestionably skillful attacks on those doctrines all the more effective. In his papers and addresses which were designed to refute what he regarded as subversive economic doctrines, Harris displayed an impressive knowledge of statistics.[38] While he was aware of some of their pitfalls, he himself did not always avoid them.

In attacking Henry George, Harris put his finger on some of the weak spots in the doctrine of the single tax. He pointed out that George made no distinction between land used for agriculture and for building sites and that his tax would actually fall with greatest severity upon the farming population. But the conclusion he himself drew from the distinction between urban and rural lands has scarcely been confirmed by subsequent events. Rapid transportation, Harris declared, would prevent city land prices from soaring by bringing them in competition with the cheap building lot carved out of the near-by country farm.

The educator also took Henry George to task for overemphasizing the amount of revenue which could be derived from ground rents. He estimated on the basis of the census of 1880 that the income in rent from privately owned land, calculated at 4 per cent, would provide but two cents revenue a day per inhabitant of the country, or $8 a year. If this pittance were added to the income of each individual, he observed, it would scarcely bring leisure or luxury to the masses who were struggling with poverty. Private property in land held no power to rob capital or labor. Furthermore, Harris insisted that, contrary to the doctrine of *Progress and Poverty,* capital actually frees

[38] Wm. T. Harris, "Statistics vs. Socialism," *The Forum,* Vol. XXIV (Oct., 1897), pp. 186–99; "The Tenth Census from an Educational Point of View," Department of Superintendence, N. E. A., *Proceedings,* 1880 (Bureau of Education, *Circular of Information,* No. 2, 1880), pp. 61–67; "The Statistical Data Required to Settle the Great Economic Questions of the Day," Harris MSS., No. 558.

labor from the tyranny of land, for under industrial capitalism other forms of wealth become a greater proportion of the total wealth.[39]

Turning his attention to Marx, Harris insisted that he likewise ignored the evidence of statistics which disproved the contention that the poor were becoming poorer and more numerous and the rich, richer and fewer. However valid the evidence Harris marshaled to show that the average wage of laborers was increasing and that a greater number of families were gaining middle-class and moderately wealthy incomes, it did not meet the Socialist argument that the increasing wealth of the owning class was, relatively as well as actually, greater than the added earnings of the proletarian class.[40] Harris ridiculed the desirability of an even division of the national income, which he considered the primary aim of Marxian economics, by estimating that it would give all workers only $34.80 a month and by asserting that every laborer who earned more at the present time had no ground for complaint but rather must be considered on the side of the "bloated bondholders."[41] With his convictions concerning private property,[42] he ignored the possibility of an increase in the total national income of a socialist state.

In his efforts to refute the teachings of Marx, Harris contended that the author of *Capital* did not understand that the largest cost to the consumer lay in the collection and distribution of commodities—the function of the market. He insisted

[39] W. T. Harris, "Henry George's Mistake About Land," *The Forum*, Vol. III (July, 1887), pp. 435–41.
[40] *Ibid*. See also "Edward Bellamy's Vision," *The Forum*, Vol. VIII (Oct., 1889), pp. 199–208, and "Statistics versus Socialism," *ibid.*, Vol. XXIV (Oct., 1897), pp. 190–99. Harris, quoting Cary and Bastiat, declared that as capital increases it draws a smaller proportion from the product as its share while labor gets a larger proportional amount. *The Forum*, Vol. VIII, p. 204.
[41] *The Forum*, Vol. III, p. 441. [42] *Ante*.

that the capitalist accumulated his wealth, not by grinding the poor, but by virtue of the fact that he or his forefathers possessed the habit of thrift or had developed methods for reducing the cost of producing or distributing goods. The captain of industry, Harris maintained, earned far more for society than he accumulated for his own profit—the savings made by big business were, in effect, socialized. He went so far as to assert that capital took only one-tenth of what it saved by virtue of its services in increasing the efficiency of the market: the other nine-tenths were distributed to producers and consumers.[43]

In using the argument of the market as the chief means of refuting Marx, Harris seemed to assume that large-scale production, cost-saving devices, and the world market would exist only under capitalism. Moreover, he did not refute the central thesis of Marx, the theory of surplus value—the argument that capitalists gained profits by the productivity of a labor day much longer than was necessary to produce an equivalent of what the worker was paid and the cost of materials and equipment. For him capitalism was sufficiently exonerated from all charges of exploitation by showing that savings had been effected during its reign.

To buttress his defense of capitalism, Harris tackled the problem of unemployment. In an article published in *The Forum* in 1898 he clearly stated the problem of technological unemployment and raised the question as to whether there could be work enough for all. Admitting that the bare necessities of life might, as the result of new labor-saving machinery, be increased beyond the needs of the community, he contended that it was impossible to overproduce in the sphere of creature comforts

[43] *Report of the Commissioner of Education* (1902), Vol. I, pp. 950–52.

and luxuries. He insisted that the entire surplus of laborers released by the application of machinery could be taken up in
the manufacture of comforts and in the production of cultural
services for everyone. This, of course, is the argument of "the
new capitalism," so frequently heard in the 1920's, and apparently so shaken by the events of 1929 and its aftermath.

Harris thought that the readjustment of vocations could be
easily accomplished if workers were intelligent. He would not
have admitted that the industrial scrap heap was due in any
sense to the profit motive of manufacturers. He ascribed it
merely to the lack of intelligence and education on the part
of workers: with a "knowledge of the rudiments" they should
be able to re-adapt themselves in new luxury industries, the
products of which they and their fellow workers were to consume. Harris believed that the vocations providing for the protection and comfort of the masses, medicine, insurance, teaching, art, drama, science, literature and religion, could expand
indefinitely, and that with increased education workers displaced by the invention of machinery could find places for
themselves in the professions designed to administer to the
protection and comfort of society.[44]

The deep-rooted antagonism which Harris felt toward socialism can be understood only in the light of the philosophy of
social evolution which he derived from Hegel. According to
this philosophy, the whole process of history had been the
emancipation of the individual from the group. Over a long
period of time the civil community, the state, and the church
had so developed as to give ever larger scope to the individual.
Church had been separated from state, and the individual had

[44] Wm. T. Harris, "Is There Work Enough for All?" *The Forum,* Vol.
XXV (April, 1898), pp. 224–36.

acquired religious freedom. The development of the Anglo-Saxon system of local government and *laissez faire* removed obstacles to the free action of the individual. Socialism, which Harris thought of as a primitive economic form flourishing in the early medieval community and guild, restricted the free action of the individual. It sought to help him, not by the removal of such obstacles as hindered his self-activity, but by so arranging matters that he might share equally in the products of the social whole without reference to his producing power. It would put a premium on weakness and incompetency at the expense of the able and the thrifty. Socialism would destroy the precious gain to the sacredness and development of person-ality that private property had brought, and would revert to the primitive and Oriental subordination of the individual to the group. It would, in short, turn the hands of the clock back-ward."[45]

Harris not only defended capitalism against its critics, but explicitly pointed out how education might serve more effec-tively the established order. In greeting the National Education Association in 1894, when the country was in the throes of labor "disorders," he observed that the school provided the people with training in those habits of regularity, silence, and industry which would "preserve and save our civil order." In the public school, the center of discipline, the pupil learned "first of all to respect the rights of organized industry."[46] In the kindergarten the child of the slum, the weakling of society,

45 Wm. T. Harris, "The Definition of Social Science and the Classification of the Topics Belonging to Its Several Provinces," *Journal of Social Science*, Vol. XXII (June, 1887), pp. 1–7; "English and German: A Study in the Phi-losophy of History," *Andover Review*, Vol. VI (Dec., 1886), pp. 590–607; *The Forum*, Vol. VIII, pp. 199–208.

46 N. E. A., *Proceedings*, 1894, p. 59. For the opposition of Harris to the demands of organized labor in the Bureau of Engraving see *Education*, Vol. XIX (Feb., 1899), p. 378.

learned self-respect, moral ideals, industry, and perseverance—
the means, in short, of conquering natural obstacles.[47]

It was, however, to higher education that Harris especially
looked for the training which would counteract economic
heresies. Although he did not realistically face the question
of the relation of the economic status of the family to the problem of selection for higher education, he did hope that more
and more young Americans would enter college. To promote
this end he favored an adjustment between the public high
school and the higher institutions of learning so that private
school training would not be necessary in order to meet college
entrance requirements.[48] While the elementary and secondary
schools were to fit the pupil for participation in the cultural
heritage and the social co-operation of the race, higher education
was to provide a critical and comparative evaluation of human
knowledge. Through the insight gained by such training,
Harris believed the college student would learn "at once to
suspect all mere *isms* and one-sided tendencies like socialism
and anarchy and anything that has the form of a universal
panacea."[49]

College graduates, being acquainted with the relation of the
many branches of human learning to the conduct of life, would
become the spiritual monitors of society: they would recognize the deep foundations of existing institutions and check the
extravagances of less educated people who took a fragmentary
view and were swept by specious arguments for radical reform into the ranks of the agitators.[50]

[47] Wm. T. Harris, "The Kindergarten as a Preparation for the Highest
Civilization," *Atlantic Educational Journal*, Vol. VI (July–Aug., 1903), pp.
35–36.
[48] N. E. A., *Proceedings*, 1891, p. 141; *Report of the Commissioner of Education*, 1893–94, Vol. I, pp. 618–19.
[49] *Education*, Vol. XVII (June, 1897), p. 583.
[50] Wm. T. Harris, "The Use of the Higher Education," *Ed. Rev.*, Vol. XVI
(Sept., 1898), pp. 147–61.

Anxious to extend to adults the methods and point of view of higher learning, Harris warmly supported the movement for university extension. In referring to its origin in England, he observed that "there is no movement . . . which has worked for the perpetuation of the power of the upper classes . . . as has this movement of university extension." Since demagogism increased in proportion to the neglect of the lower stratum of society by the highest, he contended that enlightened selfishness dictated the support of extension work in this country. In view of the demagogic and sensational appeals of the popular newspapers, it was all the more necessary to equip the masses with the ability to resist such appeals. Just as the earlier educators had advocated the free common school to preserve the established order, Harris championed university extension as a double safeguard.[51]

In his relations with educational administrators and with teachers Harris likewise gave evidence of his fundamentally capitalistic bias. He advised superintendents that in their relations with school boards they would find "the conservative business man" their best support in dealing with the members who might be classified as cranks, reformers, and demagogues.[52] Harris regarded the teachers as the most conservative group in society with the single exception of the clergy.[53] He offered with confidence the comfort of the capitalist to those who were dissatisfied with their salaries of $400 or $500 a year. The teacher must remember that her lot depended in large measure on her own efforts, that her position would be bettered if she improved her technique, her general culture, and her

[51] Wm. T. Harris, "The Place of University Extension in American Education," *Report of the Commissioner of Education,* 1891–92, Vol. II, pp. 743–51; N. E. A., *Proceedings,* 1894, pp. 133–34.

[52] *Ed. Rev.,* Vol. III (Feb., 1892), p. 169.

[53] *Education,* Vol. XII (Dec., 1891), p. 194.

skill. As in industry, so in the teaching profession, the best from the lowest ranks were certain to rise if they had ability. He did not mention the influence of politics, religion, personal charm, and the "school machines." With the advance of civilization and the increase of productive wealth, he reassured his listeners, the status of the profession in general would improve. Meantime teachers might take comfort in the knowledge that in view of the industrial progress of the country and the "economic law of increased values of vocations that have for their object the protection of culture," the future outlook for teachers' salaries was bright.[54]

II

The school child who did not learn from his teacher any of the ideas about capitalism and socialism with which the addresses of Harris in educational meetings and his papers in professional periodicals acquainted her was shielded from susceptibility to radicalism by the educational methods that he popularized. It is true that by insisting on the cardinal importance of the five traditional school subjects, literature and art, history, geography, mathematics, and grammar, Harris tended to keep such utilitarian matters as manual training from occupying an important rôle in the curriculum; and his halfhearted support of trade schools did not promote the training of a large number of skilled workers to enhance the profits of industry.

Yet in other respects Harris did influence the schools in such a way as to make them serviceable to the established order. Frankly maintaining that an important purpose of education

[54] Wm. T. Harris, "The Future of Teachers' Salaries," *Independent,* Vol. LIX (Aug. 3, 1905), pp. 255–58.

was to train the child to respect authority, he opposed the Pestalozzian concept of self-government in the schools, a concept
that Parker, Dewey, and their followers were beginning to emphasize. "The school pupil simply gets used to established order and expects it and obeys it as a habit. He will maintain it
as a sort of instinct in after life, whether he has ever learned the
theory of it or not." Instruction in the reasons for good behavior Harris considered less important than forming "habits
of punctuality, silence, and industry."[55]

While this great conservator sometimes paid qualified tribute
to educational reformers, he opposed the adoption of "fads"
and kept the schools fairly rigid in the lock-step scheme of organization, method, and point of view. He was one of the most
sturdy champions of the textbook method of teaching, which
he felt was peculiarly well adapted to the needs of American
children.[56] He believed that the Herbartian emphasis on interest as the motive force in teaching went too far and frequently
became a mere craze for novelty. Forgetting that interests were
good, bad, and indifferent, and should be furthered or repressed
in accordance with what the child was to become rather than
with what he desired at the moment, the Herbartians, Harris
thought, failed to appreciate the value of discipline.[57]

By opposing the doctrine of interest with its applications of
education through sense-perception and vocationalism and self-
government in schools, and by emphasizing the value of disci-

[55] *Education*, Vol. XII (Dec., 1891), pp. 196–97. See also "The Isolation of
the School: Its Educational Function," *Independent*, Vol. LIII (Aug. 1, 1901),
pp. 1782–86; "The Relation of School Discipline to Moral Education," *The
Third Yearbook of the National Herbartian Society*, 1897, pp. 58–72.

[56] In fairness to Harris it should be said that he recognized some of the
abuses of the textbook and did not favor mere memorization of facts. N. E. A.,
Proceedings, 1880, p. 108; 1898, pp. 127–28.

[57] Wm. T. Harris, "Herbart's Doctrine of Interest," *Ed. Rev.*, Vol. X
(June, 1895), pp. 71–80; *North American Review*, Vol. CLX (May, 1895),
p. 542; N. E. A., *Proceedings*, 1910, p. 193.

pline, will-training, textbook methods, and traditional subject matter, Harris, in the opinion of many, retarded the adjustment of the American school system to the needs of a true democracy.

Yet it would be unfair to Harris to overemphasize his rôle as a conservator of older and more authoritarian educational methods and values. If he hesitated to recommend that teachers study "the new psychology" for fear that it would negate ethical and religious convictions, he admitted that it might aid in determining the best length of study and recitation periods and in preventing fatigue.[58] If he stood for authority, discipline, and the lock step, he was too much an individualist to favor the mechanization of the child; and he advocated the short-interval system by which the brighter and quicker students were more rapidly promoted and the duller ones given more frequent chances and new incentives.[59]

Harris opposed overthorough methods of instruction, which, he held, might tend to produce arrested development in the child who must not, during his long period of infancy and helplessness, be inured to any habit or fixed form that would interfere with his ethical and spiritual development. In the spirit of *gestalt* psychology he insisted that "the absorption of the gaze upon adjustments within the machine prevents us from seeing the machine as a whole. . . . The habit of parsing every sentence that one reads may prevent one from enjoying a sonnet of Wordsworth."[60] The discipline and authority for which he

[58] Wm. T. Harris, "Fruitful Lines of Investigation in Psychology," Vol. I (Jan., 1891), pp. 8–14; "The Old Psychology versus the New," *Report of the Commissioner of Education*, 1893–94, Vol. I, pp. 433–37.

[59] Wm. T. Harris, "The Pendulum of School Reform," *Education*, Vol. VIII (Feb., 1888), pp. 347–50; *St. Louis Report*, 20th, 1873–74, p. 121; N. E. A., *Proceedings*, 1900, p. 336.

[60] Wm. T. Harris, "The Study of Arrested Development in Children as Produced by Injudicious School Methods," *Education*, Vol. XX (April, 1900), pp. 453–66.

stood was intended to be rational in character and to enable the individual *freely* to subscribe to the law of the social whole in order fully to realize his true, spiritual self. Yet in the hands of the average teacher the principles for which Harris stood doubtless encouraged discipline in the ordinary sense, rather than spiritual freedom and self-realization under the law. Certainly the educational values and methods he promoted tended to encourage, not independent thought, but devotion to the existing order.

III

Harris was no less ardent a champion of American nationalism and imperialism than he was of industrial capitalism. As a Hegelian, he believed that the national state was the greatest of human institutions, necessary for civilization and for the realization of true individualism. Only through the state could the individual be free to absorb the benefits of civilization. Since the individual *freely* accepted the sovereignty of the state in order to secure true freedom, there could be no conflict between the interests of one and the other.

As an adherent of the Hegelian interpretation of history—in 1908 he was able to say he had read the great German's *Philosophy of History* seventeen times—Harris loved to dwell on the peculiar mission of the Hebrews, the Greeks, the Romans, the Anglo-Saxons, and their American offspring. The Hebrews gave the race the realization of a monotheistic God, personal immortality, and divine will; the Greeks, individuality and beauty; the Romans, law, organization, contract, and private property; the Anglo-Saxons, local self-government, which still further emancipated the individual from authority; and the Americans carried on the process by providing the individual with an even greater freedom in local self-government, in public education, and in industry.[61]

Such enthusiastic nationalism committed the public school to the task of educating for the American state. "We educate the future citizens of the United States, not the future citizens of Prussia, France, of England, of China, or of Japan." This fundamental fact, Harris believed, must condition instruction in citizenship. Our school system, by fitting the individual for the new industrial age, offered the rest of the world an object lesson. Yet his national ideal was essentially a competitive one; Harris held that we could not compete industrially with the other nations of the world unless our children were so educated in common schools that they would, to the full extent of their capacity, utilize and improve machinery.[62]

Since the history of a nation was a commentary on its political principle—in our case, self-government, self-help, co-operative individualism—the teaching of history must emphasize that political principle. It must also show how that principle becomes entwined in all other spheres, social, æsthetic, religious, and "world-historical." Americans must be taught through history what our national ideals are and what they mean. While Harris in 1870 thought that the teaching of our history should include only the period ending with the formation of the Constitution,[63] he recommended, in the Report of the Committee of Fifteen (1895), the inclusion of the Civil War. The pupil, however, was to be taught to examine each event in history in

[61] Wm. T. Harris, "The Philosophic Aspects of History," *Papers of the American Historical Association*, Vol. V (1891), pp. 247–54; Preface to Thomas Davidson, *The Education of the Greek People* (New York, 1903), pp. v–vii; *The Arena*, Vol. XVII (Feb., 1897), p. 354; N. E. A., *Proceedings*, 1891, p. 72; "The Practical Lessons of History," Harris MSS., No. 804.
[62] N. E. A. *Proceedings*, 1910, p. 191; *Education*, Vol. V (May, 1885), p. 448.
[63] *St. Louis Report*, 18th, 1871–72, p. 152; "What the American Youth Can Learn from the History of His Own Country," Harris MSS., No. 885.

the light of "all contemporary events and to study its relation to all that has preceded it."[64] In addition, Harris thought that the study of history should train the child to discriminate between important and unimportant facts, to appreciate the ethical aspects of history, and understand the method of historical investigation.

While Harris regarded America as the culmination of the historical process which transferred government from one person to the mass of the citizens, and while he took pride in the free activity which *laissez-faire* American democracy provided for its people, he opposed the experiment of self-government through "the school city" and the notion that the child might learn civic functions by performing them.[65] The school should rest content with instilling a knowledge of the Constitution, our early history, and our great national heroes; and with providing the child with such character training as would lead him to choose the rational in preference to the irrational, to respect authority, to discipline his self-activity and to subordinate himself in voluntary co-operation with the social group for the realization of a higher and truly authentic freedom. The nationalism for which Harris stood did not lead him to favor the teaching of the patriotism expressed in the slogan, "My country, right or wrong." Patriotic sentiment, like all sentiment, could not be formally cultivated; it must, like the root of a plant, be well grounded. The teacher must encourage it, not by appeals to blind passion and to sentiment, but to reason.[66]

The philosophy of history to which Harris subscribed also prevented him from advocating the Americanization of the immigrant by steam-roller methods. As superintendent of the

[64] *St. Louis Report,* 16th, 1869–70, p. 169.

[65] Wm. T. Harris, "The School City," *School Bulletin,* Vol. XXXII (March, 1906), pp. 113–14.

[66] *Newark Evening News,* May 2, 1890, Harris MSS., No. 787.

St. Louis schools he upheld the teaching of German, pointing out that when an immigrant population broke suddenly with its past, there was apt to be a great loss in the stability of individual character. With an Hegelian respect for the ethos of each people Harris believed that the presence of our immigrant population promoted tolerance, mutual respect, and a high degree of personal liberty.[67] At the same time he warned against carrying the idea that America was an asylum for the oppressed of Europe so far as to make our country another Botany Bay.[68] As we shall see, he also regarded the immigrant as chiefly responsible for political corruption.

That his attitude toward nationalism did not prevent him from desiring education to aid in the process of promoting solidarity is plain when one considers the attitude of Harris toward the Indian and the Negro. Education, he thought, might well enable the Indian to skip over the stages of the village community (socialism) and feudalism (subordination) and quickly realize our present and higher stage of industrial nationalism. By introducing him to the printed page the school could provide the Indian with the ideals of Christianity and of civil society, which would permit him to secure the greatest possible freedom in the social whole.[69] For the Negro, he thoroughly approved industrial training, which would give discipline and habits of regularity, obedience, self-control, cooperation, and industry. "The Negro must teach himself to become a capitalist." But in addition to industrial training, the Negro must be given a cultural education which not only would

[67] *St. Louis Report*, 20th, 1893, p. 171.
[68] "Immigration and Rural Problems," address before the American Defense Association, Philadelphia, Dec., 1890, Harris MSS., No. 855.
[69] *Proceedings of the 13th annual meeting of the Lake Mohonk Conference of the Indian*, 1895, pp. 33–38; N. E. A., *Proceedings*, 1902, p. 876; "A Definition of Civilization," *Report of the Commissioner of Education*, 1904, Vol. I, pp. 1129–39.

fit him for the professions but would also introduce him to the roots of our civilization and enable him to become integrated in our national life.[70]

No American, perhaps, endeavored with greater success than Harris to put on a high and idealistic plane the imperialism on which we embarked at the end of the Spanish-American War. Expansion was held to be inevitable; it was, moreover, our duty to take a hand in the work of dividing outlying regions in order to show that we could govern backward peoples for their own benefit. It was, in short, our historical mission to help these races toward self-government. Unlike European imperialists, we would, by universal education, elevate these primitive folk into our superior industrial civilization. If we failed to lift these less advanced peoples to self-government, then our ideal would be threatened by sheer overweight of numbers in an essentially undemocratic world. We must teach the Filipinos and Porto Ricans how to command their physical environment, how to participate in the cultural achievements of the race, and how to further both. To that end we must help not one class of these islanders, but all classes, for the highest ideal of civilization demanded for the lower classes participation in all that was "good and reasonable" and increased self-activity or individuality.[71]

Just as our capitalists were helping the poor of the slums by building better tenements at cheaper rents, just as they were aiding the farmer by constructing railroads to lower freight rates, so, declared Harris, they would extend similar blessings to our newly acquired territories. There was no word of the

[70] Wm. T. Harris, "The Education of the Negro," *Atlantic Monthly*, Vol. LXIX (June, 1892), pp. 720–36; "Normal School Training for the Negro," Harris MSS., No. 866. Harris supported the Blair Educational Bill, Harris to J. R. Preston, 1889, Harris MSS., No. 519.

[71] N. E. A., *Proceedings*, 1898, pp. 49–51; "An Educational Policy for Our New Possessions," *ibid.*, 1899, pp. 69–79.

profits they might make, no hint of anything but the most altruistic behavior and motives. Blind to the arguments which Bryan and other anti-imperialists were making, Harris assumed that our capitalists would emancipate these backward peoples from unproductive methods, give them ownership of the land, and provide them with access to our cultural civilization.[72]

Harris realized that imperialism thrust new responsibilities on his countrymen and that education could not be indifferent to them. He welcomed the training that Oxford would provide, through the Rhodes scholarships, to our young men who might become administrators in our possessions and who would advance our new influence in the councils of the world.[73] "The new era is one of great portent to American statesmen. All legislation must be hereafter scrutinized in view of its influence on our foreign relations."[74] Our people must be prepared for the responsibilities of a closer union with Europe. We must study foreign literature to understand the basis of foreign opinion and foreign psychology; we must study their industry, trade, and systems of national defense; we must more adequately prepare our young men for the diplomatic service. Our elementary education, however, was not to be altered even in view of the changes involved in the emergence of the United States as a world power.

IV

However ardent a champion of industrial capitalism, nationalism, and imperialism Harris was, he was too intelligent to be blind to all the evils within the existing order. Recognizing the prevalence of political corruption, he ascribed it not to the determination of railroads, manufacturers, and cor-

[72] *Ibid.*, 1899, pp. 75–76.
[73] *Report of the Commissioner of Education*, 1902, Vol. I, p. 959.
[74] *Ed. Rev.*, Vol. XVI (Sept., 1898), p. 205.

porations to have legal immunity for their profit-making activities and legal assistance in worsting their rivals and "getting ahead," but rather to the presence of unlettered immigrants. Not being sufficiently strong in self-respect, the result of poverty and illiteracy under a monarchical government abroad, the ignorant immigrant failed to resist pecuniary offers for his vote. The temptation offered by this "lowest political stratum" was too great for the unscrupulous politician, who, as Harris explained, frequently grew up in a home where poverty and want dwarfed self-respect. When the immigrant was educated in political conscience, all would come out well. In the meantime, the higher classes must suffer *"because* the lower *are* the lower."[75] Thus Harris placed the major responsibility for political corruption upon the immigrant and only in a very qualified and left-handed way admitted that some guilt might be laid at the door of native sons or American conditions.

The slum with its squalor, degeneration, poverty, and crime was, in the eyes of Harris, the rendezvous of "the moral weaklings of society." The remedy was not charity, which could only further undermine self-respect and weaken what shreds of independence these poor wretches had left. The remedy rather was education—education which would teach these people to curb their appetites and cultivate self-respect, thrift, and decency. The kindergarten would help; the trade school would contribute to that end; instruction in domestic science would aid in stopping "the propagation of pauperism by preventing the transmission of unthrifty habits from parents to children."[76] Again and again Harris declared that it was "to the educational

[75] *North American Review,* Vol. CXXXIII (Sept., 1881), pp. 219-21. Harris recognized, however, that the political education of the adult immigrant was not a responsibility primarily of the public school.
[76] Address, Home Congress, Boston, Oct. 5, 1896, Harris MSS., No. 614; Remarks in *A Memorial of the Life and Services of John D. Philbrick,* pp. 59-61.

systems of large cities, and to them alone, that we look for the invention of more powerful and effective means to break the chain of heredity between the adult criminal and the criminal offspring, so as to eradicate the slum in the future."[77] Thus Harris continued one of the main arguments of pre-Civil War educators.

In spite of the *laissez-faire* attitude to which Hegelianism committed him, Harris was willing to lend his influence to certain reforms.[78] An early advocate of co-education, he desired women to enjoy not only the highest cultural type of learning but professional training as well. At the twenty-fifth anniversary of Smith College Harris declared that the progress of science, the conquest of nature by means of invention, the elimination of brute strength as a result of mechanical operations, and the achievements of women in higher education assured them of securing their share in the division of labor and in political control.[79]

Harris also thoroughly approved the movement for instruction in temperance in the schools, which he believed furnished a permanent and active means for disseminating correct views regarding the effects of alcohol on the human body. "It may be said that this movement is the most effective one ever devised by the friends of temperance to abate a great evil, perhaps the greatest evil abroad in the land."[80]

[77] Address, Public School Society Centenary, April 5, 1905, Harris MSS., No. 773; "Education to Regenerate the Slums," *Brooklyn Eagle*, Dec. 30, 1900, *ibid.*, No. 728; "The Old Philanthropy and the New," address at Lake Mohonk, Oct. 9, 1895, Harris MSS., No. 375.

[78] For a somewhat facetious paper on reformers see his address before the Missouri State Teachers Association, April 8, 1868, Harris MSS., No. 3.

[79] "The Relation of Women to the Trades and Professions," Smith College Anniversary, 1900, Harris MSS., No. 719; Address at the Women's Educational Association, Boston, April 18, 1872, *ibid.*; *St. Louis Report*, 16th, 1869–70, pp. 18 *et seq.*

[80] *Pall Mall Gazette*, May 14, 1894, Harris MSS., No. 291–334; *Report of the Commissioner of Education*, 1900–1901, pp. xli–xliii.

Toward the effort to eliminate international war from modern civilization Harris maintained a very interesting attitude. In an address before a peace society in St. Louis in 1873 he recognized war as a divinely appointed institution by which mankind ascended into a higher consciousness of rational principles; it would disappear only when civilization had discovered and realized other methods of attaining to this all-essential knowledge. As an Hegelian, Harris emphasized the inevitability of conflicts whenever a new and deeper idea emerged.[81]

Years later, in preparing an address for the Lake Mohonk Conference on Arbitration, Harris found a strikingly large number of legitimate causes for war.[82] As long as war was necessary, the individual must submit to the will of the social whole. But the time would come, and education would hasten the day, when each people would so participate in the thought of other nations that war would be obsolete.[83] In assuming that war was caused merely by a lack of understanding, a conflict of ideas, Harris, like the more ardent pacifists of the period, overlooked the economic conflicts out of which misunderstandings arose. Although he was opposed to a war with Spain until the very eve of its declaration, he accepted it with enthusiasm and cloaked it with noble and inspiring idealism.[84]

The conservatism of Harris is the more striking because he realized that he lived in an age of transition. He even went so far as to declare that in view of such rapid changes in industry and in social conditions, it was "indispensable that the individ-

[81] "On the Significance of Peace," *The Western,* Sept., 1873, Harris MSS., No. 800.

[82] "Sketch on the Justifications of War," *ibid.,* No. 788.

[83] *Ed. Rev.,* Vol. XXVII (March, 1904), p. 269; *Harper's New Monthly Magazine,* Vol. XC (April, 1895), p. 790; N. E. A., *Proceedings,* 1891, p. 73.

[84] Paper read at the Southern Education Association at New Orleans, Dec. 28, 1898, Harris MSS.; Harris to J. L. M. Curry, April, 1898, Curry Papers.

ual shall be educated into the power to adapt himself to his circumstances, the power to readjust himself in the case of emergencies." But for that purpose he regarded industry, courteous behavior, and mastery of the tools of thought as the essential requisites; no important changes in the school were necessary.[85]

Realizing that the school was a product of civilization and integrated with all the forces of society, Harris thought that it was less important in the educative process than the family, the church, the civil community, and the state.[86] Unlike Mann and Dewey, he did not expect that the school could contribute substantially to the creation of a new order, even had he thought one desirable. As an Hegelian, he believed that improvement would take place in any case and by necessity; that the school was an agent, not for guiding the change, but for preserving the values of the past and adjusting the individual to society.

Harris held that education, in its function of adjusting the individual to the social whole in order that he might realize his true ethical self, should be founded on sociology, "the science of a combination of men into social wholes."[87] The Hegelian found it easy to solve the conflict between the individual and society: education, which includes not only the school but the family, the church, the civil community, and the state, places the child's hands "in the hands of the great social whole, and thus he is led toward his fruition." In past ages and in the Orient the individual had existed solely for the social whole, and the result had been slavery. Freedom is the state in which the individual contributes to society his infinitesimal product

[85] *Education*, Vol. XII (Dec., 1891), p. 197; Harris, in *A Memorial of the Life and Services of John D. Philbrick*, pp. 60–61.
[86] *North American Review*, Vol. CXXXIII (Sept., 1881), p. 216.
[87] N. E. A., *Proceedings*, 1896, p. 196.

and in return participates in what the social whole produces. Education gives the individual freedom by enabling him to use the whole as his instrument.

In thus emphasizing both individuality and social obligation Harris served well the dominant forces in the America of his day. On the one hand, he preserved and, at least in theory, elevated and spiritualized the American tradition of individualism; and on the other, he reconciled it with the new forces of modernism in Christianity, nationalism, imperialism, social stratification, and industrial capitalism.

However great or however little was the influence of Harris upon American life, one is impressed by the weight his name carried in educational circles.[88] His influence can be explained by the fact that he was a representative social philosopher. In spite of the technical character of Hegelianism, it was in many

[88] The importance of Harris can in part be estimated by the character of the tributes that have been made to his influence by such educators as Ella Flagg Young, Nicholas Murray Butler, William Maxwell, James M. Greenwood, W. S. Sutton, Frank A. Fitzpatrick, George P. Brown, A. E. Winship, and James H. Canfield. For evidence of the influence of Harris see *Outlook*, Vol. XCIII (Nov. 20, 1909), pp. 611–12; *The Nation*, Vol. LXXXIII (July 5, 1906), pp. 8–9; G. Stanley Hall, *Life and Confessions of a Psychologist* (New York, 1923), pp. 496–97; *Journal of Education*, Vol. XLI (Feb. 21, 1895); *ibid.*, Vol. LXX (Dec. 16, 1907), p. 1881; *Ed. Rev.*, Vol. XXXIX (March, 1910), pp. 299–308; *ibid.* (Jan., 1910), pp. 1–12; *ibid.* (Feb., 1910), pp. 120–43; *ibid.*, Vol. XL (Sept., 1910), pp. 173–83; N. E. A., *Proceedings*, 1910, pp. 185–98; *Education*, Vol. XXX (Dec., 1909), p. 247. Canfield observed that Harris was more frequently quoted and approved by educational journals than any other American educator, not excepting Horace Mann, and that he was one of the best loved as well as the most widely known and influential educators "in this or any other country." *American Review of Reviews*, Vol. XXXIV (Aug., 1906), pp. 164–66. The influence of Harris on the curriculum, through the Report of the Committee of Fifteen, his work on other important committees of the N. E. A., his impressive contributions to educational literature, his widely read reports while superintendent of the St. Louis school system, 1869–80, and his work as Commissioner of Education, 1889–1906, was great. For additional evidence of the influence of Harris see Roberts, *William Torrey Harris*, Chaps. XI–XII. Henry Ridgley Evans, *A List of the Writings of William Torrey Harris* (Washington, 1908) contains 479 titles but is not complete. The National Education Association is the repository of the manuscripts of Harris.

ways admirably suited to the requirements of the American scene. Without sacrificing the old American ideals of self-help and *laissez faire* it seemed to lift the individual to a higher plane. Charged with idealism and optimism, it at the same time justified the existing order by declaring that whatever is, is right. It rationalized the victory of nationalism, imperialism, and industrial capitalism by insisting that true individualism could be realized only by subordinating the individual to existing institutions. It confirmed class arrangements but obscured them by idealizing class collaboration for the realization of an ethical and spiritual whole.

Who can say how far the reluctance of Americans to experiment seriously with social control, to abandon traditional *laissez-faire* individualism in spite of its patent contradiction by harsh facts, was related to the skill and plausibility with which Harris told two generations of Americans what they already believed, and what they wanted to believe? Who can estimate the influence of Harris in standardizing the school system, enveloping it with spiritual purposes, housing it in ivory towers, and excluding from its curriculum and its methods everything that did not confirm the existing economic and social structure?

X

BISHOP SPALDING, CATHOLIC EDUCATOR
1840–1916

Be taught of Him, if thou wouldst truly know.
　　　　　　　　　　　　—JOHN LANCASTER SPALDING.

Few bishops had so great an influence on the life of the people, even outside of religion and outside of the Catholic denomination, as had Bishop Spalding.

　　　　　　　　　　　　　　　　　　　—PIUS X.

I

"All serious and earnest minded thinkers engaged in solving the problems of education . . . have received help from the personal counsels or from the educational writings of the Bishop of Peoria. He is the most beloved of American educational leaders. . . . He teaches us that all physical aptitudes and all activities of man that have for an end mere creature comfort, mere bodily well-being, must yield place before the education of the immortal soul in knowing and willing and loving, and that it is man's moral nature that is made in the image of God."[1] In these words William T. Harris spoke of Bishop Spalding, the leading Catholic educator in the period between the Civil War and the World War. In his emphasis on spiritual values and in his opposition to mechanical theories of social organization, in his individualism and in his lofty conception of man's destiny, Spalding resembled Harris. But in important respects he differed from him and from most of the secular educational leaders of his time. At a time when the Catholic church was making rapid gains and arousing great antagonism

[1] William T. Harris, "Remarks introducing Bishop Spalding for Address on Higher Education of Women, at Catholic University, Washington, 1899," Harris MSS., No. 620.

in Protestant circles and among school men, Spalding exerted profound influence on the parochial and higher educational systems of his church. As Harris said, his influence also extended to non-Catholic educators.

When Spalding began his educational work at the third plenary council, which met in Baltimore in 1884, Catholic education was confronted by grave problems. Forty years had passed since Archbishop Hughes of New York had fought his great battle for state support of Catholic schools. Up to the time of that battle, Catholics and non-Catholics had been in essential agreement regarding parental responsibility for the education of children. But with the common school awakening, the gradual disappearance of religious teaching and atmosphere from the public schools, and the new conception that their work was primarily secular and designed to fit the youth of the land for the duties of citizenship, the older idea that education was a parental responsibility gave way to the belief that it was an enterprise of the state.

Catholics, however, continued to hold to the older point of view. Since they could not in conscience send their children to schools in which either Protestant sectarianism was taught or no religion at all, they demanded the continuation of the traditional policy of public support for religious schools. In spite of the precedent of the past and the political influence of Archbishop Hughes, which he did not hesitate to capitalize, and notwithstanding his willingness to compromise to the extent of using state money solely for secular instruction in Catholic schools, and of placing plant and equipment under the control of the Public School Society, the battle had been lost.[2]

With the victory of the idea of secular education, the Catho-

2 Rev. Henry A. Brann, *Most Reverend John Hughes* (New York, 1892), pp. 67–86; J. R. C. Hassard, *Life of Most Rev. John Hughes* (New York, 1866). For Mann's criticism of the parochial schools, which was based on

lic hierarchy had been compelled to establish a system of church schools independent of public support and control. Archbishop Hughes turned his attention to this task with energy, and other prelates followed his example. Communities of teaching orders were brought over from France, Germany, and Ireland. Although in general the texts used in public schools were adopted, a beginning was made in the preparation of Catholic schoolbooks.

Notwithstanding many obstacles, the persistent efforts to establish parochial schools brought substantial results. The poverty of most Catholic communities meant that schools could be maintained only at great sacrifice. In addition to the handicaps of poverty, Protestant opposition also had to be faced. In both the Know-Nothing agitation in the fifties and the anti-Catholic movement in the early nineties, which centered in the American Protective Association, parochial schools were made an especial object of attack.[3] Wisconsin in 1889 attempted, by the Bennett law,[4] to proscribe all schools which did not teach certain subjects, including United States history, in the English language; and Massachusetts and California likewise endeavored to throttle parochial schools. Litigation in regard to the right of parents to send their children to church schools was not finally settled, indeed, until the Supreme Court decided in 1924 that parents had such a right.[5]

the supposition that free discussion, an indispensable requisite of the educational process, was stifled, see *Journal of Proceedings of the National Teachers Association,* Cincinnati, Aug. 11, 1858, p. 7.

[3] For a discussion of the secular and Protestant objections to public support of Catholic schools see Joseph H. Crocker, *Religious Freedom in American Education* (Boston, 1903), p. 31. Edwin D. Mead gave a representative Protestant criticism of the parochial schools, which were upheld by Bishop John J. Keane of Washington before the N. E. A. in 1889. *Proceedings,* 1889, pp. 114–47.

[4] *Ed. Rev.,* Vol. I (Jan., 1891), pp. 48–52.

[5] Rev. James A. Burns, *The Growth and Development of the Catholic School System in the United States* (New York, 1912), pp. 217–18; *U. S. Supreme Court Reports,* 268:510.

In addition to the difficulties which Catholics had to face in establishing and maintaining their schools, other questions remained to be settled. Although in exceptional cases Catholic schools enjoyed some financial support from public funds,[6] in general the church bore the burden of carrying on its educational work. It was felt in Catholic circles, however, that it was unjust for parents to pay taxes for the maintenance of the public schools to which they could not in conscience send their children if parochial institutions were available. The hope had not been abandoned that the American public might be convinced of the injustice of the existing system, by which Catholics paid a double school tax, and might allocate tax-raised funds for the support of the secular instruction given in parochial institutions. The justice of their cause was the more patent, it was held, since the burden on the state would be increased if children in parish schools were sent to the common schools. In Poughkeepsie, New York, and in Faribault, Minnesota, public support was given to parochial schools, which were virtually incorporated in the state school system.[7]

But there was no consensus of opinion in regard to the relative rôles of parents, church, and state in the education of children. Until the practice was forbidden by the third plenary council in 1884, parents who failed to send their children to parochial schools were sometimes deprived of the sacraments. That council did not condemn public schools, but certain

[6] Burns, *op. cit.,* pp. 13, 242–45; *The Catholic School System in the United States* (New York, 1908), pp. 286, 290 *et seq.*

[7] By arrangement between the priest and local school board, parochial schools were placed under the control of the latter during regular school hours, and Sisters were listed on the payroll as public school teachers. Archbishop Ireland of St. Paul was the especial champion of this compromise by which parochial schools obtained state support. Burns, *Growth and Development of the Catholic School System,* pp. 245–47. See also John Ireland, *The Church and Modern Society, Lectures and Addresses* (Chicago and New York, 1897), pp. 197 *et seq.*

extreme apologists for the church virtually denied to the state all educational function whatever. On the other hand, efforts were being made in a number of states to put the parochial school system under the supervision of the public boards of education.

The effort to clarify theory and practice led to one of the most bitter and dramatic controversies in the history of the Catholic Church in America. In 1891 the Reverend Thomas Bouquillon, a Belgian theologian and professor at the Catholic University of America, argued in a widely read pamphlet that education was a mixed matter in which parents, the state, and the church possessed a joint jurisdiction which was to be regulated amicably by the interested parties.[8] Although an especial priority was conceded to parents, Bouquillon aroused the wrath of many ecclesiastics by contending that the civil authority had the right to use all legitimate means to diffuse human knowledge and to prescribe, even for parochial schools, certain requirements, such as instruction in English and in citizenship, which it might consider indispensable for its well-being.

Many Catholics felt that the Belgian theologian went much too far in making concessions to the state, and heated rejoinders followed.[9] The controversy affected court litigation as well as ecclesiastical circles. Even after the intervention of the Holy See, the contending parties sought to interpret the decision in a way favorable to their own point of view.[10] The whole con-

[8] The Rev. Thomas Bouquillon, D.D., *Education: To Whom Does It Belong?* (Baltimore, 1892).

[9] For example, see Rev. James Conway, S. J., *The State Last: A Study of Doctor Bouquillon's Pamphlet: Education, To Whom Does It Belong?* (New York, 1892). For a brief rejoinder by Bouquillon to his critics see *Ed. Rev.*, Vol. III (April, 1892), pp. 365–73.

[10] Burns, *Growth and Development of the Catholic School System*, pp. 232 *et seq*. The *Educational Review* summarized an encyclical of Leo XIII in which the public school was recognized and indorsed, although preference was expressed for the parochial school. The editorial concluded that no longer

troversy, apart from its immediate importance for the parochial school system, was fraught with fundamental social implications involving the older *laissez faire* theory, the newer idea of public interest and social control, and particularly such special legislation as child labor and school attendance regulations.

II

This was the background for the educational work of John Lancaster Spalding. Born in 1840 of cultured and wealthy slave-owning parents in Lebanon, Kentucky, he studied for the priesthood in several American seminaries and at Louvain and Rome. Returning to America in 1865 he was at his own request allowed to do pioneer work in building a church for Negroes in Louisville. He began his literary work by writing a life of an uncle, Archbishop Martin Spalding of Baltimore, served as assistant pastor at St. Michael's Church in New York, and in 1877 was consecrated bishop of Peoria.[11]

Brilliant and gifted, a poet, a gentleman of culture and learning, a writer of books on religion, philosophy, sociology, and education, Bishop Spalding as early as 1877 began to advocate what was later known as "Americanism." He contended that the church should, with dignity rather than in a combative spirit, enter into the living controversies of the age; should demonstrate that it was not opposed to culture and learning or the new developments in science; and that it should contribute to the literature and culture of the United States, and, in short,

could the priest or dignitary denounce and inflict penalties on Catholics who did not send their children to parochial schools. *Ed. Rev.*, Vol. VI (Sept., 1893), p. 206. For a discussion of the outcome of the controversy and for recent lierature on the subject see Manuel P. Loughran, C. S. V., "The Ethical Rights and Duties of the State in Education" (M.A. thesis, Catholic University of America).

[11] Spalding was made titular archbishop of Scythopolis in 1909, having resigned his bishopric, owing to paralysis, the previous year.

make its influence on American civilization felt.[12] To do this, the church must take into account the distinguishing characteristics of American life—its intensity, its initiative, its confidence in itself, its democracy, and above all, its faith in the future.[13] It must re-direct these qualities from the lower plane on which they commonly flourished in America to the higher level of the spirit and of religion. In 1900, only a few months after the Pope had frowned on "Americanism," Spalding, without mentioning the term, courageously preached a sermon in Rome in which he ably defended the point of view that the church must live in the present century, become a leader in criticism and in science, and within limits adapt itself to the spirit of the age.[14]

Knowing and loving America, Spalding believed, then, that it was his duty to elevate his native land, to conquer for Christ the minds and hearts of his countrymen, and that this could be done only through education. While he tactfully but courageously sympathized with the movement to adapt the church to American conditions, his outspoken criticism of what he regarded as grave faults in our national life kept him from becoming an overardent patriot.[15]

At the third plenary council which met at Baltimore in 1884 Spalding took a leading part in the decisions that were made.

[12] For Spalding's defense of Catholicism, and for his refutation of the idea that it was opposed to liberty, culture, and modern science, see his *Essays and Reviews* (New York, 1877), pp. 88 *et seq.; Lectures and Discourses* (New York and San Francisco, n. d.), pp. 43 *et seq.*

[13] F. de Hovre, *Le Catholicisme, ses pedagogues, sa pedagogie* (Bruxelles, 1930), p. 80.

[14] *The Independent*, Vol. LII (Sept. 20, 1900), pp. 2285–87.

[15] For the main outlines of Spalding's life see *Ceremonies of the Golden Sacerdotal Jubilee of His Grace John L. Spalding*, Nov. 24, 1913. De Hovre, *op. cit.*, gives an interesting discussion of Spalding, whom he regards as the leading American Catholic educator, and whom he compares with James and with Spranger, a contemporary German educator. The Reverend John J. A. Glynn, D. S. A., has written a dissertation, "The Educational Theory of Rt. Rev. John Lancaster Spalding, as Revealed in His Writings" (Catholic University of America, 1929).

It was decided to extend and improve the parochial schools and to centralize their administration under diocesan auspices. Both within and without the council, Bishop Spalding labored to impress on the Catholic mind the great importance of improving the training of Catholic teachers. In urging the importance of pedagogy and method, he did not go as far as many secular educators: technique was in his mind always to be subordinated to the character and dynamic personality of the teacher, as well as to educational and social philosophy. Yet it was due chiefly to his efforts that Catholic normal training schools were established.[16] When Sisters' College was founded at the Catholic University of America, in the organization of which Spalding was a prime mover,[17] one of his cherished ideals was realized. As president of the Catholic Educational Exhibit at the World's Fair in 1893 he stimulated Catholic teachers to make the best possible showing and at the same time familiarized secular educational authorities with the work of the parochial schools.[18] Bishop Spalding, in short, brought Catholic education from the narrow confines of race and language to the broad platform of Christian teaching.[19]

Although other leaders, such as Brother Azarias,[20] did im-

[16] *Catholic World,* Vol. LI (April, 1890), pp. 88–97.

[17] James Cardinal Gibbons, *A Retrospect of Fifty Years* (Baltimore and New York, 1916), p. 287; Maurice Francis Egan, *Recollections of a Happy Life* (New York, 1924), p. 183; *Catholic Educational Review,* Vol. XII (Oct., 1916), pp. 277–78.

[18] *Final Report, Catholic Educational Exhibit, World's Columbian Exposition* (Chicago, 1893), *passim.* Spalding also came into the public eye in connection with the World's Fair by his vigorous plea for the exclusion of all nude art exhibits, which he regarded as indecent and offensive to morality and public decency, pp. 44–45.

[19] For a description of Catholic school education at the beginning of the twentieth century, see the Rev. Morgan M. Sheedy, "The Catholic Parochial Schools in the United States," *Report of the Commissioner of Education,* 1903, Vol. I, Chap. XXI.

[20] Brother Azarias (Patrick Mullany) was born in Ireland and joined the Brothers of the Christian Schools at Utica, N. Y., in 1862. As a teacher and a college president, as a literary critic, and as a writer on educational sub-

portant educational work during this period, no one contributed
so much as Spalding to convince Catholics, and even Protestants, that the parochial school could provide a secular education
equal to that which prevailed in the best public institutions.
It was his insistence that the whole school question would be
settled by facts rather than by arguments, and that the school
which developed the best men and women would in the end
prevail, that made him such an important factor in Catholic
education and the controversies it aroused.

While Bishop Spalding was not a direct party to the bitter
dispute waged over Bouquillon's pamphlet, his influence in
clarifying the relation between family, church, and school in
educational matters was of great importance. Insisting that
Catholics did not desire to wipe out the public secular school,
he agreed with Archbishop Ireland that the state should support
denominational schools. Without compromise he upheld religious education as indispensable for the development of virtue
and for the realization of the only complete life, which was life
in God. To treat religion as an incidental phase in man's life,
as if it were not necessary for the realization of man's supernatural end, was, he urged, a blunder of most serious consequence.[21]

The importance which Bishop Spalding attached to religious
education can be understood only in relation to the main out-

jects, an editor of Catholic schoolbooks, and an ardent champion of parochial
schools, Brother Azarias exerted much influence on Catholic education. He
was also highly appreciated in many Protestant circles. He challenged the
knowledge and culture of Emerson and his disciples, opposed realism in
criticism, and emphasized, in his educational work, the complete and harmonious development of the individual. See his *Essays Educational* (Chicago,
1896), *Essays Miscellaneous* (Chicago, 1896), *Books and Reading* (New York,
1901), and Rev. John T. Smith, *Brother Azarias, The Life Story of an American Monk* (New York, 1897). Brother John, F. S. C., has written a dissertation, *The Educational Work of Brother Azarias* (Catholic University of America, 1918).

[21] J. L. Spalding, *Means and Ends of Education* (Chicago, 1909), p. 168.

lines of his general philosophy. Since man's relations to his Creator were necessarily prior to those which bound him to his fellow men, religious society naturally preceded all other types of society. This philosophy further held that the church was a sovereign society with a constitution and a government of its own. Both church and state were independent in their own sphere, and the greatest good of the greatest number was attainable only when their relations were harmonious.

According to Spalding, political society was based on the sacrifice which the individual made of a portion of his natural freedom, in order that he might thereby secure benefits which were greater than freedom. Duty was the basis of the moral, and consequently of the social, order; and duty was not possible without self-denial and self-conquest. As it was man's duty to obey God and thereby to attain to his own high destiny, he possessed a divine and inalienable right to whatever was necessary to that end; and that right was the foundation and bulwark of all his liberty. From this principle Spalding derived the spirit of freedom that led him to condemn the pagan constitution of society, by which the state assumed the right to absorb the whole activity of man, to control his private life, and to regulate his duties and even his pleasures. The tendency to attribute to the state a quasi-omnipotence at the expense of the individual, the family, and the church was invariably, Spalding thought, an evidence of the decay of Christian faith and a mark of a servile habit of thought and sentiment.

It followed that in a society where principles and morals were consonant with the law of God, government would make itself felt as little as possible: its action would be confined chiefly to enforcing respect for the rights of others and to maintenance of equilibrium among the social forces. The sense of duty would, he held, create a spirit of obedience, and obedience to law, founded in justice and equity, was liberty. Even the state could not modify the essential constitution of the family, since domestic society, like the law of God, preceded the state.

When the state organized a system of education from which the teaching of religious doctrines was excluded, "it fatally, though possibly unconsciously and negatively, commits itself to an irreligious and infidel propaganda; since to ignore religious doctrines while striving to develop the intellectual and moral faculties must result in gradual extinction of faith." Any system, continued Spalding, which tended to weaken the control of the parents over their children, or to interfere with the free exercise of their natural rights, was radically vicious. It was, therefore, the duty of both church and state to co-operate with the family in the work of education, since an incomplete and inharmonious manhood resulted when the spirit of the school was in conflict with the spirit of the home. "A state which professes to tolerate different forms of religion contradicts its own principles and becomes intolerant whenever it compels its citizens to support a uniform system of schools." If the state excluded religion from its schools, it then became the imperative duty of Catholics to maintain their own schools. Spalding, of course, preferred a denominational public system in which the state fostered education through denominational schools.[22]

Bishop Spalding agreed with Harris in thinking that the school was but one of several agencies engaged in the task of education. "It depends almost wholly for its success upon the kind of material furnished it by the home, the state, and the

---

[22] *Lectures and Discourses,* pp. 107–26. The above discussion is a summary of Spalding's lecture on "The Catholic Church." For a comprehensive discussion of the Catholic philosophy of education see Thomas E. Shields, *Philosophy of Education* (Washington, 1917). Doctor Shields was the head of the department of education in the Catholic University of America.

church." Our home life, our social, political, and religious life had, he thought, contributed far more to make us what we are than any or all of our schools. Unless the school worked in harmony with these great forces, it could do little more than to sharpen the wits.[23]

Yet in the mind of this educational philosopher the school was important in the formation of good and wise men and women and in the development of individuality. What it could do toward that end depended in large measure on its teachers. If the teacher possessed a sense of the all-importance of conduct, if he realized that what was called knowledge was but a small part of man's life, then his influence would nourish the feelings by which character was evolved. Humanity, justice, truthfulness, honor, fidelity, courage, integrity, reverence, purity, and self-respect were "higher and mightier than anything mere sharpened wits can accomplish." These virtues must be inculcated in the school, but not in a mechanical fashion.[24] Although the supernatural and explicitly religious character of this type of moral instruction differentiated it somewhat from that sponsored by such secular educators as Mann and Barnard, Harris and the Herbartians, much of the criticism that has been made of mere moral teaching, separated functionally from the pressures of everyday environment, applies also to Spalding's conception of moral training.[25]

In emphasizing the superior importance of character the Bishop of Peoria did not deprecate intellectual culture, which

[23] *Means and Ends of Education,* pp. 133–34.
[24] *Ibid.,* pp. 145, 148. Spalding opposed educational "forcing" and emulation, favored self-activity and emphasis on the meaning of what was learned rather than on the literal thing itself. "To know by heart is not to know at all, and this is one of the first lessons a child should be taught." *Catholic World,* Vol. LX (April, 1890), p. 91. Like Emerson and Channing, Spalding was an apostle of self-education and self-culture.
[25] *Ante,* p. 125.

he thought to be entirely compatible with religious life and truth. "A cultivated intellect, an open mind, a rich imagination, with correctness of thought, flexibility of view, and eloquent expression, are among the noblest endowments of man; and though they should serve no other purpose than to embellish life, to make it fairer and freer, they would nevertheless be possessions without price, for the most nobly useful things are those which make life good and beautiful."[26] His conception of intellectual culture was, however, essentially aristocratic. "Wretched is he who toils at that which nature does not intend him; and he is happy who, loving God, digs ditches or drives swine, if that is his fit work."[27] The anti-democratic implication of this doctrine, declaring as it does that nature has set off some to perform menial functions, with which station they must be entirely content, scarcely needs elaboration.

Although Spalding believed that training for political, vocational, and practical life was necessary, he gave such training a subordinate place. The tendency to regard vocations merely as means for the attainment of external ends, rather than as instruments by which mental and moral improvement was to be realized, was for him a matter of regret. "Those who speak of the soul, who thrill it with nobler thoughts, with higher views of truth and visions of a more celestial beauty, do also necessary work, for without it man would be little more than a shrewder kind of animal; and in the world by which we are surrounded, the spiritual sense, the sense for things which have no material uses, needs cultivation far more than the faculty for contriving and getting."[28] In em-

26 *Means and Ends of Education,* pp. 195–96.

27 John Lancaster Spalding, *Thirty-fourth Annual Commencement Address* (Notre Dame, 1878).

28 J. L. Spalding, *Thoughts and Theories of Life and Education* (Chicago, 1910), pp. 33–34; *Opportunity and Other Essays and Addresses* (Chicago, 1906), p. 153.

phasizing spiritual values, and especially the urge and aspiration toward "life" or spiritual energy, Spalding resembled Emerson and Bergson.

Aware of the unequal opportunities for cultural development which both heredity and environment imposed on less privileged individuals and classes, the great Catholic educator held that man was nevertheless, by reason of his free and purposive action, able to modify and to a large extent control the influence of both heredity and environment. Right education, he thought, enabled man to create his world; it taught him to live, not merely in his material surroundings but in the spiritual realms of thought and love, of hope and aspiration, of beauty and goodness, until these became his proper and abiding home, for which climate and soil merely furnished the settings and the foundations.[29] Such a belief tended in general, of course, to minimize the evils of bad environment.

Yet Spalding was too keen and observing a man to suppose that free will and education were not greatly limited by heredity and by early environment. "When we have said a thousand things in praise of education, we must, at last, come back to the fundamental fact that nearly everything depends on the kind of people of whom we are descended, and on the kind of family in which our young years are passed," he observed on one occasion. "Nearly everything, but not quite everything," Spalding continued, "and it is this little which makes liberty possible, which inspires hope and courage, which, like the indefinable something that gives the work of genius its worth and stamp, makes us children of God and masters of ourselves."[30]

[29] J. L. Spalding, *Religion, Agnosticism and Education* (Chicago, 1903), p. 199.
[30] *Means and Ends of Education*, pp. 47–48.

Realizing that the environment of the slums imposed great
obstacles in overcoming the temptations of the grog shop,
the vices of the political gang, and the grinding poverty and
weary routine of toil, Bishop Spalding saw the need of some
social action other than education. In the squalor and degradation of the slums even the proper type of education could
hardly be expected effectively to help children create their
own world of spiritual values.[31]

The years he had spent in New York had familiarized him
with the desperate situation of Irish immigrants, who lived
in the most unsanitary tenements. Exploited by their employers, desperate and goaded by adverse circumstances, they
naturally and easily persuaded themselves that heavy drinking
was necessary. A movement had been inaugurated as early
as 1856 for the colonization of the Irish immigrants on farms
in the West, but little had come of it. In 1878 the movement
was revived, and Spalding became the life and the soul of
a new colonization society. With unflagging enthusiasm he
traveled over the East and West and by inspiring lectures
aroused interest and support; he wrote a volume to popularize
the movement, and took an active part in the work of organization and administration. Eastern bishops, however,
were not easily convinced that it was a mistake to keep Irish
immigrants in urban centers. Although some capital was
raised and a few colonies founded in Nebraska, Minnesota,

---

[31] Spalding seems to have approved of eugenics in declaring that "If man
shall ever learn to do for his own kind what breeding and training enable
him to do for various strains of domestic animals, he will have discovered an
effective means for preventing crime and misery. But what he calls his
rights, which often are but his prejudices and passions, will probably continue to keep him from treating his own species with the wisdom with which
he manages inferior creatures. Reckless and senseless marriages are an inexhaustible source of evil." J. L. Spalding, *Socialism and Labor and Other Arguments, Social, Political and Patriotic* (Chicago, 1902), p. 83.

and Arkansas, far less was accomplished than had been hoped.[32]

In spite of his desire to alleviate the condition of the slum dweller, Spalding deprecated the importance of the physical basis of life. It is true that he supported the movement for temperance and especially that for better health, which he thought promised to be an effective means of moral improvement.[33] It is also true that he recognized the basic importance of food, clothing, and shelter. But he did not think that poverty was at all incompatible with the good life. One might be wise, good, happy, or foolish and wicked, whether one were rich or whether one were poor: we should be fed and housed only to grow in knowledge and virtue, in helpfulness and in holiness. "The great mass of mankind hardly lead a human life," he wrote; "they are full of ignorance and misery. Why God permits such a world to exist we cannot know. But we may know that a life of love and purity, of faith and meekness is a blessed life; and that it is as easy for the poorest and simplest as for the richest and most learned."[34] An abundance of money, fine clothes, and social success in fact distracted the mind, he believed, from the silence and strength of eternal truth and love into a world of clamor.[35]

Unlike many educators, Spalding did not claim that persistent effort and ability insured material achievement, wealth,

[32] Sister Mary E. Henthorne, *The Irish Catholic Colonization Association of the United States* (Champaign, Ill., 1932).

[33] J. L. Spalding, *The Physician's Calling and Education*, reprint from the *Journal of the American Medical Association*, Dec., 1904, *passim*. "A healthy mind can hardly be found except in a healthy body; and the greater our mental and moral power, the greater our need of physical vigor and endurance." *Aphorisms and Reflections* (Chicago, 1907), p. 103; *Socialism and Labor*, p. 164.

[34] *Aphorisms and Reflections*, pp. 85–86.

[35] *Means and Ends of Education*, p. 46. For a similar point of view see the study of a Franciscan, Father Cuthbert, *Catholic Ideals in Social Life* (New York, 1904), pp. 210 *et seq.*

and fame. But he argued that all these material values, which only a few might enjoy, were unimportant. The poor could be persuaded that they were intolerably wretched only after they had been convinced that money was the chief good. If, indeed, wealth were the highest value, then a state of society in which money was concentrated in the hands of a few was radically bad, and communism was justified. But wealth was a privilege only when it was used for just causes and for ennobling opinion; the generous heart held cheap the material comforts that money procured. "Fame and wealth and pleasure are good when they are born of noble deeds and in turn lead the way to something higher; but if sought as ends, and dwelt upon and loved for their own sake, they rot inward to the soul and moulder of all."[36]

With such an ascetic philosophy Spalding was able to combat Socialism as effectively as Harris did with his Hegelianism. In 1902 the Bishop published a book, *Socialism and Labor,* in which he endeavored to demolish the doctrines of Marx. As emotional agitators, he warned, Socialists indulged in reckless statements which were to be discredited. The theory of value which they postulated was altogether erroneous: value was created, not by labor, but by ability. He compared laborers to soldiers who conquered only when they were disciplined, equipped, and commanded by men of ability. He believed that at least two-thirds of the wealth, material as well as spiritual, produced in the nineteenth century was to be credited to such ability. Even though a railroad king inflicted financial ruin on individuals and unjustly oppressed his employees, he at the same time helped to develop the country and brought blessings to thousands. Diatribes against wealthy men, Spalding continued, sprang more often from

[36] *Thirty-fourth Commencement Address* (Notre Dame), pp. 7–9.

unworthy passions than from any real sense of wrong inflicted by the rich.[37]

The Socialist theory of class war, Spalding insisted, was as false and as dangerous as the labor theory of value. Reason as well as religion impelled those who worked and those who owned and directed to join hands in co-operation. In neither the United States nor Europe, the argument ran, was there in fact a chasm between the enormously rich and the very poor: there was rather a gradation of possession from the beggar to the great capitalist. The social gulf lay between steady, thrifty laborers, and loafers or criminals, and the cause of this disparity was moral, not economic. Hence "all real amelioration in the lot of human beings depends on religious, moral and intellectual conditions." The poor did not hate the rich, and the rich as a class were not indifferent to the needs of the poor.[38]

Moreover, Spalding believed that Socialism was in opposition to human nature—that it postulated a mechanical arrangement of society in which regimentation of the individual would crush his spontaneity and freedom. To achieve its ends, human nature would have to be changed. Selfishness, which under competitive capitalism made many employers heartless and tyrannical, would assert itself under Socialism, for a "change of government is like a change of clothes, it leaves the man what he was." Until human nature was changed, the "owner of the poorest cabin would not barter it for ·the promise of the Socialist paradise." Whatever grievances laborers suffered from under a regime of competitive production, they were not so desperate as to make Spalding willing to run the risk of jeopardizing liberty and individuality.[39] If Socialism promised

[37] *Socialism and Labor*, pp. 21, 55, 166–67.
[38] *Ibid.*, pp. 14–15, 55.   [39] *Ibid.*, pp. 18–19, 26.

a greater abundance of material things for the poor, it would, in the opinion of this prelate, lead to a general enfeeblement and lowering of human life; the sublimer moods which make men saints, heroes, and geniuses would no longer be called forth.[40]

Yet Spalding was not indifferent to the cause of organized labor. Since the laboring men were in a majority, and since we were living in an age that professed to believe in majority rule, the interest of labor could not be overlooked. In the spirit of the encyclical *Rerum Novarum* (1891) he recognized that the desire to make the poor less miserable sprang from a divine and Christian impulse. The grasping avarice and heartless methods of employers, who generally professed to be Christians, were arguments against religion that the preachers of atheism found effective in addressing the victims of the present economic system.[41] It was utterly futile to make outcries against trade unions; they existed for ends which on the whole were praiseworthy. To thwart the legitimate claims of workers was, Spalding continued, seriously to menace the prosperity of the country. Strikes and other lawful measures to secure the reduction of hours and to increase wages, to enable workers to have more opportunity for cultivating their rational and spiritual natures, were justified.[42]

In spite of his fear that labor organizations might lead working men to put too much trust in mere mechanical contrivances such as unions and strikes at the expense of their faith in "the vital sources of strength,"[43] the Catholic leader was generally looked on as a friend of organized labor when President Roosevelt appointed him to the commission which in 1902

[40] *Cf.* Father John Ryan's objections to Socialism, *Everybody's Magazine,* Vol. XXIX (Oct., Nov., Dec., 1913), pp. 488–89, 635–41, 816–24. For a Socialist refutation of Spalding's book see Arthur M. Lewis, *Ten Blind Leaders of the Blind* (Chicago, 1910), pp. 181–98.

[41] *Socialism and Labor,* pp. 27–28.

[42] *Ibid.,* pp. 58–59, 168–69.   [43] *Ibid.,* p. 67.

arbitrated a dispute between coal miners and operators.[44] In his defense of the rights of labor Spalding belongs to the small and exceptional group of educators which includes Margaret Haley and John Dewey.

While the Bishop of Peoria believed that preparation for citizenship, and especially the cultivation of political sense and conscience, was one of the most important duties of educators,[45] and while he believed that the proper sort of education would prevent violence,[46] he did not regard the protection of property and the securing of the peace of society as the most important functions of education. Believing that there was no inspiration in the ideals of plenty and stability, he declared that those alone "who look above property and the peace of society, and strive in all earnestness to live in the infinite and permanent world of truth, beauty, and goodness, can hope to rise to the full height of a noble manhood." The whole social organism was of value only in so far as it was a means of fashioning the individual in the divine image.[47]

An American of old stock, Spalding found much to admire in the civilization of his native land. He praised the good will, the loving-kindness, and the readiness of the American people

---

[44] Joseph B. Bishop, *Theodore Roosevelt and His Time* (New York, 1920), Vol. I, pp. 213, 215. In an obituary notice of Spalding *The Outlook* held that his influence was an important factor in settling the coal strike. *Outlook*, Vol. CXIV (Sept. 6, 1916), p. 12.

[45] *Aphorisms and Reflections*, p. 84. Spalding thought, however, that it was necessary that the minds of students be held aloof from "the babblement and discussions of the hour, that they may accustom themselves to take interest in the words and deeds of the greatest men, and so make themselves able and worthy to shape a larger and nobler future; but if their hours of leisure are spent over journals and reviews, they will, in later years, become the helpless victims of the newspaper habit." *Ibid.*, p. 148.

[46] *Religion, Agnosticism and Education*, pp. 216-17.

[47] N. E. A., *Proceedings*, 1901, pp. 78-79. In speaking of the discriminations against Catholics in politics Spalding in 1878 advised the graduates of Notre Dame not to enter politics to reform corruption. "Every attempt at reform is abortive, because nothing can be accomplished in politics without the aid of cliques and rings." *Thirty-fourth Commencement Address*, p. 13.

to help the weak and the suffering. He took pride in the abundant opportunities which the country afforded to the underprivileged from the Old World. He rejoiced that its citizens were so little crazed by the glitter of steel and the bray of trumpets, so little blinded by the fame of warlike glory. He was glad that American women occupied a position of dignity and importance in national life and was an enthusiastic champion of the higher education to which women were beginning to be admitted.[48] "There is inspiration in the air of America," he wrote, much in the spirit of Emerson, whom he resembled in so many respects. "Here all is fresh and young, here progress is less difficult, here there is hope and confidence, here there is eagerness to know and to do."[49]

Yet Spalding was not, like Harris, an apologist for American civilization. He regretted the lack of a single institution great enough to inspire the love and enthusiasm which, he believed, are the soul of national unity. "Our public life regards material interests alone; our theory of education is narrow and superficial, aiming chiefly to develop smartness, the least desirable quality of mind, and more sure than any other to foster vulgarity; and thus we have no ideal to elevate and guide us or fill us with faith in our destiny." There must be introduced into our public life something that appealed to minds and consciences as well as to interests: it was a disgrace that the chief concern of the nation should be the question of money, and that the significance of public contests lay in the emoluments of office. Both parties—Spalding wrote in 1902—were mills to grind the people's corn and to make bread for officeholders: both opposed the whole weight of their organized power to

[48] *Socialism and Labor*, pp. 153–55. For a patriotic appreciation of America see Spalding's poem "America," in *America and Other Poems* (New York, 1885).

[49] *Opportunity and Other Essays*, p. 28.

every honest effort to bring about a moral reformation. "The welfare of the nation demands that the one or the other cease to exist; that a new party, springing from the deep yearning of the multitudes for a purer and nobler national life, and upheld by the enthusiasm inspired by high moral aims and purposes, may take its place."[50]

In denouncing the political corruption that was especially rampant in municipal affairs, the Catholic educator declared that the machinery and institutions created to deal with violators of laws were, in large measure, the agencies whereby vice and crime were produced and diffused. Laborers and their wives and children were the chief victims of political corruption, while the rich and respectable were frequently its accomplices. The delinquents imprisoned were the poor who lacked the money to pay the fines; the heaviest punishments were often inflicted on the most helpless and least guilty. Legislation and the venal press, Spalding thought, could accomplish little unless supported by a more humane, enlightened, and Christian opinion.[51]

No one was more outspoken in condemning the imperialistic venture in the Philippines launched at the end of the Spanish-American War. We who had sympathized with all oppressed peoples, with Ireland,[52] Greece, Armenia, and Cuba, who had given our blood to emancipate our own slaves, now sent soldiers across the ocean to shoot men whose real crime was their desire to be free and to govern themselves. "Following the lead of our

[50] *Socialism and Labor*, pp. 48–49.

[51] *Ibid.*, pp. 85–87. "Reform the world within thyself, which is thy proper world; and the way to improve others shall be made plain." *Aphorisms and Reflections*, p. 199.

[52] For Spalding's sympathetic attitude toward the Irish struggle for freedom see "England's Crime," *Three Lectures Delivered in Chicago, St. Patrick's Day, 1880*, by Rt. Rev. John Hennessy, Rt. Rev. John Hogan, and Rt. Rev. John Lancaster Spalding (Chicago, 1880), p. 71.

great capitalists and trust lords, we buy at one stroke 10,000,000 human beings; beings who live in another hemisphere, who differ from us in every way, who dwell in a climate which is fatal to the white man, who can be of no advantage whatever to us, but who, if we persist in holding them, will involve us in the most serious difficulties and dangers."[53]

At bottom Bishop Spalding's quarrel with American civilization was his hatred of the spirit of commercialism and materialism. Believing that the tendency of true civilization and religion was to convert the struggle for life into co-operation for life, into work of all for all, that everybody might have those "inner goods which make men wise, holy, beautiful, and strong," this Christian leader saw and denounced the "commercial and manufacturing competition," which was becoming "a struggle for existence fiercer than that which makes Nature red with ravin in tooth and claw."[54]

Aware of the fact that we were "under the tyrannous sway of the spirit of commercialism," and that our very thought was made subservient to the ideal of success, Spalding denounced the prosperity that made us the "slaves of business and toil." The feverish pursuit of money, while it had established a great and growing inequality of possession, seemed to make the rich and the poor equal in hardness, in narrowness, in discontent, and in unintelligence.[55] Under the existing system, capitalists and captains of industry were driven to work like the laborers themselves: they became parts of the machine, mere mechanical men, victims of their own success. In short, by sacrificing men to money, wisdom and virtue to cheap produc-

---

[53] J. L. Spalding, *What Patriotism Demands, An American Catholic View,* reprint from Spalding's *Opportunity* (Chicago, n. d.), p. 4.
[54] *Ibid.,* p. 5.
[55] J. L. Spalding, "Pure Morals at the World's Fair," *Final Report, Catholic Educational Exhibit,* p. 43.

tion and the amassing of capital, "our present economic and commercial systems are subversive of civilization."[56]

Nor did Spalding hesitate to declare that the worst enemies of America were not the ranting Anarchists, but the "capitalist whose insatiate greed urges him on to crush all competitors"; the politician who sneaked into office for private gain; the buyer of votes; the demagogue who was ready to run with the crowd; and the editor who for money impugned the known truth.[57]

In the work of awakening the public to the higher values the Catholic educator counted on the aid of American women, whom he regarded as the most sober, moral, and religious portion of the people.[58] Public opinion was in their hands; and for that reason women bore the greater responsibility for the wrongs and miseries which afflicted and oppressed the modern world. The force of public opinion, which was in their keeping, was mightier than riches, armies, and laws. Woman's increasing dominion doubtless helped to arouse in public life greater sympathy and tenderness, but it must also arouse a greater sense of justice, particularly for the weak and the poor. Being the heart, as man was the mind, woman was closer to the supreme reality; she was guided by a "divine instinct to understand that the infinite need is the need of love." Nothing could be accomplished in His religion unless women put their hands to the work.[59]

The world of women, moreover, he recognized to be a constantly growing and unfolding one. They should not, as a consequence, be shut out from any career that offered an honest livelihood; and for the same work, the same wages should be paid that were given to men. For wrongdoing of whatever

---

[56] *Socialism and Labor*, pp. 172–74.
[57] *Opportunity and Other Essays*, p. 201. [58] *Socialism and Labor*, p. 49.
[59] *Ibid.*, pp. 84–85, 115–16; *Means and Ends of Education*, pp. 108–11; *Religion, Agnosticism and Education*, pp 246–51, 278–79.

kind, woman should not be made to suffer a severer punishment than that inflicted on the opposite sex. Although in 1895 Spalding seemed to think that the suffrage would hurl women into the maelstrom of selfish passion and vulgar corruption, by 1902 he recognized—considerably in advance of most educational leaders—the inevitability and even the desirability of the experiment. Since women were the natural educators of the race, their increasing influence in every sphere was to be welcomed rather than to be dreaded; and for her new duties and responsibilities an education equal to that of men should be provided.[60]

In calling on his fellow citizens to turn from dehumanizing greed, vainglory, and pride Spalding put almost his entire reliance on spiritual incentives to right-doing. Legislation, the press, trade unions, even such a measure as the inheritance tax, could, he thought, do little; schools, especially the non-religious schools, could not be effective in combating the hosts of commercialism and materialism. Only Christian character, ideals, and values could save the day, and Bishop Spalding believed that his church was called on to combat the evils that threatened the America he loved. The great moral power of the church, the reverence for authority and for spiritual values which it inculcated, and its divine and mystic character enabled it, he believed, to save America from her sins and excesses and to realize her higher destiny.[61]

Although Bishop Spalding's religious creed and faith stamped his educational and social philosophy with certain unique features, in many ways his views strikingly resembled those of his secular contemporaries. Less conservative than Harris, a critic rather than a defender of industrialism, a champion of

---

[60] *Means and Ends in Education,* p. 110; *Socialism and Labor,* p. 49; *Opportunity and Other Essays,* pp. 45–67.

[61] Introduction to John R. G. Hassard, *A History of the United States of America for the Use of Schools* (New York, 1878), pp. v–vii.

labor in its less radical demands, Spalding nevertheless agreed with the majority of secular educators in denouncing Socialism and in preaching a gospel the effect of which was to make the lowly and poor content with their station, and to minimize the advantages of leisure, social position, and a steady income. In looking to the Catholic church to save America from her ills, he was calling upon authority, the past, and the supernatural. The values for which he stood, however beautiful and engaging, nevertheless countenanced, if they did not positively encourage, social and economic distinctions and a way of life that bred vices which he condemned. The values which he with reverence and dignity popularized likewise tended to divert attention from earthly privations and struggles and from many moderate as well as radical proposals for the achievement of economic security and social democracy in this life.

XI

FRANCIS WAYLAND PARKER, DEMOCRAT
1837–1902

A wonderful century full of marvellous changes, full of progress! Nature has yielded her secrets, new worlds have been conquered, but the center and soul of all progress is the realization
of higher possibilities in the child. All things else that are new
and good or old and good sink into insignificance before the
power of the human spirit striving for a high destiny.
    —Parker to Barnard, January 21, 1899.

Colonel Parker came when the idea of the common schools
had received universal recognition; but there was little social enthusiasm, little moral idealism, embodied in the system. The
external machinery was there, but it needed to be taken possession
of by the spirit of life. It was Colonel Parker more than any
other one man who insisted that the magnificent machinery which
American democracy had created should also be made effective
for the moral aims of democracy. The timeliness of his work
is evidenced by his success.
    —John Dewey.

I

In upholding spiritual as against material values Bishop
Spalding was not alone among the educational leaders of his
time. Different in temperament, in educational philosophy,
and in social outlook, Francis Wayland Parker was in agreement with the Catholic bishop in believing that education
should be devoted, not to temporal matters alone, but to the
development of moral freedom and righteousness; that it
should be free from mechanical methods and should minister

374

to the spiritual life of the individual. As an officer of the church Spalding had to content himself with delivering challenging addresses and writing inspirational books on educational matters. Parker, as an actual teacher of the young, had a free hand to devote himself, in the atmosphere of the schoolroom, to the working out of his educational philosophy in a practical way.

The influence and significance of Francis Parker's work cannot be understood apart from his personality. The offspring of a long line of New England preachers and teachers, he was a thoroughgoing nonconformist. Intense and even vehement, Parker was at the same time tender and intuitive in his love and understanding of children. Aggressive, dominating, witty, and at times sarcastic, no one had more respect for the integrity and freedom of others than this fiery and energetic man of action. Far from being a systematic and logical thinker like Harris, Parker always showed the marks of his self-education. Contemptuous of the criticism which was unsparingly meted out to him all his life and which held him up to scorn as an ignoramus and a faddist, he remained fearless in expression, buoyant in spirit, and naïve in his faith in the goodness of human nature. Gruff and Spartanlike, Parker was none the less a pagan in his passionate love of life, freedom, and happiness. At the same time he was a son of the Puritans in his intense desire to have life more elevated, and at one with the transcendentalists in his unbounded faith that it might be richer, freer, and more abundant.

Perhaps the most important influence in the determination of Parker's personality and outlook was the poverty of his youth in rural New England. The early death of his father, a partially deaf cabinetmaker who tilled a few stony New Hampshire acres, left the family without resources, and the future educator was bound out to a farmer. Attending district school for only a few weeks each year, he pored over old almanacs, was imbued with the missionary enthusiasm of Wayland's *Life of Judson,* went through *Pilgrim's Progress* almost every month, and read the Bible several times. These books made an indelible impression on him. He also cherished all his life the education which the farm itself gave, believing that rural life tended to develop physical strength, self-control, resourcefulness, and kindly helpfulness.[1] He often said, in later years, that "the best-taught school in a densely populated city can never equal in educative value the life upon a good farm, intelligently managed."[2]

His career as a school-teacher, which he began at sixteen in New Hampshire and continued in Illinois, was interrupted by the Civil War, in which he served from start to finish. He was mustered out of the struggle with a gunshot wound in the throat, which accounted for the rasping quality of his voice. He also came out of the army with a conviction that North and South should be reconciled as quickly and as effectively as possible. His military career, moreover, confirmed his dislike of war and regimentation, and he resolved to devote his life, even when a promising career in business was within his grasp, to the development of a new kind of education, which among other things would eliminate the necessity of an appeal to the sword. In the very first school of which he took charge after the war was over he abandoned the law and gospel of old-fashioned teaching, which for him was associated with the martial spirit:

[1] Autobiographical sketch in Wm. M. Griffin, *School Days in the Fifties* (Chicago, 1906), pp. 110–37.

[2] N. E. A., *Proceedings,* 1897, p. 527; *Elementary School Teacher,* Vol. II (June, 1902), pp. 720–23. The country school, Parker urged before the N. E. A. in 1897, should not only dignify farm labor, foster an interest in farm life; it should also show that country environment develops appreciation for beautiful things and furnishes inexhaustible resources for intellectual development.

battalion drill, regimentation, discipline, and emulation, with its rewards and its incitements to fear and hatred.[3]

It is not clear in just what way Francis Parker's Christianity was molded and energized by the spirit of Emerson. But there can be little doubt that his worship of individuality, his optimistic faith in progress, his conception of the divinity and unlimited possibilities in every human being, his devotion to immutable and divine laws, and his pantheism resembled, even in the words with which he cloaked his thoughts, the philosophy of the sage at Concord.[4] Convinced that "design is the fundamental premise in all that exists" Parker believed that education was the exploration, the discovery, and the appreciation of the divine pattern of the universe. He subscribed to the doctrine of the unity of creation and the Creator: "all life for one life, and each for all."[5] In his devotion to spiritual growth, in the non-material character of his optimism, and in his conviction that self-activity was the most immutable of the immutable laws, Parker was close to Emerson. "A magnificent ferment," G. Stanley Hall described the belated and possibly unconscious exponent of the philosophy of the Concord seer. At the very time when, judged by most measures, materialism was growing in leaps and bounds, he continued aggressively to champion the cause of higher values.

In his reverence for nature and science, and in his distrust of secondhand book learning, Parker was also an Emersonian. Without really understanding the modern scientific spirit, he gave to nature study the central place in the process of educa-

3 Autobiographical sketch, *op. cit.,* p. 128; N. E. A., *Proceedings,* 1894, pp. 586–87; 1895, p. 972.
4 Colonel Parker's interest in Emerson was probably greatly stimulated by his able wife, Mrs. Frank Stuart Parker, who was an enthusiastic student of the Concord sage.
5 Francis W. Parker, *Talks on Pedagogics* (New York and Chicago, 1894), p. v.

tion; impressed by the emotions of wonder, beauty, grandeur, and sublimity to which nature gave rise, he conceived of it as the study of the Creator through his creation; it was at once reverence, love, and worship.[6] "The study of nature," he declared, "is the best and highest foundation for morality."[7] In the same vein he wrote that the unification of subjects took for its hypotheses, "first, the unity of the human being in design; second, the unity of the Creator and His creations; and third, that approximating unity of the human being to his Creator is the sublime destiny of man."[8]

In his belief that all was change, in his doctrine that the "law of human progress is infinite, and we have but started," Parker formed a link between Emerson and William James with his open-universe philosophy. In discussing the "new departure" or the "Quincy method," which virtually inaugurated progressive education in America in the last years of the seventies, Parker insisted that there never was a Quincy method or a Quincy system "unless we agree to call the Quincy method a spirit of study and the Quincy system one of everlasting change."[9] For whatever was fixed and finished, for whatever was "rounded, routinish, and efficient," he had only harsh condemnation. If he were to make a prayer, he declared that it would be "O Lord, preserve Thou me from the foregone conclusion."[10]

Parker confessed with humility that there was nothing original in his educational principles. Horace Mann was one of his earliest guides, and again and again he paid him the highest

[6] Francis W. Parker, "Syllabus of the Philosophy of Education, in Course of Study," in *Elementary School Teacher,* Vol. I (July, 1900), p. 27.

[7] *Notes of Talks on Teaching Given by Francis W. Parker,* reported by Lelia E. Patridge (New York and Chicago, 1891, 13th ed.), p. 176.

[8] *Talks on Pedagogics,* pp. 26, 158.

[9] Francis W. Parker, "The Quincy Method," Address, Apr. 20, 1900, in *Report of the Commissioner of Education,* 1902, pp 237–42.

[10] *Report of the Commissioner of Education,* 1902, Vol. I, p. 237.

tributes. He visited a school with Henry Barnard, and thought that his guide, whom he called "the keenest, truest critic of school work" he had ever known, gave him one of the most profitable days in his life.[11] In 1872, upon inheriting $5000 from an aunt, he resigned the headship of the normal school in Dayton, Ohio, and for two and a half years studied at the University in Berlin and traveled on the Continent. Although he read Hegel and became acquainted with the Herbartians, it was Pestalozzi, and especially Diesterweg and Froebel, who exerted the greatest influence on his educational thought. From Ritter he borrowed some of the ideas about the teaching of geography which he was to popularize on his return.[12] Although Parker had been working for several years at the Normal Practice School in Chicago before Dewey began his laboratory school, and although the two men seem to have reached similar conclusions independently, there can be little doubt that Dewey helped Parker to crystallize and formulate the theory which he had felt and groped toward and which he had realized in actual practice.[13] Between the two great educators of Chicago there was a very genuine friendship.[14]

II

Of the two cardinal ideas in the social philosophy of Parker, the happiness of the individual and the beauty and spiritual

[11] N. E. A., *Proceedings*, 1901, p. 408; Marion Foster Washburne, "Colonel Parker, the Man and the Educational Reformer," in *Talks on Teaching* (ed. *Kellogg's Teachers' Library*, Vol. III), pp. 11–12.
[12] Autobiographical sketch, *op. cit.*; *Elementary School Teacher*, Vol. II (June, 1902), p. 763; N. E. A., *Proceedings*, 1895, pp. 419–21, 549.
[13] For Dewey's tribute to Parker see *Talks on Teaching* (*Kellogg's Teachers' Library*, Vol. III), p. 25; *Elementary School Teacher and Course of Study*, Vol. II (June, 1902), pp. 704–8; *New Republic*, Vol. LXIII (July 9, 1930), p. 204; Ida Cassa Heffran, "A Sketch in Appreciation of the Life and Work of Colonel Francis W. Parker" (unpublished), p. 16. See also E. W. Krackourzer, *Francis Wayland Parker, Prophet and Propagandist* (Milwaukee, n. d.), p. 6.
[14] Dewey to Parker, n. d., Parker MSS.

value of democracy, the first was emphasized throughout his entire career. In his early efforts to provide an environment in which school children might be happy, he was concerned primarily with methods of teaching, and his social philosophy was scarcely crystallized. After he had achieved fame as superintendent of the schools at Quincy, Massachusetts (1875–1880)[15] and assumed the principalship of the Cook County Normal School in Chicago (1883–1899) he became increasingly aware of the social implications of elementary education. As the years passed he emphasized more and more the social and especially the democratic functions of the school. Although the two ideals were not unrelated, each may be discussed, for the sake of convenience, apart from the other.

Parker's ideal of emancipating childhood from the restrictions of discipline, authority, and regimentation was inspired by his desire to lay the foundations of a happy life for every child.[16] A lover of all small folk, an apostle of the dignity and divinity of childhood, Parker declared that the "end of all education should be to promote man's happiness, not only during his present transitory existence, but throughout the eternity which is to follow."[17] Unless the child's right to be himself was recognized, he could hardly be happy. This aim was strengthened by his sublime faith in human nature, his conviction that children do wrong only because they are "compelled to wrong doing by their surroundings."[18] In achieving freedom and spontaneity, in enjoying and profiting from the opportunity to

[15] For the Quincy period see Charles Francis Adams, *The New Departure in the Common Schools of Quincy* (Boston, 1879).

[16] Parker emphasized the importance of good health and physical training, and extended a hearty welcome to G. Stanley Hall and the child study movement. N. E. A., *Proceedings,* 1895, p. 949; 1896, pp. 844–46.

[17] Francis W. Parker, Introduction to T. Tate, *The Philosophy of Education* (Syracuse, 1884), p. 1.

[18] Lecture III, Parker MSS.

be himself, the child was not, however, to do whatever he liked. On the contrary, self-control was of prime importance, for without it true freedom was impossible. To everything that mechanized personality, to all that regimented and pressed the child into a mold, he was irrevocably opposed.

The secret of happiness, Parker thought, lay in the proper cultivation of the naturally divine motives which every child possessed. These motives, unless blighted by formal teaching methods, made every child an artist, a searcher for and lover of the truth, and an altruist. Parker found, when he assumed charge of the schools at Quincy, that the conventional pedagogy was altogether opposed to the "proper and free development" of these motives. With the zeal of a true reformer, he set himself the task of devising methods and creating a spirit in the schoolroom that would nourish rather than kill "these native endowments," which stamped every child with the image of God.

One means to that end, Parker believed, was the encouragement of art and of spontaneous activity in general. The natural desire to imitate and create made every boy and girl an artist, and the teacher must also become one if the child were to become a happy person: for the creative qualities of the artist were a true requisite of happiness. If a mere blotch on a piece of paper represented a child's sincere and best efforts, that was art and was to be respected rather than frowned upon. It was, indeed, more truly art than the painstaking and servile copying of models in drawing books.[19] The imagination of the child was to be cultivated; and to that end myths, which Parker thought of as the beginnings of anthropology, history, science, and religion, as well as of art, assumed an important

[19] Francis W. Parker, "Art in Everything," N. E. A., *Proceedings*, 1900, pp. 509–14; *ibid.*, 1895, pp. 846–51.

place in the schoolroom. The child's free play in fancy, he believed, was not only indispensable to happiness; it was also the best remedy for materialism and lack of religion.[20] Above all, the schoolroom must never become routinized. It must provide fresh adventures, new experiences. "Whatever else you do," Parker warned his teachers, "do something different. Uniformity is death; variety is life."[21]

By insisting that the teacher become an artist in order not to suppress the artist in her pupils, this dynamic leader gave her a new sense of freedom. Spontaneous enthusiasm in the work of the classroom was the quality that Parker treasured above all others in the teachers he chose for the school at Chicago. Such importance did he attach to the rôle of the teacher, that he centered the labors of his lifetime, even at personal sacrifice, upon reaching those actually teaching in America's schools.

For Parker another important means of helping the school child to realize his native capacities was to encourage shared work and to dispense with emulation as a main motive in school tasks. The child was not only an artist; he was also a natural altruist. The highest joy, after that of discovering the truth, was sharing it with comrades,[22] and the proper motive of work should be that of helping others. Emulation, with its premium on rewards for effort and accomplishment, killed this motive and lay at the root of much of the world's unhappiness. If a child were motivated by hope of reward and by fear of punishment, he could, if successful, only develop into a selfish person, never satisfied, and bent on using others for his own advancement. The child of inborn weakness, who failed under the stimulus of emulation to equal his more gifted rivals, too

[20] *Talks on Pedagogics,* pp. 9–10, 11.
[21] N. E. A., *Proceedings,* 1880, p. 50; *The Teachers' Institute and Practical Teacher,* Vol. IX (Sept., 1886), p. 6.
[22] *Talks on Pedagogics,* pp. 361–62.

often suffered a feeling of inferiority and despair.[23] With emulation as the chief incentive for work, the gulf between achievement and aspiration, instead of serving as a stimulus, could only bring frustration and unhappiness, and work too often became mere drudgery. The child should be taught to love work, and this he could do only if his altruistic motive of desiring to share the products of his toil with his co-partners in it were fully recognized.

Like Dewey, Parker not only believed in learning by doing; he also thought that the pleasure which came from manual work, as opposed to drudgery, ought to be an enriching part of the life of every teacher, clergyman, and lawyer; and that, on the other hand, conditions should be so arranged, at least in the schoolroom, that work never became drudgery.[24] To escape such a fate it must be shared by the entire group and carried on with both love and intelligence.

Work must also be socially useful. Parker was a pioneer in his efforts to unite the home and the school, to provide a school environment in which the child might see that the work he did had some bearing on the life of the community. Since the really great tasks involved man and nature they, rather than books, were made to assume prime importance. Parker was the first to establish a large garden in a public elementary school; and one of the first to make field work and visits to factories and to the country a part of instruction. Books, he thought with Emerson, were not only secondhand and artificial; they also savored of an aristocratic culture in which

[23] *The Teachers' Institute and Practical Teacher*, Vol. X (April, 1888), p. 229; *Report of the Commissioner of Education*, 1902, Vol. I, p. 240; *Talks on Pedagogics*, pp. 367–70. *How to Study Geography* (New York, 1894), p. xviii.
[24] *The Teachers' Institute and Practical Teacher*, Vol. X (April, 1888), p. 229; *Talks on Teaching*, pp. 160–61, 178–79; Bureau of Education, Circular of Information, No. 3, 1887, pp. 113–14.

mental activity had been monopolized by the few, a culture which was a contradiction of the natural motive of altruism. Only if work were freely engaged in and shared by the whole group, which was aware of its socially useful implications, could altruism find proper expression.[25]

To achieve happiness, the natural motive of love of truth must also be given abundant opportunity for realization. First-hand observation and open-mindedness were indispensable if the child were to be allowed to develop this God-given talent. Geological specimens and collections of newspaper clippings were therefore to be brought into the schoolroom to make elementary instruction more concrete. Above all, history and related subjects were not to be taught in a dogmatic fashion. Through self-activity and co-operation children were to have a chance to experience the joy of discovering truth.[26]

In his efforts to emancipate the child from the restrictions which dulled the motives of the artist, the altruist, and the truth-searcher, Parker transformed the schoolroom which came under his influence. Children were allowed to take responsibility for what was done as well as for their own conduct, and thus the lock step was undermined. They were given a new conception of work and of sharing common tasks; they no longer competed for an acquisitive and quantitative knowledge. As Bishop Spalding put it, when Parker took charge of the Quincy schools, they were "quickly transformed, as the spring rain and the sunshine transform the naked earth."[27] The 30,000 visitors who annually inspected the Quincy schools were a testimony to the fact that a new spirit had entered the schoolroom. "It is my aim to have every child as free as I am

[25] *Elementary School Teacher*, Vol. I (July, 1900), pp. 12–13; *Talks on Pedagogics*, pp. 253–55.
[26] *Talks on Teaching*, pp. 145–46, 171–72; *Talks on Pedagogics*, pp. 361–62.
[27] *Report of the Commissioner of Education*, 1902, Vol. I, p. 278.

myself," Parker said, and a keen observer added that the Colonel "was uncommonly free—free from prejudice, and free from fear."[28]

III

Parker's intense devotion to freedom and individuality was not greater than his love for democracy in all affairs of life. The weak, the defective, the erring all won his special tenderness. Himself a natural democrat after the pattern of Walt Whitman, he flayed false pride or snobbery in others.

Political democracy he believed to be the "only form of government under which the methods of freedom can be fostered." Mutual responsibility was the great, central principle of democracy. "Democracy in its essence," he wrote, "gives to each individual the liberty of becoming free; raises no artificial barriers, political or social, between him and his goal."[29] But the development of individuality through personal freedom was to be cherished, not only because of the divine character of every human being, but also because "personal liberty is the one means of making the individual of worth to the mass."[30] As the years went by, Parker came more and more to emphasize the principle that the democratic ideal, through the development of individuality in every child, in turn made each person serviceable to the state and to society in the highest degree.[31]

The aristocratic ideal, on the contrary, argued Parker, sank the individual in the state and made him subservient to organization, to the machine. Unlike democracy, aristocracy was

[28] Marion Foster Washburne, "The Educational Crisis in Chicago," *The Arena*, Vol. XV (March, 1896), pp. 611–18.
[29] *Talks on Pedagogics*, pp. 419–20.
[30] *Elementary School Teacher*, Vol. II (June, 1902), p. 754.
[31] N. E. A., *Proceedings*, 1895, pp. 428–29.

based on selfishness and on the belief that a few were born to rule over the masses who were destined to be subjects. "Its design is the complete subjugation of the masses to the domination of the few."[32] To perpetuate its power aristocracy cleverly devised various ruses and even ideals. It segregated people into classes, isolating them from each other. It employed physical force—prisons, police, and standing armies. Even as he wrote, Parker declared, standing armies were kept "more as a means of suppressing the personal right of choice than of defending the nation against foreign foes."[33]

Aristocracy also made use of charity as a means of securing the *status quo*. In one of the few passages in his writings in which he explicitly considered the economic problem Parker diagnosed charity as a Marxist might have done. The aristocracy, ignoring the fact that there was land enough, food enough, work enough, and money enough for all mankind, and that the problem of charity was only a problem of justice, of the right distribution of labor and effort, dispensed largesse as a masquerade, "a panacea, and a penance for the sins of the few against the many."[34] Parker believed "no religion or government is worthy of the name which does not give to each individual the means of self-effort, the means of self-support, the means of gaining food and a livelihood, happiness and freedom."[35]

Religion, too, had often been exploited by the aristocracy to maintain its supremacy. In the history of every great movement for good, the time came when, seeing its influence, "the dominant few grasp it and use it as a means of control." This rule, Parker declared, "is just as true today as it was centuries ago."[36]

[32] *Talks on Pedagogics*, p. 401.
[33] *Talks on Pedagogics*, p. 404.
[34] *Ibid.*, pp. 414–16.
[35] *Ibid.*, p. 416.
[36] *Ibid.*, pp. 401–2.

In addition to its use of force, religion, and charity to perpetuate its rule, aristocracy also made use of education. In times past it had popularized the notion that knowledge was an esoteric affair, a mystery that only the few could understand, and as a result the masses had trembled in ignorance. When it was no longer possible to keep them in complete darkness, aristocracy provided a quantitative and authoritative education which kept its recipients from thinking for themselves. "The problem was how to give the people education and keep them from exercising the divine gift of choice; to make them *believe* that they were educated and at the same time to prevent free action of the mind." The problem was solved by "quantity teaching."[37]

Although Parker believed that the only legitimate function of the private school was to serve as a laboratory, and although he took to task parents who thought their children "too good to mingle with the *hoi polloi* and learn to become a democrat" in the common schools, he was nevertheless a keen critic of the system of public elementary education which he often defended and which he sincerely loved.[38] "The methods of the few, in their control of the many, still govern our public schools, and to a great degree determine their management: the method of the prison, torture, police, and standing army survives in corporal punishment; the method of bribery,—in reward and prize-giving."[39] To meet the requirements of the more democratic civilization which America had developed, and to eliminate the conditions which in part still contradicted the democratic ideal, the public schools must be transformed.

Admitting that our common schools were not equal "to the

---

[37] *Talks on Pedagogics*, pp. 408–14.
[38] N. E. A., *Proceedings*, 1891, p. 88.   [39] *Talks on Pedagogics*, p. 436.

tremendous social problems that face us in the coming century," such as municipal reform, and overcoming the thirst for money and the desire to get something for nothing, Parker nevertheless believed that, elevated and democratized, the public school system was "the one central means by which the great problem of human liberty is to be worked out." The new school, he believed, could make war unnecessary, drive away poverty, misery, and unselfishness, and substitute the "ideal republic, the ideal free people."[40] It was useless, he told the members of the National Education Association, for teachers to say that the church and society must do their work, that the school could not be expected to develop every virtue. "We must gird on our armor and put into the school everything that is good in society."[41]

So much importance did Parker come to attach to the duty of the school to train the child for ideal citizenship that before the end of his life he declared that "the sole function of the teacher is the organization of sound community life, the development of sound public opinion."[42] Believing that educators, if they would learn and courageously apply "the truths that shall set us free," would lead society and mold opinion, Parker himself did not hesitate to fight the corrupt politicians who jeopardized the work he had so much at heart.[43] In spite of his unpleasant experience with the pressure of publishers while assistant superintendent and head of the teachers' training institute at Dayton in the early seventies, and notwithstanding his continual fights against the hostile politicians of Chicago, Parker never feared that the school would be so much fettered

[40] N. E. A., *Proceedings*, 1895, p. 972.   [41] *Ibid.*, p. 428.
[42] *The Course of Study*, Vol. I (Nov., 1900), p. 189.
[43] *Francis Wayland Parker: His Life and Educational Reform Work. Souvenir Issued in Honor of the Silver Anniversary of the Quincy Movement* (New York and Chicago, 1900), pp. 17 *et seq.*

by undemocratic and selfish influences that it might actually fail to elevate society to a higher and more truly democratic level.

Believing that the study of the needs of community life was infinite in its possibilities, and that altruism lay at the foundation of ideal citizenship, Parker worked out methods by which the new school might fulfill its democratic functions. The needs of society were, in fact, to determine the work as well as the atmosphere of the school; and the highest and most persistent incentive to good citizenship was the desire to help others. So altruism, which Parker also believed to be indispensable to the development of individuality, assumed basic importance in his school. Every effort was made to teach the child "how to live for others." One purpose in bringing backward children into the school was to provide an opportunity to the others for the development of altruism. All incentives to reward were ruled out, for Parker had no doubt that "many of the frauds and defalcations, so common at present in this country, may be traced directly back to the well-meant but dishonest training in the schoolroom."[44]

But Parker did not stop with the creation of an atmosphere in which altruism, freedom, responsibility, and other qualities of good citizenship were stimulated. He insisted that dogmatism and authoritarianism should not enter into teaching. While he respected the admirable intentions of the Woman's Christian Temperance Union in its desire to convert children to anti-alcoholism, he pointed out that in supposing that *words* would in some mysterious way benefit the learner, they were merely giving evidence of the fact that they too had been victimized by prevalent authoritarian methods of teaching.[45] In contending that temperance could not be taught any more than

[44] *Talks on Teaching*, p. 173.
[45] N. E. A., *Proceedings*, 1900, pp. 255–56.

righteousness, Parker maintained that it must be *lived* in the schoolroom if it were to be effective. Thus he took the ground from under the theory of formal indoctrination.

The teaching of history he also criticized because it was colored by prejudices, bigotry, and dogmatism. It should be taught rather in such a way as to enlarge and strengthen noble feelings in the soul and to quicken social sympathy.[46] Parker provided lessons which demonstrated the unjust and harsh way in which whites had treated Indians,[47] and he declared that "true patriotism embraces the whole world."[48] If, in spite of his bitter criticisms of militarism,[49] he did not provide for the definite inculcation of pacifism, he held that the teaching of history should put less emphasis on military and political events, and more on social relationships.[50] The tendency to sacrifice recent and contemporary history for the sake of the remote past was also deprecated.[51] Moreover, since history at best was but a partial record of mankind, it was to be supplemented by ethnology, anthropology, archæology, and philology, or by the myths, nature studies, and geography which were their beginning.[52]

Although Parker was less explicit in what he said about civics, he did not advocate the teaching of the law and order virtues. Indeed, he frankly declared that inhuman laws, such as those which forbade the search for truth, and filled dungeons

[46] *Talks on Pedagogics*, pp. 152–53, 340–41, 342; *Talks on Teaching*, pp. 145–46; *Elementary School Teacher*, Vol. II (June, 1902), p. 768.
[47] Lelia E. Patridge, *The "Quincy Methods" Illustrated* (New York, 1885), p. 652. Parker thoroughly approved of the educational policies of Booker T. Washington. N. E. A., *Proceedings*, 1897, pp. 586–88.
[48] N. E. A., *Proceedings*, 1894, p. 588; *Talks on Pedagogics*, p. 341.
[49] *Ibid.*, p. 404. N. E. A., *Proceedings*, 1894, p. 586.
[50] *Talks on Teaching*, p. 146.
[51] *Elementary School Teacher*, Vol. I (March, 1901), p. 600.
[52] *Ibid.*, Vol. II (June, 1902), p. 768.

and covered battlefields with countless thousands whose only fault had been a desire for liberty, were to be disobeyed. Rebellion against oppression and injustice was, in his eyes, commendable, not a crime. Although Parker did not definitely relate his defense of revolution to the American scene, he did not deny its validity here, as most of his fellow schoolmen would have done.[53]

Almost alone among the educational leaders of his day Parker remained unhorrified at the threat of anarchy and "nihilism" to law and order. They were not, he maintained, natural outgrowths from the common people: "they are the sure and deadly products of the method of the rule of the few over the many, of the minority suppressing the rights of the majority. Let us put the blame where it belongs. Not the poor men who land upon the scaffold because oppression has made them mad, but the rulers by might, secure in palace and castle, who fatten on the vitals of the people, they and they alone are responsible for political insanity."[54]

A personal friend of Jane Addams, Parker took an active interest in Hull House and often addressed gatherings there. Like Miss Addams, Parker had sympathy for the immigrant in America. While he believed that the newcomers could not safely be allowed to retain their Old World prejudices and anti-social philosophies, they were to be Americanized, not by being indoctrinated with one hundred percentism, but rather by being fused "into one crucible of common interests and brotherly love."[55] The two reformers were also united in their dislike of the spirit of business, their scorn for its money-getting ambitions. Although he recognized the desirability of carrying

[53] *Talks on Pedagogics*, pp. 403–4.   [54] *Ibid.*, p. 418.
[55] *Ibid.*, pp. 421–23.

over the efficient methods of business into the administration
of the school system,[56] Parker did not extend his general tolerance to the ideals of business enterprise.

If the emphasis which Parker put on spiritual values kept
him from subscribing to the ethics of industrial and financial
capitalism, he nevertheless scarcely understood the economic
system that was so profoundly influencing the America of his
time. In holding that the mass of children left school, not because of poverty or economic ambitions, but because the school
was less attractive than the factory and the shop, he was subscribing to a common belief.[57] Yet he did cherish certain beliefs which were in sharp conflict with the theory and practice
of the established order and at times he faintly realized that the
existing system of economics threatened his scheme of values.
"We are governed largely by money interests and machine
politicians" he is quoted as declaring.[58]

Parker not only fought publishers when, for the sake of
profits, they insisted on dictating educational policies. He held
up to scorn a Christian manufacturer who believed that his employees would be spoiled as laborers if they enjoyed better
opportunities for personal improvement.[59] No one was more
determinedly opposed to an elementary industrial education
which crippled and deformed the individual by predetermining
him to a given way of life.[60] It was, moreover, exceptional in
1891 to criticize the problems in arithmetic books on the ground
that they unduly cultivated "the sordid nature of the child."[61]
One searches in vain, moreover, among his writings and ad-

---

[56] Parker to Edward T. Steel, Dec. 6, 1890, Parker MSS.

[57] N. E. A., *Proceedings,* 1894, p. 449.

[58] *Arena,* Vol. XV (March, 1896), p. 613.

[59] *Talks on Pedagogics,* p. 439.   [60] N. E. A., *Proceedings,* 1900, p. 510.

[61] *Talks on Pedagogics,* pp. 76–77. Parker, while opposing the emphasis put
on interest, banking, and percentage, believed that teaching concerning money
might promote the higher civics by making clear its ethical relation to progress.

dresses for the denunciations of Socialism so common in the educational discussions of the period. Indeed, his belief that there was enough land, food, money, and work for all if labor and effort were equitably distributed and that what we produce should be primarily for others rather than for ourselves, was a Socialist doctrine.

But Parker did not relate these somewhat vague yet often penetrating insights to his general social philosophy or to his educational program. Aware though he was of grave social injustice, he failed to understand the economic forces that were rapidly transforming America; he did not see how seriously they conflicted with the ideals and values that he held so dear. He was trying to transform the school that it might counteract the influences of an old aristocracy which still dominated it; he only vaguely realized that a new aristocracy of wealth and power had arisen which threatened to encircle and capture the school system before democratic individualism and spiritual altruism won the day.

The shortcomings of Parker's vision, however, do not alter the fact that it represented American individualism at its best. In making social improvement a personal matter, in maintaining that character, the essence of which he defined as love for God and man, could alone save us, he resembled Emerson and the great American idealists. In his insistence on the full development of each individual, in his emphasis on spontaneity and freedom and beauty, he was likewise in the company of those Americans who have vigorously protested against acquisition and materialism. He did not essentially differ from Walt Whitman in his passionate devotion to the democratic conception of mutual helpfulness, which in its undiluted altruism was so free from the cant and sentimentality of certain "service" organizations.

Francis Parker's originality did not consist in formulating these ideals of a free and rich individuality for everyone, and of each for all and all for each; it did not consist in his advocacy of education as the instrument of social reform or as the way of achieving democracy. It consisted rather in the vivid and regenerating spirit that he brought into the schoolroom, in his power to create an atmosphere that was truly democratic. But only if this spirit of Parker should penetrate the whole of the school system, defeating opposing forces within the school and antagonistic pressures from without—only then could its promise of full development for all children be realized.

Whatever the failures of Parker, however disappointed he might be if he were to return today and measure the spread of his "new departure," his successes, difficult though they are to measure, cannot be denied. Without even trying to assess the influence of the teachers and administrators whom he inspired—people like Clarence E. Meleney, Thomas M. Balliet, Alexis Frye, Orville Bright, Florence Holbrook, Willard D. Straight, George Aldrich, Flora F. Cooke, and a great many more, it can be said that he threw dynamite into self-satisfied educational circles. It can also be said that he contributed substantially to making the school less deadening for the average child, to bringing about, not only in progressive institutions, but in the rank and file of the public schools, less routine and more spontaneity and freedom.

An impressive number of men have testified to his influence —Bishop Spalding, William T. Harris, G. Stanley Hall, Nicholas Murray Butler, and John Dewey. Hall thought that elementary education in America owed more to him during the last two decades of the nineteenth century than to any other person.[62] With the father of the child study movement, with the Herbartians whose emphasis on the organic unity of all subjects and whose revolt against conventional pedagogy enlisted his sympathy,[63] and with many other groups and forces, Francis Parker began the emancipation of the American child.

[62] For Parker's influence see A. E. Winship, "Some Who Were Influenced by Colonel Parker," *Journal of Education*, Vol. LXXXII (Sept. 30, 1915), pp. 287–88; *Francis Wayland Parker: His Life and Educational Reform Work; Elementary School Teacher*, Vol. II; *In Memoriam* (June, 1902); *Report of the Commissioner of Education*, 1901–2, Vol. I, pp. 231–84; Flora J. Cooke, *Colonel Parker, As Interpreted through the Work of the Francis W. Parker School*, reprint from *Elementary School Teacher*, Vol. XII (May, 1912), pp. 397–420; Mrs. Emmons Blaine, "Francis Wayland Parker," *Dedication of the Chicago Normal School, Apr. 20 and 21, 1906* (Chicago, 1906); Frank A. Fitzpatrick, "Francis Wayland Parker," *Ed. Rev.*, Vol. XXIV (June, 1902), pp. 23–30; Heffron, *A Sketch in Appreciation of the Life and Work of Colonel Francis W. Parker; The Nation*, Vol. LXXXIII (July 5, 1906), p. 8.

[63] N. E. A., *Proceedings*, 1894, p. 447; *ibid.*, 1895, pp. 420–21.

XII

G. STANLEY HALL, EVOLUTIONIST

1846–1924

I am an optimist root and core, not merely because an evolutionist must hold that the best and not the worst will survive and prevail, but because in most though not in all these fields, I see clearly the beginning of better things.

—G. STANLEY HALL.

America believes, as does no other country, that education must be based on a study of psychology. That this is so is due in no small degree to the influence of President Hall.

—WILLIAM H. KILPATRICK.

I

The impressionistic writings of G. Stanley Hall often seem self-contradictory, but from his fourteen books and some three hundred and fifty published papers one may glean a fairly consistent social philosophy. Four years before his death in 1924, he himself set it down in a satirical utopia, *The Fall of Atlantis.* A romantic individualist and a devout apostle of evolution, Hall was in close touch with the changing mood of his times, a mood which he passionately desired to understand and with which he sympathized in a fashion at once tender and robust. Woven in part out of his own personality and experiences, his social philosophy incorporated many characteristically American notions.

Although born of farmer stock, Hall enjoyed many of the advantages of the more privileged class of Americans. The relatively slender means of his immediate family were still sufficient to enable him to attend one of the best preparatory schools in New England, Williams College, and the Union Theological Seminary. He later enjoyed three years of study and travel in Germany as well. In his boyhood, Stanley Hall absorbed the ideals of thrift, self-help, and individuality. He acknowledged again and again the incentive he derived from the frequently expressed wishes of his parents that their children "make good." After success and admiration had come to him, it was natural to look back fondly on his early life and to idealize it, for it had given him the character and the incentive, if not the specific training and ideas, which he identified with his success.[1]

Young Stanley Hall took after his mother in her dislike of conflict and dissension. A pacifist at heart, he was glad to escape fighting in the armies of the North during the Civil War; but he was later much chagrined when he learned that his father had secured his exemption by paying a government physician a generous fee for declaring his son physically unfit for the army. Late in life, Hall believed that his life-long patriotism and idealization of the military virtues was in reality a compensation for his adolescent feeling of being a shirker and a coward. But notwithstanding his patriotism and his devotion to the ideals of aggressiveness, virility, and patriotism, he continued to feel the dread of conflict that, he believed, he had inherited from his mother. It may well be that this dislike of discord in part explains his life-long determination to see no real conflict between social groups.[2]

It is also possible that Hall may have been right in thinking that adolescent antagonisms toward his father laid the foundations for a certain independence of authority and impatience of control, as well as for his idealization of freedom in thought

[1] G. Stanley Hall, *Life and Confessions of a Psychologist* (New York, 1923), pp. 80, 85.
[2] *Ibid.*, pp. 148–49, 575–76.

and action. Whether or not he was mistaken about its explanation, this aspect of his personality helps to explain his antagonism to standardization.[3]

Hall's life on a hill farm also greatly influenced his development. The living creatures and natural phenomena all about him aroused his curiosity and laid a foundation for an interest in science. His work in the farm shop was probably one of the factors that in later life made him attach high value to motor skill, in which he himself excelled. His own versatility and capacity to do useful tasks very likely had something to do with his later devotion to utilitarian values in education. His crude initiation into a knowledge of sex, in the district school, probably accentuated a natural interest and prepared the way for his later convictions regarding its basic importance. He believed that farm life made for health, vitality, and general spontaneity, and that the country, more than the city, enabled the middle class to exert an all-controlling influence on society and to replenish civilization by its habits of industry, patriotism, conservatism, personal independence, and respectability. This belief played an important part in all his subsequent thinking on social questions. Most of all, life in a compact and homogeneous community made him feel that there was no essential conflict of interest between individuals and the group, or between one class and another.[4]

In college little happened to alter any of Hall's ideas save his religious ones. His individualism must have been confirmed by reading John Stuart Mill, his first intellectual hero. In his postgraduate year at Union Theological Seminary in 1866, he became familiar with Renan, Strauss, Tyndall, Goethe, Tom

[3] *Ibid.*, p. 86.
[4] G. Stanley Hall, "Boy Life in a Massachusetts Country Town Thirty Years Ago," *Proceedings of the American Antiquarian Society*, n. s., Vol. VII (1891), pp. 107–128.

Paine, Darwin, and Spencer. Unable by reason of his hetero-doxy to enter the ministry, he might well have stopped short of a professional career had he not been enabled to study philosophy in Germany.

In the meantime his knowledge of American life had been widened by his experiences in New York City. As a sort of pioneer social worker he became familiar with police courts, houses of ill fame, foundling homes, tenement houses, and slum life generally. He did not, apparently, ask why such conditions existed. A different side of the great metropolis was opened to him when, as a teacher in a select school, he became acquainted with the daughters of some its most wealthy citizens. Perhaps his flattering conference with Fowler and Wells, eminent phrenologists, awakened an interest in psychical life; certainly he could only have been confirmed in his individualism by an acquaintanceship with that pseudo-science.[5]

In Germany Hall did, however, discover a philosophy other than individualism. He enjoyed several pleasant talks in Berlin with the philosopher Kirschmann, who had been dismissed from the university because of his socialistic teachings. In visits to the Reichstag he listened to Liebknecht and Bebel. His writings during his second sojourn in Germany a few years later show a continued interest in these Socialist leaders and in the writings of Lassalle. He wrestled with Karl Marx and "half accepted" what he understood of him. Indeed, he was so impressed by the contribution of the worker to society as to assert, even at the end of his lifetime, that "we daily enjoy the results of the toil of generations of laborers" who have built our cities, tilled our land, and constructed our harbors and ships.[6]

On both his first and second returns from Germany Hall felt

[5] *Life and Confessions*, pp. 157 *et seq.*, 178 *et seq.*
[6] *Ibid.*, pp. 441, 222; *Aspects of German Culture* (Boston, 1881), pp. 53, 74, 88, 91.

that America did not seem to appreciate his talents and training. He fairly loathed the prosperous and smug ways of his fellow countrymen, their self-satisfaction, their inferior culture, the crudeness of their educational system. Years later, in reflecting on this period of his life, he believed that it would easily have been possible for him to "have drifted into almost any camp of radicals and to have come into such open rupture with the scheme of things as they are" that he would have been regarded as too dangerous for any academic career.

But an academic career was the only alternative to going back to the farm; and having been notified, after an appointment at the University of Minnesota, that his "German" ideas made him *persona non grata* at that institution, he must have been inclined to restrain his radical leanings. A tutorship in the family of the wealthy Seligmans, acquaintance with William T. Harris, a teaching position at Antioch, and, above all, his realization that if he was to utilize successfully his long, arduous, and expensive education, he must not express his "deeply stirred instincts of revolt"—all these tended to keep him from advertising his "rank heresies and socialistic leanings."[7]

Indeed in 1880 Socialism was an unpopular cause in America. The great strikes of the previous decade had given bad odor to all radicalism in the eyes of those who determined academic appointments. Only humble immigrants and dangerous radicals were advocating "Socialism"; the earlier American adaptation of Fourierism was, to all intents and purposes, dead and buried. If Hall was to find a place in the intellectual life of America, he was probably wise in steering clear of economic radicalism. He did write, in his *Aspects of German Culture* (1881), that business considerations had come to control politics, education, and even the church, and that American life was

[7] *Life and Confessions,* p. 223.

dominated by business. He added, however, that this materialistic basis of American culture was not so deplorable as was often assumed.

Hall saw and deplored political corruption and other evils in public life, but he did not see the love of profit as important in their explanation, and he was content to trust the integrity and political sagacity of the American people to remove the defects of the political system. Years later, when he became interested in Pavlov's early work on "food psychology," Hall reverted to a "materialistic" interpretation of history in declaring that the struggle for life was largely a struggle for food, which thus became the supreme value from which all other things derived their meaning. At about the same time he declared that unless capitalists assured their employees sufficient clothing, shelter, and food, Socialism was an imminent danger.[8]

If Socialism, with which Hall was tempted to flirt in his youthful years, was too dangerous a matter for anyone who wanted to "get ahead" in America, the doctrine of evolution was, if not entirely accepted in the most respectable circles, much less hazardous. Evolution, in fact, was the second dominant European idea with which Hall, in his German years, had become familiar. His decision to pin his faith to the doctrines of Darwin and Haeckel and not to those of Lassalle and Marx was probably due in large part to the fact that he was a student of philosophy and psychology rather than of economics and social problems. But it is also true that the decision was more acceptable to the powers that determined the fate of young academic aspirants. If there was still much opposition to evolution in clerical circles, it was by the eighties relatively "safe" in the larger and better known institutions.

[8] *Aspects of German Culture*, p. 307; *Life and Confessions*, pp. 414, 421; *Morale: The Supreme Standard of Life and Conduct* (New York, 1920), pp. 337–38, 324, 202 *et seq.*, 207.

Notwithstanding orthodox scruples against it, evolution as popularly interpreted fitted admirably into the dominant mood of America. It was an optimistic concept, and Americans believed in the future, in their future. Everything was moving fast. America had long subscribed to the doctrine of progress, and evolution gave that doctrine scientific standing. Moreover, the doctrine of evolution, while it might upset ecclesiastic authority, tended to make many who accepted it more rather than less satisfied with the existing social and economic order. Whatever ought to be, will be, ultimately. The process of change is slow, and nature has it in her keeping. Whatever is, that is a step in the process.

Hall felt that evolution, rightly and broadly interpreted, gave a new basis for our government and our type of democracy. Its fundamental assumption that the folk-soul can be trusted, that everything great and good in the world, including religion, science, and the social and industrial order, sprang out of the unfathomable depths of human nature, confirmed faith and buttressed hope.[9] To say all these things is not to say that Hall deliberately turned his back on Socialism and championed evolution because the one meant obscurity and penalization, the other fame and success. But to say that the one challenged the existing order, and that the other, for the most part, fitted agreeably into it, helps to understand his course.

So young Stanley Hall accepted a professorship at Johns Hopkins, said yes to life, and made significant contributions to American psychology and education. With James Cattell he was a pioneer in America in applying laboratory technique to the study of the mind. He became famous for his application of the doctrine of evolution, not without some metaphysical assumptions, to psychical development. He fathered the child-

[9] *Life and Confessions,* p. 363.

study movement. He translated many of the Herbartian concepts into classroom technique. He talked to teachers on the applications of the new psychology to education. Presently, in 1889, he was called to found a new university sponsored by a millionaire who insisted, with quixotic and unpredictable egotism, on interfering with what Hall supposed he had freedom to do in the interest of the institution. But these bitter experiences did not greatly modify his social philosophy. Although he later deprecated the routinized organization of research and pointed out the dangers that great wealth might bring to the search for truth, he did not question in any fundamental or critical way the existing economic structure.[10]

Of the various influences which affected the outlook of G. Stanley Hall perhaps none was so important as the spirit of romanticism, which, as Parrington has pointed out, was a dominant current of thought during Hall's young manhood. It was in the air. He could not have escaped it if he would. While in college he read the romantic poets. His early surroundings in the beautiful Berkshires made him fond of nature. His antiauthoritarianism was a part of the romantic mood. When he went to Germany, he reacted against the pious and narrow home influences, drank beer, played about with women, and began consciously to solicit experiences that gave him the raw feeling of life in all its aspects. He loved prize fights; he delighted in visits to the metropolitan "underworlds"; he took up dancing when well past middle life; he loved, in his later years, to strip and roll on Ashfield's lovely hills. He never tired

[10] G. Stanley Hall, "Research the Vital Spirit of Teaching," *The Forum,* Vol. XVII (Aug., 1894), pp. 558–70; "Contemporary University Problems," *Pedagogical Seminary,* Vol. XXI (June, 1914), pp. 242–55; *Adolescence, Its Psychology and Its Relations to Physiology, Anthropology, Sociology, Sex, Crime, Religion and Education* (New York, 1905), Vol. II, pp. 559–60; "University Research," *Pedagogical Seminary,* Vol. XXIV (March, 1917), pp. 97–113.

of talking and writing of women and of sex in a highly romantic way.

However Hall came by this romanticism, it was important in several respects. It was a vivid but ineffective protest against the increasing standardization of American life, which he cordially disliked. It also kept him from facing squarely many aspects of contemporary life, which he was anxious to face. It led him to overemphasize the mere feeling of life, and to underestimate the possibility of controlling it, especially in social ways. It led him to lose himself in contemplating feudalism and chivalry, the ideals of which he wanted to impose, through romantic literature, on every child. It accentuated his individualism, and minimized, in his thinking, the rôle played by social and economic forces. On the other hand, an examination of Hall's specific social attitudes indicates that his romanticism did not keep him from accepting, with slight qualifications, the existing social arrangements and dominant beliefs of the middle class to which he belonged and whose virtues he so highly prized.

Hall's study of evolution confirmed his individualistic belief that heredity was a far more important determining factor than environment. Consequently social institutions, and education itself, played a far less important part in his thinking than, for example, in that of Harris. He subscribed to the doctrine of the inheritance of acquired characters, and believed, in an almost mystical fashion, that feelings and impulses, transmitted from racial and even pre-human experiences of forgotten hosts of ancestors, influenced human behavior far more than ideas and institutions.

Subscribing as he did to the doctrine that nature is right and to the theories of heredity and natural selection, which he applied to psychical development, Hall thus attached far less importance to social control and reform than he did to individual virtue and to eugenics. His theory of evolution compelled him to repudiate the revolutionary concept of catastrophic leaps. To the pleas of reformers and revolutionists he replied that the proper procedure was not to sweep away or fluidize "all or even any one of our existing institutions in order to start with a *tabula rasa*," nor even to transform them. "In the whole biological field," he reasoned, "regeneration is never preceded by destruction. The scores of alluring programs of reformers are at best only palliatives, and their helpfulness is usually at best only transitory." Our own personal lives must rather be revised, "for here alone can be laid the foundations of the new kingdom of magnanimity."[11]

To check national or racial decline, Hall did, however, recommend certain things. War, sports, and a general policy of *laissez faire* might weed out the unfit and cleanse the race if it seemed on the downward incline. Sterilization and segregation of the unfit, he believed, were eminently practical measures. Although he thought that social workers and others greatly overemphasized the rôle of environment in producing the unfit, he was willing to have society assume some responsibility for them. Yet he strongly felt that, from the point of view of racial morale, pity ought not to be expended on the moribund sick, the undervitalized poor, defectives, and criminals, since by aiding them to survive the process of wholesome natural selection was unduly interfered with. Pity needed new ideals; its work was not to salvage the wreckage of humanity, but to remove the handicaps from those most able to help man to higher levels —"the leaders on more exalted planes who can be of most aid in

[11] *Pedagogical Seminary*, Vol. XXX (Sept., 1923), p. 259.

ushering in the kingdom of the superman."[12] Such an application of the theory of evolution to society, together with his
conviction that class distinctions were in large measure based on
inherited individual differences, and that the lower strata of
civilized peoples made slight progress, stamped "the American
Darwin of the mind" as a social aristocrat.[13]

Yet Hall's doctrine of the "rightness of nature" did not keep
him from believing that human selfishness must be checked.
Unlike Nietzsche, he refused to accept the creed of ruthless ex-
termination of weaklings by supermen. Like Kropotkin, he
was aware that the theory of mutual aid was a corollary of
evolution; and he consequently made a place in his social thinking for co-operation, charity, even tenderness. He became a
great advocate of "service," to which he awarded a high place
in his scale of virtues.[14] When one individual or group put its
own selfish interest above that of the entire social body, he
thought, the equilibrium was upset and catastrophe lay around
the corner.

It was his dislike of what he thought to be group selfishness
that led him to oppose lockouts and injunctions on the part of
employers, as well as boycotts, strikes and mass action on the
part of workers. It was similar dislike that made him oppose
protective tariffs, the grasping and exploiting methods of American business, and the determination of 100 per cent Americans
to ram their Americanism down the throats of our immigrants,
whose group-loyalties deserved respect.[15] It was likewise his
opposition to group selfishness that made him speak out against

[12] G. Stanley Hall, *Educational Problems* (New York, 1911), Vol. II, pp. 73,
77–79, 148, 185–86; "Pity" (with F. H. Saunders) *American Journal of
Psychology*, Vol. XI (July, 1900), pp. 534–91.

[13] *Adolescence*, Vol. II, p. 720.

[14] *Educational Problems*, Vol. II, pp. 207, 667 *et seq.*

[15] *Morale*, pp. 201, 341; *Educational Problems*, Vol. I, pp. 285, 336 *et seq.;*
Pedagogical Seminary, Vol. XXX (Sept., 1923), p. 258.

the isolationism which kept us from co-operating with the Allies in forming the League of Nations.[16]

In his last years Hall feared that stratified economic groups were selfishly endangering the social whole. He pictured in "The Fall of Atlantis" an ideal society which disintegrated because of group selfishness.[17] His belated recognition that some effective restraint must be placed on the more powerful and selfish groups marked a modification of his earlier basic assumptions of group solidarity and the desirability of *laissez faire*. This recognition, together with his desire to stimulate "morale" on the part of the worker as a safeguard against class warfare, was promoted by his fear of the "Bolshevik menace."

Hall accepted most institutions as expressions of the folk-soul, *i.e.* as representing deeply rooted instincts originally acquired at some stage or other of past human or pre-human history. In accordance with the theory of recapitulation, which was taken over from von Baer, he held that there could be no conflict between the individual and the institutions that expressed the folk-soul if the child were allowed freely to express the appropriate feelings, moods, and impulses which corresponded to the given culture-epoch of the race which he was at that time recapitulating. "If things go wrong in human affairs," Hall felt, "there must somewhere be a psychic cause" which the psychologist and educator must remove,[18] that cause being usually some repression of primitive instincts.

With the dominant institutions in America Hall had no quarrel; they were, he believed, entirely in accord with the basic instincts inherited from our remote ancestors. Notwithstanding the fact that, from an orthodox point of view, he him-

---

[16] *Life and Confessions*, p. 241.

[17] G. Stanley Hall, "The Fall of Atlantis," *Recreations of a Psychologist* (New York, 1920), pp. 1–127; *Morale*, pp. 232, 234.

[18] *Life and Confessions*, pp. 436, 438.

self was an agnostic, he valued religious institutions because he thought they were directly related to half-hidden and earlier impulses of the race. Indeed, so important did he think the church to be in answering the mystic cravings and reverberatory primal needs of most men, that he preferred to have a child brought up as a Mohammedan, a Buddhist, a Confucian, or a Catholic, rather than without any religion at all.[19]

War, like religion, was in the opinion of Hall the necessary expression of the deep-seated instinct of pugnacity—a secondary sexual trait. Nations, like individuals, might suppress legitimate anger beyond the point of well-being. While Hall did not glorify war in itself, he favored military games and military training in schools for their value in developing manly, well-rounded individuals, and naturally enough he found, when we entered the struggle to make the world safe for democracy, that it possessed many values highly desirable for the morale of individuals and the race. It broke down artificial barriers, he argued, resulted in wide and sympathetic co-operation, effected much needed discipine, and re-enforced the virile qualities so much threatened by modern urbanism and by the practice of having boys taught almost exclusively in the schoolroom by women. War, Hall thought, also lessened selfishness and held up broader, more inclusive ideals. If it was in a sense a pitiless reversion to barbarism, it called forth wholesome solidarity and gave man a superpersonal value which he could love more than his own life. War eliminated, moreover, many of the unfit; and universal military service provided much needed discipline, as well as physical culture and educational opportunities.

In disregarding the economic and social causes of war, Hall oversimplified the problem; and his psychological interpreta-

---

[19] *Ibid.*, pp. 517–18, 569–70; *Adolescence*, Vol. II, p. 700; *Educational Problems*, Vol. I, pp. 136 *et seq.*; *Eugenics Review*, Vol. I (Jan., 1910), p. 253.

tion, which gave to war a fatalistic inevitability, is not of course the accepted one among present-day psychologists. As if dimly recognizing at times the weakness of his own theory, he admitted that modern wars endangered civilization itself, and advocated our participation in the League of Nations in order to make war less likely.[20]

Private property, like war, was, in Hall's psychology, based on a fundamental instinct and must therefore be respected and protected. The instinctive character of possessiveness made Socialism and Communism unnatural, intolerable, and utterly impracticable. On the other hand, Hall said, the captains of industry must heed the fact that their workers, being human, also possess the acquisitive instinct. If employers remained arrogant and indifferent toward the legitimate and instinctive desire of workers to possess wealth and to improve their lot, they merely invited radicalism and revolution, which Hall particularly feared after the events in Russia in 1917.[21]

No existing institution met so basic an instinctive need, Hall maintained, as the family. Its function was the transmission of the "sacred torch of life undimmed"; it provided expression for "the most imperious and all-pervading instinct of man," an instinct which, more than all else, conditioned his individual and social life. Although he did not accept the more extreme doctrines of Freud and Jung, whom he brought in person to America, Hall held that sex supplied the motivation for most human behavior; nothing made art, science, altruism, moral and religious life so vivid and dynamic. He shared with Roose-

[20] *Adolescence*, Vol. II, pp. 367–68; Vol. I, pp. 216–17; "Practical Relations between Psychology and the War," *Journal of Applied Psychology*, Vol. I (March, 1917), pp. 9–16; "Some Educational Values of War," *Pedagogical Seminary*, Vol. XXV (Sept., 1918), pp. 303–7; *Morale*, pp. 142–43, 137, 16–17, 187, *passim*; *Some Aspects of the War* (Easthampton, Mass., 1917); *Life and Confessions*, p. 241.

[21] *Adolescence*, Vol. II, pp. 376, 388, 392–93; *Life and Confessions*, p. 535; *Morale*, pp. 207 *et seq.*, 213, 216.

velt the view that there was danger of race suicide, and that the better classes must do their share, and more than their share, to prevent such a calamity.[22]

The mystical and religious fervor and the biased presuppositions with which Hall regarded the whole question of sex explain his interpretation of the function of women in society. For every woman the ideal, in fact, the only full life, he said, was marriage and motherhood, and whatever interfered with that life was unethical and a sin against both the race and the highest destiny of the individual woman. Hall thought that woman differed from man in every organ and tissue, and that her mental traits were correspondingly unlike those of the opposite sex. Admitting that she possessed the ability to do high grade research, to succeed in the professions, the arts, and business, he deprecated excessive intellectualism in so far as it instilled an aversion to maternity, for which woman's body and soul were made. Without maternity, she could not hope for rest and peace. In an ideal society, education for women would center in preparation for wifehood and motherhood and seek in every way to magnify these functions and invest them with reverence and honor. "Biological psychology already dreams of a new philosophy of sex which places the wife and mother at the heart of a new world and makes her the object of a new religion and almost of a new worship, that will give her reverent exemption from sex competition and reconsecrate her to the higher responsibilities of the human race, into the past and future of which her being penetrates, where the blind worship of mere mental illumination has no place."[23]

[22] *Educational Problems,* Vol. I, pp. 388 *et seq.,* 479; *Life and Confessions,* pp. 406 *et seq.,* 532 *et seq.*

[23] *Adolescence,* Vol. II, pp. 391–92, 561–62, 609 *et seq.* For a succinct account of Hall's ideas on the education of women see his "Address on Founder's Day at Mt. Holyoke College, Nov. 5, 1896," *The Mount Holyoke News,* Vol. VI (Nov., 1896), pp. 64–72.

In adopting this mystical attitude toward women, Hall set himself against one of the dominant tendencies in modern life— the emancipation of women from traditional ideology, religious and romantic. Although he was too sensible to think that he could stay the tide of feminism, he felt it his duty to do all in his power to convince both sexes of what he believed was the true social position of women, a position derived from their biological and psychological status.

Like Parker, Hall made a gospel of childhood. Elevating the child to a new plane of importance, he focused attention upon his needs and peculiarities and insisted that the schools should meet these needs and peculiarities. The time, indeed, was ripe for declaring the intrinsic importance of the child, as an entity and in relation to a broader, more humane, and social world. In the multitudinous questionnaires which he and his students instituted, the nature of the child was investigated, and his feelings, hobbies, habits, and fancies were catalogued in an exhaustive and impressive, if sometimes dubious, manner. Science, or scientific speculation, seemed at last to be giving to the child the importance that Rousseau and his followers had preached.

In spite of the influence of Pestalozzi and Froebel, Americans as a whole had taken the child somewhat casually and had acted on the Puritan belief that what was desirable for adults was good for the young. Children had proved to be indispensable in the upbuilding of American farms and factories. With the ending of the frontier process, the incoming of hoards of cheap immigrant labor, and the multiplication of machines, however, economic conditions were emancipating children from the arduous work and discipline of former times. Moreover, new social problems demanded solution—problems arising from the extinction of free lands, from the growth of cities and of industrialism. Hall believed that the salvation of society lay, primarily, in securing for youth sound bodies and minds, in part through education and in part through eugenics.

The faith which Hall had in the strength, wholesomeness, and soundness of youth made him an optimist and at the same time led him to preach a new kind of individualism just when the old had broken down, and just when social control and intelligent collectivism seemed necessary to many observers. Hall believed that by giving the best youths, whom he frankly declared to come from the middle class,[24] more adequate educational opportunities, and by protecting society against degenerate and criminal-minded boys and girls, our problems would be well on the way to solution. Like so many of his educational predecessors, he was escaping from certain fundamental and present realities by finding satisfaction in a better tomorrow that youth was to bring into being. In so far as Hall's wide influence promoted a more tender and rational regard for children, it served humane needs; but in so far as it corroborated the belief of his fellow Americans that social problems could be solved by the mere training up of better individuals, his influence tended to postpone the solution of those problems.

Hall's attitude toward the less advanced races was not unlike that which he took toward children. His recapitulatory theory made him almost sentimental in his regard for the backward peoples, whom he thought of as in the adolescent and therefore peculiarly sacred stage of racial development, and to whom he ascribed virtues of body and soul sorely needed by civilized races.[25] He appreciated the folklore and mores of the

---

[24] *Chautauquan,* Vol. XLVII (July, 1907), p. 155.

[25] G. Stanley Hall, "The Point of View toward Primitive Races," *The Journal of Race Development,* Vol. I (July, 1910), pp. 5–11; "The Problem of Dependent Races," *Report of the Twenty-Ninth Annual Lake Mohonk Conference,* Oct. 18–20, 1911, pp. 225–32; *Adolescence,* Vol. II, pp. 649–51, 748.

Negroes and the Indians, and opposed the efforts of nationalists to thrust a standardized type of Americanism on them and on the immigrants who thronged to our shores. While many humanitarians were urging the Government to civilize and Americanize the Indians as rapidly as possible, Hall advised that they be permitted to live in their traditional way.[26]

Resenting the efforts of politicians to solve the Negro problem, Hall declared that it was a matter for sociological and anthropological experts, and for the Negro himself. He must stand squarely on his own feet and respect his unique gifts of intense emotional endowment, capacity for merriment, patience, submissiveness, mysticism, and primitive sense of rhythm, all of which Hall assumed were peculiar inherited traits. Declaring that the black man's utopia depended largely upon himself, Hall asked for no concessions from the whites in their characteristic attitudes toward him, and sympathized with Booker T. Washington's educational philosophy.[27]

Notwithstanding his acceptance of most existing institutions Hall admitted that certain recent and "artificial" ones might not be fitted to the fundamental, racial nature of man, and he believed that imperialism fell within such a category. He urged the authorities who sought military and commercial advantage in our colonies to administer them with sole reference to the interests of the natives, and above all to appreciate the peculiar racial traditions of these "child-like peoples." Quite possibly, he maintained, these races were destined so to develop as at some future time to hold the fate of the world in their hands. But

[26] G. Stanley Hall, "How Far Are the Principles of Education Along Indigenous Lines Applicable to American Indians," *Pedagogical Seminary*, Vol. XV (Sept., 1908), pp. 365–69; *Adolescence*, Vol. II, pp. 698–700.

[27] G. Stanley Hall, "The Negro in Africa and America," *Pedagogical Seminary*, Vol. XII (Sept., 1905), pp. 350–68; "The Negro Question," *Proceedings of the Massachusetts Historical Society*, 2d series, Vol. XIX (1905), pp. 95–107; "Undeveloped Races in Contact with Civilization," *Washington University Association Bulletin*, Vol. IV (1906), pp. 145–50.

Hall's romantic attitude toward imperialism was not representative.[28]

Thus Hall did not regard human institutions as fixed and
unchanging. Some, like imperialism, needed modification because they were based on mistaken ideas of human nature.
Others needed changing because, although at one time a genuine expression of a stage in racial evolution, they tended to
persist after the race was ready for a higher stage. Hence, while
his theory of evolution kept him from ascribing a large and
determining rôle to education, Hall did believe that the educator had a definite function in helping to achieve satisfactory
relations between the individual and institutions. The teacher
must, above all else, see to it that education does not obstruct,
but rather facilitates, "natural" evolution. It must make the
individual the fittest possible instrument for racial improvement.
The educator must take care that the institutions to which
he helps the child adjust itself truly square with primal human
nature. Inept institutions must be improved or melted into new
ones in accord with the primal, racial character of mankind.[29]

II

Limited though Hall believed the function of education to be,
he seems to have felt that the high school, college, and university
had an important rôle to play in readjusting and developing
institutions in such a fashion as to make them increasingly
accord with man's nature. The grammar schools, in his estima-
tion, were designed primarily to fit the child to existing institutions; but the high school and the college were to be made in

[28] *Adolescence*, Vol. II, pp. 649–51, 662–66; "The Relations between Lower
and Higher Races," *Proceedings of the Massachusetts Historical Society*,
2d series, Vol. XVII (Jan., 1903), pp. 4–13.
[29] *Educational Problems*, Vol. I, pp. x, 200; *Life and Confessions*, pp. 21,
367; N. E. A., *Proceedings*, 1902, pp. 262–63.

"the image not of the present but of the future"—they were "nests of institutions that are to be." They were to fit man for the next stage in the development of the nation and the race. It was likewise this function that led Hall to attach an almost religious significance to research.[30]

But the function of education did not stop with the contribution it made to the readjustment of institutions. With the McMurry brothers and other disciples of Herbart, Hall applied to pedagogy the culture epoch theory, a theory not now in good scientific standing. According to this theory, it will be remembered, the normal individual in his personal development instinctively recapitulates the culture epochs of the race. A curriculum enriched with the proper materials, especially in the lower grades, was to enable education to assist the child in freely expressing the appropriate feelings and impulses which correspond to the given culture epoch which he was at the time recapitulating. Unless education took care to prevent repressions of such feelings, moods, and impulses, they were likely, in Hall's opinion, to express themselves in later life in crime or other anti-social behavior. Proper education, by preventing such an unfortunate suppression and subsequent unraveling of natural and dominant instincts, was thus the great means of racial catharsis.[31]

To education Hall also ascribed the task of counteracting the dominant tendencies of standardization, an evil he believed was bound to retard the natural course of evolution. The kindergarten might help by breaking away from the formal functions which such disciples of Froebel as Susan Blow had

[30] *Pedagogical Seminary,* Vol. IX (March, 1902), pp. 89–90; *ibid.,* Vol. I (Dec., 1891), pp. 311–26; "Educational Reforms," *ibid.,* Vol. I (Jan., 1891), pp. 1–12.
[31] G. Stanley Hall, *Aspects of Child Life and Education* (Boston, 1907), pp. 266–67; *Adolescence,* Vol. I, pp. 44, 49.

fastened on it. Hall held up to ridicule symbolism and mother-play, and urged that more attention be given to music, dancing, the telling of stories, the training of the larger muscles, and, above all, to the principles of health and hygiene.[32] The grades beyond the kindergarten might help in counteracting the standardization of life by basing the curriculum and the methods of teaching on the "true needs" of the pupil as they were revealed by child study. Everything in the school, subject matter, equipment, aims, was to be measured by the supposed needs of the child at each particular stage of his development; and these needs were to be discovered, in large measure, by the inventory or questionnaire method now considered by psychologists unreliable as a means of revealing native traits.

"There is really no clue by which we can thread our way through all the mazes of culture and the distractions of modern life save by knowing the true nature and needs of childhood and adolescence," Hall declared. "I urge then," he continued, "that civilizations, religions, all human institutions, and the schools, are judged truly, or from the standpoint of the philosophy of history, by this one criterion: namely, whether they have offended against these little ones or have helped to bring childhood and adolescence to an ever higher and completer maturity as generations pass by. Childhood is thus our pillar of cloud by day and fire by night."[33]

In the prevalent "mass methods" of instruction Hall believed that the gifted child was the sufferer, and he condemned the tendency of existing schools to make children, especially those in the adolescent years, "act, feel, think and learn in platoons." The schools, he insisted, must be individualized. To promote

[32] G. Stanley Hall, "Some Defects of the Kindergarten in America," *The Forum*, Vol. XXVIII (Jan., 1900), pp. 579–91; *Educational Problems*, Vol. I, pp. 9 *et seq.*

[33] *Forum*, Vol. XXIX (Aug., 1900), p. 700.

this end, he would improve the economic and professional status of the teacher, encourage the gifted child and pay less attention to the dullard, and popularize the curriculum by introducing subjects demanded by child interest.[34]

Among the subjects which Hall favored, and for which he found social as well as individual values, was industrial training. A number of pioneers had anticipated him in this, but his influence gave great prestige to the movement. From the point of view of the individual, he argued, industrial training both evoked interest and enthusiasm and corresponded to the unfolding needs of the child. It was, moreover, perhaps the best means of cultivating truthfulness, integrity, and social solidarity. To let boys drop out of school at an early age, unequipped for factory work, was, he insisted, no less than criminal, since it condemned them to unskilled labor or to drifting. Hence boys should be taught, first how to make toys, and then how to do shop work, while girls should be instructed at an early age in the home-making subjects. In opposing education for mere culture, which he thought of as something aloof and apart from actual life, Hall resembled Dewey; but unlike him, he did not argue that industrial training was primarily class education for the children of the less well-to-do. With his belief, based on the doctrine of heredity, that class distinction corresponded to individual differences in capacity, he thought it entirely fitting that, in his own words, some should be drawers of water and hewers of wood.[35]

Hall had clear ideas as to the social importance of industrial training in the schools. It might, in the first place, supply the

[34] G. Stanley Hall, "New Departures in Education," *North American Review*, Vol. CXL (Feb., 1885), pp. 144–52; "The New Psychology as a Basis of Education," *Forum*, Vol. XVII (Aug., 1894), pp. 710–20; "The Case of the Public Schools," *Atlantic Monthly*, Vol. LXXVII (March, 1896), pp. 402–13; *Educational Problems*, Vol. II, pp. 570 *et seq.*; *Life and Confessions*, p. 550.
[35] *Educational Problems*, Vol. I, pp. 540 *et seq.*

motor training which children in a rural civilization acquired in the daily course of life and thus counteract some of the ill effects of urbanization and standardization. But he also believed that industrial, as well as commercial training in the schools was necessary to meet the needs of industry. "The new demands made on the school to help nations onward in the ever hotter competition for industrial and commercial supremacy . . . should, of course, always be welcomed."

Thus Hall did not share the alarm of certain teachers who felt that industrial education was designed by captains of industry to capture and subordinate the schools to their own interests. The enterprise of business, Hall observed, had long since subordinated the legal, to say nothing of the clerical and medical and technological professions which it supported; it was already setting new fashions in art, and now it was demanding new standards of efficiency in the school, the college, and the university. Industrial education in the school would in fact alleviate the strife between capital and labor, maintain and advance our position among our industrial and commercial competitors, and win the good will of taxpayers by convincing them that the public school could, by making workmen efficient, conserve the most precious of all capital and raw material, the individual.

As a people, Hall continued, we had trusted too much to our abundant physical resources and good luck, and it was natural for our industrial leaders to ask, "How can we make our school system, upon which we spend more money than any other people, fit the children for their life-work and furnish our industries . . . with the army of skilled and willing workers they need?" No clearer statement of the relation of the industrial class to industrial education could be desired than these words from a great educational leader who sincerely thought that scientific objectivity guided him in his educational and social, as well as in his psychological theories.[36]

Moral education Hall considered an even more important need of the schools than industrial training, and he saw and offered remedies for many of the inadequacies in the prevalent theory and practice of moral instruction. More than any of his predecessors or contemporaries, he insisted on the relation between a sound physique and morality; and he called attention to the bearing of an unfavorable environment on lying and on juvenile delinquency. Impressed as he was by the diversities of human nature, he recognized that moral education must, to a certain extent, be an individual matter, and that it was therefore difficult for the schools to tackle it. Another obstacle, he thought, lay in the fact that the basic, older traits, essentially animal in their origin, were less educable, in general, than the traits that had been more recently acquired.

A major difficulty in the way of proper moral education in the schools followed, in his judgment, from the feminization of the teaching staff. Women tended to inculcate certain qualities, such as gentleness, and neglected to instill the virile traits so vital to the adolescent boy. The woman teacher refused to depict evil and its consequences, to utilize the blunders and mistakes of others in order to prevent their intrusion into the lives of children. No real boy, moreover, could safely be taught to love his enemies; the effects of such teaching were emasculating. He must fight, whip, and be whipped. Use should also be made of prizes and rewards, since the desire to excel was a basic instinct. Unlike most of his contemporaries, Hall held a brief for flogging, which, he thought, had a place in the schools. But the greatest advance that could be made in moral instruction, this educator insisted, was to segregate the sexes, at least

[36] *Ibid.*, Vol. I, pp. 627, 634, 639.

during the adolescent period, and to provide male teachers for boys.[37]

Hall would further have the schools take advantage of the supposedly instinctive development in young children of a sense of ownership, and on its basis inculcate respect for private property and honesty in dealing with it. "Ownership is one of the best schools of responsibility, especially if of living things as pets. . . . But money is a great idealizer and quickens manifold meditations as to all its possible uses. To accumulate, lay by, and store for the future brings foresight, prudence, economy and thrift. To own also teaches respect for others' possessions; and even greed for gain by those who have much rarely prompts theft."[38]

Another moral virtue which Hall thought it important to inculcate was honor. In every emergency one should be able at least to ask the ideal course to pursue, the highest, purest, and most disinterested motive from which to act, the loftiest and not the most expedient solution—this was honor. The chivalrous, half-mythical tales of Parsifal, Galahad, Robin Hood, Tannhäuser, Lancelot, and King Arthur were, he believed, particularly calculated to inculcate a spirit of loyalty and honor. Athletics also encouraged fair play, courage, loyalty, and fraternity, virtues not unrelated to honor. Hall opposed student government, however, as a means of developing honor. Since reason, republicanism, and democracy developed only in the later stages of racial history, he argued that the child must be made docile and obedient to authority, especially in the years intervening between the kindergarten and the high school.[39] To this end he favored mechanical drill and regimentation in the pre-adolescent period.

[37] *Ibid.*, Vol. I, pp. 200 *et seq.*   [38] *Ibid.*, p. 255.
[39] *Ibid.*, pp. 279–80; *Adolescence*, Vol. II, pp. 442–44.

Perhaps, according to Hall, the most fundamental task of moral training is to develop the sense of justice, the muse of positive moral education. It culminates in "the sublime conviction that in this world nothing really evil or no failure can befall a truly good man; and, conversely, that nothing that is really good, that no true success, can ever come to a bad one. . . . By executing righteous vengeance upon others, we learn a wholesome fear that, if we are prompted to injustice, we shall expose ourselves to the same vengeance. . . . The very basis of moral inculcation is that, if we sin, we suffer in our own persons and pain helps us to right ourselves again."[40]

In the inculcation of justice, as well as in the development of other moral virtues, religious instruction and history were, Hall thought, important assets. Religion was needed to give a supernatural sanction to right. History, in his opinion, should teach the difference between good and bad, and "set forth, even if in loud colors," the law of right and wrong, justice and injustice. It should teach us, by participation, each significant step by which the present was reached. It should, in short, justify the ways of heaven to man. It is interesting to note that just at the time when leading historians were divorcing their subject from morality and making it as objective as possible, Hall insisted on its moral value,[41] and that the morality in which he believed was essentially the black-and-white morality of children and of primitive peoples.

One of the most important aspects of moral education was civic instruction, which Hall would have made universal before the high school period. Its purpose was to make the "good citi-

[40] *Educational Problems*, Vol. I, pp. 268–69.
[41] G. Stanley Hall, "The Relation of the Church to Education," *Pedagogical Seminary*, Vol. XV (June, 1908), pp. 186–96; "The Pedagogy of History," *ibid.*, Vol. XII (May, 1905), pp. 339–49; *Adolescence*, Vol. II, pp. 446–47; *Life and Confessions*, pp. 357, 517–18.

zen," and to that end visits to the city hall and to charitable and other public institutions were recommended. Something of taxation and the functions of government was to be taught. High value was attached to patriotism of the more conventional type, although, as we have seen, Hall's respect for the customs of other races and his opposition to standardization made him an enemy of the steam-roller methods by which hundred-percenters were determined to Americanize immigrant children.

Hall also favored such sex instruction as would reduce vice and disease, and increase the fecundity of the best and diminish that of the worst classes in "the interests of national efficiency and the fatherland, of the army, of industry, and success in the colonies."[42]

In the spirit of early twentieth century reform this great moralizer would have the high school give the student knowledge of court procedure, tariffs, banking, child labor, sweatshops, and other social matters. The new civics, he declared in 1911, was to be "the philanthropic social religion" of the schools. The idea of service should be inculcated in all classes. He stigmatized as anarchistic the corporation that subjected the interests of the people at large to its own, and declared that civic and moral instruction must keep grasping private interests from flourishing at the expense of the public good. "The one word now written across the very zenith of the educational skies," Hall wrote, "is the word *service*. This is coming to be, as it should be, the supreme goal of all pedagogic endeavor, the standard by which all other values are measured."[43]

[42] G. Stanley Hall, "Some Social Aspects of Education," *Pedagogical Seminary*, Vol. IX (March, 1902), pp. 81–91; "The Story of a Sand-Pile," *Scribner's Magazine*, Vol. III (June, 1888), pp. 690–96; *Educational Problems*, Vol. I, pp. 388 *et seq.*, p. 409.
[43] *Educational Problems*, Vol. II, pp. 667–82.

In the years following the World War Hall was primarily concerned that his country should avoid the pitfall of Bolshevism. He wanted laborers to be taught that Socialism violated fundamental instincts and was therefore untenable; he wished them to co-operate with capitalists rather than to endanger the social structure through strikes and mass action. This desire to make the social structure secure prompted him to declare in his *Life and Confessions* that the schools must teach youth in such a way as to leave them with "inner defenses against red propaganda," which constituted a danger only "where teachers failed of doing their duty."[44]

Thus Hall's ideas on moral education follow closely from his general social philosophy. The virtues he advocated were individual ones, and, for the most part, consonant with existing social and economic arrangements. If he attacked the methods of big business, so did the muckrakers and millions who voted for Roosevelt and Wilson in 1912. Hall might well have reminded himself of his own firm belief in the basic and enduring character of the instincts he believed to lie back of competition and profit. He might well have asked whether, in view of the importance he attached to them, moral and civic instruction such as he favored could make lions and lambs lie down peaceably together.

The argument that the type of moral and civic instruction advocated by Hall has not yet been made sufficiently general in the schools, or that it has not been given time to demonstrate its power to curb the selfish practices of corporate wealth, may to some be convincing of its potential power to accomplish the tasks allotted it. But thus far, at least, such moral and civic instruction does not seem to have restrained industrial magnates

[44] *Life and Confessions*, p. 517. See *Morale;* "The Fall of Atlantis"; "Can the Masses Rule the World?", *Scientific Monthly*, Vol. XVIII (May, 1924), pp. 456–66.

and political rulers from questionable if not anti-social practices; or to have encouraged the holders of securities to refuse dividends in order that laborers in plants might be given old-age and unemployment insurance.

Such considerations suggest the inadequacy of Hall's social philosophy, which was based on the conviction that economic and social factors were secondary to psychological ones, and which, in the opinion of leading psychologists today, failed even to discern what the really important psychological factors are. They also suggest that Hall might well have considered more seriously the criticism, with which he was indeed familiar, that education cannot rise above the existent social system and the virtues sponsored by that system. "We cannot expect any radical reforms or reconstructions of our education," he declared in 1911, "without reform and reconstruction of our social system, of which the school is essentially typical."[45] This change was to come, however, in Hall's view, by the slow process of evolutionary growth and development.

Although Hall at various times throughout his career expressed a belief that education was the only remedy for the evils of the republic,[46] and that "democracy must educate the masses who are becoming the masters of the world" if subversive doctrines such as Bolshevism are not to triumph, his influence was on the whole directed against the prevalent American conception that education is a remedy for social ills. Even when he conceded that eugenics might be a long-run remedy, and that in the meantime education must play a positive rôle, he still maintained that, heredity and the process of evolution being what they are, education cannot, even at its best, transform human nature or reverse many of its sets and trends.

[45] *Educational Problems*, Vol. I, p. xi.
[46] *Life and Confessions*, pp. 21, 521.

This anti-intellectualist and anti-rationalist attitude is, of course, in marked contrast with the faith in education held by Hall's predecessors and, particularly, among his contemporaries, by John Dewey. His devotion to the genetic principle led him to idealize the past and to find escape from those aspects of contemporary civilization that he disliked by glorifying youth and by romantically trusting to the feelings and impulses of the race rather than to the controlling power of ideas and social programs.

G. Stanley Hall was an enthusiastic and inspiring teacher. He attracted students from all over the country, and through them, as well as through his lectures and writings, his ideas became widely diffused. Probably one reason for his popularity among the teachers who flocked to him is that he gave scientific sanction to many ideas, and prejudices, and hopes which were and are very common among the plain people of America —faith in the individual and his power to get ahead, belief that the best man wins, contempt for the mollycoddle, respect for the dollar. In Hall's philosophy ideas such as these were transmuted into high-sounding and idealistic doctrines, and invested with all the dignity of science—but they were at bottom familiar American doctrines.

Aside from this popular appeal, however, there were other reasons for his influence on psychology and education. Whatever the final fate of his leading theories, it cannot be denied that he contributed much in opening up new fields for study, in emphasizing important aspects of human life hitherto largely neglected, and in encouraging research by example as well as by furnishing stimulating hypotheses. Without trying to evaluate Hall's influence on American education and social thought, attention may be called to the fact that he was the second professor of pedagogy in an American university; that he was the first modern psychologist to apply his science to education; and that for many years, at both Johns Hopkins and Clark, he lectured to teachers. He delivered perhaps 2500 extracurricular lectures in forty states; and he wrote scores of articles for popular as well as for educational magazines.[47] For forty years he took an active part in the meetings of the N. E. A., combating the ideas of William T. Harris and of other men with whom he differed.

Hall's wide acquaintance with educators still further extended his influence. His students often became heads of normal schools, colleges, and universities, teachers of education, and trainers of teachers. Among his students have been John Dewey, J. McKeen Cattell, W. H. Burnham, M. W. Swift, Phyllis Blanchard, Florence Mateer, M. H. Small, Howard Odum, E. S. Conklin, E. W. Bohannon, Edward Conradi, H. D. Sheldon, E. B. Huey, G. E. Partridge, L. M. Terman, J. H. Leuba, E. D. Starbuck, and H. H. Goddard, as well as many others. By opening his seminar to the Gilbreths he won for himself a pioneer's place in the field of industrial psychology. He was influential in the eugenics movement; and, more than any single man, was responsible in bringing public attention to the cult of childhood, with all the institutions, organizations, and investigations that have arisen from it.

Although Hall opened up new fields and emphasized new aspects of human life, his influence was largely directed to the support of individualism and *laissez faire*. This was the effect of the cult of child study, which tended to make the curriculum child-centered, and to single out for particular attention the

[47] For a list of his more than four hundred books and articles see the bibliography included in E. L. Thorndike, *Biographical Memoir of Granville Stanley Hall, 1846–1924* (National Academy of Science, *Biographical Memoirs*, Vol. XII, 1928).

gifted child. It is true, indeed, that the great importance which
Hall gave to physical health did modify, at least by implication,
a policy of extreme *laissez faire*. But the doctrines both of
laissez faire and of individualism were strengthened by the
theories of recapitulation and catharsis and the sweeping
educational applications which Hall gave them. The emphasis he put upon the basic importance of sex and the frank-
ness with which he discussed it, tended to center attention
on the individual rather than on social concerns; in helping in
the commendable work of bringing sex from behind the Vic-
torian curtains where it had concealed itself, he at the same time
obscured its social implications by accentuating its biological
ones. Even in his protests against the increasing standardization of life, his revolt was that of a romantic individualist who
failed to understand adequately the causes of the ailment and
whose prescription of living life with zeal and gusto had slight
meaning for great numbers of Americans who were insecure in
their occupations and who lived on or below the margin of
subsistence and decency.

It is true that, at the end of his life, Hall pictured the evils
of unrestrained selfishness on the part of the groups and interests between which he had before been reluctant to see conflict
or to admit cleavage. But with his well-known deprecation of
education and social reform as techniques for social control, he
left it to others to determine how these checks on rampant
selfishness were to be made effective. In spite of his "death bed
repentance," which in a certain sense "The Fall of Atlantis"
was, Hall, by his lifelong support, in the name of science and
evolution, of private property, competition, and *laissez faire,*
helped to confirm the American people in their faith in individualism. Notwithstanding his integrity and his sincerity, not-

withstanding his conviction that his work was objective, and
that what he said was in the interest of all classes of society,
he nevertheless well illustrates the relation of a great educator
to the dominant pattern of the society in which he lived, and his
unconscious subservience to the existing social system.

XIII

WILLIAM JAMES, INDIVIDUALIST
1842–1910

Religiously and philosophically, our ancient doctrine of live and let live may prove to have a far deeper meaning than our people now seem to imagine it to possess.

—WILLIAM JAMES.

Like other Americans, however, only more lyrically, James felt the call of the future and the assurance that it could be made far better, totally other, than the past.

—SANTAYANA, *Character and Opinion.*

I

Although William James was not a professional educator as was G. Stanley Hall, it could be maintained that his influence on American schools and on the outlook of educators was more profound than that of the father of the child-study movement. It was James more than anyone else who brought modern psychology into the classroom by applying it to the everyday problems of instruction. He applied it in such a way, moreover, as to center attention on the individual child. In so doing he was, with Hall, a leader in counteracting the emphasis that Harris and Parker were putting on the social purpose of education. Nowhere, in fact, in his *Talks to Teachers* did James discuss education as affecting the social order. A great individualist, James as a psychologist gave scientific standing to the individualism that had come to be a tradition and, in view of altered facts, an overbelief; and by his pragmatic philosophy, especially in the sparkling, popular lectures which spread its gospel, he gave to this individualism an exalted dignity and a spiritual validity that captured the sentiments and the ideals of middle-class America.

The grandfather of William and Henry James had left a fortune of three millions, a huge sum for pre-Civil War America, and the advantages provided by such wealth profoundly influenced the lives of his grandsons. It was not theirs to know the actual grimness and squalor of the New York City where they spent some of their childhood years; it was not theirs to experience in actuality the harshness, the deprivation, the struggle, and the defeat of the frontier. It was rather the lot of these children to enjoy rich cultural opportunities—the advantages of special schools, of foreign travel, and of life in polite, intelligent society.

William James took ten years to prepare himself in higher studies for his life work; to few Americans of his day was such a luxury possible. He tried his hand at painting and enjoyed the best instruction in it that America afforded; he tried science, philosophy, medicine. He studied at Harvard; he went to Berlin. During all these years his only problems were those of choosing a profession and of securing health. Eminent specialists seemed as little able to help him as the cures at the expensive watering places on the Continent. Finally, by disciplined reading and by speculation, in which there was an element of mysticism, he whipped himself into shape for an active career in America's leading university. He continued to travel abroad, so much that it would be wearisome to recount the crossings. He spent summers in New Hampshire and in the Adirondacks. In Cambridge he lived in a large and dignified dwelling. No wonder that he could write to Henry Lee Higginson, State Street's great banker, of his lack of anxiety about money, "beyond wishing not to live on capital."[1]

With such advantages this favorite of the gods might well be sympathetic with the existing order of things. He might well be optimistic and little disposed to take into account the darker phases of American life. It would be natural for him to minimize the importance of economic environment, against which he had never had to struggle, and to emphasize the power of the individual: for his greatest struggle had been with himself, and he had conquered.

But certain influences in the life of William James kept him from accepting everything in the America that nourished him. From his parents he acquired an intense moral earnestness, a Puritanism of sorts. He shared his father's antagonism to all that was regimented and standardized, to all that interfered with the fullest flowering of individuality. From his father, a disciple of Swedenborg and a friend of Emerson and Carlyle, he may also have derived his undying interest in the things of the spirit, in religious values.[2] In the hospitality that he showed toward psychical research, and in his concern with the psychology of religious experience, there was something of the father's sympathy for religious democracy and his come-outism.[3]

Most of his political and many of his economic ideas James took from Godkin, the brilliant Irish editor of *The Nation* and the New York *Evening Post,* under whose spell he came at

---

[1] *The Letters of William James,* ed. by Henry James (Boston, 1920), Vol. II, p. 173.

[2] C. Hartley Grattan, *The Three Jameses, a Family of Minds* (New York, 1932), pp. 1–107.

[3] Josiah Royce, *William James and Other Essays* (New York, 1911), p. 24. See also William James, *Human Immortality* (Boston, 1898), and Julius Seelye Bixler, *Religion in the Philosophy of William James* (Boston, 1926).

the age of twenty-two.[4] He shared the opposition of his mentor
to the carpetbag regime in the South, the corruption of the
Grant administration, and free silver. He sympathized with his
support of the Mugwump independent flare-up in 1884, with his
advocacy of civil service reform and a moderate tariff, and, in
general, with his moral condemnation of wickedness in politics.

If James ever asked what lay at the root of corruption, what
caused imperialism, the rise of navalism, and the increasing
standardization in our life, aspects of America to which he was
opposed, he satisfied himself with the most superficial sort of
answer. Political corruption he laid for the most part at the
door of immoral politicians.[5] In blaming our imperialistic venture on President McKinley, and in thinking that it might have
been prevented by a stronger personality,[6] he failed to see what
many of his associates in the Anti-Imperialist League did see,
that there was a relation between our acquisition of colonial possessions and the desire for new raw materials, markets, and
commercial power.

Although he believed that man was by instinct a fighting
animal, and greatly admired the martial virtues, James associated himself during the Roosevelt administration with the
movement for international peace.[7] As one means of diverting
the fighting instinct into socially useful channels without sacrificing the life *in extremis* which war symbolized he proposed,
in his famous "The Moral Equivalent for War," the conscrip-
tion of youth for constructive, but dangerous tasks.[8] He also fa-

[4] Rollo Ogden, *Life of Edwin Lawrence Godkin* (New York, 1907), Vol. I,
p. 221; *Letters of William James,* Vol. I, p. 284; Vol. II, p. 182.

[5] "The only serious permanent force of corruption in America is party spirit."
Letters of William James, Vol. II, p. 100. Letter of Sept. 11, 1899.

[6] *Letters of William James,* Vol. II, pp. 101, 88; *Springfield Republican,*
June 4, 1900.

[7] *Letters of William James,* Vol. II, p. 277; "Remarks at the Peace Banquet,"
Boston, 1904, in *Memories and Studies* (New York, 1911), pp. 299–306.

[8] *Memories and Studies,* pp. 267–96.

vored cultivating the policy of international arbitration and spoke out against jingoism and mob hysteria when the Venezuela affair threatened to involve the country in a war with England.[9] But, like most of the leaders of the peace movement, to which he gave important support, he failed to see the relation between war and economic factors, such as imperialism and the desire of munition-makers for profits; nor did he explain how, in a highly individualistic and acquisitive society, where almost every young man wanted to get into the swim of profit-making as quickly as possible, mobilization for socially useful projects could be achieved. Yet in seeing that "war becomes absurd and impossible from its own monstrosity," in looking to a "future when acts of war shall be formally outlawed as between civilized peoples," and in suggesting a psychological and moral equivalent for international fighting, James took the position of a forward-looking and intelligent individualist.[10]

Although not primarily concerned with social and economic matters, William James was by no means unresponsive to the problems presented by the increasing concentration of wealth in the hands of a few, the struggles of labor, and in his last years, the challenge of Socialism. His philosophic principles might well have made him cautious in expressing judgments about complicated social and economic matters which lay outside the scope of his own research and study; yet he made many *ex cathedra* pronouncements, as if with the authority of a scientist who knows the facts. His opinions about concrete social and economic problems were far from consistent, yet they seemed to be supported by work in his own field as he interpreted this work.

[9] *Letters of William James*, Vol. II, pp. 28–32; letter of William James to Honorable Samuel W. McCall, *Cong. Record*, 54th Cong., 1st sess., pt. I, p. 399 (Dec. 28, 1895); letter to editor, *Harvard Crimson*, Jan. 9, 1896.
[10] *Memories and Studies*, p. 286.

The fact that James had no direct experience with poverty did not keep him from saying a good deal about it. In explaining the sanctity of poverty as an adornment to a good life, he made much of the opposition between the men who *have* and the men who *are*. The gentleman had been cherished, not because he possessed land and riches but because of his personal superiority in courage, pride, and generosity. The laborer, who paid with his person day by day without any invested rights in the future, had much of the same unencumbered detachment of the soldier. Like the savage, the workingman might make his bed wherever his right arm supported him; and when his simple and athletic life was compared with that of the rich man, the latter seemed "buried and smothered in ignoble externalities, wading in straw and rubber to his knees." In other words, the claims made by *things* were "corrupters of manhood, mortgages on the soul, and a drag anchor on our progress towards the empyrean."[11]

James also found another explanation for the sanctity of poverty, something profounder still than the opposition between having and being. It was something related to the fundamental mystery of religious experience, the satisfaction found in absolute surrender to the larger power.[12]

This religious-minded scientist thus believed that the personal and spiritual values of poverty had a profound message for his contemporaries. The worship of material luxury and wealth, which seemed to constitute so large a portion of the spirit of the age, made, in his opinion, for effeminacy. He believed that we must discover something in the social realm, something besides war, which would nourish the heroic and which would counteract the ill effects of wealth and luxury;

11 William James, *The Varieties of Religious Experience* (New York, 1929, Thirty-Seventh Impression), pp. 315 *et seq.*
12 *Ibid.*, p. 320.

and he suggested that perhaps monkish poverty-worship might be a solution. In a stirring appeal to the well-to-do, James, after excoriating wealth as the chief breeder of cowardice and propagator of corruption, declared:

"Think of the strength which personal indifference to poverty would give us if we were devoted to unpopular causes. We need no longer hold our tongues or fear to vote the revolutionary or reformatory ticket. Our stocks might fall, our hopes of promotion vanish, our salaries stop, our club doors close in our faces; yet, while we lived, we would imperturbably bear witness to the spirit, and our example would help to set free our generation. The cause would need its funds, but we its servants would be potent in proportion as we personally were contented with our poverty."[13]

He himself, in spite of the admired precedent of St. Francis, continued to live in comparative luxury. We do not find him visiting the slums, the stockyards, the factories, and the mines to test his belief, to find out whether in reality the poor were as heroic, and in such good fighting shape, and as happy as he supposed. It is true that he saw a miserable North Carolina poor white who had conquered an obstinate mountain side of worn-out soil, and romanticized about the sense of triumph the feat had given to his fellow American. And, in a rare moment, this warm-hearted and inconsistent genius caught a glimpse of the possible sordidness to which poverty might deliver up a growing child. In his chapter on instinct in the *Principles* he spoke in a sentence of the gaps and even perversions that may be left in the nature of the city poor by a too-meager education.[14] But for the most part he must have remained undisturbed by such thoughts, just as in his daily living he remained aloof from the poor, whom he envied for their constant fight with diffi-

[13] *Ibid.*, pp. 367–68, 369.
[14] William James, *Principles of Psychology* (New York, 1923), Vol. II, p. 441.

culties and for the satisfactions, happiness, and sense of values which he assumed their harsh life provided.

It is for the psychologist to determine whether the attitude James took toward poverty was one of compensation and romantic escape. It may have been his alternative to Socialism—a subconscious recognition that such a way of life, if universalized, best promised the preservation of his scheme of individual and moral values.

James's attitude toward poverty and wealth helps to explain his position on labor unrest. Unlike Harris, he did not denounce strikes and agitation. In the midst of the great railway strikes of 1886 he wrote to his brother that there was no cause for alarm; that the strikes were sure "to do lots of good to all hands in the end."[15] He apparently even took Godkin to task for being too severe with the Knights of Labor; but later, retracting, wrote, "I never dare to trust myself now when you're agin me."[16] Indeed, his understanding was always limited by his individual and moral bias, which led him, for example, to the judgment that the Haymarket riot was merely to be ascribed to "a lot of pathological Germans and Poles."[17] Yet he saw that there was something to be said for labor's dissatisfaction. He believed that the growing hostility of labor to capital was largely due to the "sound sentiment of antipathy for lives based on mere having."

Thus James felt that the conflict between capital and labor was in large part due to mistaken mental attitudes. In writing of "anarchistic discontents and socialistic projects," and the conservative resistance they provoked, James declared that "so far as this conflict is unhealthy and regrettable—and I think it is so only to a limited extent—the unhealthiness consists solely

[15] *Letters of William James,* Vol. I, p. 252.
[16] *Ibid.,* p. 284.   [17] *Ibid.,* p. 252.

in the fact that one-half of our fellow countrymen remain entirely blind to the internal significance of the lives of the other half." Each group in pinning happiness and unhappiness absolutely on "some ridiculous feature of the external situation," failed to feel the moral virtue and the presence of intellectual ideals in the other camp. "They are at cross-purposes all along the line, regarding each other as they might regard a set of dangerously gesticulating automata, or, if they seek to get at the inner motivation, making the most terrible mistakes."[18]

Believing that the solid meaning of life was always the same eternal thing, "the marriage, namely, of some unhabitual ideal, however special, with some fidelity, courage, endurance, with some man's or woman's pains," James did not feel that the more equitable division of wealth, which he thought the future promised, could make any "genuine vital difference."[19] If only the inner interests of workingmen were aroused, heightened, and liberated, their external conditions of toil counted for little; if they had spiritual aims and ideals, then, by inference, wages, hours of labor, home conditions, and economic insecurity were inconsequential in their lives. "No outward changes of condition in life can keep the nightingale of its eternal meaning from singing in all sorts of different men's hearts." As an individualist, which he was before all else, James held to his belief that if poor and rich could only be tolerant and sympathetic, and realize their common inner appreciation of values, then their disputes would grow gentle, and they would be willing "to live and let live."[20]

It is the more surprising, in view of the relative unimportance which material well-being assumed in comparison with spirit-

[18] William James, *Talks to Teachers on Psychology: and to Students on Some of Life's Ideals* (New York, 1908), pp. 297–98.
[19] *Ibid.*, pp. 298–99. [20] *Ibid.*, p. 301.

ual values in James's philosophy, that toward the end of his life he gave some evidence of sympathy with Socialism. As early as 1897 he had taken Le Bon to task for regarding as "crazy" all socialistic ways of thinking.[21] A few years later, in *Varieties of Religious Experience,* he declared that utopian Socialism, in spite of its impracticability and non-adaptation to present environmental conditions, was analogous to the saint's belief in an existent kingdom of heaven and, in helping "to break the edge of the general reign of hardness," was a slow leaven of a better order.[22]

In 1910, in "The Moral Equivalent for War," James confessed a devout belief in "the gradual advent of some sort of socialistic equilibrium." He declared that while there was nothing to make one indignant in the mere fact that life was hard, there was something to make one indignant in the fact that "so many men, by mere accidents of birth and opportunity, should have a life of *nothing else* but toil and pain and hardness and inferiority imposed upon them, should have *no* vacation, while others natively no more deserving never get any taste of this campaigning life at all—this is capable of arousing indignation in reflecting minds. It may end by seeming shameful to all of us that some of us have nothing but campaigning, and others nothing but unmanly ease."[23]

Although James did not understand Socialism in any very clear way, and although he implied that it was to come about as a result of the conversion of the privileged class to a belief in its value for them as a group, it is significant that so great an individualist, so keen a critic of everything that suggested regimentation, could go so far in sympathizing with Socialism. It

---

[21] *Psychological Review,* Vol. IV (May, 1897), p. 314.
[22] *Varieties of Religious Experience,* p. 360.
[23] *Memories and Studies,* p. 290.

may have been due to the influence of H. G. Wells.[24] But it is more likely that it was the result of his increasing dislike of the money-grasping materialism of American life, which he vaguely associated with the existing economic pattern, and of his dim, half realization that without a measure of security, a decent standard of living, and some leisure, the worker could not achieve the inner and spiritual values that, James felt, should be inherent in his laborious toil.

The qualified interest that James showed in Socialism may also be explained by a certain democratic quality in his personality and outlook. Like Tolstoy and Whitman, he believed that there was something divine in the common people. "In God's eyes the differences of social position, of intellect, of culture, of cleanliness, of dress, which different men exhibit, and all the other rarities and exceptions on which they so fantastically pin their pride, must be so small as practically quite to vanish; and all that should remain is the common fact that here we are, a countless multitude of vessels of life, each of us pent in to peculiar difficulties, with which we must severally struggle by using whatever of fortitude and goodness we can summon up."[25] Even "the mediocre, comfortable, smug bourgeoisie," who attended Chautauqua and who, for James, were far less heroic and attractive than the common worker, were, he reminded himself, of the same stuff. Deep down in their souls, hidden, but potentially active, was some inner stress, some vital virtue that would be found not wanting when occasion required.[26] It was impossible, James declared, to try to keep "a

[24] *Letters of William James,* Vol. II, pp. 230–31, 259–60. These are two flattering letters from James to Wells, dated June 6, 1905, and Sept. 11, 1906. See also Walter Lippmann, "An Open Mind: William James," *Everybody's Magazine,* Vol. XXIII (Dec., 1910), pp. 800–801.

[25] *Talks to Teachers,* p. 277.

[26] *Ibid.,* p. 284; "William James's Search for the Highest Good," *Current Literature,* Vol. LIII (Nov., 1912), pp. 555–58.

man in his place," since life consisted in the process of moving out of his place and finding new ones, in obedience to a creative impulse which it would be a sin to deny, a crime to restrain.

No one could gainsay the fact that James was democratic in his tolerance of the lowly and humble; his willingness to try to find truth from their lips and in their lives and his hospitality toward new and strange-looking ideas which, to more conservative people, seemed preposterous, were noteworthy. He gave a respectful hearing to all, even to ghosts.[27] He was also democratic in his constant effort to relate his philosophy to popular meanings and experiences, and in making philosophy, as a consequence, interesting and significant to a large number of people whom the orthodox philosophers had never been able to reach.[28]

But if James was democratic, it was a conservative democracy to which he adhered, a democracy based on the best leadership, a democracy which suppressed violence whenever it threatened public order. In recognizing a certain validity in the frequent criticism that democracy was enthroning and institutionalizing vulgarity, he refused to admit its failure. "Our better men *shall* show the way, and we *shall* follow."[29] He believed that college alumni should take the place of the aristocracy of the Old World. With a sense of *noblesse oblige* they should steer democracy through its perilous and mediocre driftings.[30] The educated class must keep a "judicious pilot's hand on the tiller through all the gales of passion and forces which kept the human ship moving." Attaching great importance to this spirit of fair play, to give and take in party procedure, James held firmly that there must be "fierce and merciless resentment

[27] Lippmann, "An Open Mind: William James," *loc. cit.*
[28] Joseph Jastrow, *Ed. Rev.*, Vol. XLI (Jan., 1911), p. 33.
[29] *Memories and Studies*, pp. 317–18.
[30] *Ibid.*, pp. 319–20.

toward every man or set of men who break the public peace."[31]

In spite of his democracy James was thus in temperament and outlook an aristocrat. If in some respects he helped break down the "genteel tradition," he could write, in speaking of some religious and reforming men whom he met in 1883 at Leipzig, that *their* sphere is with the masses struggling into light, not with us at Harvard; though I'm glad I can meet them cordially for a while now and then." The condition of being a man of the world, a gentleman, carried something with it, the letter continued, an atmosphere, an outlook, a play, that made "the falsest views and tastes somehow in a man of fashion . . . truer than the truest in a plebeian cad."[32] He expressed exactly the same sentiment in his great *Principles*.[33] Years later he confessed his feeling that most of the American nation, and probably of every country, was "white trash." In spite of his recognition of the moral earnestness of the teachers he encountered at Chautauqua he was (perhaps only playfully) intolerant of their uncultured voices.[34]

Nowhere do the aristocratic feelings and convictions of James appear so clearly as in his essay "Great Men and Their Environment."[35] Here he opposed the Spencerian idea that social change was due to environment and maintained, on the contrary, that communities changed from generation to generation, because of "the accumulated differences of individuals, of their examples, their initiatives, and their decisions." The mutations of society were due directly or indirectly, not to environment, the increasing experiences of outer relations, but to the acts of individuals whose "genius was so adapted to the receptivities

[31] *Ibid.*, p. 60.
[32] *Letters of William James*, Vol. I, pp. 214–15.
[33] *Principles of Psychology*, Vol. II, p. 371.
[34] *Letters of William James*, Vol. II, p. 44.
[35] William James, *The Will to Believe, and Other Essays in Popular Philosophy* (New York, 1897), pp. 216–54.

of the moment, or whose accidental position of authority was so critical that they became ferments, initiators of movement, setters of precedent, centers of corruption, or destroyers of other persons, whose gifts, had they had free play, would have led society in another direction." Thus, although James gave a place to accident in social change, and although he ascribed to the community, the mass, or social environment the power of selecting or rejecting the genius, he weighted the scales heavily on the side of the individual.

James carried even further the implications of the rôle of the individual in society. Believing that few men live at the maximum of their energy, he held that, in the interest of national economy, it was a a social as well as an individual duty to "energize" at higher rates and levels, since a nation run at a higher pressure was superior to one filled with inferior men "energizing" below maximum. This doctrine, which resembles the "morale" of G. Stanley Hall and the "strenuous life" of Roosevelt, and might even be applied to justify such things as the speed-up in modern industry, attached especial importance to the individual gifted with high potential energy.[36]

This emphasis on the exceptional individual would have been less aristocratic in frontier America than in the America of James's mature years. The general spirit of his philosophy not only insured tolerance for all attitudes but upheld, in the words he used of religious convictions, "freest competition of the various faiths with one another, and their openest application to life by their several champions, . . . [as] the most favorable

[36] James accompanied the doctrine of energizing on high levels with the gospel of relaxation. He himself worked with alternating spurts and vacations; and though he idealized the strenuous life and energizing on high levels, which might be compared with the old qualities of frontier life as well as with those of the machine age, he had scant sympathy for the jerkiness, absence of repose, and bottled lightning aspects of American character. *Talks to Teachers*, pp. 212 *et seq.*

conditions under which the survival of the fittest can proceed."[37] This, from a social point of view, was related to *laissez faire*. But with the increasing scarcity of free elbow room in American life, the opposite conception of social control was in fact more democratic, since it insured at least minimum opportunity for development to the less gifted and to those less advantageously born and situated. Thus, the individualism of James unaccompanied by a qualifying and democratic collectivism was more aristocratic than its face value suggested.[38]

The social philosophy which has been outlined probably did not influence teachers and administrators in a greater degree than it did other Americans engaged in intellectual pursuits. Since, however, they were greatly influenced by his psychology and its applications to pedagogy, it is important to try to seek the relationship between his general social attitudes and his psychology and philosophy. It has been estimated that nine-tenths of the teachers who studied any psychology at all in the years between 1890 and 1910 read James.[39] Many of his con-

[37] *The Will to Believe,* p. xii.
[38] A discussion of the problem of the "Americanism" of William James would throw some light on his social philosophy. His generally sympathetic attitude toward his country may be contrasted with that of his brother, the novelist. *Letters of William James,* Vol. II, pp. 100; 165; *Memories and Studies,* p. 43. For the influence of American civilization on his thought see Morris Cohen, "On American Philosophy: William James," *New Republic,* Vol. XX (Oct. 1, 1919), pp. 255–57; John Dewey, "William James," *Independent,* Vol. LXIX (Sept. 8, 1910), pp. 533–36, and Dewey's later view, "William James in Nineteen Twenty-Six," *New Republic,* Vol. XLVII (June 30, 1926), pp. 163–65. See also Josiah Royce, *William James and Other Essays;* George Mead, "The Philosophies of Royce, James and Dewey in Their American Setting," *International Journal of Ethics,* Vol. XL (Jan., 1930), pp. 211–31; Horace Kallen, "The Philosophy of William James," *Dial,* Vol. LXIII (Aug. 30, 1917), pp. 141–43; D. S. Miller, "Mr. Santayana and William James," *Harvard Graduates' Magazine,* Vol. XXIX (March, 1921), pp. 348–64; R. B. Perry, "William James," *ibid.,* Vol. XIX (Dec., 1910), pp. 212–25; A. O. Lovejoy, "William James as Philosopher," *International Journal of Ethics,* Vol. XXI (Jan., 1911), pp. 127–29; Albert Schinz, *Anti-Pragmatism* (Boston, 1909); Lewis Mumford, *The Golden Day* (New York, 1926), pp. 185 *et seq.*
[39] Benjamin Gruenberg, "Student and Teacher of Philosophy," *Scientific American,* Vol. CIII (Sept. 10, 1910), p. 198. For the influence of James on

tributions to psychology, such as the physiological portion of his work, the analysis of special processes such as perception and thought, and the importance which he attached to consciousness as a process, probably had few social implications for most teachers. But some of his doctrines, especially his theories of habit and instinct, were fraught with social implications both within and without the classroom.

While the personal fortunes of James were not without effect on his psychology and philosophy, other influences probably played a dominant rôle in their formulation. The specific intellectual influences which affected him have been pointed out by others; it is necessary here only to mention that the new doctrine of evolution and other developments in biology and scientific method profoundly influenced the author of the *Principles of Psychology*. Although the British empirical tradition exerted a lasting influence, Renouvier's *Traité de psychologie rationale* (1859) converted him to a belief in moral freedom as an hypothesis actively to be adopted. C. S. Peirce provided him with concepts which became important tools in his thinking. Although he reacted against the metaphysical idealism of his father, it helps explain his antagonism to fatalism, mechanism, and "the automaton theory." It likewise throws light on his continued preoccupation with religious and spiritual values.[40]

education see: Emile Boutroux, *William James* (New York, 1912), pp. 113–23; Charles De Garmo, in *Gunton's Magazine*, Vol. XXI (Dec., 1901), p. 513; Frederick E. Bolton, "Great Contributors to Education: William James," *Progressive Education*, Vol. VII (March, 1930), pp. 82–88; Edward F. Buchner, "William James" in Monroe's *Encyclopedia of Education*, Vol. III, pp. 516–17; and especially Bird Baldwin, "William James' Contributions to Education," *Journal of Educational Psychology*, Vol. II (1911), pp. 369–82.

[40] For discussion of the influences on William James see George H. Palmer, "William James," *Harvard Graduates' Magazine*, Vol. XXIX (Sept., 1920), pp. 29–34; George Santayana, *Character and Opinion in the United States* (New York, 1921), pp. 64 *et seq.*; T. Flournoy, *The Philosophy of William James* (New York, 1917), pp. 29–30; Josiah Royce, *William James and Other*

II

James set forth his theories of instinct and habit in particularly brilliant and dramatic language. He thought of instincts as impulses to act in a particular way in response to determinate sensory stimuli and argued that human beings are equipped with even more of these blind tendencies to action than are animals. Man seems to lead a life of hesitation and choice, not because he has no instincts but because he has so many that they block each other's path. Some instincts are much more lasting and dominant than others. Some are transitory, although they are likely to give rise to powerful habits while they are ripe, and these habits may dominate throughout life just as if the instinctive basis were still present.

In his list of important human instincts James includes a number of complex social modes of response, and his discussion of these has very important social implications. While he does not tell us just which instincts are to be thought of as transitory, it is clear that he regards pugnacity, anger, appropriation and acquisitiveness, and certainly emulation and rivalry, as "intense" instincts—more persistent, more apt to become the basis of habit than others. He was inclined to believe, it seems, that the "instinct of pugnacity" is so fundamental that it can never be eliminated; and yet, in "The Moral Equivalent for War," he suggested that it might be expressed in socially useful activities.

The great emphasis on the instincts of acquisition and rivalry, and the place James gave them in education, probably confirmed most of his readers in their belief that an acquisitive economic system was inevitable. This argument has of course

Essays, pp. 13–14; John Dewey, *Reconstruction in Philosophy* (New York, 1920), pp. 37–38; Grattan, *The Three Jameses*, pp. 128 *et seq.;* Horace M. Kallen, Introduction, *The Philosophy of William James* (New York, 1925), p. 30; *Letters of William James*, Vol. II, p. 2; *Memories and Studies*, p. 14.

been often used. The more careful reader could find support for the socialistic theory of modification of the "impulse" of ownership, for James does say that "in civilized life the impulse to own is usually checked by a variety of considerations, and only passes over into action under circumstances legitimated by habit and common consent, an additional example of the way in which one instinctive tendency may be inhibited by others."[41] But he nevertheless specifically argued that the associationists were wrong in denying a blind, primitive instinct to appropriate.[42]

James's doctrine of habit, considering its influence, has probably been more important from a social point of view than his theory of instincts. In spite of his qualified adherence to the doctrine of free will, and his admission that habits *could* be changed, it is not unfair to speak of his belief in an "iron law of habit." James believed that it was practically impossible for anyone who had passed his twenty-fifth year to acquire any really new ideas or habits, except in his own specific field of work. While new habits *could* be launched, it was extremely hard for one to do so. "We are spinning our own fates, good or evil, and never to be undone." There is something almost Calvinistic about these words. It is to be observed, moreover, that it is *we ourselves* who are spinning *our* fates: our handicaps, our poverty, our malnutrition in youth, our inadequate schooling, our frustrations due to conditions over which we have slight control, are not taken into account. We are, James seems to say, morally free agents who are determining our own destiny.

If, however, it is very difficult for the individual to change his habits, we may assume that it is even harder for a class to

[41] *Principles of Psychology*, Vol. II, pp. 389, 402, 422.
[42] *Ibid.*, p. 423.

alter its habits. James specifically says that the *nouveaux riches* may seldom hope to become real gentlemen—to the manner born; and we may infer that he would have thought it even more unlikely for tenant farmers and factory workers to change their temper with their dress. But James is even more aristocratic in his conception of habit, more conservative, than this example suggests. For he goes on to say that on the whole it is best that the individual should not escape from the net he has woven for himself by the age of twenty-five or thirty. The conservative implication of his words is striking:

"Habit is thus the enormous fly-wheel of society, its most precious conservative agent. It alone is what keeps us all within the bounds of ordinance, and *saves the children of fortune from the envious uprisings of the poor*. It alone prevents the hardest and most repulsive walks of life from being deserted by those brought up to tread therein. It keeps the fisherman and the deckhand at sea through the winter; it holds the miner in his darkness, and nails the countryman to his log-cabin and his lonely farm through all the months of snow; it protects us from invasion by the natives of the desert and the frozen zone. *It dooms us all to fight out the battle of life upon the lines of our nurture or our early choice, and to make the best of a pursuit that disagrees, because there is no other for which we are fitted, and it is too late to begin again. It keeps different social strata from mixing.* . . . The man can by-and-by no more escape than his coat-sleeve can suddenly fall into a new set of folds. On the whole, it is best he should not escape. It is well for the world that in most of us, by the age of thirty, the character has set like plaster, and will never soften again."[43]

In placing great emphasis (like Tarde, whom he followed) on the idea of imitation and social heredity, James suggested that social change, if it came, must come slowly. However true this may be, it tended to discourage the idea of reform.

[43] *Principles of Psychology*, Vol. I, p. 121. [The italics are mine.]

One might expect that a true democrat who believed that habit, fixed in childhood and youth, exerts so powerful an influence on the individual's destiny, would insist on efforts to change the environment which handicapped the poor as a group and condemned them as a class to their station. His tardy references to Socialism may be considered such an extension of his democratic individualism.

James devoted much attention to pointing out to students and to teachers the more specifically educational applications of his doctrines of instinct and habit. Believing that the chief task of the teacher is to take advantage of the period when each important instinct is ripe, to instill the proper habits on its basis, he urged teachers to strike while the iron is hot, for unless instincts are thus developed at the proper and insistent moment they die and fade away. Thus teachers were to secure proper expression of the instinct of acquisition by encouraging collections of various kinds, to make use of contests, rewards, and prizes in order to satisfy the instincts of rivalry and competition, and, in general, to motivate all school work by appealing to supposedly strong inherited tendencies.

Unlike Parker and Harris, James was concerned primarily with the effect of habits upon the individual rather than upon the social order. It has been pointed out that nowhere in *Talks to Teachers* does he speak of education as a social function. Maintaining that the basis of all education is the fund of native reactions with which the child is endowed,[44] emphasizing interest as the motive power of all educational progress, and instinct as the beginning of interest, James conceived of education as the organization of acquired habits on the part of the individual in such a way as to promote his personal well-being.

[44] This view is to be contrasted with that of Judd, *cf. post*, Chap. XVI.

Nevertheless, the welfare of the individual, which education was to effect, consisted in "the organizing of the resources in the human being, of powers of conduct which shall fit him to his social and physical world."[45] This assumption that freedom was to be found by effective adjustment to things as they are, together with his emphasis on habit formation, gave sanction and support to those who regarded education as fitting for environment and adjusting the child to it. While the usefulness of habits in caring for the mechanics of life should be recognized, James's position implied a static environment. Unlike Parker and Dewey, who desired to develop "impulses" and to organize habits in such a way that the motive of altruism might be so developed as to permit the product of the schools to live creatively and co-operatively, rather than in competition, the program of James did little to make the school an agent for remolding the environment itself; little to provide an education for a changing world.

While this concept of education, as the means whereby the individual is to be fitted to his environment, is perfectly legitimate, and from many points of view, highly desirable, its social implications are conservative, since satisfied individuals must tend to make perpetual the existing stratifications of society, the existing evils. Thus the psychological pedagogy of James did not run counter, in its broad aspects, to the more conservative and aristocratic qualities of his social philosophy; nor did it threaten to transform the existing social system.[46]

---

[45] *Talks to Teachers*, p. 29.
[46] It is true that James declared that "the teachers of this country . . . have its future in their hands." But he specifically repudiated the idea which Mann, Barnard, and Harris cherished, that book learning was a panacea for the ills and vices of society. Teachers were to save the country, not as agents of social change and social control, but as the instruments for the education of better individuals. *Memories and Studies,* pp. 350–51. James attached more importance to the social function of higher education. *Ibid.,* pp. 366–67.

It is thus probable that James's doctrines of instinct and habit tended to confirm the social prejudices of teachers in addition to supporting a pedagogy which, from a social point of view, was more conservative than that of Parker.

Other psychological doctrines of this inspiring teacher also had important educational applications. The biological basis of mental development, the motor consequences of ideas, and the emphasis on training not this or that faculty but the *whole* child, by forming habits on the basis of instincts—these are the most important contributions of James to pedagogy. Although, as one writer has observed, the recognition of the importance of innate capacities, of interest, and of learning by doing and self-activity have largely been credited to others, the first clear statement of the fundamental psychology of all these theories was made by James.[47] Others, it is true, were working in the same direction; and it would be easy to overemphasize his influence in bringing about the "soft pedagogy" which relied so largely on awakening and utilizing the child's interest. James valued a certain amount of discipline and routine and warned those who bowed to the doctrine of interest that appeal must be made to the fighting instinct and if this failed to arouse the child's interest, to the prospect of personal gain.[48] The practice of emulation thus received definite support from his hands.

A new concern with the order of subjects and the increasing flexibility of the curriculum, natural consequences of the doubt he cast on the doctrine of formal discipline, were important results of the application of James's psychology to education. Until the theory of formal discipline was attacked from the psychological point of view, it was not thought nec-

[47] Frederick Bolton, *Progressive Education*, Vol. VII (March, 1930), p. 84.
[48] *Talks to Teachers*, pp. 28, 54–55, 68–69, 111, 112; *Letters of William James*, Vol. I, pp. 119, 121.

essary to teach the child in specific terms about the social order, in which he lived, since, it was felt, he could meet any situation intelligently if his mind and character had been thoroughly disciplined by a few key subjects. Without the criticism of the theory of formal discipline made by James, and especially by some of his followers,[49] the advocates of the social studies would have encountered even greater opposition. In addition James fostered a descriptive study of the data of teaching and thus hastened the coming of experimental pedagogy and the emphasis on measurements.[58] Equally important, perhaps, was the contribution that James made in opposing vague, formal, and verbalistic training and in offering as a substitute an emphasis on motor as well as intellectual responses. This gave a more practical and utilitarian flavor to instruction.

The increasing attention given psychology as the basis of education, an emphasis for which James was particularly responsible, made important and necessary contributions to the theory and practice of instruction. But this psychological emphasis tended to make the school child-centered, rather than society-centered; and by so doing gave scientific support to individualism in American life at the expense of social values. Moreover, James's general emphasis on heredity, including his idea that no amount of training could improve the general retentiveness of a child, might well make for an aristocratic conception of education. This emphasis tended to encourage the belief that genius "will out," no matter what the conditions, and that too much effort expended on the child who is below average, or even average, is time ill spent.

The anti-equalitarian aspects of James's application of his

[49] *Pos:*, pp. 466 *ff*.
[50] Monroe's *Encyclopedia of Education*, Vol. III, p. 517; Bird Baldwin, *Journal of Educational Psychology*, Vol. II (1911), pp. 369–82.

psychology are particularly evident in his discussion of the relation of education to racial and sex differences. He believed that some races, like the Italians, being most instinctive at the outset, were, on the whole, the least educated in the end. He likewise believed that girls mature earlier than boys but do not reach the level of intelligent capacity which the latter attain. Hence the masculine brain, he held, can deal with new and complex matter more effectively and over a longer period than the more limited and intuitive feminine mind.[51]

III

The philosophy of William James had less direct influence on the thinking and work of educators than his psychology. Yet because, in the eyes of so many critics, pragmatism is regarded as the typically American philosophy, and because it doubtless influenced the thinking of a great many educational workers, it cannot be omitted from a study of their social ideas.

It is now almost a commonplace that James's doctrine of pragmatism was constantly misunderstood,[52] that it was necessary for him to deny certain inferences, and that his disciples again and again have expostulated against misinterpretations. James certainly did not mean to justify anything and everything that worked, that paid, that had a cash value. He did not justify corruption, though it filled the pocketbooks of those who took bribes; or imperialism, though it paid concessionaires, exporters, and importers; or jingoism, though it brought profits to the owners of the yellow press and the

[51] *Principles of Psychology,* Vol. II, pp. 368–69.

[52] James considered pragmatism to be, in part, a philosophic generalization of scientific practice, an extension to psychology and logic of the biological conception of survival and the Darwinian principle of selection. *Nature,* Vol. LXXXVI (Sept., 1910), pp. 268–69.

stockholders of the Bethlehem Steel Company. It was often as hard to determine whether a thing was useful as to decide whether it were true; it might be useful for some purposes and to certain interests, but not for others.

Yet it must be admitted that pragmatism was entirely capable of giving aid and comfort to people whose acts he himself would have condemned. He held that emotions and wishes did and should color and condition our beliefs, and that, in the absence of other evidence, whatever gave the greatest emotional satisfaction was, within certain limits, true. From this one might infer that if employing men ten hours a day at wages that were admittedly low, if lockouts, injunctions, and the blocking of social legislation gave the greatest emotional satisfaction to the owners and managers of factories, then such practices were true for them, if on the whole and in the long run they continued to bring satisfactions. But James recognized that such practices might well also produce dissatisfactions and fail to make for the "best whole." Since there must be conflict between emotional satisfactions and ideals, since there must be victory and defeat, "the victory to be philosophically prayed for is that of the more inclusive side—of the side which even in the hour of triumph will to some degree do justice to the ideals in which the vanquished party's interests lay." James, in carrying this concept a step farther, declared that the only path to peace lay in the invention of some manner of "realizing your own ideals which will also satisfy alien demands." The course of history was nothing but "the story of men's struggles from generation to generation to find the more and more inclusive order."[53]

While it is true that a narrow application of pragmatism,

---

[53] *The Will to Believe*, p. 205. Although James was a bitter opponent of Hegelianism, this suggests the doctrine of thesis, antithesis, and synthesis.

one which obscured the long-run criterion and the concept of "the best whole" might easily justify anti-social practices and the maintenance of the *status quo,* James himself, at least in theory, would have repudiated such consequences. It is clear that for him pragmatism, from a social point of view, supported meliorism, gradual, opportunistic, and evolutionary change, a type of change which those in possession of privileges have generally considered preferable to direct action and revolution. In a truly American spirit James advocated the doctrine of co-operation, which applied, presumably, to classes as well as to individuals. "As individual members of a pluralistic universe, we must recognize that, even though we do *our* best, the other factors also will have a voice in the result. If they refuse to conspire, our good-will and labor may be thrown away."[54]

The emphasis which pragmatism put on the belief that the individual might through self-help, energy, and hope overcome nearly all if not all obstacles, and the importance which it attached to the idea that everyone should regard his own walk of life with self-confidence and pride, appeared to be democratic and in accord with American ideals and actualities. Yet as Bertrand Russell observed, pragmatism also gave sustenance to the financiers, advertisers, and successful men of action who, expecting the world to be malleable to their wishes in greater or less degree, found their expectations justified.[55] Only a partisan observer could contend that the social order had nothing to do with such success.

In its social implications pluralism also supported the existing social and economic pattern. "According to that philosophy," James explains, "the truth is too great for any one

[54] William James, *Some Problems of Philosophy* (New York, 1911), p. 229.
[55] Bertrand Russell, *Philosophical Essays* (New York, 1910), pp. 124–26.

actual mind, even though that mind be dubbed 'the Absolute,' to know the whole of it. The facts and worths of life need many cognizers to take them in. There is no point of view absolutely public and universal. . . . The practical consequence of such a philosophy is the well-known democratic respect for the sacredness of individuality,—is, at any rate, the outward tolerance of whatever is not itself intolerant."[56] The social implications of pluralism are clearly those of *laissez faire,* of live and let live.

This sort of philosophy led James, indeed, to be sympathetic with all sorts and conditions of men, to believe in their way of life, and to insist that it held for them values which others could not appreciate. But it also kept him from doing anything to change the conditions that made slum dwellers continue to live in their tenements and debtors continue to worry under the pressure of insecurity. In discarding absolute truth, James also discarded absolute justice, a doctrine which was untenable because it conflicted with the rights and energies of individuals, because it postulated a block universe. Any person repudiating absolute justice, however, might well have been charged by its proponents with a special responsibility for justice in the concrete facts of everyday life, and this James did not assume.

Without pushing the contention too far, it might be pointed out that the doctrine of radical empiricism likewise was a reflection of the individualistic way of American life. Empiricism laid stress on the part, the element, the individual, and treated the whole as a collection and the universal as an abstraction. To be radical, an empiricism, James said, must neither admit into its constructions any element that is not directly experienced, nor exclude from them any element

[56] *Talks to Teachers,* p. v.

that is directly experienced. "For such a philosophy, the relations that connect experiences must themselves be experienced relations, and any kind of relation experienced must be accounted as 'real' as anything else in the system."[57] With James radical empiricism stopped short of emphasizing the social whole, social institutions, and social justice, and concerned itself primarily with the rôle of the individual in the whole. But this was not inherent in the philosophy itself. Indeed, since relations are a part of reality, social relations are and must be included in any complete philosophy; and Dewey, as we shall see, attached great importance to them.

It would be dangerous, indeed, to assume that pragmatism, pluralism, and radical empiricism, compatible though they were with American individualism and with the inequalities in wealth and status in our national life, could be useful only in justifying our particular social and economic structure. Russian Communists might well argue that if it proved profitable for the "best whole" ruthlessly to suppress the vestiges of an exploiting class, then such suppression possessed truth and validity. Pragmatism might also be employed to justify the slogan, not science for the sake of science, but science for its practical effects. It might even be pointed out that the thrill of a collective attack on a social and physical danger, such as James visioned in "The Moral Equivalent for War," is not unlike the co-operative and heroic features of the five-year plan, save that the latter was based on an economic theory opposed to profit. The philosophy of William James, at least in its applications, was sufficiently manysided and flexible to justify incompatible schemes and values.

In neither his social opinions, his psychology and pedagogy,

[57] William James, *Essays in Radical Empiricism* (New York, 1912), pp. 41-42.

nor his philosophy, did William James consciously serve those to whom the chances of birth or the fortunes of the existing arrangements of life gave power. But the effect of his work was to support the social structure from which he derived so many advantages. If he had no heart for mere financial achievement and decried the "bitch goddess SUCCESS," if he attacked imperialism and political corruption without understanding their economic causes, he made the principles of competition, acquisition, and struggle seem psychologically sound and inevitable, and philosophically beautiful and attractive. He glorified the individualism that was the foundation stone of our economic life. He sanctified the risk, the speculation, the daring bravado that characterized it. He said repeatedly that the instinct of private property was basic and that education must take it into account.

If, in his later life, James showed some favor toward Socialism, it is not a part of the intellectual heritage which he left. Those who read him were informed that nine-tenths of the work of the world was done as the result of the instinct of competition and emulation. He deprecated a sentimental attitude toward workingmen, the softness of social settlement and uplift work. He had only scorn for anybody who tried to reform any one except himself. He outdid these "romanticists" tenfold by romanticizing far more about the workers, whom he knew less well than the most sentimental social worker. He even envied laborers their constant fight with difficulties, and by insisting that they had their own sense of happiness, their own satisfactions, offered compensations for their lot.

All this is only to say that James made the American doctrine of "rugged individualism" seem glorious, appropriate, and never to be forfeited. It is this philosophy, sprung from the twin processes of the exploitation of the frontier and the exploitation of natural and human resources, which has helped to insure the supremacy of the holders of stocks and bonds. It is this point of view which made the worker feel that co-operation with the owners of mines, factories, and tenant farms was preferable to collective organization and conflict, and which permitted high-minded Americans to support President Hoover in a policy which, they were warned, threatened starvation to out-of-work Americans. It is this doctrine of individualism which has given a halo of romance and glory to a system declared by its critics to be not only inefficient and bankrupt, but incompatible with the full development of the very individuality of the masses of Americans for which in principle James sincerely stood.

That this great individualist, in view of the importance which he attached to the concrete and the tangible, might have come to appreciate this inconsistency and have modified his views accordingly, is not improbable, because for him nothing was finished. Even his psychology and his philosophy, with their socially conservative implications, were subject to revision; and he realized that the American scene itself, including its values, was still in the process of making. There was no eternal edition, ready made and complete.[58] If the followers of James guard against limitations such as those imposed on their master by his aristocratic background and temperament; if they take care that his high regard for individuals finds realistic and inclusive expression; and if they cherish his warning against established institutions, then in the spirit of his farewell message that there is no conclusion, they may work for a radically different and better America.

[58] William James, *The Meaning of Truth* (New York, 1909), pp. 226–27; *Human Immortality*, pp. 1–2.

XIV

EDWARD LEE THORNDIKE, SCIENTIST

1874–1949

More than any other of the educational psychologists, he has
sponsored statistical method, redevised it for a hundred variable
types of inquiry, taught it to his students and headed, with a
professional associate or two, the whole movement to give educational thought and practice a scientific and dependable technique.　　　　　　　　　　　　　—HENRY SUZZALLO, 1926.

To him that hath a superior intellect is given also on the average a superior character. . . . To-day the world is being assailed
by the . . . foolish superstition that money-making is correlated
o with general intelligence and about –.80 to –1.00 with good-
will, the maker of great profits being no more fit intellectually
to run his business than his barber is, and being diabolically
eager to amass dollars at the cost of misery to anybody who gets in
his way and to all innocent bystanders.
　　　　　　　　　　　　　　　　—E. L. THORNDIKE, 1920.

I

James once said of his pupil, Edward L. Thorndike, that,
more than any other whom he knew, he had the quality most
essential to a scientific man—the ability to see things apart
from acquired perspective and personal reference.[1] Indeed,
when one inspects the titles and summaries of the thirty-some
books and three hundred-odd articles which make up Thorndike's bibliography,[2] one is impressed by their technical and
objective character. There is little to indicate, in the facts of
his life available to the student, that wealth or social position

[1] J. McKeen Cattell, in *Teachers College Record*, Vol. XXVII (Feb., 1926,
Number in Honor of Edward Lee Thorndike), p. 461
[2] *Ibid.*, p. 465.

identified him with the *status quo*. One might expect, therefore, that his work would approximate, at any rate, the high scientific ideal he himself outlines: "The methods of science are impartial, paying no heed to the immediate satisfyingness of any idea to any individual. They require verification and test by prophecy. They produce thinkers whose minds are, with respect to the problems involved, repositories of fact-systems of connections all tried and true—and so well fitted to have fruitful ideas."[3]

From the first Thorndike has insisted that the chief duty of the serious student of education is to form the habit of scientific study and to learn the logic of statistics. In 1903, in his first important educational book, he said that "it is the vice or the misfortune of thinkers about education to have chosen the methods of philosophy or of popular thought instead of those of science."[4] His influence in establishing and popularizing the fact-finding, statistical, and experimental technique in education has been immeasurable. Taking over the methods of the physical and natural sciences, and using the more quantitative devices of such pioneers as Pearson, Galton, Cattell, Rice, and Boas, Thorndike, together with Judd,[5] revolutionized American educational technique. After the publication of his *Mental and Social Measurements,* it was possible, as George Strayer has pointed out, to develop scientific work in the field of educational administration.[6] Thousands of graduate students studied with him, hundreds of thousands of classroom practitioners, principals, and supervisors heard his voice and modified their educational thought

[3] E. L. Thorndike, *Human Learning* (New York, 1931), p. 192.
[4] E. L. Thorndike, *Educational Psychology* (New York, 1903), p. 164; Arthur Gates, *Teachers College Record,* Vol. XXVII (Feb., 1926), p. 556.
[5] *Cf. post,* Chap. XVI.
[6] *Teachers College Record,* Vol. XXVII (Feb., 1926), p. 543.

and practice as a result.[7] His application of science to education also profoundly influenced the gradually changing methodology of ethics and the social sciences generally.[8]

In looking back over the period between the death of Lincoln and the outbreak of the World War it is plain that, whether it was Hegelianism, Catholicism, biological evolution, Herbartianism, or pragmatism that affected the educational philosophy of the leaders of our schools, the social implications of their philosophy, and the social opinions to which they came, were, by and large, of such a character as to fit the needs of the *status quo*. Those on top could appeal almost equally well to the social philosophy of Harris, Booker T. Washington, Bishop Spalding, the Herbartians, Hall, or James for an authoritative refutation of ideas subversive to the existing economic and social system.[9] The particular problem of this chapter is to determine whether objective science, as represented by Thorndike, is an exception to this general rule. Did Thorndike, in other words, using what seemed to him to be scientific methods, establish facts or postulate theories which supported the characteristic social philosophy of the more well-to-do Americans? Are any of his facts and theories hostile to their way of thinking and feeling? Is his work neutral, indifferent toward and aloof from social problems involving vested interests?

In short, here we have an educational leader sincerely devoted to the scientific method, and, apparently, with no axes to grind; one who comes from a humble clerical family and lives the "sheltered" academic life. What is the relation between the problems he selects and the accepted beliefs of the American social atmosphere? Are his results consonant with

[7] Henry Suzzallo, *ibid.*, p. 581.
[8] Gates, *ibid.*, p. 556.   [9] Parker and Dewey are exceptional.

that ideology? In so far as they are consonant, are they truly verified and therefore "scientific"?

A pioneer in animal psychology, Thorndike has also concerned himself with the problems of heredity, the learning process, individual differences, mental tests, educational measurements, child study, adult learning, curriculum construction, and educational administration. He has aimed, as we have seen, to answer scientifically the question of how individuals may be changed through education. These problems are of obvious importance and might seem to be chosen with no respect at all to the particular environment of early twentieth century America. Whatever the economic or social arrangements, should we not have to inquire into them? Might not research on such problems produce results either favorable toward or incompatible with a system from which a few derived far more advantages than the many? Might not these problems be truly set, not by the demands of a particular social and economic structure but by an abstract search for truth in universal terms? So it might well seem.

Yet it must be acknowledged that the time had come when the controlling spirit of business enterprise looked with favor on efforts to measure accurately the specific results of America's vast educational plant, which was both expensive and likely to be taken as a mere matter of course. The time had also come when there was a conscious need for educators to concern themselves with specific and concrete pedagogical problems. It is certainly significant that Thorndike's work led to the improving of school administration, to better classification and homogeneous grouping of students; to concern with the exceptional child; to a differentiation of courses of study, with the testing of their pragmatic value; to the carrying out of vast statistical surveys; to the critical appraisals of techniques of teaching and curriculum offerings; to methods for measuring achievement in every educational field. There was great need for these things; yet it is perhaps significant that none of them were in any sense inimical to the established economic system. In fact, they were similar to current business activities, for this was the period of the expert accountant, the scientific manager, and the efficiency engineer. Educators, patiently finding facts by scientific methods, were not, at least, raising questions that might possibly prove embarrassing.

Notwithstanding the rapid integration of economic life seen especially in the growth of big business, its directors were fond of speaking of the free individual, the opportunity for everyone to reach the top. They liked to believe that their own success was due to their talent and ability. They took little stock in the idea that social environment acted as a discriminating influence. In the nature of things, they were bound to value scientific investigations which supported that point of view.

It certainly could not be said that Thorndike, purposely hiding behind "science," selected problems for investigation which were consciously designed to serve an economic group and to discriminate against any other. Indeed, some of the problems he selected, such as the investigations into individuality, into eugenics, into the psychological basis of thrift, into the problem of initiative and originality, the intellectual status of children who were public charges, and the psychology of labor, capital, advertising, and personnel work, might have led to conclusions hostile to the business point of view. These investigations might have proved dangerous or exceedingly advantageous to the established order. We shall see whether Thorndike's conclusions were, in effect, favorable, hostile, or neutral toward the vested interests and ideas supporting them, without attempting to determine to just what extent they were influenced by personal presuppositions, defective methods, accident, or the unconscious and subtle influence of dominant intellectual and social patterns.

Despite Thorndike's predominant interest in applying the scientific method to education, his statement of general aims was determined by ethics. To make men "want the right things, and to make them better able so to control all the forces of nature and themselves that they can satisfy these wants" is the basic doctrine of his educational philosophy. The "right" thing to do in any case is the thing which a man who could foresee all the consequences of all acts, and who considered fairly the welfare of all men, would in that case choose.[10] Increased care for the welfare of others, the cultivation of impersonal pleasures, the elimination of useless and harmful wants in favor of mutually helpful ones are the chief elements in bettering the human lot. To attain them, physical health, skill, knowledge, habits of thoroughness and open-mindedness must be acquired. In upholding the ideals of co-operation and good will, in emphasizing as ultimate aims of education happiness, appreciation of beauty, utility, and service, Thorndike reminds one of Francis Parker.

But Thorndike repudiates one of the outstanding and most characteristic aims of Parker, the complete and harmonious development of the individual, or self-perfection, a doctrine upheld by Spencer and Froebel, and in keeping with the Emersonian tradition in American life. Thorndike rejects this end in part because it excuses the "too common tendency of men to educate themselves for competitive display instead

[10] E. L. Thorndike, *Education: A First Book* (New York, 1912), pp. 11-12, 29.

of co-operative work," in part because it opposes the specialization that he thinks necessary for mutual aid. Education beyond certain fundamentals, he holds, should narrow itself to fit any given man for a certain probable course of life, not for all life's possibilities. There is still some truth in the conception that the best a man can do for the world is to be the best possible man himself, but it is becoming increasingly possible, he has argued, to choose beforehand for the individual "a special line of action" of sure value to himself and to the world.[11]

In general, Thorndike's statement of educational aims has not been such as to justify the flaws of the social structure. He has condemned the competitive spirit in human relations; he has attacked those who look upon education as "a means of putting one in a position where others have to work for him, and not he for others"; he has repudiated "the leisure class" conception of culture. The manufacturers who try to fit children to be nothing except efficient workmen he has criticized as furthering narrow and unjust aims for education. He has even declared that so long as civilized nations have not learned to settle international disputes by expert judges, so long as they commit the consummate blunder of not letting all able and willing men work, education is incomplete.[12] These aims of education, while they lack James's fine sensitivity to the individual, are far more comprehensive and social than those of Thorndike's teacher.

II

Although an ethical altruism entered into the determination of Thorndike's educational objectives, they were to be

[11] *Ibid.*, pp. 31–33.   [12] *Ibid.*, p. 27.

realized by strictly scientific means. In examining his psychological theories, particularly those that directly affected educational practice, we must inquire how effectively they promoted these idealistic ends.

While Thorndike insisted that the human species could change itself for the better,[13] he also, like James, emphasized the necessity of the adjustment of the individual to his environment. This idea is implicit in his interpretation of mutual enterprise through specialization. It is confirmed by his conception of the function of the "laws" of learning (readiness, exercise, and effect) as strengthening, preserving, weakening, or abolishing original tendencies. They are "the agents by which man acquires connections productive of behavior suitable to the environment in which he lives."[14] The conservative social implications of this emphasis on adjustment to a relatively static environment have been already noted in the discussion of James.

One of the most distinctive features of Thorndike's psychology of learning is his theory of identical elements. When in 1901 he and R. S. Woodworth presented their findings concerning the problem of formal discipline or transfer of training,[15] there was only the fragmentary experimental work of James. After many experiments, Thorndike challenged the tradition of the ages, which held that there was a general transfer of training, and concluded that improvement in any single mental function need not improve the ability in others

[13] E. L. Thorndike, *Educational Psychology* (New York, 1913), Vol. I: *The Original Nature of Man*, p. 312.

[14] *Ibid.*, Vol. II: *The Psychology of Learning*, pp. 1, 4.

[15] E. L. Thorndike and R. S. Woodworth, "The Influence of Improvement in One Mental Function upon the Efficiency of Other Functions," *Psychological Review*, Vol. VIII (May, July, Nov., 1901), pp. 247–61, 384–95, 553–64.

unless very closely similar to it, and that, moreover, the amount of transfer was directly proportional to the number of "identical elements" in the two functions.[16]

In his *Educational Psychology* (1913) Thorndike did not deny the general spread of improvement, but stated that many more measurements must be made before psychology would be able to predict in general the disciplinary effect of any special forms of practice such as the "studies" of schools or the industries and games of modern life.[17] Much later, experiments in measuring educational achievements led him to conclude definitely that no particular subjects are superior to others in producing improvement in ability to think. Improvement is due not to the subject but to the original capacity of the individual; able students would become good thinkers even if they studied only physical education and dramatic art.[18] Despite this scientist's cautious statement of findings, he himself, and especially some of his followers, made extreme applications of his theory of transfer. Although there have been some criticisms by Spearman, Lashley, and other psychologists, his position has in the main been generally accepted.[19]

The educational and social implications of Thorndike's ideas about formal discipline can be at least approximately inferred.

[16] *Ibid.*, p. 386.   [17] *Educational Psychology*, Vol. II, p. 417.
[18] E. L. Thorndike, "Mental Discipline in High School Studies," *Journal of Educational Psychology*, Vol. XV (Jan., Feb., 1924), pp. 1–22, 83–98. Thorndike had for many years questioned the accepted superior value of certain subjects and had made investigations based on student and teacher opinion. See his "The Disciplinary Values of Studies: A Census of Opinion," *Education*, Vol. XXXV (Jan., 1915), pp. 278–86; "The Disciplinary Values of Studies in the Opinion of Students," *Teachers College Record*, Vol. XXV (March, 1921), pp. 134–43.
[19] Peter Sandiford, *Teachers College Record*, Vol. XXVII (Feb., 1926), pp. 528–30.

If there is no necessary transfer of learning and improvement, then there must be special training for special ends; obviously, the curriculum must be widened. If in training the intellect no subject is preferable to another, then a pragmatic or utilitarian value will determine which subjects shall make up the curriculum. This, in effect, means more science, greater attention to the social studies, and support for technical, industrial, and household subjects.[20]

With an important qualification the attack on the doctrine of formal discipline, and the position that inclusion of studies in the curriculum should be determined largely by the special information and habits which they demonstrably produce, tended to give a more utilitarian flavor to elementary and secondary education. It is true that some of Thorndike's critics, who took him to task for thus giving support to the practical and the specific rather than to the general and broadly cultural, overlooked the fact that he also included "interests, attitudes, and ideals" as transferable items; and if these are elements, then his theory is not, as so many of his critics have maintained, altogether "mechanical." But in practice the tendency to emphasize information and habits in determining the value of studies did give some basis for the criticism that his position on the question of transfer or identical elements leads straight to vocationalism, by conditioning, at too early a stage, the future life work of the masses of children. One of Bode's students, Orata, went so far as to say that the Thorndike theory leads us back to the system of apprenticeship, which is incompatible with the ideal of democracy. By robbing us of our faith in general education, Orata continued, the doctrine leaves little room for the logical organization of

[20] See Thorndike's "The Opportunity of the High Schools," *Bookman*, Vol. XXIV (Oct., 1906), pp. 180–84.

knowledge which makes for social insight and intellectual interest.[21] It means, in short, Orata argued, specific preparation for a more or less predetermined set of activities.

Since in his original statement of the general aims of education Thorndike included the improvement of the quality of human wants, mutual aid in work, and the elimination of such social evils as war and unemployment, the question may justly be asked whether the effect of his doctrine of specific elements would not be to promote ends different from if not opposite to these. If the individual is to improve his desires and his pleasures, live co-operatively with his fellows, and contribute to the elimination of war and unemployment, he must know how to meet situations for which he is not specifically trained. He must have not only the practical skills for the demands of everyday life; he will also need flexibility, the power constantly to look beyond the present practical need, the ability, in short, to do creative thinking and to help solve problems. To be sure, Thorndike in stating his general aims may not have desired such participation by the individual; in other writings he has argued against the desirability of social thinking on the part of the multitude and asked that they rely solely on the expert. Yet the point remains that dominance of the theory of specific elements in educational circles might mean that the conservation of the past and the adjustment of the individual to existing environment would gain the upper hand at the expense of social insights and the desire and ability to participate in social reconstruction.

Although Thorndike himself has not argued for indoctrination, his theory of specific elements as held by many followers might be expected to give new life to that idea. If a child

---

[21] Pedro Tamesis Orata, *The Theory of Identical Elements* (Ohio State University, Contributions in Principles of Education, No. 3, 1928), p. vi.

cannot be expected to transfer what he has learned in one situation to another, different yet similar, then it is logical to argue that he must be indoctrinated. Such a conclusion would tend to support either social conservatives or social radicals, rather than liberals or progressives who advocate tentativeness, open-mindedness, and an education designed to teach a student how to think, rather than one that tells him what to think.

In Thorndike's psychology of the learning process, the theory of identical elements is closely related to the doctrine of bonds or associations. He believes that human learning proceeds in essentially the same manner as animal learning. The evolution of mind from animal to man has no essential breaks; thinking or human self-consciousness and self-control are really secondary results of the tremendous increase in the number, quality, and complexity of associations or bonds which the human animal has acquired by virtue of the greater fineness of his neural organization. Bonds or associations that secure pleasure (satisfiers) are selected from others and retained because associated with the pleasurable situation, while contrary acts that bring discomfort are dissociated from the situation and tend to drop out. Human thought, or at least one important type of it, is a specific result of controlling impulses and thereby controlling environment.

Thorndike's maxim, "Exercise and reward desirable connections; prevent or punish undesirable connections," means that the teacher is to decide on the particular bonds or connections that are to be established, or, in short, to set the stage for the fixing process. The child would be apt to be overlooked as the result of such a procedure, in the eyes of some critics, since by insisting on the analytic and neglecting the synthetic aspects of learning, it would put a premium on skills and habits and come near to denying purposive behavior.[22] There is at least some point in the contention that such placing of the pupil at the mercy of a master designer, the teacher, means fixed and rigid reactions, not flexible ones. To the extent to which this is true, Thorndike's doctrine tends to defeat his general educational aims. It appears to some of his critics that the application of the bond theory in schoolroom practice involves neglecting the selection and organization of material to promote thinking and thus actually fits the child for an aristocratic rather than for a democratic civilization.[23]

Thorndike has not limited his work on the learning process to the young. As a result of his experiments on adult learning, he has concluded that in general nobody under forty-five should refrain from trying to learn anything because of a fear that he is too old. The conclusion that older people can learn as well as younger, a too broad and hasty generalization, as later work has shown, together with support given utilitarian subjects by his denial of formal discipline, led him to favor a mixture of schooling and productive labor. In our desire to give everyone abundant schooling, he asserts, we are apt to harm a great many who cannot profit from it by depriving them of the satisfaction which comes from commendable performance.[24] Hence he favors

22 H. Gordon Hullfish, *Aspects of Thorndike's Psychology in Their Relation to Educational Theory and Practice* (Ohio State University, Contributions in Principles of Education, No. 1, 1926), pp. 86–87, 100.

23 *Ibid.;* Boyd H. Bode, *Modern Educational Theories* (New York, 1927), p. 186; Orata, *op. cit.,* pp. vi–vii.

24 Thorndike held that those who dropped out of school did not do so primarily from economic reasons but because of incapacity for or lack of interest in the type of intellectual work demanded. See his *The Elimination of Pupils from School* (U. S. Bureau of Education, Bulletin, No. 4, 1907), p. 10; and the discussion in the book which he wrote with Strayer, *Educational Administration* (New York, 1917), p. 53.

SOCIAL IDEAS OF AMERICAN EDUCATORS

a policy of part-time productive work and part-time schooling for many children when they reach the age of fourteen.[25]

While such a program might help to bridge the gulf between education and work and life in the real world, a gulf particularly distasteful to Thorndike, it could hardly, under our system, lead to anything but class education. In practice it is almost certain to mean that, whatever their limitations or capacities, children of the well-to-do would not be put into productive work at the age of fourteen. Such a part-time arrangement would, in effect, include only the children of the poor. Although such an educational policy might help to realize Thorndike's desire to give every individual "a special benefaction," it might well defeat his declared aim of promoting concern for the welfare of others and developing high and impersonal pleasures, in so far as it tended to condemn the children of the poorer classes to a more humble station in life and to meager satisfactions.

In adult learning Thorndike has also seen a cure for technological unemployment. "The facts of adult learning," he maintains, "may also encourage industry to face changes in machinery, processes, and the like with the hope of reducing disturbances by education of the workers."[26] There is doubtless truth in the thesis that, if adult learning is as easy as Thorndike holds, the displaced worker might learn new processes. But this appears to some critics as at best an inadequate remedy for technological unemployment. In so far as it diverts attention from a more fundamental attack on the problem, it may be regarded as less conducive to "social health" than Thorndike as-

[25] Jordan True Cavan, "Have Adults Lost Their Power to Learn?", *Religious Education*, Vol. XXIV (Oct., 1929), pp. 729–32; E. L. Thorndike, "Learning from Six to Sixty," *Survey*, Vol. LX (April 15, 1928), pp. 118–20; and especially, E. L. Thorndike and others, *Adult Learning* (New York, 1928).
[26] *Adult Learning*, p. 180.

sumes. It is important, however, that an educator has offered to industrial managers, engineers, and workers a suggestion for keeping the latter employable.

Certain other social advantages, Thorndike has pointed out, are inherent in his theory of adult learning. If adults can learn as easily as the young, their leisure may be improved and the dangers consequent to a greater amount of it thereby diminished.[27] Further, since technology and science are so rapidly changing, the world view learned by the child is obsolete in adulthood; shortening the time of early schooling and making up for it later in adult learning, would remedy this lag.[28] Education of the adult, in contrast to that of the child, might make for less conformity and docility, for self-expression, self-direction, and self-government.[29] Adult education might also provide workers with a realistic acquaintance with contemporary social problems as well as with cultural subjects. Thorndike has thus encouraged the adult educational movement to provide without cost what the schools fail to provide.

These particular arguments for adult education, which are in line with the traditional American doctrine of self-help, are consistent with Thorndike's social attitudes on other questions. They are capable of lending support, of course, to those who for various reasons wish to lower the age of compulsory school attendance.

Nothing in Thorndike's psychology is so important, both in educational applications and in general social implications, as his closely related theories of heredity, environment, and individual differences. Man resembles the higher animals in original nature or in instinctive equipment, he believes, as well

[27] E. L. Thorndike, "The Right Use of Leisure," *Journal of Adult Education*, Vol. II (Jan., 1930), pp. 42–46; *Playground*, Vol. XXIII (March, 1930), pp. 713–14; Cavan, "Have Adults Lost Their Power to Learn?", *loc. cit.*, p. 731.
[28] *Adult Learning*, p. 191.   [29] *Ibid.*, p. 184.

as in the manner of learning. He reduced the number of instincts which James had listed, and particularly has argued that imitativeness is not an "original tendency" but rather the result of arousal, by the behavior of others, of special responses or impulses or ideas which, in the course of experience, have formed connections with that sort of behavior. Since the older pedagogy assumed the existence of an instinct of imitativeness and drew heavily on that assumption, this departure from earlier psychologists has important implications for schoolroom practice.

But Thorndike clings to many social instincts. "Chief in importance for education among such social instincts are gregariousness, mastering and submissive behavior, responses to approval and scorn, rivalry, motherly behavior, kindliness, teasing and bullying, and pugnacity."[30] Original nature, Thorndike holds, provides a complex interplay of activities between one human being and another with whom he has to do, whereby, as a resulting stable equilibrium, one has the attitude of mastery and the other of submission. "Submissiveness to the kind of person to whom it is a natural response, may be entirely tolerable, though it lacks the richer joys of mastery."[31] It is true, he admits, that early training modifies the crude determinants of superiority and inferiority, or who shall command and who obey, and yet they remain beneath the more rational and humane habits. This notion, it is clear, gives little support to democracy.

Believing as he does in instinctive responses to rivalry, scorn and approval, and in the satisfaction derived in mastering behavior, Thorndike might be expected to favor the use of emulation in the classroom. While he has approved of the use of grades to motivate students, he has criticized the desire to excel

[30] *Education*, p. 79.   [31] *Ibid.*, p. 81.

omeone else as "the gross form of emulation." Working or marks and for rewards is not, he holds, intrinsically bad: ts vice is its relativity and indefiniteness, the fact that a given nark does not mean any defined amount of knowledge, power, r skill. The proper remedy is not to eliminate all stimulus o rivalry and achievement, but to redirect the rivalry into the urpassing of one's past performance—into getting into a higher lass, and competing co-operatively as one of a group in rivalry vith another group. Once there is a reliable measurement of chievement, even direct rivalry with others will be "innocent nd healthy."[32]

It is a little difficult to see how the rivalry Thorndike approved vould be fundamentally different from the cruder sort of ust beating the other fellow. Neither is it clear that it would be nappropriate to an economic and social system which applauds he efforts of the individual to "get ahead." It would, in hort, hardly seem to be conducive to the altruism and mu- ual helpfulness which Thorndike postulated as an educational im.

Although he attaches great importance to the "instinct of ivalry," which is closely associated, in his thought, with the mastering and hunting instincts," Thorndike admits that the nisdirection of the latter has caused much misery in the world. The hunting and mastering instincts are so strong that they are kely to operate crudely and to extremes. "It is a bitter fact that pparently not two men in ten can be given unlimited powers s rulers, generals or school-masters without grave risk that hey will abuse it by hounding those whom they happen to dis- ke or those whom public opinion puts in a class below man, be hunted or driven."[33] In view of this recognition of the requent and disastrous effects of emulation, as well as in the

[32] *Educational Psychology*, Vol. I, p. 287.   [33] *Education*, p. 86.

light of his general educational emphasis on mutual helpfulness, it is striking that Thorndike gives even "impersonal" emulation so important a place in the schoolroom.

In his *Educational Psychology* Thorndike takes issue with McDougall's contention that anger and fighting have been blessings in disguise to mankind, by promoting higher group co-operation. He attributes social co-operation rather to hunting, agriculture, and industry than to combat. Yet, like G. Stanley Hall, he thinks it risky to cultivate tenderness and love too indiscriminately. The male's fighting instinct, he states elsewhere, is responsible for a large amount of the world's intellectual endeavor. "The financier does not think for money nor the scientist for truth nor the theologian to save souls. Their intellectual efforts are aimed in great measure to outdo the other man, to subdue nature, to conquer assent."[34]

Like his great teacher, William James, Thorndike believes, however, that the fighting instinct can and should be expressed in socially useful projects rather than in war. Shoddy patriotism, he advises, should be taken out of the school texts, and children taught that efficient labor, skillful professional service, and healthy, noble pleasures are important features of citizenship. Thus he endeavors to carry out specifically in the schoolroom his conviction that education ought to help eliminate war. It is true that only six years after he contributed *The Emotional Price of Peace* to the widely circulated International Conciliation pamphlets,[35] he abandoned his forthright pacifism, like so many others in every walk of life, and took a

34 *Educational Psychology,* Vol. I, pp. 283–85; *The Bookman,* Vol. XXIII (April, 1906), p. 212.
35 E. L. Thorndike, *The Emotional Price of Peace* (International Conciliation, No. 45, Aug., 1911). Thorndike was led to support this position, not because of the arguments of pacifists, for whom he did not entertain a high opinion, but because of his own scientific work. [Author's interview with Thorndike, Dec. 21, 1932.]

leading part in scientific personnel work as his share in winning the war.[36]

It is clear that Thorndike, unlike G. Stanley Hall, does not hold that the original tendencies of man are all good, and will probably always continue to be so. Moreover, in explaining what passes commonly for distinctively human behavior, he attaches far greater importance to adaptive behavior and to the interaction between natural forces and the capacity to learn than to instincts or original nature. With original tendencies alone, man would not feel, let alone satisfy, many of the best wants in human life. "Original nature has achieved what goodness the world knows as a state achieves order, by killing, confining or reforming some of its elements. It progresses not by *laissez faire* but by changing the environment in which it operates and by renewedly changing itself in each generation. Man is now as civilized, rational and humane as he is because man in the past has changed things into shapes more satisfying and changed parts of his own nature into traits more satisfying to man as a whole. Man is thus eternally altering himself to suit himself. His nature is not right in his own eyes. Only one thing in it, indeed, is unreservedly good, the power to make it better."[37]

Thorndike himself has been thoroughly aware that social implications of a radical character might well be drawn from such a conception of human nature. Indeed, he himself has spoken of his suspicion of the efforts of selfish interests to intrench themselves by pleading the existence of certain original tendencies in man as a species. He has opposed the plea that love of ownership in the modern sense of property rights is "the instinctive response to material objects and the instinctive

[36] E. L. Thorndike, "Scientific Personnel Work in the Army," *Science*, n. s., Vol. XLIX (Jan. 17, 1919), pp. 53–61.
[37] *Educational Psychology*, Vol. I, pp. 198, 281.

situation evoking thought and labor."[38] He has likewise warned against the unfortunate effect on social and educational reforms of the use of the term "natural" to sanction an unscien tific confusion of original and taught proclivities.[39] But while reformers and Socialists might take courage from such a theory of human nature, Thorndike himself, in his specific discussions of social issues, has arrived at conservative opinions, to which he attaches scientific validity. But since these social attitudes are also affected by his doctrine of heredity, environment, and individual differences they will be discussed later in the chap ter.

III

Recognizing the general complexity of environmental influ- ences on mental traits, and the difficulty of speaking with any degree of certainty about the problem, Thorndike has not entirely ruled out environmental influence. It would be an over-simplification, he stated in his *Educational Psychology*, to say that "original nature is at the cause of almost all of human destinies." At least in this volume he has qualified his favorite doctrine that man selects to an important extent the features of his environment which are to survive as determi- nants of his intellect and character, by admitting that the power of the original nature of the human race as a whole to affect environment does not equally hold true of one man.[40]

But Thorndike has adhered to the doctrine, always attractive to conservatives, that heredity is far more important than en- vironment. "We may even expect that education will be doubly effective, once society recognizes the advantages given to some

[38] *Ibid.*, Vol. I, p. 204.   [39] *Ibid.*, Vol. I, p. 294.
[40] *Ibid.*, Vol. III, pp. 284–85.

and denied to others by heredity." He concludes that on the whole prevalent opinions much exaggerate "the influence of differences of circumstances and training in producing the intellectual and moral differences found in men of the same nation and epoch."[41] Cattell has suggested that Thorndike's own brilliance, and the remarkable intellectual achievements of his two brothers and his children, may have something to do with his insistence on the great rôle played by heredity; but Thorndike himself believed that experimental tests were the basis of this judgment. From a study of the intellectual status of children who were public charges, this scientist concluded that "as far as our data go, equalizing opportunity, as by institutional life for five years or more for children three to nine years at entrance upon it, does not reduce original likenesses within families and differences between families to any notable extent."[42] An experiment on fatigue and improvement in arithmetic also indicated to Thorndike that equalizing opportunity does not reduce individual differences, and that individual differences of unknown causation should be attributed to original inherited characteristics rather than to differences in training.[43]

While Thorndike maintains that the influence of heredity offers no essential barrier to the real work of man for man, he

[41] *Ibid.*, Vol. III, pp. 311–13.

[42] J. L. Stenquist, E. L. Thorndike and M. R. Trabue, *The Intellectual Status of Children Who are Public Charges* (Archives of Psychology, No. 33, Sept., 1915), pp. 51–52.

[43] E. L. Thorndike, "The Failure of Equalizing Opportunity to Reduce Individual Differences," *Science*, n. s., Vol. XL (Nov. 20, 1915), pp. 753–55. For other corroborating experiments see the following articles by Thorndike: "The Permanence of Interests and Their Relation to Abilities," *Popular Science Monthly*, Vol. LXXXI (Nov., 1912), pp. 449–56; "The Relation between Initial Ability and Improvement in a Substitution Test," *School and Society*, Vol. I (March 20, 1915), pp. 429–31; "The Effects of Outside Air and Recirculated Air upon the Intellectual Achievement and Improvement of School Pupils," *School and Society*, Vols. III and IV (May 6 and Aug. 12, 1916), pp. 679–84, 260–66.

holds that it offers a barrier to the satisfaction of popular demands by education and social reform. The common man demands not absolute betterment or absolute happiness but relative superiority. Social discontent arises from the knowledge or fancy that one is less well off than others. In the actual race of life, which is not to get ahead, but to get ahead of somebody, the chief determining factor is heredity; the prizes which most men seek after are in large measure given or withheld by original nature. "For the common good it is indifferent *who* is at the top, *which* men are achieving most. The important thing for the common good, for all men, is that the top should be high, that much should be achieved."[44]

On the whole, then, intellectual and moral individuality, Thorndike asserts, seems to be due to a very large extent to germ plasm heredity rather than to similarity of home environment.[45] The relatively slight rôle which Thorndike gave to environment led him to favor eugenics. If social reform and philanthropy are, in effect, to encourage the breeding of the inferior and unfit, then, he argues, just in that degree are social reform and philanthropy to be deprecated. Science must teach man to control his own future nature as well as the animals, plants, and physical forces among which he will have to live.[46]

Every one of the score or more important studies on the causes of individual differences, he declares, gives evidence that "if the thousand babies born this week in New York City were

44 *Educational Psychology*, Vol. III, pp. 311–12, 313–14.

45 E. L. Thorndike, *Individuality* (Boston, 1911), p. 43.

46 E. L. Thorndike, "Eugenics: with Special Reference to Intellect and Character," *Popular Science Monthly*, Vol. LXXXIII (Aug., 1913), pp. 125–38; and "The Decrease in Size of American Families," *ibid.*, Vol. LXIII (May, 1903), pp. 64–70. Thorndike seems to have subscribed to the doctrine that, on the basis of the fertility of college trained men and women, some nations are on the "up" and some on the "down." The social implications of this doctrine are suggestive, especially in relation to national competition and rivalry, the "yellow peril," chauvinism, and international relations.

given equal opportunities they would still differ in much the same way and to much the same extent as they will in fact differ." These thousand babies, he continues, would in large measure each create his own environment by cherishing this feature and neglecting that among those which the circumstances of life offer. "We must remember that one of these babies, if of mean and brutal nature, can by enough pains avoid industry, justice and honor, no matter how carefully brought up; and that one of them of intellectual gifts can, if he cares enough, seek out and possess adequate stimuli to achieve in art, science, or letters, no matter how poor and sordid his home may be."[47] The fact that these words were probably written within a few blocks of Harlem and within two or three miles of the East Side slums, did not lead their author to make qualifications. As late as 1932 he said that such experiments as those of Freeman showing the influence of different home environments on the tested intelligence of identical twins did not affect his position.[48]

From experiments which indicated that equalizing opportunity in the practice of arithmetical processes, such as mental multiplication, left unimpaired the gross variability between individuals, or even accentuated their differences in excellence, Thorndike made the broad generalization that "it is unsafe to assume that the differences found among individuals in intellect, character, and skill are due chiefly to the different opportunities which the individuals have enjoyed."[49]

On the basis of similarly limited evidence, this hereditarian has maintained that native ability and moral worth go to-

[47] *Popular Science Monthly*, Vol. LXXXIII (Aug., 1913), pp. 127, 128.
[48] Interview, Dec. 19, 1932; Frank N. Freeman, Karl J. Holzinger, and Blythe C. Mitchell, "The Influence of Environment on the Intelligence, School Achievement, and Conduct of Foster Children," *Twenty-Seventh Yearbook of the National Society for the Study of Education*, 1928, Pt. I, pp. 103–217.
[49] *School and Society*, Vol. I (March 20, 1915), p. 431.

gether, even though the correlations are not perfect.[50] "History records no career, war or revolution," he declares, "that can compare in significance with the fact that the correlation between intellect and morality is approximately .3, a fact to which perhaps a fourth of the world's progress is due."[51] This position, together with his insistence upon the large selective power over environment exercised by an individual's original nature, can certainly have offered no encouragement to work for fundamental changes in the social *status quo,* and despite his occasional qualification of the importance of original nature, must have supported the dominant American notion that here, in America, at least, people get what they are worth to society.

Thorndike's doctrine of heredity is thus in line with the philosophic defense of the existing social pattern which William T. Harris popularized. In view of more recent researches, Thorndike was unjustified in asserting such claims for heredity and in so deprecating the effects of circumstances and opportunities.[52] But he did make them, and he made them in the name of science. He made them sincerely and, as he thought, objectively. It would be hard to determine whether his really unscientific generalizations on this subject were due more to the crude state of scientific technique, to the fact that the brilliance of his family may have been an unconscious factor in his hereditarianism, or to the dominant trend of American thought, which was congenial to his conclusions regarding the relative unimportance of handicaps resulting from environment. Certainly there is good evidence that all thinking is influenced,

[50] *Psychological Bulletin,* Vol. XV (May, 1918), pp. 158–59; *Harper's Monthly Magazine,* Vol. CXL (Jan., 1920), p. 233.

[51] *Science,* n. s., Vol. XXXVII (Jan. 24, 1913), p. 142.

[52] *Twenty-Seventh Yearbook of the National Society for the Study of Education,* 1928, Pt. I; H. S. Jennings, *The Biological Basis of Human Nature* (New York, 1930); and, for a general critical analysis of the concept of inherited intelligence, H. A. Carr, *Psychology* (New York, 1925), Chap. XVI.

consciously or unconsciously, by the previous ideas, habits, and emotional attitudes of the thinker; and especially where the thinking has important social implications but is not subject to clear-cut verification, must such influence be important. If this is true, educators particularly, in utilizing the data and results of experimental science, need to keep such considerations in mind, and to be honestly self-critical.

Thorndike's doctrine of individual differences has had important educational consequences, and these have not been without social implications.[53] Greater specialization of instruction and a specialization of the curriculum for different classes and individuals have probably been promoted by Thorndike's attitude on individual differences as well as by his rejection of the doctrine of formal discipline. After arriving at the conclusion that the interests of an individual in childhood are a reliable indication of his permanent interests and abilities, Thorndike states that the importance of his findings are obvious for all those who direct students' choices of schools, studies, and careers.[54] Despite the usefulness and benefit of the whole concept of specialization based on individual interests and ability, it is not without its undemocratic character, as Bode has pointed out.[55]

Strayer has declared that "all our investigations with respect to the classification and progress of children in the elementary schools, in high schools, and in higher education are based upon Professor Thorndike's contribution to the psychology of individual differences."[56] The present trend toward individualization among progressive thinkers, according to Doctor Augusta Bronner, has received support and justification from Thorn-

---

[53] *Individuality*, pp. 23–26.
[54] *Popular Science Monthly*, Vol. LXXXI (Nov., 1912), p. 456.
[55] *Modern Educational Theories*, pp. 307–8, 325.
[56] *Teachers College Record*, Vol. XXVII (Feb., 1926), p. 542.

dike's experiments.[57] His emphasis on adjusting the school to the needs of the child, his idea that the person to be educated decides in part what the proximate aims of education are to be, his consideration for the gifted child, all this has doubtless given an impetus to the progressive education movement as well as to reclassification within the more conventional school systems.

Admirable in many respects, these tendencies in education have nevertheless, it may be argued, placed a disproportionate emphasis on the training of the intellectually superior. Indeed, the sort of adjustment to the individual child which Thorndike's work has stimulated should be contrasted with the more democratic interpretation of this adjustment by the Dewey school of educators.

In fact Thorndike has at no point in his career been an advocate of educational equality. In reviewing Ward's *Applied Sociology* he took exception to the thesis that the one chief efficient means of social improvement is equal distribution of knowledge and held that it is much more important to supply added opportunity to the gifted few who can add to the world's knowledge than to attempt "intellectual communism."[58] Writing much later, he deplored the ill effects of the half education of the American masses. He saw grave dangers, such as the tendency to believe in magic or luck, the lack of impersonal thought with rationalization as a substitute, and the inability to think through a problem.[59] Real education, in contrast with

[57] *Ibid.*, p. 535.

[58] E. L. Thorndike, "Education: A Sociologist's Theory of Education," *Bookman,* Vol. XXIV (Nov., 1906), pp. 290–94.

[59] It should be noted in passing that he used as illustration of such dangerous half education the workingmen who asked why they should not have as much as $50 weekly, a question which, according to Thorndike, signified their ignorance of the fact that if every worker had so much there would not be enough to go around and also indicated the inability of the half-educated worker to rise above the personal equation and really think the problem through in a disinterested way.

half education, he stated, involves recognition of one's ignorance and willingness to consult the expert. The intelligent remedy for America's educational shortcomings is for each individual to refuse to think beyond his own limited field and to spend his energy in finding out what the expert thinks, whether the subject be chemistry or government.[60]

The doctrine of innate individual differences has led Thorndike, in the name of scientific psychology, to challenge the traditional American notion that in order to hand on to the next generation a richer life, education must not only be available, but compulsory for all. His attack on compulsory education and school attendance laws is based on his feeling that they do not take into account the ability of the individual to profit by equality of opportunity. School laws which distribute schooling to those least able to profit from it seem to him "intolerably unjust." Education, he contends, should be so distributed that those who can use it best have the most of it. Since at present (1932) the five per cent intellectually ablest boys are in school only four months longer than the least able, a rearrangement should be made which will create an intellectual aristocracy. This doctrine follows naturally from his idea that more advantageous environment does not greatly benefit those whose fortune it is to have been born with ordinary I. Q.'s.[61]

If it were true, as Thorndike has held, that the wealth of parents has little to do with the length of time children stay in school and that unequal environment does not greatly handicap the brighter children of the poor, then it might be argued that there is nothing essentially undemocratic in Thorndike's suggestion. But these contentions have by no means been satisfactorily established, and it has seemed to some critics that his

[60] E. L. Thorndike, "The Psychology of the Half-Educated Man," *Harper's Monthly Magazine*, Vol. CXL (April, 1920), pp. 666–70.
[61] *New York Times*, March 20, 1932, Sunday educational supplement.

doctrine of individual differences has led him to overestimate individual interest and inclination, and to underemphasize so-cial opportunities and economic restrictions. Unequal though opportunities were even in frontier America, they have come to be far more unequal in urban America; so much so, in fact, that in the eyes of many observers these inequalities cannot be overlooked in any discussion involving democracy, education, and successful achievement.[62] Moreover, educators who attach less importance than does Thorndike to the measurement of intelligence or who disagree with his belief that improvement of society depends largely upon the achievements and direction of the intellectually gifted, would question on other grounds also the desirability of weighting educational opportunities on the side of the intellectually most able.

The concern of Thorndike and his followers with tests and measurements represents another application of his psychology of individual differences which has important social implica-tions. In spite of his cautious warnings about the application of tests and their fallibility, he has attached great importance to their use. He has not hesitated to apply them as a substitute for college entrance examinations; he instituted what were perhaps the first industrial psychological tests, for the Metropolitan In-surance Company; and he took a leading part in standardizing and applying the army tests during the World War.[63] Thorn-dike must take much responsibility for the popularization of intelligence tests together with the concept of intelligence as

[62] Professor Thorndike does not believe that any observable social and eco-nomic changes during the last ten years give any important ground for alter-ing his conviction that the able individual, in spite of environmental handicaps, may and will still come to the top. The auto, the radio, the movie, aviation, and other inventions seem to him to compensate for the loss of opportunities which the frontier formerly provided. [Interview, Dec. 19, 1932.]

[63] See Thorndike's "Fundamental Theorems in Judging Men," *Teachers College Record*, Vol. XIX (May, 1918), pp. 278–88, and "Scientific Personnel Work in the Army," *Science,* n. s., Vol. XLIX (Jan. 17, 1919), pp. 53–61.

something in which individuals differ by original nature "as in stature or eye color."[64]

In education the intelligence test has been an important instrument in making influential Thorndike's attitude toward specialization and his insistence on the importance of native intelligence and heredity as against training and environment.[65] He has held that a knowledge of abstract intelligence, once it was adequately measured, might be used to predict and direct the individual's career.[66] The mental testing movement has enhanced individualism as a belief and a practice at the same time that a modification of individualism has come to seem imperative to many students of American life. In calling attention to individual differences in ability and achievement, the movement at least offered no opposition to the growing concept of a stratified society.

In business and industry also, Thorndike has argued, mental tests, and especially a knowledge of the relationships between mental traits, would be of enormous importance for the utilization of man power by employers and the state. "When we have such exact knowledge, we shall be able to make up a bill of specifications of the sort of intellect and character required for a certain job, select men efficiently instead of haphazard, and train them according to their individual needs instead of indiscriminately."[67] He assails as a foolish superstition the notion that there is no correlation between the making of great profits and intelligence. He believes measurements show that superior intellect also in general carries with it a superior character.

[64] *Harper's Monthly Magazine*, Vol. CXL (Jan., 1920), p. 231.
[65] Thorndike believes that events since 1920 offer no ground for modifying his judgment, published in that year, that good or bad training does not greatly disarrange the order or decrease the differences of individuals in respect to intellect. [Interview, Dec., 1932.]
[66] *Harper's Monthly Magazine*, Vol. CXL (Jan., 1920), p. 232.
[67] *Ibid.*, p. 234.

Hence there can be little truth in the popular misconception that the maker of great profits amassed his dollars "at the cost of misery to anybody who gets in his way and to all innocent bystanders."[68]

Observing that knowledge of the correlation of mental traits is a "protection against many unsound, impracticable theories of business and government," Thorndike declares that it has paid the masses to be ruled by intelligence. The assumption is that the social order which resulted in the evils that should have been obvious in 1920, corruption, war, slums, poverty, and unemployment, has been guided and directed by men of intelligence and superior character. "Furthermore, the natural processes which give power to men of ability to gain it and keep it are not, in their results, unmoral. Such men are, by and large, of superior intelligence, and consequently of somewhat superior justice and good-will. They act in the long run, not against the interest of the world, but for it."[69]

Such a popularization of the intelligence tests implies that the men who govern and control the business and political life of America are, on the whole, intelligent, charged with good will, and bent on exercising their power, not in their own interest, but in the interest of "all." It also assumes that the men on top in the economic and political world have achieved their position by sheer talent, and ignores such environmental factors as family influence, the inheritance of wealth, and the aid given by a corrupt political machine or by unscrupulous business practices. This one-sided assumption is an error common to many Americans, but the error is the more serious when given "scientific" support by a leading American psychologist. Well intentioned though Thorndike's popular article was, it can only

[68] *Ibid.*, pp. 234–35.   [69] *Ibid.*, p. 235.

serve to intrench the privileged in their advantageous position.

Measurements of educational achievement have proved in some respects to be quite as important an application of the psychology of individual differences as the mental testing movement.[70] Since it is the task of education to make changes in human beings, it is clearly necessary, this scientist believes, to provide definite and exact knowledge of what changes it actually makes, and what changes it ought to make. Thorndike devised objective measurements to determine the efficiency of methods of teaching reading, arithmetic, algebra, writing, and spelling. He resents the criticism that such measurements are incompatible with the finer, more spiritual aspects of education, observing that "if any virtue is worth seeking, we shall seek it more eagerly the more we know and measure it."[71] Such a belief is in line with the tendency of modern business civilization, which has particularly influenced America, to desire quantitative measurements. It is fruitless, Thorndike says, to keep only the debit account of time and money expended, of teachers, books, supplies, buildings, courses of study, and methods of teaching: the credit side, the results achieved, the products of this expensive education, must be measured if we are to know what we are actually getting, and where we are going.[72] Education should be put on a more businesslike basis.

Americans have long trusted to education, somewhat blindly perhaps, as the social cure-all, as the road to utopia. Realism requires a scientific effort, Thorndike urges, to measure results,

[70] E. L. Thorndike, *Empirical Studies in the Theory of Measurements* (New York, 1907), *passim*.

[71] E. L. Thorndike, "Measurement in Education," *Teachers College Record*, Vol. XXII (Nov., 1921), pp. 371–79.

[72] E. L. Thorndike, "The Measurement of Educational Products," *School Review*, Vol. XX (May, 1912), pp. 289–99.

to determine whether in actuality education, as it is, can really accomplish what we have expected and trusted it to achieve. Thorndike's work in measurements might conceivably have the social effect of qualifying the American faith in education by presenting reliable data as to its achievements. If the results of the educational measurement movement have been to discredit the effectiveness of education in the eyes of the public, particularly if this be the effect of measurements now being made, designed to determine the effect of teaching on social attitudes, the American people may be more willing to turn to more direct methods of achieving social and economic reform. On the other hand, concern with the measurement of educational achievement together with the emphasis on mental testing seems actually, so far, rather to have helped divert attention from fundamental social aims and from a consideration of the philosophy of education.

Another matter of general social interest involved in this psychologist's attitude toward individual differences is the importance which he attaches to the two factors of sex and race. He holds that the worth of any man or woman is in great part the result not of sex or race but of individual variation. The aid which this position gives to the effort to secure equal treatment for women is counteracted in part by wide acceptance of Thorndike's findings that the male group is the more variable, thereby containing many more brilliant minds than are found among women. He believes that education should "recognize" this restriction of women to the more mediocre grades of ability, as well as the fact that marriage and family are desirable for most members of the sex. Women will, on the whole, he argues, profit much less from graduate work, though more from high school work, than men; education should train them for nursing, teaching, medicine, and architecture rather than for statesmanship, philosophy, and scientific research.[73]

Thorndike likewise believes that race differences, though small, are sufficiently important to compel attention in government, business, industry, marriage, friendship, and almost every other feature of human instinctive and civilized life. The experiments on Negro and white children in New York high schools, which show the white children superior in scholastic intelligence tests, are cited by him as evidence for the important generalization that racial differences in "original nature" are not mere myth.[74]

Thorndike's doctrine of individual differences has still other social implications apart from education itself. In the concluding paragraphs of *Individuality* he declares that "the most pitiful waste and unreason in human affairs is behavior whereby one makes himself suffer to secure for another a good which is to the other a nuisance or a pain. . . . A parent who sacrifices his own joys to protect his children against the healthy, beloved, and noble struggles of life; a philanthropist who lessens his own welfare to teach factory workers refinements, knowledge of which can only embitter their inability to secure them . . . in such gratuitous miseries, false diagnosis of human hearts is prolific."[75] Here Thorndike seems to contradict his statement that an important aim of education is to elevate human wants. Here experimental psychology upholds the doctrine of rugged individualism.

[73] *Individuality*, pp. 30–34; *Education*, pp. 158, 160; "Sex in Education," *Bookman*, Vol. XXIII (April, 1906), pp. 211–14; "The Influence of Men Teachers upon the Enrollment of Boys in Public High Schools," *Ed. Rev.*, Vol. XXXVII (Jan., 1909), pp. 71–85.

[74] *Individuality*, pp. 33–39; "Intelligence Scores of Colored Pupils in High Schools," *School and Society*, Vol. XVIII (Nov. 10, 1923), pp. 569–70; *Educational Psychology*, Vol. III, pp. 207 *et seq.*

[75] *Individuality*, p. 51.

This theory of individualism is also applied in an analysis of democratic political theory. Distribution of traits shows, as Thorndike's innumerable figures indicate, great frequency of mediocrity and the rareness of both especially low and especially high degrees of a trait. This is approximately a rule, he writes, for both the original individualities of mankind and for many traits throughout the course of life. In many traits a very small difference in ability or attitude near the middle point of the scale includes a great many individuals, and this fact explains much in social behavior.

Social and political movements, Thorndike goes on to say, are often instigated by individuals who are at the extremes of the scale with respect to some doctrine. But the deciding votes are almost always cast by individuals who have no very pronounced inclination in either direction. The attractiveness of some hero, the suggestive power of some battle-cry, an affront to a sense of fair play, a year of hard times, a moderate expenditure of money, even the mere desire for novelty may sometimes turn the balance, because only a slight addition to the attractiveness of one proposal is needed to move a great number of those near the point of neutrality. To overturn a large majority requires only a small change in opinion. This interesting argument suggests a psychological basis for pressure groups and propagandists, and its aristocratic implications are clear.[76]

IV

Although Professor Thorndike does not believe that he has incorporated in his classroom instruction specific applications of his educational psychology to economic problems, he has

[76] *Ibid.*, p. 17.

made such applications in a number of popular papers. In his opinion, his general reading on social and economic questions has not influenced him in what he has said in these papers; to him they represent an objective application of his scientific work to contemporary problems. He has been pleased, however, when the studies of social scientists have corroborated him.[77]

For the fundamental characteristics of the existing economic system and for the business class itself, whose representatives Thorndike came to know as his academic distinction attracted more and more attention, he has entertained high regard. While he is willing to grant that the "instinct of pugnacity" may be modified and redirected, he has refused to admit that the "competitive instinct" may be similarly modified.[78] With such convictions it is natural that he should have applied his scientific knowledge in such a way as to serve business enterprise.

In 1911 an article appeared from the scientist's pen which illustrated in a practical and vivid way how certain psychological principles might be useful in the field of business advertising. Nothing was said, however, of the possible psychological and social abuses of advertising; it was not hinted that social values might be made to suffer as a result of this type of application of science to profit-making.[79]

In an address before the American Association for the Advancement of Science in 1932 Thorndike declared that capital is "largely an expression of personality." Minimizing the contributions of labor and ignoring those of the system itself to the creation of new capital, he characterized as a "dangerous

---

[77] At Wesleyan University, from which he took a Bachelor's degree in 1895, Thorndike studied economics and later read Adam Smith and Alfred Marshall, as well as Veblen and Carlton Parker. [Interview, Dec. 19, 1932.]
[78] *Ibid.*
[79] E. L. Thorndike, "Psychology and Advertising," *Scientific American,* Vol. CV (Sept. 16, 1911), pp. 250—51.

myth" the idea that manual labor is the creator of capital and that capital as such is the oppressor of labor. These two myths, he continued, are standing excuses, almost an invitation for any worker who wished to commit robbery without self-reproach.[80] Thus does Thorndike dispose of sabotage, strikes, and labor boycotts. In assuming that critics of capitalistic production do not recognize the contributions of intelligence and managerial skill in the creation of socially useful wealth, and in his misunderstanding of the theory of surplus value, Thorndike merely shares the misconceptions of most American business men. His misunderstanding of the psychology of the worker who indulges in sabotage and strikes is, however, scarcely a tribute to the insight of one of America's most influential psychologists. Certainly he was not adhering strictly to his experimental data when he made these remarks before America's leading scientists, nor when he wrote, in 1920, that Communism is merely an example of the half-educated man's belief in magic.[81]

Thorndike has offered employers advice which he believes will make their laborers more contented. We have seen that he regards as pitifully wasteful and unreasonable such behavior on the part of a philanthropist as "lessens his own welfare to teach factory-workers refinements, knowledge of which can only embitter their inability to secure them."[82] In a popular article which appeared in 1922 he developed much more explicitly the usefulness of psychology in business. Welfare schemes for laborers, as well as labor laws and labor disputes, all confirm, he wrote, the erroneous view that labor is a necessary and evil curse to be endured only to prevent the greater evil of lacking what its wages will buy. Labor is not, he observed, more intrinsically objectionable than the same activity when

[80] *New York Times,* June 21, 1932.
[81] *Harper's Monthly Magazine,* Vol. CXL (April, 1920), p. 667.
[82] *Individuality,* p. 51.

undertaken for sport, and there is hardly a gainful occupation which is not cherished as a pastime by many men and women. While unskilled labor, such as bed-making, dish-washing, and ditch-digging, would be uncongenial to an economist, such labor is often a real pleasure to those performing it. Many workers, in fact, are paid by their love for their menial work, by the sociability it occasions, or by the friendliness of the boss.

In this article are listed five fundamental trends in human nature which, the argument runs, could be capitalized by the employer in making his employee happy in his work. Many of these devices, moreover, would not cost a cent. Work, to be satisfying, must not demand more skill and intelligence than the laborer possesses: finding the right man for the right job would eliminate much labor discontent, and the psychologist can help the employer in this matter. Another fundamental trait is the satisfyingness of submission to the right kind of man. But by far the most important trait for the employer to utilize, he continues, is the satisfyingness of approval, which is one of the great motives in human life. The wise employer will give the worker as much personal dignity and importance as possible in order to minimize the disapproval that attaches to certain kinds of labor.

The employer, according to this article, is justified in his abomination of the labor agitator, who harms everyone concerned "by replacing a general peacefulness and content and good feeling with irritability and suspicion." Thorndike, assuming that we know what the actual natures of laboring people are, declared that, "other things being equal, the American worker will be efficient and happy in proportion as general life for him, his parents, his wife, and his children, is desirable. . . . This desirability should, however, be such as fits their actual natures, not necessarily such as a philanthropist or social philosopher might choose."[83]

Thorndike is too intelligent to say that business capitalism is without crudenesses and faults. But he holds that injustice in business would be largely eliminated by higher schools of business administration, whereby "the crude tendencies to respond to the situation, a business opportunity, with acts productive of success at any cost, will be replaced by tendencies to do the work in question as efficiently as possible in the spirit of science."[84] This harks back to the old idea that mere knowledge is virtue. While Thorndike recognizes that the "crudenesses" characteristic of big business during the primacy of John D. Rockefeller were found to antagonize the public to such an extent that they "paid" less well than smoother tactics, his argument shows little real insight into the actual workings of the profit-making motive.[85]

Thorndike has only rarely spoken in definite terms of the appropriateness of *laissez faire* in our modern life. He has, however, in his plea for reliance on the expert in all departments of life, suggested that in the future the old individualism and *laissez faire* might give way to "deliberate learning to do the nation's work, obey the nation's creed, and live as the nation decrees." But nothing need be lost "for American independence, initiative, and originality by greater emphasis on obedience to the right masters, imitation of the right models, and learning of the right facts in our schools." If the masters,

83 E. L. Thorndike, "The Psychology of Labor," *Harper's Monthly Magazine,* Vol. CXLIV (May, 1922), pp. 799–806.

84 *Education,* p. 201.

85 A recent investigation has convinced Thorndike that there is no nepotism in the modern corporation, and that, in the city at least, the son of the rabbi has no better chance to get a job with a good income than the son of the street cleaner. The positive correlation between the father's occupation and the income of the son was found to be surprisingly small. [Interview, Dec. 21, 1932.]

models, facts, creeds, and ideals were impartially chosen in the light of pure reason as best for the nation's welfare, if the child were given special training to judge leaders and impartial experts, then, Thorndike argues, our citizenship would be efficient and our democracy preserved.

As scientist and idealistic altruist Thorndike would place the fate of mankind in the hands of the impartial expert but would also have every child, man, and woman taught that he, as well as the highest of his rulers, is free—in so far as he is able—to change customs, masters, and creeds for the better, and that the highest of the high is not free to change them except for the better. Thorndike is here relying on the individual's will to be good and the expert's ability to be impartially efficient, without adequately reckoning with economic and social forces, as well as personal factors, as important causes of inefficiency and lack of virtue.[86]

It has been pointed out that Thorndike's general statement of the aims of education and his specific influence on classroom procedure are not entirely compatible. It is also plain that his emphasis on the scientific and on the measurement of educational results tends to put in the background the determination of purposes by sociological and economic factors; there has thus been a tendency unconsciously to take these purposes from the existing social and economic environment, without critical examination. The emphasis on scientific technique, however necessary and valuable, has made much educational thought and practice less searching, less potentially critical of the existing cultural and economic equilibrium, than under different leadership it might have been.

But an even more serious criticism of Thorndike lies in the

[86] E. L. Thorndike, "Education for Initiative and Originality," *Teachers College Record*, Vol. XXIX (Nov., 1927), pp. 92–100.

fact that, while his social beliefs seem to be buttressed by the findings of experimental science, his generalizations frequently, according to other workers in his field, go beyond his data. In his social thinking he is an example, moreover, of his own doctrine of specificity. He has seemed in practice to be unaware of his contention that the discipline and meanings acquired in one field do not necessarily and automatically apply to others. One must question to what extent his social opinions are truly related, scientifically, to his experimental work, and to what extent they are determined by his own unconscious participation in the prejudices of our own time.

XV

JOHN DEWEY

1859–1952

Democracy has to be born anew every generation and education is the midwife.

—John Dewey.

Like Socrates he too has brought philosophy down from the clouds to dwell among men.

—William H. Kilpatrick.

I

John Dewey's work covers a range much broader than that of Thorndike, or indeed of any other psychologist or educator. So vast is it and so impressive in extent and quality that only a limited aspect can be treated here. We can merely attempt to explain his more important social ideas in terms of his own development; to ask how his conception of the social purposes of education differs from those of other educators, and in what manner the educational methods he has sponsored vary from those of his predecessors and contemporaries; and finally, to evaluate the main criticisms that have been made of his social and educational ideas.

It has been one of the most striking contentions of Dewey that philosophy has in considerable measure reflected, idealized, and justified some of the tendencies of its own age, that it has made much of the apparatus of reason and proof in order the better to justify rationally the "things that had been previously accepted because of their emotional congeniality and social prestige." In *Reconstruction in Philosophy* the position was frankly advanced that what philosophy had been unconsciously, it must henceforth become openly and deliberately—an instrument to clarify men's ideas as to "the social and moral strifes of their own day." Since Dewey accepts the idea that philosophy is made not out of intellectual but out of social and emotional material, and since he recognizes its functional character in actual life, we may well ask at the outset what social and emotional material has conditioned his own philosophy, and the uses to which he has dedicated it.[1]

Persons and situations, Dewey has told us, probably influenced his intellectual development more than books. All his forefathers earned "an honest living as farmers, wheelwrights, and coopers." The son of a merchant in Burlington, Vermont, he spent a share of his youth on a farm, and it was a rural rather than an urban culture that molded his early years. A democratic neighborliness and a sort of nonconformist individualism modified the social conservatism of the Vermont community in which he lived, factors that may well have contributed to his independent and democratic temper. Residence in Michigan and in Chicago during his formative period gave him a first-hand acquaintance with a type of life still colored by the pioneer heritage of social democracy.[2]

While young Dewey was a student at the University of Vermont in the late seventies, Professor H. A. P. Torrey turned his thoughts to the study of philosophy as a life pursuit; and William T. Harris, to whom he sent contributions for *The*

[1] John Dewey, *Reconstruction in Philosophy* (New York, 1920), pp. 25–26; *Character and Events* (New York, 1929), Vol. II, p. 437; "The Rôle of Philosophy in the History of Civilization" in Daniel Sommer Robinson, *An Anthology of Recent Philosophy* (New York, 1929), pp. 47–63.

[2] Author's interview with Dewey, Dec. 21, 1932.

Journal of Speculative Philosophy, encouraged him in this bold course. The New England culture which was Dewey's heritage was marked by a gap that set off labor from leisure and knowledge from practice, and by divisions that isolated the self from the world, the soul from the body, and nature from God. These cleavages, we are told in his philosophical autobiography, were an "inward laceration" from which arose an intense emotional craving that only an intellectualized subject matter could satisfy. In his junior year in college a book of Huxley's, used in a non-laboratory course in physiology, awakened intellectual stirrings that led to a partly conscious desire for a world and a life possessing the same unified properties as the human organism described by the English scientist. Running across Harriet Martineau's exposition of Comte, he became impressed by the idea of the disorganized character of modern culture, which the French sociologist ascribed to disintegrative "individualism"; and he was deeply struck by Comte's notion of a synthesis of science that should be a regulative method of organized social life.[3]

Dewey did not discover until many years later that Emerson had achieved a synthesis which tested ideas and values by the service rendered to present and immediate experiences; and that the philosopher of Concord, moreover, stood "for restoring to the common man that which in the name of religion, of philosophy, of art and of morality, has been embezzled from the common store and appropriated to sectarian and class use."[4] Although transcendentalism had in a real sense originated at the University of Vermont some fifty years

[3] John Dewey, "From Absolutism to Experimentalism," in George P. Adams and William Pepperell Montague, eds., *Contemporary American Philosophy, Personal Statements* (London, 1930), Vol. II, pp. 16–20.
[4] John Dewey, "Emerson—The Philosopher of Democracy," *Journal of International Ethics,* Vol. XIII (July, 1903), pp. 405–13.

earlier, it was no longer a strong influence in Dewey's student days.[5]

When Dewey embarked on graduate work at Johns Hopkins University in 1884, he found there much enthusiasm for the work of Thomas Hill Greene and other English neo-Hegelians; and Professor George Sylvester Morris re-enforced his newly awakened interest in their stimulating criticisms of atomic individualism and sensationalistic empiricism.[6] The German philosopher's synthesis of subject and object, matter and spirit, the divine and the human, as well as his treatment of human culture and institutions, fascinated the young Vermonter.[7] Although the next fifteen years marked a gradual drifting away from Hegel, Dewey himself has admitted that his acquaintanceship with this absolute idealist left a permanent mark on his thinking.[8] The Hegelian conception that the social as well as the moral process is one without fixed origins and fixed ends, and Hegel's location of reason within the struggles of life, rather than somewhere outside, were never abandoned. The American philosopher's method of resolving apparent contradictions by pointing out the elements of truth in them and then envisaging the larger whole that embraces the contradictions has at least faint resemblance to the Hegelian dialectic.

Perhaps an evidence of Dewey's contention that philosophy is more largely made up of social and emotional than of intellectual material is found in the fact that, even during his Hegelian period, the conservative social implications of that

[5] Marjorie Hope Nicolson, "James Marsh and the Vermont Transcendentalists," *Philosophical Review*, Vol. XXXIV (Jan., 1925), pp. 28–50.

[6] R. M. Wenley, *The Life and Work of George Sylvester Morris, A Chapter in the History of American Thought in the Nineteenth Century* (New York, 1917), pp. 146, 151, 302, 313 *et seq.*

[7] *Contemporary American Philosophy, Personal Statements*, Vol. II, pp. 19, 21.

[8] *Ibid.*, p. 21. See also John Dewey, *German Philosophy and Politics* (New York, 1915), p. 95.

formal and schematic system did not win his allegiance. It is, of course, true that, unlike Harris, he had come under the influence of the more socially liberal English neo-Hegelians.[9] Rousseau's writings had also, apparently, made him explicitly aware of the influence of economic conditions, needs, and struggles on social institutions and relations.[10] Yet his own temperament and the Jeffersonian and anti-authoritarian elements in the American life around him, to which he sensitively responded, and which in a measure he expressed, may very likely have been in large part responsible for the surprisingly radical character of his social thought even at the height of his Hegelian period.

The fact that Dewey entertained a thoroughly democratic and even radical social point of view as early as 1888 is shown in his paper *The Ethics of Democracy*. At this time in America, in spite of the momentary popularity of *Looking Backward* and *Progress and Poverty,* it was not common to hold that civil and political democracy was meaningless without economic and industrial democracy. Yet this was the upshot of the argument of Dewey's paper. If democracy is to achieve the higher and more complete unity for every single human being, he wrote, it can fulfil that destiny only by substituting economic democracy for the existing economic aristocracy.[11]

Subsequent experiences confirmed Dewey in this forward-looking point of view. He was familiar with the Fabian movement in England, and when he went to Chicago in 1894 he became closely associated with Hull House and saw at first hand some of the evil effects of an industrial aristocracy. But it was

---

[9] John Dewey, *Outlines of a Critical Theory of Ethics* (Ann Arbor, 1891), Preface and p. 131.
[10] *Political Science Quarterly,* Vol. IX (Dec., 1894), p. 743.
[11] John Dewey, *The Ethics of Democracy* (Ann Arbor, 1888), pp. 25–28.

not until the muckraking revelations in the first decade of the twentieth century that he came to be more fully and definitely concerned with the contradictions imposed by the existing economic order on the ideal of democracy. Years later the failure of the World War to achieve an extension of democracy by political and military action, together with the Russian Revolution, was to confirm him in his conviction that economic democracy was an indispensable basis for political and cultural democracy.[12]

Meantime, for reasons not entirely clear, Dewey was, as he himself describes it, drifting away from Hegelianism and developing an integrated and yet growing philosophy and psychology which was applied first to education and then to an increasing number of other social fields. Possibly discontent with the socially conservative philosophy of the master Hegelian in America, William T. Harris, may have rankled in his democratic heart. Quite likely the increasingly obvious challenges to the democratic tradition which the rapid transformation from an agrarian to an industrial civilization offered, a transformation suggesting the need of conscious effort to realize democratic values on a new and almost miraculously changing stage, made Dewey discontented with the *laissez faire* implications of Hegelianism. But the power exerted by the theory of evolution, the increasing influence of all the sciences, and the biological psychology of William James in particular, probably did most to modify his thinking.[13]

In some respects the step between Hegel and Darwin was a

[12] Interview, Dec. 21, 1932.

[13] As late as 1887, however, Dewey was convinced that the "physical interpretation of the universe is one which necessarily shuts out those ideas and principles which are fundamental to ethics." Further, "we believe that the cause of theology and morals is one, and that whatever banishes God from the heart of things, with the same edict excludes the ideal, the ethical, from the life of man." *Andover Review*, Vol. VII (June, 1887), pp. 576–77.

short one: both conceived the universe in dynamic rather than in static terms. Yet Darwinism went even further than Hegelianism in substituting the concept of the process and the concrete "natural" elements of the world for the fixed, the final, and the transcendant. Moreover, the method of science, with its spirit of investigation and experiment, differed markedly from the dialectic of Hegel.[14] Thinking itself, instead of being considered the means for arriving at objective truths, became a secondary, functional process, a means of adjustment and an instrument for the control of the process of life. "The biological point of view," Dewey declared, "commits us to the conviction that mind, whatever else it may be, is at least an organ of service for the control of environment in relation to the ends of the life process."[15]

Above all, Dewey came to feel that, in the light of the doctrine of evolution, moral judgments are to be regarded as hypotheses for experimentation rather than as absolute principles.[16] In an essay on "Darwinism and Philosophy" he declared that Darwinian logic transforms intellectual problems by shifting them from an "intelligence that shaped things once for all to the particular intelligence which things are even now shaping; shifts from an ultimate goal of good to the direct increments of justice and happiness that intelligent administration of existent conditions beget and that present carelessness or stupidity will destroy or forego."[17] In other words, he

[14] In 1891 Dewey believed that Hegel represented "the quintessence of the scientific spirit." *The Monist*, Vol. II (Oct., 1891), p. 14.

[15] John Dewey, "Interpretations of the Savage Mind," *Psychological Review*, Vol. IX (May, 1902), p. 219.

[16] John Dewey, *The Influence of Darwin on Philosophy, and Other Essays in Contemporary Thought* (New York, 1910), pp. 1–19. See also Royal G. Hall, "The Significance of John Dewey for Religious Interpretation," *Open Court*, Vol. XLII (June, 1928), pp. 331–32.

[17] *Influence of Darwin and Other Essays*, p. 15; "Evolution and Ethics," *The Monist*, Vol. VIII (April, 1898), pp. 326–28.

threw overboard absolute, "idealistic" conceptions of reality and unembodied, transcendental values in favor of the colors and sounds, the joys and sorrows which constitute the concrete, meaningful experience of men and women.

But Hegelianism still influenced him. Four years before the publication of James's *Principles of Psychology* in 1890, Dewey's *Psychology,* which was primarily Hegelian, had nevertheless shown an awareness of the Wundtian principles and methods which Hall was making known to Johns Hopkins students. Dewey had praised "the new psychology" for bearing "the realistic stamp of contact with life" and for its rejection of formal logic and the legal fiction of mathematical analogies,[18] and he accepted the idea of the mind as a unit in its action. But it was Hegelianism that led him to cherish certain concepts which, notwithstanding the great influence exerted on him later by the *Principles,* were to be modified rather than abandoned. "In social feeling," he wrote in his *Psychology,* "we merge our private life in the wider life of the community, and, in so doing, immensely transcend self and realize our being in its widest way." The functionalist psychologists, with James and Dewey as forerunners, were presently to develop, on a scientific level, the Hegelian concept of the impossibility of separating the individual mind from the social *milieu.* Dewey's early doctrine of habit, formulated in his *Psychology* (1887), is a striking evidence of transition between Hegelianism and an objective biological psychology.[19]

Dewey himself has made a great point of the "new direction and quality" which James's *Principles of Psychology* gave to

[18] John Dewey, "The New Psychology," *Andover Review,* Vol. II (Sept., 1884), pp. 287–88. In an article written in 1886, "Soul and Body" (*Bibliotheca Sacra,* Vol. XLIII, April, 1886, pp. 239–63), Dewey declared, however, that the physiological psychology had revealed no new truths concerning the relations of soul and body.

[19] *Cf. post,* pp. 515 ff.

ßis thought. James's way of thinking of life in terms of ac-
ßion, together with his objective, biological conception of
ßhought, led him to see the importance of distinctive social
ßategories, especially those of communication and participa-
ßion.[20] It remained for the sometime Hegelian, with this fresh
ßutlook, to make concrete the social concepts of communica-
ßion and participation; and, with his own democratic tempera-
ßnent and background, the applications that he gave, in his
ßthics and in his social philosophy, were scientific and at the
ßame time humane and anti-aristocratic.

II

The influence of evolution, of science in general, and of
ßames's objective, biological psychology in particular, not only
ßontributed to Dewey's drifting away from Hegelianism; they
ßvere also important factors in his development of a new syn-
ßhesis. Having long felt troubled by the dualism in tradi-
ßional conceptions of science and morals, Dewey developed
ß'instrumentalism" as a critical method for inquiry into morals,
ßwhich, in the spirit of Hegel, are thought of as social rather
ßhan as individual. The philosophy of instrumentalism is an
ßttempt to adapt the scientist's technique of hypothesis, checked
ßhrough experiment and experience, to the problems of so-
ßiety. Existing morals and institutions, as well as new pro-
ßosals, are to be tested by their effectiveness in promoting the
ßullest development of all individuals in free association and
ßo-operation. Dewey argued that the very character of the
ßAmerican environment with its constant beginning over again
ßand its comparative lack of a traditional background of law
ßand social institutions, demands a philosophy of experiment,
ßf intelligently directed trial and error, rather than one based

[20] *Contemporary American Philosophy, Personal Statements*, Vol. II, p. 25.

upon *a priori* principles. But the chief argument for instru
mentalism, and its great value, according to Dewey, lies in th
fact that it supplies practical wants which traditional philos
ophy and science, in their aloofness from practical morality
have failed to supply.[21]

Any discussion of Dewey's social objectives must be both
prefaced by and penetrated with his unqualified repudiation o
fixed goals. Yet in spite of his adherence to the idea of a
open universe in which change and growth are the paramoun
characteristics, Dewey, in the concrete and realistic spirit o
instrumentalism, has concerned himself with proximate goal
or next steps. These proximate goals may be best understoo
by the specific criticisms which he has made of actualities i
the world about him.

Underlying Dewey's criticisms of practices in politics, in
dustry, education, and the realm of culture is a basic faith in
human nature and in the necessity of sharing values. As early
as 1888, as we have seen, he had sharply criticized the existing
industrial order for its fundamentally aristocratic character and
had expressed the belief that without economic democracy, social, cultural, and political democracy must remain barren
ideals. The following year, in a paper pleading for the application of statistics in the field of industry and finance, he noted
the tendency of wealth to breed wealth and of extreme poverty
to plunge the children of the poor into still deeper poverty.[22]
At the same time he made the uncommon statement that while
the attaining of wealth bore some relation to personal industry
and foresight, it also depended in large part upon forces of

[21] John Dewey, *The Significance of the Problem of Knowledge* (University
of Chicago Contributions to Philosophy, Vol. I, No. 3, 1897); *German Philosophy and Politics,* p. 129; *Reconstruction in Philosophy,* pp. 26, 124; *The
Quest for Certainty* (New York, 1929).

[22] *Publications of the American Statistical Association,* n. s., Vol. I (Sept.,
1889), p. 334.

ature and of society which the individual could not govern.[23]

With such a conviction it was for Dewey a natural step to egard charity and existing altruism as efforts to regulate the onduct of its recipients. In his *Outlines of a Critical Theory of Ethics* (1891) he declared that it would be far better to pro- ide conditions which, instead of postulating continual "social nequality and social slavery," would secure for the poor the neans of getting along without charity and altruism.[24] Al- hough he recognized that this could be done only by trans- orming the existing environment instead of by reproducing nd perpetuating it, he suggested no specific plans for such a ransformation.

Twenty years later, at the height of the muckraking period nd of Rooseveltian reformism, Dewey collaborated with his olleague, James Tufts, in the writing of a more systematic nd comprehensive *Ethics* (1908), which is equally drastic in ts criticism of existing economic arrangements and more con- rete in its diagnosis of actual social relations. In this book he aristocratic and class character of cultural values as well as f the economic system was criticized and the inadequacy of aissez faire clearly pointed out. In one of the chapters writ- en by him, Dewey stated that, in the name of democracy and ndividual freedom, the few, as a result of superior possessions nd powers, had in fact made it impossible for the masses of nen to realize their personal capacities and to count in the social order. As against the *a priori* claims both of individu- lism and of socialism the authors recommended measures to neet what appeared to be the needs of the hour, experiments hat seemed to be realizable and to be demanded by an analysis f the concrete situation. Dewey expressed approval for cer-

[23] John Dewey and J. A. McLellan, *Applied Psychology* (Boston, 1889), p. 151.
[24] *Outlines of a Critical Theory of Ethics*, p. 108.

tain measures restricting property rights, such as child labor laws, old age insurance, the recognition of the legal right of labor to organize, sociological jurisprudence, and other ameliatory measures. He probably shared the view of his associate who held that if capital evaded government regulation in the interest of society, public ownership of the great agencies for the production of the necessaries of life would be demanded by the public conscience.[25]

In the years since the publication of the *Ethics,* Dewey has not softened his criticisms of the class character of our civilization, and in some respects his analysis of its shortcomings and tensions has become more concrete and incisive. While many critics quarrel with machine civilization, he holds that the crux of our economic and cultural shortcomings lies in the fact that machine production is "harnessed to the dollar." Intelligently controlled for the benefit of the entire population, the machine, he believes, is capable of releasing from drudgery the bulk of human energies for the pursuit of æsthetic, intellectual, and spiritual values. He explicitly condemns the commercialization of recreation and spares no words in denouncing the prevalent tolerance of ugliness if at the same time it pays the owners. The high value he attaches to science does not blind him to the fact that it is frequently exploited by vested interests for the multiplication of profits. For example, as special interests and pressure groups elaborated increasingly effective types of propaganda for the advancement of private profits, he pointed out the grave dangers involved for critical inquiry and constructive social thinking and even admitted that true experimentalism cannot flourish when so many obstacles stand in the way.

[25] John Dewey and James H. Tufts, *Ethics* (New York, 1908), pp. 443–45, 461, 474–76, 481, 485, 540–41.

As the years went by, Dewey also became increasingly pointed in calling attention to the slender basis of security for the individual in the existing order, and in illustrating by concrete examples his idea that political democracy in America has become a shell that does not even hide the existing contradictions. The "hypocritical religion of prosperity" during the nineteen twenties did not mislead him. At the time he exposed its insubstantial and partial character and fought against its materialistic values. But he discriminated carefully between the common confusion of economic and materialistic values. In defending the priority of the first, he suggested that until there is something like economic security and economic democracy, æsthetic, intellectual, and social concerns will be subordinated to an exploitation by the owning class which carries with it the commercialization of culture.[26]

By 1920 the American philosopher freely admitted a belief that the class struggle is a reality in American life but deprecated it as a method for remedying undemocratic actualities. Yet he has missed no occasion to denounce what he thought was class injustice, as in the Sacco and Vanzetti case, or to promote a more effective and democratic organization and education of labor.

Perhaps Dewey's most clear-cut proposals for meeting the social problem are found in his political activity. Notwithstanding his conviction that the American people are becoming increasingly indifferent and cynical toward political action, he has courageously devoted his energy to the work of educating public opinion for a new party to be based on

[26] John Dewey, "The House Divided against Itself," *New Republic,* Vol. LVIII (April 24, 1929), pp. 270–71; William H. Kilpatrick, ed., *The Educational Frontier* (New York, 1933), Chaps. II and IX. See also *Human Nature and Conduct* (New York, 1922), pp. 116, 126–27, 146.

existing economic realities.[27] In 1928 he supported Al Smith, not because he supposed that the Democratic party could effect the economic reconstruction he believed to be necessary, but because he felt that his fellow citizens were not sufficiently educated to the need of the democratic collectivism for which Norman Thomas and the Socialists stood.[28] In a characteristically experimental way the League for Independent Political Action, with which he identified himself, called upon Senator Norris to form a new political party based on the concept of social planning and control, in contradistinction to rugged individualism and *laissez faire,* and devoted to human rights rather than to property interests.[29] When the Nebraska enemy of the power trust failed to heed the call, the League for Independent Political Action tentatively endorsed the Socialist candidates and most of the measures they advocated in the campaign of 1932. Above all, Dewey sought for the cooperation of people of all shades of opinion and of all groups who claimed to be devoted to the ideal of democratic collectivism and international organization for the riddance of militarism and war.[30]

Notwithstanding the more exact character of his recent political activity and of his remedies for the undemocratic evils he deplores, Dewey is still, as a true experimentalist, unwilling to regard his ideals and methods as final. Believing that the situation and the future bristle with unknowns, he trusts to education as the most far-reaching and fundamental method

[27] John Dewey, "Is There Hope for Politics," *Scribner's Magazine,* Vol. LXXXIX (May, 1931), pp. 483–87.

[28] Dewey also believed that Smith should be supported because of his humane spirit, his freedom from hypocrisy on the prohibition question, and because of the religious intolerance directed against him. "Why I Am for Al Smith," *New Republic,* Vol. LVI (Nov. 7, 1928), pp. 320–21.

[29] *Outlook and Independent,* Vol. CLVII (Jan. 7, 1931), p. 10.

[30] John Dewey, "The Future of Radical Political Action," *The Nation,* Vol. CXXXVI (Jan. 4, 1933), pp. 8–9.

of correcting economic evils and meeting social issues. Even in his latest writings, which seem clearly to recognize the need for changing the currents of social life that run outside the school if the school itself is to function adequately, Dewey gives to education a rôle of the first importance.[31]

Before asking how it happened that Dewey came to pin his faith primarily to education as the means of achieving his proximate goals of a more democratic society, the character of his relative objectives may be clarified by comparing them with those of his predecessors. Mann had visioned a society in which each person, regardless of his family circumstances, was to have an economic competence, in which education was to eliminate crime, economic insecurity, poverty, and misery. His attacks on the aristocratic and class character of society, and his denunciations of industrial capitalism, were hardly less explicit than those of Dewey. Barnard, without postulating an economic democracy, nevertheless resembled Dewey in his insistence that, through education, cultural values could be shared by everyone. Spalding had likewise recommended education as the cure for the rampant spirit of commercialism and economic exploitation. Parker, sensing the fact that there was "enough for all" if tasks and rewards were co-operatively and democratically arranged, advocated education as the means to that end. Among the great educational leaders we have treated, Harris, in his belief that the individual could fully realize his true self by accepting and identifying himself with existing institutions and arrangements, stands out in notable contrast to Dewey.

Yet none of Dewey's predecessors discerned so clearly as he the economic influences that govern social relations; none of them so firmly believed that cultural and social democracy is

[31] *The Educational Frontier*, pp. 318–19.

impossible without economic democracy, that existing attitudes and institutions in America are inadequate for the realization of economic democracy. Dewey, it is true, has had the advantage of living in a period when the relative equality of opportunity of frontier America was more visibly vanishing, and the forces of industrialism more rapidly crystallizing along undemocratic lines, than was true even in the time of Harris.

While Dewey's difference from other educators consists in part in his more realistic economic interpretation of institutions and culture, it must be in considerable part measured by his more comprehensive idea of the educational process and by his more specific development of its possibilities in "remaking social conditions into something worthier of man and of life."[32] But one can hardly understand how he came to rely upon education as a technique for social improvement, or what he means by the educational process, without having clearly in mind the basic principles of his psychology and philosophy.

When he brought together the individual theory of the mind which was current in the early nineties and the biological theory of society which Spencer popularized, Dewey modified both in a new synthesis. On the one hand he clearly saw the need of reconstructing the static theory of mind, which isolated it from the actual contents of life. On the other, he recognized the need of admitting impulse, emotion, and intellect into the biological theory of society, which frequently became atomistic and mechanistic. In thus recognizing that mind is conditioned by social institutions, an idea so often overlooked by those psychologists who concern themselves largely with reactions to the immediate physical environment, Dewey preserved the

[32] John Dewey, "Philosophy and Education," in Paul A. Schilpp, ed., *Higher Education Faces the Future* (New York, 1930), pp. 282–83.

Hegelian and Spencerian contributions. Because of this social conception of mind which he has consistently maintained, and because of his emphasis on the dynamic influence of intelligence in changing social institutions, Dewey has more logical ground for his faith in education than any of his predecessors.

Experimentalism accepts the functional conception that human needs and ends are the controlling factors in the acquisition of knowledge of objective things. For Dewey thinking is the means of achieving these ends.[33] Ideas are tentative, experimental plans of action. Thinking involves the seeing of the relationships between what we do and what happens in consequence, the means, in short, by which experience is reconstructed. All thinking originates, then, in a problem or a conflict, which exists because a felt need is unsatisfied. Of the hypotheses or suggestions for solution that occur, one is accepted and is, ideally, held tentatively until thoroughly tested. Thinking is complete only when tested through further observation and experiment.[34] It is this last feature that especially distinguishes effective and scientific thinking from dogmatic or makeshift thought; and for Dewey the problem of problems in education is to discover the means for making scientific thought more widespread and for giving it an ever deepening hold among the people.[35]

While Dewey's psychology has by no means remained static throughout his whole intellectual career, it is noteworthy that, even before he drifted away from Hegel, his conception of habit

[33] John Dewey, "The Bearings of Pragmatism upon Education," *Progressive Journal of Education*, Vol. I (Dec., 1908), pp. 1–3.
[34] John Dewey, *How We Think* (Boston, 1910), pp. 68–78.
[35] John Dewey, "Science as Subject Matter and Method," *Science*, n. s., Vol. XXXI (Jan., 1910), pp. 121–27. In this article Dewey also insisted that science must not only have something to say about *how* to do, but also about *what* to do. "Science as yet has had next to nothing to do with forming the social and moral ideals for the sake of which she is used."

was already clearly outlined—a conception quite as important in his theory of education as a technique for social betterment as is his theory of thinking. After speaking of the important function of habits in enabling the individual to make smooth adjustments to the relatively permanent necessities of life, he attached far more importance than James to the corollary: the mechanics of life being taken care of, the residual freedom enables the individual to have greater scope for conscious and purposive adaptation to new circumstances. "We want change, variety, growth. . . . [and] the ability to grow requires the conscious effort of intelligence and the active direction of will, and this can be given only upon condition that the automatic mechanism of the soul attends to all demands made [habit]."[36] Dewey was shortly to declare that if one were merely fitted by habit training to survive in the existing environment, he would not be fitted to survive at all, for social environment is changing and progressive. "Everyone must have his fitness judged by the whole, including the anticipated change; not merely by reference to the conditions of today, because these may be gone tomorrow."[37]

Dewey believed that the dependency and plasticity of the child can be in part preserved by education if the habits formed out of the flexible native impulses are weighted on the side of the formative and the dynamic. The original plasticity of impulse, which has no specific, necessary consequences, may be intelligently guided; on the basis of impulses new habits "more sensitively percipient, more informed with foresight, more aware of what they are about, more direct and sincere, more flexibly responsive than those now current," may be formed by means of proper education. The malleability of native impulses, the sole stock of original human nature, might also be

36 John Dewey, *Psychology* (New York, 1891), p. 115.
37 *The Monist,* Vol. VIII (April, 1898), p. 328.

prolonged if care were taken, in education or the reconstruction of experience, to prevent habits from becoming so fixed that they are incapable of being adapted to new ends suggested by new situations. Habits, in short, can and must be so manipulated that they remain co-operating factors in the conscious reconstruction of experience for human betterment.[38]

The doctrine that conflicting impulses or desires may be utilized, by intelligent readjustment and synthesis, for the formation of new habits, and the belief that old habits may be so modified as to become adequately serviceable under novel conditions, is given some important applications in *Human Nature and Conduct.* Unlike many leading Americans, Dewey maintains that capitalism is a social or habitual, not an instinctive matter, and that, therefore, it possesses no irrevocable basis in human nature. Similarly war is a function of social institutions and customs, rather than something natively fixed in the human constitution: pugnacity and fear are no more natively fixed than pity and sympathy.[39] Even romantic love is a definite sign of specific, historic conditions to a greater degree than it is an expression of an original, single psychic force or libido.[40]

Dewey's faith in the formative or dynamic quality of habit, intelligently guided, does not blind him to actual obstacles in the way of social reconstruction by the educative process. If conditions do not permit continuous and intelligent renewal of the pattern of habits to meet new demands, he says the renewal may take place by revolution. Unfortunately, according to the author of *Human Nature and Conduct,* far more energy is spent by intrenched interests in censuring reformers than in criticizing obsolete institutions. "The primary accusation

[38] *Human Nature and Conduct,* Part I.
[39] *Ibid.,* pp. 109–10, 116, 122 *et seq.*   [40] *Ibid.,* pp. 153–54.

against the revolutionary must be directed against those who, having power, refuse to use it for ameliorations. They are the ones who accumulate the wrath that sweeps away customs and institutions in an undiscriminating way."[41]

The short-cut revolutionist, on the other hand, Dewey argues, fails to realize the full force of the habits embodied in the institutions he would destroy. While a social revolution may effect abrupt and deep changes in external customs, in legal and political institutions, the habits of thought and feeling behind these institutions, which have been shaped by objective conditions in a willy-nilly way, are not so easily modified.[42]

Dewey's repudiation of class war is not based on pacifist scruples against force, since he justified its use to achieve democratic ends in the World War.[43] He admits that what is frequently condemned as recourse to mere violence may, under given circumstances, represent an intelligent utilization of energy. His objection to the use of class warfare to effect the goals he shares with Socialists is based in part on his horror of *a priori* principles which are incompatible with experimentalism, but more fundamentally on his belief that his doctrines of thinking and of habits afford a better means for eliminating classes and promoting social betterment.

III

Dewey's conception of education follows naturally from his belief that mind is a function of organic life and conditioned by the totality of that organic life including basic occupational

---

[41] *Ibid.*, pp. 167–68.   [42] *Ibid.*, pp. 107–9.

[43] "I have been a thorough and complete sympathizer with the part played by this country in this war, and I have wished to see the resources of this country used for its successful prosecution." *The American Teacher*, Vol. VII (Jan., 1918), p. 8.

activity, and from his conviction that mind plays a part in controlling, directing, and reforming social organization. The existing pattern of social arrangements, according to Dewey, is based on an orderly system of reactions to existing stimuli; hence that pattern may be modified by an intelligent change of the stimuli. The change is to be achieved by education, or "the continuous reconstruction of experience." Experience, or trying and undergoing the consequences of activity, provides the organism with intelligent foresight and is fundamental in the educative process.[44]

This psychological conception of experience and education is intimately associated with the theory of democracy. In fact, Dewey has regarded psychology as a tool both for understanding and attaining that ideal. For him, as for Emerson and Whitman, democracy is far more than a form of government or an expression of popular sovereignty;[45] it is an associated method of living together in such a way as to break down the barriers which separate the class which works with its hands from the class which occupies itself with matters of the mind.[46] It is, in other words, a way of life in which affairs are so ordered that the æsthetic as well as the intellectual and social self-realization of the individual in a community involves necessarily the equal self-realization of every other person.[47] In a democracy, Dewey urged in an early article, the determination of ethical values lies, not in any set or class, however superior, but in the workings of the social whole.[48] The needs of the

[44] John Dewey, *Democracy and Education* (New York, 1931), pp. 89–90.

[45] Dewey, in discussing political democracy, repudiated Austin's idea that sovereignty could be found in a certain definitely limited portion of society. *Political Science Quarterly*, Vol. IX (March, 1894), p. 42. For a critical discussion of Dewey's pragmatic conception of politics see W. Y. Elliott, *The Pragmatic Revolt in Politics* (New York, 1928).

[46] *Ed. Rev.*, Vol. XXI (May, 1901), p. 471.

[47] *Outlines of a Critical Theory of Ethics*, p. 131.

[48] John Dewey, "Psychology and Social Practice," *Psychological Review*, Vol. VII (March, 1900), pp. 105–24.

moment, in accordance with the ascertained truth of the moment, are to be met through "the free and mutual harmonizing of different individuals," the precaution being constantly taken that every person share in determining the conditions and aims of his own work.[49] When Dewey asserted that psychology is "a conception of democracy" he seems to have had in mind the communicative and participative processes through which individualization proceeds.[50]

The rôle of education in promoting social change can now be better understood. Every ideal, according to Dewey, is preceded by an actuality; but "the ideal is more than a repetition in inner image of the actual. It projects in securer and wider and fuller form some good which has been previously experienced in a precarious, accidental, fleeting way."[51] The ideal, for Dewey, is never an abstraction. The diversion of intelligence from attaining concrete, particular ends, desirable for the common good, to upholding vague moral ideas, has done more to establish inequality and injustice among men than brute love of power. In reality, he argues, the championship of the bare precepts of categorical imperatives has resulted in the use of intelligence to incorporate class standards of conduct, based upon uncriticized customs and established habits, into professed ideal codes of morals.[52] If intelligence were, instead, freely and effectively used, and tested by concrete results, then it might become far more potent than force for achieving true democracy.

If the reconstruction of habits be systematically pursued in a new type of education, then the class codes of morals which, under the caption of ideals, sanction the *status quo* would be,

---

[49] *The Influence of Darwin on Philosophy,* pp. 266 *et seq.*
[50] *Ibid.,* p. 268.
[51] *Human Nature and Conduct,* p. 23.
[52] *The Influence of Darwin on Philosophy,* pp. 74–76.

according to Dewey, criticized and finally eliminated; new and more democratic habits, based on the same impulses, would arise. Thus new needs of society could be met in an intelligent way. If asked for more specific indications of exactly how psychology and philosophy are to serve these functions, Dewey would refer the questioner to his concrete criticisms of existing schools and to his definite proposals for their reconstruction.

When in 1894 Dewey left Ann Arbor to become head of the department of philosophy and education at the University of Chicago he had already given evidence of his interest in the school. Possibly three years of high school teaching was the foundation of that interest. As early as 1885 in a paper on health and sex in higher education he had applauded the tendency to apply the exact methods of science to the problems of education and had called attention to the importance of environment, broadly speaking, in its various relations to education.[53] Four years later he had collaborated with James Alexander McLellan in writing *Applied Psychology: An Introduction to the Principles and Practice of Education*. In Chicago Francis W. Parker and Ella Flagg Young not only provided him with suggestions for the organization of his own laboratory school but often helped him translate his philosophic conceptions into their empirical equivalents.[54] By 1895 he was participating in the discussions of interest, which the Herbartian movement had aroused, interpreting the culture epoch theory,

[53] John Dewey, "Education and the Health of Women," *Science,* Vol. VI (Oct. 16, 1885), pp. 341–42; "Health and Sex in Higher Education," *Popular Science Monthly,* Vol. XXVIII (March, 1886), pp. 606–14. In contrast to Hall, Dewey concluded that the data at hand did not bear out the common belief concerning the injurious effects of higher education on women.

[54] John T. McManis, *Ella Flagg Young* (Chicago, 1916), pp. 120–21. Dewey is quoted as saying, "More times than I could well say I didn't see the meaning or force of some favorite conception of my own till Mrs. Young had given it back to me—I am referring even more to association with her as a colleague than when she was a student."

which the American disciples of Herbart were popularizing, and showing an alert interest in the child study movement. A few years later he was challenging the educational doctrines of William T. Harris, which he believed to be a fairly adequate statement of existing practice.[55]

The upshot of Dewey's criticism of existing practice in school education was that it overemphasized the mere symbols of knowledge; that it did not make ample use of positive and first-hand contact with experience; and, above all, that by failing to equip its pupils with the scientific and co-operative methods by which the spiritual interests of society are conserved, broadened, and deepened, it fitted the child to the pattern of accepted social attitudes rather than making him a conscious center for the criticism and reconstruction of social life. Existing classroom methods only partly succeeded in helping the small child to develop physically, to get along with other people, and to develop expanding interest in the new and the changing. Too much attention was paid, he urged again and again, to the acquisition of information, and too little to the development of responsiveness and sharing in common and pleasurable tasks.

The dominant position occupied by book learning in school education, while once justifiable, was, Dewey thought, no longer defensible. When a single small class had access to the exclusive knowledge of books, it was natural and justifiable for the new public schools to concentrate on providing the masses with reading and writing, tools essential to their participation

[55] John Dewey, "The Results of Child Study Applied to Education," *Transactions of the Illinois Society for Child-Study,* Vol. I (Jan., 1895), pp. 18–19; "Interest as Related to Will," *Second Supplement to the First Yearbook of the National Herbart Society,* 1895, pp. 209–55; review of Harris's *Psychologic Foundations of Education, Ed. Rev.,* Vol. XVI (June, 1898), pp. 1–14.

in the knowledge of the past. Now, however, the universal diffusion of cheap reading matter and the democratization of literacy did not justify such exclusive attention in the schools to mere book knowledge. In former generations the child, participating constantly in household and community activities, almost automatically acquired capacities for self-direction, leadership, and independent judgment. Now, however, social and economic conditions had so changed that he no longer developed these qualities outside the schoolroom, and education must devise new methods to inculcate them.[56]

Although the Herbartians were emphasizing moral education in a new and more realistic way, prevalent practice still assumed that the term "moral" designated some special and transcendental region or portion of life. But Dewey in those years at Chicago developed his doctrine that the school must relate morality to the actual conditions and problems of community life if it is to enable the child to contribute to the betterment of society. Character is to be thought of as social insight, social executive power, and social responsiveness—the organized capacity for social functioning. The common separation between intellectual and moral training must be broken down; the isolation of what is moral in the school must be so transformed as to be identical with what is moral in the social relations of the world.[57]

To effect this end, the school must be made into a social center capable of participating in the daily life of the community.[58] The way to prepare for a moral social life in the

[56] John Dewey, "The Primary-Education Fetich," *Forum*, Vol. XXV (May, 1898), pp. 315–28.

[57] John Dewey, "Ethical Principles Underlying Education," *Third Yearbook of the National Herbart Society*, 1897, pp. 7–33.

[58] John Dewey, "The School as Social Center," N. E. A., *Proceedings*, 1902, pp. 373–83.

world is to engage in a moral social life in school. In its function as a social center the school must, according to Dewey, develop morality by interpreting to the individual the intellectual and social meaning of the work in which he is engaged; it must further provide for bringing people and their ideas and beliefs together in such ways as to lessen friction and to introduce deeper sympathy and understanding. In addition, the school in its capacity as a social center must make up in part to the child for the decay of dogmatic and fixed methods of social discipline and for the loss of reverence and the influence of authority.

This idea of the school as a social center had been at least faintly anticipated by Barnard. For Dewey, as for so many of his predecessors, the school was to break down class barriers and distinctions. The new note is his insistence that these barriers are due to the traditional and false separation between knowing and doing, and that by their fusion such class distinctions can be in part obliterated; and that, particularly, the school is to reconstruct society by concentrating on existing, developing factors in community life which are not yet dominant.

The belief that school rewards and fear of punishments, with their undemocratic and competitive social implications, will not be necessary if children feel the glow of positive achievement in doing things together resembles that of Parker. The assumption is that co-operative activity will develop, not only the positive virtues of energy and originality, but also those of sharing and helpfulness.[59]

In Dewey's opinion another crying evil of the day was to be found in the existing curriculum. The Herbartians, as he

[59] John and Evelyn Dewey, *Schools of Tomorrow* (New York, 1915), pp. 298–99.

was aware, had brought to the front questions connected with the material of study, but their attitude reflected the pedagogue's view of life rather than the child's.[60] Slurring over the fact that the environment involves a personal sharing in common experiences, they exaggerated beyond reason, he thought, the possibilities of methods consciously formulated and used in the teaching technique; and one infers that he believed this to be true of their organization of the curriculum as well. The actual interests of the child must be discovered, Dewey wrote, if the significance and worth of his life are to be taken into account, and if his full development, the aim of a democratic and progressive society, is to be achieved.[61]

In his specific considerations of the curriculum Dewey, both on the elementary and secondary levels, has repudiated narrowly utilitarian criteria. Each subject is to be cherished for its capacity to fulfill the present needs of growing children— a principle which Rousseau was probably the first to lay down. The business of education is not, for the presumable usefulness of his future, to rob the child of the intrinsic joy involved in living each single day. Yet coupled with this emphasis on growth as an end in itself is the equally important consideration of the effect which a given subject produces in promoting social insight, interest, and responsibility for social improvement, qualities which bulk largest of all in the individual's full development. The curriculum, in short, like the methods and spirit of the classroom, must be designed to further the mental and moral growth of everyone in the group toward a full and rich personality.[62]

[60] *Democracy and Education*, p. 83.
[61] *Ed. Rev.*, Vol. XIII (April, 1897), p. 363.
[62] *Democracy and Education*, pp. 59–61, 226. "We are no longer concerned," Dewey wrote in *The Educational Situation* (University of Chicago, Contributions to Education, No. 3, 1902, pp. 78–79), "with the abstract appraisal of

Although no subjects possess inherent value, geography and history, according to Dewey, are the two great school resources for "bringing about the enlargement of the significance of a direct personal experience"—the two most effective means in an education which furthers growth in individual and social terms. Properly taught, geography and history provide "the most direct and interesting roads out into the larger world of meanings." History makes human implications explicit; geography makes natural implications explicit. History is to be an indirect study of sociology, "a study of society which lays bare its process of becoming and its modes of becoming."[63] Its ethical value, Dewey claimed as early as 1897, is to be measured by the extent to which it develops powers of observing, analyzing, and making inferences with respect to the factors making up a social situation and the agencies through which it is modified.[64] This social conception of history is to be contrasted with that of Harris and the report of the Committee of Fifteen;[65] and it is also to be kept in mind in judging Dewey's conviction that the school may become an agency for the remaking of social institutions.

Dewey is not among the radical educators who, under the influence of the doctrine of specificity and the apparent failure of the social studies to give students a realistic understanding of contemporary problems, support the claims of indoctrination. He has held that neither social nor economic isms should be taught in the social studies; but he has insisted that subject matter be made sufficiently specific and explicit to

studies by the measuring rod of culture or discipline. Our problem is rather to study the typical necessities of social life, and the actual nature of the individual in his specific needs and capacities."

[63] John Dewey, "History for the Educator," *Progressive Journal of Education,* Vol. I (March, 1909), pp. 1–4.

[64] *Third Yearbook of the National Herbart Society,* 1897, pp. 22–24.

[65] *Cf. ante,* pp. 337–38.

bring the student into gradual contact with the actual realities and democratic needs of contemporary life.[66]

Although not a pacifist, Dewey has disapproved of chauvinistic patriotism in current instruction in civics. His advanced views on international questions, including his pioneer work for the outlawry of war, led him in 1923 to favor a school program designed to promote international friendship. For such a program, considering the determined policy of isolation of the federal government and the reactionary nationalism of the K. K. K., friends of peace felt much need; but Dewey hardly went much farther than Mann and Parker in suggesting effective means for realizing the ideal of international peace through the schools.

In commenting upon the important place he gives to science in the curriculum, a place for which the technological character of the age, as well as the influence of leaders such as Spencer, is responsible, Dewey has been on his guard against making a fetich of laboratory methods. Recognizing that they may become a meaningless ritual, he has insisted that the function of science in the curriculum is to modify "the habitual attitude of imagination and feeling" in such a way as to create "an intelligence pregnant with belief in the possibility of the direction of human affairs by itself."[67] Science, in accordance with the philosophy of instrumentalism, is to be applied to social problems for the determination of objectives as well as for discovering techniques. Its findings, as the teacher should make evident, are to be used for the democratic promotion of human well-being. The dislike of employing scientific knowl-

[66] John Dewey, "The Schools as a Means of Developing a Social Consciousness and Social Ideals in Children," *Journal of Social Forces*, Vol. I (Sept., 1923), pp. 513–17; "Freedom in Philosophies" in H. H. Kallen, *Freedom in the Modern World* (New York, 1928). For Dewey's most recent and specific attitude toward indoctrination see *The Educational Frontier*, p. 71.

[67] *Democracy and Education*, pp. 262–63.

edge as it functions in men's occupations, Dewey says, is a survival of an aristocratic culture in which "applied" knowledge
was held less worthy than "pure knowledge." But in actuality
science is one of the most humanistic of subjects, since knowledge is humanistic in quality, not because it is about human
products in the past, but "because of what it *does* in liberat-
ing human intelligence and human sympathy."[68]

With such a conception of science, and with his insistence
that the curriculum is to be evaluated by its contributions to
present growth and joy in participation in group activity,
Dewey has naturally opposed whatever is narrowly utilitarian
in the theory and practice of industrial education.[69] To the
chaotic body of opinion regarding the usefulness or harmful-
ness of manual and industrial training, he brought, largely as
a result of the laboratory school he founded in Chicago in 1896,
an orderly and constructive theory.

Froebel, Ruskin, and Heusinger had anticipated Dewey in
his belief that industrial occupations in the school are psychologically and educationally sound. Dewey argued that, if the
child's knowledge began by doing, then industrial education
satisfies his native tendencies to explore, to manipulate tools
and materials, and to construct and create.[70] But such a training also provides that play for the creative impulse which in
the pre-industrial period the home had offered; it affords the
child the knowledge of the industrial world and of the funda-

[68] *Ibid.*, p. 269; N. E. A., *Proceedings*, 1916, p. 734. Dewey's faith in science
as an agent for the solution of social problems is well expressed in his remark
that "there is no industrial question that has not arisen in some new
discovery regarding the forces of nature and whose ultimate solution does not
depend upon some further insight into the truths of nature—upon some scientific advance." *The Educational Situation*, p. 86.

[69] For the development of industrial education in the United States see
Charles A. Bennett, *History of Manual and Industrial Education up to 1870*
(Peoria, Ill., 1926), and Lewis F. Anderson, *History of Manual and Industrial
School Education* (New York, 1926).

[70] *Democracy and Education*, p. 368.

mental processes of economic life that in times past could be obtained in the community.[71] Industrial training in the schools, as opposed to the factories, further offers a natural and therefore an interesting avenue to the study of the physical, biological, and social sciences.[72] The resulting culture provided by modern industrial occupations, based as they are on the latest discoveries of science, is not necessarily inferior, Dewey has held, to that of the traditional disciplines.

Dewey was more original in discussing the social effects that he believed might result from industrial training, which included commercial subjects as well.[73] Motives for acquiring information could be provided which, instead of leading to habits of competition and rivalry, would result in co-operative planning and sharing. Industrial occupations in the schools, if related to the cultural pattern, would bring intellectual culture within the reach of the masses; and in doing this, would help to break down feudally inherited barriers separating the vast majority who toil with their hands from the few who enjoy the more creative activities of the mind and the spirit.

But Dewey saw grave dangers as well as advantages in industrial training. When industrial interests began to demand special trade schools for the training of skilled workmen he was the first to sound an alarm. Educators, he declared, must insist upon the primacy of educational as opposed to mere industrial values, because the educational values represent the more fundamental interests of a society organized on a demo-

---

[71] John Dewey, *School and Society* (Chicago, 1900), pp. 21–26.

[72] *Democracy and Education*, p. 372. An important aspect of industrial education was found in the fact that it provided a correlating medium for other subjects.

[73] *The Educational Situation*, pp. 76–77; *School Review*, Vol. X (Jan., 1902), pp. 26–27. "There is nothing in any one study or any one calling which makes it in and of itself low or meanly practical. It is all a question of its isolation or its setting."

cratic basis. The place of industry in education is not to hurry the child of the poorer classes into his individual trade: "the ideal is not to use the schools as tools of existing industrial systems, but to use industry for the reorganization of the schools."[74]

To the argument of the National Manufacturers' Association that secondary and higher education infected students with "Bolshevism," and that therefore they would better be put into trade schools, Dewey made no soft answer. "The moral is evident," he declared. "The sooner the children leave school . . . the more they will be protected from these dangerous bolshevistic college professors, and the less dangerous will they be to 20 percent or more annual dividends in the textile industries of the United States, and hence less dangerous to the future of America."[75]

Fearing that industrial and commercial interests would dominate special trade schools if they were erected into a system separate from the ordinary public schools, Dewey fought tooth and nail the movement for "splitting up the school system."[76] It seemed to be an overt attempt to have the public school system legally and actually recognize the stratification of classes and adapt its administrative machinery, its course of study, and methods of instruction to perpetuate that stratification. The constant references by industrialist champions of a separate system of trade schools to the advantages Germany had derived from such a policy seemed to Dewey to be additional evidence that the captains of industry wished to exploit industrial education in the interests of the employing class and

[74] *Schools of To-morrow*, pp. 311–12.
[75] *Journal of the N. E. A.*, Vol. XVII (Feb., 1928), p. 62.
[76] John Dewey, "Splitting up the School System," *New Republic*, Vol. II (April 17, 1915), pp. 283–84; "Industrial Education, a Wrong Kind," *ibid.* (Feb. 20, 1915), pp. 71–73; "Learning to Earn," *School and Society*, Vol. V (March 24, 1917), pp. 331–35.

to condemn the children of the less well-to-do to a permanently inferior economic and social status. He believed that unless care were taken, the older divisions of "master and subject class" were about to be reinstated in a new and subtle form. Social and economic mobility, the wide and varied distribution of opportunities, the fullest development of the capacities of every individual regardless of his parents' status, these essential characteristics of democracy were, according to Dewey, threatened by the proposed segregation of poorer children in narrowly vocational schools.

A fear that industrial training, if it were segregated from the rounded education of the public schools, would duplicate and perpetuate some of the most unfortunate effects of factory work, also guided Dewey in his insistence on a broad type of industrial education. Schooling must not model itself upon the "automatic repetitiousness of machines." It must be broad and comprehensive, so that, in the inevitable monotonous stretches of work, the imagination might have worthy material of art, literature, and science upon which to feed, instead of being "frittered away upon undisciplined dreamings and sensual fancies." Industrial training, if integrated with cultural education and with progressive methods in the schoolroom, might help produce the type of laborer who would be capable of assuming greater directive power in his work and thus prepare for the democratization of industry itself. Although Dewey recognized that at best certain types of labor must be of a routine character, he believed that even these could be made more significant if the importance of such labor were realized and if those who performed it had greater control over the circumstances of their work.

In short, if the effort to isolate at an early age the children of the less well-to-do in narrowly vocational schools succeeded, if industrial education merely reproduced the automatic and efficient worker, without furthering his knowledge of and control over his work, then education would certainly fail to promote the social and cultural democracy which, at best, it promised. Education alone could guarantee a community of interest and aim, a free circulation of experiences and ideas, a "lively and ardent sense of common life"; for this reason it was the midwife of democracy, which had to be born each generation anew. If it were to perform its function, then the schools must become more, not less, democratic.[77]

Dewey did not stop with a criticism of narrow, vocational education; he has also opposed a close and literal application of science to educational measurements. Without denying the value of ratings, ideals of efficiency, classifications of students and the like, he has pointed out many of the shortcomings of the mania for measurements. Even if it be true that everything which *does* exist could be measured if we only knew how, that which does *not* exist cannot be measured; and it is no paradox to say that the teacher is deeply concerned with what does not exist. Primarily concerned with growth, change, and the transformation of existing capacities and experiences, the school has less interest in what already exists in the form of native endowment and past achievement than with what such endowment and achievement may become. Only if we are satisfied with the aims and progress of existing society, only if the schools are to perpetuate the existing order, is the attempt to determine objectives and select subject matter by the wide collection and accurate measurement of data a commendable procedure.[78]

[77] John Dewey, "The Need of an Industrial Education in an Industrial Democracy," *Proceedings of the Second Pan-American Scientific Conference,* Vol. IV (1915), pp. 222–24.
[78] *Progressive Education,* Vol. V (July, Aug., Sept., 1928), pp. 199–200.

In his latest work Dewey has pointed out that the application of factual science to education in general results in an educational philosophy which simply transmits and reproduces existing institutions, merely making them more efficient. In addition, it has had the effect of reducing personality to impersonal terms—with the result, in practice, of encouraging an anti-social philosophy.[79] In taking the individual out of the medium of associations and contexts in which he lives, in ignoring social bearings, narrowly factual science invites an educational policy in line with "an outworn philosophy of individualism."

IV

Before attempting to evaluate Dewey's faith in the school as an agency for the promotion of the proximate goals which his analysis of contemporary America demands, it is necessary to call attention to the qualifications he himself has made. The schools, although they are formal agencies for producing mental and cultural attitudes and values, do not, in his view, constitute the basic formative force. "Social institutions, the trend of occupations, the pattern of social arrangements, are the finally controlling influences in shaping minds."[80] But while the school changes in a reflex fashion with changing social conditions, it need not passively accommodate itself to exigencies forced upon it from without: it may by accentuating the more desirable of existing attitudes and ideals take a position in actively determining the movement of social forces.[81]

Education and radical social change, in short, are for Dewey correlative and interactive. Every improvement in the social

[79] *The Educational Frontier*, pp. 289–90.
[80] John Dewey, *Individualism, Old and New* (New York, 1930), p. 128.
[81] N. E. A., *Proceedings*, 1898, p. 336.

structure releases the educative forces of mankind and "gives them a better opportunity to enter into normal social processes so that the latter become themselves more truly educative." On the other hand, no social change, however slight or however revolutionary, can endure save in so far as education causes it to permeate the desires and purposes of the people.[82] In other words, by searching out and re-enforcing concrete patterns to remake society and enable each individual to realize his full potentiality in the changing and the new society, the school could become increasingly a dynamic, and decreasingly a reflexive, agency.[83]

To exert this leverage, Dewey has recognized, along with a host of educational predecessors and contemporaries, that education must be made more truly universal. His personal activity as well as his influence has been given generously to the movement designed to enlist federal aid for equalizing educational opportunities throughout the land.[84]

But unlike all of his predecessors, save Parker, Dewey has insisted that there must be certain fundamental qualitative changes in the schools. The schools on the whole have reflected the prevalent cultural division between knowledge and conduct. "Only the acknowledgment, first in idea and then in practical fact, of the intimate union of theory and practice, knowledge and action, can create a society having foresight and the capacity to plan so as to regulate the inevitable processes of change."[85] Even when lip service is paid to the new educational and social philosophy, Dewey writes, it too often means simply a new vocabulary for old practices and attitudes

[82] *The Educational Frontier*, p. 318.   [83] *Ibid.*, p. 36.
[84] John Dewey, "Nationalizing Education," N. E. A., *Proceedings*, 1916, pp. 183–89; "Federal Aid to Elementary Education," *Child Labor Bulletin*, Vol. VI (May, 1917), pp. 61–66; "Our Illiteracy Problem," *Pictorial Review*, Vol. XXXI (Aug., 1930), p. 28.
[85] *The Educational Frontier*, p. 302.

and a new means for justifying them.[86] Relegated to a formal plane, even Dewey's new theories are not, as he himself has regretted, applied concretely to the America of today.

According to Dewey the teacher must assume social leadership as a fundamental part of her office if she is to promote, through education, the democratic goal. Aware of the difficulty of resisting the pressure of conservative influences in a community, Dewey has, in word 'and deed, urged teachers to organize themselves in associations sufficiently strong and militant to protect their freedom to work for their larger and more difficult purposes.[87] After visiting the schools of Soviet Russia, he became even more deeply convinced that the large part played by personal competition and desire for profit in our economic life is the greatest possible obstacle to the selection of the embryonic forces of democracy for accentuation in the school—a selection and an accentuation necessary if the school is to accelerate the victory of the democratic ideal.[88] In his most recent words on this problem, Dewey explicitly recognizes that the experimental way of life cannot be fully established unless the right of every person to the realization of all his potential capacities, æsthetic as well as social and intellectual, is effectively recognized.[89]

Finally, Dewey himself, in the spirit of his philosophy of instrumentalism, has worked for his ideals outside the schools. As an educator and an organizer, his influence has been important in the League for Independent Political Action, which has embarked on the task of educating public opinion to the need of a realignment of parties, and in the People's Lobby,

[86] *Ibid.*, pp. 33–35.
[87] John Dewey, "Professional Organization of Teachers," *American Teacher,* Vol. V (Sept., 1916), pp. 99–101.
[88] John Dewey, "Soviet Education" in George A. Coe, *Am I Getting an Education?* (New York, 1929), pp. 39–46.
[89] *The Educational Frontier,* p. 317.

which has championed progressive policies at Washington. In an impressive number of journalistic articles he has also promoted proximate goals by fighting, as in the Sacco and Vanzetti case, for what appeared to liberals as more humane and democratic solutions of pressing issues.

But even with these qualifications, it has been the school upon which Dewey has especially relied to promote his concept of democracy. The analysis made of his specific recommendations for the transformation of the school, in materials and technique of instruction as well as in spirit, suggests that unless these changes become widely prevalent, they can, in themselves, only very inadequately promote Dewey's proximate goals. It is at least open to question whether the schools, representative as they are of dominant interests, can function on an extensive scale in a way sufficiently effective to counteract the opposition inherent in the existing environment to the principles of experimentalism and radical social change.

Critics of widely different points of view have raised their voices against both the aims and methods of instrumentalism and experimentalism.[90] The inclusive, democratic, and socially radical purposes of Dewey's philosophy have been questioned by a wide variety of interests which refuse to accept his fundamental hypothesis of the desirability of these purposes. Those philosophers who have insisted that the primary function of philosophic discipline is to provide a haven of escape from the immediate and actual cruelties of the world represent a considerable body of opinion.[91] Avowed aristocrats and exponents

[90] *Elementary School Journal,* Vol. XVII (Sept., 1916), pp. 13–17; N. E. A., *Proceedings,* 1919, p. 718; Margaret Naumberg, "A Challenge to John Dewey," *Survey,* Vol. LX (Sept. 15, 1928), pp. 598–600; G. Stanley Hall, *Life and Confessions of a Psychologist,* p. 499.

[91] M. Cohen, review of *Essays in Experimental Logic, New Republic,* Vol. VIII (Sept. 2, 1916), pp. 118–19. R. B. Perry, in his review of *Reconstruction in Philosophy,* offers another type of philosophical criticism. *Dial,* Vol. LXX (April, 1921), pp. 454–57.

of the genteel tradition have been vigorous opponents,[92] and to the man in the street, as well as to a great number of teachers, the voice of science, as expressed in the work of leading educational psychologists and biologists, seems to condemn as a will-o'-the-wisp the democracy for which Dewey stands.[93]

Conservative individualists, however obsolete their position in the light of recent events, have been outspoken in condemning Dewey's democratic purposes;[94] and representative Catholics have likewise questioned some of his fundamental aims as well as his methods.[95] His own tilts with manufacturers' associations over the question of industrial education may be taken as a reminder of the fact that powerful, if not dominant, economic groups conceal beneath a lip service to democracy a fundamental opposition to it.[96]

In addition to the opposition of people who do not agree with his fundamental assumptions as to what is desirable, Dewey has also encountered the opposition of liberals who, while in general sharing his objectives, doubt the efficacy of experimentalism as a method for their achievement. Randolph Bourne, for example, in view of Dewey's support of the World War, wondered whether the tentativeness of experimentalism, its very interest in next steps, its concern with methodology,

[92] Professor W. H. Sheldon, in declaring that "we do not want the 'all-round' growth of everybody" and that Dewey's idea of participation of all in directing would be fatal to unique achievement, the beauty of division of work, and progress, is representative. "Professor Dewey, The Protagonist of Democracy," *Journal of Philosophy*, Vol. XVIII (June, 1921), pp. 309–20.

[93] John L. Childs, *Education and the Philosophy of Experimentalism* (New York, 1931), reviews and criticizes these arguments.

[94] Warner Fite, in Adams and Montague, *Contemporary American Philosophy, Personal Statements*, Vol. I, pp. 362–68.

[95] Joseph T. Barron, "Professor Dewey and Truth," *Catholic World*, Vol. CXVI (Nov., 1922), pp. 212–21; William Turner, "Pragmatism," *Catholic Encyclopedia*, Vol. XII, pp. 333–38; F. De Hovre, *Philosophy and Education*, pp. 103 *et seq.*

[96] Edwin C. Cooley, "Professor Dewey's Criticism of the Chicago Commercial Club and Its Vocational Education Bill," *Vocational Education*, Vol. III (Sept., 1913), pp. 24–29.

its very freedom from unyielding standards were not responsible for betraying it into a justification of a war which convinced pacifists and doctrinaire Socialists refused to support on the ground either that war under all circumstances is ethically wrong or that this war was in the interest not of democracy but of imperialism, nationalism, and profits.[97]

What has happened once, these critics say, may happen again. A willingness to take what can be got, they feel, often results in obtaining considerably less than is expected. A willingness to accept war in 1917 brought far less than the Wilsonian promises; a willingness to accept Al Smith in 1928 did not prevent the election of Hoover. Willingness to work with powerful forces, to look for next steps, assumes, it is maintained, that there is a strong desire for progress and change on the part of these powerful forces.[98]

Other critics have contended that Dewey has underestimated the power of "the cultural lag" and overemphasized the potency of deliberative and intelligent aspects of individual and social life.[99] Overlooking his own criticism of eighteenth century rationalism for its separation of thought and action, they have contended that he offers little more than the "philosophes" who expected reason to reform the world. One may suggest that a more serious obstacle to his conception of education than these critics have urged lies in the hindrances imposed to scientific solving of social problems by the pressure groups and propaganda methods. Dewey, although aware of the sinister character of propaganda, has possibly underrated its strength.

[97] Randolph Bourne, "Twilight of Idols," *Seven Arts Magazine,* Vol. II (Oct., 1917), pp. 688–702.

[98] For Dewey's denial that his philosophy is opportunistic see *The Educational Frontier,* p. 313.

[99] Ross Finney, *A Sociological Philosophy of Education* (New York, 1928), p. 478.

Still other critics have seen in Dewey's devotion to the democratic method of promoting human betterment an idealization and prolongation of the tendency of Americans to form mutual associations, such as the log-raising, the sewing bee, and the co-operative harvest, associations which at the time were spontaneous and truly functional. Now, however, it is maintained, commercial interests and pressure groups exploit this habit for the purpose of profits; and urban conditions have transformed the old neighborliness into the objective indifference of apartment-house dwellers. There is a good deal of truth in such a criticism. Indeed, it might be suggested that Dewey, in spite of the originality and great value of his interpretations of American life for the student of the social sciences, has underestimated the force of the aristocratic or Hamiltonian tradition in American life. Even the frontier, relatively democratic though it was, very quickly came to know social distinctions based on the differences in economic status of its early pioneers.

Other critics have contended that, with production and distribution based as they are on a desire for profits, Dewey's ideal of breaking down the separation between the more creative and the more routine tasks cannot be realized by so simple a device as a new type of school and adult political education. They have wondered whether unskilled labor, such as the necessary work in sewers, the care of blast furnaces, and the disposal of garbage, to say nothing of the monotonous tending of a machine, could be made as pleasurable as Dewey supposes by enlightening the participants concerning its social value and increasing their control, within the given system, of the conditions of their work. These critics, however, have partly misunderstood Dewey; and he himself has lately become more clearly aware of the obstacles imposed by the profit motive to the realization of his democratic conception of work and life.

Dewey has recently answered his liberal critics with much effectiveness.[100] It may still be questioned, however, whether in view of the power of certain of the conservatives who have challenged his fundamental hypotheses regarding democracy as a goal and intelligence as a means to that end, the cards may not be in some measure stacked against both the objective and the method. At least certain critics have felt that if the hypotheses of democracy and intelligent action are to be given a fair chance in the actual framework of competing situations and forces, a championship more militant than education may be required.

Dewey himself has faced this question and given an answer. Admitting that, in specific instances, to be determined in an experimental way, other and more immediate techniques, including mass action and even revolution, may be utilized,[101] he has insisted that judgments in regard to proximate courses of action must be determined, not by prejudged philosophies, but by the best available knowledge of actual conditions and the concrete situations at hand.[102] In other words, goals, to be effective, must be able to guide one to the next mileposts. Ends are continuous with means: ends stated without verifiable consideration of the immediate means are utopias to which no known paths lead.

Dewey would admit that the philosophy of instrumentalism, and the weight it attaches to education as the technique of

[100] *The Educational Frontier*, pp. 310–19. Sidney Hook has also answered the critics of Dewey in an engaging manner. *New Republic*, Vol. LXVII (June 3, 1931), p. 73.

[101] Dewey has recalled that both Jefferson and Lincoln believed in the right of the people to change their institutions by revolution for the promotion of the common good. *The Educational Frontier*, p. 43.

[102] For Dewey's most recent analysis of American experience in relation to his objectives and methods see *The Educational Frontier*, Chap. II.

social betterment, involves risky experiments and the possibility of failure. He would admit, with Mann, that sometimes short-run contingencies arise when the battle of human betterment cannot be fought effectively with formal education as the instrument. But he has not discovered a promising revolutionary situation in contemporary America. He is unwilling to say at the present time just what means must be utilized to achieve democracy in America. The quest for certainty, he feels, when all is said and done, leads too often to a mistaken and barren kind of assurance. At best, creative statecraft in education, politics, and industry may without revolutionary violence transform the possibilities of the present into the actualities of the future. And Dewey, whether by decree of the gods or by sensitiveness to the American mood, takes an optimistic view.

POST–WAR PATTERNS

For some two decades now the dominant stress in study and research has been laid upon the scientific and impersonal aspects of education, with a resulting accumulation of techniques and procedures which largely ignore any social outlook and bearing. Indeed the net effect has often been anti-social in that many have been led to believe that a scientific and statistical treatment of facts as such would supply all needed direction and aim.

—WILLIAM H. KILPATRICK, 1933.

The social thought of American educational leaders was appreciably influenced by our participation in the World War and by its aftermath. Some of the tendencies which the war accelerated and heightened were already definitely in the air and undoubtedly would have attracted increasing attention had the decision of 1917 been otherwise. Some issues that arose during the war proved to be temporary in character. Others continued, long after the armistice, to concern and sometimes to confuse educational leaders.

Of the tendencies which the war heightened and acceler-ated, none were so important as the concern with child health and welfare, with the greater efficiency of the school plant, and with the promotion of training for citizenship and espe-cially for the more obviously practical vocations. The pre-war movement for Americanizing the immigrant was given great impetus after the war by the demand for the elimination of "hyphenated Americans." In general, the states and the schools took over the Americanization work which had been in considerable part in the hands of such voluntary organizations as the Y. M. C. A.

Other issues which consumed much energy and thought, such as the problem of military training in the schools, proved to be temporary. This was also more or less true of the virulent reaction against German standards and influences in American education, although it seemed likely that never again would so much deference be paid to the educational system of any foreign country.

While the contributions of teachers and pupils to the winning of the war necessarily came to an end with the armistice, the war undoubtedly served to give the inculcation of patriotism a larger and a continuing place in the schools. After having expressed opposition to military training and devotion to internationalism in its resolutions of 1915, the National Education Association swung over to one hundred per cent patriotism in its next two annual conventions.[1] Throughout the war educators rallied with whole-hearted loyalty to the crusade preached by President Wilson. Even the most independent and liberal leaders, who had always insisted on the truth-searching function of education, men like John Dewey, welcomed the opportunity for an actual and a spiritual cooperation of the schools with society in the major problem of winning the war.

By instilling into school children the desire to help win the war by food conservation and by heightening general morale, by encouraging hatred of the Germans and devotion to the stars and stripes, teachers and leading educators gave evidence

[1] N. E. A., *Proceedings,* 1915, pp. 25–28; 1916, pp. 27–28; 1917, pp. 26–27; Erwin Steveson Selle, *The Organization and Activities of the National Education Association* (Teachers College, Columbia University, Contributions to Education, No. 513, 1932), pp. 167–72.

of their undiluted patriotism.[2] The N. E. A., in a resolution typical of American educational thought at the time, demanded the employment of only those teachers who proved their loyalty to our national ideals.[3] While the more hysterical aspects of this patriotism subsided after the war, the impetus given to the patriotic function of the schools has, on the whole, proved to be persistent.[4]

Just as educators after the Civil War felt and assumed responsibility for reconstruction and for the prevention of a similar catastrophe in the future, so after the struggle to make the world safe for democracy did other educators take on their shoulders the task of building a more truly democratic order. This was to be an order in which war was to be eliminated, in which illiteracy, a festering sore uncovered by draft statistics, was to be wiped out, and in which the challenge presented to democracy by the low I. Q.'s of so many enlisted men, the rise of Bolshevism and Fascism in Europe, and the slump of Wilsonian idealism everywhere, was to be met and answered. The proceedings of the N. E. A. and reports of general educational activity throughout the country indicate a more alert and persistent concern with certain social reformist movements, such as the abolition of child labor and the creation of international good will than was evident in the earlier period.[5]

In short, educators were stimulated to take stock, to re-

[2] Report of the Commissioner of Education, 1917, Vol. I, pp. 1–16; N. E. A., Proceedings, 1918, pp. 23–24; Arthur D. Dean, Our Schools in War Time and After (Boston, 1918).

[3] N. E. A., Proceedings, 1918, p. 25.

[4] Bessie Pierce, Civic Attitudes in American School Textbooks (Chicago, 1930), p. 254.

[5] For the relation of schools to the peace movement see Daniel Alfred Prescott, Education and International Relations (Harvard Studies in Education, No. 14, 1930); and Spencer Stoker, The Schools and International Understanding (Chapel Hill, N. C., 1933).

examine educational objectives and ideals. They were led, not-withstanding the general confusion in their own ranks and in the country at large, to wage a campaign for converting equality of opportunity from an ideal to an actuality. As a result, the concept of the social function of the school, an idea which, as we have seen, was by no means born with the war, was invigorated and given new significance and standing.[6]

This concern with the educational promotion of democracy expressed itself in a number of concrete movements, none of which was better organized than the N. E. A.'s Commission on the National Emergency in Education. Appointed in 1918 to co-ordinate the various types of war-time service work assigned to the schools, to find means for solving the problem of the shortage of teachers, and to study the relation of the educational system to the outstanding weaknesses of our national structure and life which the war crisis had revealed, the Commission continued its work after the armistice by framing a program and by embarking on a spirited "drive" for its realization.

Both program and campaign were more largely the work of George D. Strayer, professor of educational administration at Teachers College, than of any other single person. Attention was directed toward the securing of Federal aid for the removal of illiteracy, the promotion of health through the schools, the furthering of Americanization activities and civic education generally, the improvement of the status of the educational profession through universal and more effective teacher training, and, above all, the equalization of educational opportunity throughout the land. It also embraced the

6 N. E. A., *Proceedings,* 1919, pp. 22–27, 31–32, 81–88, 381–82, 545–47, 552–54, 717–39; 1920, p. 176; 1922, pp. 44, 215–16, 245–52, 683–85; 1923, pp. 447–83; *School and Society,* Vol. VII (April 20, 1918), p. 465; Vol. IX (Jan. 4, 1919), pp. 1 *et seq.;* Vol. X (July 12, 1919), pp. 33 *et seq.*

idea of a Federal Department of Education, with a secretary in the Cabinet.[7]

A movement for Federal support of schools in the poorer and more illiterate sections of the country and for a national Department of Education had enlisted the support of many educators and political leaders in the decades following the Civil War. But the crusading "drive" of the Emergency Commission, utilizing as it did statistical evidence and the various war-time methods of publicity, was much more comprehensive and took on something of the character of an effort at educational planning on a national scale. Various forces, among them the tradition of localism and the fear of national centralization, the opposition of Catholics to the extension of secular education, the resistance of large taxpayers, and the "return to normalcy" with its glorification of *laissez faire* defeated the bills in Congress; but the movement was of great importance.[8] It marked the frank recognition of the need for expansion in the schools if anything like true equality of educational opportunity were to be achieved. It insisted that education was a national interest and a matter for national planning. It gave more exact and scientific character to the traditional belief that democracy was to be realized through more and better education.

[7] George Strayer, "The Emergency in Education," *School and Society*, Vol. VIII (Oct. 5, 1918), pp. 416–17; "Why We Need a Secretary of Education," *Elementary School Journal*, Vol. XX (April, 1920), pp. 593–99; "A National Program for Education," N. E. A., *Proceedings*, 1920, pp. 41–48; W. C. Bagley, "Professor Strayer and the Emergency Commission," *School and Society*, Vol. XXXI (May 24, 1930), pp. 713–14.

[8] Report by Mr. Towner from the Committee on Education, "Create a Department of Education," 66th Congress, 3d session, *House Report*, No. 1201; L. T. Baman, compiler, *The Towner-Sterling Bill* (*The Reference Shelf*, Vol. I, No. 5, New York, 1922); George Strayer, A Reply to the Arguments against the Smith-Towner Bill," *Ed. Rev.*, Vol. LXI (Jan., 1921), pp. 65–70; *School and Society*, Vol. X (Aug. 9, 1919), p. 167; author's interview with Professor Strayer, Dec. 19, 1932.

If the Emergency Commission failed to realize its aims through Congressional action, it did promote the expansion of the N. E. A. by giving it a positive and an appealing program, and by resorting to the technique of the successful "drive." The great increase in membership involved the reorganization of this conservative association along somewhat more democratic lines; and this response to the general identification of democracy and education was at least a limited gain for the ideal of a more democratic organization of the profession.[9] The N. E. A. proceeded to establish elaborate headquarters at Washington, to edit an official journal, to institute researches into educational problems, and to assume a more energetic professional leadership.

This leadership, however, failed to satisfy all elements in the profession. One group of critics attacked the leaders of the Association for their alleged spirit of commercialism and desire for expansion in terms of dollars and cents, their evangelical and inspirational interference in questions of public morals such as prohibition, and their tendency to make a fetich of "professionalism."[10] Other groups, some of which found expression in the Progressive Education Association, attacked the Association for its social conservatism and educational traditionalism. They particularly took the directors of the N. E. A. to task for their refusal to keep the 1933 convention from convening in Chicago as a protest against the failure of that city to pay its teachers.[11]

[9] Fred M. Hunter, "Report of the President on the Program and Development of the Association," N. E. A., *Proceedings,* 1921, pp. 184–208; Selle, *op. cit.,* Chap. III. The representative assembly met for the first time in 1921.
[10] M. E. Bucholz, "The Pedagogues Leap to Save Us," *American Mercury,* Vol. XXVI (July, 1932), pp. 328–45; and "The Pedagogues at Armageddon," *ibid.,* Vol. XXIX (June, 1933), pp. 129–38 (by the same author).
[11] Clyde R. Miller, "Is the N. E. A. Missing Its Opportunity at Chicago?" *School and Society,* Vol. XXXVII (June 17, 1933), pp. 778–83.

The movement for the more active participation of the teacher in the administration generally, which was also stimulated by the war, encountered much opposition. Ella Flagg Young, who was a pioneer in her efforts to secure for the teachers of Chicago a greater share in administration, protested in vain in 1917 when the Illinois Supreme Court ruled that a city school board had the absolute right to decline to employ or re-employ an applicant for any reason whatever, including participation or non-participation in a teachers' council or trade union. The pre-war feeling that teachers' organizations should not affiliate with the American Federation of Labor was strengthened and given what appeared to be the scientific prestige of the expert when such an influential authority on administration as Strayer expressed clear-cut opposition to affiliation.[12]

Increasing reliance was placed upon the social studies as the means of realizing the social and democratic function of the schools. While conservative and reactionary pressure groups spared no pains in endeavoring to capture for their own ends the wider interest in the social studies, many educational liberals attempted to translate into practice the injunction of President Wilson, who had called attention to the part that the school must play in the post-war task of "purging and ennobling the life of the world." Partly as a result of the war enthusiasm over current issues and problems, the earlier sporadic interest in the democratic function of the social studies was now given an increasingly definite and at the same time comprehensive rôle in the thought of educators and in the schools themselves.

In 1922 the National Council for the Social Studies was

[12] N. E. A., *Proceedings*, 1920, pp. 93–99; 1917, pp. 292, 350–54; 1919, pp. 47–48.

established to correlate work in the field. Committees sprang up to further interest in the social studies and to work out concrete techniques and materials as well as objectives. Professional periodicals and educational programs gave increasing space to these studies, and it came to be a more general conviction that history, community civics, sociology, and economics could teach the rising generation to think more realistically and constructively on international as well as on domestic problems, and that the perspective and methods of history and the other social studies promised to equip the student with keener insight and discrimination. The increasing growth of educational sociology, which David Snedden had stimulated at least a decade before the war, and the social emphasis which Judd had long placed both on psychology and on its applications in schoolroom practice, seemed now to threaten, at least, the hegemony that had been held by educational tests and measurements and administrative engineering since the opening of the century.

The increased interest in the social and democratic objectives of school education is symbolized by the more explicit emphasis which Dean James Earl Russell seemed to attach to it during and subsequent to the war. Dean Russell, who became head of Teachers College in 1898, was more than any one else responsible for the development and emphasis of the educational institution which, it may be safely said, trained more leaders and exerted more influence on American education than any other American institution. Working through other men rather than directly, Dean Russell suggested and guided much of the distinctive work of the institution over which he presided.

Russell's pre-war work was primarily directed toward the professionalization of education. Thinking and planning in advance of current practice, he, together with Judd in the Middle West and Cubberley on the Pacific Coast, virtually transformed the character of secondary and elementary education. While other men and many complex forces in American life co-operated in this task, these three were chiefly responsible. They insisted on the introduction of research in the solution of educational problems. They set high standards for teacher training, for supervision, for administration. They attracted students and colleagues whose work departmentalized the theory and practice of education. The ideals of scientific precision, professional leadership, and ever more refined and controlled techniques in the whole educational process were translated, by their own work and by that of their colleagues and students, into practice. In short, in addition to what they themselves did, they symbolized the whole movement for the professionalization of education, which, in practice, resulted in specialization in the application of scientific methods to the study and practice of education, and in a concern for standards, methods, and techniques.[13]

These three leaders, it is true, had not ignored the social objectives and functions of education. Cubberley, as early as 1909, had forthrightly declared that, in the vastly more complex civilization that had developed, the school must grasp the significance of its social connections and relations, and must realize that "its real worth . . . lies in social efficiency."[14] In his contributions to the field of rural education he particularly illustrated the social possibilities of the school. Judd, who

[13] James Earl Russell, *The Trend in American Education* (New York, 1922), *passim; School and Society,* Vol. XXIV (Nov. 13, 1926), pp. 607–8; (Nov. 20, 1926), pp. 643–44.
[14] Ellwood P. Cubberley, *Changing Conceptions of Education* (Boston, 1909), p. 55. For an evaluation of Cubberley's educational work see William G. Carr, "Ellwood P. Cubberley: His Message for America," *School and Society,* Vol. XXXVII (June 10, 1933), pp. 738–39.

had built upon the psychology of institutions rather than upon the prevalent biological psychology, had been outstanding in his concern with the social implications of language and number, and had, in specific curriculum work, translated some of his social concepts into practice.

Even Dean Russell, who had been less social-minded than either of his colleagues and more narrowly bent upon the professionalization of education, had not overlooked the social aspects of the schools. He had given generous support and sympathy in Teachers College to the work of the pioneer sociologist, Snedden, and had not slighted educational philosophy as represented by Dewey and Kilpatrick. In his own writings, he had pointed out that existing practice did not in actuality give equality of opportunity to all and had suggested how this equality might be achieved. He had favored such vocational training as best promised to equip children with the means of earning a decent livelihood; but he had also, in the spirit of Dewey, insisted on making sure of the educational and cultural value of such training. He had by his words and more particularly by his deeds, furthered the concept that the schools must provide an education more completely adapted to everyday life. He had expressed the hope that the development of such a trend in education might help to solve such social problems as that of the conflict between capital and labor. The culture of today as opposed to that of a bygone period found in him a staunch friend. "The ethical import of professional service," he declared in 1908, "requires that the professional man maintain a healthy interest in his fellows." But in spite of these words and the early sympathy he had expressed toward the social function of higher education in Germany, Dean Russell had in practice subordinated social and democratic objectives to the ideals of specialized knowledge and technical skill, and to the ethical standards that he associated with the professional spirit.[15]

In 1918, however, Dean Russell clearly formulated a more definitely democratic and social objective for education. So long as we cling to our old habits of thinking and acting, he wrote, we shall never solve the problems of our new democracy. The new order demands a new philosophy, a new mode of attack. The democratic conception, which is engaged in an epic struggle with the autocratic ideal, imposes on each citizen the duty of being his brother's keeper. A survey of the recent history of education, Russell continued, raised considerable doubt regarding our pedagogical contribution to democracy; there had been too great concern with curricula, administration, standardization, and too little with "the relative worth and moral significance of the facts at our command." The new education must find and secure "justice for all" and guarantee to each "the attainment of what he deserves."

In wrestling with a new set of social and pedagogical problems, schoolmasters were reminded by the dean of Teachers College that "a government that shows it can take over the railroads and commandeer shipping fleets, will never again be helpless in the regulation of transportation; the power that can fix the prices of coal and wheat, will have the chance to try it again on a larger scale, when the majority so decrees; if subsidies can be provided to buy farms, build workmen's houses, and supply luncheons for school children, it is only a short step to public largesses for all who are hungry or in need of financial aid."

The era of free competition, Russell concluded, had passed;

[15] Russell, *op. cit.*, pp. 76, 83, 87, 97, 113, 119, 175, 199; *German Higher Schools* (New York, 1905), pp. 421–22.

the individual could no longer stand on his own rights, defining them to suit himself. The fundamental problem of the democratic state, in which the ideal of justice for all must be realized, is an educational one: "the problem of teaching the proper appreciation of life values and of training citizens to act in accord with the precepts of the Golden Rule."[16]

While it would be easy to overemphasize the social and democratic aspects of Dean Russell's declaration, it clearly expresses the conviction he had reached that the mere professionalization of education is inadequate. In subsequent addresses and writings he gave the social and democratic aspects of education still further attention. Unless teachers in the public schools and colleges, teachers in the press, the church, and the home, and teachers in business and industry assume new responsibilities, he wrote, discontent will develop and, like a fatal disease, infect great groups of our citizens hitherto exempt from the woes of the Old World, with the consequent failure of our experiment in democracy.[17]

After his retirement in 1927 from the deanship of Teachers College, Russell, who has been primarily a man of action rather than of words, expressed his conviction of the importance of promoting social and democratic values by himself enlisting in the cause of adult education, a movement which the war had greatly stimulated.[18] He regarded the movement as a means of solving the problem of technological un-

16 James Earl Russell, "Education for a Democracy," *Teachers College Record*, Vol. XIX (May, 1918), pp. 219–28.
17 *School and Society*, Vol. XVI (Oct. 7, 1922), p. 408.
18 For the adult education movement see the publications of the American Association for Adult Education, organized in 1926. An important aspect of adult education is that which is endeavoring to discover the objectives for American economic life with special reference to the consumption of food, shelter, and clothing. See Henry Harap, *The Education of the Consumer, A Study in Curriculum Material* (New York, 1924).

employment and thus preventing the "breakdown" of the existing system and consequent social revolution.[19]

Charles H. Judd, head of the School of Education at the University of Chicago, must have seen in the new emphasis on the social function of education a vindication of a position he had long held.[20] Unlike most of the other American students of Wundt, he had chosen to emphasize the social rather than the individual psychology of the great German master and, partly, no doubt, because of the religious and missionary atmosphere of his boyhood, he had sympathized with the critics of the theory of evolution who insisted on man's time-honored separateness from the animal world of instinct.[21] Although, as we have seen, Judd stood with Russell for the scientific procedure in education and for its professionalization, and with Cubberley for the development of school administration, he had in addition been an outspoken advocate of the social concept in psychology, a concept which led him to maintain that institutions are a product of man's mentality and a controlling factor in his present life of far greater importance than his instincts and impulses.[22]

Although Judd's emphasis upon the co-operative character of intelligence and social life contrasted with the extreme individualism of many of his educational colleagues, his social

[19] James Earl Russell, "Education as a Remediable Factor" in M. A. Cartwright, ed., *Unemployment and Adult Education* (New York, 1931), pp. 58–59.

[20] In addition to his emphasis upon the social studies and his important work in elaborating techniques for school surveys, Judd has stood out against the segregation of technical from academic high schools, the making of curriculums by legislatures and pressure groups, and the more individualistic aspects of progressive education. He has also concerned himself with studies designed to gauge the social implications of standard school subjects.

[21] Carl A. Murchison, ed., *History of Psychology in Autobiography* (London, 1930–32), Vol. II, pp. 207, 218–19.

[22] See his *Psychology of Social Institutions* (New York, 1926).

thinking nevertheless lacked the radical character of Dewey's instrumentalism. This was doubtless in part due to the fact that his very concern with the more general and abstract cooperative elements in life, such as the evolution of weights, measures, numbers, and languages, led him to underestimate actual strifes and specific struggles in the America of his own day. His conception of existing institutions as embodiments of the accumulative intelligence of the past might easily lead many who came under its influence to support the *status quo* out of respect for the established practices of mankind.

The World War not only led Judd to criticize severely certain undemocratic aspects of American education, which he insisted had been unfortunately borrowed from autocratic Prussia; it also enlisted his efforts to provide new and concrete materials for the promotion of democratic and social objectives through the schools.[23] In editing, with Professor L. C. Marshall, a series of pamphlets, *Lessons in Community and National Life* (1918), Judd endeavored to give concrete illustrations of the co-operative character of intelligence and social life. While most of the material was non-controversial and designed to familiarize the student with the social aspects of American life, the *Lessons* also dealt frankly with the question of unemployment and critically considered some of the more ticklish problems of a profit-making society.[24] As a result the Industrial Conference Board vehemently protested

[23] Charles H. Judd, "Industry and the Liberal Arts," *School and Society,* Vol. VIII (Aug. 10, 1918), pp. 151–64; "The Teaching of Civics," *School Review,* Vol. XXVI (Sept., 1918), pp. 511–32; *Democracy and American Schools* (Chicago, 1918); *Evolution of a Democratic School System* (Boston, 1918); N. E. A., *Proceedings,* 1920, p. 168; "Some Constructive Principles of Reorganization," *Elementary School Journal,* Vol. XXIII (Feb., 1923), pp. 413–22.

[24] Charles H. Judd and L. C. Marshall, eds., *Lessons in Community and National Life* (Washington, 1918), pp. 51–60, 84–85, 88, 90, 96, 241, 243–44, 248.

that the *Lessons* inculcated radical ideas in young Americans, and their protests sounded the death knell of the *Lessons*.[25] It was at about the same time that Judd commended the platform of the British Labor Party.[26] After the decline of Wilsonian idealism, his own attitude toward economic problems became less definite if not more conservative.[27]

In his subsequent pleas that the social studies be made the backbone of the curriculum in the seventh, eighth, and ninth grades, Judd called attention to the fact that business organizations might oppose the introduction of controversial material affecting their interests. He suggested the importance of creating some agency of objective investigation strong enough to cope with the forces which might inhibit the introduction of controversial and radical material in the social studies. Yet his own essentially ambiguous attitude toward concrete economic problems was illustrated when he declared that the pro-power trust propaganda in the schools was less harmful than the exclusion of all discussion of public utilities.[28]

Other exponents of the social studies in the schools have been less content with emphasizing the social significance of such elementary and non-controversial material as the development of weights, measures, money, and numbers, and to a much greater extent have campaigned for material definitely

25 *School and Society,* Vol. XV (Jan. 7, 1922), p. 7; Vol. XVII (March 17, 1923), p. 282.

26 *Ibid.,* Vol. VIII (Aug. 10, 1918), p. 164.

27 Judd's remarks in Carlton Washburne, *Remakers of Mankind* (New York, 1932), pp. 313–14; "Programs of Social Studies for the Schools of the United States," *Elementary School Journal,* Vol. XXXII (Sept., 1932), pp. 17–24.

28 Charles H. Judd, "Scientific Techniques of Curriculum Making," *School and Society,* Vol. XV (Jan. 7, 1922), pp. 1–11; "Curriculum: A Paramount Issue," N. E. A., *Proceedings,* 1925, pp. 805–11; "Method of Securing National Educational Standards," *Educational Record,* Vol. IX (April, 1928), pp. 81–95; "Place of Research in a Program of Curriculum Development," *Journal of Educational Research,* Vol. XVII (May, 1928), pp. 313–23; *School and Society,* Vol. XXXV (Jan., 1932), p. 105.

critical of existing economic arrangements. Without emphasizing less than Judd the co-operative character of past and
present achievements, Harold Rugg, for example, has sought
to demonstrate in his textbooks how concrete lessons may be
taught in such a way as to develop a social attitude that is
critical toward the existing order as well as appreciative of
some of its achievements, an attitude that places higher value
on human interests than on profits. At the same time, in cele-
brating, sometimes in a rhapsodic manner, the need of such
social conditions as permit and encourage the free and creative
expression and directing power of all individuals,[29] Rugg has
supplemented the content of Judd's social thought, which, like
that of Harris, has paid less attention to the needs, values, and
aspirations of the individual than to his adaptation to the social heritage. It should be added that Rugg's position was
hardly typical of the advocates of greater emphasis upon the
social and democratic objectives of school education: for the
most part, especially in the reactionary years following the
war, they roundly denounced anything that seemed even
faintly to savor of "Bolshevism."[30]

One of the most significant developments to which the
World War gave marked impetus was that of vocational education. The pre-war movement was definitely inaugurated by

[29] See Rugg's *Culture and Education in America* (New York, 1931), particularly Chap. XVIII.

[30] N. E. A., *Proceedings*, 1918, p. 119; 1920, pp. 165, 244–45, 428; 1921,
pp. 275, 279; 1922, p. 45; 1924, p. 177; 1926, p. 657. An exception was the
statement of Edward O. Sisson that anyone who had "obtained even a glimpse
of unemployment and poverty, of the grinding hardships of industrial situations, can see that I. W. W. and sabotage are the ulcerous symptoms of deep-
seated evils in the body politic, and cannot be solved by jails and machine
guns." *Proceedings*, 1917, p. 283. The findings of the N. E. A.'s first Committee on the Teaching of Democracy, despite avowed opposition to "Bolshevism," were less socially conservative than those of the committee which replaced it in 1925. The latter turned to moral training and teachings that would
offset "dangerous political isms." *Proceedings*, 1919, pp. 717 *et seq.;* 1923, pp.
447–83; 1924, pp. 400–15; 1925, pp. 193 *et seq.*

the report of the Massachusetts Commission on Industrial and Technical Training (1906) and the organization of the National Society for the Promotion of Industrial Education in the same year, and culminated in the 1914 report of the Commission on National Aid to Vocational Education. These advocated government support for vocational training on the ground that such training is indispensable for national industrial efficiency, that private enterprise is no longer adequate to provide it, and that it will help eliminate labor troubles and social unrest.[31]

Even in the period before the war some of the exponents of vocational education maintained that it is necessary in order to realize in fact our much-vaunted claim that our schools provide educational equality to all children. As early as 1897 the existing school system was criticized for its functionally aristocratic character by William Hawley Smith, whose famous *Evolution of Dodd* had interested thousands of teachers in a type of education which could more flexibly serve the real, everyday needs of the average boy.[32] Others, like Dean Russell and above all, David Snedden, agreed with Smith in criticizing the schools for assuming that all children would profit by bookish training, which at best could equip a mere handful for academic culture and the professions.[33] The democratic implications of vocational education were increasingly emphasized, partly because of the trenchant criticisms of those

[31] *Report of the Commission on Industrial and Technical Training* (Boston, 1906); *The Prospectus of the National Society for the Promotion of Industrial Education* (1910); *Vocational Education: Report of the Commission on National Aid to Vocational Education,* 63d Congress, 2d session, *House Document,* No. 1004 (Washington, 1914).

[32] William Hawley Smith, "An Interview with the Shade of Socrates," *Ed. Rev.,* Vol. XIII (March, 1897), pp. 273–90.

[33] James Earl Russell, "The Place of Industries in Public Education," N. E. A., *Proceedings,* 1908, pp. 155–58; "The Trend in American Education," *Ed. Rev.,* Vol. XXXII (June, 1906), pp. 28–41.

who, suspecting the capitalistic inspiration of the movement, maintained that in effect it threatened to foreordain the children of the less well-to-do to the group into which they were born.[34] It was perhaps to meet this type of criticism that the official report to Congress of the Commission on National Aid to Vocational Education, after elaborating at great length the economic arguments in its behalf, insisted on its democratic character.[35]

While the war stimulated vocational education by identifying it with preparedness and the more efficient production of munitions and ships, it enabled the friends of the movement to gain wider support by maintaining also that it is necessary to achieve true democracy at home.[36] The alleged democratic implications of such education were especially upheld by the two most outstanding pioneers of the movement, Charles A. Prosser and Charles R. Allen. For years they had conscientiously worked for the extension of vocational education. Both contributed substantially to the organization of the new federal board which the Smith-Hughes Act of 1917 created to stimulate vocational education by the allocation of national funds to the states. Allen, although trained as an engineer, had engaged in school work only to find that the conventional curriculum failed to equip the vast majority of children for the earning of a decent livelihood, and as a result he began his active work for the cause in a New Bedford school in 1906.[37]

[34] William Noyes, "Some Objections to the Industrial Education Movement," *Progressive Journal of Education*, Vol. I (Feb., 1909), pp. 1–5.

[35] *Report of the Commission on National Aid to Vocational Education*, pp. 23–24.

[36] Charles Prosser, "Education as Preparedness," *School and Society*, Vol. III (June 3, 1916), pp. 796–98; G. F. Arps, "National Supremacy, Industrial Education and Co-operation," *ibid.*, Vol. X (Nov. 1, 1919), p. 503; David Rosenstein, "Recent Developments in Industrial Training," *ibid.*, (Aug. 9, 1919), pp. 155–63.

[37] *Charles Ricketson Allen, A Testimonial in Recognition of Service Rendered the Cause of Vocational Education* (compiled for the National Association

Prosser, whose father was a trade-union official, acquired, as a teacher, superintendent, judge in a juvenile court, and student of Snedden, a militant interest in vocational education as a means of rendering service to those who worked with their hands.[38]

These men agreed in their social and educational philosophy. While they emphasized the economic advantages of vocational education, they also believed that it is the best means of promoting social efficiency, the well-being of the masses, and democracy. Frankly accepting the existing economic system as it was, they maintained that adequate training for the household, for agriculture, commerce, and industry would permit wage-earners to find and hold better jobs, and, in accordance with their talent and skill, to move ahead. Unlike Dewey and Judd, they have promoted a type of vocational training designed to provide wage-earners with practical skills rather than with the sociological and cultural background of their vocations. They have also held that vocational schools must avoid the discussion of all controversial social and economic questions, including that of collective bargaining.[39] The practical effect of this position was to align them with the *status quo*.

Without discussing the perplexing technical questions that have arisen in connection with industrial training, it may be pointed out that it has become increasingly concerned with adult wage-earners rather than with the training of adolescent

of State Directors of Vocational Education, n. p., n. d.); Charles A. Prosser, "A Tribute to Charles R. Allen," *Industrial Education Magazine,* Vol. XXX (Oct., 1928), p. 121; interview with Doctor Allen, Dec. 21, 1932.

[38] Editorial, "Charles A. Prosser," *Manual Training and Vocational Education,* Vol. XVI (June, 1915), pp. 636–37; statement of Doctor Prosser.

[39] Statement of Doctor Prosser and interview with Doctor Allen. For an exposition of their educational and social philosophy see their joint writings, *Vocational Education in a Democracy* (New York, 1925) and *Have We Kept the Faith?* (New York, 1929).

workers, an emphasis supported by Thorndike's findings on
the ineffectiveness of "general training" and on the ability of
adults to learn new techniques. It is also noteworthy that, in
its work with pre-occupational training, it has, in what has
seemed to its exponents a spirit of realism, endeavored to provide typical rather than ideal shop conditions. It has also, by
necessity, confined its attention to the skilled and semi-skilled
trades, thus leaving out of account the vast numbers of unskilled workers. In solving its technical problems, and in adjusting itself to the existing economic organization, leaders of
the movement continued, in the years of relative prosperity following the collapse of Wilsonian democracy, to talk in terms of
democracy without making any pretense of helping to democ-
ratize industry or even of alleviating any of its shortcomings.[40]

With a few notable exceptions, the tone of educational
thought lost its social liberalism as the country swung "back
to normalcy" and as relative prosperity, at least for the more
favored groups, pushed back stage the high ideals of democracy
which Wilson's leadership during the war and immediately
after the armistice had stimulated. Educators again concerned
themselves with problems of expansion, administration, tests
and measurements, and curriculum making. Even the increasing interest in educational sociology, like that in the social
studies, revealed, on the whole, a conservative philosophy.

It is true that the liberal social philosophy of Dewey was, due
in large part to the influence of such men as Kilpatrick, Counts,
and Newlon, making itself felt among teachers. Kilpatrick,
exploring democratic ideals and ethics, unhesitatingly showed
how they are emasculated by traditions and by vested interests,

[40] *Vocational Education in a Democracy,* pp. 201–2, 134–36; Charles Pros-
ser, "Industrial Education and the Changing Job" in N. Riccardi and Ira W.
Kibby, *Readings in Vocational Education: Trade and Industrial Aspect* (New
York, 1932), pp. 552–59.

and insisted that creative, integrated personalities can be achieved only through genuine sharing of social activities. If his call for humane and intelligent control over a rapidly changing world was too general to endow many with militant and socially effective zeal in basic economic and cultural conflicts, his teaching definitely challenged the social structure as well as existing educational aims and procedure.

It is also true that a small group in the camp of progressive education began to criticize that movement for its class character and for its primary concern with the spontaneous expression and rich development of individual children, and to insist that its ideals of democracy cannot be realized without more explicit attention to the actual social and economic setting in which schools function. It is also noteworthy that trenchant critics called attention to what they termed the lock-step character of the public schools, the concern with materials and expansion, and the mediocre results from educational efforts. But until the depression, educators who failed to crystallize their social philosophy in explicit terms, or who were frankly anti-democratic, enjoyed the widest hearing.

Many examples might be cited to illustrate the anti-democratic social philosophy which during these years found expression in high places. There can be slight doubt that the imposing researches and generalizations of Professor Lewis M. Terman carried great weight notwithstanding the questioning of his interpretations by some educators, psychologists, and other writers.[41] "We have been too much swayed by the all-American feeling for the fellow at the foot," Terman declared. Insist-

41 Among early critics of Terman's anti-democratic teachings regarding the relative influence of inherited and acquired traits in determining intelligence, achievement, and character were Walter Lippmann (*New Republic,* Vol. XXXII (Oct. 25–Nov. 15, 1922), pp. 213–15, 246–48, 275–77, 297–98, 328–30; William C. Bagley, *Determinism and Education* (Baltimore, 1925); Margaret

ing that his data show that superior children are superior because of their heredity, and minimizing environmental factors in low intelligence test scores and in educational achievement, he urged the curriculum makers to keep primarily in mind the needs of the gifted child.[42]

The social philosophy of the group controlling the publications of the N. E. A. was, if less scientific in its documentation than that of the psychologists, equally conservative. One widely distributed pamphlet declared that "the free public school and American business are partners, each supplementing and strengthening the other." The pamphlet defended the dominant economic system and denounced as distorted the view which looked upon business as "a merely materialistic acquisitive enterprise." It "demonstrated" with an abundance of fresh examples the stock arguments that education trains efficient leaders and followers for the business world, promotes profits by making better customers of the masses, and secures the safety of property by creating an environment free from strife and otherwise favorable to business. "Setting aside all the important cultural, civic, and social values of education," concluded the argument, "the schools can easily justify themselves in their contributions to business."[43]

Even where educators did not deliberately set out to "contribute to business," many of them, by their use of business methods as well as their generally conservative social attitudes, ministered indirectly to business interests. This was particularly true of many educators who developed the field of admin-

Wooster Curti, *Scientific Monthly*, Vol. XXII (Feb., 1926), pp. 132–38, and *Journal of Criminal Law and Criminology*, Vol. XVII (Aug., 1926), pp. 246–53; and J. E. W. Wallin, *Problems of Subnormality* (Yonkers-on-Hudson, N. Y., 1917), Chap. II.
  [42] Lewis M. Terman, "The Conservation of Talent," N. E. A., *Proceedings*, 1923, pp. 152–58.
  [43] *The Schools and Business* (Washington, n.d.), pp. 22 and *passim*.

istration. Their work, which was in part a wholesome reaction against the corrupt and inefficient consequences of lay administration, possessed many merits. There was a place for fact-finding school surveys which determined educational needs. Much of the work of these educational engineers, who concerned themselves with the equipment and efficient management of school plant, the classification and progress of school children, the salaries and functions of teachers, and the effectiveness of existing curriculums and teaching technique, was admirable. It was natural for the educational administrators to borrow from business the efficient methods it had developed, such as division of function, centralized responsibility and control, and elimination of politics and special favoritism.[44]

The business character of educational administration had, however, certain undemocratic effects. As Doctor V. T. Thayer has pointed out, leading administrators have, in the name of efficiency, adopted policies that tend to eliminate the influence of the teacher in the formation and even in the execution of educational policies, to cement the alliance of the schools with socially conservative business interests, and to encourage the oversimplification of the educational process. They have tended to "view the school as an organization devoted to the dispensing of ready-made knowledge, much as a wholesale establishment prepares and assorts packages for distribution, grading them according to the needs of different types of consumers."[45] The administrators have also, according to Doctor Thayer, more or less unwittingly fostered the isolation of the school from life and encouraged "the conduct of education in such wise that children attend autocratically managed schools

[44] For a brief discussion of the early history of school surveys, an important aspect of administration, see Leonard Ayres, "School Surveys," *School and Society*, Vol. I (April 24, 1915), pp. 577–80.
[45] William H. Kilpatrick, ed., *The Educational Frontier*, pp. 226, 254.

where they receive formal instruction in what is deemed essential for participation in democratic citizenship."[46] All but the most far-seeing administrators were certainly under the temptation to become mere engineers who, in believing in the adequacy of scientific and statistical treatment of facts, overlooked direction and aim, and, by thus ignoring important social problems, became in effect anti-social.[47]

While the development of educational sociology as a special field represented a reaction against the emphasis on both administration and psychology, its most outspoken leader, David Snedden, regarded the problems of post-war America with eyes scarcely less conservative than those of administrative and psychological experts. Educational sociology, which was at first concerned with such special problems as the relation of education to crime, children in industry, racial groups, and unusual family conditions, came, largely as the result of Snedden's leadership, to claim far more inclusive objectives. Reacting strongly against what he called "the wilderness of aspirations, theories, and unco-ordinated facts" in which educators found themselves when they considered democracy, culture, social control, and the educative process, he has endeavored to develop an educational-sociological science which can concretely determine the objectives and techniques functionally valuable in the actualities of modern living.

Educational sociology, according to this leader, must point the way by providing educators with certain criteria and attainable goals, by analyzing concrete social groups, and by recommending specific curriculums for particular children. It must determine, through case and group studies and other sociological techniques, not only educational objectives with reference to postulated adult and social needs, but the means by

46 *Ibid.*, p. 228.   47 *Ibid.*, p. 257.

which these are to be realized. In opposing abstractions, such as "school and society," "the child," "education," and "learning," and in battling for "sharp, hard thinking" about the factors making up general categories, Snedden has emphasized a pluralistic approach to educational problems.[48]

In neither the analyses which Snedden has made of contemporary American society, however, nor in his specific educational recommendations, has he in any way challenged the existing social and economic pattern. Aware of some of the defects of political democracy and of industrial capitalism, he has admitted, it is true, that desirable improvements might be made in both. But these admissions have been moderate in character.[49] He has deprecated class struggles as a means of effecting improvements; he has decried anti-militaristic teachings on the ground that experts have not yet determined the deeper causes, the contributive processes, and the final social values or "disvalues" of war;[50] and he has insisted that the teacher has no right to teach anything contrary to the collective opinions or valuations of society, or its controlling majority.[51] In accordance with his belief that the function of the school is to diffuse knowledge on social problems which has already been determined by sociological experts, Snedden has believed that the social studies should be concerned with concrete and minor problems rather than with major and controversial issues.[52] The *Charter for the Social Sciences* failed to meet with his approval because it seemed to assume that the social studies

[48] David Snedden, "Sociology, A Basic Science to Education," *Teachers College Record,* Vol. XXIV (May, 1923), pp. 95–110; *Cultural Educations and Common Sense* (New York, 1931), pp. viii–ix.

[49] David Snedden, *Educations for Political Citizenship* (New York, 1932), p. 23; *Sociology for Teachers* (New York, 1924), pp. 216–18, 242–43, 270; *Towards Better Educations* (New York, 1931), p. 369.

[50] *Educations for Political Citizenship,* pp. 173, 180–81.

[51] David Snedden, "Liberty of Teaching in Social Sciences," *School and Society,* Vol. XIII (Feb. 12, 1920), pp. 181–91.

[52] *Educations for Political Citizenship,* pp. 10–11.

are ends in themselves, rather than "deliberatively functional means to the production of the insights and motives which may confidently be expected to produce desirable civic behaviors."[53]

Snedden's criticism of the educational philosophy of Dewey, Kilpatrick, and Bode for its failure to formulate sufficiently definite educational programs has not been the only point on which he has differed from these educators. In his attitude toward cultural and vocational education, he has shown an unwillingness to concede the possible cultural value of vocational training. In vocational education, which he thinks of in plural terms, Snedden visions man the producer; in cultural education, man the consumer. He separates the two, not because of any personal preference, but because he believes their separation an inescapable condition of modern life and industry, and that efforts to unite the two are utopian and unrealistic. The whole tendency of industry he sees as one of specialization; the cultural tendency of modern life is toward generalization. His conception of culture is not aristocratic or traditional; an ideal culture would differ for individuals according to their various abilities and interests, and it would be intimately connected with the actual world rather than with the particular processes in which the individual is engaged as a producer.[54] But Snedden's position is undemocratic in so far as it does not try to counteract the effects of unfavorable economic circumstances, which often prevent less well-to-do children from following vocations suitable to their talents and interests.[55]

[53] David Snedden, "The Social Studies—for What?" *School and Society,* Vol. XXXVI (Sept. 17, 1932), pp. 358–62.
[54] David Snedden, *The Problem of Vocational Education* (Boston, 1910); *Vocational Education* (New York, 1920); *Cultural Educations and Common Sense; Towards Better Educations,* pp. 418–19.
[55] For the expositions of educational sociology at the hands of other leaders, some of whom represent a more conservative, others a more radical social phi-

Using fact-finding techniques to investigate the actual relations of the schools to their social and economic setting, George S. Counts came to a social philosophy essentially different from that of Snedden. As early as 1922 Counts, struck by certain shortcomings in the existing economic pattern, challenged his colleagues to face the fact that American industry was, according to recent studies, honeycombed with inefficiency and waste; and that at the same time statistical investigations proved that incomes were not only grossly unequal, but, for the masses of the people, inadequate for the maintenance of a decent standard of living. Educators, Counts insisted, must concern themselves with the problem of the distribution of wealth; in his opinion the existing inequality of wealth is justified neither by ethics nor by economics.[56]

In a series of documented monographs Counts subjected to a searching scrutiny the generally accepted idea that the American school system is democratic in its control and in the opportunities it offers to all classes. He presented factual evidence, for example, to show that "in a very large measure participation in the privileges of a secondary education is contingent on social and economic status."[57] If the high school is really to serve every class without distinction, and at the same time to render the largest service to the entire community, it must, Counts maintained, either open its doors to all children, taking

losophy than Snedden, see Alvin Good, Sociology and Education (New York, 1926); C. C. Peters, Foundations of Educational Sociology (New York, 1930); Daniel H. Kulp, Educational Sociology (New York, 1932); Ross Finney, A Sociological Philosophy of Education (New York, 1928); John Kinnemann, Society and Education (New York, 1932).

[56] George S. Counts, "Education for Vocational Efficiency," The School Review, Vol. XXX (Sept., 1922), pp. 493–513.

[57] George S. Counts, "The Selective Character of American Secondary Education" (School Review and Elementary School Journal, Supplementary Educational Monographs, No. 19, 1922), pp. 148, 149.

care that all enter without favor, or else frankly close its doors to all but a chosen few, to be selected by objective methods and to be taught the meaning of social obligation.

In his monograph, *The Social Composition of Boards of Education,* Counts showed that, for the most part, their members were drawn from the more favored economic classes. This not only helped to explain the growing distrust of the labor movement for the public school. It also furnished important evidence that educational policies and their execution, so long as they were in the hands of the dominant interest in the community, a group likely to exaggerate the merits of the prevailing order and to fear agitations favoring any fundamental change in the social order, tend to result in the maintenance of the *status quo.* To prevent the school from functioning as the partisan and conservative tool of commerce and industry, Counts recommended that all important groups be represented in boards of education.[58] The significance of his analysis of forces influencing public education was enhanced in the study he made of the Chicago schools and the forces that controlled them.[59]

In another study, *The Senior High School Curriculum,* Counts studied the extent to which the public high school curriculum was being adjusted to the altered purposes of secondary education. Although significant changes were shown to have been made in some schools, nowhere, in 1926, had a program been developed in the light of the needs of American civilization as a careful analysis revealed those needs. A plea was made for comprehensive, critical, and careful experimen-

[58] George S. Counts, *The Social Composition of Boards of Education* (School Review and Elementary School Journal, *Supplementary Educational Monographs,* No. 33, 1927), pp. 81, 95–96.
[59] George S. Counts, *School and Society in Chicago* (New York, 1928).

tation to remedy the selective and undemocratic character of the secondary school curriculum.[60]

Feeling that a rapid transition from an individualistic to a collectivistic society was actually being made, Counts also considered the meaning of the traditionally American conception of "education as an individual right." His explanation of this conception in terms of the concrete forces in the American past was a significant contribution to an understanding of our cultural history. From his investigation he concluded that in practice American higher education is selective in a thoroughly undemocratic sense. The more fortunate classes enjoy educational privileges which the unfortunate, in their capacity as ultimate taxpayers by virtue of their consumption of goods and services, help to provide. The educated man, according to Counts, is not necessarily an asset to the community; he is in no sense a trustee of society. The individual of superior talent and special training should adopt an attitude of "thankfulness toward the great rank and file of common folk who till the soil, harvest the crops, delve in the mines, fell the forest, guide the locomotive, and in shop and factory and office fabricate the goods and render the services that society requires. To them he is indebted in considerable measure for that wider view which they must forego. If he sees farther than they, it is at least in part because he enjoys the privileges which they have provided."[61]

In addition to standing for the fashioning of an educational and social philosophy that would exalt all forms of socially useful labor and endeavor to effect a social reconstruction in the

[60] George S. Counts, *The Senior High School Curriculum* (School Review and Elementary School Journal, *Supplementary Educational Monographs,* No. 29, 1926), pp. 46–47.
[61] George S. Counts, "Education as an Individual Right," *School and Society,* Vol. XV (April 22, 1922), p. 436.

light of both the specific kind of democracy in America, and of a rational ideal, Counts was a pioneer in calling the attention of American educators to the educational and social experiments of the Soviet Union.[62] Perhaps it was his interest in the Communist theories of education and social change that led him, as early as 1926, to consider the relation of the school to social change.[63] The school, he observed, is not the sole or even the most powerful educational institution, and unless it is regarded in its proper perspective, its importance is bound to be exaggerated by school men. The school may, however, in a certain sense, play the rôle of censor, critic, and judge of social and other educational values and agencies; it may seek to correct the functioning of other institutions. While in general the school, being controlled by conservative social forces, may be expected to assume a conservative rather than a progressive rôle, while it may even be used by the privileged classes as a means of preventing social change, still it might bring about such change on a limited but important scale. To effect even that modest function, the school must, however, be given a freer hand in determining its policies and in selecting for emphasis the embryonic forces which might develop a better future.

In 1932 in the pamphlet, *Dare the School Build a New Social Order?* this point of view was explicitly elaborated. Counts maintained that, in view of the new economic and technological conditions which enabled sufficient goods and services to be produced for all, the age-long basis for property and the struggle for its possession is no longer rational; and that in consequence shifts in economic power might possibly be effected by other than violent means. He also argued that, with proper

[62] George S. Counts, "The Educational Program of Soviet Russia," N. E. A., *Proceedings,* 1928, pp. 593–602.
[63] George S. Counts, "The Place of the School in the Social Order," *ibid.,* 1926, pp. 308–15.

leadership, the militant organization of teachers for furthering social change, and the recognition that indoctrination of some sort is inevitable and may as well be used for broader social ends, the schools might, notwithstanding the limitations imposed by dominant forces, guide and even accelerate an improvement in the social order. This is the more possible, he urged, because of the revolutionary changes in economic life actually under way.

The very fact that in the pre-depression years of devotion to individualistic success and to materialistic prosperity such a challenging critic of the American school system as Counts did gain a wide hearing is itself evidence of his contention that education might at least help to shape policies and clarify ideals.

It would be a mistake, however, to suppose that the position of Counts was at all typical. In an objective study of the social attitudes of American educators published in 1927, M. H. Harper has disclosed much conservatism in the ranks of education and a notably greater conservatism among educators generally than among those educators who have had graduate work at institutions of higher learning. Even among a representative group of the latter, however, 51 per cent believed that among the poor many more fall short of highest satisfaction on account of too many desires than on account of lack of income; 41 per cent held that the practice of democracy as developed in the United States has no serious nor far-reaching defects; 33 per cent were of the opinion that in teaching the vital problems of citizenship teachers should so impress on students the approved opinions in these matters that life's later experiences can never unsettle or modify the opinions given; and 84 per cent agreed that teachers should strive to give students in our public schools an abiding faith in the Constitution of the United States in all its parts and principles.[64] A similar investigation of the social beliefs of school children revealed not only a marked conservative bias but also a lamentable lack of understanding of important social concepts.[65]

The depression of 1929 and subsequent years not only further supported Counts's contention regarding the class character of American education and the inadequacy of its control by business; it also, like the World War, made educators of every shade of opinion more socially conscious and more willing to assume new responsibilities for building a better and more truly democratic order. The depressions of 1837 and 1857 had stimulated some educators to assume special responsibility for preventing such catastrophes in the future, but the debacle of 1929 had more far-reaching effects.[66] The economic crisis, as Judd reminded his educational colleagues, "has made us all aware in a new and vivid way that schools are a part of the general social order and that the curriculums of schools and their methods of dealing with pupils are largely determined by the conditions of life outside the schools." In the past, Judd continued, educational leaders have looked upon business and politics as subjects outside their circle of interests.[67]

While such judgments expressed a good deal of truth, it should be pointed out that it was only in the later stages of the depression, when business support was increasingly withdrawn from the schools, that educators were thoroughly aroused regarding the educational, social, and economic crisis; and that

[64] Manly H. Harper, *Social Beliefs and Attitudes of American Educators* (Teachers College, Columbia University, Contributions to Education, No. 294, 1927), pp. 4–9, 80.
[65] Hyman Meltzer, *Children's Social Concepts* (Teachers College, Columbia University, Contributions to Education, No. 192, 1925).
[66] *Cf. ante,* pp. 78–9.
[67] Charles H. Judd, "Education, the Nation's Safeguard," *Educational Record,* Vol. XIII (April, 1932), pp. 99–111.

even then their attitude and program, with some exceptions, was more conservative than that which the Federal Council of Churches took in September, 1931.[68]

The reaction of leaders of the progressive education movement was more incisive and more explicit than that of their more conservative colleagues. Even before their schools or their work were appreciably touched in an immediate and concrete way, they faced boldly some of the most fundamental issues in the crisis. In general the depression accentuated the social tendency within the ranks of progressive education, the tendency for which Parker and Dewey had always stood, and to which some others, notably Kilpatrick, were responsive even before 1929. Leaders now realized that the concern of progressive education for projects unrelated to the actual economic and social conflicts of modern life had been carried too far; and, above all, that the concern of progressive education for the rich cultural and intellectual development of the individual child had overlooked the consideration that mere flexibility, the capacity to adjust to a changing world, left out of the picture social security, without which there can be no true individual happiness.

Many leaders of the progressive education movement accordingly followed Counts in giving up their opposition to what they had called the indoctrination of social attitudes more concrete than general good will and willingness to co-operate with others in matters touching no vested interest.[69] Kilpatrick, in a plain-spoken book, *Education and the Social Crisis,* declared that "reconstruction of experience" and the bogy of indoc-

[68] See addresses before the N. E. A. in *Proceedings,* 1930, p. 224; 1931, pp. 105–10, 111–12, 127–34, 177–81, 452–53, 626.
[69] *Progressive Education,* Vol. VIII (April, 1931), pp. 287–93; (Nov., 1931), pp. 543–49; Vol. IX (Dec., 1932–Jan., 1933), pp. 3–7, 8–11; Vol. X (May, 1933), pp. 268–72.

trination as well as aloofness from the urgent struggles of the day must be replaced by a more explicit social philosophy.[70] Counts himself redoubled his efforts to develop a socially militant attitude and organization of educators and teachers for guiding and accelerating a transition to a new democratic and collectivist order in which the "Jeffersonian" ideals of liberty, life, and happiness might in fact be realized in a dynamic way and on an inclusive scale.

While leaders outside the ranks of progressive education somewhat more hesitantly took a liberal and even rather radical social position, their reactions to the depression betray much confusion of thought. They seemed at first to be rudely shocked by the discovery that the promises of business leaders of a new and permanent era of prosperity had been so frail and so utterly without justification. But their attitude toward business, which in general they had frankly supported and even imitated as far as they could, did not become militantly critical until business had in many communities slashed school appropriations to the bone, until educational services were sloughed off and salaries drastically reduced, until teachers found themselves sharing their reduced pay with relief organizations, until much vaunted professional standards were thrown to the winds, until business leaders, their former heroes, derided educators for having overexpanded their plant and their services. It was indeed upsetting to find bankers, brokers, and industrialists making educators scapegoats for their own economic sins.

In no uncertain voice educators now decried the use of the pruning knife and organized a vast propaganda to spare the schools in the popular drive for economy. They demanded new systems of taxation and promised more economical consoli-

[70] William H. Kilpatrick, *Education and the Social Crisis* (New York, 1932).

dation of school units and more efficient administration. But disillusionment with business did not reach its maximum until 1932 and 1933, when 11,000 teachers in New York City found themselves out of work; when the pay of Chicago instructors of the young was $28,000,000 in arrears; when newspapers reported that 85 per cent of the schools of Alabama were closed; and when it was announced that, since 1927, malnutrition of children in New York schools had increased 55 per cent.[71] Then even the conservative leadership of the N. E. A. denounced the New York banker-power trust in words which would have sounded less strange had they come from militant farmers or left-wing labor leaders. The Chamber of Commerce was denounced in bitter terms as an enemy of the schools; while "greedy manufacturers" fared no better.[72] Outspoken educators, in words resembling those of Mann during the lean years following the panic of 1837, excoriated the rich, who, it was said, shearing the public schools of democracy, sent their own children to private "and far-distant centers of snobbery."[73]

But the sharp words and militant tactics of the former friends of big business did not conceal their confusion, a confusion the more understandable in view of the fact that educators had confidently preached the power of the schools to solve all manner of social problems, and in view of the further considera-

[71] *New York Times*, April 16, 1933; March 19, 1933; Dec. 3, 1932; Dec. 18, 1932; April 2, 1933. See also the N. E. A. publication, *Childhood and the Depression, A Look Ahead* (Washington, Nov., 1931).

[72] For typical criticisms and denunciations of bankers and business men see *Journal of the N. E. A.*, Vol. XXII (April, 1933), p. 109; Vol. XX (Jan., 1933), pp. 1–2; *School Review*, Vol. XLI (March, 1933), pp. 161–67; N. E. A., *Proceedings*, 1932, p. 68.

[73] Wm. Bogan, N. E. A., *Proceedings*, 1929, p. 151; John Dewey, *School and Society*, Vol. XXXVII (April 15, 1933), p. 475; Henry L. Smith, N. E. A., *Proceedings*, 1932, p. 27. A recent study shows that in former depressions legislative and financial support of the schools was maintained, and frequently was even increased. See R. S. Pitkin, *Public School Support in the United States during Periods of Economic Depression* (Brattleboro, Vt., 1933).

tion that they had been, at least in many areas, generously supported for their work. Their confusion was shown in their bitter denunciations of business while at the same time they made overtures to business for continued financial support. They declared that the schools, if they were not shorn of their worldly means, could help solve complex economic problems.[74] They asserted that the schools could prevent depressions by creating a still higher standard of living and cultural wants, by producing, in short, a mass of high-grade consumers.[75] Moreover, in words resembling those used by their predecessors a hundred years earlier, educators were again heard to contend that public schools, properly supported, were the best preventives of revolution.

The President of the N. E. A. and the United States Commissioner of Education expressed essentially this attitude, which one prominent leader voiced in the warning that the "ugly visage of revolt on a national scale will never appear in America unless our educational system is hampered and crippled so that eventually it can not adequately serve the needs of the many millions of boys and girls attending it." The remarkable lack of violence in the present crisis was claimed as evidence of the "intelligence and rightmindedness of the people" and as a reflection of "a high level of schooling."[76] The editor of *The Journal of the National Education Association* declared, in the spring of 1933, that whether America ultimately shall take the path of revolution or "the commonsense road of patient readjustment through political and social reform . . . depends in the last analysis upon the schools, upon the ability of the

[74] N. E. A., *Proceedings*, 1931, pp. 134–40, 110–12; 1932, p. 673.
[75] *Ibid.*, 1931, p. 133.
[76] E. C. Holland, *School and Society*, Vol. XXXVI (Dec. 24, 1932), p. 809; Joseph Rosier, N. E. A., *Proceedings*, 1931, pp. 177, 178–79; Wm. John Cooper, "Education and Business," *ibid.*, pp. 127–34.

lower schools to guide and stabilize the neighborhood and community; upon the ability of the higher schools to lead and enlighten the nation."[77]

In assuming new social responsibilities for a better ordered economic life, leaders of Catholic education did not lag behind. Under the guidance of the National Catholic Welfare Conference the liberal social philosophy of Father John Ryan, of the Catholic University of America, was translated into explicit materials for the parochial schools. In some respects, the social attitude and program of these alert if not entirely representative Catholic leaders was more tangible and consistently thought out than that of their secular colleagues.[78] An inspection of much of the material for instruction in the social studies in parochial schools, however, makes it clear that, in practice, the Catholic schools have taught a conservative social philosophy and a narrow patriotic type of civics; that, in short, a dichotomy of opinion on social questions has existed within the ranks of the church.

The parallel between the social thought of educational leaders during the World War and in the later stages of the depression is striking. In both cases, educators declared their readiness to assume new responsibilities for building a more just, democratic, and humane social order. In 1919 they had declared their intention of preventing the recurrence of war and of building a sound and beautiful international order; in 1933 they

[77] *Journal of the N. E. A.,* Vol. XXII (March, 1933), pp. 71–72.
[78] Reverend R. A. McGowan, "The School and the Industrial Commercial System" in *Bulletin of The National Catholic Educational Association,* Vol. XXVI (Aug., 1930), pp. 15–28; Doctor George Johnson, "The Need for a Catholic Philosophy of Education" in C. A. Hart, ed., *Aspects of the New Scholastic Philosophy* (New York, 1932), pp. 292–303; Reverend George Johnson, "The World Crisis and Its Challenge to Catholic Education," *Bulletin of The National Catholic Educational Association,* Vol. XXVIII (Aug., 1932), pp. 18–32; and sermon of Most Reverend John T. McNicholas, *ibid.,* pp. 6–17.

vouchsafed their desire and their readiness to prevent the recurrence of depressions, to eliminate technological unemployment, and to bring about, by means of economic security and, above all, by national planning, a rational order in which traditional American ideas were to be realized on a new and quite different stage.

Even the specific methods they proposed, as late as the spring of 1933, resembled those of 1919. More attention was to be given to the social studies. Some educators, as in the days of Wilsonian reformism, emphasized the presentation in the schools of present social and economic problems. Judd, however, in 1932, reiterated his conviction of earlier years that increased emphasis upon the social significance of numbers, weights, and languages would be of far greater permanent value than specific indoctrinations regarding the causes of ailments in the existing economic system;[79] and new lessons were prepared with that purpose by a committee of the American Council on Education. Adult education, which was called for in and immediately after the World War, was now to be resorted to on an increasing scale; and character education was to be informed with social insight and given more direction.[80] Even the brief statement of the committee of the N. E. A. on social-economic goals for America offered little that was new in its discussion of the kind of education necessary to realize its democratic and enlightened social, economic, and cultural objectives.[81] Perhaps the most striking difference in the methods proposed during the depression was the suggestion now made that educators

[79] Charles H. Judd, "Programs of Social Studies for the Schools of the United States," *Elementary School Journal*, Vol. XXXIII (Sept., 1932), pp. 22–23.
[80] *Department of Superintendence, Official Report*, 1933, pp. 241–45.
[81] *Tentative Report of the Committee on Social Economic Goals of America of the National Education Association* (Washington, 1933), pp. 19–22.

should sponsor the proposal for a national deliberative assembly of social and economic experts to pass objective judgments on questions which the country faced.[82]

Whether the spirit of revolt and social consciousness was more widespread among the rank and file in 1933 than in 1919; whether the disillusionment with business leaders had truly severed the ancient alliance between educators and business men; or whether, if prosperity returned, if the "new deal" of Roosevelt succeeded in its purposes, educators would forget their heated words and noble aspirations—these questions the future alone could answer.

[82] *Ibid.;* Fred J. Kelly, "The Place of Education in Social-Economic Planning," *School and Society,* Vol. XXXVI (Oct. 29, 1932), pp. 545–53.

CONCLUSION

Contrary to a quite general impression, educational leaders in every period of American life have thought of the school as a social institution as well as an agent for transmitting culture and for equipping individuals with the rudiments of knowledge. For the most part, however, the school system was not planned by its leaders in reference to other institutions, or on the basis of a realistic analysis of social actualities and social needs. Most educators advanced their arguments for increased public support and control of the schools, for certain types of instruction, for particular studies in the curriculum, and for given schemes of administration, without clearly defining or understanding how their proposed educational policies were to affect our social institutions.

Certain qualifications must be made, however. Immediately after the Revolution, educational theorists did consciously plan a system of schools based on the idea of a functional relation to other institutions and designed to further national and democratic ideals. In recent times the more systematic social thinkers, such as Harris and Dewey, have urged that the schools be more closely related to our social, economic, and cultural institutions; and the educational sociologists have strongly approved a similar program. Yet it remains true that, for the most part, educators have followed politicians and men of affairs, rather than endeavored to help initiate and direct public policies.

In order to build a publicly supported system of schools early educators were, indeed, compelled to initiate a campaign for modifying the prevalent conception of *laissez faire,* and in so doing they established a precedent for the abridgment of private enterprise and the extension of social interest and control. With some exceptions, however, they were content with this victory. If critics are tempted to condemn educational leaders for isolating the schools from the actualities of American life, for unrealistic assumptions and procedures, they must remember that American leaders in other fields have seldom tried to think out the relationship between their own problems and the problems and institutions of the country as a whole. General planlessness, a love of freedom, of individual enterprise, and of open goals have been characteristic of American life.

While, with some exceptions, educators have proceeded in their work with slight conscious reference to other institutions, they have, as this report demonstrates, thought during our whole history in social rather than in merely individualistic terms. Concerning whatever promoted the established social and economic pattern, they have spoken in definite rather than in general terms. But concerning whatever cut across the *status quo,* they have been either cautious or else nebulous and extremely general in their use of words. From the colonial period, when educational spokesmen urged planters and merchants to support their work on the ground that it would prevent internal dissensions and upheavals, to the depression of 1929, when business was urged not to cut school appropriations on the ground that provision for broad educational opportunities was the best insurance against radicalism, there has been a constant tendency for educators to insist that schools are the most certain means for preventing violent overturns in the social order. At certain periods, particularly in the years following the French Revolution and in the bitter years of struggle between capital and labor in the seventies, eighties, and nineties, this idea was expressed not only with great frequency, but with much intensity.

With equal definiteness educators, particularly since the days of the common school awakening, have advocated the ideal of a classless society and the ideal of co-operation between economic groups, and have argued that the schools promote these ends. The great majority have further contended, somewhat inconsistently, that in actuality there are no cleavages, no contradictions in interest between different social groups. But their words, while explicit, have been general in character.

While most educational spokesmen have aligned themselves with the established order and have asked for support from the dominant classes on the ground that they were protecting those classes from possible or even probable danger, some have looked to education as an instrument for social reform. In large degree, the reforms advocated have been of a conservative and highly moral sort, such as temperance. In almost all social crusades, as in those for woman's rights and for international peace, educators have, with some notable exceptions, lagged behind the more progressive groups in American society. For fear of alienating powerful and conservative support, even liberal leaders like Mann refused to permit the schools to concern themselves with certain ticklish and controversial issues.

Yet, beginning with Jefferson, there have been outspoken leaders of education who have stood uncompromisingly for a democratic conception of life. Later educators, with an even broader democratic ideal for education than Jefferson proposed, have looked upon the schools as an instrument for defeating the aristocratic and plutocratic elements in the national life, and for achieving a rich and happy life for all Americans. It is noteworthy that the three leaders who have especially stood for this point of view, Mann, Parker, and Dewey, came from less privileged groups than many who emphasized the conservative function of the schools.

Although Dewey did a great deal to translate the Jeffersonian ideal of education as an instrument for the realization of democracy into concrete terminology and schoolroom practice, most educators who have stood for his point of view have been less specific than those who frankly desired to have the schools perpetuate the established order. Only in the last decade have the democratic leaders sensed this situation and tended to become more explicit in their words and acts.

For those who have wished to bring about reform and the realization of democracy through the schools, the method chiefly relied upon has been that of individual action, rather than mass action or the alleviation of environmental conditions contradicting democracy. In depending upon individual good will for the transformation of conditions, educators have expressed their faith in a characteristically American idea, which sprang out of our own experience. This study has suggested some of the inadequacies of this sort of faith in the individual.

Of the various individualistic techniques for realizing democratic ends, none has played a larger rôle in the thinking and practice of educators than character training. It has, for the most part, depended upon religious sanctions, which have themselves constantly tended to become less effective as American life became increasingly secularized. The prizes in actual life frequently have gone to men who violated the moral precepts which the schools tried to inculcate; and these men have not infrequently received general social approval.

Educational reformers who have hoped that the schools might achieve a better and more democratic order have also contended that a co-operative spirit in the classroom might, by acting on individual children, promote that end. Hence they have stood out against the prevalent spirit of emulation which more conservative educators have defended on psychological grounds.

Arguments for the social studies, like those for character education, have for the most part been based on the assumption that reforms might be effected and democracy realized simply by acting through the individual. Whether their purpose was to acquaint the child with the workings of the Constitution, to imbue him with reverence for the high ideals of the fathers, or to inoculate him with distrust of mass action, violence, and economic radicalism, the assumption has been that knowledge is virtue, and that if only our social problems were understood, faults in the existing structure would *ipso facto* be remedied by a new generation of upright and intelligent citizens.

Another method which democratic educators have relied upon to effect the transformation of America has been the fusing of learning and doing, theory and practice, culture and vocation. They have believed that, if the school could break down the traditional and aristocratic separation between these antitheses, true democracy would be realized. In addition to the general force of tradition, which has militated against their proposal, certain actualities in American life have also stood in the way. In point of fact, children of the less well-to-do classes have, by reason of economic necessity, been compelled or at least encouraged to prepare themselves in school for a narrowly vocational life; and the influence of business has not been conducive to a truly cultural conception of the more humble vocations.

Closely connected with this proposal has been the argument, first popularized by Mann and Barnard, but frequently heard even today, that a single system of schools would break down class barriers, and, by intimately acquainting children of all social groups with each other, promote understanding and sympathy and hasten the day of a classless society. Here again the technique has been the individualistic one, and its weakness lies in the fact that it underestimates the hold and influence of undemocratic forces in the environment outside the school-room.

Finally, educational reformers have been individualistic in their effort to promote democracy and the good life for all. The schools were to further this end by placing emphasis upon training the individual to achieve personal security. Earlier educators believed that schooling in childhood would save the adult from the poorhouse and the prison, and that, as a conse-quence, crime and poverty would be wiped out. Later leaders have assumed that the individual, if he is educated for a changing world, in which he knows how to make the neces-sary, successive adjustments which change compels, will find his individual salvation; and that somehow, social salvation will follow. This conception has assumed that individual se-curity in a changing world can be achieved without social security.

If educational reformers who have visioned the realization of democracy through the school have relied on individual action to achieve that end, conservative leaders have aimed to secure the *status quo* by similar methods. The emphasis placed on the adjustment of the individual to his environment, on achieving his intelligent and voluntary subordination to existing institu-tions, and on inculcating in him the ideals of efficiency and suc-cess, has enhanced competitive individualism. By encouraging children to believe that their own development as leaders and their own achievement of success are identical with the social good, these conservative educators have doubtless lessened the influence of the reformers.

But an even greater handicap to the democratic leaders in their individualistic approach to their goal has been the fact that they themselves have tended to underemphasize the inequalities in American life, the actual social stratification and the existence of class conflicts. It is true that there is substantial ground for their doctrine of co-operation and mutual help-fulness, which have been real elements in American life. But they have failed to see that the ideal of voluntary co-operation of individuals has less validity in a highly industrialized society based on the profit motive than in a simpler type of economy in which subsistence agriculture played an important part, and in which the frontier neighborliness that expressed itself in log-raisings and husking bees kindled social sympathy. Hence the general character both of the objectives in which educational re-formers have expressed their ideal of achieving democracy and a better order through the school, and of the techniques they have employed, has run counter, not only to the ideas and prac-tices of conservative educational leaders, but to many important tendencies in American life. The reformers have failed to see that while the Jeffersonian tradition has supplied the words and ideals, the Hamiltonian tradition of aristocracy and the spirit of business enterprise have with greater frequency governed prac-tices.

Some few educators, however, particularly in the recent period, have been aware of the intensity of undemocratic forces in the actual environment. Expecting less from the schools, these educators have tended to narrow the circle within which they thought the school could effectively realize democratic purposes. They have tended to emphasize adult education and workers' education, and to advocate militant organization of teachers and their alliance with the more radical rather than the more con-servative groups in American life. They have with increasing frequency admitted that the school, being the reflex of existing institutions, could play a less important rôle than they would like in the transformation of American life. Still, they have believed that, with certain reforms in the schools, educators might, if they would learn to look more realistically at the forces and factors in our civilization, and if they would assume a more militant attitude, exert an appreciable influence in the direction of social change.

It is not possible to speak with assurance on the relationship between the social ideas of educational leaders and various factors in their environment. No one can doubt that their early surroundings and personal experiences have greatly influenced their social thinking. No one can doubt that religion, humanitarianism, philosophy, and science have also been powerful factors. But it appears that different elements in the climate of opinion have exerted quite different degrees of influence. Attitudes and opinions growing out of the existent economic pattern of American life, and helping to sustain it, have cut across other influences and have even tended to shape their expression. At times the influence of dominant economic forces is unmistakable. Humanitarian though Mann was, for example, he was unwilling, while engaged in school work, to alienate economic powers that were sympathetic toward slavery; and he reserved his most trenchant criticisms of industrial capitalism until he entered Congress.

In other instances the relationship has been more subtle. Mann's justification of the use of violence for certain purposes, and his refusal to tolerate its use on the part of the underprivileged for the improvement of their economic status, was probably related to the prevailing disinclination of the American middle class, having arrived at power through one revolution, to allow the same weapon to those who had secured less. Thus the democracy and humanitarianism which played so large a part in the social thinking of Mann aligned him, on certain test issues, with the essentially conservative Barnard. In the later period, also, it seems to have made little difference, so far as certain important attitudes on social questions were concerned, what philosophical, religious, or scientific theories influenced educational leaders. Harris was inspired by Hegelianism, Hall by Darwinism, Spalding by Catholicism, Thorndike by the idea of scientific experimentation. Yet all agreed in taking a conservative or at most a liberal, rather than a radical, position on questions involving capital and labor. Among scientists, the hereditarians were on the whole more socially conservative than the environmentalists; yet some of the latter took a social position almost equally consonant with the established order. It would seem that science, religion, and philosophy were less important in determining the social thinking of educators than the pressure, however unconscious it may have been, of the dominant economic forces of the day.

A few educators, however, transcended the conservative pattern in their social thinking. While their personal experience was probably an important factor in this, it is also likely that they were influenced by the more democratic elements in American life; and it is equally probable that the hearing they have gained is due to the influence of the same elements. With the logic of recent events on their side, and with the aid of other liberal groups, they have demonstrated, not only the contradiction in theory and fact between our democratic aspirations and achievements; they have also stimulated others to think of education, past and present, as a relatively ineffective instrument for promoting a more equitable distribution of the amenities and comforts of life.

In so far as these educators have helped in spreading such a point of view, and in so far as they have shown how education may at least help in dealing with our social ills of war, racial hatreds, economic depressions, and the like, and in realizing for all Americans the purposes of the Declaration of Independence, they bear witness to the power of ideas, which, growing out of certain minority interests and actualities, may exert a dynamic influence when the times are ripe. This report has not attempted to measure the effectiveness or extent of that influence; it has, however, shown some of its limitations and analyzed specifically some of the factors which have impeded and promoted it.

While the school structure itself, in origin and in growth, has been much less the expression of humanitarianism and democracy and much more the result of, and dependent upon, dominant economic interests than is commonly supposed, it is also clear that virtually all educational leaders have assumed that they have great social responsibilities and power. In assuming these responsibilities and in claiming a social influence, they have, with few exceptions, paid a sincere, if nebulous, tribute to the ideal of a rich and full life for all Americans. There has been a common tradition of idealism, and the eighteenth century revolutionary tradition has come down continuously in the social theory of educators. Nevertheless, there has been the same cleavage between fact and ideal in educational circles as in other groups in American life, the same tendency to discover the achievement in the aspiration.

What educators will do to resolve this conflict largely depends, if this study may be drawn upon for an inference and a prophecy, on the changing economic and cultural forces outside the schools. Within the circle in which educators may effectively work for the realization of the ideals to which conservative as well as liberal leaders have, with some exceptions, subscribed, much depends on the recognition of actual conflicts and cleavages in American life and on the alliances educational leaders and teachers make in those conflicts. Much also depends on the extent to which educators realize that they, like the men and women whose social ideas have been considered in this book, are deeply influenced by a point of view which they have unconsciously absorbed from their social environment, by a frame of reference which constantly limits their thought. Only by recognizing this source of error in their work, only by analyzing the influences which have determined this frame of reference, can they hope to rise above the limitations of their class and personal backgrounds and the more or less obsolete ideas and emotional attitudes related to these. Only by so doing can they become whole-hearted pioneers in the building of a better social order. Even more depends, perhaps, on their realization of discrepancies between aspirations and existing conditions, and on avoiding the methods, within and without the schools, which past experience has shown to be ineffective in translating the ideal into the real.

BIBLIOGRAPHICAL NOTES

Although many materials not specifically cited in the footnotes of the text were consulted in this investigation, no attempt will be made to indicate these materials in any complete way or to duplicate the specific references which have been fully cited. This bibliographical note will merely indicate the places in which the manuscripts used may be found and give a general description of the types of materials that may be useful to scholars interested in this field of research.

Several bibliographies should be mentioned, particularly S. E. Davis, *Educational Periodicals during the Nineteenth Century* (Bureau of Education, *Bulletin* No. 28, 1919), *Bibliography of Horace Mann* (*Report of the U. S. Commissioner of Education for 1895-1896,* Vol. I, pp. 897-927), Will S. Monroe, *Bibliography of Henry Barnard* (Boston, 1897), Henry Ridgely Evans, *A List of the Writings of William Torrey Harris* (Washington, 1908), Ralph Barton Perry, *Annotated Bibliography of the Writings of William James* (New York, 1920), "Bibliography of the Published Writings of G. Stanley Hall" in Edward L. Thorndike, *Biographical Memoir of Granville Stanley Hall, 1846-1924* (National Academy of Sciences, Washington, 1928), Milton Halsey Thomas and Herbert Wallace Schneider, *A Bibliography of John Dewey* (New York, 1929), *Bibliographies on Educational Sociology* (*First Yearbook of the National Society for the Study of Educational Sociology,* State Teachers College, Buffalo, N. Y., 1928), and *Locating Educational Information in Published Sources* (Bureau of Educational Research, College of Education, University of Illinois, *Bulletin* No. 50, 1930).

MANUSCRIPTS

While all the manuscript collections consulted contained much material irrelevant to this study, research in these collections yielded fruitful results. The personal letters of educators frequently made explicit the social ideas which one could only infer from their published writings; and frequently these letters also helped explain the position taken on social questions. Naturally the more intimate correspondence was also very helpful in illuminating the personality of the writer.

One of the largest collections of unpublished correspondence consulted was the Mann Papers in the possession of the Massachusetts Historical Society. The papers include many letters written by Mann and a larger number written by others to him. The educational leader and his correspondents not only discussed the schools and social issues, but, frequently, the relations between them. Mann's letters written when he left the law for educational work, and when he retired from the Massachusetts Board of Education for the political fight against slavery in Congress, throw a good deal of light on his motives, and on his attitude toward the possibilities and limitations of the two methods of achieving social reform.

The Watkinson Library in Hartford, Connecticut, possesses a chest of Barnard papers, which include materials Barnard collected for an autobiography or biography, drafts of his addresses, sketches for his *American Journal of Education,* letters written by himself as well as letters he received, and many newspaper clippings. The more important collection of materials, however, is in the possession of Professor Will S. Monroe of Richmond, Vermont. This collection is made up of some forty packages of letters received by Barnard from almost every important contemporary in the educational world, and the letters which Barnard wrote to many colleagues, particularly to Daniel Coit Gilman, Elisha Potter, and W. S. Baker. The fifteen or twenty Barnard letters in the Wilkins Updike Papers in the Rhode Island Historical Society did not prove to be particularly important in revealing or explaining the social ideas of Barnard.

The papers of William T. Harris have been in part deposited in the library of the National Education Association. This collection contains about a thousand manuscripts, consecutively numbered and more or less chronologically arranged. The papers include the manuscripts of some addresses which were delivered but apparently not printed, as well as the original drafts of the published papers. Indeed, many items, some fairly important, are to be found which are not included in Doctor Evans's *A List of the Writings of William Torrey Harris.* While the collection contains some personal letters, the largest part of these is still in the possession of Doctor Harris's daughter, Miss Edith Harris of Walpole, New Hampshire.

The Library of Congress possesses the voluminous correspondence of J. L. M. Curry. This collection, like the Harris collection, contains many of the addresses which appeared in periodicals not easily accessible, as well as original drafts and notes for lectures. It also contains many newspaper clippings which give some indication of the influence of Curry. But the greatest value of the collection lies in his letters to Robert Winthrop and in Winthrop's replies. These letters, which were of a confidential nature, throw a great deal of light on Doctor Curry's social attitudes. Curry also corresponded with a great many educators, and their letters to him make the collection a very valuable source for understanding the development of public education in the South in the decades following the Civil War.

The papers of Robert Ogden are also in the Library of Congress; and although the collection is not as important as that of Curry, it should be consulted by any student of the post-Civil War movement to improve the public schools in the South. Professor Samuel C. Mitchell's valuable unpublished life of Ogden is deposited with the collection.

Mrs. Edna Shepard of Brookline, Massachusetts, has in her possession some letters from Colonel Francis W. Parker, as well as some of his unpublished addresses and many interesting newspaper clippings.

PERIODICAL LITERATURE: EDUCATIONAL

Notwithstanding the fact that the educational periodicals, particularly in the nineteenth century, contain few articles which formally discuss social ideas, the periodicals proved to be one of the most important sources for this study. Social attitudes sometimes appeared in the periodicals in the most unexpected places; the context of articles often permitted one to infer the social beliefs and assumptions of the writers. But almost all the periodicals consulted also contained many explicit expressions of the social beliefs of educators. Although the sampling of these educational periodicals was fairly wide, particularly for the first part of the nineteenth century, nothing like an exhaustive study of them was made. Among those which proved to be most useful were *The Academician* (1818–1820, edited by Albert and John W. Pickett), the *American Journal of Education* (1826–1830, edited by William Russell, and succeeded by the *American Annals of Education and Instruction*, 1831–1839, edited by W. C. Woodbridge and others), *The Common School Journal* (1838–1852, edited by Horace Mann and William

B. Fowle in Boston), *The Connecticut Common School Journal* (1838–1866, edited by Henry Barnard and others), the *Journal of the Rhode Island Institute of Instruction* (1845–1849), edited also by Barnard), the *North Carolina Journal of Education* (1858–1861, edited by Calvin Wiley), and, particularly, Henry Barnard's *The American Journal of Education* (1855–1882). For the period after the Civil War, the *Educational Review* (1891–   , edited by Nicholas Murray Butler and others), the *New England Journal of Education* (1875–   , edited by T. W. Bicknell and A. E. Winship), and *School and Society* (1915–   , edited by J. McKeen Cattell) were selected.

PERIODICAL LITERATURE: NON-EDUCATIONAL

In order to compare the social thought of non-educators who at times concerned themselves with the schools, many periodicals were sampled. The following titles suggest the range of this type of material: *The North American Review, Southern Literary Messenger, Journal of Man, DeBow's Commercial Review, Niles' Weekly Register, Gunton's Magazine.*

EDUCATIONAL REPORTS

While the reports of superintendents and commissioners of education, state and city, as well as national, contain a vast amount of material with slight bearing on the problems of this investigation, such reports indicated the interests of educational administrators, and also often included material very relevant to this research. The reports most extensively used were those of the United States Commissioner of Education (1867–   ), of the secretary of the Massachusetts Board of Education for the years 1837–1848, and of the state commissioners of education in Connecticut, North Carolina, Indiana, and Illinois in the pre-Civil War period. The *Annual Reports of the Public Schools of St. Louis* (1868–1880), prepared by William T. Harris, were important, not only for that educator's ideas on school organization, subjects in the curriculum, and methods of teaching, but because of the wide circulation and influence these reports enjoyed. *The Addresses and Proceedings of the National Education Association* (1871–   , title varying) were examined, and these documents provide a rich store of material on the subject of this investigation. The *Proceedings of the Trustees of the Peabody Educational Fund* (Jan., 1868–) were also consulted, particularly during the years when J. L. M. Curry acted as general agent.

WRITINGS OF EDUCATORS

Fortunately, some educational leaders wrote formal treatises on education in which, either explicitly or implicitly, their social ideas in relation to their educational theories appear. Typical of this category are G. Stanley Hall's *Educational Problems* (New York, 1911) and his *Adolescence, Its Psychology and Its Relations to Physiology, Anthropology, Sex, Crime, Religion and Education* (New York, 1905). William T. Harris summarized his philosophic, psychological, educational, and social ideas in *Psychologic Foundations of Education* (New York, 1898), while E. L. Thorndike's *Educational Psychology* (New York, 1913, 3 volumes) is a monumental work and of fundamental importance in understanding Thorndike's social philosophy.

From more informal and less systematic writings on pedagogy one may also gather the social assumptions of the writers. George B. Emerson and Alonzo Potter collaborated in writing *The School and the Schoolmaster. A Manual for the Use of Teachers, Employers, Trustees, Inspectors, etc., of Common Schools* (New York, 1873), a book which probably is typical of the social philosophy, for the most part implicit in the discussions of discipline, moral training, and administration, of a great many teachers in the middle decades of the last century. Jacob Abbott's *The Teacher, Moral Influences Employed in the Instruction and Government of the Young* (New York, 1856) is even more conservative, religious, and moral in tone. David Page's *Theory and Practice of Teaching* was one of the most widely used manuals but has fewer precepts capable of a social interpretation. Charles Brooks, *Elementary Instruction* and Hall's *Lectures on School Keeping* were pioneer works. In the later period, the number of such books, which become increasingly specialized in character, is so large that it is hardly possible to make typical suggestions. Francis W. Parker's *Talks on Pedagogics* (New York and Chicago, 1894) and William James's *Talks to Teachers on Psychology, and to Students on Some of Life's Ideals* (New York, 1899) should be supplemented by the extremely popular *Evolution of Dodd* (Peoria, Ill., 1884) by William Hawley Smith.

A few educators wrote autobiographies that throw much light

on their social philosophy and on the influences that determined it. One of the best is John Swett's *Public Education in California* (New York, 1911), which is especially valuable in enabling one to understand a chapter in the transit of New England culture to the Coast, with its subsequent modification. George Emerson's *Reminiscences of an Old Teacher* (Boston, 1878), and William A. Mowry's *Recollections of a New England Educator* (New York, 1908) and Francis W. Parker's autobiographical sketch in William M. Griffin's *School Days in the Fifties* (Chicago, 1906) are useful, but do not compare in importance with G. Stanley Hall's *Life and Confessions of a Psychologist* (New York, 1923) and the autobiographical writings of Booker T. Washington, *Up from Slavery* (New York, 1901) and *My Larger Education* (New York, 1911).

Although the speeches, addresses, and essays of educators often reveal their social outlook, the list of such materials used in this study is much too long to indicate in this bibliographical note. To illustrate the general character of this category, however, a few titles may be indicated. Thaddeus Stevens's "Speech against the Repeal of the School Law" (*Report of the Commissioner of Education for 1898–1899,* Vol. I, pp. 518–24) is a justly celebrated address. Any one who wishes to understand the social and cultural appeals of an influential Middle Westerner during the middle period should read Caleb Mill's *First Address on Popular Education to the Legislature of Indiana, 1847* (Indiana Historical Society Collections, Vol. III (1905), pp. 447–49. The Reverend F. A. Packard severely criticized the public schools and expressed in the strongest terms the extremely orthodox religious point of view in regard to education in his *Thoughts on Popular Education* (Philadelphia, 1836). Special attention should be called to Horace Mann's *Lectures on Education* (Boston, 1845), *A Few Thoughts for a Young Man* (Boston, 1850), and *Lectures on Various Subjects* (New York, 1859). A fairly adequate understanding of Bishop Spalding's social philosophy may be gained from his *Means and Ends in Education* (Chicago, 1909) and from his *Opportunity and Other Essays and Addresses* (Chicago, 1906). A succinct account of Booker T. Washington's educational philosophy, with its social implications, may be gathered from his *Selected Speeches* (edited by E. Davidson Washington, Garden City, N. Y., 1932).

No effort was made to study in anything like a comprehensive manner the school texts. But Caleb Bingham's *The Columbian Orator* (Boston, 1812) and Noah Webster's various editions of

The Elementary Spelling Book represent the Jeffersonian and Hamiltonian positions in the early republic. Calvin H. Wiley's *The
North Carolina Reader* (Philadelphia, 1859) abounds in state patriotism, and the McGuffey "Readers" illustrate the prevalent type
of moral education.

SECONDARY MATERIALS

There are biographies for most educational leaders, varying in
merit and in usefulness for an understanding of the social ideas of
their subjects. Mary Tyler Peabody Mann's *Life and Works of
Horace Mann* (Boston, 1865–1868) contains many extracts from
her husband's correspondence. Bernard C. Steiner's *Life of Henry
Barnard* (Department of Interior, Bureau of Education, Bulletin
No. 8, 1919) gives the essential facts of Barnard's life and work,
without suggesting very definitely his social philosophy, and this is
similarly true of many competent lives of other educators. John S.
Roberts's *William T. Harris, A Critical Study of His Educational
and Related Philosophical Views* (Washington, 1924) is a systematic account of the philosophical, educational, and social thinking of Harris, but it is not adequately related to the cultural and
economic pattern of American life. Adequate biographies exist for
several women educators: Mae Elizabeth Harveston, *Catherine
Esther Beecher: A Pioneer Educator* (Philadelphia, 1932), Mary
Garvey, R. S. C. J., *Mary Aloysia Hardey, Religious of the Sacred
Heart, 1809–1886* (New York, 1925), and Alma Lutz, *Emma
Willard, Daughter of Democracy* (Boston, 1929) are representative.

Several monographs on special problems have been drawn upon.
Allan Oscar Hansen's *Liberalism and American Education in the
Eighteenth Century* (New York, 1926) is an admirable study of
the first efforts at educational planning. Royal J. Honeywell's *Educational Work of Thomas Jefferson* (Harvard Studies in Education,
No. 16, Cambridge, 1931) supersedes earlier studies of this phase
of Jefferson's thought. Raymond B. Culver's *Horace Mann and
Religion in the Massachusetts Schools* (New Haven, 1929) sets a
high standard and ought to stimulate similar studies of this aspect
of the work of other educators. H. H. Reeder has written a very
useful study, *The Historical Development of Early School Readers*
(Columbia University, Contributions to Philosophy, Psychology and
Education, Vol. VIII, No. 2, May, 1900); and particular attention
should be called to Thomas Woody's monumental and extremely
valuable *History of Women's Education in the United States* (New

York, 1929, 2 volumes). Philip R. V. Curoe, *Educational Attitudes and Policies of Organized Labor in the United States* (Columbia University, Teachers College, Contributions to Education, No. 201, New York, 1926) ascribes less influence to organized labor in the upbuilding of the public schools than does Frank Tracy Carlton, *Economic Influences upon Educational Progress, 1820–1850* (University of Wisconsin, Bulletin No. 221, Madison, 1908). In his *Molders of the American Mind* (New York, 1933) Norman Woelfel has brilliantly analyzed the social and educational philosophy of seventeen contemporary educators.

While many other admirable studies exist, there are great gaps. Studies of the schools in the various frontier areas, and in the southern colonies, comparable to Walter Herbert Small's *Early New England Schools* (Boston, 1914) would be valuable contributions. Investigations of the social ideas of minor and obscure though representative educators and teachers are especially needed.

INDEX

Abbott, Jacob, school discipline and citizenship, 60; freedom of teaching, 61

Abolition, attitude of Mann toward, 130–31; Barnard on, 141; views of women educators on, 190

Academies, class character of, 22, 27

Addams, Jane, quoted on business man's concept of education, 203; criticizes educators for lack of zeal in fighting child labor, 234; on exploitation of immigrants and political corruption, 256

Administration, business ideals in, 230–31; conservative social influence of most leaders of, 563–64; advanced by Thorndike's work, 462; criticisms of emphasis on, 242, 564–66; rôle of teachers in, 548

Adult education, beginnings of, 240–41; favored by Harris, 332; Thorndike's attitude toward, 471–73. *See also* Davidson, Thomas; Russell, Dean James Earl; Lyceum; Chautauqua

Agricultural education, in pre-Civil War period, 213 n., 216 n.; promoted by Morrill Act, 212–13, and by Grange and Farmers' Alliance, 213–14; views of Populists on, 214; improvements of as means of solving rural and urban problems, 214, 216–18. *See also* Knapp, Dr. Seaman

Alcott, A. Bronson, on self-government in school and state, 60

Allen, Charles R., leader in industrial education, 559–60

American Federation of Labor, views on education, 236–37

American Philosophical Society, prize essay contest, 47

American Revolution, as a social movement, 24; Mann and Barnard on, 161

Americanization, schools as instrument for furthering, 11, 39, 62, 255; steam-roller methods criticized by

Harris and Hall, 338–39, 422; promoted by World War, 542–43

Anarchists, public education as preventive of growth of, 57–58, 135, 146, 220; understood by Francis W. Parker, 391; views of toward schools, 237; William James on, 436. *See also* Revolution, Violence

Anthony, Susan B., quoted on exclusion of women from professions, 189–90

Apprenticeship system, influence of, on education, 22–24, 25

Armstrong, John, free schools a preventive of revolution, 80; of migration westward, 71

Armstrong, Gen. Samuel C., social and educational views, 289–91

Aydelott, Rev. B. P., education a preventive of Socialism, 19, 83; citizenship training, 57–58

Azarias, Brother, Catholic educator, 355–56 n.

Babson, Roger, quoted, 203

Baldwin, William Henry, education of Negro, 299

Barnard, Henry, class background, 144, 152; religious orthodoxy, 142 ff.; humanitarian sympathies, 139 ff., 147–49; education as security for *status quo*, 15, 145–46; uninfluenced by socialist critic, 151–52; exponent of capitalism, 154 ff.; social conservatism, 140–41, 143 ff.; schools and a democratic culture, 147 ff.; education and reform of social evils, 147, 150, 161; citizenship training, 161–63; private schools, 27–28; lack of interest in politics, 163–64; political neutrality, 167–68; education of women, 178; favors practical subjects, 158–59, 168; tribute of Francis W. Parker to, 379

Beecher, Catharine, social status, 179; religious fervor, 182; female education a preparation for wifehood and motherhood, 184-85; favors substitution of women for men teachers, 186-87; fear of Western radicalism, 186-87; opposes employment of girls in factories, 187; conservative attitude toward abolition, 190; anticipates John Dewey, 184-85

Benefactors of public education, 77, 228; criticized by S. Y. Gillan, 229. *See also* Mann, Horace

Bicknell, George, quoted on class struggle, 239

Bingham, Caleb, textbook compiler, 18; promotes cultural nationalism, 54

Blair, Senator Henry, federal funds for public schools, 270-73

Bouquillon, Rev. Thomas, on relation of parochial schools to family, church, and state, 352

Bray, Dr. Thomas, quoted, 5; educational work, 8

Bronner, Dr. Augusta, on relation of psychology of individual differences to progressive education, 483-84

Brooks, Charles, moral training and mob action, 59

Brougham, Lord, on popular education and labor disputes, 84; class differences, 94 n.

Buehrle, R. V., critic of capitalism, 243-44

Burroughs, Charles, promotes advanced education of girls, 176-77

Business enterprise, influence on schools and educational thought, 227 ff. *See also* Hall, G. Stanley; Harris, Wm. T.; Spalding, Bishop John L.; Thorndike, E. L.; Administration; Capitalism

Butler, Nicholas Murray, opposes Bryan in 1896, 215; views on Spanish-American War, 225; on schooling and productive capacity, 227

Capitalism, upheld by educators, 154 ff., 321 ff., 493-94; criticized by educators, 113-17, 243, 244, 370-71, 509-10. *See also* Business enterprise, Socialism, Working class

Carter, James, befriends common schools, 106-7

Catholic schools, in colonial period, 13; growth of , 19-20, 207, 349-50; Protestant opposition to, 350; relation to public schools, 351-53; social views of leaders of, 578. *See also* Hardey, Mother; Friess, Mother; Seton, Mother; Spalding, Bishop John L.

Cattell, J. McKeen, pioneer in testing movement, 208, 402; on Thorndike, 479

Character education, *see* Moral training

Chautauqua, William James on, 439. *See also* Adult education

Cheever, Ezekiel, colonial schoolmaster, 12

Child labor, in New England, 98; defended by Alexander Hamilton, 98; Jane Addams on, 234; Lawton B. Evans on, 235; N. E. A., 235

Citizenship training, 56 ff.; uncritical of faults in political structure, 62; advocated as cure for political corruption, 253-54; limitations of, 254-56, 423; views of Mann, 135; Barnard, 161-63; Harris, 337 ff.; Parker, 390-91; Hall, 421-22; Thorndike, 476; Dewey, 525; John B. McMaster, 251; N. E. A. Commission on Teaching of Democracy, 557 n.

Civil service reform, advocated by Barnard, 140; N. E. A., 253

Class structure of society, influence of on schools, 4 ff., 21 ff., 25 ff.: promoted by slavery, 75; endangered by mass education, 78 n., 88, 206 n.; to be eliminated by common schools, 94-95, 122, 148-50, 184, 232-33; criticized by Dewey, 511

Class struggle, denial of, by educators, 233, 365; philanthropy as solution of, 239; Dewey on, 511. *See also* Mann, Barnard, Coe

Clinton, De Witt, promotes Lancastrian schools, 25; free schools and free institutions, 56; education of girls, 176

Coe, George A., quoted on class tensions, 233

Commercial education, business efficiency and, 223-25

Commission on the National Emergency in Education, 545 ff.

Constitution, citizenship training in, 61, 162

Corson, Oscar T., quoted on business ideal in educational administration, 231

Counts, George S., on unequal distribution of wealth, 568–69; undemocratic character of school system, 568–69; high-school curriculum, 569–70; education as an "individual right," 570; interest in education in Soviet Union, 571; *Dare the Schools Build a New Social Order?* 571–72; organization of teachers, 575

Crime, preventable by education, 118 n.; 415

Crockett, David, disparages book education, 67

Cubberley, Ellwood P., advances professionalization of education, 550; child labor, 235; opposition to teachers' unions, 243; emphasis on social functions of schools, 550

Cultural independence of the United States, education to effect, 51; desire for reflected in texts, 54–55; influence of idea of, on Barnard, 161

Culture, promotion of among poor advocated by educators, 147, 238–39; Harris on relation of machines to, 319–20

Curricula, in colonial and early national periods, 28; in female seminaries, 175, 182; influence of publishers on, 229–30; views of labor, 236–37, 240; Harris on, 315 ff.; Dewey, 524–55; Counts, 569–70

Curry, J. L. M., background, 264–65; work for public schools in South, 266 ff.; interpreter between North and South, 267; educational views, 267–68; political and social philosophy, 268 ff., 276 ff.; exponent of the New South, 268–69; minister to Spain, 269–70; illiteracy and free institutions, 271; befriends Negro education, 271, 278 ff.; opposes Populism, 273–74; and Socialism, 274–76; favors Northern invest-ments in South, 276–77; quoted on Booker T. Washington, 298

Curtis, George William, *see* Civil service reform

Davidson, Thomas, pioneer in workers' education, 241

De Garmo, Charles, favors criticism of social evils in civic education, 256–57 n.

Deism, growth of, 13–14; reaction against, 18; opposition of Barnard to, 142

Democracy, Jefferson's educational scheme and, 41–42; Mann's conception of, 134–35; not supported by Thorndike's psychological theories, 474 ff.; economic basis for urged by Dewey, 503, 519

Depressions, ascribed to popular ignorance, 78–79; social studies as safeguard against, 79; influence of on educational thought, 573 ff.

De Tocqueville, religion in U. S., 16 n.

Dewey, John, background, 500 ff.; influences on intellectual development of, 500–507; educational and social objectives compared with those of other educators, 291 ff., 379, 513–14; views on habit, 515–17; thinking, 513; instrumentalism, 507; repudiates fixed goals, 508; early insistence on necessity of economic democracy, 503, 511; criticizes class character of culture and private benefactions to education, 229, 510; rôle of education in promoting social change and democracy, 519 ff.; limitations of, 534–35; deprecates class struggle as instrument of solving social conflicts, 511, 518; views on force and war, 518, 543; political activities, 511–12, 535–36; views on moral education, 523–24; importance of history, geography, and science in curricula, 526–27; opposes narrowly utilitarian industrial education, 528–31; calls attention to influence of publishers on curricula, 229; favors teachers' unions, 243; criticisms of tests and measurements, 532–33; criticisms of, 536 ff.

Dock, Christopher, colonial schoolmaster, 12

Donnelly, Ignatius, educational work, 214

Dorr War, free schools to prevent similar outbreaks, 80, 165–66

Drawing and design, commercial and æsthetic values of, 223

Drunkenness, education as preventive, 122. *See also* Temperance

Du Bois, Dr. W. E. Burghardt, background, 304–5; emphasis on cultural values in Negro education, 305, 309; views on Booker T. Washington, 305 ff.

Duchesne, Mother, interest in education of the lowly, 174

Dwight, Edward, subsidizes normal school, 113

Dwight, Timothy, fears "atheism," 13; criticism of education of upper class girls, 28, 175

East, fear of West, 68; desire to control West through education, 68–70; to prevent migration westward by increasing educational advantages, 70–71

Eaton, John, U. S. Commissioner of Education, 211; advocates education of Indian, 211; education a preventive of strikes, 219; favors commercial subjects, 223; education and prosperity, 227

Edwards, Jonathan, schools and evangelistic piety, 10

Edwards, Richard, on duty of educators during Reconstruction, 209–10

Efficiency, goal of educators, 230–31

Eliot, Charles W., advocates teaching of economics, 222; better training for consuls, 223; influence of education on business and profits indirect, 227; low regard for intellectual ability of women, 251; on political corruption, 256

Emerson, George, citizenship training, 57, 60; respect for property, 86

Emerson, Ralph Waldo, quoted, 50; on Mann, 126 n.; anticipated John Dewey, 501

Emulation, regarded as socially undesirable, 59, 123. *See also* Parker, F. W.; Thorndike, E. L.

Eugenics, advocated by Spalding, 362 n.; Hall, 412, 424; Thorndike, 480

European influences on American education, 4, 56. *See also* Pestalozzi, Spencer, Herbart, Calvin E. Stowe, Locke

Everett, A. H., quoted on schools as preventives of migration westward, 70

Everett, Edward, quoted on Eastern responsibility for education of West, 69; education of mechanics to prevent class conflict, 86–87

Evolution, doctrine of, influence on American educational thought, 207–8; influence of, on G. Stanley Hall, 401–2, 404–7; on William James, 444; on John Dewey, 504–5

Family, views of Bishop Spalding on, 357–58; instinctive basis of in Hall's psychology, 409–10; importance of, in Harris's social philosophy, 314

Federal support of public schools, movement for, 546–47

Fisher, Jonathan, textbook compiler, 17

Folwell, W. W., promoter of agricultural and secondary education, 212

Formal discipline. *See* Transfer of training

Franklin, Benjamin, influence of middle-class outlook on education and social philosophy of, 35 ff.; opposition to classics and useless knowledge, 35; devotion to science, 36; self-education, 37–38; attitude toward education of poor, 38; humanitarianism of, 39; nationalism of, 39

Free schools, conservative opposition to, 87 ff., 195; arguments for, 76 ff.; victory for, 194–95; extension to South and West, 206. *See also* Socialism, Anarchism, South, and Individual educators

Freedom of expression, defended by Mann, 127–28; Barnard on, 140; qualified by Jacob Abbott, 61

French Revolution, influence of, on American educational thought, 51, 55, 81

Friess, Mother Caroline, Catholic Educator, 186

Frontier, and religion, 15; distinctive educational system desired on, 64 ff.; antagonism to schools on, 67–68; Eastern fear of, 68–70, 135, 186; social cleavages on, 124

Gallaudet, Thomas, educator of deaf, 147; attacks one-sided memory training, 177

George, Henry, on education and wages, 245; ideas of opposed by W. T. Harris, 326–27

Girls, education in Colonial and early national periods, 169–72, 176–78; educational privileges at New Harmony, 67; class character of education, 174–75; curricula in female seminaries, 175; Dr. Benjamin Rush's plan for "an American education for American women," 176; better schooling for favored by De Witt Clinton and other friends of education, 176–78; educational and social philosophy of pioneers of female education, 178 ff.; conservative attitude of toward feminism, 189–90; contributions to emancipation of women, 193. See also Women; Beecher, Catharine; Lyon, Mary; Willard, Emma; Wright, Frances; Mother Hardey; Mother Seton; Mother Friess

Godkin, E. L., influence of on William James, 431–32

Gompers, Samuel. See A. F. of L.

Grant, Elijah P., socialist critic of Barnard, 151–52

Great Awakening. See Revivals

Greeley, Horace, education not a substitute for social reform, 91–92; condition of the working class, 97

Hadley, President Arthur, quoted on individual success, 259

Haley, Margaret, pioneer in teachers' union movement, 242; criticizes regimentation of teachers, 242–43; fights tax evasion, 253

Hall, G. Stanley, background, 396 ff.; education, 398 ff.; influenced by Romanticism, 402–3; interest in Socialism, 399 ff.; criticism of America, 400–401, 404; enthusiasm for theory of evolution, 402–3; contributions to education, 402–3; dislike of group selfishness, 406–7; social implications of theory of recapitulation, 407; institutions an expression of the folk-soul, 407–8; religion, 407–8; views on war, 408–9; on private property, 409; family, 409–10; sex and women, 409–11; primitive races, 412–13; Negro problem, 413; opposes imperialism, 413–14; culture epoch theory, 415; proper education a remedy for standardization, 415; advocates industrial education, 417–18; and moral education, 419 ff.; value of history, 421; of education in effecting social control, 419 ff.; popularity as a teacher, 425; influence, 426–27

Hall, James, compiler of The Western Reader, 66

Hardey, Mother, Catholic educator, 174, 179, 183, 189; engages in relief work in Civil War, 192

Harper, M. H., investigates social ideas of educators, 572–73

Harris, William T., background, 311 ff.; embraces Hegelian philosophy, 312; importance of, 312 ff.; views on institutions, 314; defends religion, 314–15; advocates sharing of cultural values, 315; educational views, 315 ff., 324, 331 ff.; defends cultural as against vocational subjects, 316 ff.; favors science, 318; advocates kindergarten for salvaging children of wealth, 324, and of slum-dwellers, 352; favors university extension, 332; views on administration and teachers, 332 ff.; respect for authority to be inculcated, 330, 333–35; criticizes educational fads, 334; opposes mechanization of child, 335–36; citizenship training, 337 ff.; history, 337–39; views on education of Indian and Negro, 339–40; educational methods for alleviation of slum conditions, 342–43; favors temperance instruction, 343; sociology basis of education, 345–46; justifies machine age, 318–20; apologist for urbanization of American life, 321–22; defends capitalism, 321 ff., 330 ff.; idealizes doctrine of self-help, 325; refutes ideas of Henry George, 326, and of Karl Marx, 327–29; views on technological unemployment, 328–29; relation of individual to group, 329 ff.; criticizes steam-roller methods of Americanization, 338–39; ascribes political corruption to immigrants, 341–42; high regard for women, 343; attitude toward peace and war, 344–45

Health, child, concern of educators for, 185, 246–48; views of Harris on, 316; Hall on, 412; promoted after World War, 542

Henry, James, criticizes class education, 27

Herbart, influence on American educational practice, 207–8, 254, 415; ideas of criticized by Harris, 334; by Dewey, 524–25

Hereditarianism. *See* Hall, G. Stanley; Thorndike, E. L.; Terman, Lewis M.

High schools, checks on socialism, 220–21; means by which poor improve status, 239

Higher education, function of to check radicalism, 331–32

History, in citizenship training, 61–62; conventional character of deprecated by Mann, 162; favored by Barnard, 162; opposition of N. E. A. to teaching of recent history, 222; emphasis on political, military, and constitutional, 222; views of John B. McMaster on, 251; of Harris, 337–39; of Parker, 390–91; of Hall, 421; of Dewey, 526

Howe, Dr. Samuel Gridley, opposes statutory limitation of working day, 119

Howell, Clark, quoted on Booker T. Washington, 297

Howerth, I. W., criticizes capitalism, 244

Howison, G. W., quoted on private schools, 206 n.

Hughes, Archbishop, battle for state support of parochial schools, 349

Humanitarianism, sources, 95; inspires movement for free schools as instrument for social ameliorization, 99; Mann and, 103 ff.; Barnard and, 139–40

Hunt, Mary Hanchett, work for indoctrination of total abstinence. 248–49

Identical elements. *See* Thorndike, E. L.

Immigrants, blamed for political corruption, 255–56, 314–42; sympathy for, 256. *See also* Americanization

Imperialism, views of educators on, 225–27, 340–41, 369–70, 413–14, 432

Indians, justice toward, 62; education of, 211–12, 339, 413

Individualism, Mann's faith in, 123–25; Barnard's devotion to, 153; strength of faith in, 256–57; criticized, 259; justified by Harris, 329 ff.; buttressed by William James, 429–30, 441–43, 455 ff.; Thorndike's theory of individual differences, 473 ff., 483 ff., 490–91

Indoctrination, Mann's inconsistent attitude toward, 126 ff.; Thorndike on, 469–70; Dewey, 526–27; Counts, 571–72

Industrial education, a means of breaking down class barriers, 240; dangers in, 233; narrow conception of opposed by Dewey, 528–29; advocated by Hall, 417–19; favored by Thorndike's attack of theory of transfer of training, 468; promoted by World War, 557 ff.; controversy regarding democratic or undemocratic character of, 558–59. *See also* A. F. of L., Working classes, Washington, Booker T., Manual training

Industrialism, creates social and educational problems, 76 ff., 204–5; education to be functional to, 159–60

Jacksonian democracy, free schools a safeguard for excesses of, 79, 135

James, William, applies psychology to education, 429–30; confirms American faith in individualism, 429–30; privileged background, 430 ff.; religious influence of father, 431; political influence of Godkin, 431–32; views on corruption, imperialism, war, and peace, 432–33; idealizes poverty, 434–35, 438; deprecates worship of prosperity, 434–35, 437; holds conflict of capital and labor to be merely psychological, 437–38; sympathy with Socialism, 438–39; tolerance of lowly, 440; opposes sentimental attitude toward workers, 457; faith in leadership and noblesse oblige, 440–42; aristocratic sympathies, 441–42, 446–47; influenced by hereditarianism, 441; influence of American environment on philosophy of, 443–44 n.; other influences on, 444; conservative social implications of teachings on instinct, 445 ff., and on habit, 446–47; educational applications of, 448–50; adjustment of individual to environment, 449; criticizes formal discipline theory, 450; educational implications of, 451–52; views on race and sex differences, 452; social implications of pragmatism, 453 ff.; relation of pluralism to *laissez faire* and individualism, 544–46; radical empiricism, and social implications of, 455–56; influence, 443–44; significance, 456–58; quoted on Thorndike, 459

Jefferson, Thomas, relation of education to liberty, 3; Bill for the More General Diffusion of Knowledge, 26, 40; education a means of breaking down class barriers and promoting social reform and democracy, 41 ff.; class limitations of educational program, 45–46; defeat of educational program by conservatives, 45–46; influence of educational philosophy of, 46 n.; warns against education of Southerners in North, 72

Jones, Hugh, quoted, 3

Judd, C. H., advances professionalization of education, 550–51; emphasizes psychology of institutions, 551; favors social studies, 555–56; co-operative character of intelligence and social life, 554–55; reaction to depression, 579

Kilpatrick, W. H., quoted on Dewey, 499; on administration and technique, 542; social philosophy, 561–62; *Education and the Social Crisis*, 574–75

Kindergarten. *See* Harris, W. T., and Hall, G. Stanley

Knapp, Dr. Seaman, co-operative demonstration work, 285; idealizes the commonplace, 286

Knights of Labor, favor practical studies, 236; oppose high schools, 239

Laissez faire, belief in checks growth of free schools, 74; hinders health work in schools, 247; educators establish precedent for abridgment of, 581–82; defended by Harris, 338, Hall, 407, Thorndike, 496–97

Lancastrian schools, teachers in, 29; emulation in, 59

Lawrence, Abbott, befriends popular education, 77–78; on wages, 97–98

Leisler Rebellion, effect on freedom of teaching, 8–9

Lewis, Dio, advocates physical culture in schools, 246

Lincoln, Abraham, quoted on education, 198; importance of knowledge of history, 62 n.

Lloyd, Henry D., views on economic ills and education, 245

Locke, John, influence of on American education, 36; acquisition of habits conditions character of society, 56

Luther, Seth, and working class, 89, 93

Lyceum, promotes education of girls, 173

Lyon, Mary, quoted, 169; interest in middle-class girls, 174, 179; humble origins, 179–80; religious ideals of education, 181–82; preparation for motherhood an educational aim, 185; ideal of social service, 188

McGuffey, William H., religious orthodoxy, 19

McMaster, John Bach, quoted on history, 251

Machine age, defended by Mann, 121, Harris, 318–19; capitalistic dominance of criticized by Dewey, 510

Madison, James, popular intelligence necessary for free institutions, 55–56

Mann, Horace, formative influences on, 101 ff.; moral earnestness, 102; utilitarianism, 102–3; humanitarianism, 103–6; Secretary of Mass. State Board of Education, 107; work for improvement of common schools, 108–9; self-sacrifice, 109–10; unjustly criticized, 109; controversies, 109–10; espouses phrenology, 110–11, 123; universal education and prosperity, 112 ff.; criticizes capitalists, 113–17; responsibilities of property owners, 114–15; attacked for "socialist" doctrines, 117; sympathy for working class, 118 ff.; attitude toward child labor, 119–20; opposes revolutionary action, 120–21; defends machine age, 121; common schools a remedy for pauperism, 122–23; for a class society, 122; character education, 122 ff.; inconsistent attitude toward indoctrination, 126 ff.; defends freedom of expression, 127–28; opposes war, 128; advocates temperance instruction, 128; attitude toward violence, 128–30; toward abolition, 130–31; interest of school and society identical, 132; advocates education for changing world, 133–34; excesses of democracy to be checked by education, 135; limitations of education in political crises, 135 ff.; education of women, 177

Manual training, as preventive of migration westward, 70–71; as preventive of labor troubles, 221; criticized by W. T. Harris, 317. See also Industrial education

Marshall, Chief-Justice, importance of elementary free schools, 46 n.; a preventive of labor troubles, 87

Martineau, Harriet, on Southern movement for educational independence of North, 72

Marx, Karl, anticipated by Thomas Skidmore, 91; views of opposed by W. T. Harris, 327 ff. See also Socialism

Mather, Cotton, education and theocracy, 9–10; eulogizes Ezekiel Cheever, 12

Maxwell, William H., relation of personal efficiency to poverty, 231; favors free school lunches, 240; fights school politics, 253

May, Samuel J., on opposition of wealthy to free schools, 87; criticized by Mann for abolitionist activities, 130–31

Mayo, Rev. A. D., education as preventive of radicalism, 219; breaks down Southern opposition to school taxation, 262 n.; on Southern educational and industrial development, 210

Memminger, C. G., common schools as solvent of class distinctions, 94; tribute to Barnard, 141 n.

Methods of teaching, social implications of, 30–31; mass methods criticized by G. Stanley Hall, 416–17

Middle class, ideas of in educational theories of Franklin, 35 ff.; devotion to of Mary Lyon, 174, 179; of G. Stanley Hall, 404, 412; James criticizes smugness of, 439

Mills, Caleb, father of Indiana's public schools, 19; free schools responsible for New England's prosperity, 78; for security of investments, 82; public education an instrument for furthering social democracy, 94–95

Mobs. See Violence

Moral training, necessity of in a republic, 59–60; influence of, 60–61; a safeguard to property, 82; Barnard's religious conception of, 142–43; urged by Herbartians, 254, by Bishop Spalding, 372, by Hall, 419–20; limitations of, 125

Mormons, regard for science and its applications, 65

Morrill Act. See Agricultural education

N. E. A., reorganization and growth of after World War, 547–48; criticisms of, 547; alliance with business, 563–64; leaders of denounce business in depression, 576–78

Nationalism, educational programs for promotion of, 47–48; retarded by sectional loyalties, 63; attitude toward of educators during and after Civil War, 209–10; championed by W. T. Harris, 336 ff.

Negroes, education of in colonial period, 7, 39; during Reconstruction, 261–62; promoted by Slater Fund, 266; befriended by J. L. M. Curry, 271; Hall on, 413; inferiority of claimed by Thorndike, 491. *See also* Armstrong, Gen. S. C.; Washington, Booker T.; Du Bois, Dr. W. E. B.

New England Primer, religious tone, 16; becomes more worldly, 32

Newlon, Jesse, liberal social philosophy of, 561

Newspapers, educational value of, 318

Northeast, sectional pride in educational enterprise, 75; affected by rise of capitalism and industrialism, 76; humanitarianism in, 95 ff.

Ogden, Robert, background, 282–83; social philosophy, 283–85; befriends Hampton Institute, 283; helps organize Southern Conference on Education, 284

Orata, Pedro Tamesis, attacks antidemocratic implications of Thorndike's position on transfer of training, 468–69

Ordinances of 1785 and 1787, and free schools, 68 n.

Owen, Robert, sponsors Pestalozzian ideas in New Harmony schools, 66–67; favors free public schools as boon for labor, 89–90; Barnard on, 155

Packard, Frederick, quoted on education and *status quo*, 83; opposes Mann, 109

Page, David, respect for property, 85–86

Page, Walter Hines, agitation for improvement of public schools, 281–82

Paine, Thomas, "heretical" ideas feared, 13, 14

Parker, Col. Francis W., personality, 375; background, 375–76; reverence for nature and science, 377–78; belief in idea of progress, 378; educational philosophy not original, 378–79; relation to Dewey, 379, 521; "the Quincy method," 378, 380; apostle of dignity and divinity of childhood, 380; learning by doing, 383–84; views on private schools, 387–88; democratic functions of public schools, 388–89; criticizes dogmatism, 389; views on teaching of history, 390; citizenship training, 390–91; sympathy for immigrants, 391; scorn of money-making values, 391–92; sympathy with socialist doctrines, 392–93; represents American individualism at best, 393; influence of, 394–95

Parker, Theodore, on Horace Mann, 110

Patri, Angelo, views on immigrant school children, 256

Patriotism. *See* Citizenship training

Patten, Simon N., relation of morality and culture to economic status, 239

Peabody, George, promotes public education in outh, 262 ff.

Peace, inculcation of love for, 62, 128; views of educators, 128, 139–41, 249–50, 344–45, 432, 476–77, 529

Peers, Rev. B. O., free schools and social democracy, 95

Periodicals, educational, advocate moral training, 18; criticize authoritarianism in classroom, 30

Pestalozzianism, and spontaneity in classroom, 29–30; regarded as suitable to Western needs, 65; at New Harmony, 66; as instrument for social amelioration, 99; influences Mann, 123–24; Barnard, 143, 152; high regard for women teachers, 178; Francis Parker, 379

Philbrick, John D., quoted on Mann, 113

Phrenology, influences Mann, 110–11, 122; interest of G. Stanley Hall in, 399

Potter, Alonzo, training for citizenship, 57; schools and industrial prosperity, 77–78; schools and labor, 94

Potter, Elisha R., on Barnard's work in Rhode Island, 166

Poverty, preventable by education, 122, 147

Pragmatism, social implications of, 452 ff.

Pressure groups, 205, 492, 538

Private schools. *See* Class character of education

Progress, idea of, and education, 48; identified with West, 64; Mann, 133; Harris, 345

Progressive education, anticipated by Booker T. Washington, 291 ff.; relation to theory of individual differences, 483–84; emphasis on individualism, 562; increased social consciousness of leaders in, 574–75

Propaganda, endangers critical inquiry, 510

Property, secured by popular education, 79, 80, 81–83, 85–86; Mann's views, 114–15; Curry's defense of, 275; Harris, 323; Spalding, 367; Hall, 409, 420; Thorndike, 477

Prosperity, education and, 7–8, 77–78, 227–28, 238; worship of deprecated by James, 434

Prosser, Charles A., leader of industrial education, 559–60

Psychology, relation to education, 317, 355. *See also* James, Hall, Thorndike

Quakers, 10–11; influence Franklin, 39; education of girls, 172

Quincy, Josiah, political functions of popular education, 57

Randolph, Edward, education and loyalty to British Empire, 9

Rantoul, Robert, Jr., free schools as guaranty of social justice, 89–90; friend of labor, 119

Recapitulation theory. *See* Hall, G. Stanley

Reconstruction, views of educators on, 209–10

Reform, attitude of educators in pre-

Civil War period toward, 99–100, 103 ff., 139 ff., 180; in post-Civil War period, 234 ff., 246 ff.; Hall on, 405. *See also* Peace, Temperance, Abolition, Child labor, Health, Working class, Women, Civil service, Americanization, Socialism, Indians

Religion, influence of on colonial schools, 6–13; prolonged into later period, 14–21; relation to class structure of colonial society, 5 ff.; relation to maintenance of civil authority, 5 ff.; importance in female education, 181 ff.; upheld by Harris, 314 ff., Hall, 407–8

Republican institutions, free schools and maintenance of, 55–56, 271

Revivals, a stimulus to education, 10, 13; at Troy Female Seminary, 181

Revolution, education as preventive of, 79–80, 81, 191, 302; Mann on, 128–29; opposition of Hall to, 405, 423; views of Dewey on, 518

Romanticism, influence on G. Stanley Hall, 403–4

Rugg, Harold, social and democratic objectives of education, 557

Rural life, educational value of, 376, 398, 418

Rush, Dr. Benjamin, friend of female education, 176

Russell, Dean James Earl, work for professionalization of education, 549–50; early interest in social effects of education, 551; accentuated by World War, 551; advocates better rural schools, 216; interest in adult education, 553–54; influence, 549

Science, relation of to economic pattern, 461–63; Dewey on teaching of, 527–28. *See also* Thorndike, E. L.

Sears, Dr. Barnas, agent of Peabody Fund, 263–64

Sectionalism, to be promoted by regional systems of education, 63 ff. *See also* Frontier, South, Northeast

Secularization of American life, influence of on education, 13, 16

Seton, Mother, Catholic educator, 174, 179, 183; quoted, 185

Sex, Hall's mystical views on, 409–10; beginnings of instruction in schools, 247–48; Ella Flagg Young on, 248 n.

Simpson, Steven, quoted on class character of education, 89

Skidmore, Thomas, on limited capacity of education to improve condition of labor, 90–91

Slavery, problems created by, 53; retards growth of free schools, 74–75; criticized by Mann, 136–37

Smith, Adam, popular education and respect for authority, 85, 93

Smith, Dr. William, quoted, 6, 11

Smith, William Hawley, author of *Evolution of Dodd*, 558

Snedden, David, exponent of educational sociology, 565 ff.; social ideas, 566 ff.; criticizes *A Charter for the Social Sciences*, 566–67; criticizes Dewey, Kilpatrick, and Bode, 567

Social studies, advocated as checks on radicalism, 221–22; as means of understanding social tensions, 233 n.; greater emphasis on requested by A. F. of L., 237; relation of theory of transfer of training to, 467–68; increased emphasis on after World War, 548–49; Judd on, 555–56

Socialism, inspires criticism of schools as agent of social change, 151–52; denounced by educational leaders, 218 ff., 274–75, 302–3, 364–65; leaders of demand free clothes and lunches for poor children, 237–38; ideals of advocated by F. W. Parker, 392–93; John Dewey, 503; qualified sympathy of William James with, 439–40; early interest of G. Stanley Hall in, 399 ff., 423

Society for Propagation of Gospel in Foreign Parts, educational work, 5, 8, 11, 12

Sociology, influence of on educational thought, 257–58; advocated by Harris as basis of education, 345–46. *See also* Ward, Lester; Snedden, David; Spencer, Herbert

South, education and sectional self-consciousness, 72 ff.; public school movement in post-Civil War period, 210–11, 228, 261; effect of Civil War and Reconstruction on schools of, 261–62; Peabody Fund, 262 ff.; educational revival, 281 ff. *See also* Page, Walter Hines; Knapp, Dr. Seaman A.; Curry, J. L. M.; Sears, Barnas; Ogden, Robert; Washington, Booker T.

Spalding, Bishop John Lancaster, background, 353–54; adjustment of Catholic Church to American spirit, 353–54; better training of Catholic teachers, 355; educational philosophy, 355 ff., 372; conception of intellectual culture, 360; training for practical life subordinate, 360; relation of education to heredity and environment, 361–62; colonization of Irish slum-dwellers in West, 362–63; deprecates importance of physical basis of life, 363–64; criticizes Socialism, 364–65; favors organized labor, 366–67; appreciation of American civilization, 367–68; criticizes American life, 368–69; favors education of women and women's rights, 371–72; quoted on Francis Parker, 384; William T. Harris on, 348

Spencer, Herbert, health basic in education, 246; harmonious development of individuals, 464; opposed by W. T. Harris, 312

Status quo, education for, 61, 80 ff., 146, 154 ff., 165–66, 333 ff.; upheld by educators of varying types, 461; education to undermine favored by Dewey, 521–22

Stevens, Thaddeus, favors public schools, 76–77

Stowe, Calvin E., Report on education in Prussia, 65–66

Strayer, George D., directs work of Commission on National Emergency in Education, 545 ff.; opposes affiliation of teachers' organizations with A. F. of L., 548; on Thorndike's contribution to classification and progress of school children, 483. *See also* Administration

Strikes, opposed by educators, 218 ff., 330

Success, education as means of achieving, 31, 124; influence of idea of on G. Stanley Hall, 397

Suffrage, dangers of preventable by popular education, 79, 81

Sumner, Charles, on political opposition to Horace Mann, 117

Suzzallo, Henry, quoted on E. L. Thorndike, 459

Swett, John, California educator, 196, 209 n.; fights school graft, 253

Swift, Edgar James, criticizes capitalism, 244

Sylvis, William H., educational and economic problems of workers, 235-36

Teachers, social status of, 28-29, 220, 252, 332-33; restrictions in selection of, 8, 11-12, 20, 61; unionization of, 242-43; Dewey on social leadership of, 535. See also Women; Beecher, Catharine

Teachers College, William T. Harris on, 324-25

Temperance, 128; work of Mary H. Hunt for, 248-49; sympathetic attitude of educators toward, 248-49, 343. See also Drunkenness

Tennent, Rev. William, 13

Terman, Lewis H., aristocratic implications of psychological work, 562-63

Tests and measurements, social implications of, 230, 486 ff.; Dewey on, 532-33

Textbooks, religious character, 16-18; utilitarian tone, 31 ff.; nationalism, 54-55; sectional self-consciousness, 66, 73; profits of publishers, 229-30

Thayer, V. T., criticizes business character of educational administration, 564-65

Thorndike, E. L., scientific ideal, 460-63; popularizes statistical technique in education, 460; general educational aims determined by ethics, 464-65; rejects self-perfection as educational ideal, 464-65; emphasizes adjustment of individual to environment, 466; on specific elements and transfer of training, 466-69; indoctrination, 469-70; bond theory, 470-71; adult learning, 471-73; compulsory school attendance, 472, 485; individual differences, 473 ff.; undemocratic implications of theory of instincts, 474 ff.; views on war, 476-77; possible radical interpretations of his theory of human nature, 477-78; conservative implications of theory of heredity and environment, 481-82; tests and measurements, 486-90; women, 490-91; promotes psychology of advertising, 492; views on labor, 494-95; laissez faire, 496-97; respect for expert, 497; influence, 460-61; criticisms of, 497-98

Thrift, training for, 231-32. See also Webster, Noah; Franklin, Benjamin

Transfer of training, questioned by James, 450-51; criticized by Thorndike, 466-67; social implications of, 467-68

Tufts, James, collaborates with Dewey, 509

Unemployment, relation to Thorndike's theory of adult learning, 472-73; Harris on, 328-29

Unions, teachers', favored by Margaret Haley and John Dewey, 242-43; opposed by leading educators, 243, 253, 548

Unitarianism, social gospel of, 15

Violence, education as preventive, 79 ff.; attributed to lax school discipline, 86; inconsistent attitude of Mann toward, 128 ff.; Rev. A. D. Mayo tolerant of, 241; Dewey on, 511, 518, 543. See also Revolution, Anarchy, Socialism

Vocational education. See Industrial education

War, psychological basis of defended by Hall, 408-9; alternative for suggested by James and Thorndike, 432, 476-77; Dewey on, 517-19. See also World War

Ward, Lester, 257-58; criticized by Thorndike, 484. See also Sociology

Washington, Booker T., quoted, 261; background, 288 ff.; project method, 291-94; founds Tuskegee, 291 ff.; emphasizes educational value of solving practical problems, 293-94; appeals to self-interest of Southern whites, 294 ff.; views on political and social rights of Negroes, 294 ff., 303; address at Cotton States Exposition, 297-98; admires business men, 298-300; enlists aid of Northern financiers, 298-99; compares man "farthest down" in Europe with Negro, 301 ff.; opposes Socialism, 302-3; social views similar to those of average American, 303-4; criticized by Dr. W. E. B. Du Bois, 304 ff.; evaluation of social and educational principles, 309

Webster, Daniel, free schools society's police protection, 86; denounced by Mann, 137

Webster, Noah, religious and political views, 14, 48; *Elementary Spelling Book*, 17; social philosophy, 32-4

West. *See* Frontier

Western Literary Institute and College of Teachers, 18-19, 65

Wickersham, J. P., views on Reconstruction, 210

Wiley, Calvin, North Carolina educator, 71; education and westward migration, 71; free schools and unification of Southern people, 74

Willard, Emma, background, 178; religious ideals in education, 181; favors science and mathematics, geography and history, 183, 188; interest in peace movement, 188, 192; denounces "vain amusements," 188; favors teaching as career for women, 189; attitude toward slavery, 190; toward Socialism, 192; works for common schools in Connecticut, 193

Winthrop, Gov. John, quoted on education of women, 171

Winthrop, Robert, and Southern education, 273

Women, restrictions on freedom of, 53, 170 ff.; education of defended by educators, 140, 343, 371-72; handicaps in teaching profession, 178; Catharine Beecher on women teachers, 186 ff.; effect of machine age on, 320; Hall's romantic attitude toward, 410, 419-20; James and Thorndike on mental differences of, 452, 490-91; Dewey on, 521 n. *See also* Girls

Woodbridge, W. C., education and good citizenship, 58; female education, 177

Working class, education of to prevent subversive action by, 79, 83, 84, 86, 423-24; attitude of toward public schools, 88 ff., 235 ff.; views of educators on, 118-21, 145-46, 238, 240, 241, 242, 277 ff., 301-2, 319, 367-68, 423-24, 434, 436-37, 493-95; condition of, 96 ff.; problems of, 204. *See also* Unions, A. F. of L., Knights of Labor, Socialism, Anarchism

World War, influence on social thought of educators, 542 ff.; accepted enthusiastically by most educators, 543-44; idealistic desire of educators to build new social order, 578

Wright, Frances, radical social philosophy, 180-81

Young, Ella Flagg, favors sex instruction, 248 n.; elected president of N. E. A., 252; aids Dewey, 521; pioneer in movement to increase rôle of teachers in administration, 548